THE ROUTLEDGE COMPANION TO GLOBAL INTERNET HISTORIES

The Routledge Companion to Global Internet Histories brings together research on the diverse Internet histories that have evolved in different regions, language cultures and social contexts across the globe. While the Internet is now in its fifth decade, the understanding and formulation of its histories outside of an anglophone framework is still very much in its infancy. From Tunisia to Taiwan, this volume emphasizes the importance of understanding and formulating Internet histories outside the anglophone case studies and theoretical paradigms that have thus far dominated academic scholarship on Internet history. Interdisciplinary in scope, the collection offers a variety of historical lenses on the development of the Internet: as a new communication technology seen in the context of older technologies; as a new form of sociality read alongside previous technologically mediated means of relating; and as a new media "vehicle" for the communication of content.

Contributors: César Albarrán-Torres, Ilhem Allagui, Rajiv Aricat, Bunty Avieson, Niels Brügger, Anissa Daoudi, Stuart Davis, Charles Ess, Alisa Freedman, Martha Fuentes-Bautista, Ivo Furman, Shihui Gui, Fernando Gutiérrez, Tim Highfield, Larissa Hjorth, Arthur Hou-ming Huang, Dongwon Jo, Nicholas John, Rhys James Jones, Katarzyna Kamińska-Korolczuk, Fumitoshi Kato, Barbara Kijewska, Kwang-Suk Lee, Li Shao Liang, Rich Ling, Sarah Logan, May O. Lwin, Hayes Mawindi Mabweazara, Robin Mansell, Teodor Mitew, Christopher Moore, Kana Ohashi, Elisa Oreglia, Sari Östman, Camille Paloque-Berges, Chitra Panchapakesan, Petri Saarikoski, Susana Salgado, Valérie Schafer, Nishant Shah, Jeremiah Spence, Christina Spurgeon, Joe Straubhaar, Jaakko Suominen, Joseph Suwamaru, Takanori Tamura, Benjamin G. Thierry, Endah Triastuti, Riikka Turtiainen, Andrew Whelan, Ling Yang, Lin Yi-Ren, Hu Yong, Haiqing Yu, Baohua Zhou.

Gerard Goggin is Professor of Media and Communications and ARC Future Fellow at the University of Sydney. He is widely published on mobile technologies and the Internet, including *The Routledge Companion to Mobile Media* (with Larissa Hjorth, 2014), *New Technologies and the Media* (2012), *Global Mobile Media* (2010), *Internationalizing Internet Studies* (with Mark McLelland, 2009), and *Cell Phone Culture* (2006).

Mark McLelland is Professor of Gender and Sexuality Studies at the University of Wollongong, and author or editor of ten books focusing on issues to do with the history of sexuality, popular culture, and new media in Japan and East Asia, most recently: *Love, Sex and Democracy in Japan during the American Occupation* (Palgrave Macmillan, 2012), and *The Routledge Handbook of Sexuality Studies in East Asia*, edited with Vera Mackie (Routledge, 2015).

THE ROUTLEDGE COMPANION TO GLOBAL INTERNET HISTORIES

Edited by
Gerard Goggin and
Mark McLelland

Routledge
Taylor & Francis Group

LONDON AND NEW YORK

First published 2017
by Routledge

2 Park Square, Milton Park, Abingdon, Oxfordshire OX14 4RN
52 Vanderbilt Avenue, New York, NY 10017

Routledge is an imprint of the Taylor & Francis Group, an informa business

First issued in paperback 2019

Library of Congress Cataloging in Publication Data
Names: Goggin, Gerard, 1964– editor. |
McLelland, Mark J., 1966– editor.
Title: The Routledge companion to global internet histories /
edited by Gerard Goggin and Mark McLelland.
Other titles: Global internet histories
Description: New York: Routledge, Taylor & Francis Group, 2017. |
Includes bibliographical references.
Identifiers: LCCN 2016038503| ISBN 9781138812161 (hbk) |
ISBN 9781315748962 (ebk)
Subjects: LCSH: Internet—History. | Telecommunication—
History—20th century. | Telecommunication—History—21st century.
Classification: LCC TK5105.875.I57 R727 2017 | DDC 384.309—dc23
LC record available at https://lccn.loc.gov/2016038503

ISBN: 978-1-138-81216-1 (hbk)
ISBN: 978-0-367-87075-1 (pbk)

Typeset in Bembo
by Florence Production Ltd, Stoodleigh, Devon, UK

CONTENTS

FIGURES AND TABLES

Figures

Tables

CONTRIBUTORS

César Albarrán-Torres is a lecturer in Media and Communication at Swinburne University of Technology in Melbourne, Australia. He has been widely published in academic and non-academic publications as a film and literary critic, author, and translator. His current research focuses on what he calls "gamble-play media", hybrid platforms where gambling and digital interactive media intersect.

Ilhem Allagui is Associate Professor-in-residence in the Journalism program at Northwestern University in Qatar. She earned her Ph.D. (2006) and MSc (2000) in Communication from the University of Montreal, Canada. Her research interests include the social integration of new media, Internet studies, Internet adoption and development in the MENA region, digital transformations and social empowerment in the MENA region, the Arab cultural industries, as well as entrepreneurship, advertising, and public relations practices in the MENA region. Dr. Allagui joined the World Internet Project network in 2007, and launched the Emirates Internet Project (2007–2014) that was awarded the National Research Foundation grant (UAE) in 2009. The results of this research are discussed in a forthcoming book, *Technology and the Stresses to a National Community: The Case of the United Arab Emirates*. Ilhem Allagui serves on the editorial board of the *International Journal of Communication* (USC).

Rajiv Aricat is a research associate in Wee Kim Wee School of Communication & Information, Nanyang Technological University, Singapore. For his Ph.D., he studied the impact of mobile phones on South Asian migrant workers' acculturation to Singapore. During 2014–2015, he was part of a research project that investigated the adoption, usage, and impact of mobile phones in Myanmar. Originally from Kerala, India, Rajiv has an M.Phil. in Semiotics (Jawaharlal Nehru University, New Delhi) and a Master's in Communication & Journalism (University of Kerala).

Bunty Avieson is a lecturer in the Department of Media and Communications at the University of Sydney, where she teaches news writing. A former journalist, she has also published three novels, a novella, and two memoirs. The most recent, *The Dragon's Voice: How Modern Media Found Bhutan*, was about the year she spent in Bhutan as a media consultant funded by the UN.

Niels Brügger is Professor of Internet Studies and Digital Humanities at Aarhus University, Denmark; Head of the Centre for Internet Studies, and of NetLab. His research interests are Web historiography, Web archiving, and digital humanities. Recent books include

Web History (ed., Peter Lang, 2010) and *Histories of Public Service Broadcasters on the Web* (co-ed. with M. Burns, Peter Lang, 2012), and he is editing a special issue of *New Media & Society* about the first 25 years of the Web's history, as well as the following forthcoming books: *The Web as History: Using Web Archives to Understand the Past and the Present* (co-ed. with R. Schroeder, UCL Press, 2016), *Web 25: Histories from the First 25 Years of the World Wide Web* (Peter Lang, 2016), and the *Sage Handbook of Web History* (co-ed. with M. Anderson and I. Milligan, Sage, 2017). Finally, he is preparing the monograph *The Archived Web: Doing History in the Digital Age* (MIT Press, 2017).

Anissa Daoudi is a lecturer in Arabic and Translation Studies. She is Head of Arabic Section and Specialist for the Translation Studies (Arabic–English–Arabic) program. She recently won the Leverhulme Fellowship for her project on "Narrating and Translating Sexual Violence in Algeria in the 1990s," which is in the areas of translation studies, memory and narrativity. She is the author of *Cultural and Linguistic Encounters: Arab EFL Learners Encoding and Decoding Idioms* (2012) and other edited books and articles in linguistics and discourse analysis.

Stuart Davis is Assistant Professor of Communication and Director of the graduate program in Latin American Communication and Media Studies at Texas A&M-International University. He has articles published or forthcoming in *Communication Theory*, *Digital Journalism*, *International Journal of Communication*, and *Journalism Practice*, as well as edited collections including *Civic Media: Technology, Design, Practice* (MIT Press), *Inequity in the Technopolis: Race, Class, Gender, and the Digital Divide in Austin, Texas* (University of Texas Press), and *Protests in the Information Age: Social Movements, Digital Practices, and Surveillance* (Routledge). In 2013, he was a William J. Fulbright Scholar in the Department of Sociology at the Federal University of Rio de Janeiro. In 2015, he was a post-doctoral fellow in the graduate program in Media and Technology, Department of Social Communication, State University of São Paulo.

Charles Ess works at the intersections of philosophy, computing, applied ethics, comparative philosophy, and media studies, with particular focus on research ethics, digital religion, and virtue ethics in media and communication, specifically social robots. He serves as a research ethics consultant for the *VOX-Pol* Network of Excellence and the H2020 ICT-project HUMANE. His recent guest positions include Aarhus University (2009–2012), University of Vienna (2013–2014), University Institute of Lisbon (ISCTE-IUL—2015, 2016), and the Vienna University of Economics and Business (2016).

Alisa Freedman is Associate Professor of Japanese Literature and Film at the University of Oregon. Her books include *Tokyo in Transit: Japanese Culture on the Rails and Road* (Stanford University Press, 2010), an annotated translation of Kawabata Yasunari's *The Scarlet Gang of Asakusa* (University of California Press, 2005), and the co-edited volumes *Modern Girls on the Go: Gender, Mobility, and Labor in Japan* (Stanford University Press, 2013) and *Introducing Japanese Popular Culture* (forthcoming from Routledge). She has published articles and edited special journal issues on Japanese modernism, Tokyo studies, youth culture, gender, television, humor as social critique, teaching pedagogies, and intersections of literature and digital media, along with translations of Japanese literature. She is Editor-in-Chief of the *US–Japan Women's Journal*.

Martha Fuentes-Bautista is Senior Lecturer and Director of Engaged Research & Learning, in the Department of Communication at the University of Massachusetts, Amherst. Fuentes-Bautista's research focuses on social stratification of digital media systems, and the role of advocacy networks, media activism, and media reform movements in shaping media democracy and digital inclusion efforts in the U.S. and ILatin America. Her areas of interest include: media technologies and social inequality; community media policy; media reform and justice movements; community broadband and digital inclusion; empowerment evaluation and participatory action research.

Ivo Furman is a post-doctoral researcher at the Turkish Science and Technology Foundation (TUBITAK) and part-time lecturer at the Faculty of Media and Communications at Istanbul Bilgi University. He completed his Ph.D. in Sociology at Goldsmiths College, University of London in 2015. Furman is currently part of a research project that aims to build an open access Twitter research platform for social science researchers interested in social media analytics. The system, Bilgi-TCAT, will be fully operational by the end of 2016. Furman also teaches a course in digital methods, wherein students are taught how to collect, clean, and visualize data from social media platforms such as Twitter, Instagram, and Facebook. He will also start teaching a data journalism course next year. Furman's research has been supported by the Istanbul Bilgi University, Freedom House, European Corporation in Science and Technology (COST) Goldsmiths College, the Arts and Humanities Research Council (AHRC), Goethe Institut in London and Berlin, the Central Research Fund, the British Sociological Association, Administratia Fondului Cultural National (AFCN), the Museum of Contemporary Art in Bucharest (MNAC), British Sociological Association, and the British Institute in Ankara (BIAA). Furman's current research interests include digital methods focusing on Twitter and Instagram, social network analysis, data visualization, digital sociology, and data journalism.

Gerard Goggin is Professor of Media and Communications and ARC Future Fellow at the University of Sydney. He is widely published on mobile technologies and the Internet, including the books *Locative Media* (with Rowan Wilken, 2015), *The Routledge Companion to Mobile Media* (with Larissa Hjorth, 2014), *New Technologies and the Media* (2012), *Global Mobile Media* (2010), *Internationalizing Internet Studies* (with Mark McLelland, 2009), and *Cell Phone Culture* (2006). Gerard has a longstanding interest in disability, media, and technology, with key volumes being *The Routledge Companion to Disability and Media* (with Katie Ellis and Beth Haller, 2017), *Disability and the Media* (with Katie Ellis, 2015), and *Digital Disability* (with Christopher Newell, 2003).

Shihui Gui was born in Shanghai in the 1990s and received her BA from Peking University in 2014, majoring in English Literature. She is expected to receive her MA in New Media Communication from Fudan University by June 2016. Due to her strong interest in social media, she chose *The Influence of WeChat on Intergenerational Relationships in China* as her graduation thesis. Shihui will start her career at IBM China and will continue to focus on the TMT industry.

Fernando Gutiérrez is Dean of the School of Social Sciences and Humanities at the Monterrey Institute of Technology and Higher Education (Santa Fe Campus). He earned a Master's degree in Information Technologies, and a Ph.D. in Design and Data Visualization from the Metropolitan Autonomous University (UAM). He also serves as a member of the board of directors of the Media Ecology Association, is Head of the World Internet Project in Mexico, and a member of the Mexican Academy of Communication. His research focuses on "The Exploration of Flows to Predict Shapes: A Constructal Approach to Understand the New Media Ecology in the Digital Age." He was the coordinator of the Alfaomega collection "Ciudadan@ de Internet" (Internet Citizen) and author and associate editor of the following Spanish titles: *La Comprensión de los medios en la era digital*; *Internet como herramienta para la investigación*; *Explorando el ciberperiodismo Iberoamericano*; *.com probado Modelos exitosos de Internet en México*; *Internet: el Medio Inteligente*. Fernando has received the Louis Forsdale Award, 2015 from the Media Ecology Association; the National Research Award, 2012 from the Federation of Private Mexican Institutions of Higher Education (FIMPES); and the Gunther Saupe Award, 2009 from the Communication & Marketing Industry Confederation (CICOM), among other honors.

Tim Highfield is Vice-Chancellor's Research Fellow in the Digital Media Research Centre at Queensland University of Technology. He is the author of *Social Media and Everyday Politics* (Polity, 2016). His current fellowship project is "Visual Cultures of Social Media", and his research draws together social media, popular culture, politics, activism, Internet cultures, and more. Full details are available at timhighfield.net.

Larissa Hjorth, Professor, is an artist and digital ethnographer in the School of Media & Communication, RMIT University. She has co-edited *The Routledge Handbook to New Media in Asia* (with O. Khoo), *The Routledge Companion to Mobile Media* (with G. Goggin), *Gaming Cultures and Place* (with D. Chan), *Mobile Technologies* (with G. Goggin), *Art in Asia-Pacific* (with N. King and M. Kataoka), *Mobile Media Practices, Presence and Politics: The Challenge of Being Seamlessly Mobile* (with K. Cumiskey), and *Studying Mobile Media* (with I. Richardson and J. Burgess). Hjorth is currently first CI on two Australian Research Council (ARC) grants: one Linkage with Intel, *Locating the Mobile*, on locative media in Japan, China, and Australia (with S. Pink and H. Horst) (LP130100848); one Discovery (with I. Richardson), *Games of Being Mobile*, on mobile gaming in Australian everyday life (DP140104295). Since 2000, Hjorth has been researching the gendered and socio-cultural dimensions of mobile media and play cultures in the Asia-Pacific. These studies are outlined in her books *Mobile Media in the Asia-Pacific* (Routledge, 2009), *Games & Gaming* (Berg, 2010), *Online@AsiaPacific* (with Arnold, Routledge, 2013), *Understanding Social Media* (with Hinton, Sage, 2013), *Gaming in Social, Locative and Mobile Media* (with Richardson, Palgrave, 2014), *Haunting Hands* (with K. Cumiskey, Oxford University Press, 2016), *Digital Ethnography* (with Pink, Horst, Postill, Lewis, and Tacchi (Sage, 2016), and *Screen Ecologies* (with Pink, Sharp, and Williams, MIT Press, 2016).

Arthur Hou-ming Huang is Associate Professor of the Department of Sociology, National Chengchi University, Taiwan. He has been a heavy user of the Internet, and has engaged in studies of the Internet culture of Taiwan since 1994. He is currently conducting a study on Ingress from the viewpoint of phenomenology of technology. He is now on the editorial boards of the *Journal of Cyber Culture and Information Society*, and *Societas: A Journal of Philosophical Study of Public Affairs*.

Dongwon Jo is a post-doctoral researcher at Flinders University, Adelaide, Australia in 2016. He has recently researched on socio-cultural histories of information technologies in Korea and East Asia, particularly on the history of electronics markets, (micro)computers,

BBS, the Internet, and their users. His present projects include a comparative history of the the Internet and Videotex in France and Korea; a comparative archiving project for microcomputer users' experiences and memories in Australia and Korea; and a study on the practices of microcomputer cloning and circulation of that knowledge, parts, and products across the electronics markets in the early 1980s in Japan, Taiwan, Hong Kong, and Korea.

Nicholas John is Assistant Professor at the Department of Communication and Journalism, the Hebrew University of Jerusalem, Israel. He has written extensively about the arrival of the Internet to Israel and its diffusion there. Other research projects include a large study of sharing in the digital age, and pioneering work on Facebook unfriending, especially in relation to political disagreement. Find more at http://nicholasjohn.huji.ac.il.

Rhys James Jones is Senior Lecturer in Digital Media in the Department of Media and Communication, Swansea University. He researches Wales and the Welsh language in contemporary and historical online contexts, and is currently investigating the use of Welsh on social media by political parties during election campaigns.

Katarzyna Kamińska-Korolczuk, Ph.D., is a lecturer at the Political Science Institute at the Faculty of Social Science at the University of Gdańsk, Poland. Her main area of research is political and party systems, including relations between political actors and the media. She is especially interested in the party and media systems in Estonia and Latvia. From 2012 to 2016, she was the Deputy Director of the Institute of Political Science, University of Gdańsk, where she was responsible for raising the quality of teaching and modernizing the study programs, and she also co-created a new field of study: diplomacy. She is the scientific editor of four books, and the author of many book chapters and scientific articles.

Fumitoshi Kato, Ph.D. Communication, is currently working as a professor at the Faculty of Environment and Information Studies, Keio University, Japan. His research interests include communication theory, media studies, socio-cultural impacts of new technologies, and qualitative research methods. He is especially interested in the use of camera phones in the context of community development. For the past few years, he has been conducting field research in various local communities in Japan, with a primary focus on the notion of "mobile learning".

Barbara Kijewska is Assistant Professor at the Institute of Political Science, University of Gdańsk (Poland). She has been involved in international projects in the societal aspects of energy technology. Her research has been mainly concerned with issues of gender, especially women's political activity and mass media research. She is the author of numerous papers and communications. She is an expert of the Polish Ecological Club and member of the WAGA Association promoting equality between women and men.

Kwang-Suk Lee is Director of IT Convergence Policy Research Institute and Assistant Professor in the Graduate School of Public Policy and Information Technology at Seoul National University of Science and Technology. Lee earned his Ph.D. in the Radio-TV-Film Department of the University of Texas at Austin. He has been an Australian Research Council (ARC) post-doctoral research fellow. His recent publications include the following books: *Aesthetic Notes from the Edge* (Seoul, 2016), *New Art Activism* (Seoul, 2015), *Digital Barbarism* (Seoul, 2014), *IT Development in Korea: A Broadband Nirvana* (London: Routledge, 2012), and *The Art and Cultural Politics of Cyber Avant-Gardes* (Seoul, 2010).

Shao Liang Li is Master of the Department of Sociology, National Chengchi University, Taiwan. He is interested in science and technology studies, the sociology of technology, and cyber culture and the information society. He is currently working in the digital marketing industry.

Rich Ling is the Shaw Foundation Professor of Media Technology, Wee Kim Wee School of Communication and Information, Nanyang Technological University, Singapore. His work focuses on the social consequences of mobile communication.

Sarah Logan is an honorary research fellow in the Department of Government and International Relations at the University of Sydney. She was previously the inaugural digital politics research fellow in the Department of State, Society and Governance in Melanesia at the Australian National University. Her research interests include the political and social impact of the Internet on emerging democracies, and the impact of the Internet on international politics.

May O. Lwin is Associate Professor in the Wee Kim Wee School of Communication and Information, Nanyang Technological University. Concurrently, Lwin serves as the Associate Dean at NTU's College of Humanities, Arts, and Social Sciences. Lwin specializes in strategic and health communication. Her projects involve the assessment and development of digital media systems to tackle societal and health concerns. In Myanmar, she is currently involved in projects studying how technology can improve public health. She has published widely in journals such as the *Journal of Communication*, the *Journal of Consumer Research*, and the *Journal of Adolescence*. Email contact for Lwin: mailto:tmaylwin@ntu.edu.sg.

Hayes Mawindi Mabweazara, Ph.D., is Senior Lecturer in Journalism Studies at Falmouth University, UK. He is Associate Editor for *African Journalism Studies* (Routledge) and edits the journal's Special Annual Issue titled *African Digital Media Review*. Mabweazara serves on the editorial boards of *Digital Journalism* (Routledge), *Journalism Practice* (Routledge) and the *Journal of Alternative and Community Media* (Griffiths University). He edited *Digital Technologies and the Evolving African Newsroom* (Routledge, 2015), as well as co-edited *Online Journalism in Africa* (Routledge, 2014). He also guest-edited a special issue of *Journalism: Theory, Practice & Criticism* (Sage, 2011), titled "New Media and Journalism Practice in Africa: An Agenda for Research" (with Prof. Chis Atton). Mabweazara is currently working on a monograph, titled *Africa's Mainstream Press in the Digital Era*, due for publication by Palgrave Macmillan.

Robin Mansell is Professor of New Media and the Internet in the Department of Media and Communications, London School of Economics and Political Science. She has been Head of the LSE Media and Communications Department, President of IAMCR, and Scientific Chair of EUROCPR. She is the author of numerous academic papers and books including *Imagining the Internet: Communication, Innovation and Governance* (Oxford University Press, 2012).

Mark McLelland is Professor of Gender and Sexuality Studies at the University of Wollongong, and author or editor of ten books focusing on issues to do with the history of sexuality, popular culture, and new media in Japan and East Asia, most recently *Love, Sex and Democracy in Japan during the American Occupation* (Palgrave Macmillan, 2012), and *The Routledge Handbook of Sexuality Studies in East Asia*, edited with Vera Mackie (Routledge, 2015).

Teodor Mitew specializes in actor network theory and ambient socio-digital systems. His current research includes the implications of the Internet of Things for sociability and memory, maker communities, and object-oriented ontology. His recent research explores the application of actor network theory to the study of mobile socio-technical assemblages. He is a senior lecturer in Digital Media and Communication at the University of Wollongong, Australia.

Christopher Moore is a lecturer in Digital Communication and Media Studies at the University of Wollongong, Australia. His research in game studies examines the affective dimensions of multiplayer and first-person experiences. He is currently focused on the appropriation of game engines and virtual reality interfaces for archival curation and knowledge production in open and collaboratively assembled spaces. Most recently co-editing the journal of *Persona Studies*, his research in the digital humanities explores the role of digital objects in the presentation and personal surveillance of the public self online.

Kana Ohashi is a doctoral student at the Graduate School of Media and Governance, Keio University, Japan. She graduated from Keio University and completed a documentary film-making program at Met Film School. Her research interests are mobilities studies, sociology of families, and video ethnography. She is especially interested in how people experience migration and how they maintain long-distance relationships with their family members. Currently, she is making ethnographic videos on transnational lives in Japan.

Elisa Oreglia, Ph.D., UC Berkeley, is a lecturer in Global Digital Media at the Centre for Media Studies, SOAS, University of London. She studies the appropriation of digital media among marginal users in China and Myanmar, with a particular focus on local knowledge production and information-sharing practices in markets.

Sari Östman, Ph.D., Researcher, Digital Culture, University of Turku. Her Ph.D. study (defended in 2015) analyzed the appropriation of life-publishing, the phenomena and a concept which unites all the practices and motives for telling about ourselves and our lives online. She has published multiple scholarly articles about life-publishing and research ethics.

Camille Paloque-Berges holds a Ph.D. in Information and Communication sciences with a thesis on the cultural history of Internet folklore. She is the author of *Poétique des Codes sur les Réseaux Informatiques* (2009) and co-editor of *Histoires et Cultures du Libre* (with C. Masutti, 2013). Today, she is a research engineer at the lab for History of Techno-Sciences (HT2S) at the Conservatoire National des Arts et Métiers in Paris and an associated researcher at the "Trajectoires numériques" cluster of the Communication Science Institute of CNRS (ISCC).

Chitra Panchapakesan is a doctoral candidate in the Wee Kim Wee School of Communication and Information at Nanyang Technological University, Singapore. Her research interest focuses on mobile communication, media effects, gender roles, and civic engagement.

Petri Saarikoski, Ph.D., Docent, University Lecturer, Department of Digital Culture, University of Turku. Saarikoski has studied the history of computer hobbyism and home computer culture in Finland.

Susana Salgado, Ph.D., 2007, University of Lisbon, is a researcher and Professor of Political Communication and Media and Politics at the Institute of Social Sciences, University of Lisbon, Portugal. Her research work is currently sponsored by the Portuguese Foundation for Science and Technology (IF/01451/2014/CP1239/CT0004).

Valérie Schafer is a researcher at the French National Center for Scientific Research (Institute for Communication Sciences). She specializes in the history of computing and telecommunications. Her current research deals with the Internet and Web history in France and Europe.

Nishant Shah is the co-founder of the Centre for Internet & Society, Bangalore, India, a guest professor of Culture and Aesthetics of Digital Media (ICAM) at Leuphana University, Lüneburg, Germany, and the Dean-Research at ArtEZ University of the Arts, in the Netherlands. His work is at the intersections of digital technologies, social justice, and new modes of knowledge production and intervention making.

Jeremiah P. Spence, Ph.D., is Assistant Professor of International and Global Communications in the Department of Media & Communication at the Erasmus University in Rotterdam, Netherlands. Spence completed his doctorate in 2015 in the Department of Radio, TV & Film at the University of Texas at Austin with a dissertation on the theme of TV audience research in Brazil from 2004 to 2014, with significant findings regarding the theorization of cultural proximity in the field of international media flows. Spence is currently researching the media consumption habits of recent migrants and refugees within the European Union countries, with a specific focus on questions related to acculturation.

Christina Spurgeon lectures in Journalism, Media and Communication in the Creative Industries Faculty at the Queensland University of Technology, Brisbane, Australia, and is an active media studies researcher and postgraduate supervisor. Christina serves on the editorial board of Media International Australia and edits *3CMedia: Journal of Community, Citizens, and Third Sector Media*. Her book, *Advertising and New Media*, was published by Routledge in 2008.

Joe Straubhaar is the Amon G. Carter Sr. Centennial Professor of Communication in the Radio-Television-Film Department, and Director of the Latino and Latin American Media Studies program at the University of Texas at Austin. His current research concerns the globalization of television and new media, the BRICs, television in Brazil, the digital divide in Brazil and Texas, media and migration, and ICTs and development in Brazil and Texas. He is co-author of *Television in Latin America* (BFI, 2013), the author of *World Television: From Global to Local* (Sage Publications, 2007), and editor of *Inequity* *in the Technopolis: Race, Class, Gender and the Digital Divide in Austin* (University of Texas Press, 2011), and numerous journal articles and conference papers on these topics.

Jaakko Suominen, Ph.D., Professor of Digital Culture at University of Turku. With a focus on cultural history of media and information technologies, Suominen has studied computers and popular media, the Internet, social media, digital games, and theoretical and method-ological aspects of the study of digital culture. He has led several multidisciplinary research projects, funded by the Academy of Finland, Tekes, companies, and municipal bodies, and has over 100 scholarly publications. Currently, Suominen leads the Mindscapes24 research project (Academy of Finland funding #293460), where the digital culture research group is studying the history of social media in Finland.

Joseph Suwamaru earned his Ph.D. for research on aspects of mobile phone usage in socio-economic development in Papua New Guinea (PNG). Prior to completing his Ph.D., he was the Executive Director of the Engineering Department within the former ICT regulator in PNG, PANGTEL. He also served as Vice Chairman of the Asia Pacific Telecommunity Study Groups. On completing his Ph.D., Dr. Suwamaru became a senior lecturer within the Department of Information Systems at the Divine Word University in Madang, PNG. He currently sits on the board of directors of a new state-owned enterprise in PNG, DATACO, tasked with rolling out terrestrial and undersea submarine fiber-optic cables across PNG and Melanesia.

Takanori Tamura is a lecturer at H sei University in Tokyo. He studies human interaction in computer mediated communication (CMC). Starting from studies of a pre-internet domestic networking system in Japan, he is interested in the self presentation and interaction of people via CMC based on a narrative approach. He has written on religion, privacy and social movements' use of CMC. He is the author, along with Tamura Daiyu, of "Reflexive Self Identification of Internet Users and the Authority of Soka Gakkai: Analysis of Discourse in Japanese BBS, Ni-Channeru", pp. 173–195 in *Japanese Religions on the Internet: Innovation, Representation, and Authority*, New York, Routledge, 2011.

Benjamin G. Thierry is Assistant Professor at Paris-Sorbonne University. He teaches media and technical history. He is a specialist in interactivity and computer interfaces from the 1960s. Recent publications include *Le Minitel, l'Enfance Numérique de la France* (The Minitel, the French Digital Childhood) (Nuvis, 2012), co-authored with Valérie Schafer.

Endah Triastuti is a researcher at the Communication Research Centre and a lecturer in Media Studies at the University of Indonesia. Her interests are in convergent media practices, including the anthropology of the media. Her current work is designing research-based policy to establish in broadband villages in disadvantaged areas throughout Indonesia for the Ministry of Telecommunications and ICT.

Riikka Turtiainen, Ph.D., University Lecturer, Digital Culture, University of Turku. Her doctoral thesis (defended in 2012) illustrated the multiplicity of the uses of digital technologies and services including games in the context of media sport. She has published multiple scholarly articles about digital media sports and online cultures, and specializes in online research ethics.

Andrew Whelan is a sociology lecturer at the University of Wollongong. He has written previously about "extreme" music and underground electronic music subcultures, sampling aesthetics and canonical samples, the cultural politics of digital media, Australian media regulation policy, peer-to-peer file-sharing, and online interaction about music. His work has been published in *First Monday*, *Sociological Research Online*, *Sites*, and the recent edited volumes *Music at the Extremes* (2015) and *Researching Music Censorship* (2016). He is co-editor of *Networked Music Cultures* (2016).

Ling Yang is Assistant Professor of Chinese at Xiamen University, P.R. China. She is the author of *Entertaining the Transitional Era: Super Girl Fandom and the Consumption of Popular Culture* (China Social Sciences Press, 2012) and the co-editor of *Fan Cultures: A Reader* (Peking University Press, 2009). She has published on Chinese fan culture, popular culture, and Web literature in both English and Chinese.

Lin Yi-Ren is a doctoral student at the Graduate School of Interdisciplinary Information Studies, University of Tokyo. Originally trained in economics and sociology, he is now focusing on media studies with a sociological perspective, and is currently writing a Ph.D. dissertation on Taiwanese Internet users, their roles in the recent political power shift in Taiwan, and how they help form an emotional public culture. For more information, please visit http://villagersociety.info.

Hu Yong is Professor of Journalism and Communication at Peking University's School of Journalism and Communication. Prior to joining the academy, Professor Hu was a journalist, social activist, entrepreneur, and translator. He is a founding director of the Communication Association of China (CAC) and China New Media Communication Association (CNMCA). He is a member of the China Information Economics Society (CIES), and the World Economic Forum Global Agenda Council on Social Media, as well as the steering committee of the Chinese Internet Research Conference (CIRC). He is the author of 13 books, including *Network Politics: Contemporary Chinese Society and Media Options for Action* (National School of Administration Press, 2014).

Haiqing Yu is Senior Lecturer in Contemporary Chinese Media and Culture at the University of New South Wales, Australia. Haiqing is the author of *Sex in China*, with Elaine Jeffreys (Polity, 2015) and *Media and Cultural Transformation in China* (Routledge, 2009). Her research covers two broad disciplines: media studies and cultural/sociological studies, focusing on the political economy of digital media and communication in China, contemporary Chinese youth culture and sexuality, and social movements. Haiqing has published widely in these areas in refereed academic journals.

Baohua Zhou is a professor and Assistant Dean at the School of Journalism, Fudan University. He is Director of the New Media Communication Master's program and Associate Director of the Media and Public Opinion Research Centre at Fudan University. He was a visiting scholar at the University of Pennsylvania. He was awarded the Changjiang Young Scholar by the Ministry of Education of China. His research focuses on digital media, media effects, and public opinion. His current research projects include social differentiation, media use, and citizenship engagement in China; ICTs and migrants workers; social media and journalism; and public opinion on social media, among others. His research has been published in the *Asian Journal of Communication*, the *Chinese Journal of Communication*, *Communication & Society*, and various communication journals in China.

ACKNOWLEDGEMENTS

We thank the Australian Research Council (ARC) for the award of a Discovery grant, *Internet History in Australia and the Asia-Pacific* (DP1092878), of which this volume is a key output. We are very grateful to Emily van der Nagel for her excellent editorial assistance in the preparation of the manuscript. It has been our pleasure to once again work with the talented and consummate publishing professionals at Routledge. Special thanks to Erica Wetter for her commissioning of the project and thoughtful feedback, and also to Simon Jacobs and Mia Moran for all their help.

INTRODUCTION

Global Coordinates of Internet Histories

Gerard Goggin and Mark McLelland

Nearly five decades since the Internet's official launch in 1969, its historical study is finally gathering momentum. As this book appears, so too does a new scholarly journal devoted to the area entitled *Internet Histories*.[1] Other markers of development include several significant edited volumes and journal special issues, many more academic papers, and dedicated book-length studies. In the spirit of the medium, and the emergence of digital humanities and social sciences, and associated e-research, we can also point to growing digital resources, online history sites, resources, archives, and data sets.

Arguably, however, it is still the case that available Internet histories in the anglophone world have predominately focused on North American or European experiences, and then only some aspects of these. For instance, scholarly work on the early history of the Internet in the United States has been established for some time. In her *Inventing the Internet*, Janet Abbate charts the origin of the Internet, especially through the ARPANET, and how the technology developed in conjunction with its meanings (Abbate 1999). Patrice Flichy takes up the heyday of 1990s US cyberculture, best symbolized by the avidly read *Wired Magazine* (Flichy 2007). In his *From Counterculture to Cyberculture: Stewart Brand, the Whole Earth Network, and the Rise of Digital Utopianism*, Fred Turner explores the linking of military-industrial research culture with counterculture in the emergence of computer networks and digital cultures—something that developed long before the Internet appears publicly (Turner 2006: 9). William Aspray and Paul E. Ceruzzi's edited volume *The Internet and American Business* (2008) brings together perspectives on important trajectories in the design and use of the Internet by American business.

Research on Internet histories is still emerging in European countries. The Oxford Internet Institute was founded in the UK in 2001, and has been an important center supporting research into European and global Internet cultures. Elsewhere, a pioneering European figure in Internet histories is Niels Brügger, having instigated an important case study of Web history in Denmark (see Brügger, this volume) and inaugurating the area of Web histories (Brügger 2010, 2013; Burns and Brügger 2012; Brügger 2016a, 2016b; Brügger and Schroeder 2016; Brügger this volume; Brügger *et al.* 2017). Other leading figures include: French researchers, such as Valérie Schafer (Schafer and Tuy 2013), Benjamin Thierry (Schafer and Thierry 2012), and Camille Paloque-Berges (Masutti and Paloque-Berges 2013) (also with chapters in this volume); researchers at the University of London, such as Jane Winters leading the Big UK Domain Data for the Arts and Humanities (BUDDAH; http://buddah.projects.history.ac.uk/) project which will generate a history of the UK Web; and researchers from the University of Amsterdam's Digital Methods Initiative, including Anat Ben-David (2010, 2012, 2016), Anne Helmond (2015), and Ester Weltevrede (Weltevrede and Helmond 2012), not to mention Richard Rogers's germinal book *Digital Methods* (Rogers 2013). There is as yet, however, no comparative survey of Internet histories across the European Union, although there are many local case studies.

When it comes to histories of the Internet in other countries and regions, especially systematic, scholarly histories, there are few. In many countries, technical and technology expert communities strongly affiliated with the Internet, especially those actors in organizations such as the Internet Society, or governance bodies such as the Internet Corporation for Assigned Names and Numbers (ICANN), were the first to contribute participant histories, and encouraged or sponsored institutional histories. We have few published book-length accounts available that focus upon countries outside the US or Europe (China and Korea being exceptions – for instance, Zhou 2006 and Lee 2012), and even fewer, if any, multi-country, comparative studies that focus on network history. The first insights about the histories of diverse careers of the Internet internationally came from the many studies that focus upon the Internet in particular countries (for instance, many of the volumes published in Steve Jones's excellent *Digital Formations* series, published by Peter Lang). In offering accounts of the Internet in particular settings, scholars inevitably need to grapple with the specific characteristics of the local or regional Internet—even if only to relate these to the "received" histories of the global Internet. There is also a second wave of research from the various scholarly disciplines that, for some time, have had to grapple with the Internet, because it has become central to the dynamics of media, communications, culture, and technology across so many parts of the world (for instance, Bruijn and van Dijk 2012; van Dijck 2013). So the widening body of research on, for instance, countries across every region, including the "Global South", has drawn our attention to the ways that the Internet is developing internationally when it comes to Web 2.0, social media, mobile Internet, as well as other data technologies and infrastructures (for instance, see Donner 2015).

However, although there are some studies written in the local languages that look at the early development of the Internet in nations outside of North America and Europe, these have not been translated into English, nor are they generally referenced in English-language scholarship about the histories of the Internet in these countries. Japan is a particular case in point. Despite having a rich literature about early BBS and Internet culture in Japanese, dating back to Shumpei Kumon's groundbreaking 1988 *Nettowāku Shakai* [The Network Society], commentary in English about Japan's adoption of Internet communication throughout the 1990s was largely reliant on accounts of Americans either living in or visiting Japan who necessarily had particular preconceptions about what networked communications should look like (see McLelland's chapter in this volume). Although from the early 2000s especially, there was pioneering scholarship available in English on Japanese computer technology (Gottlieb 2000), cybercultures (Gottlieb and McLelland 2003), and mobile media (Ito *et al.* 2005), real gaps still remain—in the research, as well as the ways in which it is acknowledged and taken up in the nascent field. In general, this lack of reference to local histories is a significant stumbling block, given the recognition of the importance of understanding communications, media, digital technology, and culture in genuinely international, global contexts. As Internet histories mature as a discipline, we can expect to see existing early accounts of Internet cultures in non-Euro-American contexts substantially revised as first-hand accounts in the local languages are made more available.

Against this backdrop of burgeoning research on, and interest concerning, Internet histories, this chapter introduces the particular angle and contribution of this reference work—the imperative to grasp the *global* character of Internet histories.

Internet History as Media History

The area of Internet histories has been frustratingly slow to develop and gain acceptance—at least, in the eyes of those of us involved in it. It can sensibly be contended that the Internet has still very much been under construction, and, like other communication and media forms, and technologies also, the grounds, warrants, and necessities of doing histories simply take time.

After all, newspaper and press histories might be relatively well-established now, but will not be exhausted for some time to come. Not only is the press itself complex and compelling—even if its demise is regularly predicted—but it holds great significance for wider histories. A good recent example of an area of histories really hitting its straps is television history. Television is a medium that has had several decades' development. The infrastructure that enables research has been slowly built up—private collections and archives, now being supplemented by popular and commercial archiving. Concepts, methods, and approaches have diversified, and programs of research are well underway.

There are many other examples of contiguous forms, not least computing. There has been a strong interest in history among those engaged in computing, information science, information technology disciplines, science and technology studies, including historians. This interest has resulted in a strong set of resources and supports, including dedicated scholarly and professional groups, prizes, awards, and bursaries, significant collections and archives, and evolving, distributed expertise with a widening pool of interested researchers developing the field and maintaining the momentum. It also includes significant journals, including *IEEE Annals of the History of Computing*,[2] and *Information & Culture: A Journal of History*.[3]

Not all Internet research occurs in universities alone. Rather like the Bell Labs in the heyday of the telephone, or the US Defense Advanced Research Projects Agency (DAPRA) or Japanese Nippon Telegraph and Telephone Corporation (NTT) in the histories of Internet and mobiles (Goggin *et al.* 2016), in contemporary Internet research, significant, high-value research is being produced and circulated by researchers in leading industry research labs—notably, Microsoft Labs and Intel Corporation. Yet many aspects of the Internet are not the subject of such industrially and commercially supported research; for instance, communities of use that developed around certain applications may differ from the ways in which the technology was intended to be deployed by its designers or sponsors (as we see in McLelland's chapter on early computer networking in Japan, Jo's chapter on early online culture in South Korea, and Schafer and Thierry's chapter on the Minitel in France).

Histories of the telephone and telecommunications are another useful example. Here work is more dispersed, not as systematically brought together and nurtured, and, since the deregulation of telecommunications in the 1980s and 1990s, the funding and impetus from the industry has dried up. Nonetheless, important studies have been undertaken, across various disciplines, including history, economics, law, sociology, and communications (Moyal 1984; Fischer 1992; Rens 2001; Hills 2007). As yet, however, there has been little systematic work on histories of mobile communications, especially in a global context (Agar 2003), although there is a wide range of work by scholars charting the evolution of mobile communication (such as the chapter here on mobiles in Myanmar/Burma by Rich Ling and collaborators). This work is particularly important given that it is via mobile phones (increasingly smartphones) that hundreds of millions of people around the world have their only or primary access to the Internet, something underscored by the 2015 Internet Society's report on the *Mobile Evolution and Development of the Internet* (Internet Society 2015).

What is most surprising is that the well-established area of communication and media histories has taken a while to include Internet histories on their roster of research interests. Partly, this is to do with the vibrancy of the technology itself that is undergoing constant change and development, with new and significant applications appearing regularly that require analysis and interpretation. As new applications and content appear at a rapid pace, existing applications and content are being revised or deleted. As Brügger points out in his chapter, the archiving of Web sources is full of challenges, not least the impossibility of capturing and preserving all the hyperlinks that comprise the dense and highly intertextual "content" of a page at any specific point in time. For example, a media historian wanting to give an account of the important role that the GeoCities Web hosting service played in familiarizing the first generation of public Internet users with the affordances of a personal home page would have difficulty in accessing all the 38 million web pages reportedly available when the service was finally closed down in 2009 (Shechmeister 2009)—despite efforts made to archive these sites.

Another issue that bedevils Internet histories—and, to an extent, constitutes a general problematic in general media history—revolves around the definition of the medium. In its relatively short lifespan, the Internet has supported a wide range of uses and applications. We wouldn't be the first to point out that the term "the Internet" is used to indicate many things. The best recurrent definition remains the technical stipulation: that the Internet revolves around a protocol at the heart of the technology as a system—that is, the layers, elements, and applications pertaining to the TCP/IP (Transmission Control Protocol/Internet Protocol). What the Internet used to look like was relatively easy to determine—from a conventional view of technology history, at least—when the focus was upon its invention and launch in the context of a limited number of institutions, sectors, countries, and societal groups from the 1960s through to the mid-1980s. Here, recourse to histories of computing, and telecommunications infrastructure and governance, has been the reflex response and often most relevant. With the Internet's popular uptake from the early to mid-1990s, we are confronted with trying to understand a new media form, with an increasingly decisive effect upon what we understand media to be, and do. Surely, the Internet has arrived *as* media. And so media history needs to grapple with the Internet, as a media form worthy of study alongside histories of speech, the press, cinema, radio, television, and so on.

The process of Internet histories being acknowledged as a bona fide part of media history is a work in progress. As the Internet is comparatively recent as media, and so its specialized historical study is in its infancy, so too are the particular conceptual, methodological, and archival challenges involved in its study. Here those undertaking Internet histories have an opportunity to learn from, and indeed deploy and inter-mix, other kinds of media histories. For example, when we consider the rise and rise of the Internet from the late 1980s, we are confronted with a bewildering array of technologies, applications, formats, and uses. True, the TCP/IP still can be used to rule in and out what is and is not the Internet—or so it might seem. With developments such as the Internet of Things, or the hybridity of the Internet's intersections with wireless, mobile, broadcast, sensor, and other networks and technologies, however, the decision about what kinds of Internet, and what particular histories matter for these, becomes all important.

A further problem is that dominant notions of the Internet, like those of media or culture generally, are still modelled on a limited range of experiences, deployments, and conceptions of the Internet, largely based on the perspectives of Anglophone users, especially North Americans, who featured prominently among early pioneers (as well as some European nations). The cultural, linguistic, and social values of such anglophone users have had a strong influence—even in the inscription of such values at the level of technical protocols, as in the centrality of English to domain names, for instance. At the present time, however, English is already a minority language on the Internet, with the rapid rise of Chinese, Japanese, Korean, Spanish, Russian, and other language communities figuring heavily in the development and domestication of various Internet technologies, applications, and cultures. Consequently, as the field of Internet histories constitutes itself, we argue that it must be born—or at least, rebirthed—global in scope.

Internet Histories—Born Global?

To some extent, Internet technology is different from other media forms such as the newspaper, radio, cinema, and television that originated in multiple national settings and experienced several decades of development before becoming a part of global circuits of communication. The history of film is a case in point, with independent film industries arising in England, Germany, France, and the United States around the same time at the end of the nineteenth century. The early history of the Internet is, however, very much tied up with innovations in the United States due to the role played by the US military in funding the necessary infrastructure that provided the backbone for computer networks. For many nations (but not all—Japan and France being exceptions), the beginning of computer networks involved signing up for a connection with the infrastructure already established in the US. This necessarily required those nations, as well as computer manufacturers based outside the US, to accept the protocols and terms of use already established there. Although there had been independent national computer networks set up in the early 1980s in countries such as France (see Schafer and Thierry in this volume), Japan (see McLelland in this volume), as well as the non-Internet-based computer networks of the US (Aspray and Ceruzzi 2008; Carey and Elton 2010), these systems were superseded when connections to the international Internet became available at the close of that decade. It is therefore understandable that early histories of the Internet have focused on developments in the US, and that many histories of the Internet outside of North America have emphasized these first connections with the US technological backbone in their own local histories.

We often forget that unlike early film, which was silent and able to be subtitled for diverse audiences, in the late 1980s and early 1990s, the vast majority of material available on the Internet was in the English language and hence mainly of interest to those university-based scholars and computer hobbyists who were the early adopters in non-anglophone countries. English remained the predominant language on the Internet until the late 1990s, when its percentage of overall language use was reduced by the rapid upsurge in Japanese-, Spanish-, and Chinese-speaking users. The preference for English was not simply an artefact of the technology's cultural antecedents in the US, but was also built into the very computer code necessary in order to input and display text. The American Standard Code for Information Exchange (ASCII) originally developed in 1963 provided only for the input and display of the Roman alphabet, and the numerals and punctuation marks associated with English. The input of specialized diacritics and the accommodation of non-Roman alphabets, and especially character-based scripts such as Chinese and Japanese, was a significant problem that took another two decades of research and innovation to overcome (see, for example, the discussion in Charles Ess's chapter on "ASCII imperialism"). It is still somewhat astonishing that the QWERTY keyboard—originally developed to avoid the jamming of commonly occurring letter combinations in English words (such as "th" and "st") in nineteenth-century typewriters—is *still* the main human/computer interface even in countries like Japan where the Roman alphabet is not used for daily communication. The very close connection between language (including writing systems) and culture means that certain nations were better placed than others to take advantage of early Internet networks, pointing to the fact that a technology is never neutral in its design and application. A global history of Internet technologies, then, cannot assume the neutrality of technology, but needs to address local cultural and social conditions from the beginning.

The main point of this reference work, then, is to consolidate the proposition that to understand the Internet, especially, research needs to embrace, respond to, study, and be in long, deep dialogue with the local factors that informed the early uptake of Internet technology in diverse locations and that continue to structure and shape the Internet cultures of different nations and language communities even today. Internet histories have global coordinates that are simultaneously located in the local and particular; without understanding this diversity, we have, at best, an incomplete picture. This volume aims to guide and stimulate a radical expansion of Internet histories, across a wider range of global, international, and comparative dimensions. The reason for this is not simply because this will mean better, more accurate, and richer histories. It is also because such histories will help us gain a deeper understanding of the Internet itself. Developing a better sense of global Internet histories, our argument goes, will equip us for understanding the uses and abuses of history in understanding the Internet at the present time, and in the future. Hence, this collection continues a developing theme in Internet research: the need to understand the technology and its cultures in an international perspective.

Internationalizing Internet Studies

The interdisciplinary field of Internet studies and research is now in its third decade (Jones 1999; Consalvo and Ess, 2011; Dutton 2013). It has attracted researchers from across the world, and has been centered, especially, in North America, and, increasingly, Europe. IR1, the first conference of the Association of Internet Research (AoIR; http://aoir.org/), was held in Lawrence, Kansas, in 2000, under the rubric of *The State of the Interdiscipline*. With two Asia-Pacific exceptions, IR7: Internet Conferences (Brisbane, Australia, 2006), and IR15 (Daegu, Korea, 2014), the venues for the 18 IR conferences between 2000 and 2017 have been located in the US (7 in total); Europe (5); UK, still officially part of the EU at the time of writing (2); and Canada (2). In many ways, Internet research as a field has been open and welcoming to perspectives and research on the Internet from across different countries, languages, and cultures. Yet often still, the framing—for instance, at the AoIR conferences—is centered in US, European, and anglophone perspectives (we say this, noting that Australians have loomed large in the development and identity of Internet research, not least with Matthew Allen's founding of the first Internet studies program at Curtin University in 1999). Most of the participants in Internet research, and IR, belong to multiple scholarly communities and associations, so would bring other experiences and repertoires for exchanging internationally.

Mindful of the anglophone bias in much early reporting on Internet cultures, in 2009 we published our volume *Internationalizing Internet Studies: Beyond Anglophone Paradigms* (Goggin and McLelland 2009), to accent and support the multicultural, multilingual, and international plurality of work in Internet research. This earlier collection built upon a body of other work on the relationship between language and technology (in relation to the Internet, notably Danet and Herring 2007), theorization of the strong links between culture and technology (by which we mean productive links, as opposed to the prevalent view in many publics that some kind of unitary and backward "culture" of non-Western others is the great obstacle blocking technology), and research on the international dimensions of Internet technology (Hunsinger, Klastrup, and Allen 2010).

The "internationalizing" turn is well established now and has its limitations as well as advantages. It sits alongside—uneasily at times—approaches such as "de-Westernizing", "post-colonial", "cosmopolitan", and others. However, as it is approached, in recent years the genie is well and truly out of the bottle when it comes to Internet research. We could point to the complex rise of the emerging powers such as China and India, in particular; the return of Russia; the various resurgences of other parts of the world—if it's not the "Chinese Century", then it's the "Asia Century", needing a pivot towards "Asia Pacific" (for the United States); or it's the "Latin American Century", "Africa Rising", the rise and waning of the "BRICS", and the continuing pivotal importance and development of the Arab world, among other regions. Slogans aside, it is evident that there is a long, sustained process underway of geopolitical, as well as intraregional, intranational, subnational, and diasporic reconfiguration. This poses many challenges as well as fabulous opportunities for Internet research.

A key challenge lies in the organization of research and universities internationally, and their economies for undertaking, valuing, and rewarding research and researchers (and building infrastructure). For some time, universities have been orienting themselves around "competing" in a global marketplace, especially for students, but also for research funding, prestige, and influence. National systems, still decisive on many, if not most, universities, have deepened their reliance on a relatively small number of research quality and esteem indicators. These tend to assume English as *the* global language of scientific diffusion and exchange. The best known journal lists are the Thomson Reuters Web of Science journal rankings, joined by Scopus, and, more recently, the Google Scholar list. In all of these, most of the journals accepted for ranking use the English language. This English dominance is being increasingly challenged, with major scholarly associations responding to imperatives to internationalize. The International Communication Association (ICA) has sought to move beyond its North American heartland to become genuinely international, holding regional ICA conferences in Latin America, Asia, and elsewhere; and has undertaken an initiative to endorse and support two journals in Chinese and German respectively, as part of its prestigious stable of scholarly publications. For its part, the International Association of Media and Communications Research (IAMCR), as signaled by its founding association with the UN's UNESCO, has long been committed to multilingual, genuinely cosmopolitan research, especially driven by its "majority world" members—though it too struggles with the practical and material difficulties of holding conferences in its three official languages (French, Spanish, English), as well as its conference hosts, let alone the various languages of its members— many of whom do continue to operate and publish in journals and presses in languages other than the dominant European languages, little recognized outside their communities and spheres of influence. There is also rich existing practice in different areas of research (for instance, area studies, or particular tendencies such as Inter-Asia Cultural Studies, where inter- and cross-cultural approaches and frameworks, as well as multilingual, multiscript publishing efforts, are common).

This backdrop is largely taken for granted. There are many who would argue that universities have been eminently cosmopolitan, global institutions, where research—especially in the age of the Internet—is undertaken, circulated, and drawn upon by teams and communities distributed around the world, using whatever languages come to hand. We agree with this vision, but there are many little noticed or discussed gaps, losses, labor, and terms of agreement at play here. When it comes to the Internet in particular, lack of acknowledgement and working through of the global coordinates of Internet histories means we have a highly impoverished, or at least partial sense of what the Internet has meant, and what it might become.

What we seek to do through this *Global Internet Histories* Companion is provide a challenge to the conception of "the Internet" as a "deterritorialized" technology, via chapters that offer detailed, comparative histories of how the Internet has actually developed in strategically important nations and regions. As Ito points out, technologies are not universal; rather, it is necessary to attend to "the heterogeneous co-constitution of technology across a transnational stage" (Ito *et al.* 2005: 7). Thus the Internet should, in fact, be understood in relation to different cultures of use, which are very much influenced by language, culture, and geographical location. Our hypothesis is that once such a detailed, variegated picture of the Internet is assembled, it will be possible to achieve a deeper appreciation of the technology's global or international character, via what might be called its "glocal" (or global/local) imaginaries. As this Companion illustrates, "global Internet histories" is a handy term for enriching, expanding, integrating, and catalyzing a wide range of resources, inquiries, concepts, and conversations about the Internet.

We often fail to acknowledge and appreciate that Internet histories that have been written are circulated and put into use in framing and imagining the Internet. Strangely, people have done and are doing Internet histories, not just in the English language. So, a foundational task, across Internet, media, communications, culture, and technology research, is translation of such "missing narratives" (Campbell-Kelly and Garcia-Swartz 2013). In this volume, although our lack of resources has meant that we have only been able to arrange translation of one chapter, we have sought out where possible scholars who work in the language of the country or area they specialize in. These authors draw on, present, and translate scholarship in languages other than English, helping make available the vocabularies and worldviews of groups, communities, and publics not figuring prominently, if at all, in existing Internet histories research.

Overview of the Volume

One advantage of the Companion model is the scope that it provides for gathering together a comparatively large number of specific area studies and for getting the chapters in conversation with each other. To encourage the reading of specific chapters alongside other cognate chapters we have organized the contents across seven broad thematic areas.

Chapters in Part 1, *Framing Concepts and Approaches*, explore some of the problems, methods, biases, and ethical issues that arise when researching the diverse histories of the Internet. Authors deploy a high degree of methodological and epistemological self-consciousness in elucidating the points of contact and divergence that arise when Internet applications are taken up and integrated into specific local contexts. **Robin Mansell**, for instance, considers how different "social imaginaries" surrounding what the Internet means or signifies affect key government or industry players whose decisions impact on the roll-out and governance of the technology. Yet an Internet history that focuses solely on these key players overlooks the multiple ways in which technology is reimagined by its various stakeholders; instead, she encourages us to account for how individuals imagine themselves as active agents and not simply as users of a technology. Also drawing attention to the manner in which cultural framings of technology are important is key to the ways the Internet is appropriated and understood, **Charles Ess** in his chapter looks at how Internet research has been framed in the CATaC (Cultural Attitudes towards Technology and Communication) conference series since 1998. Pointing to a tendency, particularly in studies based in the United States, that tend to rely on information available in a single language (English), he notes how holding the first CATaC conference in Oslo, Norway, forced the US participants to consider aspects of Internet configuration that proved a problem for local participants. This included the fact that three common Norwegian vowel sounds (ø, æ, å) were not available in the ASCII script of the time, requiring Norwegians to transliterate their own names in order to become visible on Internet search engines.

Nishant Shah provides a panorama of Internet histories in India, drawing on the landmark project he led, supported by the Bangalore-based Centre for Internet & Society. Reflecting upon a number of these histories, Shah offers provocative and rich reflections concerning Internet historiographies. Shah proposes three entry points for approaching the history of Internets in India, which are also extremely productive for thinking about Internets globally: body, affect, and the state in transition. Shah observes that to "write the history of the Internet in India is to write the history of India", a lapidary formula that resonates across the striations of global Internet histories.

Niels Brügger, in his chapter, looks at the difficulties of content archiving on the Internet, taking as his example efforts in Denmark to archive the entire national .dk web domain. As he points out, web pages are entirely unlike traditional media such as books or films, because they are made up of hyperlinks that result in a dense "strata" rather than a single medium. Yet, as he argues, the establishment of such archives is necessary not just for understanding past Web developments, but for gaining an enhanced understanding of what is happening on the Web today.

Part 2, *Rethinking Internet Evolution*, offers a set of perspectives on how we approach and understand the unfolding of the Internet, drawing our attention to the need to construe and situate narratives of the technology's development with precision and care. **Valérie Schafer and Benjamin G. Thierry** take up the fabled case of the French Minitel system, often presented as the alternative to North American commercial visions of computer networking. Schafer and Thierry offer a fascinating discussion of the parallel, entwined, and yet distinct ways in which the French development of the Internet threaded its ways in and out of the kinds of technical systems, ecosystems, business models, and uses that were associated with Minitel. Charting the "multiple reversals" at play in visions of Minitel and the Internet respectively, they conclude, *inter alia*, that time "will tell whether this Internet Minitelisation is only a fleeting moment in the evolution of digital economies, or a lasting model initiated by the Minitel and brilliantly promoted by Apple some years after".

Nicholas John follows on with a detailed study of the emergence of the Internet Service Provider (ISP) in Israel, a very interesting case given the country's reputation as a high-tech pioneer. John discusses the ways in which particular actors in this process had very different ideas concerning the Internet, as well as distinctive ideas about the "Israeliness" of the Israel context. Drawing on the work of Pierre Bourdieu, John argues that this period was exemplified by overlapping elements: the shift from "technological capital" to purely "economic capital"; the productive tension between the "local habitus" and "global field", as investment came in from overseas interests and members of Israel's economic elite. In dialogue with accounts of the Brazilian Internet (see Davis *et al.*'s chapter), John contends that we cannot "take the arrival of the Internet to new countries for granted, thereby resisting a simple deterministic narrative . . . and second, we recognize the place of struggles between different institutional bodies in shaping the Internet". Invoking Mansell's notion of imaginaries (see her chapter in this volume), John argues that "the range of possible imaginaries available to social actors (and, indeed, researchers) is a function of their social and cultural positioning".

This point is borne out in **Fernando Gutiérrez**'s chapter on the evolution of the Internet in Mexico. As Gutiérrez shows, universities were pivotal in early connection, but a crucial moment came with one of the most famous and best known examples of Internet appropriation anywhere—that of the Zapatista National Liberation Army (EZLN), taking its struggles online on 1 January 1994, including a website while hosted in a US university which achieved great notoriety and visibility in Mexico. Mexico's "Year of the Internet" in 1995 saw the prestigious *La Jornada* newspaper establish itself on the Web, and a boom underway that also engaged Mexican governments and civil society in the project of building infrastructure and extending access. Drawing on data from the World Internet Survey, Gutiérrez discusses the paradoxes of connection and connectivity in a country riven by notable inequalities, where such uneven patterns of knowledge, capacity, and use sit alongside deepening diffusion, innovation, and significance of the Internet in a dynamic, redefinition of Mexican media and culture.

Stuart Davis, Joe Straubhaar, Martha Fuentes-Bautista, and Jeremiah Spence provide another Latin American case study, drawn from the contrasting case of Brazil. Davis *et al.* dissect the social shaping of the Brazilian Internet, arguing that here "ICT diffusion was largely driven by creative innovations in diffusion from below by NGOs who sought to create new forms of access to the Internet to fulfill demand by users". However, as they point out "these efforts were heavily influenced by national policies regarding public access, liberalization of regulations governing the national telecommunications market, as well as attempts by private corporations vying for consumer access".

In the final chapter in Part 2, we shift to Eastern Europe, with **Katarzyna Kamińska-Korolczuk and Barbara Kijewska**'s fascinating comparative account of the evolution of the Internet in Poland and Estonia, in the period when both countries gained independence from the Soviet Union and sought to re-establish free media systems. They note that "[y]oung generations are today rooted in the network that they use in their private, social, and professional lives"; however, that it is "difficult to predict whether the increase in the number of users will translate into the increase in trust in the use of the Internet in the process of strengthening of civil society". Here, distinct approaches can be discerned between Poland, where caution concerning the Internet's societal role is especially a concern, and Estonia, where Kamińska-Korolczuk and Kijewska note that "Estonians saw in the development of innovative technologies the chance to strengthen their sovereignty".

In Part 3, *Early Computer Networks, Technology, and Culture*, chapters consider specific case studies of pre-Internet and early Internet computer-mediated communications systems in order to shed light on how the experience of these early adopters helped shape mainstream roll-out of Internet technologies in specific locations. Given that "the Internet" is so often spoken of as a "global" and "deterritorialized" technology, it might be supposed that specific cultures of use can be replicated anywhere that has Internet connectivity. Yet as the case of BBS reveals, this is often not so. What Internet technologies are available and preferred depends upon cultural factors, including language use, as well as market and policy factors such as government regulation, competition, and pricing.

Camille Paloque-Berges looks at a revealing and little known part of the French Internet story, the development from 1983 onwards of Fnet, an informal infrastructure, dedicated to supporting the open Unix-based communication networks. As Paloque-Berges notes, Fnet was a kind of "shadow infrastructure"—"an informal, experimental, and unacknowledged network of machines annexed to the existing telecom network, as well as a network of peers using and rerouting public resources from the academic world". As such, it elicited many of the qualities attributed later to the guiding spirits of the Internet, such as those of being "[o]pen, decentralized, collaborative, heterogeneous, and worldwide".

In his chapter, **Mark McLelland** looks at the social and cultural shifts that had to take place in Japan before the use of computers for the input, display, and communication of the Japanese language could be widely accepted. Japan's highly complicated and hybrid writing system initially proved difficult to input and transmit via CMC. The fact that early BBS systems were pioneered by different computer companies (and not the government) meant that different companies offering "personal computer communication" developed their own protocols. This led to a series of proprietary "intranets" where up to a million Japanese users first gained exposure to the affordances of CMC in their native language. In the early 1990s, the preponderance of English on the Internet, the fact that some familiarity with English was necessary to connect with overseas servers and high dial-up charges meant that accessing the Internet was seen as having little application for most users in Japan. In addition, the relatively low penetration rate of personal computers meant that Internet use in Japan did not accelerate rapidly until the release of Internet-enabled cellphones in the late 1990s.

In their chapter, **Li Shao Liang, Lin Yi-Ren and Arthur Hou-ming Huang** also stress the importance of an early BBS phase for the development of Internet cultures in Taiwan. Similar to the situation in Japan, early CMC networks were not supported by government initiatives but developed by small groups of computer hobbyists and early adopters on university campuses. Unlike the slow dial-up options offered in Japan, however, from 1992 Taiwanese university connections were offered using a TCP/IP model that allowed many more users to access the system at the same time and at faster speeds. The fact that Taiwanese universities offered students free access to these services via their campus dormitories and recruited administrative staff from among the student body enabled the BBS networks to expand rapidly among the student body. The large scale of student participation in these networks encouraged the use of the BBS system for social activism, a characteristic that remains constant today.

Dongwon Jo's chapter investigates the first public e-mail service in Korea, H-mail, provided in 1987 by the Korea Data Communications Corporation (DACOM), and examines how the contentious relations between the technology provider and its users set the stage for early online activism, prefiguring features of Korea's present-day Internet culture that sees high levels of user activism even in the face of state surveillance.

From East Asian studies, we move to Turkey, where **Ivo Furman** provides an engrossing study of the vibrant bulletin board system (BBS) ecology centered around the *Hi! Türkiye* Network (known colloquially as Hitnet), which had its heyday between 1992 and 1996. Spanning the nation, Hitnet was based on Fidonet network protocols, and as Furman explains: "Although BBS communication networks rapidly disappeared with the arrival of the Internet, early BBS users were the first in Turkey to engage in networked publications and experienced long-distance collaboration via electronic communication". Furman's account shows how such BBS pioneers and users played a key and enduring role in shaping local Internet communication ecologies in Turkey.

Chapters in Part 4, *Imagining Community via the Internet*, look at how the Internet and its affordances have allowed users to imagine community in the context of specific language and national communities. The case studies point to how the paths of Internet adoption have been multiple and divergent—China being a relatively early adopter in Asia where users made a switch from PC-based to mobile devices, whereas in Bhutan and Papua New Guinea, where the Internet was introduced much later, the majority of those accessing Internet applications have been via mobile devices. Understanding the state of existing communications systems in a society prior to the adoption of Internet technology is vital in accounting for the meanings given to this emergent technology among users as well as across local media including government reports, science journalism, popular journalism, and advertising.

Part 4 opens with **Anissa Daoudi**'s reflections on the rise of e-Arabic. Daoudi's chapter is significant as her description of how Arabic works reveals a situation unfamiliar to most native English speakers, wherein two distinct varieties of the same language exist within the same language community but are used for different purposes. Known as diglossia, there are high status (grammatically more complex and often used in writing) and colloquial versions of Arabic (in addition to local dialects). Hence, alongside coding differences for the input and display of the distinctive script, the use of Arabic as a means of informal written communication via computers was not a straightforward proposition. Daoudi outlines the gradual development of a third linguistic form that she terms e-Arabic that involves both orthographic as well as hybrid dialect transformations, including borrowings from other languages. This has led to tensions between largely younger, online users and older cultural gatekeepers who see this new dialect as incorrect and uncanonical. Daoudi argues that this "new" language form, which is not constrained by canonical language practices, has been instrumental in young people developing a voice and expressing their ideas and concerns.

Haiqing Yu in her chapter affirms that more can be learned about the Internet in China through a focus on how it has come to be conceived and understood by its everyday users than by a timeline of infrastructure, governance measures, and software roll-outs. Contrary to much negative reporting about the social and political situation in China, particularly a stress on the "Great Firewall", Yu points out how there is much optimism among Chinese people themselves about the future. She explains how narratives about the Internet and its capacity to break down hierarchical boundaries, share information, and build connections between people is a key part of this optimism, suggesting that impediments such as online censorship are evaluated differently by those inside and outside the People's Republic.

Rhys James Jones's chapter on how the early days of the Internet were represented in Welsh-language media takes us back to a time when there were strong fears that Internet technology, still very much associated with the United States, would further enhance the hegemony of the English language, especially at the expense of minority languages such as Welsh. Yet at the same time there was push-back against this claim by users who saw a great opportunity for CMC to connect Welsh speakers globally and thus enhance the use of the language—as was seen in the early translation into Welsh of key computer and Internet terms, a process also notable in the early days of the Korean Internet use (see Jo's chapter in this volume).

The Internet's impact on language practices is also a key issue picked up on in **Bunty Avieson**'s chapter on Bhutan. She notes that the introduction of the Internet in that country took place at a time when widespread democratizing changes were impacting on the media more generally. While access to print media is limited due to the fact that many local vernaculars do not have a written form, the introduction of CMC, usually via mobile devices, has opened up new ways of connecting via voice—an illiterate farmer only needs to learn how to navigate apps via a few basic icons in order to connect up with other users. The affordances for text communication, too, have served as an incentive for users to familiarize themselves with Roman script which they use to transliterate and communicate in the local language.

Sarah Logan and Joseph Suwamaru, in their chapter on Papua New Guinea (PNG), point out that although slow dial-up connections were available between some PNG educational institutions and university networks in Australia, it was not until deregulation of the mobile phone market in 2005 that accessibility rose from 3 percent to 80 percent of the population across the ensuing decade. As the authors point out, PNG is a largely oral society and the affordances of mobile Internet, particularly status updates via Facebook, have proven extremely popular. Facebook also provides a platform for the sharing of news in a media context lacking in any truly national outlets. Like PNG, Myanmar (Burma) is also a case where the Internet has only arrived very recently, and then preceded, paralleled, and, in important ways, interwoven with the mobile phone and mobile communication—and is the subject of **Rich Ling, Chitra Panchapakesan, Rajiv Aricat, Elisa Oreglia, and May O. Lwin**'s chapter. Ling *et al.* draw on studies of the adoption of mobile phones and digital access among the Myanmar people, to point to a highly significant phenomenon of the "digital imagination" in shaping images, meanings, knowledge, and potential uses of the Internet, even before people have an opportunity to experience it directly. Discussing the adoption and impact of mobiles among a range of business sectors and social groups —trishaw operators, rag pickers and scrap handlers, brick makers, an Indian Tamil enclave, and farmers—Ling *et al.* invoke digital imagination as a concept that "helps us to see how the adoption process draws on a set of insights, folklores, second-hand techniques, and cultural appropriations in their imagining of digital access".

Part 5, *Histories of Social Internets*, provides historical perspectives on one of the defining characteristics of early twenty-first-century developments—the global penetration of social networking systems and the emergence of social media. Chapters explore a range of local-language and fan- and community-based networking systems. In addition, to grasp the significance of an application's take-up requires an acknowledgement of the kind of already existing media cultures influential upon users, as well as the industry, policy, and social contexts, and the ways that imported—and local—technologies are domesticated. Takanori Tamura takes a historical perspective on human interaction in how the Internet comes to be imagined. Specifically, he explores the striking phenomenon of *self-narratives* (that is, talking about ourselves) via computer-mediated communication (CMC) in Japan, that take shape in the pre-Internet era. Tamura makes the case that communication on self-narratives on the pre-Internet domestic networks provided a context for later Web and social media developments. In particular, such narratives, and the earlier models of CMC, helped develop a defining sense of intimate citizenship that made possible the social movements that have emerged in the recent crises in Japan after the earthquake and nuclear power disasters in 2011.

Tim Highfield provides an indispensable history of blogging, which, as he remarks, now seems very old hat: "blogging's moment as an innovative and popular social medium—before 'social media' became a thing—seems, in Internet time, like the distant past". In his "brief sketch of the history of blogging, as platform, genre, and influence", Highfield argues that "the blogosphere was never just a space for talking about politics or celebrity gossip, or acting as an online version of personal diaries". Rather, he suggests that the

> history of blogging is part of the wider development of the mediasphere, for bloggers were not just bloggers, posting their own thoughts: they were readers of other blogs and media sources, commenting, linking to, and sharing other content, and using other platforms in addition to their own blogs.

For their part, **Jaakko Suominen, Petri Saarikoski, Riikka Turtiainen, and Sari Östman**'s chapter also opens up perspectives on histories of the present and future, with their archaeology of the various, largely forgotten, national Finnish social media services and platforms such as IRC-Galleria (a photo gallery whose majority of users were teenagers), Jaiku and Qaiku (microblogging services), and Vuodatus (a blog platform). Actually, national and regional social media platforms are very much alive and well in the complex global–local mix of contemporary Internets, and Finland, it should be remembered, played an important role in global Internet culture, as well as mobile phone cultures, with such technology experiments. Our three main examples show that there has been a need for national social media services, meaning Finnish developed platforms for Finnish users, in a relatively small country as well. Yet the trajectories, significance, and experience of the great diversity of social media platforms globally is something we still know little about. Suominen *et al.* suggest, for instance, that in their case study "what is difficult to estimate, is that the unique something 'Finnish' in these case services, and their life-cycles are not greatly comparable to large states or populated states such as China, Russia, South Korea, or Japan". As such, their call for "more comparative studies between similar types of national cases" is a point well made.

Baohua Zhou, Shihui Gui, Fumitoshi Kato, Kana Ohashi, and Larissa Hjorth in their chapter explore the very much alive and scaled-up cases of social media in two of the world's biggest markets, Japan and China. With special attention to convergent mobile messaging platforms, WeChat and LINE, Zhou *et al.* contrast two very different histories of the rise of the Internet, and its transformation into the smartphone phase. They suggest that the "development of the Internet in China took place in a rather staged way—from Web 1.0 . . . to Web 2.0", compared to Japan where "access to the Internet from both PC and mobile phones converged early thanks to the existence of *keitai*"; add to which the different roles that government played in incubating and promoting such Internet technology. Also focusing on the Chinese Internet, **Ling Yang** provides an account of the history, practices, and issues associated with Chinese online fan communities. Yang starts with the evolution of Internet platforms and technologies that have facilitated the formation and development of networked fan communities, such as bulletin board systems (BBS), Baidu Post Bar, Sina Weibo, and Tencent QQ, then discusses fansubbing (foreign-language media subtitled by fans) and shipping ("*peidui*" in Chinese, meaning "pairing" or "coupling" of celebrities or media characters in original stories), two Web-based practices that have far-reaching impacts on Chinese fan cultures and society at large. Yang argues that while such online fandoms provide agency, identity, and belonging, they also constitute a site of fierce contestations, often caused by gender-related issues and government censorship.

Part 6, *Internets and New Media Forms*, opens with **Christina Spurgeon**'s chapter providing a lucid and admirably concise overview of the main currents and dynamics of the global development of online advertising. In an area of particular need of extensive international research, Spurgeon issues a call for research to pay "greater attention to the influence of advertising in accounting for Internet history". With **Hayes Mawindi Mabweazara**'s chapter, we move to the African region, and the case of the evolution of Internet-based digital journalism and its associated research. Mabweazara's comprehensive and illuminating account offers an alternative understanding of how digital journalism and its research has taken shape and flourished quite apart from the dominant body of knowledge emerging from Western scholarship. In doing so, he shows that

> the history of Internet-based journalism, as well as research into the connections between the Internet and journalism in Africa, has in many ways taken the path of

research in other contexts outside journalism itself, which is largely characterized by mixed, and occasionally contradictory, opinions on the opportunities and challenges offered by the Internet in Africa.

Alisa Freedman's chapter looks at another media form, digital literature, as represented by the celebrated emergence of mobile phones and Internet novels in Japan. For Freedman, such Internet-based digital literature "reaffirmed, rather than undermined, the cultural significance of the print book in Japan and provided models for the commercialization of fan-produced culture worldwide". Moreover, what is evident in cellphone and Internet novels is the way that they capture and are driven by nascent "conventions of Japanese Internet use, including access patterns, visual languages, user identifications, and corporate tie-ins". Also pivotal is the way in which such Internet cultural developments "encouraged discussions about groups on the fringes of Japanese society, particularly delinquent girls and male *otaku* (avid fans of hobbies)".

César Albarrán-Torres offers a rare study of online gambling, with its complex locations and meanings, stretching from the Global South to the Global North. With a focus on the important case of Costa Rica, where online casinos were established in the early 2000s, Albarrán-Torres shows how gambling via the Internet needs to be understood as an instance where "longstanding cultural practices and industries adapted to online spaces, traversing spatial and jurisdictional borders". He pays close attention to these processes of adaptation, drawing our attention to the legal and labor issues that emerged from the expansion of online gambling practices in developed countries and the hosting of casino servers in developing nations—something he puts on the research agenda for the first time.

With **Andrew Whelan**'s chapter, we take up the vastly popular realm of music and the Internet. Rather than a remix of the usual themes, Whelan explicitly eschews "a standard sequential history of the emergence of digital music, or of the antecedent cultures of music production, distribution, and consumption on the Internet". Instead, Whelan's chapter works "around" some of the central dynamics and processes of music online—aiming to "highlight how the standard histories work to legitimate or obscure particular sets of concerns". In particular, Whelan focuses on two key dynamics: "configurations of practice around music sharing as a mediated social activity . . . longstanding, durable, and open to encounters with new distributive forms and formats"; "the sociability of digital audio [whereby] 'music online talks to itself', largely because, from its emergence, digital music has by design and affordance been miniature and open to manipulation and reassembly".

In the final chapter in Part 6, **Teodor Mitew and Christopher Moore** also take up an enormous area of Internet histories—games and play. Similarly to Whelan, they focus their efforts in a historiographic and theoretical vein, focusing on game spaces, game techniques, and game modalities as a "prism through which the historicity of Internet play is to be approached". They address the

> contention that the Internet has simultaneously facilitated the dematerialization of the physical copy associated with accessing games, and rematerialized play as investment in the new global market in a mix of official and unofficial channels of consumption, from licensed merchandising to fan-produced cosplay and other expressions of participatory media culture.

Mitew and Moore note that the

degree to which the technologies of the Internet, especially the diffusion of high-speed broadband Internet connections, have made new game spaces possible, including those for the reconfigurations of the modalities of play, is matched only by their enclosure within the formalized modes of industrial production, as beta-testers, mod-creators, community leaders, and so on.

In Part 7, *Publics, Politics, and Digital Societies*, the volume concludes with a set of chapters that register and evaluate issues about the health of the body politic that are highly prominent in debates and research on the Internet, yet where the understanding of how these are shaped by Internet histories is still largely absent. **Ilhem Allagui**'s chapter provides an overview and retrospective of the histories and roles of the Internet and associated digital media in the Arab region, where much recent attention has focused, especially in relation to democratic struggles. Allagui dissects the highlights of Internet history in the Arab region in relation to its social and political transformations, arguing that the celebrated uprisings are a construct of several *actors* and not *technologies*. Allagui notes that such "insurrections were the work of activists online and offline; those who survived and others who martyred themselves for their countries". Declaring that "people trusted that the 'revolutions' would carry on for themselves", Allagui observes that

> They did not. The technology is *enabling* and leading to collective actions in inconsistent ways. It enabled popular movements to overthrow authoritarian regimes, and is also now enabling the Mujahidin of the Islamic State (IS) to expand their troops and achieve the objectives of their socio-political agendas.

In her chapter, **Endah Triastuti** charts the emergence of Indonesia as a "digital nation". Triastuti examines the various factors that contributed to the ongoing development of the Internet in Indonesia. She especially draws our attention to the "circulations of power through media culture after the collapse of the authoritarian regime [of former President Suharto] especially in the era of ICTs". For Triastuti, "engagement with the Internet in Indonesia involves struggle, forms of appropriation, oppression, and resistance to the former regime's effort to impose the idea of the nation using traditional media such as radio and television".

Susana Salgado's chapter explores the Internet and political communication in the especially interesting and telling cases of the countries of Lusophone Africa: Angola, Cape Verde, Mozambique, and Sao Tome and Principe. With a common language, a historical background of Portuguese colonization, and varying claims to be "new democracies", Salgado's starting point is that these "four countries also share the particular feature of having started their democratization processes simultaneously with the worldwide expansion of the Internet". Salgado's chapter provides a very suggestive discussion of such online political communication opportunities in countries experiencing democratization processes, addressing the role of independent online news media outlets and blogs, as well as the use of the Internet in citizens' participation and political change.

Kwang-Suk Lee's chapter aims to provide an "integrative historical approach" to digital or e-resistance in South Korea, yoking together analysis of the "top-down historical engines driving technological futures—such as information technology (IT) policies, governmentality, market activities, and other power conditions influencing digital technologies"—as well as the "evolving phases of digital culture autonomously constructed by Internet users from below". Drawing attention to the subcultural histories of the Internet and activism in Korea, Lee explores Korean digital activism, highlighting how "political tension has existed between the codification of power and social influences". The Companion concludes with **Hu Yong**'s chapter on tracing the shift from *yulun* (public opinion) to *yuqing* (public intelligence) in the development of the Chinese Internet, and information management. In a powerful critique, Yong contends that the "operations of the *yuqing* monitoring system reflect the paradox of China's Internet management regime: there is more information available to average Internet users, but less authenticity on the real sentiments of the masses". He suggests that the "change of lexicon and practice from *yulun* to *yuqing* is a result of the change in China's information governance and social management". As much as *yuqing* signifies a move by the Chinese Party-State to keep up with the zeitgeist of good governance, it also serves as a handy tool to control the masses, rather than contemplating any fundamental democratic and political transformation.

Conclusion: The Futures of Internet Histories

In the introduction to their 2015 special issue on "Histories of the Internet" Thomas Haight *et al.* note:

> Looking at both scholarly histories and popular myths, we suggest that the expanding scope of the Internet has created a demand for different kinds of history that capture the development of the many technological and social practices that converged to create today's Internet-based online world.
>
> (Haigh, Russell, and Dutton 2015)

As Internet histories develops as a field it will increasingly need to take account of how the Internet actually developed in particular places and among certain groups; explore dominant narratives, myths, and metaphors; pay attention to "minor" and alternative histories of the Internet; investigate histories of the Internet across different language and cultural groups; histories of the Internet across different demographics ("old" people as well as "young" people; excluded and marginalized groups, and minorities, as well as majorities); histories of the Internet in the Global South as well as the Global North; cross-fertilization of Internet technologies and cultures across regions; and Internet circuits and exchanges in unexpected trajectories, locally, translocally, and internationally. As we shall see, and has been well established in theories of global and international media, this can often mean a renewed, intense, and focused attention on local spaces and places, specific subcultures, one particular platform or technology from a teeming Internet media and communication ecology.

What has become clear to us after engaging with the 36 different national, regional, and thematic case studies presented in this Companion is that although "the Internet" is now a technology with "global" range and impact, it is not the case that specific cultures of use, particularly those that might be most familiar to users resident in the anglophone West, can be replicated anywhere that has Internet connectivity. What Internet technologies are available and preferred depends upon many factors including geography and resulting infrastructure, as well as market and policy factors such as government regulation, competition between providers, and pricing. As important as these considerations are, there are also many complex cultural factors that are much more difficult for outsiders to discern—especially if they have no access to accounts of Internet culture in local languages. These less tangible influences include local understandings governing what communication means, what constitutes information and how it should be used and shared, issues around privacy and security, and, most important, literacy. By "literacy" we don't just mean the ability to read and decipher a conventional written text—but the whole range of "new literacies" that are involved in the effective use of today's convergent media devices.

An aspect of this need for enhanced literacy requires us to step outside of our own culturally coded set of assumptions about what the Internet is or means, and to recognize the significance of alternative Internet histories and cultures of use. Rather than view other localities as engaged in a process of "catch up" with current Western models, we need to appreciate how local instances of Internet culture enhance our understanding of the technology and its affordances as a whole. We hope that the chapters offered here will be useful in moving this ongoing conversation and much needed research forward.

Acknowledgements

This chapter is an output of *Internet History in Australia and the Asia-Pacific*, an Australian Research Council Discovery grant (DP1092878).

Notes

1. *Internet Histories: Digital Technology, Culture & Society* is published by Taylor & Francis from 2017. Its remit is "research on the cultural, social, political and technological histories of the Internet and associated digital cultures". A key aim of the journal is "its desire to publish and catalyse research and scholarly debate on the development, forms, and histories of the Internet internationally, across the full global range of countries, regions, cultures, and communities". Founding editors of *Internet Histories* are Niels Brügger, Megan Ankerson, Gerard Goggin, and Valérie Schafer.
2. *Annals of the History of Computing* is a longstanding journal, published by the IEEE (Institute of Electrical and Electronics Engineers), an association of 420,000 professionals across engineering, computing, and technology information. The *Annals*: "covers the breadth of computer history. Featuring scholarly articles by leading computer scientists and historians, as well as firsthand accounts by computer pioneers, the Annals is the primary publication for recording, analyzing, and debating the history of computing. The Annals also serves as a focal point for people interested in uncovering and preserving the records of this exciting field" (www.computer.org/web/computingnow/annals/about).
3. *Information & Culture* is a journal based at the University of Texas Austin. It was established in 1966 as *The Journal of Library History*: "The journal honors its (45+ year) heritage by continuing to publish in the areas of library, archival, museum, conservation, and information science history. However, the journal's scope has been broadened significantly beyond these areas to include the historical study of any topic that would fall under the purview of any of the modern interdisciplinary schools of information" (www.infoculturejournal.org/about).

References

Abbate, J. (1999) *Inventing the Internet*, Cambridge, MA: MIT Press.

Agar, J. (2003) *Constant Touch: A Global History of the Mobile Phone*, London: Icon Books.

Aspray, W., and Ceruzzi, P. E. (eds) (2008) *The Internet and American Business*, Cambridge, MA: MIT Press.

Ben-David, A. (2010) "Palestine's Virtual Borders 2.0: From a Non-Place to a User-Generated Space", *Réseaux*, 159: 151–179.

Ben-David, A. (2012) "The Palestinian Diaspora on the Web: Between De-Territorialization and Re-Territorialization", *Social Science Information*, 51(4): 459–474.

Ben-David, A. (2016) "What Does the Web Remember of its Deleted Past? An Archival Reconstruction of the Former Yugoslav Top-Level Domain", *New Media & Society*, published online first, 26 April, 1461444816643790.

Brügger, N. (ed.) (2010) *Web History*, New York: Peter Lang.

Brügger, N. (2013) "Web Historiography and Internet Studies: Challenges and Perspectives", *New Media & Society*, 15: 752–764.

Brügger, N. (ed.) (2016a) "The Web's First 25 Years", special issue of *New Media & Society*, 18.

Brügger, N. (ed.) (2016b) *Web 25: Histories from the First 25 Years of the World Wide Web*, New York: Peter Lang.

Brügger, N., and Schroeder, R. (eds) (2016) *The Web as History: Using Web Archives to Understand the Past and the Present*, London: UCL Press.

Brügger, N., Ankerson, M. S., and Milligan I. (eds) (2017) *Sage Handbook of Web History*, London: Sage.

Bruijn, M., and van Dijk, R. (2012) *The Social Life of Connectivity in Africa*, New York: Palgrave Macmillan.

Burns, M., and Brügger, N. (eds) (2012) *Histories of Public Service Broadcasters on the Web*, New York: Peter Lang.

Campbell-Kelly, M., and Garcia-Swartz, D. D. (2013) "The History of the Internet: The Missing Narratives", *Journal of Information Technology*, 28: 18–33.

Carey, J., and Elton, M. C. J. (2010) *When Media Are New: Understanding the Dynamics of New Media Adoption and Use*, Ann Arbor, MI: University of Michigan Press.

Consalvo, M., and Ess, C. (eds) (2011) *The Handbook of Internet Studies*, Malden, MA: Wiley-Blackwell.

Danet, B., and Herring, S. C. (eds) (2007) *The Multilingual Internet: Language, Culture, and Communication Online*, New York: Oxford University Press.

Donner, J. (2015) *After Access: Inclusion, Development, and a More Mobile Internet*, Cambridge, MA: MIT Press.

Dutton, W. (ed.) (2013) *The Oxford Handbook of Internet Studies*, Oxford: Oxford University Press.

Fischer, C. (1992) *America Calling: A Social History of the Telephone*, Berkeley, CA: University of California Press.

Flichy, P. (2007) *The Internet Imaginaire*, Cambridge, MA: MIT Press.

Goggin, G., and McLelland, M. (eds) (2009) *Internationalizing Internet Studies: Beyond Anglophone Paradigms*, New York: Routledge.

Goggin, G., Ling, R., and Hjorth, L. (2016) "'Must-Read' Mobile Technology Research: A Field Guide", in G. Goggin, R. Ling, and L. Hjorth (eds), *Mobile Technologies: Major Works*, New York: Routledge, 1, pp. 1–16.

Gottlieb, N. (2000) *Word Processing Technology in Japan: Kanji and the Keyboard*, Richmond: Curzon.

Gottlieb, N., and McLelland, M. (eds) (2003) *Japanese Cybercultures*, Oxford: Routledge.

Haigh, T., Russell, A. L., and Dutton, W. H. (2015) "Histories of the Internet: Introducing a Special Issue of *Information & Culture*", *Information & Culture: A Journal of History*, 50(2): 143–159.

Helmond, A. (2015) "The Platformization of the Web: Making Web Data Platform Ready", *Social Media + Society*, 1(2), DOI: 10.1177/2056305115603080.

Hills, J. (2007) *Telecommunications and Empire*, Urbana, IL and Chicago: University of Illinois Press.

Hunsinger, J., Klastrup, L., and Allen, M. (eds) (2010) *The International Handbook of Internet Research*, Dordrecht and London: Springer.

Internet Society (2015) *Global Internet Report 2015*, available at: www.Internetsociety.org/globalInternetreport/

Ito, M., Okabe, D., and Matsuda, M. (eds) (2005) *Personal, Portable, Pedestrian: Mobile Phones in Japanese Life*, Cambridge, MA: MIT Press.

Jones, S. (ed.) (1999) *Doing Internet Research: Critical Issues and Methods for Examining the Net*, Thousand Oaks, CA: Sage.

Lee, K-S. (2012) *IT Development in Korea: A Broadband Nirvana?*, New York: Routledge.

Lee, K-S. (2016) "On the Historiography of the Korean Internet: Issues Raised by the Historical Dialectic of Structure and Agency", *The Information Society*, 32(3): 217–222.

Masutti, C., and Paloque-Berges, C. (2013) *Histoires et Cultures du Libre: Des Logiciels Partagés aux Licences Échangées*, Raleigh, NC: Framasoft.

Moyal, A. (1984) *Clear Across Australia: A History of Telecommunications*, Melbourne: Nelson.

Rens, J-G. (2001) *The Invisible Empire: A History of the Telecommunications Industry in Canada, 1846–1956*, Montreal: McGill-Queen's University Press.

Rogers, R. (2013) *Digital Methods*, Cambridge, MA: MIT Press.

Schafer, V., and Thierry, B. G. (2012) *Le Minitel: L'Enfance Numérique de la France*, Paris: Nuvis, Cigref.

Schafer, V., and Tuy, B. (2013) *Dans les Coulisses de l'Internet: RENATER, 20 Ans de Technologie, d'Enseignement et de Recherche*, Paris: Armand Colin.

Shechmeister, M. (2009) "Ghost Pages: A Wired.com Farewell to GeoCities", Wired.com, March 11, available at: www.wired.com/2009/11/geocities

Turner, F. (2006) *From Counterculture to Cyberculture: Stewart Brand, the Whole Earth Network, and the Rise of Digital Utopianism*, Chicago: University of Chicago Press.

van Dijck, J. (2013) *The Culture of Connectivity: A Critical History of Social Media*, Oxford: Oxford University Press.

Weltevrede, E., and Helmond, A. (2012) "Where Do Bloggers Blog? Platform Transitions Within the Historical Dutch Blogosphere", *First Monday*, 17(2), available at: http://firstmonday.org/ojs/index.php/fm/article/view Article/3775

Zhou, Y. (2006) *Historicizing Online Politics: Telegraphy, the Internet, and Political Participation in China*, Stanford, CA: Stanford University Press.

Part 1

FRAMING CONCEPTS AND APPROACHES

1

IMAGINARIES, VALUES, AND TRAJECTORIES

A Critical Reflection on the Internet

Robin Mansell

The history of the Internet is in urgent need of critical reflection. Most historical accounts suggest that there has been, and will continue to be, a relatively homogeneous trajectory of innovation. Examples are the widely cited accounts provided by Abbate 2000; Flichy 2007; Katz *et al.* 2001; Leiner *et al.* 1997; Leiner *et al.* 1998; and Murphy 2002. These neglect the heterogeneity of choices taken by decision makers around the world. It is these choices which have shaped what the Internet is, notwithstanding a common set of technical protocols. Some scholars have examined the "localization" of the Internet (Figueroa and Hugo 2007; Miller and Slater 2000; Postill 2011), but their accounts tend to focus on user appropriation of the Internet, and less so on its development. John Postill notes that many analysts regard the "rest of the world", beyond the United States, simply as being impacted by "the Internet".

A South Korean doctoral thesis by a student in the United Kingdom brought the importance of diverse trajectories of Internet innovation to my attention in the early 2000s. He had worked in the telecommunications industry in a senior capacity and participated in discussions about how the Internet should be deployed in his country. His research drew attention to the way the Internet was implemented in South Korea and his account departed from those originating in the United States (Kim 2005). He argued that those accounts persistently focused on a relatively small number of actors, assuming that their remarkably homogeneous cultural values would extend unproblematically to other regions of the world. He further suggested that these accounts favored a particular vision of the Internet, making implicit claims to universal accuracy. These accounts should not be generalized, he said, because the way the Internet (and other digital technologies) actually came to be embedded beyond the United States was substantially different.

Over time, the word "Internet" has come to be treated as a proper noun—that is, as a term designating something unique and singular. This usage limits inquiry into the variety of possible trajectories of technological innovation. The designation of "the Internet" as unique, timeless, and placeless is especially effective in deflecting attention away from contests over the socio-technical relationships that are fostered through its development. This notion of a unique configuration of technical and social relations, propagated through a largely US-centric historical record, is very effective in diminishing the visibility of the variegated character of the innovation process.

I reflect in this chapter on how the scholarly community might contribute to a much more variegated history of the Internet. I start in the next section by considering the prevailing social imaginaries that have been in contention from the earliest days of the Internet. The following section turns to additional narratives that are indicative of a broader range of social imaginaries that underpin studies of technological innovation generally. These perspectives are taken as a starting point for considering an approach to developing alternative histories of the Internet that are more likely to acknowledge the diverse, or variegated, nature of the innovation process in different parts of the world. In the final section, I conclude that critical reflection on the Internet's history may encourage new social imaginaries to emerge. This might encompass a more variegated set of guiding principles that is consistent with governance arrangements that are not indifferent to people's rights to access information, to experience some semblance of individual privacy, and to be relatively safe from intrusive surveillance.

Contending Social Imaginaries

One alternative to conventional individually oriented accounts of the Internet's history is to start with reflections on the configuration of the social imaginaries that influence technological innovation and its governance. Taylor's (2004) notion of social imaginaries can be applied to problematize widely cited Internet histories, so that the variety that characterizes its development trajectory in different geographical places is acknowledged.

For Charles Taylor, social imaginaries are "deeper normative notions and images", referring to the expectations, or common understandings, that people have about how collective practice in a given society is, or should be, organized and governed. He suggests that social imaginaries are what enable people to make sense of practices at the individual and institutional levels. Social imaginaries include people's expectations about governance arrangements, the locus of authority, and how it is, or should be, constituted institutionally. Taylor emphasizes that there are always multiple conflicting social imaginaries in play. These are articulated in the form of narratives or stories that people can tell about any feature of human endeavor. Thus, for example, if the prevailing narrative about the Internet insists that the technology's design favors individual rights and freedoms, then this is likely to become a taken-for-granted assumption that is very widely held.

Although Taylor's construct of social imaginaries is concerned with how people imagine that authority operates, or should operate, in a given context, he makes no a priori claims about the specific arrangements for governance that constitute a just or moral order (Mansell 2012). Applying the construct of social imaginaries as a basis for reflecting on narratives about the Internet's history, it becomes clear that multiple narratives have been in play, notwithstanding the fact that only a very few of these are reflected in the most frequently cited accounts. This approach can sensitize researchers and other stakeholders to the existence of diverse narratives. This is essential when investigation of the Internet's history is extended beyond the individuals and institutions that played a formative role in the United States.

Approaching a critical reflection on the Internet's history in this way immediately yields insight into a prevailing narrative account (Mansell 2012). This account is underpinned by a social imaginary that informs many received histories of the Internet. It privileges techno-logical innovation and the diffusion of digital technologies on a world scale. The imaginary is of exogenous impacts of technological innovation, guided by key individuals who value progressively more intense connectivity via networks, specifically supported by the Internet's technical protocols. This social imaginary is consistent with a notion of autonomous technology and it privileges increasing quantities of information over the messy world of situated meaning construction. This narrative is principally concerned with the impacts of technological innovation and massive increases in capacities to produce, process, distribute, and store digital information. The main focus is on how society adjusts to the shock of rapid technological innovation. The narrative emphasizes outcome assessment to calibrate the effects of shocks such as measures of the rate of investment in Internet-related infrastructure. Scholarship is preoccupied with tracking transformations in computational capacity or with indicators of the intensity of use of the Internet (Katz *et al.* 2014).

In this narrative, the historical account focuses on individual behaviors in response to technological change with little attention to their distinctive features in different societies. As mathematician/philosopher Norbert Wiener argued, any activity involving digital information involves a complex interactive process: "information is a name for the content of what is exchanged with the outer world as we adjust to it, and make our adjustment felt upon it" (Wiener 1950: 17). This narrative acknowledges that technological and human systems interact, but it is presumed that there is some "higher authority" that controls the outcomes. It is an easy step from here to a universal account of the trajectory of the Internet's development. This social imaginary arguably underpins programmatic visions of scientific research, engineering, and mathematics that focus on feedback systems and automation as control systems for military and non-military applications. The prevailing narrative is derived from a social imaginary that discounts the socio-cultural and political character of technology. It comes in two principal favors, consistent with Taylor's view that there are always multiple narratives in play.

One variant of this social imaginary privileges a "higher authority" in the form of the market. In this account, efficient markets and individual choice are said to have guided change in the Internet system. This imaginary invokes a market-led diffusion of technology model. In the case of the Internet, the distinctive expectation is that all countries and people eventually will benefit from a "single global digital economy" (Aspen Institute 2012). The narrative underpinning this imaginary envisages a "catching up" process whereby decisions are taken to "leapfrog" generations of technology to reap economic benefit. Innovation is seen as being responsive to market demand, which is assumed to maximize individual choice, leading to evermore intelligent machines that are increasingly responsive to human needs, most recently for instance, through the development of the Internet of Things. The expectation is that investment in the digital technology system (including the Internet) has uniform positive impacts, unless "residual" factors skew the development trajectory in unexpected ways. The factor deemed most likely to detract from widespread economic benefit is interference in the marketplace through intrusive governance or regulation. The social imaginary of the digital world is one in which "thing-like" information products enlighten people's lives. The idea that technological progress could be benign or harmful becomes simply "too obvious to mention" (Taylor 2007: 176).

The second variant of the prevailing social imaginary is very similar to the first. It also privileges technological innovation and the diffusion of digital technologies on a world scale. It differs mainly in its expectations with regard to where any "higher authority" is, or should be, located. In this case, there is an expectation that horizontal or collaborative models of authority, enabled by decentralized networks, are the optimal means for organizing and governing society (Mansell 2012). In this social imaginary, authority may reside with the commercial market, or it may be located in a host of non-market arrangements. In either case, however, the narrative focuses on how Internet technology-supported, non-hierarchical models of authority, most notably, peer-to-peer online interaction, favor the exchange or sharing of digital information.

This social imaginary underpins the notion that an open, emergent, and collaborative culture is favorable to collective decision making (Benkler 2009; Jenkins 2006; Lessig 2006). Like its counterpart, it insists that the Internet should not be regulated so as to give free rein to innovators, often, but not exclusively, in an open information commons. Inspired by a commitment to open access to information, and to minimal restraints on freedom of expression and the preservation of privacy, the historical narrative is about the benefits of horizontal institutions of governance, the empowering characteristics of user-generated content and mass-self communication (Castells 2009). Scholars whose work is informed by this variant of the prevailing social imaginary may criticize intrusive corporations and state exploitation of Internet users and highlight power asymmetries (Mosco 2014), but their accounts treat digital information primarily as a "thing" to be circulated and diffused. This second variant of the prevailing technologically deterministic social imaginary fits with the notion that the Internet should not be formally regulated.

In both variants of the prevailing social imaginary, the resulting accounts of the innovation process eschew a consideration of the variability of meaning construction. The accounts are therefore apparently universally applicable. In both cases, the appropriate locus of authority is assumed to be diffuse, consistent with the end-to-end architecture of the Internet. Over time, this architecture comes to be seen as a technological given, no longer one with multiple possibilities and potential trajectories. Proponents of the two variants of the prevailing social imaginary of the Internet are pitted against each other in policy debates. One group advocates reliance on the emergent properties of a complex market system as the means to achieve universally positive outcomes. The other advocates reliance on the generative activities of decentralized technology designers and a growing mass of online participants to achieve these outcomes. In both, the overall narrative about the history of the Internet is remarkably similar. Claims to universal applicability invoke a "higher authority", whether market or dispersed members of civil society. This means that detailed attention to differences in the values and commitments of stakeholders to market-, government-, or civil society-led innovation go largely unexamined.

If this prevailing social imaginary of a technologically undifferentiated Internet was simply a narrative account with no bearing on the future, we might conclude that scholarship on the distinctive ways in which the Internet has been "localized" is all that is needed to correct the historical record. It is this prevailing social imaginary, however, that gives rise to expectations that predominate in contemporary debates about the future of the Internet. Today, computing experts are referring to "social machines". A world of Web 3.0 technologies is expected to diffuse throughout the world. The contemporary imaginary is one of "metaverses" embracing social media and information, drawing in data from virtual (physical) spaces. Social computing, Web science, and social computation focus on combining citizen participation with machine-based computation. Higher authority here rests with key individuals who are responsible for ensuring that security and privacy are designed into these machines (Smart and Shadbolt 2014).

The prevailing social imaginary is of machines that can "think" and make "choices" on behalf of human beings. Manuel DeLanda's (2011) work on simulation, for example, is illustrative of attempts to employ computerization to explain the emergent properties of systems, including the social. Self-organizing "meshworks" are depicted as alternatives to hierarchy in a socio-technical system that increasingly privileges the potentialities of "intelligent" computing. This is seen either as enhancing the prospects for economic growth through information markets, now designated as "big data", or as facilitating increasingly decentralized societal governance (Mayer-Schönberger and Cukier 2013). These expectations are being inscribed into algorithms (boyd and Crawford 2012). With companies storing terabytes of data for scrutiny, the emphasis is on machine learning to harness the power of the social Web, resting on an open Internet.

This diffusion of technology narrative differs remarkably little from that which informed the work of earlier generations of scientists and engineers. Vannevar Bush (1945), for example, hoped that social machines would be better able to review their "shady past" and to analyze social problems. As Philip Mirowski (2002: 19) asserts: "If there was one tenet of that era's particular faith in science, it was that logical rigor and the mathematical idiom of expression would produce *transparent agreement* over the meaning and significance of various models and their implications" (emphasis added).

Little has changed. The prevailing expectation is that by searching, tagging, and reviewing, digital information is being harmoniously aligned with the pursuit of commercial gain or with the pursuit of fairness and justice; the same technology is universally invoked.

This is not only a Western (or American) narrative. China's Baidu is estimated to be investing US$1.6 billion in big data centers and in automation. Social media platforms from Twitter to Facebook or Google and non-commercial open source online tools (Ushahidi or OpenStreetMap) are supporting massive data collection and aggregation for commercial or social application. This digital information, generated as a by-product of electronic services, is discussed in terms of the quantities of data/information available for algorithmic processing and pattern recognition. In the prevailing social imaginary, the innovation trajectory is not discussed in terms of its implications for meaning construction or how it may differ across cultural, social, or political contexts (Couldry and Powell 2014).

Additional Distinctive Imaginaries

Other traditions of research on digital technology innovation suggest additional social imaginaries. These continue to be in play, and are especially visible when the Internet's development is considered on a world scale. These contrast with the individualistic, technology-centric, and diffusion-oriented social imaginary discussed above, even if they go largely unnoticed in much Western scholarship.

In the 1930s, "technics" was assumed by Lewis Mumford (1934) to encompass people's diverse wishes, ideas, goals, and habits, as well as their tools and machines. It was assumed that people do not simply adjust to the exigencies of digital technological innovation. The social imaginary in this context gives rise to the expectation that socio-technical transformation is not simply a response to digital tools. Instead, in these narratives it is the heterogeneous interfaces between the material and informational or symbolic world that matter; human agency gives rise to heterogeneity. The emphasis in historical accounts is often on specific tactics for accommodating or resisting digital technologies (Silverstone 2007). In these narratives, ethical and moral differences, and contested symbolic meaning, are given a central place.

Andrew Feenberg (1992: 319) argues, for instance, that "individuals who are incorporated into new types of technical networks have learned to resist through the net itself in order to influence the powers that control it". The history of such resistance cannot be told when the focus is on individuals and their technical choices about the functioning of technology. In these accounts the social imaginaries about the locus of "higher authority" are that digital information should not be presumed to be "innocent" (Escobar 1995). This is because asymmetrical power relations and disparate cultural, social, and political contexts inevitably mediate people's lives in heterogeneous ways. When digital technologies are not privileged as "sentient" actors (Latour 2005), but, instead, as the embodiment of "propensities", attention in the historical narrative can be drawn to the non-linearity of innovation and to the variety that guides interactions between technologies and human beings. As Steven Jackson and Laewoo Kang (2014: 9) suggest, if the expectation is that technologies add "weight, shape and direction to some lines of action while subtracting it from others", it is easier to see that the Internet's history is more variegated than it appears when its history is narrated in line with the prevailing social imaginaries. Critical reflections on the history of the Internet are more likely to display a variegated development trajectory when digital technologies are seen as embracing propensities that can accommodate a wide variety of expectations about how they are, or should be, developed and used.

The persistence of the technology-led diffusion narrative is not attributable only to the influence of the scientific and engineering-led communities or to the privileged position of the economics discipline. Notably, some strands of economic analysis are open to the notion that digital technology innovation differs around the world, as does the invocation of a "higher authority", with respect to governance. For example, Christopher Freeman (1974; Freeman and Louçã 2001), Carlota Perez (1983) and other economists who bring micro- and macro-level empirical analysis of technological innovation into a dialogue argue that a technological "style" or "techno-economic paradigm" comes to predominate. A close reading of this tradition indicates, however, that in suggesting that a new "common sense" with respect to governance might take hold in parallel with technological innovation, they insist that choices are never fixed and final; they are not the only ones available at a given time or in a particular context (Lundvall 1996; von Hippel 2005). Even within the mainstream of economics in the United States, there has been awareness of the variety that characterizes the innovation process. Timothy Bresnahan and Manuel Trajtenberg (1995: 84), who coined the term General Purpose Technology (GPT) to designate innovative technologies with pervasive impacts on all areas of social and economic life, comment, for instance, that "most GPTs play the role of 'enabling technologies', opening up new opportunities rather than offering complete, final solutions". The notion that there could be an innovation trajectory that is generalizable across countries is not, therefore, present in the broader literature on innovation with respect to digital technologies. Additionally, research on technological innovation in the economics tradition sometimes has been concerned with knowledge, its construction, and its multiple meanings. For instance, Martin Bell (1979: 45) observes that "we are concerned with technical knowledge which is rooted and embedded in (indigenous to) specified social groups". This is not a view that treats information as a "thing-like" object as in the prevailing social imaginary.

Towards Alternative Histories of the Internet

It is, nevertheless, the prevailing social imaginary that gives rise to Internet histories with an implied technological, cultural, political, and social homogeneity. In contrast, research on the malleability of technology is more likely to privilege meaning, and the asymmetry of power relations articulated through technological systems. Contemporary histories of the Internet are needed to map the diverse social imaginaries that shape the process of technological innovation in the case of the Internet. The scholarly community has an obligation to "construct different alternatives for the future" of the Internet, and to recognize "that no culture has a monopoly on the factors for successful socio-economic development" (Albagli and Maciel 2010: 18).

Research that does reveal the complex narratives that are indicative of contested social imaginaries of the locus of a "higher authority" with respect to the Internet rarely pay attention to governance institutions (Gagliardone *et al.* 2012; Geldof *et al.* 2011; Smith and Elder 2010; Tacchi 2010). It tends to examine micro-level innovation processes and to emphasize knowledge asymmetries (Kleine 2013). The vast literature on Internet governance tends to focus on specific conflicts over arrangements for the Internet's governance. Differences in notions about the appropriate "higher authority" typically are ascribed to the architecture of the Internet (Brown and Marsden 2013; Cohen 2012; DeNardis 2014), rather than to more deeply rooted social imaginaries. Manuel Castells and Pekka Himanen (2014) have recently sought to treat technological innovation and governance from a global perspective. They begin to probe the normative commitments that underpin internationally diverse trajectories of technological change. There is, nevertheless, a relatively limited body of research on the distinctive ways the Internet has become embedded in societies. Most historical accounts simply do not yield comparative insight into how the Internet and other digital technologies are "structurally integrating communities into wider, uneven networks of power" (Thompson 2004: 2).

How can the historical record of the Internet be sensitized to sustained variety in the social imaginaries about where authority is located and how it should be institutionalized? One approach is to emphasize contests over the "guiding principles" (Freeman 1992) that inform the innovation process. Historical accounts that are less Internet-centric and which focus on the Internet's role within the capitalist formation are needed to emphasize similarities and differences around the world (Jessop 2014). A focus on how neoliberal market values are accommodated or resisted and on whether or not governance arrangements perpetuate asymmetrical power relationships (Lash and Urry 1987) is essential if competing social imaginaries are to be acknowledged.

Competing social imaginaries become embedded in texts (laws, regulations, treaties), in technical standards, and in the norms influencing the micro-practices of designing or implementing technology. The way these enable or constrain the development of the Internet should be reflected in future narratives about how the Internet is developing. Digital technology innovation is provoking globally contested debates, and stakeholder commitments to different styles of governing authority are influenced by social imaginaries about who has the authority to act to "get things done" in a given context (Nelson and Sampat 2001). However, research on the Internet invariably focuses on implementing prefigured digital applications such as social media, mobile phone apps or e-government platforms, or on individual or intra-organizational use (Kallinikos 2010). Studies of formal governance institutions and regulation are often specific to domains of digital innovation such as the audiovisual industry, data protection, or copyright enforcement (Puppis 2010). Research on participation in multi-stakeholder deliberation (Raboy *et al.* 2010) and on the institutions that specifically govern the Internet (Brown and Marsden 2013) also pays relatively little attention to how contested social imaginaries are instantiated in authority relationships.

Historical accounts acknowledging the variegated nature of technological innovation trajectories and their governance are needed to compare where it is that a wide range of actors expect (imagine) authority to be located. A key question is where preferences for specific governance arrangements relying on the market or on its alternatives originate. Put another way, critical reflections on the Internet's history need to be based on investigations of stakeholders' preferences for constituted (formal) or adaptive (flexible informal) authority and how these are combined in various contexts around the world (Mansell 2013).

Such histories would have considerable contemporary relevance especially in a time of global instability. Increasingly strong commitments are being made to specific governance arrangements for the Internet. This is exemplified in debates about the future remit of the Internet Corporation for Assigned Names and Numbers (ICANN) at the time of writing at the beginning of 2015. The narrative in this instance is often about the respective roles of government, companies, and civil society actors. Civil society representatives frequently assert a commitment to non-market collective action and a variety of hybrids, implicitly invoking commitments to where authority is best located and institutionalized. A key assumption in this and similar debates is that the Internet will provide access to empowering information *if* appropriate governance arrangements are in place (Gigler *et al.* 2014). This is a big "if", and it is far from clear that there is likely to be a lasting consensus.

A profusion of multi-stakeholder deliberations has been yielding policy statements and principles about Internet governance since the 2003/5 United Nations World Summit on the Information Society (WSIS) (Mansell 2014). These invariably assert that the Internet can be governed to ensure that it contributes to justice and equity. At the Global Multistakeholder Meeting on the Future of Internet Governance in Brazil in 2014 it was asserted that "human rights are universal as reflected in the Universal Declaration of Human Rights" (NETmundial 2014). When applied to rights such as access to information, freedom of expression, privacy and surveillance, or other pressing issues, we need a deeper understanding of the social imaginaries that inform stakeholder approaches to institutionalizing governance. We need comparative research on how entrenched they are, and on whether they are converging over time. Studies that systematically map the Internet's variegated development trajectories within the context of global capitalism would reveal whether emerging governance arrangements are likely to better secure people's entitlements to digital information (Mansell 2002; Sen 1999).

Conclusion

Such histories would provide insight into whether emerging Internet trajectories and governance are likely to be consistent with "another development" (Dag Hammarskjöld Foundation 2006 [1975]). These could yield insight into "struggles for recognition" (Honneth 1996) in the Internet domain, as is the case in many of the chapters in this volume. When the technology diffusion narrative, underpinned by the prevailing social imaginary, is universalized, it suppresses alternatives and it negates people's abilities to account for themselves and to conceive of themselves as active agents (Couldry 2010). Historical accounts that focus principally on the choices of key individuals in the United States make it appear that "the Internet" establishes the conditions for the production, circulation, and use of information. Since the end of World War II, this prevailing social imaginary has influenced commitments to investment in digital hardware and software for stimulating economic growth. It is more recently supporting initiatives to foster multi-stakeholder forums for democratic decision making. It is also fostering, whether intentionally or not, an expectation that progressively widespread automation of digital information processing is to be valued. This is because the narrative is consistent with the perception of digital information as a thing to be quantified and then acted upon.

If the prevailing social imaginary that gives rise to this narrative can be challenged effectively, it may be that new social imaginaries will emerge. These will start to influence the trajectories of technological innovation and the practice of governance. A more variegated, yet still viable, set of guiding principles might then emerge that is not indifferent to people's lives—that is, to their rights to access information, to experience some semblance of individual privacy, and to be relatively safe from intrusive surveillance. In applying the social imaginaries construct in research on the history of the Internet, taken-for-granted expectations are inevitably challenged. This arguably is an essential contribution to the understanding of the Internet's past and its future development.

References

Abbate, J. (2000) *Inventing the Internet*, Cambridge, MA: MIT Press.

Albagli, S., and Maciel, M. L. (eds) (2010) *Information, Power and Politics: Technological and Institutional Mediations*, Lanham, MD: Lexington Books.

Aspen Institute (2012) *Toward a Single Global Digital Economy: The First Report of the Aspen Institute Idea Project*, Washington, DC: Aspen Institute.

Bell, M. (1979) "The Exploitation of Indigenous Knowledge or the Indigenous Exploitation of Knowledge: Whose Use of What for What?", *IDS Bulletin*, 10(2): 44–50.

Benkler, Y. (2009) "Technology Policy, Cooperation and Human Systems Design", in D. Foray (ed.), *The New Economics of Technology Policy*, Cheltenham: Edward Elgar Publishers, pp. 337–357.

boyd, d., and Crawford, K. (2012) "Critical Questions for Big Data", *Information, Communication and Society*, 15(5): 662–679.

Bresnahan, T. F., and Trajtenberg, M. (1995) "General Purpose Technologies 'Engines of Growth?'", *NBER Working Paper Series*, w4148.

Brown, I., and Marsden, C. T. (2013) *Regulating Code: Good Governance and Better Regulation in the Information Age*, Cambridge, MA: MIT Press.

Bush, V. (1945) "As We May Think", *The Atlantic Monthly*, 176(1): 101–108.

Castells, M. (2009) *Communication Power*, Oxford: Oxford University Press.

Castells, M., and Himanen, P. (eds) (2014) *Reconceptualizing Development in the Global Information Age*, Oxford: Oxford University Press.

Cohen, J. E. (2012) *Configuring the Networked Self: Law, Code, and the Play of Everyday Practice*, New Haven, CT: Yale University Press.

Couldry, N. (2010) *Why Voice Matters: Culture and Politics after Neoliberalism*, London: Sage.

Couldry, N., and Powell, A. (2014) "Big Data from the Bottom Up", *Big Data & Society*, 1(2): 1–5.

Dag Hammarskjöld Foundation (2006 [1975]) "The 1975 Dag Hammarskjöld Report on Development and International Cooperation", 5th printing, *Seventh Special Session of the United Nations General Assembly*, 1–12 September, Motala: Dag Hammarskjöld Foundation.

DeLanda, M. (2011) *Philosophy and Simulation: The Emergence of Synthetic Reason*, London: Continuum International Publishing Group.

DeNardis, L. (2014) *The Global War for Internet Governance*, New Haven, CT: Yale University Press.

Escobar, A. (1995) *Encountering Development: The Making and Unmaking of the Third World*, Princeton, NJ: Princeton University Press.

Feenberg, A. (1992) "Subversive Rationalization, Technology, Power, and Democracy", *Inquiry—an Interdisciplinary Journal of Philosophy*, 35(3–4): 301–322.

Figueroa, A., and Hugo, A. (2007) "Collective Construction of Identity in the Internet: Ethical Dimension and Intercultural Perspective", in R. Capurro, J. Frauhbauer, and T. Hausmanninger (eds), *Localizing the Internet: Ethical Aspects in Intercultural Perspective*, Munich: Fink, pp. 229–241.

Flichy, P. (2007) *The Internet Imaginaire*, Cambridge, MA: MIT Press.

Freeman, C. (1974) *The Economics of Industrial Innovation*, 1st edn, London: Pinter.

Freeman, C. (1992) "Technology, Progress and the Quality of Life", in C. Freeman (ed.), *The Economics of Hope: Essays on Technical Change, Economic Growth and the Environment*, London: Pinter Publishers, pp. 212–230.

Freeman, C. and Louça, F. (2001) *As Time Goes By: From Industrial Revolutions to the Information Revolution*, Oxford: Oxford University Press.

Gagliardone, I., Stremlau, N., and Nkrumah, D. (2012) "Partner, Prototype, or Persuader? China's Renewed Media Engagement with Ghana", *Communication, Politics & Culture*, 45(2).

Geldof, M., Grimshaw, D. J., Kleine, D., and Unwin, T. (2011) "What Are the Key Lessons of Ict4d Partnerships for Poverty Reduction? Systematic Review Report", *Department for International Development*, London, available at: http://r4d.dfid.gov.uk/PDF/Outputs/SystematicReviews/DFID_ICT_SR_Final_Report_r5.pdf

Gigler, B.-S., Custer, S., Bailur, S., Dodds, E., Asad, S., and Gagieva, E. (2014) *Closing the Feedback Loop: Can Technology Amplify Citizen Voices*, Washington, DC: World Bank.

Honneth, A. (1996) *The Struggle for Recognition: The Moral Grammar of Social Conflicts*, Cambridge, MA: MIT Press.

Jackson, S. J., and Kang, L. (2014) "Breakdown, Obsolescence and Reuse: HCI and the Art of Repair", *CHI 2014, 26 April–1 May, Toronto*.

Jenkins, H. (2006) *Convergence Culture: Where Old and New Media Collide*, New York: New York University Press.

Jessop, B. (2014) "Capitalist Diversity and Variety: Variegation, the World Market, Compossibility and Ecological Dominance", *Capital & Class*, 38(1): 45–58.

Kallinikos, J. (2010) *Governing through Technology: Information Artifacts and Social Practice*, Basingstoke: Palgrave.

Katz, J. E., Rice, R. E., and Aspden, P. (2001) "The Internet, 1995–2000: Access, Civic Involvement, and Social Interaction", *American Behavioral Scientist*, 45(3): 405–420.

Katz, R., Koutroumpis, P., and Callorda, F. M. (2014) "Using a Digitization Index to Measure the Economic and Social Impact of Digital Agendas", *Info*, 16(1): 32–44.

Kim, B.-K. (2005) *Internationalizing the Internet: The Co-Evolution of Influence and Technology*, Cheltenham: Edward Elgar.

Kleine, D. (2013) *Technologies of Choice? ICTs, Development, and the Capabilities Approach*, Cambridge, MA: MIT Press.

Lash, S., and Urry, J. (1987) *The End of Organized Capitalism*, Cambridge: Polity Press.

Latour, B. (2005) *Reassembling the Social: An Introduction to Actor-Network-Theory*, Oxford: Oxford University Press.

Leiner, B. M., Cerf, V. G., Clark, D. D., Kahn, R. E., Kleinrock, L., Lynch, D. C., Postel, J., Roberts, L. G., and Wolff, S. S. (1997) "The Past and Future History of the Internet", *Communications of the ACM*, 40(2): 102–108.

Leiner, B. M., Cerf, V. G., Clark, D. D., Kahn, R. E., Kleinrock, L., Lynch, D., Postel, J., Roberts, L. G., and Wolff, S. (1998), "A Brief History of the Internet", *Internet Society*, available at: www.Internetsociety.org/Internet/what-Internet/history-Internet/brief-history-Internet.

Lessig, L. (2006) *Code: Version 2.0*, New York: Basic Books.

Lundvall, B.-Å. (1996) "Information Technology in the Learning Economy—Challenges for Development Strategies", *Memorandum for United Nations Commission for Science and Technology and its Work on Information Technology and Development*, Department of Business Studies, Aalborg: Aalborg University.

Mansell, R. (2002) "From Digital Divides to Digital Entitlements in Knowledge Societies", *Current Sociology*, 50(3): 407–426.

Mansell, R. (2012) *Imagining the Internet: Communication, Innovation and Governance*, Oxford: Oxford University Press.

Mansell, R. (2013) "Employing Crowdsourced Information Resources: Managing the Information Commons", *International Journal of the Commons*, 7(2): 255–277.

Mansell, R. (2014) "Power and Interests in Developing Knowledge Societies: Exogenous and Endogenous Discourses in Contention", *Journal of International Development*, 26(1): 109–127.

Mayer-Schönberger, V., and Cukier, K. (2013) *Big Data: A Revolution That Will Transform How We Live, Work and Think*, London: John Murray.

Miller, D., and Slater, D. (2000) *The Internet: An Ethnographic Approach*, London: Berg.

Mirowski, P. (2002) *Machine Dreams: Economics Becomes a Cyborg Science*, Cambridge: Cambridge University Press.

Mosco, V. (2014) *To the Cloud: Big Data in a Turbulent World*, Boulder, CO: Paradigm Publishers.

Mumford, L. (1934) *Technics and Civilization*, London: Routledge.

Murphy, B. (2002) "A Critical History of the Internet", in G. Elmer (ed.), *Critical Perspectives on the Internet*, Lanham, MD: Rowman & Littlefield, pp. 27–48.

Nelson, R. R., and Sampat, B. N. (2001) "Making Sense of Institutions as a Factor Shaping Economic Performance", *Journal of Economic Behavior & Organization*, 44(1): 31–54.

NETmundial (2014) "Netmundial Multistakeholder Statement", *Global Multistakeholder Meeting on the Future of Internet Governance*, available at: http://netmundial.br/wp-content/uploads/2014/04/NETmundial-Multistakeholder-Document.pdf

Perez, C. (1983) "Structural Change and the Assimilation of New Technologies in the Economic and Social System", *Futures*, 15(4): 357–375.

Postill, J. (2011) *Localizing the Internet*, Oxford: Berghahn Books.

Puppis, M. (2010) "Media Governance: A New Concept for the Analysis of Media Policy and Regulation", *Communication, Culture & Critique*, 3(2): 134–149.

Raboy, M., Landry, N., and Shtern, J. (2010) *Digital Solidarities, Communication Policy and Multi-Stakeholder Global Governance: The Legacy of the World Summit on the Information Society*, New York: Peter Lang.

Sen, A. (1999) *Development as Freedom*, Oxford: Oxford University Press.

Silverstone, R. (2007) *Media and Morality: On the Rise of the Mediapolis*, Cambridge: Polity Press.

Smart, P. R., and Shadbolt, N. R. (2014) "Social Machines", in M. Khosrow-Pour (ed.), *Encyclopedia of Information Science and Technology*, 3rd edn, Hershey, PA: IGI Global, pp. 6855–6862.

Smith, M. L., and Elder, L. (2010) "Open ICT Ecosystems Transforming the Developing World", *Information Technology and International Development*, 6(1): 65–71.

Tacchi, J. (2010) "Open Content Creation: The Issues of Voice and the Challenges of Listening", *Open Development: Technological, Organizational and Social Innovations Transforming the Developing World*, IDRC, 6–7 May, Ottawa.

Taylor, C. (2004) *Modern Social Imaginaries*, Durham, NC: Duke University Press.

Taylor, C. (2007) *A Secular Age*, Cambridge, MA: Belknap Press.

Thompson, M. (2004) "ICT, Power, and Developmental Discourse: A Critical Analysis", *Electronic Journal on Information Systems in Developing Countries*, 20(4): 1–26.

von Hippel, E. (2005) *Democratizing Innovation*, Cambridge, MA: MIT Press.

Wiener, N. (1950) *The Human Use of Human Beings: Cybernetics and Society*, New York: Houghton Mifflin.

2

WHAT'S "CULTURE" GOT TO DO WITH IT?

A (Personal) Review of CATaC (Cultural Attitudes towards Technology and Communication), 1998–2014

Charles Ess

Expect the unexpected—for it is hard to find, and difficult.

(Heraclitus)

What became known as the CATaC (Cultural Attitudes towards Technology and Communication) conference series began at a specific time in Internet studies—and in a very specific experience of culture shock. I describe these beginnings as an introduction to the conferences for three reasons. One, the experience of culture shock illuminates both the conceptual and normative dimensions that came to shape the conferences. Two, this culture shock rests on a kind of ethnocentrism[1] that remains difficult to avoid, even among those of us who are privileged to research and reflect in these domains. Overcoming such ethnocentrism is a core goal of the CATaC series—and articulating it clearly from the outset is helpful. Finally, we will see in the conclusion that this kind of ethnocentrism—despite the kinds of developments and advances in understanding that I detail in the second section—remains intransigent, if not predominant. As it does so—specifically among those of us who study and to some degree may shape the histories and nature of the Internet—such ethnocentrism remains a core problem and danger.

In the second section, I describe the first CATaC conference (1998) in somewhat more detail, in order to bring forward the contributions that shaped what became defining themes and threads of the series. These began with demonstrating that "culture" (whatever it is) makes a difference in our design, implementation, and responses to information and communication technologies (ICTs), including those constituting the Internet. Both initially, and then throughout the series, the role and impact of "culture" can be seen especially in terms of four core threads: embodiment and gender; democracy and freedom of expression; the role and processes of design; and our understandings of selfhood and identity. Last, but certainly not least, the foundational notion of "culture" itself becomes problematized. I take up each of these from their beginning expressions in 1998 and trace their development through the subsequent 15 years of the conference series, including affiliated publications and most recent Ph.D. theses.

The third section begins with some brief summary remarks on the broad shape and trajectory of the series, identifying some distinctive moments and developments, along with some of the impacts of the conferences. I conclude with what lessons can be gleaned from the conferences—most especially for those of us who seek to foster both our histories and the future shape of the Internet in ways that overcome intransigent ethnocentrisms for the sake of protecting and fostering diverse cultural identities in an Internet-entangled and interwoven world.

CATaC Genealogies: The First Age of Internet Studies and Culture Shock

The first CATaC conference was inspired by a specific history and set of experiences that co-emerged in 1997. To begin with, I had come to Oslo, Norway, to participate in a conference on "Technology and Democracy—Comparative Perspectives", organized by the Centre for Technology and Culture, University of Oslo. I was invited because of my work on the democratization potentials and realities of computer-mediated communication—which, by then, had been subsumed under the larger name and notion of the Internet. Barry Wellman has described this "first age" of Internet studies as one in which "punditry rides rampant" (2011: 18). Broadly, in the absence of what we now enjoy—well-established literatures, documenting an extensive array of disciplinary and interdisciplinary research that provides us with at least some reliable empirical foundations for our claims—much of the available literature and debate reflected what James Carey characterized as a Manichean debate (1989). On one hand, pundits, and what we later came to call technology evangelists, boosted a picture of the Internet as "wiring the world" in ways that would inevitably bring about a McLuhanesque "global village" defined by democratic discourse, freedom of expression, and economic prosperity. On the other hand, anticipations of various cyber-hells ran the gamut from "McWorld" to jihad—that is, either the complete homogenization of all peoples and cultures under the pressures of globalization and multinational capitalism, and/or local—and if need be, violent—resistance to such imperialism and colonization (Barber 1995).

I had come to Oslo to discuss a Habermasian-feminist version of democratization via the Internet. Briefly, the hope was that the affordances of Internet-facilitated communication could help us better realize the conditions of an ideal speech situation, beginning with freedom and equality between participants, whose discourse would be guided by rational argument rather than familiar sorts of force. Extensive feminist critique of Habermas helped extend the discourse model to include, e.g. narrative and emotion, thereby fostering the participation of those too frequently excluded from classical notions of rationality—namely, women and children (Ess 1994; cf. Thorseth 2011). And, for its part, the conference collected a remarkable range of diverse viewpoints and approaches to questions of technology and democracy. But even more importantly, my trip to Oslo was the first time I had left the United States in some 20 years. I was not entirely unprepared for the visit: in the 1970s, I had enjoyed considerable experience of life and work in Germany, France, and Switzerland—that is, I knew something of these diverse cultures, their defining languages, values and traditions, the practices of everyday life, and so on. Moreover, partly because of my own Cherokee heritage, and partly because I had witnessed some of the devastating consequences of imperialism and colonialism, I thought I was acutely aware of the grave dangers of falling into ethnocentrism, and thereby complicity, however tacitly and naively, with cultural imperialism.

But in the meantime, of course, the personal computer revolution had broken out in the early 1980s, bringing computing technologies and their near-infinite possibilities to the desktops of scholars, businesses, and the homes of everyday consumers and citizens. It was on the wave of this revolution that I had come to Oslo. So it was no small shock to come to recognize during my first days in Oslo that I had, despite my earlier experiences and sensibilities, also fallen into an easy ethnocentrism—this time, with regard to computing technologies, networks, and computer-mediated communication (CMC). By this, I mean that I had simply assumed that my Norwegian colleagues and their cohorts would be using CMC more or less as I and my cohorts in the United States did. In part thanks to patient and understanding colleagues from Norway and elsewhere, I quickly began to see that this was not the case. For example, as compared with their US counterparts, my Norwegian colleagues appeared to spend considerably less time on email and more on face-to-face communication in the course of their work days. On the other hand, I had the strong sense that young people in Norway were far more intensive users of MUDs (multi-user domains), MOOs (MUD object-oriented), and other then-prevalent forms of CMC than were their US counterparts. However spotty and inaccurate these initial impressions may have been, they nonetheless brought home the critical truth and insight that *culture made a difference*.

This recognition—however commonplace it may be for us today—was something of a heresy, however. In 1998, the vast majority (about 84 percent) of those using the Internet were physically, and thereby (with some exceptions) culturally, located in North America (GVU 1998). This cultural dominance was manifest in many ways, beginning with the predominance of US-based scholarship on CMC. Still more importantly, much of the discourse—especially coming from the side of the boosters—reflected underlying and usually tacit assumptions that in turn were grounded in North American cultures and traditions. Some of these were obvious, beginning with the insistence on democratic processes and norms such as freedom of expression. More subtly, however, there was also a prevailing assumption regarding *technological instrumentalism*—that is, that technologies, including the technologies of the Internet and CMC—are somehow neutral: they are "just tools" that embed or carry no particular values, norms, or preferences. Against this orthodoxy, the suspicion that CMC and the Internet might indeed embed specific cultural norms and culturally variable communicative preferences was tantamount to heresy. To go further and suggest that the ostensibly beneficent vision of "wiring the world" in the name of democracy, etc., might rather risk becoming yet one more expression of cultural (and thereby, political and economic) imperialism was even more outrageous.

These were nonetheless the growing suspicions and worries that emerged for me over the two days of the conference. And, to make matters worse, a first look for research that sought to explore matters of culture vis-à-vis CMC and the Internet turned up, to put it kindly, very little indeed.

As noted in the introduction, these personal beginnings are significant in three ways. One, this genealogy explains the defining focus of the CATaC conferences on the complex intersections between "culture", technology, and communication. Two, our conference series began from specific *normative* grounds and commitments. These normative grounds popped up first in my background work on the democratization and emancipatory potentials of the Internet—a core theme of Internet studies both then and certainly now. But these normative grounds were made all the more manifest—as perhaps they only can be—in the *collision* between two cultures, and the resulting personal shock in the face of important cultural differences in our use of the Internet. Such shock was (and remains) critical for recognizing my own ethnocentric assumptions about the nature of Internet-based technologies and their uses—and for further recognizing how these ethnocentrisms prevented me from anticipating important differences rooted in culturally variable norms, traditions, practices, and communicative preferences. Three, in the following section we will see that uncovering and seeking to find ways to avoid such ethnocentrism—both for the sake of more balanced and informed research and scholarship, and for the sake of avoiding complicity in the sorts of colonization (both overt and covert) that begins with ethnocentrism—in turn is a defining norm and goal of the conference series as it unfolds.

The CATaC Conference Series: Unfoldings and Developments

Following my culture shock in Oslo, I sought to explore these new insights and interests in terms of research and scholarship. I approached Teri Harrison at SUNY Press, who had shepherded me through my first anthology, *Philosophical Perspectives on Computer-Mediated Communication* (Ess 1996). Teri offered the possibility of developing a special issue for the *Electronic Journal of Communication* (*La Revue Electronic de Communication*) (EJC (REC))—with the strong suggestion that organizing an international conference would serve better to attract good papers. Gulp. While I had had some experience with organizing regional conferences, an international conference seemed entirely beyond my depth. Most fortunately, Teri put me in touch with Fay Sudweeks at Murdoch University. Fay was a pioneer in CMC studies in her own right (see, for example, Sudweeks, McLaughlin, and Rafaeli 1998)—and further had extensive experience in such organization. Most happily, Fay accepted my request for help and set to work on organizing our first conference.

It is hard to overstate Fay's contributions to the conference series, and this at all levels. First of all, she had as comprehensive an overview as anyone at the time of CMC studies, especially from a non-US perspective. Her work in Australia was also key in helping us take up research and scholarship on indigenous communities—those peoples and cultures most distant from US centers of ICT development and CMC scholarship. (These Australian linkages are manifest in the cover design of our 2001 anthology (Ess 2001), which incorporates an Aboriginal map that both reveals and conceals important information, especially with a view towards protecting vital information from white outsiders.) Fay was also especially attentive to every detail of logistics, including venue, accommodation, catering, and excursions—all of which contributed to an overall conference experience of warmth and hospitality. This was neither a small accomplishment nor an incidental detail, precisely because the conferences brought together scholars and researchers from across diverse disciplines and cultures, providing the most comfortable and enjoyable context for both formal and informal interactions that was critical to establishing the atmosphere and conference culture required for those interactions to succeed.

Through a series of additional happy connections and fortunate circumstances—including colleagues who helped us line up our conference venue, other colleagues who helped us acquire a substantial grant from the Swiss Office of Technology Assessment, along with many other helping hands—we were able to greet the 60 or so colleagues who attended the first conference at the Science Museum of London on 1–3 August 1998. The conference participants represented some 17 diverse countries and cultures, including Australia, Europe and

Scandinavia, Russia, Africa, the Middle East, Asia (Japan, Thailand), Latin America (Venezuela), as well as the United Kingdom and the United States.

Culture Makes a Difference

As it happened, our conference began at the cusp of what Wellman characterizes as the second age of Internet studies—marked precisely by a turn from punditry to more systematic, empirically oriented research (Wellman 2011: 19f.). And in fact, both individually and collectively, the conference contributions powerfully documented—far beyond my original suspicions and intuitions—that indeed, culture makes a difference. As a first example, Daniel Pargmann documented what he later called "ASCII imperialism"—the difficulties presented for Scandinavians who sought to use the Internet for both work and play, but whose distinctive three vowel sounds (ø, æ, å) were not available in the standard ASCII encoding at the time. This meant, for example, that researchers and libraries in Scandinavia would be forced to rewrite even their very names in order to be searchable from a "global" perspective (Hård af Segerstad 2002). And, of course, these foundational mismatches only grew more dramatic the further one moved away from the English and US centers.

For instance, Lorna Heaton demonstrated the profound differences between the low-context/high-content cultures of the US and (northern) Europe on one hand, and the high-context/low-content culture of Japan: these differences more or less forced Japanese engineers to design their own CSCW systems that could capture the essential communicative elements of gesture, gaze, and body distance—elements essential in a culture whose communicative preferences emphasize the non-verbal, in contrast with Western (northern) emphases on direct communication via bare texts (Heaton 1998).

Soraj Hongladarom reiterated Pargmann's point regarding ASCII imperialism, as now faced all the more powerfully by Thai users of CMC. At the same time, however, Hongladarom offered a helpful middle ground between the prevailing binaries of jihad vs. McWorld. That is, he suggested that "Internet culture" would emerge as indeed a homogeneous one—one that would span and conjoin the globe, but primarily as a "thin" culture. By contrast, "thick" cultures—ones preserving core values, practices, and traditions defining cultural identity—would likewise remain (Hongladarom 1998). Such "thick" cultures were manifest, for example, in the *resistance* to reshaping via CMC documented in many of these first and subsequent CATaC conference presentations.

To cite just one example from CATaC'02: James Piecowye documents how young women of the United Arab Emirates consciously chose what elements of global cultures they wished to appropriate while they simultaneously insisted on preserving their own cultural values and practices (2003). As this example suggests, moreover, one can trace through the CATaC conference presentations and proceedings a strong thread of focus on the Arabic world, including women.

Later on, in fact, we would adopt the phrase from Ulf Hannerz (1989)—"the peripheries talk back"—to point to this dialectical relationship between thin and thick cultures. Finally, some ten years later, Soraj would return to CATaC to review his notions of thick and thin, to argue that the boundary between these two was becoming "fuzzier"—in part, because CMC technologies had, in fact, developed in ways that were more culturally sensitive and adaptable, while users themselves (in the Thai example at least) had likewise developed new communicative abilities, precisely through the ongoing dynamics of globalization and cultural change. Risk to cultural integrity and identity remain, however; as he put it, "the thick is probably getting thinner, and the thin is becoming thicker" (Hongladarom 2008: 85).

In particular, the conference contributions helped crystalize how the ostensibly cosmopolitan and beneficent visions of an "electronic global village" rested on several assumptions, namely:

> belief in communication as a sufficient condition for bringing about global understanding and democracy; belief in some sort of technological determinism, so that providing the infrastructure of CMC technologies will encourage, if not inevitably lead to, the appropriation of democratic and egalitarian values; and belief in a universally shared humanity, one more or less transparently communicable via CMC.
>
> (Ess 1998: 12f.)

Of course, from a contemporary perspective, these assumptions are profoundly suspect. But in 1998, these assumptions were not usually articulated, much less called into question. One of the primary accomplishments of the first CATaC conference, then, was to focus on these assumptions—and then further highlight their questionability, not simply on philosophical grounds, but on strongly *empirical* grounds—that is, as critically illuminated precisely by the wide range of experiences and analyses brought together at the conference.

The conference experience further helped us highlight what would become characteristic questions and themes, beginning with:

> Do CMC technologies embed or encourage the appropriation of a given set of cultural values, and/or do pre-existent cultural values resist and reshape the use of such technologies?
>
> What culturally-related factors, including attitudes toward gender and gender roles, encourage and/or discourage the appropriation and use of CMC technologies?
>
> (Ess 1998: 12)

Embodiment and Gender

In these directions, the venerable Steve Jones emphasized for us the importance of attention to embodiment and gender (Jones 1998). Again, from a contemporary perspective, this may seem obvious. But much of the 1990s discourse surrounding the Internet emphasized ostensibly sharp contrasts between online and offline experiences—between virtual and real worlds—in what I later characterized as Augustinian and Cartesian dualisms as central to, for example, William Gibson's *Neuromancer* (1984), the science fiction novel that shaped much of our thinking about "cyberspace" in the 1990s (Ess 2011). Such dualisms underlay Gibson's rapturous accounts of "bodiless exultation in cyberspace" (1984: 6)—an escape from the body that some feminists took up as a much needed escape from real-world violence and exploitation. These dualisms seem largely dead—first of all, as more empirical research through the 1990s and early 2000s increasingly demonstrated the inextricable interconnections between online and offline (Ess and Consalvo 2011: 3f.). Indeed, these interconnections are now so thoroughly documented as to have reached policy-oriented documents in the European Commission (Broadbent *et al.* 2013). But in 1998, foregrounding the body represented a still novel and courageous call.

The same must be said, unfortunately, for gender. On one hand, 1990s' concerns about how we might encourage more women to make use of what began as a set of technologies almost exclusively dominated by males (Ess 1996: 6f.) now seem quaint in the face of the many ways and venues in which women have taken up and sometimes dominate in turn

Internet-based communication technologies and venues. At the same time, however, as the most recent explosions over "Gamergate" make clear, hostility towards women—both overt and covert—remains deeply engrained in some communities and circles. The CATaC focus on gender thus remains centrally relevant.

Four further thematics emerged from CATaC'98 to become definitive of subsequent conferences.

Democracy and Freedom of Expression

To begin with, the utopian hope that wiring the world would thereby automatically bring in its trail greater democracy and freedom of expression was strongly challenged by both Hongladarom's observations and those of Michael Dahan (1998). Dahan drew on several episodes in Israel highlighting both the potentials and clear limitations of CMC to foster greater freedom of expression and democracy, with less than optimistic conclusions. With the advantage of some 18 additional years of research and exploration, we are acutely aware these days of how far CMC and the Internet may—and may not—foster greater democracy and freedom of expression. Examples abound of regimes around the world, including ostensibly more democratic ones, that achieve considerable, if not total, degrees of success in censoring diverse forms of content, often coupled with Internet-facilitated surveillance of their own populations that can result in jail, torture, or death for those who speak out. To be sure, a kind of Internet arms race is on—with those who, for example, develop new technological appliances to help counter government surveillance and censorship (e.g. Al-Saqaf 2014). However, all of this continues to unfold—especially recent revelations of the comprehensive surveillance capacities of the US National Security Administration, along with ongoing successes of repressive regimes in limiting citizen access to Internet-based content and exchange, make clear that 1990s' optimism regarding an inevitable democratization and emancipation via the Internet was profoundly open to question once we began to look seriously at culture, technology, and communication.

At times, of course, the themes of democracy and gender intersect: a striking example of this was Rasha Abdulla's keynote speech and conference presence in 2012, following soon after the so-called Arab Springs (Abdulla 2012).

Design

Second, CATaC'98 introduced a thematic that has, however gradually, developed into one of the most important foci for those of us motivated by normative commitments to democratic processes and norms, the importance of protecting cultural diversity, equality and gender equality, and so on—namely, the central role of the *designers* who shape and build the devices and their applications that constitute our communicative universe. CATaC'98 called attention to the possibility of design as embedding cultural elements, and thus risking cultural imperialism. To be sure, we were not the first to notice that design is not value-free—for example, something that ostensibly seeks to proceed from what Lucy Suchman has called "the view from nowhere" (2002). Very importantly, since the 1990s attention to these dimensions of ICT design has continued to grow and expand. In particular, José Abdelnour-Nocera—whose 1998 conference presentation examined Latin American virtual communities—went on to found the SOCIOTECH-INTERACTIONDESIGN mailing list in 2006, followed by *The International Journal of Sociotechnology and Knowledge Development* in 2009. (This is a first example of what I describe below in terms of the centrifugal effects of

CATaC—that is, how persons and their research, as first presented and developed at a CATaC conference, moved on to help shape and influence research and publication in specific disciplines and communities.) Indeed, the most recent CATaC conference (2014) took up design precisely as a central focus. Many good developments can be celebrated from this conference—along with ongoing recognition of how difficult it remains, in some quarters at least, to help bring deep awareness of culturally variable norms and communicative preferences into the design process.

Selfhood and Identity

Especially from a philosophical perspective, among the most foundational components of human existence as shaped by "culture" are our conceptions of selfhood and identity. This theme is, of course, older than CATaC—(see, for instance, Goonasekera 1990, cited in Ess 2001: 33). At the same time, the philosophers among us in particular sought to foreground identity and selfhood vis-à-vis diverse cultures, including long-time CATaC participant Soraj Hongladarom (for example, Hongladarom 2007). In my own case, attention to how foundational conceptions of selfhood and identity are changing in conjunction with changing media technologies and practices, especially across "East" and "West" differences, has become a prominent focus in recent years (for example, Ess 2014a).

Culture Makes a Difference—But What is "Culture"?

Finally, "culture" emerged as both more articulate and more problematic as a concept. On one hand, the foundational works of Gert Hofstede (for instance, 1980) and E. T. Hall (1976) made their appearance here—thereby beginning a defining thread for the series. Indeed, the first phase of the conference series was marked by an ever-increasing use of Hall and Hofstede, coupled with rising critique and resistance. In 1998, one of the first criticisms launched against (at least the use of) what were becoming widely used frameworks was just that "culture" tended to be understood here as something static and monolithic, if not strongly deterministic (see, for instance, Maitland 1998). Moreover, whatever "culture" might be, we as individuals represent the intersection of multiple layers and levels of "culture", most especially in a world marked not only by ever increasing cultural exchanges and encounters via CMC, but also by increased mobility, immigration, diasporas, and thereby the emergence of "third" or hybrid identities that mix two or more strong cultural backgrounds.

Subsequent CATaC conferences in this first phase saw increasing use of Hofstede, Hall, and others—sometimes conjoined in creative and expansive ways so as to identify, for instance, 29 culturally variable factors (Baumgartner and Marcus 2004, cited in Cantoni *et al.* 2006), or more than 70 (Reeder, Macfadyen, and Chase 2004). At the same time, however, critiques of any sort of simple notions of "culture" likewise developed and expanded—for example, Kamppuri and Tukiainen (2004). This critical thread continued both beyond the boundaries of the conference series and within, so as to reach a kind of crescendo in our 2008 conference in Nîmes, France. Here, CATaC veterans Connie Kampf (Aarhus University) and José Abdelnour-Nocera (University of West London) organized a panel titled "Beyond Hall, Hofstede, and 'culture': Understanding diversity from the top-down to the bottom-up and back!" The various critiques and alternatives to Hofstede and Hall consolidated here thereby continued the problematization of notions of "culture" that began in 1998.

Our conferences in 2010 and 2012 continued both the critical and constructive uses of "culture"—and by 2014, something of a synthesis of views could be discerned. On one hand, in his presentation, Abdelnour-Nocera summarized the now familiar criticisms of the term, but argued that "culture" could still be used as a "can-opener". And in these directions, a number of striking examples were presented of research that presumed one or more of these now (overly) familiar frameworks, so as to demonstrate—still and yet once again—how conflicts between the cultural norms, values, and practices, including communicative preferences that (still) shape the design and implementation of contemporary ICTs (now including mobile devices) and those of "target" cultures, (still) generated friction and conflict. Perhaps most strikingly, Gwyneth Sutherlin developed an experimental inquiry carried out among the Acholi people, using Western-based ICTs such as computers and mobile phones, in order to discern the communicative impacts of the differences between: narrative structures (linear vs. circular), time/space conceptions (abstract vs. concrete), and identity/agency (individualistic vs. relational) as rooted in chirographic ("literate") vs. oral cultures. She found that these contrasts resulted in a narrative distortion from what the informants could convey orally and thereby within their indigenous conceptual framework, and what they then could convey by way of texting through a mobile device. The upshot was that important information was left out and/or distorted in the move from one to the other—information that could be critical especially in crisis management and relief efforts (Sutherlin 2014a, 2014b).

At the same time, other long-term CATaC participants such as Patrizia Schettino (2014a, 2014b) have continued efforts to develop new analytical categories that capture our intuition that "culture makes a difference", but in ways that move beyond the limitations of earlier frameworks. Schettino does so by developing notions of "home" and "place" that build on post-colonial concepts of "hybridity" (Appadurai 1996; Bhabha 1994) in order to identify important culturally variable dimensions of a museum installation intended to be accessible to visitors from a wide range of cultural backgrounds. As such hybrid identities become more and more commonplace in the contemporary world as a result of immigration and mobility, such conceptualizations are likely to prove more fruitful for both analytical and design purposes.

The CATaC Conferences: Summary Observations

Perhaps the most surprising outcome of CATaC'98 was its success as a conference: the first participants convinced us that we should do this again. Conferences then followed on a biennial basis, accompanied by a number of publication ventures that succeeded in bringing this new research and reflection into the light of print and online publication. These included several special issues (Ess and Sudweeks 1998), including in such flagship journals such as *New Media and Society* (Ess and Sudweeks 2001) and the *Journal of Computer-Mediated Communication* (Ess and Sudweeks 2003, 2005; Ess, Zhu and Sudweeks 2002) as well as an edited volume (Ess 2001). In addition, the conference proceedings themselves constitute a rich archive of papers: the most recent ones are available online (catacconference.org) and we plan to make earlier ones accessible over the next year or so. I think of these outcomes as centripetal, as the conferences worked to focus and make available research and scholarship from a wide range of disciplines, gathered under a single banner. In this direction, the conferences also gained recognition from the Australian Research Council as "B" level—that is, in the top 20 percent of conferences analyzed in terms of impact and significance.

As these earlier publications indicate, the conferences managed to collect research from a very wide range of disciplines and interdisciplinary conjunctions, representing research and reflection from an exceptional range of peoples, cultures, and locales. Specifically, in their analysis of the first ten years of the CATaC conferences, P. Clint Rogers, M. Brooke

Robertshaw, and Javier López-González noted that the conferences attracted participants from 38 different countries, whose research focused on at least 52 different countries (2008: 9). Research methods represented were equally diverse, covering the gamut of qualitative, quantitative, and mixed-method approaches (ibid. 2008: 5). Despite our best efforts at moving beyond especially US-centric work, however, "Europe, Australia, and North America are much better represented than Asia, South America, the Middle East, and Africa" (ibid. 2008: 3).

Broadly, then, the CATaC conferences were growing in scope and impact, along with the Internet itself, of course, and thereby what we have come to call Internet studies more broadly. There are two moments in this (second) age of Internet studies and the growth of CATaC that are worth noting. The first is that, while it was certainly heartening to see more and more participants and publications with each conference—in 2004 (Karlstad, Sweden) CATaC attracted nearly 100 participants, and such large participation might seem like a strong advantage—especially those colleagues who had participated in previous conferences uniformly agreed that a critical component of the conference series was lost—namely, the informality and warm hospitality that we had managed to establish from the beginning. These characteristics were not simply important: they were indispensable. That is, a uniform chord across the conference series has been that the collocations we focus on—"culture", technology, communication—require an exceptional commitment to interdisciplinarity. For interdisciplinarity to succeed—especially in a conference setting, especially for younger scholars and researchers—it is essential to set a tone of informality and warmth that fosters respect and gentleness when raising an essential critique of a given presentation. Such a tone and atmosphere are equally critical to the manifold informal interactions that take place during the conference, where we are always newcomers and amateurs vis-à-vis someone else's deep expertise and specialization. Unlike other conference series, then, we made an explicit decision to keep the CATaC series comparatively small—on average, roughly 60-plus participants. While clearly limiting our finances (the conferences are self-funded) and potential impact, we nonetheless recognized that such a limitation was essential to maintaining the distinctive atmosphere and mood that were so prized by participants.

However justified from our perspective, this decision also guaranteed a kind of marginalization vis-à-vis other larger conferences. At the same time, however, the CATaC series was proving to be fruitful in a second, more centrifugal way—that is, as conference participants would take their work back into their more disciplinary orientations. In my own case, for example, I published a series of journal articles and chapters within philosophy, attempting to highlight the importance of cultural perspectives within the domains of information and computing ethics (for example, Ess 2002a, 2004), while simultaneously attempting to take up central matters of computer-mediated communication within comparative philosophy (Ess 2002b, 2003).

Following the 2004 conference, we undertook fewer and fewer CATaC-specific publication projects (for instance, Ess, Kawabata, and Kurosaki 2007), but it seems clear that the CATaC conferences continued to foster further publication and collaboration in more centrifugal directions. In this way, our development paralleled that of the conference many of us were also intimately engaged with—namely, the Internet Research conferences of the Association of Internet Researchers (AoIR), which began in 2000. In particular, Wellman argues that 2004 marks the shift into the (current) third age of Internet studies. In this age, he notes that Internet studies continues to develop into a field in its own right (however interdisciplinary)—that is, in what I have called a centripetal direction, as manifest, for example, in several handbooks and volumes devoted to Internet studies (for example, Ess and Consalvo 2011; Dutton 2013; Tsatsou 2015). These developments are accompanied by a second, complementary trend—namely, "the incorporation of Internet research into the main-stream conferences and journals of their disciplines, with projects driven by ongoing issues" (Wellman 2011: 21). Wellman's additional comment here is also critical: "This brings the more developed theories, methods, and substantive lore of the disciplines into play, although sometimes at the cost of the adventurous innovativeness of interdisciplinary Internet research" (2011: 21).

In this light, it may well be that the CATaC conference series, especially as it remains comparatively small for the sake of fostering highly interdisciplinary engagement and dialogue, will thereby enjoy impact enough in centripetal directions, but will prove productive in more diffuse centrifugal ways as participants take their findings and insights back into their own more disciplinary departments, research, and publications.

Concluding Observations

With the benefit of more than 15 years of research and reflection, it is clear that "culture" indeed makes a difference vis-à-vis design, implementation, and responses to ICTs, including the Internet as the medium that connects ever greater percentages of the world's populations. At the same time, just as the technologies themselves undergo constant development and transformation, so our most foundational conceptions likewise continue to develop and transform—most especially notions of what counts as "culture" and the culturally variable elements that need to be brought to the foreground in our analyses (Schettino 2014a, 2014b, among others).

More broadly, perhaps we can say with some confidence that the once heretical questions of "culture" vis-à-vis communication and technology are now increasingly mainstream and diffuse, driven not only by whatever impacts the CATaC conferences may have had, but also certainly by the inescapable confrontations with cultural differences brought about by Internet-based communications themselves, most especially as a result of the dramatic expansion of Internet access via mobile devices in developing countries.

Beyond CATaC, however, my impression is that still a relatively small percentage of work within Internet studies takes up explicitly cultural dimensions. To be sure, there is now considerably more work on Japan and China as well as within Arabic-speaking cultures (represented early on at CATaC, as we have seen, e.g. Heaton 1998; Piecowye 2003; see also the chapters in Goggin and McLelland 2009). But attempting to publish research and scholarship in these directions very often falls into an uncomfortable pattern. On one hand, as Goggin and McLelland observe (2009: 13), work sent to many of the top-ranked English-language journals—namely, those whose own cultural centers remain focused on the United States, Europe, and (perhaps) Australia—is often sent back with the critique that the research fails to speak to prominent US or European theorists. Of course, it is not unreasonable to request, in effect, a dialogue between such prevailing views and theories, and the research and scholarship that in some ways may deeply challenge the culturally shaped assumptions that underlie such ostensibly central frameworks and perspectives. At the same time, however, this request appears to rest on and reinforce the (ethnocentric) assumption that these theories are indeed the center and the default—the paradigms against which all other work must be measured. The upshot is that, apart from, say, the occasional anthology, theme issue, or conference proceedings (such as those from CATaC), much of our work has to be fitted into more specialized domains and publication venues. In my case, for example, we have been able to place important cross-cultural analyses of privacy vis-à-vis CMC and ICT in first-rank journals (e.g. Lü 2005; Nakada and Takanori 2005). But however heartening, significant, and influential this work may be, it thereby remains quarantined within a comparatively specialized domain, one that puts, in this example, the specifics of privacy above what for us are the more central and compelling matters of culture. In these ways, "culture" remains subordinated, if not marginalized, thereby reinforcing the ethnocentrisms that our work seeks to directly confront and overcome. To borrow from Hannerz (1989), our efforts still resemble those of the peripheries to talk back. While I have argued that culturally oriented research has managed to move from the heretical to a somewhat more mainstream status over the past 16 years or so, it seems there is still much work to be done to overcome the tendencies of even our best colleagues and institutions towards an ethnocentrism that continues to privilege US and European models and frameworks.

There are, no doubt, multiple reasons for this—beginning with the complexities of "culture" itself. At the same time, there are multiple additional pressures working against these CATaC foci. To begin with, while there is still much discourse in the academy praising the critical importance of interdisciplinary work—there are also many and familiar pressures working against such interdisciplinarity. In particular, resources in the academy are always limited, and have been more so since the financial crises of 2009 forwards.

At a more foundational level, it seems to me that a primary blockage remains the one I highlighted from the outset—namely, our own tendencies towards ethnocentrism, despite our best efforts to the contrary. A key factor in this direction is our tendency—most especially in the United States, which remains at least somewhat dominant in these domains—to remain within a single language. To state the obvious, crossing cultures requires acquiring facility in new languages and the correlative skills required for research and dialogue in multilingual environments. In the case of CATaC, our most manifest success in this direction was the 2008 conference in Nîmes, France, organized as a bilingual conference with particular emphasis on thereby attracting participation from both France as well as the many and strikingly diverse francophone countries around the world. The challenges in making this conference work, however, were also exceptionally high, beginning precisely with the demands on many of us to work with some fluency in at least two and often more languages (English, French, Arabic, and so on). Par contra, there appears to be a counter move away from more international towards more nationally focused scholarship (for instance, Ess 2014b). Perhaps this should not be surprising, both in light of the difficulties of moving beyond our own linguistic and cultural homes, and in light of shrinking resources in the academy that weigh against international travel, etc.

Most fundamentally, perhaps, it may be that the explicitly normative commitments that have defined CATaC from its inception also represent obstacles. That is, whatever one's personal ethical and political commitments may be—especially within the social science disciplines that tend to dominate both Internet studies broadly and CATaC work in particular—the positivist roots of these disciplines weigh heavily against taking up explicit normative commitments or goals as definitive of one's work. (There are, to be sure, many and important exceptions to this, along with important, ongoing debates over the appropriate role of normativity in these disciplines: Ess 2015.)

Nonetheless, it seems clear that the temptations of ethnocentrism and thus the correlative risks of colonization and imperialism remain, whether in more overt or more covert forms, especially as these ethical and political concerns are marginalized in Internet spaces driven more by commercialization and commodification, including self-commodification (for example, Fuchs and Dyer-Witheford 2012). Insofar as this is true, then it seems equally clear that the signature concerns and foci of the CATaC conferences remain as critical as ever.

Acknowledgements

The CATaC conference series has benefited from far more individuals and institutions than can possibly be named here individually. But here I must recognize the multiple contributions of Herbert Hrachovec (University of Vienna). Herbert was among the first in 1998 to point out that our presumptions about "culture" were problematic, and he has served through subsequent CATaC conferences as an exemplary critic—one who conjoins exceptional background and insight with sharp but collegial and constructive critique. Herbert has also provided much of the IT resources and support for CATaC over the years—a task also ably shared by Leah Macfadyen (University of Vancouver).

Deepest thanks further go to the many local organizing committees who worked with our organizing and program committees to make each conference possible, fruitful, and enjoyable. Especial thanks to my colleagues who have served as our organizing and program committees in recent years: Herbert Hrachovec, Leah Macfadyen, Michele Strano (Bridgewater College, US), and Maja van der Velden (University of Oslo).

Note

1. By "ethnocentrism" here I refer to the more or less universal human cognitive and emotive maneuver to simply assume that the norms, practices, beliefs, behaviors, etc. of our home culture(s) and society are universally the same for all peoples at all times in all cultures. When stated so baldly, it is blindingly obvious that such a maneuver is deeply mistaken. But part of my point here is just that such ethnocentrism is stubbornly difficult to avoid, even among those of us who—well educated, well travelled, experienced in diverse languages and cultures, etc.—do our best to avoid and overcome it.

References

Abdelnour-Nocera, J. (1998) "Virtual Environments as Spaces of Symbolic Construction and Cultural Identity: Latin American Virtual Communities", in C. Ess and F. Sudweeks (eds), *Proceedings Cultural Attitudes Towards Communication and Technology'98*, University of Sydney, Australia, pp. 149–151.

Abdulla, R. (2012) "Lessons from Egypt: The Roles and Limits of Social Media in Political Activism and Transformation (Keynote Address)", *Proceedings Cultural Attitudes Towards Communication and Technology'12*, Aarhus, Denmark, June.

Al-Saqaf, W. (2014) "Breaking Digital Firewalls: Analyzing Internet Censorship and Circumvention in the Arab World", Ph.D. thesis, Örebro University.

Appadurai, A. (1996) *Modernity at Large: Cultural Dimensions of Globalization*, Minneapolis, MN: University of Minnesota Press.

Barber, B. (1995) *Jihad versus McWorld*, New York: Times Books.

Baumgartner, V. J., and Marcus, A. (2004) "A Practical Set of Culture Dimensions for Global User-Interface Development", *Proceedings APCHI 2004: 6th Asia-Pacific Conference on Computer-Human Interaction*.

Bhabha, H. (1994) *Location of Culture*, London: Routledge.

Broadbent, S., Dewandre, N., Ess, C., Floridi, L., Ganascia, J-G., Hildebrandt, M., and Verbeek, P-P. (2013) *The Onlife Initiative*, Brussels: European Commission, available at: https://ec.europa.eu/digital-agenda/sites/digital-agenda/files/Onlife_Initiative.pdf

Carey, J. W. (1989) *Communication as Culture: Essays on Media and Society*, Boston, MA: Unwin Hyman.

Cantoni, L., Fanni, F., Rega, I., Schettino, P., and Tardini, S. (2006) "Localization of Blended Courses in Salvador De Bahia. A Localization Case Study. A Path for Integrating National Cultural Dimensions and Social Frameworks", in F. Sudweeks, H. Hrachovec, and C. Ess (eds), *Proceedings Cultural Attitudes Towards Communication and Technology*, Murdoch University, Australia, pp. 202–216.

Dahan, M. (1998) "National Security and Democracy on the Internet in Israel", in C. Ess and F. Sudweeks (eds), *Proceedings Cultural Attitudes Towards Communication and Technology*, Sydney: University of Sydney, pp. 145–148.

Dutton, W. (ed.) (2013) *The Oxford Handbook of Internet Studies*, Oxford: Oxford University Press.

Ess, C. (1994) "The Political Computer: Hypertext, Democracy, and Habermas", in G. Landow (ed.), *Hyper/Text/Theory*, Baltimore: Johns Hopkins Press, pp. 225–267.

Ess, C. (1996) "Introduction: Thoughts Along the I-way: Philosophy and the Emergence of Computer-Mediated Communication", in C. Ess (ed.), *Philosophical Perspectives on Computer-Mediated Communication*, Albany, NY: SUNY Press, pp. 1–12.

Ess, C. (1998) "First Looks: CATAC'98 (Introduction)", in C. Ess and F. Sudweeks (eds), *Proceedings Cultural Attitudes Towards Communication and Technology '98*, University of Sydney, Australia, pp. 1–17.

Ess, C. (2001) "What's Culture Got to Do with It? Cultural Collisions in the Electronic Global Village, Creative Interferences, and the Rise of Culturally-Mediated Computing", in C. Ess (ed.) with F. Sudweeks, *Culture, Technology, Communication: Towards an Intercultural Global Village*, Albany, NY: State University of New York Press, pp. 1–50.

Ess, C. (2002a) "Cultures in Collision: Philosophical Lessons from Computer-Mediated Communication", *Metaphilosophy*, 33(1/2): 229–253.

Ess, C. (2002b) "Electronic Global Village or McWorld? The Paradoxes of Computer-Mediated Cosmopolitanism and the Quest for Universal Values", in R. Elberfeld, J. Kreuzer, J. Minford, and G. Wohlfart (eds), *Komparative Ethik: Das gute Leben zwischen den Kulteren* (Comparative Ethics: The Good Life between Cultures), Munich: Wilhelm Fink Verlag, pp. 319–342.

Ess, C. (2003) "Cultural Collisions and Collusions in the Electronic Global Village: From McWorld and Jihad to Intercultural Cosmopolitanism", in P. D. Herschock, M. Stepaniants, and R. T. Ames (eds), *Technology and Cultural Values on the Edge of the Third Millennium*, Honolulu: University of Hawai'i Press and East-West Philosophers Conference, pp. 508–527.

Ess, C. (2004) "Computer-Mediated Colonization, the Renaissance, and Educational Imperatives for an Intercultural Global Village", in R. Cavalier (ed.), *The Internet and Our Moral Lives*, Albany, NY: SUNY Press, pp. 161–193.

Ess, C. (2011) "Self, Community, and Ethics in Digital Mediatized Worlds", in C. Ess and M. Thorseth (eds), *Trust and Virtual Worlds: Contemporary Perspectives*, Oxford: Peter Lang, pp. 3–30.

Ess, C. (2014a) "Selfhood, Moral Agency, and the Good Life in Mediatized Worlds? Perspectives from Medium Theory and Philosophy", in K. Lundby (ed.), *Mediatization of Communication*, Vol. 21, *Handbook of Communication Science*, Berlin: De Gruyter Mouton, pp. 617–640.

Ess, C. (2014b) "Zwischen zwei Stühlen sitzen—oder drei, oder . . .", in I. Baxmann, T. Beyes, and C. Pias (eds), *Soziale Medien—Neue Massen?* (Social Media—New Masses?), Berlin: Akademie Verlag, 357–363.

Ess, C. (2015) "The Good Life: Selfhood and Virtue Ethics in the Digital Age", in H. Wang (ed.), *Communication and the Good Life*, ICA Themebook 2014, New York: Peter Lang, pp. 17–29.

Ess, C., and Sudweeks, F. (eds) (1998) "Cultural Attitudes toward Technology and Communication (Comportement Culturel en vers le Progres Technique et la Communication)", *Electronic Journal of Communication (La Revue Electronic de Communication)*, 8(3 & 4), available at: www.cios.org/www/ejc/v8n398.htm (accessed 24 January 2015).

Ess, C., and Sudweeks, F. (2001) "On the Edge: Cultural Barriers and Catalysts to IT Diffusion among Remote and Marginalized Communities (Introduction)", *New Media and Society*, 3(3): 259–269.

Ess, C., and Sudweeks, F. (2003) "Technologies of Despair and Hope: Liberatory Potentials and Practices of CMC in the Middle East", *Journal of Computer-Mediated Communication*, 8(2).

Ess, C., and Sudweeks, F. (2005) "Culture and Computer-Mediated Communication: Toward New Understandings", *Journal of Computer-Mediated Communication*, 11(1): 179–191.

Ess, C., and Consalvo, M. (2011) "Introduction: What is 'Internet Studies'?", in M. Consalvo and C. Ess (eds), *The Handbook of Internet Studies*, Malden, MA: Wiley-Blackwell, pp. 1–8.

Ess, C., Zhu, J., and Sudweeks, F. (eds) (2002) *Internet Adoption in the Asia-Pacific Region*, special issue of *Journal of Computer-Mediated Communication*, 7(2). (NB: only the articles of this special issue are still available online.)

Ess, C., Kawabata, A., and Kurosaki, H. (2007) "Cross-Cultural Perspectives on Religion and Computer-Mediated Communication", *Journal of Computer-Mediated Communication*, 12(3).

Fuchs, C., and Dyer-Witheford, N. (2012) "Karl Marx @ Internet Studies", *New Media and Society*, 15(5): 782–796.

Gibson, W. (1984) *Neuromancer*, New York: Ace Books.

Goggin, G., and McLelland, M. (eds) (2009) *Internationalizing Internet Studies: Beyond Anglophone Paradigms*, Oxford: Routledge.

Goonasekera, A. (1990) "Communication, Culture and the Growth of the Individual Self in Third World Societies", *Asian Journal of Communication*, 1(1): 34–52.

GVU (Graphic, Visualization, and Usability Center) (1998), "GVU's 10th WWW user survey", *Georgia Technological University*, available at: www.cc.gatech.edu/gvu/user_surveys/survey-1998-10/graphs/general/q50.htm

Hall, E. T. (1976) *Beyond Culture*, Garden City, NJ: Doubleday.

Hannerz, U. (1989) "Culture Between Center and Periphery: Toward a Macroanthropology", *Ethnos*, 54: 200–216.

Hård af Segerstad, Y. (2002) "Effects of Mobile Text Messaging on the Swedish Written Language", in F. Sudweeks and C. Ess (eds), *Proceedings Cultural Attitudes Towards Communication and Technology*, Murdoch University, Australia, pp. 355–360.

Heaton, L. (1998) "Preserving Communication Context: Virtual Workspace and Interpersonal Space in Japanese CSCW", in C. Ess and F. Sudweeks (eds), *Proceedings Cultural Attitudes Towards Communication and Technology'98*, University of Sydney, Australia, pp. 163–186.

Hofstede, G. (1980) *Culture's Consequences: International Differences in Work-Related Values*, Beverly Hills, CA: Sage.

Hongladarom, S. (1998) "Global Culture, Local Cultures, and the Internet", in C. Ess and F. Sudweeks (eds), *Proceedings Cultural Attitudes Towards Communication and Technology*, Sydney: University of Sydney, pp. 187–201.

Hongladarom, S. (2007) "Analysis and Justification of Privacy from a Buddhist Perspective", in S. Hongladarom and C. Ess (eds), *Information Technology Ethics: Cultural Perspectives*, Hershey, PA: Idea Group Reference, pp. 108–122.

Hongladarom, S. (2008) "Global Culture, Local Cultures and the Internet", in F. Sudweeks, H. Hrachovec, and C. Ess (eds), *Proceedings Cultural Attitudes Towards Communication and Technology*, Murdoch University, Australia, pp. 80–85.

Jones, S. (1998) "Understanding Micropolis and Compunity", in C. Ess and F. Sudweeks (eds), *Proceedings Cultural Attitudes Towards Communication and Technology*, Sydney: University of Sydney, pp. 21–33.

Kamppuri, M. and Tukiainen, M. (2004) "Culture in Human-Computer Interaction Studies: A Survey of Ideas and Definitions", in F. Sudweeks and C. Ess (eds), *Proceedings Cultural Attitudes Towards Communication and Technology*, Murdoch University, Australia, pp. 43–57.

Lü, Y-H. (2005) "Privacy and Data Privacy Issues in Contemporary China", *Ethics and Information Technology*, 7(1): 7–15.

Maitland, C. (1998) "Global Diffusion of Interactive Networks: The Impact of Culture", in C. Ess and F. Sudweeks (eds), *Proceedings Cultural Attitudes Towards Communication and Technology*, University of Sydney, Australia, pp. 51–69.

Nakada, M., and Takanori, T. (2005) "Japanese Conceptions of Privacy: An Intercultural Perspective", *Ethics and Information Technology*, 7(1): 27–36.

Piecowye, J. (2003) "Habitus in Transition? CMC Use and Impacts among Young Women in the United Arab Emirates", *Journal of Computer-Mediated Communication*, 8:0.

Reeder, K., Macfadyen, L. P., and Chase, M. (2004) "Falling Through the (Cultural) Gaps? Intercultural Communication Challenges in Cyberspace", in F. Sudweeks and C. Ess (eds), *Proceedings Cultural Attitudes Towards Communication and Technology*, Karlstads Universitet, Sweden, pp. 123–134.

Rogers, P. C., Robertshaw, M. B., and López-González, J. (2008) "Analysis of CATAC: What Do We Know? Where Do We Next Go?", in F. Sudweeks, H. Hrachovec, and C. Ess (eds), *Proceedings Cultural Attitudes Towards Communication and Technology*, Murdoch University, Australia, pp. 1–10.

Schettino, P. (2014a) "Rethinking Immersive Cultural Experience in Museums: A Crosscultural Analysis of Visitors' Behaviors Based on Roles", in M. Strano, H. Hrachovec, S. Fragoso, C. Ess, and M. van der Velden (eds), *Proceedings Culture, Technology, Communication*, University of Oslo, Norway, pp. 83–97.

Schettino, P. (2014b) "Re-Thinking the Immersive Intercultural Design Process in Museums: A Qualitative Study Based on the Embodied Constructivist GTM Digital Ethnography in Situ", Ph.D. thesis, Università della Svizzera italiana, Lugano, Switzerland.

Suchman, L. (2002) "Located Accountabilities in Technology Production", *Scandinavian Journal of Information Systems*, 14(2): 91–105.

Sudweeks, F., McLaughlin, M., and Rafaeli, S. (eds) (1998) *Network and Netplay: Virtual Groups on the Internet*, Cambridge, MA: MIT Press.

Sutherlin, G. (2014a) "Groupthink: ICT Design with Culture in Mind", in M. Strano, H. Hrachovec, S. Fragoso, C. Ess, and M. van der Velden (eds), *Proceedings Culture, Technology, Communication*, University of Oslo, Norway, pp. 116–132.

Sutherlin, G. (2014b) "The Myth of the Universal User", Ph.D. thesis, Bradford University, Bradford, UK.

Thorseth, M. (2011) "Virtuality and Trust in Broadened Thinking Online", in C. Ess and M. Thorseth (eds), *Trust and Virtual Worlds: Contemporary Perspectives*, New York: Peter Lang, pp. 162–173.

Tsatsou, P. (2015) *Internet Studies: Past, Present and Future Directions*, Farnham, Surrey: Ashgate.

Wellman, B. (2011) "Studying the Internet Through the Ages", in M. Consalvo and C. Ess (eds), *The Blackwell Handbook of Internet Studies*, Oxford: Wiley-Blackwell, pp. 17–23.

3

THE STATE OF THE INTERNETS

Notes for a New Historiography of Technosociality

Nishant Shah

History is generally perceived to be a narrative of time. However, when it comes down to the nuts and bolts, history is actually about the sequencing of time but focused on space. Histories are both wedded to the geography and confined to the areas that they emerge from. It is in the nature of historiography that it simultaneously provincializes and globalizes locations. Thus, a cursory glance at almost any history project of the Internet focuses on the Euro-American unfolding of the Internet, positing that narrative as the de facto history and also the global history of the Internet. This becomes such a powerful metaphor that the world gets separated into the West versus the Rest (Postill 2011), where the West is the location of the Internet and the Rest becomes the site to be rescued by the Internet.[1]

These histories are informed by three presumptions that are often critiqued, and yet fiercely reinforced, in history writing. The first is the genesis paradigm. There is a deep conviction that things begin from a single point that can be marked as the beginning. The Internet has had many and multiple beginnings, like Charles Babbage and Ada Lovelaces's differential and analytic engines to the production of the ENIAC that mark the emergence of the computer, as well as the industrial–military complex of the Second World War that propels computing into the networked era, allowing for an encrypted circulation of digital traffic to emerge (Markoff 2006). More contemporary histories of the Internet might focus on the personaliza-tion of the Internet and the countercultures that led to the visions of the World Wide Web (Berners-Lee and Fischetti 2000; Turner 2006), or the production of global information structures and infrastructures that make the physical spread of the Internet possible (Hafner and Lyon 1996). While these beginning points can be multiple, defined by the inquiry and the intention of the historian, identifying the different layers of technology and usage that the Internet embodies, they are all marked by a single point origin that always resides in the Global North, thus initiating the prevalent imagination of the world where some geographies are where the Internet is built and some other geographies are where the Internet gets applied.

They acknowledge and allow for multiple interpretations and disarticulations of the Internet, but they still tie it to single origin points that allow for these histories to be the de facto and global histories of the Internet, located in provincial towns that become the global hubs for talking about the Internet. Thus, Silicon Valley, for instance, doesn't become a West Coast American History of the Internet. Instead, it becomes such a powerful genesis story, like the garden of Eden and man's fall from grace, that any other location around the "flattened world" becomes a mere mimicry or pale imitation of that Silicon Valley (Friedman 2005). Thus, even when producing a new history, a new narrative, a new geography and genealogy for the history, the original Silicon Valley remains the unquestioned reference point, shaping all the other histories as alternative or derivative. The genesis history of the Internet remains the only measure by which all other histories are to be written, and it becomes the burden of the alternative historian to qualify and justify the new locations and stories as measuring up to the rubrics established by these monolithic historical narratives of the Internet. Such an history mimics what Donna Haraway (1991) calls the romantic imagination of the human that "depends on the myth of original unity, fullness, bliss and terror" (1991: 151). Indeed, taking a cue from Haraway, the quest would be to write a (cyborg) history of the Internet that is "resolutely committed to partiality, irony, intimacy, and perversity. It is oppositional, utopian, and completely without innocence" (1991: 151).

The second presumption that marks all these histories of the Internet is the idea that they know exactly what the Internet is. While there is a recognition that the Internet is ubiquitous, intertwined with socio-cultural and economic–political processes, the Internet is also produced as a discrete, complete, and concrete object which can be traced in all its forms, formats, and functions through time and space. The attempt of historicizing the Internet is often to understand its contemporary practices and structures. However, ironically, the history writing demands that a clear understanding of the Internet as we know it now be presented in order for the historical narrative to emerge. This strange paradox where the historiography is in the service of understanding the object, but simultaneously demands a clear understanding of the object in order for the history writing to begin, often leads to the reduction of the Internet to its technological materiality and specificity. Such a process is an attempt at what Bruno Latour in *An Inquiry into Modes of Existence* (2013) describes as "making history systematic" when it isn't. Latour argues for a contingent history that is assembled by different modes of inquiry where each mode is differentiated and yet interlinked. However, in the absence of this, the Latourian Internet is reduced to its technology infrastructure or rendered through gadgets and devices; it is located in corporations that build it or in the users that consume it; it is contained in spaces where it becomes manifest or in the networks that configure it. The demand for a clear idea of what the Internet is does not discount the many and contesting meanings of the Internet, as well as the conflicted interpretations that are around us. However, it does make it imperative for the historical narrative to still produce a coherent and consolidated vision of the Internet that would synthesize and stitch together these different fragments, producing the Internet as a monolithic structure that has expected and accepted practices, processes, and people who embody and illustrate it (Bagga, Keniston, and Mathur 2005). The diversity of the Internet is replaced by the scale of the Internet (Shah 2015a). And any history writing, no matter how alternative the approach or how unusual the location, is expected to follow this trope where it distills the Internet into a clear object, removing its messiness and its untowardness to create gentrified histories that reduce the scope of what the Internet is and how it could be studied.

The third presumption that is prevalent in the dominant histories of the Internet is the role of the Internet in defining subjectivities in and outside of these global provinces. It is clear that the Internet allows for and enables a multitude of practices for different users. However, the practices of the Internet are not global, and the location of the user often gives it meanings and values. Thus, a global community of Facebook users might be constructed as homogeneous because they all perform similar functions designed by the interface and algorithms of that platform. However, as Jonas Löwgren and Bo Reimer in their coining of "collaborative media" (2013) show, the homogenization of design that is often considered as the prerequisite for collaborative work is actually a fallacy. This idea easily gets exploded when we locate it in the context of protests and activism, as we realize that the Like button has a very different function when it is being used to spread messages of political solidarity than when it is being used to share pictures of cute cats.

The geographical context of the user and the intention of usage obviously inform the value of such a practice. These differences are accounted for in these histories. However, these differences are not about the technological, but social, usages. Even when these differences are accounted for, the technological protocols and the subjectivity of the 'liker' are considered to be uniform and homogeneous. Kavita Philip (2005), in her work on the history of the technological pirate, shows how the difference becomes stark when the same practice, using the same technologies, towards the same intentions, still constructs some users as creative entrepreneurs and artists as it penalizes others as criminals and pirates. Philip takes up an advertisement from Apple, which branded its iMac and the introduction of iTunes with the slogan "Rip. Mix. Burn", encouraging its privileged users to share files, to override copyright, to eschew licenses, to mix and burn new discs with music, movies, and software, thus realizing the true potential of the digital and connected technologies. In the same year, following mounting pressures from American companies that were exploring India as the new digital market and off-shore processing hub, the Indian government cracked down on local markets that were ripping licensed software, mixing Hollywood music and movies, and burning discs to sell in the "grey" market, labeling these practices as acts of piracy, and introducing criminal proceedings against the users and distributors involved in these processes.

This chapter is an attempt to look at the three different entry points that introduce new locations, objects, and frameworks by which the history of the Internets in India can be told. These are histories which are not about names and numbers, dates and events, gadgets and usage. They are also not shaped to mimic either the military state's development of the Internet or the neoliberal market's appropriation and escalation of these technologies. Instead, they root the Internet firmly in the Indian context and propose that the history of the Internets in India is the history of its interaction with the Indian state. Firmly drawing attention away from the market-driven rhetoric of India as an emerging economy, as the largest untapped consumer base, and as the new frontier of frugal innovation known as jugaad (Rajdou, Prabhu, and Ahuja 2012), the approaches, instead, identify three blank spaces in the unfolding of the state and the Internet in India to help understand the trajectories and terrains that have formed and informed the making of the technosocial contemporary.

The Missing Body

Different attempts at historicizing the Internet in India have pointed at the electrification of the country, the telecommunication revolutions, and the mass adoption of the personal computer and the mobile phone as landmarks where it can all be supposed to have begun. However, in citing these beginnings, the histories largely focus on technological inventions, infrastructure building, and governmental policies, developing a persistent blind spot when it comes to the body and its interactions with the Internet. Even within the discourse and implementation of the Information and Communication Technologies for Development (ICT4D), which has a strong rooting in the bodily conditions of its subjects, engaging with a range of issues from poverty, illiteracy, gender-based discrimination, health, etc. the body remains on the fringes or as unaffected by the presence of the digital technologies and the Internet. The body, when invoked, is thought of merely as the infrastructure that can be accounted for in quantifications of usage, access, inclusion, and adoption.

Asha Achuthan (2011), writing a feminist history of the epistemology of the Internet titled *Re:wiring Bodies*, argues that this discrete production of the body and its dissociation and extraction from the developmental practices leads to two pre-wired responses that are characteristic of post-colonial societies that depend on these technologies as a form of rebuilding their nations. The body is either thought of as fragile, ready to be saved by the emergence of these technologies, thus rendered without agency or choice; or the body is understood as unclean and corrupt, unable to realize the potentials of these technologies and hence in need of correction and rehabilitation by these technologies.

Drawing particularly from the intersections of digital technologies and their penetration in women's bodies through contemporary healthcare practices in India, Achuthan shows how digital technologies of connectivity in their interaction with the state policies and operations produce the body in a condition of aporia. In explaining her characterization of aporia, Achuthan argues that when it comes to intersections of body with the digital, it offers a pre-wired set of responses. The first step is to fetishize access and insist that the sexual invisibility and inequity will be corrected by connecting everybody in the digital networks. Once access infrastructure building is initiated, there is recognition that access is uneven and does not guarantee presence. Efforts are made to train these identified minorities to be habilitated into the existing practices, making them "subjects" of technology. Presence proves to be inadequate, because in the burgeoning information sets of the digital Web, it is highly possible to be present, but not be visible. The next step is to think of inclusion and set up corrective mechanisms by which the underserved communities can be included in discourse, practice, and policy. This immediately establishes corrective mechanisms of control and regulation, where only certain kinds of bodies and identities can be created as occupying these positions of power, eventually amplifying the same inequalities that the entire process was set up to address. Aporia, then, becomes a trope by which the technology states are pitched against each other, and each shares a common blind spot where the body itself slips into a black hole.

Achuthan locates this aporetic body as being at the heart of the ICT4D movement that ensured that the Internet came in as yet another tool for the development state, and is in the service of fulfilling the indices of development which have equally been critiqued for being systems of accounting which do not take the individual or the body into account. The history of the Internet in India, for Achuthan, then, is a history of the state's encounter with science and technology and the ways in which the original impulses of the "scientific temperament" that construct the modern Indian nation state as a post-colonial country continue to shape both the spread of the Internet and the invisible ways in which it rewires the body in conditions of precariousness and neglect. In her comprehensive thesis, Achuthan argues that the technoscience industry in India predates the national industry. In fact, looking at the conversations between Mohandas Gandhi and Rabindranath Tagore, two of the most prominent architects of the Indian freedom revolution and the new nation state, reveals how much faith was invested in the production of the nation state as a technosocial artifact. For Gandhi, the economic nationalist, the new nation state was to be constructed through the spinning wheel, which was not only the embodiment of an indigenous technology of production, but also a metaphor for the "swaraj" (self-governance) that was at the heart of the call for independence.[2] It is not a coincidence that in 2015, when the new right wing Hindu nationalist party BJP forms the government, one of their first projects, Make in India (n.d.), which seeks to reconstruct India into becoming a digital superpower that attracts foreign investment and infrastructure building, invokes Gandhi's notions of swaraj as the historical antecedent to this project.

However, for Tagore, the Oxbridge-educated spiritualist, this reliance on technology and science to build our national identity and society was problematic. Tagore, Achuthan points out, introduces the idea of a "yantra danava" (demonic machine) in his nationalist writing, as a metaphor for a technology that will engulf the nation and neglect the very bodies that it seeks to protect and uplift. For Tagore, the technological had to be superseded by the humanism of nation building, demanding that these machines are not just things that we use, but that they write us, create and construct us, that as we spin the wheel to produce cotton, we spin ourselves into becoming subjects of and to the technologies. Tagore's fear of putting all our faith in the resilience of technologies is often reflected in contemporary debates where the problems of development are often turned into problems of information technologies.[3] Achuthan looks at the production of technologized healthcare for women in India, where a wide range of social and political factors that contribute to poor reproductive health, like poverty, corruption, illiteracy, ignorance, etc. are now reduced to becoming a problem of the informational subject's incapacity to receive, interpret, and act upon the information that is given out to them. She points out that the reliance on the Internet and its connectivity as the solution to some of the most historically endemic national problems replaces lived reality with informational reality. When faced with a problem that is both bodily and messy, these healthcare systems produce either a call for better data or more data, and eventually write the ill body as an unclean body which cannot be accommodated for or is not intelligible to the technogovernmental systems. This body then either has to be cured or corrected to become worthy of these Internet regimes and its failure to adapt exfiltrates it from the domains of care and support that these digital systems build.

Achuthan argues that the history of the Internet will have to begin with the history of the body, not in its use of technologies, but as it is written by the technological apparatus and the scientific industry of the nation state. She shows that the body is created, contained, corrected, cured, and celebrated as the state interacts with technologies, and that the contemporary digital body has its unshaken roots in the first model of the nationalist body that has remain unchanged, even as technologies transitioned into new political discourses from the nationalist to the Marxist, from the Marxist to the subaltern, and from the subaltern to the contemporary neoliberal digitality. This history of the changing technologies and the unchanging bodies, of the cleaned-up technologies and the body that remains dirty, of mobile digitality and the rooted biology, is a cyborg history of how the body becomes the site where the interaction between the political state and the scientific technologies become reified, thus offering a critical questioning of the digital that we otherwise access only as a suite of tools rather than a "set of attitudes" which define the very ways in which the body is conceived and controlled. Achuthan's approach is to think of the body as the Internet, as opposed to the body as merely the use agent of the Internet, and thus brings in questions of politics, justice, equality, and equity that are often lost in the interactions between the developmental state and the developing technologies.

The Place of Affect

If Achuthan's argument was to recenter the body and its rewirings as crucial to the telling of the history of the Internet as a technogovernmental artifact, for Namita Malhotra (2011), the history of the Internet is in rehumanizing its practices. Working at an intersection between law, affect, and digital technologies, Malhotra, in her work on "Pleasure, Pornography and the Law", brings forth a conundrum of the non-computational in contemporary Internet practices. Malhotra begins by positing law and affect, in this case pleasure, as unable to interact with each other. The incapacity of law to perceive pleasure, argues Malhotra, is akin to the digital systems' inability to compute it. Both the digital and the legal systems are systems of counting, accounting, and accountability. They access phenomena by producing them as informational and data sets, which are then cross-referenced, correlated, and collated in order to form normative templates of subjectivity, ethics, and regulation. That which does not compute or cannot be parsed through the reified logical systems of law becomes problematic and pathologized.

Pornography, then, becomes the common ground where the digital and the legal coincide, as it perplexes and bewilders both these systems. As the popular meme goes, the Internet was made for porn, and guesstimates offer that 40 percent of the indexed Web is devoted to the production, distribution, and consumption of pornographic material (Tancer 2008). In India, the pornographic object has also been at the heart of great legal debates around questions of obscenity, prurience, morality, and the regulation of gendered and sexualized practices. However, when it comes to the regulation of pornographic images, both the law and the digital remain confounded on identifying and regulating it. The resistance that pornography offers is at three different levels.

The first is in the fuzziness of what constitutes pornography. As the famous court judgment from the USA has suggested, you can't name it, but when you see it, you know it.[4] The attempts on digital regulation of pornography through flesh detection algorithms, index of obscene words and actions, or even user-generated classification have all failed to varying extent. It is perhaps safe to assume that almost anything can be rendered pornographic, and that the proof of the pornographic pudding is in the eating of it. The second resistance that pornography offers to these two systems is in producing an externality to the meaning of porn. Malhotra argues that the final pornographic meaning resides in the visceral, the bodily, the affective responses that the user of pornography experiences. The same object, through repetition or through lack of interest, might become non-pornographic in time. The pornographic principle, as I have argued elsewhere, is not in the content or the representation, but in the acts of transgression, titillation, and trepidation that digital objects produce. This external location of the meaning of pornography, which resides in the pleasure it affords the user and the intentions, which render it pornographic, produce a stalemate for the digital and the legal systems. Hence, the law and the regulatory structures of the Internet produce draconian measures of dealing with the pornographic object, resulting in censorship, bans, and naturalizing and normalizing some sexual practices and bodies over others.

Looking at this common blind-spot, Malhotra suggests that the history of the Internet in India has to be written as the history of the non-computational and the affective. In her work, she draws the history of the Internet from the history of the law's interaction with affect within the Indian context. The Internet, for Malhotra, has to be seen as emerging from and building upon the larger technological conflict where the very technologies that the nation state has invested in, to create new opportunities of legible and legitimized practices, have always been used to construct spaces of affect, of experience, of pleasure, which get rendered pathological or criminal because of the legal and the technological apparatus' failure to read them.

In her analysis of an early case that was one of the first instances of Internet pornography in India—the DPS MMS case—Malhotra shows how the Internet and the law collectively fail to comprehend pleasure, and in this incomprehension, produce draconian measures that seek to reduce the scope of expression and penalize any articulation that is not legible to these systems. The story of the DPS MMS case is as simple as it is now common. Two under-aged adults in a Delhi public school in 2005 made a multimedia clip of their sexual encounter, where the male was holding the camera and hence not identifiable, whereas the female was visible in her actions. This clip was leaked onto the Internet as an act of "revenge porn" by the guy after he was dumped by the girl. It went viral; it was shared illicitly as one of the first instances of "authentic" porn; it was sold in grey markets of pirated pleasures, and it was sold online on an auction site. When the clip came in the cognizance of the court, it led to a strange judgment where a crime was committed but none of the people identified with the crime were found punishable. The girl was pardoned because she was considered to be the victim, the guy was discharged because his error was attributed to his inexperience. The person who was trying to auction the clip online did not have an actual sale or proof of possession, but merely the intention of distribution, and the owner of the auction site where the clip was intended to be distributed was protected by Terms of Service.

In this case, as Malhotra argues, the court decided that this is a crime of the technology and decided to set up a committee that would regulate the Internet to decide what it can or cannot do. This idea of the Internet as doing things beyond the purview of the law was historical, because it started a dialogue between the Internet and the law to bring their systems of accounting and counting into sync. Furthermore, the role of the Internet and the law was then to produce limitations on pleasure and crack down on the affective realms of experience, which the pornographic object merely signifies. Through the regulation of these connected pornographic objects, both algorithmically and legally, there was an attempt to regulate and regularize bodies that will be allowed the space of pleasure, expressions which will be charged with obscenity, and the processes and practices which, even when innocent of sexual content, will be punished through decoding intentionality and affect.

As I have written elsewhere (Shah 2015b), this produces a cultural history of the Internet which is not about the Internet as a space of endless possibilities, but rather as a space that normalizes and contains the possibilities, allowing only a limited set of expressions, articulations, and practices online. By looking at the debates that have accompanied the growth of the Internet, and the alarming rate at which innocent users have been turned into criminalized pornographers, Malhotra argues that we need to understand the incapacity of the Internet to compute affect, and build new strategies by which this lack of computation does not result in culpability for the users drenched in their affective and sensory practices online. She calls for a history of the Internet which is not to look at the expansive penetration of the digital technologies, but the limitations of form and the constraints of computing when it comes to shaping and regulating human practices. Her work builds a case for examining the contours of the Internet instead of thinking about it as a seamless, global, and extensive connectivity network and argues that the limits of what cannot be computed need to be studied in conjunction with that which cannot be passed by law to form historical frameworks that question the centrality that the Internet has garnered in our contemporary human and affective practices.

The State in Transition

In both the approaches as suggested by Achuthan and Malhotra, there is a sense that the history of the Internet cannot be about the visible manifestations of the technology or about its apparent interactions with the state. While the state has to be a more powerful interlocutor in the analysis—much more than the market which, in the rhetoric of innovation, experimentation, and upscaling, is often considered the primary benefactor of the digital—it is also important to understand that the alternative histories need to begin with that which is not easily legible. For Achuthan, it was the body in a state of aporia that is often left out of the state-technology dialogue, but is made to bear the burdens of their finality and imagined subjectivity, which was the location of the Internet and its history in India. For Malhotra, it was the affective, which the state apparatus of the law as well as the digital systems of regulation are unable to parse or compute respectively, and thus produce criminal positions for those engaging with the possibilities and potentials of the Internet that exceed and transgress the authority and the gambit of both these systems.

Ashish Rajadhyaksha (2011), in his work on "The Cultural Last Mile", proposes that the focus does not always have to be on things that are dropped out of the state–Internet conversations. In fact, Rajadhyaksha, working his way through the sites of television, telecommunication, networked higher education, and biometric governance, proposes that what is often left out of the state–Internet equation is the changing nature of the state and its reconfigured capacities. Looking at the production of new social rights, of public–private partnerships, and of the rise of state-like institutions which dislocate the centrality of the state in the imagined model of India, Rajadhyaksha proposes that the idea of a technogovernmental state is caught in a paradox.

On one hand, the state—especially the Indian state, which has so extensively used technologies of cinema and telecommunication to imagine itself as a massive geographical entity that is diverse but united—is a technological artifact. Rajadhyaksha argues that the modern nation state follows a communication model of transmission where it resides at the center and governs through the management and distribution of information between its different units and with the citizens. The state is conceptually structured by the then-contemporary models of information and communication, and the different technologies of state-craft before the arrival of the Internet might have changed the formats and forms of state governance but not its fundamental structure. On the other hand, the state is an unrealized or a failed instance of the communication model—something that Rajadhyaksha coins as the "last-mile problem". The technologically produced state has always been unable to make the information reach to the very remote and interior parts of the country, and its investment in different communication technologies has been in an attempt to bridge this last mile so as to reach the full potentials of its technologized statehood. The state, thus, is constructed by a model which it believes in, but this is also the model that the state is not able to implement in its entirety, and hence requires the technological mainframe to help in its evolution.

With the Internet and networked technologies, though, the Indian state seems to be able to escape this paradox for the first time. Even as it embraces these new networked technologies of peer-to-peer distribution, it does not seem to reconfigure itself through that model. In fact, through a series of contemporary problems of specious bans, of futile efforts at filtering and censoring the Web, at errors in regulating content, and in producing effective models of accountability, the state has often appeared as a buffoon, unable to catch up with the changed models of information and communication. However, this conflict is not merely about a state that is unable to change with the times, but a state that is realizing that the communication model that it embodies no longer needs to find its validation in the practices of the state. The practices of the digital and networked state, with the Internet at the forefront, in fact allow for the state to invest in these technologies not to justify itself but to build new structures of regulation, governance, arbitration, and adjudication which transcend the state's own perception of itself.

In Rajadhyaksha's thesis, the history of the Internet in India, while it needs to be in dialogue with the state, has to recognize that the ambitions of the state with regard to the Internet are different. While the earlier investment of the state in different technologies was to validate itself, with the Internet the state no longer bears the burden of making the technologies work to affirm its status. Instead, it allows for the state to disinvest, to privatize, to enfranchise new entities that would take up state-like responsibilities and powers in the construction of new networked societies. The transformation of the last-mile problem that the Internet brings, replacing distance with speed and connectivity with access, is a new configuration of societies and the language of rights, safeguards, protection, responsibilities, and reprisals that we were able to deploy in the earlier technological practices of the state will no longer be adequate to address these changing structures.

The argument ends by analyzing the biometric governmental project Aadhaar,[5] which promises to be the one-point technologized solution to a range of problems like poverty, corruption, inefficient delivery of public resources, widespread illiteracy, poor healthcare, etc. Rajadhyaksha points out that with the Aadhaar system, the legitimizing functions of the state have been taken over by the verification systems of the digital, operationalized by private registrars within the system. Similarly, the authority of the state to intervene and negotiate identities for its citizens have been outsourced to big data algorithms that create quantified profiles based on actions and identifications, as opposed to the historically rooted identity politics of caste, language, religion, etc. In both these instances, we see the ways in which the Indian state's interaction with the Internet is simultaneously a self-professed dislocation of its centrality as well as the creation of new proto-state structures, which are often invisible but need to be unpacked to understand the contemporary nature of the Internet in the country.

Rajadhyaksha ends with the claim that in the interaction between the state and the Internet, we often imagine that the Internet is under the patronage of the state and is being used to reproduce statecraft as it has been done historically through other technologies. However, the Internet produces a new moment for the state's capacity and interest in reproducing itself. The Internet is not a continuation of older state practices—not merely a digital rendering of old records and archives—but a digitization that reimagines the state within which these new digital technologies would be accommodated. Rajadhyaksha, particularly looking at the Aadhaar project, calls it the "cog that has to imagine the system", within which it makes sense, thus arguing that the history of the Internet is not about building the future of the state, but of the state of the future, eventually hoping for the state as we understand it to disappear and new structures to replace it.

Towards Technosocial Historiography

To write the history of the Internet in India is to write the history of India. As Ravi Sundaram (2010) would have it in his formulation of "Cyber Publics", the Internet needs to be understood not only as a tool for change but as the catalyst for transformation—a force that doesn't just create a new public sphere on the cyberspace, but radically constructs all publics into cyber publics. Extricating one from the other reinforces the two presumptions that have always marked post-colonial developing countries in their relationship with technologies. It presumes that the Internet is made outside and enters India only as a foreign tool, overriding the material practices and historical structures of embedded technologies and governance. It also emphasizes a romantic argument about the new frontiers in the erstwhile colonies that are seen as the panacea that will cure the problems of the powerful hubs. In telling the story of the Internet through the story of India, in establishing the Internet not as a commodity or a product, but as a powerful force that enters into conversation with the Indian state, we produce a different vision of the Internet as well as of India. In thus embedding the Internet into the history and negotiation with the state, its apparatus, and affects, posits the Internet as a reconciliation force. It imagines the Internet as a point of convergence where multiple actors, interests, histories, technologies, impulses, ambitions, stakes, and values enter into a state of negotiation and contestation, thus providing new opportunities of localization which are more than acts of prosthetic translation.

In Achuthan's triangulation of the body, state, and the Internet, we see how the body becomes precarious and is made invisible in the negotiations between the other two, thus becoming the site where the technosociality is operationalized. In Malhotra's argument about the mutual blind spots of the law as the state apparatus and the digital as the new logic of networked governance, we see affect as being regulated through commodities that cannot be made legible to the intertwined systems of law and the Internet. Rajadhyaksha's description of the state in transition, as a state that is finally free to escape its older centralized transmission structures in an attempt to replace itself and the imagination of the new social rights and the new subject, allows us to write the history of the Internet as a history of how technologies have been central in imagining not only the future of our states but the states of our future.

Our project to document the histories of the Internet(s) in India[6] was an attempt at alternative historiography rather than merely writing traditional histories of alternative spaces. We wanted to move away from the tropes of writing about the Internet that, even as they examine the effects and causes of the Internet, always think of it as a discrete, complete, and absolute object which can be disentangled from the larger industries of nation building. The alternative sought to simultaneously resist the imperial historicization where the new, the exotic, and the local are made legible and intelligible to a global gaze, as well as questioning the seamless expanse of history writing that subsumes more geographies, values, and people under the reified ideal origin that is nailed to particular spaces of power.

These approaches to the history of the Internet, in positing body, affect, and a state that is seeking to dislocate itself, offer disjunctures and disruptions to how we understand the Internet and how we embed it in our global provinces. These approaches are not comprehensive and complete, but they signal towards a technosocial historiography that defies provenance, refuses clarity, and overturns temporality, which is at the heart of traditional history making. They offer histories that will need to find beginnings that are not the genesis, locations which are outside the narrowed understanding of the Internet as digital technology, and help rethink the Internet as a technosocial process, thus expanding the scope and method of writing histories of Internets and the structures of governance, regulation, and statecraft that form and inform them.

Notes

1. An extremely telling example of this is a legal and public policy battle that is unfolding in India even as this chapter is written, where the social media and data aggregation giant Facebook is promoting a FreeBasics campaign through its non-profit organization Internet.org that seeks to overturn and undermine the principles of net neutrality that have long since been heralded as embodying the foundational values of the Internet. The imagination of India as a country with huge digital divide and Internet access as a way of correcting its perceived problems allows Facebook to propose a differential, preferential, and discriminatory Web access for the potential new users in the country. Facebook's attacks on net neutrality and its promotion of such bandwidth-shaping practices go completely against its self-avowed commitment to a responsible and fair Internet support in the developed countries. For an exhaustive coverage on the current net neutrality debates in India, see Medianama (n.d.).

2. An exhaustive compilation of the dialogue between Gandhi and Tagore is in Sabyasachi Bhattacharya's edited anthology, *The Mahatma and the Poet* (1997).

3. This caution of techno-utopianism and a certain reluctance to celebrate technological advancements which is a characteristic of left-leaning, post-colonial politics has had a strong presence in Indian history. Even when

Jawaharlal Nehru, the first Prime Minister of modern India, declared that he sought to build a new India through a "scientific temperament", there was always resistance to these technological solutions. It is only with the emergence of the Internet that the country could reimagine itself using the tropes of technology as the strokes to paint the new contours of the country. Nandan Nilekani, one of the strongest advocates of technogovernmental policies and structures in the country, writes in his book *Imagining India* (2009) that digital connectivity offered a way by which the new India could dissociate from the old India, and start building a future that is not just going to use the digital technologies but also be constructed by them.

4. Potter Stewart famously stated in *Jacobellis v. Ohio 278 US 184 (1964)*: "I shall not today attempt further to define the kinds of material I understand to be embraced within that shorthand description [hard-core pornography]; and perhaps I could never succeed in intelligibly doing so. But I know it when I see it, and the motion picture involved in this case is not that." This has been used, since then, as one of the strongest comments on questions concerning free speech, expression, artistic intent, and pornographic material. More about the case can be found at Wikipedia (n.d.).

5. In his other work, Rajadhyaksha has edited an anthology called *In the Wake of Aadhaar* (2013), where, along with a set of critical scholars, Rajadhyaksha shows how the project needs to be understood both as a crucial point of departure from informational governance in India, as well as a continuation of the technogovernmental structures that have shaped the idea of a citizen and their right to interact with the state.

6. In 2008, at the then newly started Centre for Internet & Society, Bangalore, where I was a co-founder and the Director of Research, we started a project on the *Histories of the Internet(s) in India*, which produced seven alternative monographs and frameworks of unraveling the layers of the Internet, as well as the ways in which these could be studied through a technosocial framework. This chapter draws from the conversations that framed that project, and owes its intellectual debt to Asha Achuthan, Ashish Rajadhyaksha, Namita Avriti Malhotra, Rochelle Pinto, Aparna Balachandran, Nithya Vasudevan, Nithin Manayath, Zainab Bawa, Anja Kovacs, and Arun Menon, who all contributed to this project and helped in developing the critical knowledge summarized in this chapter. To stay within the size constraints of this chapter, I have drawn from three of the inquiries initiated by the project. The larger research publications and discussions can be accessed at the Centre for Internet & Society (n.d.).

References

Achuthan, A. (2011) *Re:wiring Bodies*, Bangalore: Centre for Internet & Society, available at: http://cis-india.org/raw/rewiringpdf/view (accessed 10 November 2015).

Bagga, R. K., Keniston, K., and Mathur, R. R. (eds) (2005) *The State, IT and Development*, New Delhi: Sage Publications.

Berners-Lee, T., and Fischetti, M. (2000) *Weaving the Web: The Original Design and Ultimate Destiny of the World Wide Web*, New York: HarperCollins.

Bhattacharya, S. (ed.) (1997) *The Mahatma and the Poet: Letters and Debates between Gandhi and Tagore 1915–1941*, New Delhi: National Book Trust.

The Centre for Internet & Society (n.d.) *Internet Histories*, The Centre for Internet & Society, available at: http://cis-india.org/raw/internet-histories

Friedman, T. L. (2005) *The World is Flat: A Brief History of the Twenty-First Century*, New York: Farrar, Straus & Giroux.

Hafner, K., and Lyon, M. (1996) *Where Wizards Stay Up Late: The Origins of the Internet*, New York: Simon & Schuster.

Haraway, D. (1991) "A Cyborg Manifesto: Science, Technology, and Socialist-Feminism in the Late Twentieth Century", in *Simians, Cyborgs and Women: The Reinvention of Nature*, New York: Routledge, pp. 149–181.

Latour, B. (2013) *An Inquiry into Modes of Existence: An Anthropology of the Moderns*, Cambridge, MA: Harvard University Press.

Löwgren, J., and Reimer, B. (2013) *Collaborative Media*, Cambridge, MA: MIT Press.

Make in India (n.d.) *Make in India*, available at: www.makeinindia.com/

Malhotra, N. A. (2011) *Porn: Law, Video, Technology*, Bangalore: Centre for Internet & Society, available at: http://cis-india.org/raw/histories-of-the-internet/porn-law-video-technology (accessed 10 November 2015).

Markoff, J. (2006) *What the Dormouse Said: How the 60s Counterculture Shaped the Personal Computer Industry*, New York: Penguin.

Medianama (n.d.) *Net Neutrality*, available at: www.medianama.com/tag/net-neutrality/

Nilekani, N. (2009) *Imagining India: The Idea of a Renewed Nation*, New York: Penguin Press.

Philip, K. (2005) "What Is a Technological Author? The Pirate Function and Intellectual Property", *Postcolonial Studies*, 8(2): 199–218.

Postill, J. (2011) *Localizing the Internet*, Oxford: Berghahn Books.

Rajadhyaksha, A. (2011) *The Last Cultural Mile: An Inquiry into Technology and Governance in India,* Bangalore: Centre for Internet & Society, available at: http://cis-india.org/raw/histories-of-the-internet/last-cultural-mile.pdf (accessed 10 November 2015).

Rajadhyaksha, A. (ed.) (2013) *In the Wake of Aadhaar: The Digital Ecosystem of Governance,* Bangalore: Centre for the Study of Culture and Society.

Rajdou, N., Prabhu, J., and Ahuja, S. (2012) *Jugaad Innovation: Think Frugal, Be Flexible, Generate Breakthrough Growth,* San Francisco, CA: Jossey-Bass.

Shah, N. (2015a) "Of Heathens, Perverts, and Stalkers: The Imagined Learners in MOOCs", in *The Europa World of Learning 2016*, Oxford: Routledge, pp. 21–25.

Shah, N. (2015b) "Sluts 'R' Us: Intersections of Gender, Protocol and Agency in the Digital Age", *First Monday,* 20(4), available at: http://firstmonday.org/ojs/index.php/fm/article/view/5463/4415 (accessed 10 January 2016).

Sundaram, R. (2010) *Pirate Modernity: Delhi's Media Urbanism*, New York: Routledge.

Tancer, B. (2008) *Click: What Millions of People Do Online and Why It Matters*, New York: Hyperion.

Turner, F. (2006) *From Counterculture to Cyberculture: Stewart Brand, the Whole Earth Network, and the Rise of Digital Utopianism*, Chicago: University of Chicago Press.

Wikipedia (n.d.) *Jacobellis v. Ohio*, available at: https://en.wikipedia.org/wiki/Jacobellis_v._Ohio

4

PROBING A NATION'S WEB DOMAIN

A New Approach to Web History and a New Kind of Historical Source

Niels Brügger

Introduction

The World Wide Web—or simply "the Web"—is an important object of study which could be integrated in many studies of the recent history of our (media) culture, just as it constitutes a gold mine as a historical source. The Internet emerged as a network of computer networks in the early 1980s, but it was not until the advent of a specific set of protocols in the beginning of the 1990s—namely, the World Wide Web—that the Internet in the form of the Web gained currency. Since then, it has constituted an integral element of the communicative infrastructure of most societies. Thus, if we want to understand the Web, as well as the media and society at large, the history of the Web may prove to be pivotal.

The Web is not only something which can be studied in itself; it also constitutes an important historical source in its own right, potentially to be used within all kinds of historical studies, along with handwritten or printed documents, film, or broadcast media (cf. Brügger 2012a). However, when the Web is considered as an historical source, the focus is usually only on the parts of the Web that look like traditional documents—that is, individual web pages or websites, whereas other web entities such as an entire national Web are not taken into consideration.

By focusing on a nation's Web domain—that is, the space related to a given nation on the Web—this chapter investigates a new way of approching the Web within communication and media history—including Internet history—and within historiography in general. Focusing on the national Web domain is just one of the ways of using the Web within historiography. But it is an important one, since the national Web domain constitutes the backdrop of other forms of Web uses, and studying it can thus constitute an important first step in an in-depth analysis of more specific elements of a national Web.

This chapter aims at scrutinizing how an entire national Web domain and its developments over time can be studied. After a discussion of some of the fundamental methodological challenges that this new type of historical study puts on the research agenda, an outline of an analytical design follows. With a view to illustrating the main points, a recurring case is used—namely, Denmark and the material in the national Danish web archive Netarkivet. However, the methodological challenges, as well as the analytical design, are generic to a large extent and will therefore apply to most countries.

The term "web archive" is used throughout the chapter, although web archives are usually not archives in the traditional sense of the word—that is, a collection of unpublished material— but rather libraries—that is, a collection of published documents in the broad sense of the word. However, since the late 1990s "web archiving" has been coined as the term used for collecting and preserving the Web, in the main referring to the publicly available Web, and this is, in a large number of countries, performed by (national) libraries. Therefore, "web archive" is used here, although "webrary" may be considered a more appropriate term.

Characterizations of National Webs

National Webs have been studied since 2000 (cf. the overviews in Baeza-Yates *et al.* 2005: 5, and in Miranda and Gomes 2009: 146–147), and even the Web domain of an entire continent has been studied—namely, the African Web as early as 2002 (Boldi *et al.* 2002). These national studies follow the more general Web's development (O'Neill *et al.* 2003). But, in contrast to the present analytical design, the rationale of the above-mentioned studies has mainly been to gain knowledge about the national Web with a view to either improving the Web (e.g. browsers, link structure, interaction design, processing of specific media types such as music; cf. Miranda and Gomes 2009: 147–149) or the web archives (e.g. archiving software, required storage resources, archiving strategies; cf. Miranda and Gomes 2009: 148, 150). These studies have merely focused on the Web's technological information from an application-oriented perspective, and few have adopted an historical perspective on a national Web (one example of the latter is Miranda and Gomes 2009; others are mentioned in the overview in Miranda and Gomes 2009: 147).

Recently, a few articles with a social science and humanities approach to national Web studies have been published (Rogers *et al.* 2013; Ben-David 2014; Hale *et al.* 2014). In contrast to the present approach, these studies are mainly concerned with the study of a national Web at a given point in time and not with studying developments; and when a temporal dimension is added, only material archived by the scholars is used, not material in web archives (Rogers *et al.* 2013: 150–151). The exception is Hale *et al.* 2014 which is clearly a historical study, based on an archived web; however, it is limited to studying nodes and hyperlink networks.

The present chapter argues that a nation's Web domain can be considered a relevant object of study for historiography as well as a genuine and valuable historical source. Therefore, a temporal dimension with focus on developments and trends has to be added to studies of a nation's Web, just as an archived web has to be at the core of the study. Although a number of the measurement points put forward below are shared with the existing literature, these points have to be reinterpreted and reframed within the discipline of historiography, and, in addition, a number of measurement points should be added with a view to establishing a comprehensive historiographical analytical grid.

A National Web Domain

In the present context, the idea of a nation's Web domain builds upon a typology of how the Web can be studied where five web strata are distinguished: the web element, the web page, the website, the web sphere, and the Web as a whole (Brügger 2009: 122–125). This typology shares a number of similarities with the stratified model in Baeza-Yates *et al.* 2007: 2–3). The Web element is defined as a distinct semantic entity that appears on a web page (an image, written text, background, etc.), the web page itself is whatever is present within a browser window, the website comprises the interlinked web pages, the web sphere is all the material on the Web deemed relevant to a concept, a theme, or an event (political elections, sports events, catastrophes, etc.), and the Web as a whole is taken to be the Web in its totality (e.g. everything that transcends all the other strata such as the technical infrastructure of the Web). Each of these web strata can be considered an object of historical study and an historical source in its own right, and Web histories focusing on each of these have been written (cf. the overview in Brügger 2010: 3–4). Taking this typology as a point of departure, a national Web domain can be understood as the web sphere related to a given nation.

However, a national web sphere plays a particularly important role vis-à-vis the other strata since it constitutes a mostly unacknowledged backcloth for all other types of web entities and activities within the national Web area, be that websites or smaller web spheres within the national boundaries. For instance, if a given website or group of websites is studied and one wants to know if a website is small or big, flat or deep, containing many/few outlinks, or the like, this cannot be determined if there is no overview of how small/big, flat/deep, or outlinking websites usually are on a national scale at this point in time. Likewise, one may want to know the status of a website or cluster of websites in terms of how central they are, based on the number of links pointing to them from the entire national web sphere—such a study acquires knowledge about the most central websites of the national area as such (see e.g. Ben-David 2014 about the Arabic national webspace within the Israeli webspace). Thus, it is important to study a nation's web sphere with a view to establishing a baseline of a nation's web environment.

Constructing a National Web Domain

The historian who sets out to identify a nation's web sphere has to acknowledge that this web sphere did not exist as such beforehand. On the contrary, it has to be constructed as is the case with any web sphere (cf. the definition of a web sphere in Foot and Schneider 2006: 20). This is particularly important when studying a web sphere of the past (Brügger 2013: 759–761). Therefore, methodological considerations are to be taken into account with a view to documenting the construction of the historical web sphere and to explaining possible biases, sources of error, and limitations. In the following, the most relevant methodological topics are outlined.

Archived Web

The main challenge when setting out to analyze the developments of a nation's Web domain is that the Web of the past is gone. It is often maintained that the average lifetime of a web page is two months (cf. Brügger 2012b: 318). Therefore, studies of the past Web must be based on the Web which can be found in web archives. However, the Web in web archives is in many ways not only different from other kinds of digital material, but also from what was once on the online Web, before it was archived (Brügger and Finnemann 2013: 74–78). As a consequence, an analysis of a nation's Web domain has to deal with the general methodological issues related to web archiving and to the use of archived web material for analysis (Brügger and Finnemann 2013: 75–78), some of which will be touched upon in the following.

Although the archived web in itself constitutes a main source for the mapping of a nation's web sphere, it is not the only relevant source. It can be supplemented with user statistics and other types of web statistics, but unfortunately, in many cases web user statistics from the past are not preserved systematically (cf. Brügger 2013: 757). However, in this chapter, the focus will be exclusively on the archived web in national web archives.

The National Web Sphere Is Not a Mirror Image: Spatial Delimitation

When setting out to delimit a nation's web sphere in space, the main concern is that the nation's presence on the Web is not a mirror image of the geographical extension of the nation (like with traditional analogue broadcasting, for example). There is not a one-to-one relation between the physical borders of the nation and the nation's borders on the Web (how to define a nation (or a nation state) is not discussed in the following; for an overview of literature about media and nation, see Rogers *et al.* 2013: 145). This gives rise to a fundamental methodological question: How can a nation be delimited on the Web?

As debated by Anat Ben-David (2014: 137–138) and Richard Rogers *et al.* (2013: 145–153), various demarcation criteria and technical solutions can be used when delimiting a national Web domain (whois lookups, Google AdPlanner, PageRanks, etc.). However, in the main, these criteria and solutions are aimed at studying the Web here and now, based on immediate collecting and preserving of the Web performed by the scholar (Rogers *et al.* 2013: 153). But, on one hand, these techniques cannot be used retrospectively on archived web material (cf. Brügger 2013: 757, 759–761), and, on the other, material in web archives has already been archived by others—namely, the archiving institutions, based on their strategies and practices for collecting and preserving, and independently of the historian who thus has no influence on the form of the material—on the contrary, the material must be studied as is. Therefore, other demarcation criteria have to be taken into consideration.

When looking for relevant criteria for spatial delimitation of a national Web domain, an obvious point of departure is the criteria used to identify the material in the first place—that is, the criteria used by national web archives (these criteria are also discussed in Rogers *et al.* 2013: 145–146). For more than a century, librarians in national libraries have used a set of rules to help them establish a national collection which transcends national borders. For instance, the Royal Library of Denmark has collected material that was printed outside the borders of the nation, but was aimed at a Danish audience or treated themes of relevance for a Danish readership (this material is called "Danica"). In continuation of this approach, the national Danish web archive Netarkivet (introduced more in detail below) uses the following set of rules to determine what should be included in its collections:

> Material published in electronic communication networks is considered to be Danish when 1) it is published from Internet domains etc. which are specifically assigned to Denmark, or 2) it is published from other Internet domains etc. and is directed at a public in Denmark.
>
> (Act on Legal Deposit of Published Material n.d., §8, 2)

Regarding the material from other Internet domains aimed at a Danish public, this material is tracked down manually or is semi-automated (man-made choices, based on an automatically generated gross list of possible websites to include), based on the following criteria: Is the material written in Danish? Is the person registered as the owner of a domain name a Danish resident? Does the material concern Danish affairs? Is the author a Danish citizen? Are the performing artists Danish? (Netarkivet.dk 2005; for how these criteria are operationalized, see Schostag and Fønss-Jørgensen 2012: 111).

If these archiving criteria are also applied to delimit the national Danish web sphere as an object of study, the Danish Web domain is all material published on the national country code top-level domain name assigned to Denmark—that is, .dk, and material published on other domain names aimed at a Danish audience. The advantage of using these criteria is that they were initially used when archiving the national Web, which tends to make the material more complete. However, the disadvantage is that the historian is dependent on the curatorial practice used for the "Danica" material (resources, strategies, individual choices, technical solutions, etc.), and he or she has to acknowledge that these practices probably come with a history of their own.

However useful this approach may be in countries where a national web archive exists, it comes with a number of shortcomings when applied in nations with no national web archive that have to construct their national Web domain based on transnational web archives such as the Internet Archive or national web archives in other countries. First, this approach is not very useful in countries where the country code is rarely used, especially the US where most websites are registered on generic top-level domains such as .com, .gov, .net, .org, and the like; thus, regarding the US, the manual/semi-automated method is the only option, which makes the delimitation of the national web sphere less systematic, especially backwards in time. Second, language cannot always be used as a delimitation criterion, if it is spoken extensively outside a given nation (e.g. English, Spanish, Portuguese, Chinese).

The National Web Sphere Is Not a Clear-Cut Point in Time: Temporal Delimitation

A nation's web sphere also has to be delimited in time. This is not an issue when studying the online Web, but there are several challenges related to this when using material in web archives.

First, that web archiving takes time, which affects the archived web material's temporality. For instance, it takes two to three months to archive a national top-level domain such as .dk. This entails that the web content may change several times during the archiving with the consequence that, for instance, the link structure in its totality becomes temporally inconsistent—web pages may link to material which has been removed or deleted during the two to three months in which the archiving was performed. This uncertainty as to the updating of the web content is constitutive of any kind of web archiving, and it can only be diminished, never totally eliminated. However, it is obvious that the larger the amount to be archived, the more time-consuming it is, and thereby the greater the chance that something has been changed or removed. Therefore, the impact of this constitutive problem is in particular affecting large-scale web archiving such as the archiving of a national domain, even if archiving speed increases—for instance, in 2005, Netarkivet took six months to archive the entire .dk domain, whereas the same task only took two months in 2012, with a domain twice the size of that in 2005 (cf. Netarkivet.dk n.d.b).

Second, archiving strategies may have been changed between two archivings, or they may have been different from the outset, which affects the possibility of temporally delimiting the nation's web sphere. For instance, when the Danish web archive collects the .dk domain, the archiving starts with a list of all .dk-domain names, and when all domain names on the list are archived, the archiving is stopped. In contrast, the US-based Internet Archive's strategy is primarily based on following links from what has already been archived. Thus, this cumulative strategy is not limited to a certain period of time with clear-cut start and stop times. The consequence is that it can be difficult to compare material archived with precise start and stop times to continuously archived material with overlapping temporalities and with start and stop time inserted more or less randomly by the scholar or by the archiving institution. These temporal inconsistencies may be the result when combining material archived by the use of different archiving strategies, which is the case when web collections are mixed in the same archive. This is exactly what has happened in the UK Web Archive, as well as in the Danish web archive, since both archives have acquired versions of their national Web domains dating before they were established, and this material was extracted and acquired from the Internet Archive's collection.

Netarkivet, the Danish Internet Archive

Before outlining an analytical design for the study of a national Web domain, the national Danish web archive Netarkivet has to be briefly introduced since it is used as an illustration in the following. Netarkivet was established in 2005, and it aims to collect and preserve the Danish part of the Internet. It is a joint venture between the two national libraries—the State and University Library and the Royal Library—and the legal framework for its activity is the legal deposit law (revised in 2004; for an introduction to Netarkivet, see Andersen 2006; Schostag and Fønss-Jørgensen 2012).

With a view to preserving as much of the Danish Internet as possible, three strategies are used: 1) a snapshot strategy where the entire .dk domain and Danica are archived (four times per year); 2) a selective strategy where approximately 100 of the most dynamic websites are archived (e.g. news sites, on a daily/weekly basis); and 3) an event strategy where selected websites in relation to events are preserved (elections, disasters, sport events, etc., three to four events per year). In 2015, Netarkivet's collection is approximately 500 terabytes (TB).

In the present context, where the aim is to characterize a nation's web sphere, the snapshots are of special interest. Each snapshot is based on a complete list of domain names within the domain .dk supplied by the administrator of the country code top-level domain; to this is added a list of relevant domain names outside .dk (cf. about Danica above, and Schostag and Fønss-Jørgensen 2012: 111). In 2013, there were approximately one million .dk domain names, and 50,000 domain names outside .dk (Netarkivet.dk n.d.a). Concerning archiving depth—that is, the number of page levels below the front page—a snapshot is set to 25 levels. Between 2005 and 2013, Netarkivet has made 18 snapshots (Netarkivet.dk n.d.b).

In terms of spatial completeness, each snapshot has the possibility of becoming close to complete, partly because it is based on the official list of domain names, partly because of the archiving depth; as for the domains outside .dk, it is difficult to judge their completeness. However, that the archiving is based on a complete list and a high archiving depth does not imply that the result is a complete collection—for instance, technical problems may occur during the archiving, and specific types of material are known to be impossible to archive (javascripts, streamed sound and video, etc.). Regarding temporal completeness, the constitutive inconsistency related to possible updates during the archiving remains, but apart from this, the snapshots are complete in terms of time.

As for the material which has been integrated from the Internet Archive (2000–2004), the differences in archiving strategy imply challenges regarding spatial, as well as temporal, delimitation. First, it is difficult to determine if all active Danish domain names are part of the material, and therefore all web addresses have to be correlated with the official lists of top-level domain names from each period if such lists still exist; second, a policy has to be developed as to how an adequate time period can be delimited, and what to do with duplicates of the same website within this time period. Despite these shortcomings, the snapshots in Netarkivet are as close as it is possible to get to a complete construction of the Danish web sphere of the past.

Characterizing the Development of a Nation's Web Sphere: An Outline of an Analytical Design

Assuming that the national web sphere has been succesfully delimited in a web archive, the next step is to set up an analytical design with a number of points to be measured and examined. Such measurement points can be considered probes, each of which gives information about specific elements of the web sphere and contributes to completing a fuller picture (Rogers *et al.* use the term "metrics"—e.g. Rogers *et al.* 2013: 144).

The following is an outline of some of the probes which could be taken into consideration. The overall focal points are volume, space, structure, "aliveliness", and content. Other types may also be included, and each of the points mentioned below can be granulated and detailed depending on the specific research question to be investigated. Each way of probing is briefly presented, followed by a short discussion of limitations and relevant methodological challenges as well as possible solutions.

Volume: Bytes

The most obvious measurement point is volume: How small/big is a nation's web sphere? Volume can be measured in a number of ways, the most simple being the total amount of bytes; for instance, in 2006 Netarkivet's snapshot of the Danish web sphere was 8.9TB, in 2009 it was 22–24TB, and in 2012 21–28TB (Netarkivet.dk n.d.b). These figures indicate that in terms of bytes the Danish Web has not been growing significantly since 2009.

The size of different file types, and of file types in general, could also be measured—that is, how big/small different file types such as html, txt, pdf, img, jpg, swf, avi, etc. are, the average size of all file types, and how this has developed. In Netarkivet's first snapshot from 2005, the average file size was 40KB, which is an increase of 17 percent compared to 2001 where tests were made before Netarkivet was established. This increase could indicate that the bandwidth in Danish households has increased in this period (Andersen 2006: 6).

Websites also come in different sizes, and it could be relevant to know how big/small websites were on the national Web—for instance, the average size, the top 100 biggest/smallest websites, and the number of websites between certain intervals such as sites with only one page, sites between 1 and 10MB, 10 and 100MB, 100MB and 1GB, and websites bigger than 1GB. Such figures can indicate whether a nation's web sphere is dominated by many small websites and a few large ones, or if the size of websites is more evenly distributed. In Netarkivet's snapshot from 2006, 85 percent of all .dk registered domains were smaller than 10MB, and fewer than 1 percent were bigger than 500MB (Netarchive.dk 2006: 2). The number of web pages on each website could also be examined, indicating, for instance, whether websites have one page, 2–100 pages, or 100+ pages.

And, finally, it could also be relevant to know the number of websites/domain names per web server—that is, how many websites were located on each web server. This could indicate how widespread the use of, for instance, web hotels has been—that is, web servers hosting more than one domain name (cf. Miranda and Gomes 2009: 151).

Space: Geolocation

The geographical distribution of websites could also be a relevant indicator of how the nation's web sphere looks. Geolocation is usually made either by using the web server's IP address, running it through an IP geographical locator (GeoIP) with a view to revealing where the host is located, or by gathering information from a whois database—for instance, the contact address of the correspondent domain registrant (or by using both approaches).

When using the archived web, many of the above-mentioned approaches cannot be used because the required information is no longer available. Thus, focus has to be on the actual content on the web pages—for instance, by correlating postcode information and other geographic references with the content on each individual web page such as postcodes or names of cities in a footer or in the body text of web pages with contact information. This approach has been used by the UK Web Archive and is explained as follows:

> The ~2.5 billion 200 OK responses in the JISC UK Web Domain Dataset (1996–2010) have been scanned for geographic references—specifically postcodes. This set of postcode citations found at particular URLs, crawled at particular times, forms an historical GeoIndex of the UK web.
>
> (GeoIndex n.d.)

Geolocating the websites of a nation's web sphere by searching the content on the websites' web pages may indicate whether websites are "located" in the big cities or in the countryside, in specific regions, or the like, and it may contribute valuable historical information to discussions of "the geography of the Internet" and its interrelation with the geophysical world (cf. the discussion of these issues in Castells 2001: 207–246).

Structure: Networks of Hyperlinks

One of the main features of the Web is the hyperlink, and mapping the structures of hyperlink networks can be a highly relevant way of probing the national web sphere.

Usually, a distinction is made between internal and external hyperlinks—that is, hyperlinks pointing only within the boundaries of a given web entity (e.g. a website), or outside the web entity, respectively. In the present context, this distinction can be applied to the individual website as well as to the entire national web sphere.

Regarding individual websites, the internal and external links could be calculated with a view to determining to what degree the national Web domain is composed of websites cutting themselves off from the Web outside their own boundaries, or of websites being open towards the rest of the Web. Website internal links are also relevant to measure—for instance, by calculating the depth of the websites, which would indicate how flat/deep the websites of the national Web domain are (e.g. Tolosa et al. 2007: 17–18).

Regarding the national web sphere's hyperlink networks, its internal as well as the external link structure could be examined. Analyses of the hyperlinks from one web page/website to another within the national domain (web sphere internal linking) could result in a number of mappings. First, one could map the top 100 most central domains, based on an analysis of each node's in-degree level—that is, the number of hyperlinks pointing to it from the rest of the national Web—the more in-links from the entire network, the more central is the node (cf. Baeza-Yates et al. 2005: 19–20, 40–41; and Ben-David 2014: 140–154, about the mapping of internal ties within the Arabic-language web space/s in Israel). Second, another way of mapping the hyperlinked network of a national web sphere is to make a "bow-tie" analysis, where each web page can be located in one of six web regions (so-called Strongly Connected Components), indicating how well linked it is to the rest, and thereby how internally well connected the entire national web sphere is (cf. the analyses of the Argentinian Web in Tolosa *et al.* 2007: 12–14; cf. also Baeza-Yates *et al.* 2007: 18–21).

These types of hyperlink analyses which are dependent on outgoing as well as incoming links to a website are part of the analysis that are challenged by the possible inconsistency of the entire archived web sphere mentioned above; due to the fact that archiving a nation's Web takes several months, a subsequent hyperlink analysis may be influenced by an asynchrony between link source—the web page where the link is found—and link target—that is, the web page to which the link points (cf. above, and Brügger 2012a: 113–114).

Analyses of the hyperlinks from one web page/website to a web page/website outside the national domain (web sphere external linking) is also highly relevant, and it will indicate how international the national web sphere is—that is, how linked it is to the rest of the Web. This analysis could, for instance, include examinations of how connected one nation's web sphere is to other national web spheres (specific countries, clusters of countries), or to which degree it is linking to non-country-specific top-level domains such as .com, .nu, .net, etc. (e.g. Baeza-Yates *et al.* 2005: 43–44). Or the analysis could identify the top 100 most linked-to websites outside the national domain.

"Aliveliness": Domain Names and Updating

A nation's web sphere can also be characterized by investigating how "alive" it is, either by focusing on the domain names or on the frequency of updating. A simple comparison of the lists of domain names that are used to launch the archiving in two subsequent snapshots can indicate how many domain names (and which domain names) are new, and how many have disappeared. And by studying the so-called response codes that the web servers have rendered when requested for a specific web page, the response codes "404, Not Found", "500, Internal Server Error", and "503, Service Unavailable" indicate that either the website is no longer active, or it is not well-maintained (Rogers *et al.* also investigate these response codes as well as the "freshness" of websites; Rogers *et al.* 2013: 156–157, 160–161). In Netarkivet's snapshot from 2005, 479,000 websites of 579,000 were active. In 2011, the numbers were approximately one million active of 1.1 million registered domain names (Andersen 2006: 7; Netarchive.dk 2011: 2).

With a view to examining the frequency of updating, it could be calculated how many of the websites have been changed from one snapshot to another (in absolute numbers and as a percentage of the total number of websites; cf. Tolosa *et al.* 2007: 6–7). These numbers could also be used to identify the frequently/non-frequently updated segments of the national Web, thereby indicating not only to what extent the entire national Web is alive, but also if some parts of it are more alive than others.

Content: Closedness, File and Software Types, Language, Textual Elements, and Semantics

A nation's web sphere can be characterized by going more into detail with the content that is actually found on the web pages. Such analyses could address issues such as openness/closedness, file types, software types, language, and words and semantics. Each of these will be briefly elaborated on.

If a web page is not open to the public, it may render a response code such as "403, Forbidden" or "401, Unauthorized". These response codes attest that a given website is closed—for instance, because a password is needed, and the number of these response codes within a nation's web sphere may indicate how open or closed it is. Another type of closedness of a national Web domain is state-initiated censorship (see reflections on how this can be studied on the live Web in Rogers *et al.* 2013: 157–160).

The number of specific file types such as text, image, and video files may also indicate what the web sphere looks like and how it has developed—for instance, if written text, images, or video prevail (Rogers *et al.* 2013: 155 also mention media, document, and image formats). One of the more significant changes between 2005 and 2006 in Netarkivet's snapshots is that the number of jpg-pictures has increased from 25 percent to almost 32 percent of the total amount of files, just as video formats have become more widespread in the same period (Netarchive.dk 2007: 4; cf. also Brügger 2012a: 114). However, there are at least two methodological challenges related to using file types as indicators of the actual content on web pages. First, all file types are not unambiguously either written text or images—for instance, pdf and Powerpoint files may contain text as well as images. Thus, quantitative analyses of file types could be supplemented with qualitative random checks of a selection of websites. Second, content on the actual web pages may not necessarily be based on files that were archived. This is especially the case with images, audio, and video where the actual media file is not necessarily part of the website, but can be hosted elsewhere (e.g. on image or video services such as Flickr or YouTube), and it is only made part of the website by an embedding command. Therefore, if only the number of files in the archive is calculated the picture may be biased. As a solution to this, a list of all the commands referring to images, audio, and video could be generated and compared to what is actually in the archive and what is not.

The presence of specific software types can also inform an analysis of the content in a nation's web sphere. The number of websites using a specific software language such as PHP, ASP, or the like indicates how dynamic the content is since these software languages are used to generate content from a CMS as opposed to "flat" HTML-pages (cf. Baeza-Yates *et al.* 2007: 24–26; Tolosa *et al.* 2007: 18–19). And the presence of certain software types such as WordPress and blogger.com, or WikiWikiWeb and MediaWiki, indicates that the content is in the form of a blog or a wiki. The limitation of this approach is that specific software types do not necessarily entail specific types of content—for instance, WordPress or MediaWiki may be used as a CMS-system for producing any kind of website content; and blogs may also exist as embedded in web pages, constructed by other software types than usually used for stand-alone blogs.

The use of specific languages on a nation's web pages can be examined (cf. O'Neill *et al.* 2003: 7–8; Baeza-Yates *et al.* 2005: 15; Baeza-Yates *et al.* 2007: 7–8; Tolosa *et al.* 2007: 5–6; Rogers *et al.* 2013: 155–156), and it can tell something about the linguistic composition of a nation's web sphere—for instance, how linguistically "national" it is (does the national language prevail?), how "regionalized" it is (how dominant are different regional languages such as Catalan, Galician, and Basque in Spain?), or how international it is (how dominant are foreign languages?).

The textual elements which can actually be found on each web page can also be investigated. For instance, this could include analyses of the most widespread background colors (based on the code for background color or image), of the most used font types, of the length of web pages, or of the most common way of placing the menu items (left aligned, placed vertically, top aligned, placed horizontally).

And, finally, the actual words on the web pages can help characterize the national web sphere. A number of word-based analyses can be performed, from simple countings of word frequencies (with lists of stop words carrying no individual meaning ("and", "the", etc.))—for instance, presented as a top 100 list, as a tag cloud, or as an N-gram search—to more sophisticated semantic analyses of specific issues or topics, aiming at identifying where discussions of these topics can be found on the national web, and how the topic spreads (e.g. sentiment analysis, topic modelling, issue crawl). Examples are the analysis of most frequently used terms in Gabriel Tolosa et al. 2007: 4–5, and the UK Web Archive's possibility to search for individual words over time and to visualize the result as an N-gram (UK Web Archive n.d.).

Comparative Studies

Comparative studies of two or more national web spheres are also possible (e.g. Baeza-Yates et al. 2004; Baeza-Yates et al. 2007). On one hand, the different national web spheres could be mutually compared with a view to examining differences and similarities, and on the other hand, their actual interrelations could be investigated. The latter point would be an examination of the national web spheres' internationalization—for instance, aiming at identifying to what extent the United Kingdom and Denmark link to each other, or whether the United Kingdom links more to Denmark than the opposite.

The main challenge with any kind of transnational comparison is that the national web archives involved may have used different archiving strategies or settings (different archiving depth, inclusion/exclusion of specific file types, etc.; cf. Brügger 2013: 759–761). Thus, the material in the archives may be very different on a number of variables, and the comparisons may be biased. In addition, different legal frameworks may apply (regarding copyright, data protection/privacy) and thereby make comparisons impossible or difficult, but since analyses of a nation's web sphere are not focusing closely on individual websites or content, the legal challenges are probably minor.

Conclusion

As has been discussed in this chapter, studying a nation's Web domain encompasses a number of general challenges revolving around the spatial and temporal nature of the Web, and especially of the archived web. These general challenges affect the more detailed ways of probing the national Web outlined in the analytical design.

The next steps are to test the analytical design, to develop the adequate analytical software to analyze large amounts of archived web material, as well as to visualize the results, and, finally, to perform actual analyses of the archived web material, thus establishing the baseline of national historical studies of the Web.

Depending on the quality of the archived web material, the probing of a national Web may provide valuable knowledge about a nation's Web in general, as well as of the changing patterns and trends, which could eventually be summed up in a national "web trend index". Based on this type of knowledge about yesterday's web developments, we may gain a better understanding of what is happening on the Web today; this may help qualify broad discussions of culture, sociality, and technology, or more application-oriented approaches to the Web— for instance, among web producers. And last but not least, the interplay between a national Web and the nation's life outside the Web could be investigated—for instance, by comparing geographical distribution of the population with the distribution of websites in the national web sphere, by comparing the development of outgoing links from the national Web domain with migration, immigration, travelling, and trade on the ground, or by comparing changes over time in linking practices within a second-level domain such as the academic sub-domain ac.uk with institutional affiliation, league table ranking, and geographic location, as demonstrated in Hale *et al.* 2014. Thus, historical studies of a national Web domain may open a totally new array of investigations within Internet studies—and outside.

References

Andersen, B. (2006) *The DK-Domain: In Words and Figures,* available at: http://netarkivet.dk/wp-content/uploads/DK-domaenet-i-ord-og-tal.pdf

Baeza-Yates, R., Castillo, C., and Efthimiadis, E. (2004) *Comparing the Characteristics of the Chilean and the Greek Web,* available at: http://chato.cl/papers/baeza04_comparing_chilean_web_greek_web.pdf

Baeza-Yates, R., Castillo, C., and Efthimiadis, E. (2007) "Characterization of National Web Domains", *ACM Transactions on Internet Technology,* 7(2), available at: www.chato.cl/research/

Baeza-Yates, R., Castillo, C., and López, V. (2005) "Characteristics of the Web of Spain", *Cybermetrics: International Journal of Scientometrics, Informetrics and Bibliometrics,* 9(1), available at: www.cindoc.csic.es/cybermetrics/articles/v9i1p3.html

Baeza-Yates, R., Lalanne, F., Castillo, C., and Dupret, G. (2004) "Comparing the Characteristics of the Korean and the Chilean Web", *Korea-Chile IT Cooperation Center ITCC, Technical Report,* available at: http://chato.cl/papers/baeza_04_comparing_chilean_web_korean_web.pdf

Ben-David, A. (2014) "Mapping Minority Webspaces: The Case of the Arabic Webspace in Israel", in D. Caspi and N. Elias (eds), *Ethnic Minorities and Media in the Holy Land,* London: Vallentine-Mitchell Academic, pp. 137–157.

Boldi, P., Codenotti, B., Santini, M., and Vigna, S. (2002) "Structural Properties of the African Web", *Proceedings of the 11th International World Wide Web Conference,* Honolulu, Hawaii, May, available at: www2002.org/CDROM/poster/164/

Brügger, N. (2009) "Website History and the Website as an Object of Study", *New Media & Society,* 11(1–2): 115–132.

Brügger, N. (2010) "Introduction: Web History, an Emerging Field of Study", in N. Brügger (ed.), *Web History,* New York: Peter Lang, pp. 1–25.

Brügger, N. (2012a) "When the Present Web Is Later the Past: Web Historiography, Digital History, and Internet Studies", *Historical Social Research,* 37(4): 102–117.

Brügger, N. (2012b) "Web History and the Web as a Historical Source", *Zeithistorische Forschungen,* 9(2): 316–325.

Brügger, N. (2013) "Web Historiography and Internet Studies: Challenges and Perspectives", *New Media & Society,* 15(5): 752–764.

Brügger, N., and Finnemann, N. O. (2013) "The Web and Digital Humanities: Theoretical and Methodological Concerns", *Journal of Broadcasting and Electronic Media,* 57(1): 66–80.

Castells, M. (2001) *The Internet Galaxy: Reflections on the Internet, Business, and Society,* Oxford: Oxford University Press.

Foot, K. A., and Schneider, S. M. (2006) *Web Campaigning,* Cambridge, MA: MIT Press.

GeoIndex (n.d.) *GeoIndex of the JISC UK Web Domain Dataset (1996–2010),* available at: www.webarchive.org.uk/ukwa/visualisation/ukwa.ds.2/geo

Hale, S. A., Yasseri, T., Cowls, J., Meyer, E. T., Schroeder, R., and Margetts, H. (2014) "Mapping the UK Webspace: Fifteen Years of British Universities on the Web", *WebSci '14 Proceedings of the 2014 ACM Conference on Web Science,* 62–70, ACM New York, NYdoi 10.1145/2615569.2615691.

Miranda, J., and Gomes, D. (2009) "Trends in Web Characteristics", in E. Chavéz, E. S. Furtade, and A. L. Morán (eds), *2009 Latin American Web Congress. LA-WEB 2009,* pp. 146–153

Netarchive.dk (2006) *Newsletter—Year-1,* available at: http://netarkivet.dk/wp-content/uploads/Newsletter_Net archive_dk_august2006.pdf

Netarchive.dk (2007) *Newsletter—March 2007,* available at: http://netarkivet.dk/wp-content/uploads/Newsletter_Netarchive_dk_march2007.pdf

Netarchive.dk (2011) *Newsletter—August 2011,* available at: http://netarkivet.dk/wp-content/uploads/Newsletter_Netarchive_dk_august2011.pdf

Netarkivet.dk (2005), *Pligtaflevering af Dansk Materiale, Offentliggjort på Internettet fra 1. Juli (Legal Deposit of Danish Material Published on the Internet from July 1, 2005),* available at: http://netarkivet.dk/til-webstedejere/pligtaflevering/

Netarkivet.dk (n.d.a) *Statistik*, available at: http://netarkivet.dk/om-netarkivet/statistik/

Netarkivet.dk (n.d.b) *Tværsnitshøstninger (Cross-section Harvesting Inger)*, available at: http://netarkivet.dk/om-net arkivet/tvaersnitshostninger/

O'Neill, E. T., Lavoie, B. F., and Bennett, R. (2003) "How 'World Wide' Is the Web?: Trends in the Evolution of the Public Web", *D-Lib Magazine*, 9(4), available at: www.dlib.org/dlib/april03/lavoie/04lavoie.html

Pitkow, J. E. (1998) "Summary of WWW Characterizations", *Computer Networks and ISDN Systems*, 30(1–7): 551–558, http://citeseer.nj.nec.com/article/james98summary.html

Rogers, R., Weltevrede, E., Borra, E., and Niederer, S. (2013) "National Web Studies: The Case of Iran Online", in J. Hartley, J. Burgess, and A. Bruns (eds), *A Companion to New Media Dynamics*, Oxford: Blackwell, pp. 142–166.

The Royal Library: National Library of Denmark and Copenhagen University Library (n.d.), *Danish Collections (The National Collections)*, available at: www.kb.dk/en/nb/samling/ds/index.html

The Royal Library: National Library of Denmark and Copenhagen University Library (2004) *Act on Legal Deposit of Published Material*, Act No. 1439 of 22 December, available at: www.kb.dk/en/kb/service/pligtaflevering-ISSN/lov.html

Schostag, S., and Fønss-Jørgensen, E. (2012) "Webarchiving: Legal Deposit of Internet in Denmark, a Curatorial Perspective", *Microform & Digitization Review*, 41: 110–120.

Tolosa, G., Bordignon, F., Baeza-Yates, R., and Castillo, C. (2007) "Characterization of the Argentinian Web", *Cybermetrics*, 11(1): 1–25, available at: www.cindoc.csic.es/cybermetrics/articles/v11i1p3.html

UK Web Archive (n.d.), *N-gram Search*, available at: www.webarchive.org.uk/ukwa/ngram/

W3C (2001) *Web Characterization Activity Statement*, available at: www.w3.org/WCA/Activity

Part 2

RETHINKING INTERNET EVOLUTION

5

FROM THE MINITEL TO THE INTERNET

The Path to Digital Literacy and Network Culture in France (1980s–1990s)

Valérie Schafer and Benjamin G. Thierry

When France Telecom retired its Transpac data network in June 2012, it put a definitive end to the Minitel. This "intermediate technology", as historian Pascal Griset once put it (Griset in Schafer and Thierry 2012: 7), was an early alternative to the public Internet, and a vestige of French voluntarism—both state and industrial—as well as an important, but often overlooked, tool for digital education that died in France.

At its birth in the early 1980s, the Minitel had been far from an isolated project for countries in the Organisation for Economic Cooperation and Development. The convergence between telecommunications and computers, in what was known as telematics, seemed to be promising. With state support, the monopoly of the telephone lines, the packet-switching network Transpac that opened in 1978, and an electronic telephone directory project, the powerful French Telecommunications Administration made a bet on services. The Minitel was a small terminal in typical 1980s design that supported Télétel traffic and met many challenges successfully. First, there were technical challenges, such as the creation of a massive database for the electronic telephone directory, the development of an affordable terminal, the invention of original interfaces, and interactive devices. Second, it responded to economic challenges, as with the creation of a business model, a telematics market, and profitability. Third, it also dealt with political challenges, as when it faced initial hostility by the media, which brought some members of parliament along with it. And, finally, it met the social challenges of introducing screen-and-keyboard devices into the home, attracting new users.

Yet, far from being a success story, in the mid-1990s, the Minitel gradually went from a symbol of modernity and industrial voluntarism to becoming synonymous with outdated, centralized technology, a "dumb terminal" blamed for "France's Internet delay". This "little French box" entered history as it exited French quotidian life. It is time to consider the original innovation that it helped bring about, and identify and evaluate the intersections and divergences that unite telematics and the Internet, to try to understand digital culture as one of constant reinvention and surprising continuities.

The Minitel: A French Exception

From Captain in Japan, to Bildschirmtext in the Federal Republic of Germany, to the British Prestel, to the Canadian Telidon, numerous videotex experiments were conducted in the late 1970s, but none enjoyed the success or longevity of France's Minitel. The Minitel did little to heed the wishes of the French Telecommunications Administration to export its product. This failure, which was caused by several factors, from the battle for a common European display standard, to the Directorate-General of Telecommunications' (DGT) desire to export a turnkey system, doesn't diminish the originality of the device that was developed in the 1980s and 1990s, and which remains the chief symbol of the successful implementation of a public telematics project. These lasting choices would set the Minitel apart, as well as the Télétel interactive system more generally.

After the Phone Catch-up

In the first half of the 1970s, before the idea of launching a large-scale telematics public project was ever put forth, the DGT, under Presidents Georges Pompidou and Valéry Giscard d'Estaing, made a last attempt at bringing the telephones up to date. Indeed, for nearly a century, France had been cursed with a state of poor equipment and chronic breakdowns linked to high costs, lack of planning, and mismanagements. This even became a laughing matter, giving rise to the saying, "Half of France waits for the phone, the other half waits for the tone". A total of 442,000 applications for a phone line were awaiting treatment in 1966, in rural and urban areas.

To remedy the situation, the DGT, led by Gérard Théry from 1974, undertook Delta LP, an unprecedented plan to upgrade the telephone lines and infrastructures. From 1970 to 1975, the telephone lines had increased from four to seven million. In parallel, the DGT, which held the monopoly, was already brainstorming how to recoup its investment after the upgrade. It would be what wasn't yet known as telematics, but was at this time called "téléinformatique"—a contraction of the French words "telecommunications" and "informatique"—that later generated the establishment of new services with high added value.

From the beginning of the decade, the National Centre for the Study of Telecommunications (CNET) and the Joint Research Centre for Broadcast and Telecommunication (CCETT) worked on implementable services on the telephone and its network. To this end, the CCETT's Bernard Marti developed Antiope, a standard for videographic data production and dissemination, and then Titan, a first draft for interactive data broadcasting. The first TV-based service, the Antiope Exchange, was founded in 1977.

For its part, CNET worked on a phone-based desktop computing system in 1970 that allowed for simple operations to be completed from long distance on a computer that delivered results using voice, and, later, graphics. The arrival on the market of the first American and Japanese pocket calculators disappointed any expectations of marketing that service, but the same team soon developed the Tic-Tac system (*Terminal intégré comportant un téléviseur avec appel au clavier*) (Thierry 2013), an integrated terminal composed of a monitor and a keyboard—similar in principle, but not limited to arithmetic. The system went public in 1975, allowing for databases to be queried and their responses displayed on the screen.

In the late 1970s, France's Antiope and Britain's Prestel developed similar, but competing, "videotext" systems (a term denoting a telecommunications service allowing pages of text and simple graphics to be sent in response to a user request). In September 1977, at Berlin's Funkaustellung, the French presented Antiope, and Gérard Théry, fully aware of his system's

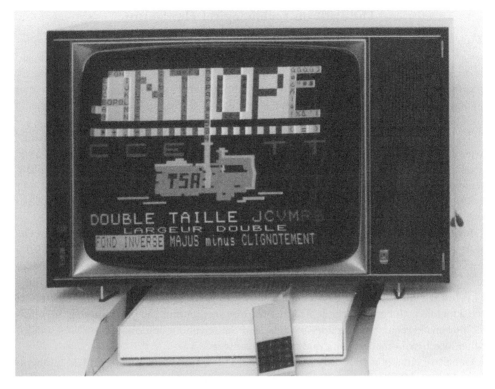

Figure 5.1 An Antiope page (created around 1980 by Bernard Marti). Attribution: I, Liagushka, CC-BY-SA-3.0 (http://creativecommons.org/licenses/by-sa/3.0/)

capabilities, but taking note of Britain's heavy promotion of their own system, decided to ask his government to support further development of the new services. On 30 November 1978, the Cabinet agreed to a "full-scale" test of telematics, which would take the form of an experiment in the Parisian suburbs. In 1981, this experiment, which later became known as Télétel 3V, connected 2,500 users to 200 content providers under the aegis of the Telecommunications Administration.

The year 1978 was thus pivotal. The opening of the Transpac network gave birth to an infrastructure allowing for data transfer. The government decided on experiments with new telephone services and manifested its political will. The Nora-Minc Report, named for its authors, two finance inspectors, provided the modernizing ideology and accompanying discourse on the necessity of the "informatisation de la société" (Nora and Minc 1978), meaning the necessity for society to adopt computers on a wide scale, towards which end DGT would be the central actor. Through its monopoly, the Telecommunications Administration was able to claim not only a special role in the data networks, but also in services, all the while supporting innovative work within the parameters of traditional activities. In effect, the development of public telematics came through a flagship service that lent legitimacy to the DGT, which was inspired notably by an experiment led on a much smaller scale in the United States: the replacement of the paper telephone directory—a costly service that was becoming overwhelmed by the growing number of subscribers, while telephone information services were inundated with requests—by an "electronic directory" made available online.

The Path of Technological Humanism

While having one or more interactive screens in the home or the workplace is now common-place, it was not so at the end of the 1970s. The widespread adoption of screen-and-keyboard devices providing access to databases, and later to "interactive services", seemed highly uncertain at the time. Would the French accept this terminal into their homes? And, another question, partly contained in the first: even if they accepted telematics, would they understand how to use it?

To simultaneously ward off the risk of early rejection, and allow for a user-friendly experience, CNET and CCETT did not limit themselves to technical concerns during the system's design phase, but also initiated a comprehensive human-centered development process, beginning in 1978. The first concern was to define an interface that could facilitate user interaction with the services. This initial interaction actually developed right within the digital telephone directory.

In 1979, its specifications, drafted by Jean-Paul Maury's team, placed average users at the heart of the discussion. The dumb terminal model and videographic standards imposed a display simplicity that would impede neither the legibility nor the immediate intelligibility of function. Instead of a scoring system, the screen displayed fields for the user to fill in using a keyboard whose function keys could access help, get clarifications, or submit queries. It was a middle path between the logic inherited from computing and programming, in which the user made requests using lines of code, and the telephone information service's model, which was based on alternating questions and answers.

Definitive choices were finally made in 1982, following several rounds of field testing in Saint-Malo and Rennes (in the Western part of France), in the context of a concrete, and rather unusual, collaborative construct: average users drove innovation from the design phase forward. This logic of active user participation led to a "full-scale" test of the first services, which were offered beginning in July 1981 to 2,500 "guinea pigs" in the Parisian suburbs. This experiment, known as "Télétel 3V", lasted until December 1982, and allowed for the exploration of the terminal's first uses: digital sales, synchronous and asynchronous messaging, and information consulting. It also ensured the possibility of imagining early public adoption of telematics.

This test phase was a critical step in the development of French telematics. The human-centered approach was particularly striking in the changes it brought to the keyboard and its layout, to the way forms were formatted, and to the various services that were provided in response to participant/user feedback. It also strengthened this characteristically French approach to developing the telematics interface. Text-based, without a scoring system, and based on the most "natural" user-system interaction possible, it diverged with US experiments conducted in the same period that led to the appearance of graphics interfaces like Windows, Icons, Menus, Pointing devices (WIMP), which had been popularized by the microcomputer.

A Winning Economic and Technical Bet

At the same time, an economic model was emerging. Very quickly, telecommunications agreed that the terminal, whose cost ranged between 500 and 1,000 francs (from US$80 to $160, approximately) when produced in bulk, should be provided to customers free of charge.

It was a risky bet. Tacked onto the cost of the network infrastructure, it transformed the project into a real gamble. The evaluation of the overall financial requirements is complex, but from 1984 to 1995 it required an investment of around 17 billion francs (approximately US$3 billion).

Figure 5.2 Minitel 1 (France, 1982). Attribution: I, Deep silence, CC–BY–SA–3.0 (http://creativecommons.org/licenses/by-sa/3.0/)

Nevertheless, the break-even point seems to have been reached shortly after the early 1990s (Cats-Baril and Jelassi 1994). In 1993, 6.5 million Minitel terminals, and nearly half a million modem cards allowing network access via computers, generated revenue to the tune of 6.7 billion francs, of which three billion went to service providers. This success was partly thanks to a novel pricing model called the "Kiosque". Developed in 1983, introduced in 1984, and extended to the whole country in 1985, this system was based on paying for service use according to duration as indexed across several different pricing levels. The amount was directly applied to the customer's phone bill, and 60 percent of it on average was paid to service providers. For most services, the cost for one hour of use was between 50 and 70 francs (approximately US$9–12).

This pricing led the entire ecosystem towards very fast growth: profitability was viewed favorably by service providers, who were multiplying and increasing the variety of services offered, which in turn increased the number of users, and so on. Between 1984 and 2000, net revenue was about four billion francs, for a total cost of 60 billion francs, with a rate of return oscillating between 11 and 15 percent, according to various interpretations. From an industrial standpoint alone, the national effort served its purpose, injecting 5.5 billion francs into the components industry (Masset 1986). Content providers also reaped rapid and significant rewards, and new market entrants stood out, like AGL, whose famous pink Ulla messaging service earned US$16 million profit in 20 years.

The Telecommunications Administration could congratulate itself for having made a successful economic bet, and for accomplishing a technical feat. The Transpac network encountered some very occasional difficulties in supporting the Minitel traffic as it grew exponentially in the mid-1980s, but it was a robust network, secure and capable of adapting and evolving with its customers. The system was based on PAVI (videotex access points), which used modems to established links between the telephone network and Transpac, as well as data conversion between analogic and digital modes. These achievements were made possible with industrial support such as, in this case, that of Alcatel. At the end of 1991, the network included 120 PAVI with 61,000 access ports, 20,000 of them pointing to the electronic directory.

From a technical point of view, the electronic telephone directory was not the least of its challenges: it included an access point connecting to the network, a "query center", and a database benefiting from a distributed architecture. The main challenge was to support the large number of simultaneous connections entering from the front end of the query center and the database. Service development and implementation, as well as information storage, were also key technical goals. For services, page creation moved gradually from a traditional method to an industrial system—at times, it took as long as eight days to build the first pages, working bit by bit. For accommodation, the Administration allowed service providers to choose between operating using the dedicated informatics service provided by the Administration, the CITV (Computer Centre in Velizy Télétel), or their own system, like a service company or an internal computer system. Most providers were happy to use CITV, although some large companies preferred the second option to maintain control over their technical developments.

When it came to developing the electronic telephone directory, the main challenge was scale, even if the numbers might inspire a chuckle by today's standards: the database in use at the time was the world's largest, identifying the information of 23 million individuals, making 40,000 queries per day, for a daily update requiring nearly 20 gigabytes. In 1987 alone, the electronic telephone directory generated ten million hours of queries and 294 million calls in 1987 alone.

The Emergence of a Digital Culture in France

The development of a viable infrastructure and a free terminal, together with the wide availability of services, brought France into its digital childhood earlier than other developed countries. Indeed, a real culture *for* and *by* the digital settled permanently within equipped populations. Many of the users were young people (25–45-year-olds), employed in the service sector, with a post-Baccalaureate education. While exceptions to this profile may apply, the Minitel was a medium widely and mainly disseminated in the middle class.

Email communication was a salient feature of this gradual digital acclimatization. Following research on email conducted at CCETT in 1977, several services were offered to Minitel users like Velizy's messaging system, M3V. Others paved the way for "chatting", like Gretel, launched by the newspaper *Les Dernières Nouvelles d'Alsace*. They were followed by the so-called "pink" chat rooms in the middle of the decade. Both the most popular "pink" messaging services were Aline and Cum. They allowed online dating and erotic live chat between two or more users, and they made many headlines by questioning the place of sex and the regulation of trade in this new medium. Those who were attracted to direct communication with other Minitel users were the biggest consumers, generating up to 50 percent of Kiosque traffic. Some "amateurs" collected astronomical bills. The great freedom that prevailed in these virtual discussion spaces does not alone explain their success. "Taxi Girls"—hostesses who maintained the interest of Minitel users with enticing usernames and unambiguous subjects of discussion—also generated higher and stable attendance. These professionals, pretending to be users, often assumed several identities simultaneously to stimulate conversation, keep men (the main users) online and increase the benefits of the service providers. Moderate users, the vast majority of Minitel users, did not participate in these discussion boards, and focused on more directly practical messaging services.

Orders for merchandise via digital correspondence, especially textile, played a major role in generating interest in telematics. Not only did the sector's big names quickly seize upon this new tool, but the shortening of order and delivery time, in comparison to traditional postal logistics circuits, also won over customers. In 1983, the famous French mail order company Trois Suisses launched its service, generating 400,000 connections annually, which represented 3.5 percent of the company's total revenue in 1986, and over 10 percent in 1988. These practices became a permanent part of the French consumer landscape in 1994, when 1.2 million households placed orders on a Minitel mail order site. In that same year in the United States, only 800,000 homes engaged in similar online shopping on the Internet.

In terms of information search, the Minitel also found success. Despite the press criticism when the project was announced at the beginning of the 1980s, by the end of 1983 the daily newspaper *Libération*, soon followed by others, had created a digital information service. Similarly, banking and travel services settled permanently into the French telematics landscape. The SNCF (railway company), which had been involved in Velizy's early experiments, provided access to ticket booking and viewing train schedules. The French bank Banque de la Cité was the first institution to offer online accounts in 1985; five years later, this type of service took up 11 percent of online traffic.

For companies, Minitel also became an everyday tool. From the end of 1978, a number of infrastructure projects were in development. In the banking sector in 1980, following the first experiments transmitting stock information, the Bank Message Switching Centre (CCMB) (Centre de commutation de messageries bancaires) opened, offering a complement to SWIFT international banking—the transmission of payments and wire transfers. In the field of transportation, the Tourist Teleinformatics Service allowed travel agencies to interact with the reservation systems of major transport companies, beginning in 1979. More generally, supplies were increasingly traded via Minitel. In 1992, the telematics business generated more than 12 million connection hours, while other services generated 65 million.

Nevertheless, a slowdown in the growth of the number of terminals began to be felt at the beginning of the 1990s. Numbers fell in 1995, when the Internet and the World Wide Web began to generate discussion. The era of competition had begun.

Rethinking the Minitel's Role in the "French Internet Delay"

In 2000, the report of the Working Group on the Future Internet highlighted the French delay in general Internet use. Indeed, as of November 1999, the country had only 5.7 million Internet users in private or professional settings, as compared with 110.8 million in the United States, 12.3 million in Germany, and 13.9 million in the United Kingdom. An exacerbating factor was the low market penetration of computers into France: only 26 percent of households owned a microcomputer at the end of 1999, compared with about 50 percent of American homes in December 1998.

In this context, many identified the Minitel as a slowing, or impeding, factor. In late 1999, the Médiamétrie Institute stressed:

> The Minitel is [. . .] a serious competitor with the Internet in the field of online services, but by having encouraged French familiarization with these services, it may be a future ally when the Internet offers an interface as simple as the Minitel interface, access tools to effective information, and richer and more attractive services tools.

Was the Minitel an ally or an obstacle to the implementation of the Internet? It was noted at the time that:

> The French have paid a price by using a system that the rest of the world does not support. France is caught in a paradoxical situation. The Minitel has led to France's being behind the rest of the world in technology, the same problem Minitel was created to fix.
>
> (Kerr 1999: 11)

The whole matter is certainly a little more complex.

Did France Miss the Internet in the 1970s?

In 2013, Louis Pouzin, a French pioneer of research on data networks and the head of Cyclades, a packet-switching network developed at IRIA (Institut de Recherche en Informatique et Automatique), now INRIA (the French Institute for Research in Computer Science and Automation) in the 1970s, received the Queen Elizabeth Prize for Engineering alongside Vinton Cerf, Robert Kahn, Tim Berners-Lee, and Marc Andreessen for his participation in the creation of the Internet. The French discovered with amazement that France might have passed by the invention of the Internet in the 1970s. While it is also tempting to hold the Minitel primarily responsible for France's peripheral role in Internet development during the 1990s and 2000s, such a statement is in need of greater nuance and contextualization.

Above all, it is important to emphasize that Louis Pouzin was undoubtedly a figurehead in data networks, and the French contributed to the history of the Internet protocol (including the genesis of TCP/IP), but this missed opportunity concerned the pre-Web Internet, rather than its mainstream development. It should also be underscored that any historian uncomfortable with alternative or counterfactual histories should be careful in responding: without the Minitel, would France have gained faster uptake of the Internet? This is a possibility, but by no means certain.

Undeniably, in any case, we can highlight France's contribution to the genesis of the Internet, and the role of Louis Pouzin and the Cyclades team at IRIA from 1971 to 1979 in developing what became TCP/IP. In an email to David Reed, Vinton Cerf himself called Louis Pouzin the "guru of datagrams" (Net History 2014)—one of the foundations of the TCP/IP protocol which circulates data packets according to adaptive routing. Vinton Cerf also mentioned Hubert Zimmermann, another member of the French Cyclades team, who was one of the main designers of the first version of OSI, the seven-layer open architecture that was presented in the 1980s and early 1990s as a serious alternative to TCP/IP.

Cyclades was thus a milestone in the history of the Internet. In effect, it maintained a real technical and relational proximity with the achievements of the US teams who worked on ARPANET. In addition to inventing datagrams, its members participated in discussions within the International Network Working Group to work out open protocol specifications. They were also present at the first official demonstrations of ARPANET in 1972, and Gérard Le Lann was at Stanford in 1973 alongside Vinton Cerf, who defined TCP, with Robert Kahn.

Yet, despite these important achievements, Cyclades bore the brunt of the competition with Transpac, a network which, as mentioned above, later allowed the traffic generated by Minitel services. Indeed, beginning in 1972, the Cyclades and Transpac teams, which both developed packet-switching networks, attempted to collaborate, but were unable to agree on a joint project. Disagreements focused on the packets routing. Cyclades preferred an adaptive model, while telecommunications, which was sensitive to the service quality, criticized this "best effort" model and its potential pricing difficulties. This view led telecommunications to opt for virtual circuits, whereby all of a message's packets followed together to ensure a safe delivery. Louis Pouzin called this a "belt and suspenders" model. The conflict led to open criticism on the international scene, and a race towards standardization that telecommunications won by standardizing virtual circuits to CCITT in 1976 (Després 2010). However, it also meant the extinction of Cyclades in 1979. This was partly due to the influence of the Telecommunications Authority, with its monopoly on the phone lines, and the ability to offer both a network and a suitable commercial supply to businesses. After Cyclades was buried, the Internet undoubtedly lost the battle in France: telematics and its thousands of services reached the majority of users, while the Internet remained inaccessible to the mainstream public for many years. Noting this paradoxical situation at the beginning of the 1980s, the historian can only conclude with a question that remains largely open: did getting it right too early ultimately mean getting it wrong?

The Internet from Early Adopters to the General Public: Birth of a Market

In France, telematics allowed some scientific communications in the 1980s (Thierry 2013), but it was not really a suitable tool. A small community of early adopters came together to explore their interest in the "network of networks" via personal and institutional links within the North American Internet space. Indeed, from the 1980s on, some researchers at INRIA who worked or had links with the United States lamented not having the opportunity to receive emails or news from the Usenet community, particularly those based on UUCP and the Unix operating system. They found technical and organizational solutions enabling access to these services. In 1983, when Berkeley Unix 4.2 joined with the TCP/IP protocol, more users moved toward the Internet. This was not only the case in the United States, but also a few years later at INRIA with FNET. FNET was the French branch of EUnet, the European Unix community. It benefited from its membership by having access to the newsgroups of the UNIX community through an agreement with CWI, a Dutch computing center. FNET converted from UUCP to TCP/IP in 1986.

Later, in 1988, INRIA's Christian Huitema used his relationships with US researchers to obtain a direct liaison with Wisconsin (Griset and Schafer 2012). And in 1993, INRIA was one of the co-founders of RENATER, the network for research and higher education, which provided a backbone connecting the regional university hubs. In 1995, INRIA became the second host, after MIT, of the consortium W3C that Tim Berners-Lee, founder of the Web, created to manage specifications and protocols (Griset and Schafer 2011), since in the meantime, the Internet had changed scale.

The world of research, especially computer science research, comprised early Internet adopters, but it is from the angle of service providers that we have to look for the driving force that allowed the Internet to mutate from a tool for the happy few to a genuine communication market. Although France Telecom didn't launch Wanadoo, its public Internet access, until 1996, several Internet service providers (ISPs) had already begun to explore the new market. EUnet (as we have seen, its French branch, FNET, was part of INRIA) was the first, claiming 53 percent of connected companies and laboratories; RENATER was the second (37 percent of French Internet), followed by Oléane, a division of the IT company Apysoft and member of the European commercial network Pipex (4 percent). Internet-Way, created in 1994, should also be mentioned. It targeted professionals and was connected to the European network Ebone. Other ISPs like Calvanet, Calvacom's Internet branch that was born in the Apple universe, as well as Francenet and Worldnet, offered Internet access for the consumer market. And we can't leave out the myriad of small regional ISPs born before the Minister of Telecommunications wished that every French citizen could connect to an ISP for the price of a local phone call (Rebillard 2012). This favored the establishment of a mass national Internet market concentrated around a few large ISPs. And, indeed, the Telecommunications Administration took the technological turn at that moment, after hesitating about the Minitel's possibility for evolution, as well as with offering proprietary services like CompuServe and AOL.

Télécom Multimédia was a structure led by Gérard Eymery and associated with France Telecom Group, at a time when two teams merged. The first was an "Innovation" team led by Daniel Sainthorant at the Ad Agency, who had helped develop the marketing campaign for the electronic phone directory during the 1980s, and who now carried out a fairly typical reapplication of his telematics expertise to the Internet. His team worked on a "mall" project. The second team was led by Jean-Jacques Damlamian from France Telecom's Sales department. It acquired skills by participating in the construction of RENATER. The ambitious goals of this new entity, which was baptized France Telecom Interactive under the chairmanship of Roger Courtois in early 1996, included launching Internet access for the general public, marketing complete Internet offerings (electronic phone directory and online services), and evolving the Minitel. In fact, the page did not turn quite so easily, and for users it was still a time of caution, no less than for the service providers at first.

For most service providers familiar with telematics' Kiosque and profitability, the transition to the Internet, without a clear payment system or business model, seemed like a leap into the unknown. They complained of poor service performance, network vulnerability, and subscriber turnover, then estimated at 40 percent. In comparison with the multiple problems highlighted (Internet saturation, crashing, hacking, unstructured supply), online services that were crossed between Télétel and the Web (Prodigy, CompuServe, and AOL) seemed reassuring. With the Web:

> The user is "spoiled with choices" in the negative sense of the term: the first Internet users even speak of "surfing the Net", that expression [which] aptly characterises such random navigation.
>
> (Grellier 1995: 67–68)

Offerings were still dominated by the idea of a portal guiding navigation, which "stream-lined" and thus maintained an influence, however small, on the consumption of services. On the supply end, the delay seems therefore to be explained by Minitel's ability to create value, while the Internet of the day had a less clear economic model. While Minitel users paid both a base fee and an additional tariff for the length of time they spent consuming services, the Internet promoted a certain amount of free use and services (paid through advertising or an extra cost). As Henri de Maublanc, President of the Association for Online Trade and Services, explained in the newspaper *Le Monde* on 30 May 2001: "Today, when all the publishers on the Internet are searching for a way to get paid by Internet users for content, the Minitel's surcharged line model now passes for a stroke of genius." However, at that time, the general French consumption of telematic services had begun to decline, and the Web was able to find its place in homes and businesses.

Continuities of Usage and Updating Through Practices

Some service providers joined the bandwagon, displaying remarkable adaptability. Such was the case of the iconic owner of Free, Xavier Niel, who continues to make headlines today. His first steps in pink chat rooms allowed him to build up a "war chest" that he reinvested in the acquisition of a 50 percent share of Fermic Multimédia in 1990, which soon became Iliad. Niel then embarked on a transition phase with his gateways to the Internet beginning in 1994, before obtaining the right to operate his own network, and founding Free in 1999.

There were others who transitioned successfully from the Minitel to the Internet (for example, Denys Chalumeau's Seloger.com and Jean-David Blanc's Allociné.com). A true digital entrepreneur community had made telematics its classroom, and would invest in the Internet market in the 1990s when it was still embryonic.

For users, the transition also came in the second half of the 1990s. While the cost of using the Minitel was high, averaging around 60 francs per hour, the terminal itself was free. This was not the case for Internet access, which not only was sold on a per-minute basis until "unlimited" packages became available in 1999, but also required an initial investment of several thousand francs to purchase equipment, specifically a computer that could connect through its modem. From a logistical standpoint as well, the use of the Minitel had nothing in common with the difficulties of dealing with a micro-computer whose emerging graphic interfaces had not yet eliminated bugs and complexities (Thierry 2012).

During the 2000s, the catching up proceeded more quickly. In 2004, Europe's average monthly residential connection rate was 47 percent, with France located in the upper half at 49 percent. By the last three months of 2007, 72 percent of the French population was connected at home and 40 percent at their workplace. By 2009, 19.8 million people, out of a total population of 64 million, were connecting to the Internet every day, and daily connection time approached one hour and twenty minutes.

Even more than these overall connection figures, usage continuities were updated, from telematics habits to practices reinvested in the Internet. In 2008, one in five people in France purchased movies, music, books, periodicals, or software online, while 10 percent of movie, concert, theater, opera, dance, and sporting event tickets were purchased online (Berret 2008). France led Europe in terms of connections leading to the purchase of a cultural product, while it was tied for third place with Iceland, behind Germany and the United Kingdom (which each claimed 8 percent) for purchasing movies and music delivered or updated online (it claimed 7 percent). It is difficult not to see here the beneficial effects of online ordering that had been popularized in the 1980s by the Minitel. The Minitel was an indisputable pathway for French digital development, and it maintains multiple and complex relationships with the Internet that are resistant to single factor analysis.

As the outcome of political will and a pioneering vision of modernity enabled by teleinformatics communication networks, telematics was an alternative to the world of networking driven by the United States. The standards used, the "dumb terminal" model, and the technological humanism that governed its introduction to all users, borrowed from a professional culture specific to French telecommunications. The early success of services, enabled both by the bet made on the free terminal and the pricing system that favored the emergence of a rich and vivid ecosystem, makes France a pioneering nation in enabling the immense possibilities of data networks available to the greatest number of people. As President Jacques Chirac enjoyed recalling in 1997, the Aubervilliers baker could check the balance of his bank account from home, while his equivalent in New York could not. This early start should generate reflection about a society's pathways to innovation. Although one emphasizes the bottom-up model of Internet development, the model of entry into society from below is symbolized by the Minitel, a "dumb terminal" whose ease of use and operation was part of its initial success, but inhibited later its ability to evolve. On the contrary, at its beginning, the Internet was a model of entry from above. Born in labs, designed as a tool for its own designers, and progressively adapted for the consumer market, its plasticity guarantees its continuity.

Today, while the Transpac network has definitively ended, the study of telematics is revealing the winding and multicentered nature of innovation trajectories. The Minitel's history is, too often, briefly summarized or overlooked as an "intermediate innovation" in relation to the technological winners of the day (Campbell-Kelly and Garcia-Swartz 2013). Telematics also examines long-term continuities, beyond the boundaries of the object alone. We can thus investigate the perpetuation of billing models initiated by telematics, which have re-emerged today in mobile telephony and software sales—for example, with Apple's App Store, which is in some ways reminiscent of the DGT's Kiosque. In an irony of history's turnarounds, isn't today's Web in the midst of a "Minitelization" of sorts, with its quasi-monopolistic actors and its increasingly closed service offerings? A model widely denounced by the various technical clergy of enlightened amateurs who argue for an open Internet while denouncing the gilded cage that, nevertheless, the great majority of users call for through their purchases? Time will tell whether this Internet Minitelization is only a fleeting moment in the evolution of digital economies, or a lasting model initiated by the Minitel and brilliantly promoted by Apple some years after. For today's historian, these multiple reversals are a reminder not to indulge presentist analysis, but to question the foundations of acquired positions, and never to mistake the winners of the day for those of yesterday, and still less those of tomorrow.

Archives

This chapter is based on archives that we consulted at INRIA and CCETT, on the French National Archives and France Telecom Archives, on audiovisual and press archives. We also had an interview campaign with around 30 protagonists of this history.

Further Reading

Ponjaert, M., Georgiades, P., and Magnier, A. (1983) "Communiquer par Télétel. Les Acquis de l'Expérience de Télétel 3V et de l'Annuaire Électronique en Ille-et-Vilaine" (Communicating through Télétel: Skills Acquired with Télétel 3V and the Electronic Telephone Directory in Ille-et-Vilaine), *France Télécom Historical Archives*, 99026/03 (a detailed study of Teletel experiments).

References

Berret, P. (2008) "Diffusion et Utilisation des Tic en France et en Europe" (Distribution and Use of ICTs in France and Europe), *Culture Chiffres*, 2: 1–15.

Campbell-Kelly, M., and Garcia-Swartz, D. (2013) "The History of the Internet: The Missing Narratives", *Journal of Information Technology*, 28: 18–33.

Cats-Baril, W., and Jelassi, T. (1994) "The French Videotex System Minitel: A Successful Implementation of a National Information Technology Infrastructure", *MIS Quaterly*, 18(1): 1–20.

Després, R. (2010) "X.25 Virtual Circuits: Transpac in France—Pre-Internet Data Networking", *IEEE Communications Magazine*, 48(11): 40–46.

Grellier, C. (1995) "Internet et ses Concurrents" (The Internet and its Competitors), *Communication et Langage*, 105: 67–68.

Griset, P., and Schafer, V. (2011) "Hosting the World Wide Web Consortium for Europe: From CERN to INRIA", *History and Technology*, 27(3): 353–370.

Griset, P., and Schafer, V. (2012) "Make the Pig Fly! l'Inria, ses Chercheurs et Internet des Années 1970 aux Années 1990" (Make the Pig Fly! Inria, its Researchers and Internet from the Seventies to the Nineties), *Le Temps des Médias*, 18: 41–53.

Kerr, R. (1999) "Minitel versus the Internet in France", *Senior Research Projects,* Paper 86, available at: http://knowledge.e.southern.edu/senior_research/86

Masset, M. (1986) "La Télématique en Plein Boom" (Telematics in Full Swing), *La Revue du Minitel*, 5: 24–29.

Net History (2014) *On the Design of TCP/IP*, available at: www.nethistory.info/Archives/tcpiptalk.html (accessed 14 April 2014).

Nora, S., and Minc, A. (1978) *L'Informatisation de la Société* (The Computerization of Society), Paris: Seuil.

Rebillard, F. (2012) "La Genèse de l'Offre Commerciale Grand Public en France (1995–1996): Entre Fourniture d'Accès à l'Internet et Services en Ligne Propriétaires" (The Genesis of the Consumer Commercial Offering in France (1995–1996): Between Internet Access Provision and Online Service Owners), *Le Temps des Médias*, 18: 65–75.

Schafer, V., and Thierry, B. (2012) *Le Minitel: L'Enfance Numérique de la France* (The Minitel: The French Digital Childhood), Paris: Nuvis.

Thierry, B. (2012) "'Révolution 0.1': Utilisateurs et Communautés d'Utilisateurs au Premier Âge de l'Informatique Personnelle et des Réseaux Grand Public (1978–1990)" ('Revolution 0.1': Users and User Communities in the First Age of Personal Computing and Public Networks (1978–1990)), *Le Temps des Médias*, 18: 54–64.

Thierry, B. (2013) "De Tic-Tac au Minitel: La Télématique Grand Public, Une Réussite Française" (From Tic-Tac to the Minitel: Mainstream Telematics, a French Success), in *Actes du Colloque Les Ingénieurs des Télécommunications Dans la France Contemporaine. Réseaux, Innovation et Territoires (XIXe–XXe Siècles)*, Paris: IGPDE, pp. 185–205.

6

THE EMERGENCE OF THE INTERNET SERVICE PROVIDER (ISP) INDUSTRY IN ISRAEL

Nicholas John

Introduction

This chapter focuses on the emerging Internet service provision (ISP) industry in Israel in the mid-1990s. It deals with the formation of an Israeli ISP industry, a development that we could also term the commercialization of the Internet, referring to the fact that the Internet ceased to be a service provided for free by academic institutions for its members, becoming instead a commodity purchased from private enterprises (Press 1994). In particular, it argues that a shift took place within the field of Internet service provision in Israel that saw the Transnational Capitalist Class (Sklair 2000) usurp the Netizen (Hauben and Hauben 1997). Put differently, part of the history of the Internet in Israel concerns the very definition of the Israeliness of the Israeli context, which itself is subject to struggle and contention. In this sense, the history told below offers some of the variety that Robin Mansell (this volume) calls for concerning "social imaginaries about where authority is located and how it should be institutionalized". As we shall see, the various actors had quite different ideas about who had, or should have, power in the field of Internet provision. Moreover, and similarly to Byung-Keun Kim (2005, cited by Mansell, this volume), not only do I *not* assume that the actors involved in institutionalizing the Israeli ISP industry had homogeneous cultural values, I actually take their diverse cultural values and outlooks as the object of my research, and relate them to broader socio-political changes afoot in Israel at the time that Israel was being diffused there.

In presenting my argument, I deploy theory developed by Pierre Bourdieu and conceptualize the ISP industry as a *field* and analyze the relations between different actors in that field in terms of their *habitus* and the different types of *capital* at their disposal. A field is "a space of conflict and competition" (Bourdieu and Wacquant 1992: 17), in which power relations are a function of the possession of different types of capital (social and cultural, for instance, and not only economic). One of the major struggles is that between "groups or individuals [attempting] to determine what constitutes capital within that field" (Webb *et al.* 2002: 43–44), or, adopting Bourdieu's game metaphor, what rules apply in settling struggles within the field. The notion of habitus is defined as "the durable and transposable systems of schemata of perception, appreciation, and action that result from the institution of the social in the body" (Bourdieu and Wacquant 1992: 126). As we shall see below, it was not only the possession of financial capital that gave certain actors advantages in the field of Internet service provision in Israel, but their habitus too, or a particular way of orienting the self in relation to society.

Indeed, the main argument advanced here is that the actors with what can be called a *global habitus*—defined as "a cognitive and emotional disposition to move easily and smoothly from one national context to another, to quickly adapt and adopt different cultural outlooks, and to think of [oneself] as an agent operating in the world as a single unit" (Illouz and John 2003)—were those who captured the key positions in the field. In other words, the shape of Internet service provision in Israel was influenced by the extent to which the various actors in it were associated with the processes of neoliberal globalization that were sweeping over Israel in the 1980s and 1990s (Ram 2007; Shafir and Peled 2002). However, and significantly, it is not argued that the formation of the Israeli ISP industry was shaped by global actors who overcame more locally oriented actors, but rather that *different versions of the global* were given expression by different actors.

Method

As part of my broader study into the diffusion of the Internet to Israel and its institutionalization there, I interviewed the founders, CEOs, and other senior executives of all of the ISPs founded in Israel at the time of the commercialization of the Internet. The purpose of these semi-structured in-depth interviews was to ask the people who, in an important sense, had brought the Internet to people's houses and businesses in the mid-1990s whether they saw themselves as involved in the processes of globalization that were going on at the time.

The data collected for this chapter come from a larger project on the diffusion of the Internet to and within Israel from the mid-1980s to the mid-1990s. The main methodology behind the collection of data presented here is interviews with key actors in the arrival of the Internet to Israel. Thirteen members of the Israeli ISP industry were interviewed, covering all but one of the ISPs founded in Israel at the time of the commercialization of the Internet. Ten of them had set up ISPs and served as the CEO of their own company. The other three interviewees from the ISP industry had held very senior positions in ISPs that they themselves did not found or run. The interviews were semi-structured in-depth interviews and based on a pre-prepared basic interview schedule (Fontana and Frey 1994). The interviews were recorded and transcribed.

There were two main reasons for conducting these interviews. The first was to document the processes of the arrival and institutionalization of the Internet in Israel. The second reason was to do with matters beyond the historical record. I did not only want to know what had happened (this is presented in John 2011a), but I also wanted to know what the people who had been involved *thought about* what had happened (see John 2011b). Before describing and analyzing the consolidation of the Israeli ISP industry, though, I offer a very brief history of the arrival of the Internet to Israel and its institutionalization in that country.

The Internet Comes to Israel, 1984–1994

Israel's first connections to overseas networks were made in 1984. As was the case with the diffusion of the Internet to many other countries outside of the United States, the first connections were made between academic institutions (for examples from South Africa, Ghana, and India, see Brown *et al.* 2007; Foster *et al.* 2004; Wolcott and Goodman 2003). In February 1984, the School of Computer Science at the Hebrew University of Jerusalem initiated a linkage with the emerging CSNET network in the United States, funded by the Ministry of Science. Later that year, on 13 August 1984, MACHBA (the Hebrew acronym for the Inter-University Computation Center) connected to EARN (the European Academic Research Network; see Ein-Dor *et al.* 1999: 7).[1]

Israel was relatively early in joining these new academic networks (it was the first international node of CSNET), and it was also one of the first countries to secure its Country Code Top Level Domain (ccTLD) suffix—namely, the two-letter code allocated to individual countries (for instance, .fr for France, or .de for Germany). The first two ccTLDs to be allocated were those of the United States—.us—and the United Kingdom –.uk—in 1985. Israel's .il suffix was the third, also in 1985. In this regard, it is also worth noting that in 1995, Israel became only the second country outside the US (after Japan) to set up a local chapter of the Internet Society (ISOC-IL).

As soon as Israeli universities were connected to CSNET and EARN, the country's network grew apace, though at first it was limited to academic institutions and their affiliated members. The Israeli network and its connections with the world outside were managed by MACHBA, which after a number of years began to feel that it was not able to perform the huge task it found itself responsible for, as more and more people were finding their way online. Indeed, in 1990, a joint committee of representatives of the Ministries of Science and Communications approved the formation of the Israeli Research and Education Network (IREN, modeled on the American National Research and Education Network), leading to the network being opened up to organizations outside of the academy.

A further step in this direction was taken in June 1991, when representatives from three ministries—Industry and Trade, Science, and Communications—asked MACHBA to start connecting commercial companies to the Internet via its infrastructure. However, MACHBA had no interest in becoming what for all intents and purposes would have been a nationwide ISP. It saw itself as responsible for research-based networking, and did not want to dirty its hands with commercial dealings. It was at this point that the idea of licensing commercial ISPs was first floated.

In the period between 1992 and 1994—when non-academic organizations could use the Internet, but before full licenses were issued—there was a rather curious mechanism for deciding who would and would not be able to get onto the network. This mechanism was a committee in the Ministry of Communications to which applications for network access were made. The main criterion was that the connection was required for research and development purposes, and although the criterion was properly applied, getting past the committee was not very difficult.

Still, though, there was no way for the private individual to attain Internet access from his or her home. This was finally enabled in May 1994, when three companies—Elron, Darcom, and NetManage—were given full Internet licenses by the Ministry of Communications (this was covered in the local press by, among others, Gabizon 1994).

For the purposes of this chapter, it is interesting to compare the list of ISPs given permission to connect research arms of commercial enterprises in 1992, and the ISPs given permission to connect all and sundry in 1994. In 1992, four ISPs provided dial-up services: Actcom, Dataserve, Kav Mancheh, and Bezeq Zahav. Of these companies, one operated until 2007 before being acquired by another ISP (Actcom); one disappeared entirely quite quickly

(Dataserve); and the other two never became fully fledged commercial providers for home usage (Bezeq Zahav and Kav Mancheh, which provided mainly business services, such as live stock exchange data). So, while there were some companies working at this time, they did not really constitute the foundations of Israel's future Internet industry. By contrast, of the three companies to receive the first full Internet licenses in 1994—Elronet, NetManage, and Darcom—two went on to enjoy supremacy in the ISP market for a number of years. Darcom never actually provided services, and Elronet and NetManage merged to become NetVision. Notably, all three entities were founded by Israelis who were either immigrants or returning from long periods of time in the US, and it is they who should really be considered Israel's first commercial ISPs.

Elsewhere, I have analyzed the arrival of the Internet to Israel in terms of globalization (John 2011a). In the following, I turn to a closer examination of the consolidation of the Internet service provision industry in Israel.

A Bourdiean Analysis: Shifting Types of Capital

According to Bourdieu, a large part of the struggles in a given field are over which type of capital will be considered valid (Bourdieu and Wacquant 1992). Actors with large amounts of a certain type of capital will try to ensure that possession of that capital is the deciding factor in the position of actors in the field. Actors with other types of capital will try to resist this, asserting the validity of the capital in which they are wealthy instead. This kind of struggle is clearly visible in the Israeli ISP field during its first few years; today, however, it would seem that this particular struggle has been settled.

More specifically, I contend that in the ISP field there was a shift from the dominance of what I call "technological capital" to purely economic capital, and that this shift was the source of much of the bitterness expressed to me by the medium-sized ISP owners towards the institutions that they perceive as being responsible for it. By "technological capital" I mean technological knowledge itself and the symbolic capital associated with it as a resource. The importance of technological capital in the early days of the Internet can be seen in the fact that the dominant actors were computing experts, and that all but one of the ISPs were set up by people with a rich background in computer networking, bulletin boards, and so on.[2] For instance, one medium-sized ISP founder brought knowledge and experience from the military, where he had served as an officer in the Communications Corps; another had worked in a university computing department prior to founding his company; another had jointly set up a large and successful network of computer stores. In other words, the dominant players were those with deep knowledge and experience of computers, which earned them recognition and enabled them to stake a claim in the field. Just as this had been the case with the invention of the Internet in the US, so it was also the case in the early days of the Internet in Israel.

With time, however, this knowledge became less and less valuable, especially because of the introduction of standardized broadband Internet connectivity technologies. One ISP owner put it like this:

> Not long ago, before the age of broadband, my knowledge had real value. [. . .] Every ISP would buy its equipment and set up network technologies between his dialing areas. Today[3] that doesn't exist anymore. Today Bezeq [at the time the state-owned telecoms monopoly] controls the market with all sorts of monopolistic practices. One of these is that actually there is no difference between the ISPs.

[. . .] I can't give you a different technical service even if I want to; even if you pay me more, I won't give you better or worse service than [another ISP].

The technological capital of the medium-sized ISP owners, then, seriously declined in value. Moreover, the contrast between actors rich in technological capital and the figures dominant in today's ISP industry in Israel is striking. For instance, Internet Gold represented the first major financial involvement in the Israeli Internet. If most ISPs had been set up with virtually no investor backing whatsoever, and if NetVision was remarkable at the time with a starting investment of around $3 million, then we can appreciate the novelty of Internet Gold, which started providing Internet connectivity in 1997, by the size of its $10 million initial investment. By means of comparison, let us recall that the smaller ISPs had been set up by people who had worked at a university computing department, for instance, or who had a long history of involvement in BBSs (online bulletin boards). Let us compare these backgrounds with that of Eli Holtzman, co-founder and CEO of Internet Gold. This is how he was described on the Internet Gold website in 2006:

> Serving Internet Gold since 1992, Eli Holtzman co-founded Internet Gold and is its Chief Executive Officer. From 1988 to 1992, Mr. Holtzman provided independent marketing consulting services to a number of enterprises. From 1986 to 1988, Mr. Holtzman served as CEO of the Israeli franchisee of the U.S. fast-food chain Wendy's, and from 1984 to 1986, he was general manager of Arieli Advertising Ltd., a leading Israeli advertising company. In 1977, Mr. Holtzman co-founded Super-Pharm, Israel's largest pharmacy chain, and was its CEO until 1984. Mr. Holtzman holds a B.Sc. in chemistry and pharmaceuticals from Illinois University.

It is immediately obvious that Holtzman's credentials as the head of an ISP are entirely different from those of previous ISP owners. Holtzman is first and foremost a businessman, and not an engineer, like virtually all other ISP CEOs up until then. Moreover, he is a businessman with global ties (a degree from an American university, the Israeli franchisee of an American fast-food chain), also unlike most of the ISP owners in Israel at the time. In this context, then, he represents the shift from "technological capital" to global financial capital.

It would appear that Abe Peled and Ruth Alon, as the CEOs of Elronet and NetManage respectively, whose companies quickly merged to become NetVision, represent a half-way stage in this process. Both are technical people who came to their positions in Israel from many years of working in the United States; indeed, Peled came from a very senior position in IBM. They were both connected to Uzia Galil, one of Israel's foremost and longstanding technological entrepreneurs, sometimes referred to as the father of the Israeli high-tech start-up industry (Elronet was a daughter company of Elron; Alon is Galil's daughter). Alon founded NetManage on the basis of an extremely strong commitment to customer service, a value that she quite explicitly declares she brought with her from America, and a fact which she sees as lying at the root of NetManage/NetVision's success. In other words, they would seem to lie between the owners of the small and medium-sized ISPs on one hand, and Holtzman and others like him on the other. As the ISP field changed, Alon and Peled were able to stay at the center of it. Their counterparts at the smaller ISPs, however, were left behind. Their technological capital was losing its value, but they were unable to supplement it with any other kind of capital, particularly the global financial capital required to compete with companies that could afford to lose money on their customers. The fact that they were extremely able engineers became increasingly irrelevant.

This, I maintain, is the source of the comments made by one ISP owner who, in interview, accused Bezeq of behaving monopolistically, and who described the imposition of a certain type of router as "undemocratic". He said: "This is an undemocratic country here. Israel is an undemocratic country. Why? Because, what can you do? Bezeq belongs to the government, and the government defends itself in all sorts of ways."

Another interviewee saw the Ministry of Communications (MoC) as giving unfair advantages to other actors:

> It's not [the government's] job to decide who will earn more money and who will earn less. [. . . But] the Ministry of Communications only deals with who will earn more money and who will be given more advantages and who will be given less, whom will it damage and whom will it help.

By the time I interviewed them, these and other interviewees in a similar position in the field had lost the game. Their technological knowledge no longer gave them any advantage: they could not convert it into financial gain, as financial capital was no longer distributed in the field according to holdings in technological capital. Hence, all that was left to do was to bemoan the situation and decry its rules—in this instance, by terming them monopolistic and undemocratic. This, then, is a major part of the explanation for the critical comments made by the owners of the mid-sized ISPs: they could see the dominant type of capital in the field changing in front of their eyes, and were powerless to halt that process.

Bourdieu and Loic Wacquant say:

> players can play to increase or to conserve their capital, their number of tokens, in conformity with the tacit rules of the game and the prerequisites of the reproduction of the game and its stakes; but they can also get in it to transform, partially or completely, the immanent rules of the game.
>
> (Bourdieu and Wacquant 1992: 99–100)

By entering the field of Internet provision, Internet Gold, and later the international telephony companies, Barak and Bezeq International, changed the rules of the game beyond the "dumbing down" of the sector described above. One of the ways they did this was through a practice known as cross-subsidizing—namely, using the profits from one branch of the company to cover losses in another. Another was by embarking on extensive marketing campaigns, including television adverts, something which the small and medium-sized ISPs could never do, quite simply because they lacked the finances. Third, they sold Internet connectivity packages at a loss, on the grounds that it was worth losing money today in order to gain customers for the future. Again, the smaller and medium-sized firms were simply unable to do this for the most rudimentary of cash-flow reasons.

So far, then, I have argued that the indignation directed towards the MoC and Bezeq by the medium-sized ISP owners can be explained in terms of the decline in value of the capital in which they were richest—technological capital. In other words, the large holdings of financial capital of other actors were enabling the latter to undercut the significance of technological capital in the field. This in turn should be seen as the outcome of changes in the field of power—that is, the state, and in particular the trend towards liberalization and decentralization in telecommunications in Israel (Levi-Faur 1999a, 1999b), for it is this which encouraged and enabled large concerns to enter the ISP industry.

Local Habitus, Global Field

Another way to explain the consolidation of the ISP field is in terms of the habitus of the actors in it. This is to go beyond a purely economic argument based on market forces (see also Davis *et al.*, this volume), and to bring into play certain dispositions, worldviews, and modes of action that also had an important part in enabling what I have termed the large ISPs to become so, and in preventing the medium-sized ISPs from fully exploiting their seniority in the field. For instance, I have already cited the CV of the CEO of Internet Gold and Ruth Alon's emphasis on American-style service as examples of the global orientations of the large companies. Perhaps the owners of the medium-sized ISPs lacked a sufficiently global outlook in order to successfully play the game in the ISP field. As I shall explain, the ISP field began to be populated by large economic concerns backed by money from overseas and by members of Israel's economic elite. The senior managers in these companies were people with global business ties and experience. In this context, the owners of the mid-size ISPs were simply left behind: their technological capital became worthless; their financial capital was not only limited in size, but also in its sources, all of which were local; and their social capital too was entirely locally based.

However, this is not to say that the medium-sized ISP owners entirely lacked a global perspective and that the story of the ISP field is simply one of the global overwhelming the local. Instead, we can see the medium-sized ISP owners as having a global outlook in two ways: first, in an important sense, their technological expertise was most definitely global in nature; and second, they identified with a political ideology of the Internet that must certainly be seen as global.

Regarding technological expertise, I asked my interviewees where they got their knowledge from. One of them said:

> It doesn't matter where. I don't check what country I get my information from. I don't check it, and it could come from all sorts of countries [. . .]. The geographical location of the knowledge is not what interests me. Geographic space has no meaning, there is no meaning at all in how it got to Israel.

This man truly seems to enter a different kind of space when surfing for information, a space without national borders. This is surely to do with a quality of such kinds of knowledge— it is extremely easily lifted out of context (see, for instance, Hannerz 1990). Of course, almost all of the knowledge possessed by these ISP owners comes from the United States, a fact which they are quick to recognize. In other words, to describe these people as lacking a global perspective of any kind would clearly be inaccurate: by working in the Internet industry, they are necessarily tied into global networks of both computers and knowledge. So, technological capital is itself a kind of global capital.

Turning to the interviewees' political ideology of the Internet, or what Mansell (2012 and this volume) would call their imaginary, it can also be argued that their perception of the place of the Internet in the world was more global than local. Given their sense of borderlessness when using the Internet, and given their strongly expressed sentiments regarding the state's perceived over-involvement in the field, we can fruitfully see the attitudes of the owners of the medium-sized ISPs as being rooted in the habitus of the "Netizen", taken here as synecdochic for a kind of broadly bottom-up, user-focused, non-hierarchical, and fundamentally utopian view of the Internet; this is the "open, emergent, and collaborative" Internet (Mansell, this volume). Michael and Ronda Hauben (1997) coined the term to refer to users of Usenet and the Internet who made a positive contribution to them:

There are people online who actively contribute towards the development of the Net. These people understand the value of collective work and the communal aspects of public communications. These are the people who discuss and debate topics in a constructive manner.

(Hauben 1996a)

Moreover, the "Proposed Declaration of the Rights of Netizens" starts by recognizing "that the net represents a revolution in human communications that was built by a cooperative non-commercial process", and goes on to assert that "[t]he Net is not a Service, it is a Right. It is only valuable when it is collective and universal" (Hauben 1996b). Relatedly, John Perry Barlow's "Declaration of the Independence of Cyberspace" adopts a similar, if more boldly stated, rhetoric:

We are creating a world that all may enter without privilege or prejudice accorded by race, economic power, military force, or station of birth. We are creating a world where anyone, anywhere may express his or her beliefs, no matter how singular, without fear of being coerced into silence or conformity.

(Barlow 1996)

In particular, and in a way that perhaps resonates with the dynamics presented in this chapter, he rails against the involvement of "Governments of the Industrial World", which he terms "weary giants of flesh and steel", telling them not "to invade our precincts".

In other words, ignoring the ways that "public policy and regulation have important direct and indirect implications for Internet access" (Bauer *et al.* 2002: 123), these writers saw the Internet as the perfect instantiation of distributed power—"decentralization, openness, possibility of expansion, no hierarchy, no centre, no conditions for authoritarian or monopoly control" (Sassen 1999: 54)—subscribing to what Saskia Sassen sees as the utopianism characteristic of the "first era of the Internet" (Sassen 1999: 50), or to the "utopian, communal, and libertarian undercurrents" that Manuel Castells identified in the first generation of Internet developers in America (Castells 1996: 357). It would be overstating the case to argue that the owners of the medium-sized ISPs whom I interviewed identified whole-heartedly with the ideology of the Netizen and Barlow's "Declaration of Independence". However, their comments definitely resonated with certain aspects of that ideology—in particular, disparaging talk of monopolistic practices; a sense that the government was interfering where it had no right to (deciding who could and could not get online, for instance); the suggestion intimated to me in an interview that business information submitted as part of the ISP license bureaucracy would be (illegally) passed on to Bezeq by the MoC; the allegation that Bezeq was (illegally) approaching customers who had asked for Internet connectivity to be provided at their home or office in order to offer them connectivity packages; and the more general charge that the field was being run undemocratically, all resonate with the kind of statements referred to above. At the risk of putting words in their mouths, we might say that the medium-sized ISP owners were asking themselves, as Robert McChesney was asking at about the same time, whether "the emerging communication technological revolution, particularly the Internet, [can] override the antidemocratic implications of the media marketplace and foster more democratic media and a more democratic political culture?" (McChesney 1996: 99).

So their technological capital was global, and they shared a global ideology of the Internet, but what, however, of the management styles adopted by the medium-sized ISPs? Can they shed light on the relative localism or globalism of their habitus? In order to gauge the extent to which other aspects of globalization had penetrated the way they run their businesses, I asked the ISP owners where they learnt how to manage; whether they read management journals or books, and if so which; and whether they implemented a specific kind of management philosophy in their companies. None of them had studied management formally, and nor did they read up on it. Not one of them ran their companies in line with a distinct management philosophy, rather making the decisions that seemed the right thing to do at the time. Indeed, in sharp distinction to the Israeli high-tech sector of which they form a part, they were quite detached from and unaware of global trends in management practices. For instance, the following is taken from an interview with the founder of a medium-sized ISP:

QUESTION: So where do you know about management from? Did you study it, read books about it, or from experience?

ANSWER: Only from experience and the fact that I worked with people better than me [. . .].

QUESTION: And do you follow developments in management in America, management trends in the United States?

ANSWER: No. I know, the truth is that I [. . .] I just do what I do.

This should be compared with how a former VP of NetVision talked about the management philosophies in that company, in particular, the belief in open-space offices:

QUESTION: You say that you had an American attitude about providing support.

ANSWER: Absolutely.

QUESTION: Were there other American aspects about how the company was managed?

ANSWER: Yes. The company was managed as an American firm in every way.

QUESTION: How did that manifest itself?

ANSWER: First of all the workers were completely involved in everything. It was the employees' company [. . .] and when someone had an idea or something they would knock on [the CEO's] door, it was open space. I sat in the open space, out of principle. I didn't want to move to a room; until my last year when they made me move into an office, I sat with everyone in the open space.

QUESTION: You say that you were always looking at what was happening in America.

ANSWER: All the time.

In other words, this large ISP was consciously applying management ideas, such as having an open-plan office, that had been imported from the US, in contrast to the medium-sized ISPs, which were managed on a much more ad hoc basis, and whose owners had minimal formal knowledge of management. It should be noted, of course, that these views were present from the outset, and were not a function of the firms' growth and success. I suggest that this lack of a global managerial outlook goes some way to explaining why the medium-sized ISPs failed to turn themselves into very large ones.

This view—that the owners of the medium-sized ISPs lacked the global orientation that could be found among the senior staff of the larger companies—is reinforced by their answers to questions about their Israeli identity in relation to their working in what is, in important ways, a global industry. This, too, reflects on the absence of what we might call a global habitus, defined above as:

> A cognitive and emotional disposition to move easily and smoothly from one national context to another, to quickly adapt and adopt different cultural outlooks, and to think of [oneself] as an agent operating in the world as a single unit.
>
> (Illouz and John: 2003)

For instance, when I asked an interviewee from one of the large ISPs whether he saw himself as a "world citizen", he replied:

> I feel at home in America. The place I lived in France [for three years] I feel very at home. I don't know what a world citizen is. *I feel versatile. Wherever they put me I'll live*, I won't have a problem.

Despite claiming not to know what a world citizen is, this interviewee shows that he surely is one.

Compare this to the medium-sized ISP owners, one of whom said he was no more a "world citizen" than his car mechanic (because they are both equally exposed to global culture), while another defended his Israeli identity in extremely strong terms:

QUESTION: Have you become less Israeli [through working in this global industry]?

ANSWER: No, no. [. . .]

QUESTION: There is an idea that people talk about today of world citizens. Are you one of them?

ANSWER: No.

In sum, the medium-sized ISP owners held large stocks of global technological knowledge that came to be devalued. As the field shifted, they lacked the global habitus that characterized those who succeeded in the field. Their approach to managing their firms, for instance, was entirely isolated from trends in global or American management, just as high-tech companies in Israel were assimilating American management practices as a matter of course (Frenkel 2005). This notion that the medium-sized ISP owners were locals in an increasingly global field was reinforced by their own descriptions of themselves as not being world citizens. On the contrary, they saw themselves as just belonging to the specific locality of Israel as much as, if not more than, their fellow citizens. As the field in which they operated became more global, their local orientation became inappropriate. In the following section I point to an additional way in which the field was becoming global—namely, via the entrance of global capital.

Zooming Out

So far, my focus has been at a very micro level, taking into account the individual biographies of the specific actors involved. This strategy is possible because the field itself is small, with relatively few people involved. However, as I hope it has become increasingly clear throughout, this analysis of the field of Internet provision has been conducted in the shadow of macro-level processes, in particular the globalization of Israeli society and the liberalization of the country's economy. Indeed, it is in this regard that the field under study has become increasingly global, thus gradually squeezing out the small and medium-sized firms.

Both of these processes—globalization and liberalization—are reflected in the ownership of the ISPs that appeared in Israel in the second half of the 1990s, and which basically put paid to the hopes of the medium-sized ISPs to make their businesses very successful. For instance, in 2007 Barak's[4] website described the company as follows:

> 013 Barak was established in 1997 by three of the world's leading telecommunications companies—Sprint, France Telecom and Deutsche Telecom—and two major Israeli companies—Clalcom and Matav. 013 Barak has grown rapidly and is now Israel's leading provider for international calls. In 2005, the company was acquired by IDB (81.5%) and Matav (18.5%).

And Internet Zahav[5] was described in an external site at the same period in the following way:

> INTERNET GOLD is a leading Internet service provider (ISP) in Israel in number of subscribers, based on recent surveys. Established in 1996, the Company is controlled by two of Israel's most reputable corporations, Eurocom Communications and Arison Investments.

Two aspects of these companies' ownerships are immediately clear: first, the involvement of foreign investment; and second, the involvement of the Israeli economic elite. Barak was founded by three foreign communications firms, in conjunction with two large Israeli companies. Clalcom is itself a subsidiary of IDB, whose CEO is Nochi Dankner, who for years has been one of the most influential figures in Israeli business. Eurocom Communications, which shares in the holdings of Internet Gold, was bought by the Elovitch brothers in 1985. Until that point, the company had manufactured and marketed telecommunications systems, though within a year, the new owners set up Eurocom Marketing, with the aim of importing telecommunications equipment to Israel, quickly becoming a major player in the retail communications market in Israel, exclusively representing firms such as Panasonic and Nokia in the Israeli market. The other corporation with a holding in Internet Gold is Arison Holdings, owned by Shari Arison, Israel's richest woman.

After a few years in the early to mid-1990s during which companies such as Actcom, Aquanet, Israsrv, and Shani could command a decent portion of the market share along with NetVision, then the dominant actor, the Internet provision industry started to attract the attention of some of the biggest players in the Israeli economy, not to mention concerns from overseas as well. Many of the holding companies and firms that began to take an interest in the ISP industry had been active in the Israeli economy for quite some time, such as the Dankner family.[6] What was new, however, was their ability to access the telecommunications industry following its liberalization. For Internet provision to become an attractive investment, the prices of overseas connectivity had to come down drastically, and Bezeq, which then still had a monopoly on telecommunications within Israel, had to begin operating more efficiently and with a stronger emphasis on customer support.

These two processes took place during the mid-1990s in a way that would seem to have been unconnected to party politics—that is, the MoC pressed ahead with an agenda of liberalization in quite a uniform way regardless of which party the minister belonged to. This suggests that, while the drive to liberalization has been associated with Israeli left-wing secular elites, who were also behind the Oslo agreements with the Palestinians (Levy 2007; Shafir and Peled 2002), it is actually an issue with broad support, at least vis-à-vis telecommunications.[7] Indeed, the perceived apolitical nature of telecommunications policies can also be seen in the appointments of Shlomo Waxe and Danny Rosenne as Directors-General of the Ministry of Communications, both of whom told me in an interview that they had been "professional"—as opposed to political—appointments.

As with Davis et al.'s contribution to this volume about the Brazilian Internet, I do not wish to present an economically reductionist account of the failure of the medium-sized ISPs and the success of the large ones, with their impressive financial backing. The ISPs in the field in the mid-1990s, before "big business" arrived on the scene, had a chance to entrench their positions, but, NetVision excluded, did not manage to do so. This is not for merely economic reasons, though they too are surely relevant. It is my contention that the men heading those companies lacked the necessary background that would enable them to accurately read the field and leverage their position as pioneers in the field into one of dominance. Lacking the social capital of, say, Uzia Galil or Abe Peled, they could not gain access to representatives of the field of power (in the form of the Ministry of Communications),[8] and were thus unable to influence the changing rules of the game, or at the very least, make the changes in the rules work to their advantage. They no doubt lacked the financial clout of the newer members of the field, but as their comments on management showed, they were ill equipped in other ways to make their companies very much larger.

Conclusion

In the above, I have described the forces that shaped the ISP field in Israel at the time of its consolidation. On the face of it, the story is one of big global businesses elbowing small local businesses out of the way. However, on closer inspection, or indeed when observed from a broader perspective, the story appears riddled with contingencies, from certain people being in the right place at the right time,[9] to the Internet arriving in Israel just as that country began to undertake a massive reformation of its political economy.[10]

This talks to a broader issue regarding the way we write the histories of the Internet. Davis et al. (this volume) use a different theoretical framing (social shaping of technology) from mine in their analysis of the Brazilian Internet, but a number of similarities in our modes of analysis and the stories we subsequently tell emerge. First, we do not take the arrival of the Internet to new countries for granted, thereby resisting a simple deterministic narrative. Moreover, and second, we recognize the place of struggles between different institutional bodies in shaping the Internet. However, the composition of the research population cannot be known in advance, and the tensions between the institutional actors can only be uncovered during the research process itself. Thus, for instance, questions of reaching geographically remote areas were not relevant in the Israeli case (Brazil is over 400 times larger than Israel), but issues to do with the spread of neoliberal economic ideology throughout the world during the 1980s and 1990s certainly were. As with the Brazilian case, in seeking to understand the development of the Israeli Internet, one must pay close attention to both the local and the global simultaneously. Adopting Mansell's (2012; this volume) notion of imaginaries, we might say that the range of possible imaginaries available to social actors (and, indeed, researchers) is a function of their social and cultural positioning.

While one may know ahead of time that the state, the university system, and some parts of the private sector are likely to be relevant to an historical analysis of the consolidation of the Internet in a given country, as just mentioned the precise actors involved only emerge through research. The key to the topography of the field as presented in this analysis lay with the medium-sized ISPs: while the small ISP owners accepted that they could not be serious players in the field, and while the large ISP owners were quite naturally pleased with their location in it, the medium-sized ISP owners expressed a strong sense of indignation at how the field had developed. Indignation is an emotion that arises when one reads reality through a certain moral lens.[11] The reality I described was one whereby technological capital was losing its ability to structure the field to the mid-sized ISP owners' advantage. With the globalization of the Israeli economy and the liberalization of the telecommunications regime, global financial capital was coming to play a much more dominant role. The actors with what I have called a "global habitus" were those in a position to take advantage of this state of affairs.

This is not to say that the medium-sized ISP owners were entirely local. As I noted above, I do not assert that this is a simple victory of the global over the local. Indeed, the ISP owners were tied into significant global processes. However, their affiliations with globalism—in terms of technology and a political ideology of the Internet—were of the "wrong" kind. They were being usurped in the field of Internet provision by actors who were enmeshed in global networks in an entirely different way. These were people with access to global capital and ties with multinational corporations. Their habitus was that of the Transnational Capitalist Class (Sklair 2000), and not that of the Netizen.

Epilogue

In the 21 years since the Internet was made accessible to all Israelis, it has been quite enthusiastically adopted. World Bank and OECD data show that 71 percent of the population uses the Internet (slightly less than Spain and Hungary; slightly more than Malaysia and Croatia), and that Israel ranks 33rd in the world for fixed broadband Internet connections, and 24th in the OECD (per 100 people; around the same proportion as in Singapore and Spain).[12]

The processes described above in the ISP industry have continued. Today, there are three main Internet service providers, all of whom were around in the second half of the 1990s, and all of whom have grown considerably since then. In particular, we note that all three companies offer international telephony as well as Internet access. In the case of Bezeq International, Internet provision was added to its initial mandate of offering competition in the field of international telephony; 012 Smile and 013 NetVision were both created in the mid-2000s following the merging of an international telephony company and an ISP, as the dynamic in the field was one of mergers and acquisitions (for a detailed analysis of concentration trends in the electronic media industries in Israel over the last 30 years, see Schejter and Yemini 2015).

Along with this process of concentration, the Israeli Internet service provision industry has become increasingly embedded in the global economy, and it is now led by businessmen with MBAs rather than engineers with M.Scs. Moti Elmaliach, CEO of Bezeq Benleumi, came to the company from Eurocom Digital Communications, the Israeli representative of Panasonic, and he holds an MBA; Haim Romano, CEO of Partner which owns 012 Smile, served previously as CEO of Israeli airline El Al, and attended the Advanced Management Program at Harvard Business School (Partner 2015); finally, Nir Sztern, CEO of Cellcom, owner of 013 NetVision, has a background in marketing in the telecoms sector and an MBA from the Israeli branch of Manchester University.

These figures, and their colleagues in senior management positions throughout the Internet industry in Israel, work for companies whose ownership structures tie them to international concerns, and whose qualifications are in management, not technology. They are able to move around between telecommunications companies, airlines, and the import industry because their skills are sector non-specific. There would appear to be no way back into the leadership of the ISP industry for the Netizen engineers of the 1990s.

Notes

1. As early as 1982, a UUCP (Unix-to-Unix Copy Protocol) link was made between the Hebrew University of Jerusalem's School of Computer Science and that of the University of Maryland. However, this connection does not really constitute a network—it was only available to people within the Hebrew University, and certainly there was no network of Israeli universities.
2. Without having conducted extensive comparative research, this would seem to apply to other countries too. To take a particularly notable example, Julian Assange, founder of WikiLeaks, was the founder of Australia's first ISP.
3. This interview was carried out in January 2004.
4. Barak later merged with NetVision, and the company is now 013 NetVision.
5. Internet Zahav is now 012 Smile.
6. On the place of large holding companies in the Israeli political economy, see Maman 2000; for descriptions of the part of the Dankners and other families in the Israeli political economy, see Nitzan and Bichler 2002.
7. More recently, the mobile telecommunication market was comprehensively reformed by former Likud parliamentarian, Moshe Kahlon, when serving as Minister of Communications.
8. Abe Peled, the CEO of the ISP, Elronet, helped the MoC to write the licenses issued to ISPs.
9. Such as Ruth Alon returning to Israel from Silicon Valley so that her children could attend high school in Israel.
10. I am referring here to the Economic Stabilization Plan of 1985.
11. This is what Peter Lyman is referring to when he states that moral indignation is created by "[d]etaching the self-righteousness of anger from the self and re-attaching it to a political ideology" (Lyman 2004: 137).
12. The World Bank (2014). When interpreting these data one must remember that Israel has two large and relatively poor populations who are less likely to be online (albeit for quite different reasons): Palestinian citizens of Israel, and ultra-Orthodox Jews. The Broadband Commission of the International Telecommunication Union and UNESCO ranks Israel 30th in the world for fixed broadband subscriptions (Broadband Commission 2014).

References

Barlow, J. P. (1996) "A Declaration of the Independence of Cyberspace", 8 February, *Electronic Frontier Foundation*, available at: www.eff.org/cyberspace-independence (accessed 28 March 2015).

Bauer, J. M., Berne, M., and Maitland, C. F. (2002) "Internet Access in the European Union and in the United States", *Telematics and Informatics,* 19(2): 117–137.

Bourdieu, P., and Wacquant, L. J. D. (1992) *An Invitation to Reflexive Sociology*, Chicago: University of Chicago Press.

Broadband Commission (2014) "The State of Broadband 2014: Broadband for All, a report by the Broadband Commission", *United Nations Educational, Scientific and Cultural Organization*, available at: www.broadband commission.org/documents/reports/bb-annualreport2014.pdf (accessed 28 March 2015).

Brown, I., Collins, T., Malika, B., Morrison, D., Muganda, N., and Speight, H. (2007) "Global Diffusion of the Internet XI: Internet Diffusion and its Determinants in South Africa: The First Decade of Democracy (1994–2004) and Beyond", *Communications of the Association for Information Systems*, 19(1): 9.

Castells, M. (1996) *The Rise of the Network Society*, Malden, MA: Blackwell Publishers.

Ein-Dor, P., Goodman, S., and Wolcott, P. (1999) *The Global Diffusion of the Internet Project: The State of Israel*, The Global Diffusion of the Internet Project.

Fontana, A., and Frey, J. H. (1994) "The Interview: From Structured Questions to Negotiated Text", in N. K. Denzin and Y. S. Lincoln (eds), *Handbook of Qualitative Research*, Thousand Oaks, CA: Sage Publications, pp. 645–672.

Foster, W., Goodman, S., Osiakwan, E., and Bernstein, A. (2004) "Global Diffusion of the Internet IV: The Internet in Ghana", *Communications of the Association for Information Systems*, 13: 1–46, available at: http://cais.aisnet.org/articles/13-38/default.asp?View=pdf&x=76&y=11

Frenkel, M. (2005) "The Politics of Translation: How State Level Political Relations Affect the Cross-National Travel of Ideas", *Organization*, 12(2): 275–301.

Gabizon, Y. (1994) "Elron—Green Light for the Information Superhighway", *Ha'aretz*, 8 June, p. C6.

Hannerz, U. (1990) "Cosmopolitans and Locals in World Culture", *Theory, Culture & Society*, 7(2–3): 237–251.

Hauben, M. (1996a) "What Is a Netizen?", in *Netizens: On the History and Impact of Usenet and the Internet* (draft), available at: www.columbia.edu/~rh120/ch106.txt (accessed 28 March 2015).

Hauben, M. (1996b) "Proposed Declaration of the Rights of Netizens", in *Netizens: On the History and Impact of Usenet and the Internet* (draft), available at: www.columbia.edu/~rh120/netizen-rights.txt (accessed 28 March 2015).

Hauben, M., and Hauben, R. (1997) *Netizens: On the History and Impact of Usenet and the Internet*, Los Alamitos: IEEE Computer Society Press.

Illouz, E., and John, N. (2003) "Global Habitus, Local Stratification and Symbolic Struggles over Identity: The Case of McDonald's Israel", *American Behavioral Scientist*, 47(2): 201–229.

John, N. A. (2011a) "The Diffusion of the Internet to Israel: The First Ten Years", *Israel Affairs*, 17(3): 327–340.

John, N. A. (2011b) "Representing the Israeli Internet: The Press, the Pioneers and the Practitioners", *International Journal of Communication*, 5: 1545–1566.

Kim, B-K. (2005) *Internationalizing the Internet: The Co-evolution of Influence and Technology*, Cheltenham: Edward Elgar Publishing.

Levi-Faur, D. (1999a) "The Dynamics of Liberalisation of Israeli Telecommunications", in E. A. Kjell and S. Marit (eds), *European Telecommunications Liberalisation*, London: Routledge, pp. 173–190.

Levi-Faur, D. (1999b) "More Competition, More Regulation: The Israeli Communications Revolution and the Role of the State", *Politika*, 4: 27–44.

Levy, Y. (2007) *Israel's Materialist Militarism*, Lanham, MD: Lexington Books.

Lyman, P. (2004) "The Domestication of Anger: The Use and Abuse of Anger in Politics", *European Journal of Social Theory*, 7(2): 133–147.

McChesney, R. W. (1996) "The Internet and US Communication Policy-Making in Historical and Critical Perspective", *Journal of Communication*, 46(1): 98–124.

Maman, D. (2000) "Who Accumulates Directorships of Big Business Firms in Israel? Organizational Structure, Social Capital and Human Capital", *Human Relations*, 53(5): 603–630.

Mansell, R. (2012) *Imagining the Internet: Communication, Innovation, and Governance*, Oxford: Oxford University Press.

Nitzan, J., and Bichler, S. (2002) *The Global Political Economy of Israel*, London: Pluto Press.

Partner (2015) "Management Team", *Partner*, available at: www.orange.co.il/en/Investors-Relations/lobby/company-information/Management-Team# (accessed 29 March 2015).

Press, L. (1994) "Commercialization of the Internet", *Communications of the ACM*, 37(11): 17–21.

Ram, U. (2007) *The Globalization of Israel: McWorld in Tel Aviv, Jihad in Jerusalem*, New York: Routledge.

Sassen, S. (1999) "Digital Networks and Power", in M. Featherstone and S. Lash (eds), *Spaces of Culture: City, Nation, World*, London and Thousand Oaks, CA: Sage, pp. 49–63.

Schejter, A. M., and Yemini, M. (2015) "'A Time to Scatter Stones and a Time to Gather Them': Electronic Media Industries Concentration Trends in Israel 1984–2013", *Telecommunications Policy*, 39(2): 112–126.

Shafir, G., and Peled, Y. (2002) *Being Israeli: The Dynamics of Multiple Citizenship*, New York: Cambridge University Press.

Sklair, L. (2000) *The Transnational Capitalist Class*, Malden, MA: Blackwell.

Webb, J., Schirato, T., and Danaher, G. (2002) *Understanding Bourdieu*, London: SAGE Publications.

Wolcott, P., and Goodman, S. E. (2003) "Global Diffusion of the Internet-I: India: Is the Elephant Learning to Dance?", *Communications of the Association for Information Systems*, 11(1): 32.

The World Bank (2014) "World Development Indicators: The Information Society", *The World Bank*, available at: http://wdi.worldbank.org/table/5.12#; www.oecd.org/sti/broadband/1.2-OECD-WiredWirelessBB-2014-06.xls (accessed 28 March 2015).

7

THE EVOLUTION OF THE INTERNET IN MEXICO (1986–2016)

Fernando Gutiérrez

A Brief History of the Internet in Mexico

Mexico's largest private university, Monterrey Institute of Technology and Higher Education, generated its first shared connection to the telecommunications network called BITNET in 1986, followed a year later by the National Autonomous University of Mexico (UNAM).

In June 1986, Monterrey Institute of Technology and Higher Education joined the BITNET network (EDUCOM) through a line connecting at 2,400 bps to the University of Texas in San Antonio. In 1987, the National Autonomous University of Mexico (UNAM) set up a connection with BITNET. The main universities were the first institutions to establish Internet connections in Mexico, just as in the United States. This event would mark the history of the Internet in Mexico, which properly began in 1989 when Monterrey Institute of Technology and Higher Education set up the first connection for the network of the National Science Foundation (NSF) through the School of Medicine of the University of Texas in San Antonio (UTSA) using Internet connection protocols. Thus, the first equipment was connected to the Internet via the domain.mx: dns.mty.itesm.mx with the address 131.178.1.1. On 28 February 1989, NSFnet officially recognised the connection with Mexico (Islas and Gutiérrez 2000). Soon after, a second node was established at UNAM's Astronomy Institute, connecting to the National Centre for Atmospheric Research (NCAR) in Boulder, Colorado, USA. Later, Monterrey Institute of Technology and Higher Education at the Mexico State Campus connected to the NSF network through NCAR, using a digital link via satellite.

According to the Network Information Center (NIC) Mexico, other educational institutions were connected to the NSF network, including Las Americas University (UDLAP), a private university located in the city of Puebla; the Instituto Tecnológico y de Estudios Superiores de Occidente (ITESO) (Western Technological and Higher Studies Institute), a Jesuit university in Guadalajara; Guadalajara University (UAG); the National Science & Technology Council (CONACYT, the body responsible for drawing up science and technology policies in Mexico); and the Department of Education itself (Network Information Center 2011). As in the United States, in Mexico the major universities were the first institutions to decide to set up their own Internet connections.

According to a study conducted by NIC Mexico, in 1991 the services most used by academics and researchers at that time were remote access (Telnet), file transfer (FTP), email,

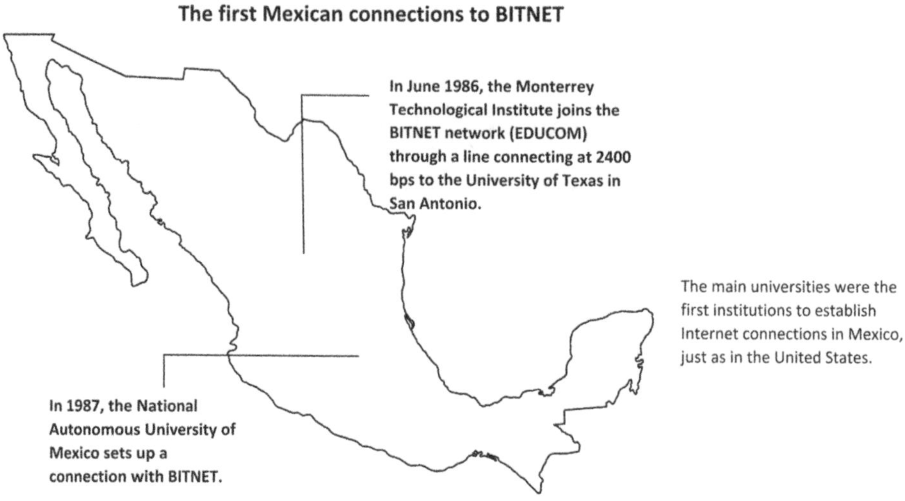

The first Mexican connections to BITNET

In June 1986, the Monterrey Technological Institute joins the BITNET network (EDUCOM) through a line connecting at 2400 bps to the University of Texas in San Antonio.

The main universities were the first institutions to establish Internet connections in Mexico, just as in the United States.

In 1987, the National Autonomous University of Mexico sets up a connection with BITNET.

Figure 7.1 The first Mexican connections to BITNET (prepared by the author with information from Network Information Center Mexico: www.nic.mx/es/NicMx.Historia)

and Gopher (in 1992). As the World Wide Web (WWW) did not exist for the public at that time, the demand for connections to the network was not large, nor was it seen as attractive.

MexNET, a civil association promoting discussion on policies, statutes, and procedures to govern and guide the development of the communications network in Mexico, was established in 1992. The following institutions formed part of that association: Monterrey Institute of Technology and Higher Education, Guadalajara University, Las Americas University, ITESO, the Postgraduate College, the National Lab for Advanced Computer Studies, the Applied Chemistry Research Institute, Guanajuato University, Veracruzana University, the Ecology Institute, the Ibero-American University and the Technological Institute of Mexicali. Through this network one could access the Internet for free via broadband at 56 kilobytes per second. MexNET, however, turned out to be just an ambitious short-term project of good intentions that never could consolidate, and after a time it became part of the National Technological Network (RTN).

The National Polytechnic Institute (IPN) and the Department of Education formed an association known as the Network of Technical Universities and Centers, and a year later, in 1993, Las Americas University began to experiment in the environment called the Web. It developed Mexico's first electronic page of information available for the Internet's international community. From then on, news about the Internet began to circulate more intensely in specialized Mexican newspapers and magazines.

RedUNAM was created in 1994, in an effort by Mexico's oldest university to commercialize the connection service. RedUNAM was the first Internet service provider. Later, CONACYT and MexNET established the National Technological Network (RTN), with an E1 connection (two megabytes a second). Infotec was in charge of administering the RTN in Mexico, and at that time it began to offer lines and rent the service to individuals. PixelNET became the first commercial enterprise in Mexico to have a server connected to the Internet. The year 1994 saw the end of the Internet as a technological tool exclusive to academic institutions. The commercial age of the Internet in Mexico had begun.

The first organizations to take advantage of the Internet were not government bodies. The Zapatista National Liberation Army (EZLN) established a solid Internet presence from early 1994, and thus created serious political problems for the government of President Ernesto Zedillo. Many sectors in international public opinion circles considered the EZLN website a primary source of information about Mexico. As a result, uncertainty about the national situation spread rapidly around the world. This situation arose because of the absence of a governmental Internet information strategy, at a time when millions of people across the globe were already using the Internet.

The EZLN website, created in 1994 by Justin Paulson, a teacher at the University of California in Santa Cruz, sought to provide information about the uprising in Chiapas. The site was set up for people living outside Mexico who wanted reliable information about the conflict, and thus, at the beginning, almost all the information was published in English, but more and more Mexicans began to use the site as a primary source of information. The EZLN website gained popularity because it offered the widest range of news items, media releases, and articles about the conflict in Chiapas that could be found on the Internet (or in other media). At the time, newspapers like *La Jornada* and *Reforma* published articles about the website that lent it a certain notoriety. The visibility of the page in Mexico was so great that Jose Angel Gurría (then Foreign Affairs Minister) declared that the war in Chiapas was nothing more than "a war of ink and Internet" (De la Guardia 1999). The main governmental institutions took almost a year to realize the importance of the Internet and to start to develop their respective strategies to learn about the new media and publish their own pages. By 1995, UNAM had two ways of connecting to the Internet, one towards Houston and the other through the Rice University in Texas. The Mexican newspaper *La Jornada* appeared on the Web for the first time on 6 February 1995, thus demonstrating the new possibilities of the Internet to transform conventional communications media. This kind of occurrence helped promote a real increase in national connections to the Internet.

Monterrey Institute of Technology and Higher Education was officially named the Mexican Information Networks Center (NIC-Mexico) in December 1995. The Center was set up to assign IP addresses and domains located under ".mx". In early 1995, educational institutions outnumbered commercial entities connected to the Internet, but by the end of this same year the number of commercial companies greatly outnumbered the educational institutions. The registration of commercial domains (com.mx) grew 1,000 percent in just nine months.

The year 1995 was considered "the year of the Internet in Mexico". This tag originated because of the intense activity observed in the sector during those 12 months. From then on, the Internet spread to the masses. Commercial companies developed Internet strategies similar to those of academic, governmental, and non-governmental institutions (Islas and Gutiérrez 1996).

According to NIC Mexico, in 1996 cities such as Monterrey registered nearly 17 connections of the "E1" type (two mbps) for private use, through the recently privatized phone company Teléfonos de México. This company, once owned by the state, was sold in 1990 by the national government to a consortium headed by the Mexican businessman Carlos Slim (Cortés 2010). The opening up of the telecommunications industry, set in place by the government of Carlos Salinas de Gortari, led to a boom in infrastructure for Internet connections during the government of President Ernesto Zedillo (1994–2000).

The main national providers of Internet services in the country were firmly established by 1996. Around this time, the Mexico chapter of the Internet Society was formed, part of the international non-government organization working on global Internet coordination and cooperation. Between October 1995 and January 1996, an average of 30 domains were added

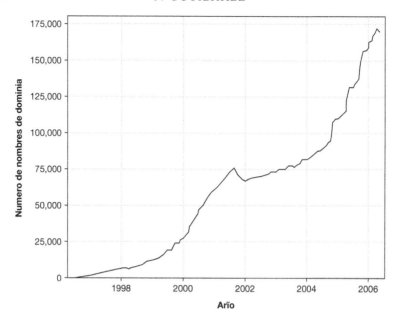

Figure 7.2 Growth of domains .mx (Network Information Center Mexico)

each month. By 1997, there were more than 150 Internet service providers offering services throughout Mexico, located in the main urban centers like Mexico City, Guadalajara, Monterrey, Chihuahua, Tijuana, Puebla, Merida, Nuevo Laredo, Saltillo, Oaxaca, etc.

The official site of the presidency of the Republic was launched on 1 September 1996, in the framework of President Ernesto Zedillo's Second State of the Nation Report (Islas and Gutiérrez 2003a). This constituted a major reference point for other governmental institutions, which saw themselves obliged to develop their own Internet-based information strategies. The Chamber of Deputies, the Senate, and the Federal Judicial Council were among others to publish their first pages on the Internet from 1996 onwards. At the same time, academic and journalistic bodies and social groups were also setting up their own information servers. This was a positive development, as it gave rise to the creation of the first online information service centers for the general population. Since then, the Internet has become a key element in the new national environment.

The Effects of the Ink and Internet Wars

In January 1997, while the database "WHOIS" for the domain ".mx" was beginning to operate, the three main candidates for election to the government of Mexico City, Alfredo del Mazo (Institutional Revolutionary Party), Carlos Castillo Peraza (National Action Party), and Cuauhtémoc Cárdenas (Party of the Democratic Revolution) all used the Internet as a propaganda tool in their campaigns. Without a doubt, this helped confirm the Internet's worldwide importance in the development of political campaigns by candidates in election contests. From 1998, the websites of several government institutions were targeted by organized groups of hackers. On 4 February 1998, X Ploit Team, a group of "proudly Mexican" hackers, replaced the Treasury's official logo with an image of the charismatic revolutionary leader Emiliano Zapata. The image was accompanied by the following text: "We do not belong to any group, we do not belong to the EZLN, we exercise our right of free expression as Mexicans" (Avilés 1998). This was the welcome received by José Angel Gurría, who had just been named Treasurer. Years before, when he was Foreign Affairs Minister, Gurría had declared that the armed uprising in Chiapas was just "a war of ink and Internet". Hacker attacks also occurred on the websites of the National Statistics Institute, the National Water Commission, the Senate of the Republic, and the Health Ministry, all these public institutions of the federal Mexican government. However, in statements made to the Mexican weekly *Proceso*, the well-known expert Miguel de Icaza made light of these hacker attacks. He declared that it was not a matter of any organized cyber war, but only "children playing *techno-pirates*", whose main purpose was that of "gaining notoriety in public opinion" (De la Vega 1998). Intense activity by hackers was not in any way limited to the public sector. It extended to the websites of companies and education institutes such as Bancomer, IPN, and various campuses of Monterrey Institute of Technology and Higher Education. Hackers in Mexico also attacked a wide group of non-government organizations.

The Internet and Elections of Change in Mexico

The pivotal importance of the 2 July elections in 2000 favored the intense use of the Internet as a propaganda tool. Thousands of supporters of the candidates Cuauhtémoc Cárdenas, Francisco Labastida, and Vicente Fox carried out ingenious and remarkable campaigns on the Internet with a great deal of autonomy from the online information systems provided by the candidates themselves. These supporters became effective independent transmitters who took the electoral battle to cyberspace. By 31 January 2000, the last year of President Ernesto Zedillo's government, the number of ".mx" domains had reached 30,748, while estimates of the number of Internet users fluctuated between two and three million (Network Information Center Mexico 2011).

The electoral campaigns of the National Action Party, and its candidate Vicente Fox, in 2000 were noteworthy for their intensive use of Internet technologies. In fact, Fox declared that the historic change of power of 2 July was possible because he and his team had managed to connect with citizens all over the country. And during his first year of government, he also announced that the country would enjoy a great upturn with the e-Mexico program, as it would move Mexico from 70th or 80th in development terms to 10th or 12th place (Fox 2001).

As Carmen Gómez Mont suggests, 2000 was also a year of great changes in the telecommunications sector, marked by the end of the great communications monopolies in Mexico, Televisa and Telmex (Gómez Mont 2000). The monopoly held by these two companies in the radio broadcasting and telecommunications sector resulted in a policy of limited development for the nation. But once these two areas were opened to competition, benefits were won for the service user in terms of both cost and quality. New actors appeared in the market, such as Iusacell (owned by the Salinas Group, owner of Mexico's second largest commercial television chain), Nextel, and Telefónica Española in the mobile phone segment, along with other companies in landline phone services that entered the market later. The ground was also prepared for the provision of various levels of multi-services, such as "triple play" and "quadruple play" (video, voice, data, mobile).

The e-Mexico Project at the Beginning of the 21st Century

The Mexican government presented its National e-Mexico System to the public early in 2001. According to its coordinator Julio César Margáin (2001), this comprehensive project would join together the interests of various levels of government from different states and public offices, of telecommunications operators, and of many other public and private institutions, with the aim of extending the provision of services in health, education, commerce, government, and any other area of interest for the community.

The e-Mexico project consisted of four subsystems: technologies and interconnection; contents and programs; legal and price frameworks; and administration and management. The program aimed to reduce Mexico's digital divide; increase the provision and coverage of telephone, Internet, and similar services; eliminate obstacles to accessing information, knowledge, and markets; facilitate access to various services such as health, education, commerce, and government procedures; incorporate small and medium-sized companies, as well as micro-producers of arts and crafts, and of various other regional activities into the so-called digital economy; eliminate chains of intermediaries who did not add value to companies' productive and commercial activities; and, finally, give publicity to Mexico's multicultural wealth and its natural and tourist attractions (Margáin 2001).

As it happened, on 1 August 2001, F. Bartolomé, in his column "Templo Mayor" in the newspaper *Reforma*, raised critical questions about the development of the National e-Mexico System:

> It's nearly five months since the consultation forums on the e-Mexico program were held, and now no one can remember anything about what was supposed to be a grand network to conduct transactions with the new government. The speeches are there, on the Internet as they should be, but the Communications & Transport Department headed by Pedro Cerisola has not said a word on the subject. The serious problem here is that, even when e-Mexico was supposed to be something like the doorway to modernity in government, in reality, the Foxists have not found the locksmith to open the door. Because it is one thing to offer access to government procedures and applications, to information, education and even health services on the Internet, and it's something very different that the network of networks only serves as another way of publicizing government actions, as it does currently *ad nauseam* . . .
>
> (Bartolomé 2001)

On 17 April 2002, the government of Mexico signed a collaboration agreement with Microsoft in Seattle, Washington, to install 2,473 digital community centers which formed part of the National e-Mexico System. Pedro Cerisola y Weber, Head of the Communications & Transport Department, and Rick Belluzzo, then-President of Microsoft, signed the agreement in the framework of the Fifth Government Leaders Conference, an event organized by Microsoft. President Vicente Fox himself could not attend the conference, as the Senate of the Republic did not grant him permission to travel to the US (Notimex 2002). This agreement was widely criticized, especially by people who promoted and defended the use of free software, and who considered it a mistake to create any kind of technological dependence of the National System on Microsoft.

Miguel de Icaza had this to say:

> If e-Mexico is not forged with free software, then the said national plan risks becoming a technological hostage of the great transnationals, as it would create full dependence in matters like computing security and technological improvements, while some are even daring to make references to our national sovereignty.
>
> (Islas and Gutiérrez 2003b)

In Mexico, the matter of regulations concerning the state's software unfortunately represented yet another of the subjects on the "to-do" list for the so-called "government of change".

Miguel de Icaza, who promoted the use of free software in the country, reckoned that the Mexican government would have to pay $3.5 billion to Microsoft for licenses and the renewal of computers that would be installed in 1,200 public libraries across the country as part of the initiative "towards a nation of readers", which formed part of the National e-Mexico System. He also declared that the millions of dollars paid for licenses to use Microsoft software could well have been saved, and used to train and employ an entire generation of programmers, which would have meant the creation of a Mexican software industry (De Icaza, quoted in Islas and Gutiérrez 2004).

The National e-Mexico System was without a doubt a very interesting and ambitious project of the Fox administration, but it could not be executed during his six years of government as planned, and thus its stipulated goals were not met. The effects of this can be seen in various studies on information and communication technologies carried out by the United Nations, where Mexico appeared after 30 other nations (United Nations Public Administration Country Studies 2005).

Panorama of the Internet in Mexico

During the six-year term of President Felipe Calderón, the telecommunications sector did not register any considerable growth. In fact, the country regressed 25 places in the e-government development index, reaching position number 55. Although market inertia surpassed the levels expected by the Mexican government, the telecommunications sector was left behind when compared with other regional economies. Due to the absence of public policy in this area, and a total lack of definition in the field of telecommunications, the development the Internet could have had in Mexico compared poorly with that of other nations.

That said, the development of the Internet in Mexico up to the present time has been noteworthy. Currently, the number of Internet users in the country is estimated at nearly 60 million, which means the Internet is reaching just over half the population. Details by region can be seen in Figure 7.3 showing projections from the World Internet Project in Mexico.

Given the grave economic constraints faced by a majority of the population, we could suppose that the main reason given by those who do not use the Internet would be financial. However, in spite of the high costs presumably involved in having access to the Internet in Mexico, the main reason is not economic, but one of lack of interest and of knowledge. Non-users of the Internet simply do not see significant advantages to make them become users. This statement can be studied in detail in Figure 7.4.

The distribution of Internet users by age is interesting. Most users are people younger than 26 (42 percent, equal to 33.8 million people). In contrast, the number and percentage of older adults using the Internet is still very low (2,400,000 in the age range from 54 to 70, and 400,000 users older than 70). Figure 7.5 shows the general distribution of Internet users by age.

Social groups with more purchasing power (levels A, B, and C+) register the highest percentage of Internet users in Mexico, confirming the great digital divide defined by socio-economic factors. Social classes with greater purchasing power have more information available to them about the advantages that Internet access might give them—for example, online banking and shopping, and electronic operations with the government. In 98 percent of Mexican homes of higher socio-economic levels, there is at least one Internet user.

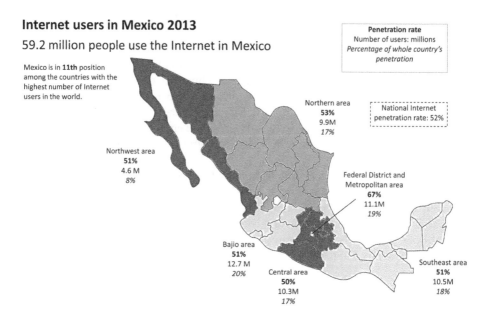

Internet users in Mexico 2013

59.2 million people use the Internet in Mexico

Penetration rate
Number of users: millions
Percentage of whole country's penetration

Mexico is in **11th** position among the countries with the highest number of Internet users in the world.

Northern area
53%
9.9M
17%

National Internet penetration rate: 52%

Northwest area
51%
4.6 M
8%

Federal District and Metropolitan area
67%
11.1M
19%

Bajio area
51%
12.7 M
20%

Central area
50%
10.3M
17%

Southeast area
51%
10.5M
18%

Figure 7.3 Internet users in Mexico (World Internet Project, Mexico, 2013)

Reasons limiting Internet use in Mexico

Ignorance and lack of interest are the main reasons why Mexicans don't use the Internet

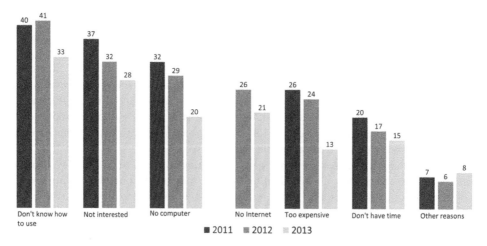

Figure 7.4 Reasons limiting Internet use in Mexico (World Internet Project, Mexico, 2013)

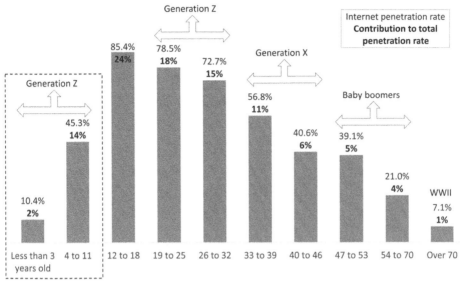

More than nine million users are younger than 12

Figure 7.5 General distribution of Internet users by age: more than nine million users are younger than 12 (World Internet Project, Mexico, 2013)

Levels	2009	2010	2011	2012	2013
A,B, C+	53	59	67	73	73
C	35	40	51	65	60
D+	21	23	31	40	47
D	20	21	24	37	39

Figure 7.6 Internet penetration by socio-economic level, 2009–2013 (World Internet Project, Mexico, 2013)

Mexican Internet users possess a wide range of devices. However, not all of these are used to connect to the Internet, as can be seen in Figure 7.7.

In any case, it can be observed that consumers are increasingly using smartphones, tablets and smart TVs to access the Internet. And these devices will probably continue to make up an important part of the growth in Internet users in Mexico in the next few years. These devices are ideal for the most common online activities, which are: accessing social networks (88 percent); sending emails (80 percent); conducting research using search engines

Laptop	Smartphone	Desktop	Mobile	Tablet	Video game console	Smart TV	Portables (wearables)	Portable video game console
76	68	53	50	42	38	38	27	18
70*	62*			35*	18*	22*		

* Percentage of users who use the device to access the Internet

Figure 7.7 Devices of Internet users in Mexico in percent (Interactive Advertising Bureau Mexico 2015)

(73 percent); listening to music (56 percent); reading news items (46 percent); and watching videos (44 percent) (Interactive Advertising Bureau Mexico 2015).

With the arrival of the concept of Web 2.0, a second generation of Internet services appeared in Mexico, and this led to a range of communities of active participants who not only consume information but also produce it. First, there was a boom in blogging, which broke the passivity of the simple web page and enabled the common user to post content within a given community. Users did not have to possess great technical skills to create a blog. The systems were so designed that anybody could set up a blog in a matter of minutes and at no cost. Today, blogs constitute a very important source of information on the Internet. Companies use them for testing their products, to conduct surveys to see how a brand is perceived, for post-sales services, and in general for direct and constant contact with their clients. Some people use them as an alternative source of information to conventional news sources. Blogs were first seen as structured Internet systems that allowed anybody to publish personal information in a way similar to a diary or logbook, with the additional capacity to register email addresses, add images, and for asynchronous interaction. Now they also function as important digital newspapers, offering different viewpoints on particular events, and they compete strongly with the established conventional media: press, radio, and television. Information production on these digital platforms is now firmly in the hands of the users, as can be seen in Figure 7.8.

These diverse digital platforms (instant messaging, forums, blogs, and social networks) have proven to be a good tool for consolidating large volumes of all kinds of (structured and non-structured) information produced by users. Figure 7.8 also shows a decrease in the time spent on the first instant messaging apps (ICQ, Messenger). However, this can be explained by the fact that these applications lost their share of the market with the arrival of new applications like Whatsapp. In general, all these tools show clear growth trends in their use. Platforms such as Facebook, Twitter, YouTube, and LinkedIn, among others, have contributed to a new revolution on the Internet, giving creativity and decision-making powers to the service users. Figure 7.8 shows sustained growth of these platforms over time.

The effects of Internet-related digital technologies within cultural contexts have also been important. Mexicans are now exposed to different cultural expressions that combine with local ones, and this phenomenon gives rise to new hybrid forms of expression that are empowered thanks to digital technologies. For example, users today access all kinds of music

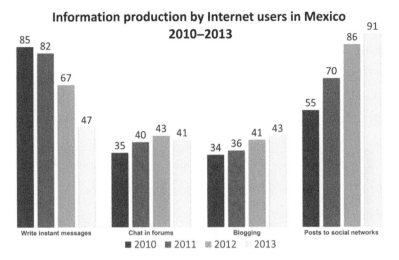

Figure 7.8 Information production by Internet users in Mexico, 2010–2013 (World Internet Project, Mexico, 2013)

through platforms such as iTunes or Spotify, and gradually abandon the ways they used to listen to music (on the radio or with compact discs). According to results obtained by the World Internet Project, Mexico (2013), 80 percent of Internet users in Mexico listened to music online through digital platforms. This figure increased gradually from 2011 (77 percent in 2011, 79 percent in 2012 and 80 percent in 2013). This not only shows a change in terms of cultural habits, but also in ways of doing business. Internet users now spend less and less on CDs because they prefer to access large musical catalogues from their various devices, rather than buy a CD for an amount similar to what a year's subscription to a digital platform might cost. Given such low demand for their traditional products (CDs), recording and production companies are exploring new avenues to find new concepts to generate income and keep their businesses going. Something similar is happening with conventional television.

People with access to the Internet prefer to consume content from various regions around the world through new digital platforms like Netflix, because the catalogue is very large and there is greater independence in choosing times and types of content consumption compared with traditional television. These new technologies are changing customs and traditions that were well established in cultural practice, as Neil Postman (1998) indicates.

Figure 7.9 shows how the Internet has helped reconfigure certain cultural practices in the country. As can be seen in Figure 7.9, Internet users' free time is spent on cyberspace activities that are slowly forming new cultural habits. Most users spend most of their time listening to music online, a large percentage surfs the Web with no apparent purpose, others look for jokes and cartoons, while others divide their time between online games (52 percent), reading blogs (49 percent), studying online courses (34 percent), and visiting sites of explicit sexual content. Some of these new cultural practices are mixed with traditional ones (such as listening to music) and are only modified, while others (surfing the Internet with no apparent purpose) are simply gradually displacing conventional practices.

Conaculta (the National Council for Culture & Arts) published the results in 2010 of a National Survey of Cultural Habits, Practices and Consumption in each state of the federation.

Cultural practices of Internet users in Mexico 2011–2013

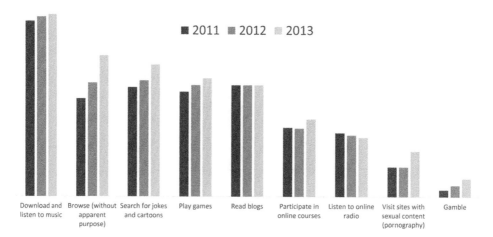

Figure 7.9 Cultural practices of Internet users in Mexico, 2011–2013 (World Internet Project, Mexico, 2013)

The results of the survey in the Federal District (DF) show that some cultural consumer activities, such as going to the movies, are in decline. For example, 43 percent of people in the DF said that they can spend three months without going to see a movie (Conaculta 2010). The survey also shows that the Internet has greatly contributed to the reshaping of cultural practices among the population throughout the country (Conaculta, 2010).

The Internet and the 2012 Federal Elections

During 2012, it was possible to assess the impact of the Internet on the presidential elections, where social networks played an interesting role. Figure 7.10 shows how the presidential campaigns were followed on the Internet, and Figure 7.11 shows the influence this media had on the vote, according to the World Internet Project, Mexico (2013).

As can be seen in Figure 7.10, nearly six of every ten users followed the presidential campaigns on the Internet. However, in Figure 7.11, one sees that only 43 percent of these admitted any considerable influence of the Internet on their voting intentions.

According to the Mexican users, the most commonly used platforms for following the 2012 election campaigns were Facebook, YouTube, email, Twitter, blogs, websites, and instant messaging. And users were using the same platforms to follow the social phenomenon known as #YoSoy132 (I'm (number) 132), which was reviewed and analyzed in numerous journalistic articles, in Mexico as well as in various other countries (Galindo and González-Acosta 2013). The movement #YoSoy132 began one Friday, 11 May 2012 in the Ibero-American University, when a group of 100 people gathered in the auditorium for the visit of then-candidate Enrique Peña Nieto, and challenged him with negative messages. Galindo and González-Acosta (2013) state that during the candidate's intervention in this event, which lasted about an hour, some students questioned him on topics like the violation of human rights in the Atenco case, his relationship with the former governor of Coahuila state,

Have you followed the development of the (2012) presidential elections online?

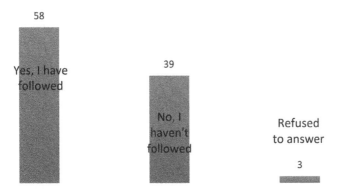

Figure 7.10 Following the presidential campaigns on the Internet, 2012 (World Internet Project, Mexico, 2013)

Influence of the Internet on voting intentions in the 2012 presidential elections

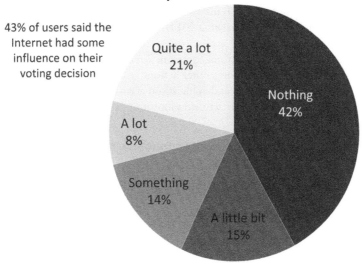

Figure 7.11 Influence of the Internet on voting intentions in the 2012 presidential elections (World Internet Project, Mexico, 2013)

Humberto Moreira, then undergoing a public inquiry, and his closeness to the ex-president Carlos Salinas de Gortari, among others. The unpleasant climate faced by the candidate led him to cancel his participation in a radio interview on the university's Radio Ibero 90.9, and this was rapidly made known on the social networks, especially on Twitter, where the hashtag #EPNlaIBEROnoTEquiere (EPN—the Ibero doesn't love you) became a trending topic worldwide within a few minutes. Later, the candidate Peña Nieto's campaign team condemned the event, saying that those who began the protest actions that day had been paid thugs, supporters, and operators of the left-wing candidate Andrés Manual López Obrador. In response to these accusations, a group of 131 students from the Ibero-American University posted a video on YouTube on 14 May 2012, where they stated that they were students of the university, they had not been taken there, they were not thugs, and they had received no training for the event. This video was also then condemned by the candidate's campaign team and certain communications media, which said that it was just a matter of 131 opinions of students at one university. This gave rise to various demonstrations of support from different student communities around the country that joined the campaign of the Ibero-American University students, standing up as student #132. And so the movement #YoSoy132 (#I am 132) was born.

Galindo and González-Acosta (2013) say that the video posted on YouTube by the students shook up the electoral atmosphere more than anything else had done up to that point in time. The social media and the very ecology of the Internet enabled the students to spread their messages and unite across the country to stand against those opposing their ideas.

Figure 7.12 shows the platforms most used to follow the campaigns, as well as the level of presence of each of these during the official campaign period of 2012.

The most commonly used platforms were Facebook, YouTube, and email. Twitter, the micro-blogging platform (140 characters maximum) hardly had any presence during the development of the campaigns, at just 19 percent. All this fits perfectly with the figures reported by the directors of these companies. By 2014, Facebook reported a figure of 49 million users with an active profile, according to Jorge Ruiz Escamilla, Director General of the company in Mexico (quoted by Sánchez in *El Economista* 2014). YouTube and Twitter appear later, with smaller levels of participation.

Enrique Peña Nieto finally won the electoral contest in 2012, and a year later he established the National Digital Strategy, which, among other actions, would enable the digitalization of more than 7,000 government processes and applications across Mexico. Up to the present day, the National Digital Strategy seeks to activate innovation, competition, and prosperity

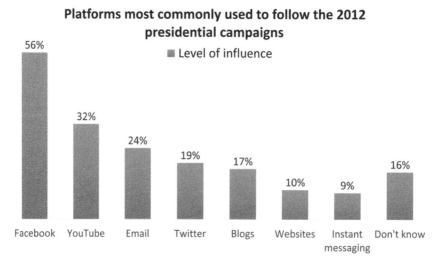

Figure 7.12 Platforms most commonly used to follow the 2012 presidential campaigns (World Internet Project, Mexico, 2013)

for Mexico, and has five stated main purposes: government change; digital economy; quality education; effective universal health; and security for the population.

The federal government has set itself the goal to get Mexico to first place in the digital arena among Latin American nations that form part of the Organisation for Economic Co-operation and Development (OECD) by 2018. Currently, Mexico is in the last place with respect to Internet use, according to the report *Measuring the Digital Economy* (OECD 2014). Looking at the adult population (aged 25 to 64) and youth (15 to 24), the OECD puts Mexico in 34th place, and for the population of older adults (65 to 74), Mexico ranks 33rd, ahead of just one other nation, Turkey.

Figure 7.13 shows the position of Mexico with regard to the other 33 nations making up the OECD. The first vertical bar in the three graphics shows exactly the place occupied by Mexico (on the extreme left). The second bar highlighted in the graphics shows the OECD average.

The number of Internet users in Mexico continues to grow, and if this tendency continues, in five years' time (2020) the country could reach the average in the OECD ranking (79 percent), because the number of Internet users is growing by 5 percent every year.

The last five years of the World Internet Project's research in Mexico have helped better understand the social effects of the Internet on the Mexican population. Mexico was able to connect to the Internet for the first time 30 years ago, and Internet penetration is currently estimated at 52 percent, which means that just over half the population can connect via an electronic device and through various options. With more than 60 million users, Mexico is in 11th place among countries with the greater number of Internet users in the world. These figures can be seen as evidence to support what Marshall McLuhan declared last century. When a technology, medium, tool, or artifact successfully enters a society, it transforms it dramatically (McLuhan and Fiore 1967). Just as radio and television helped modify perceptions and habits of people in contact with these media in the twentieth century, now the new digital communications technologies are again reshaping social visions and actions in this new era.

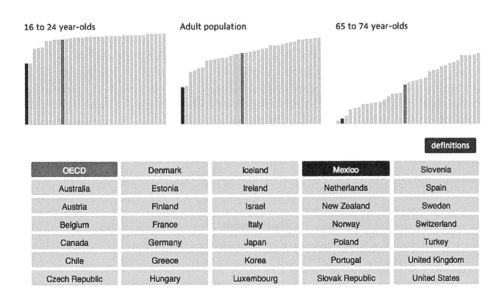

Figure 7.13 Internet penetration in Mexico according to the OECD (2014)

The Future of the Internet in Mexico

The new Internet-linked communications media create new ways of associating and facilitate new kinds of knowledge. They are slowly contributing to an ecological change that transforms the interdependent elements of a system. This change leads to the complete redefinition of processes taking shape with the establishment of new conditions in the society. Thus, every technology brings with it a new concept of the environment. As the Internet gains importance in the country's culture, it is to be expected that certain elements defining that culture will be drastically redefined. The new culture will be shaped as a result of the interaction with the new technologies and its evolution processes. Values, sentiments, perceptions, and forms of knowledge will surely be modified as a result of technological change.

Markedly, the perceptions and actions of the younger generations forming part of the new digital culture differ greatly from those held, or that used to be held, by earlier generations (Generation X and Baby Boomers). New reference points, meanings, inspirations, aspirations, and motivations appear, stimulated to a great measure by technological development. What was once important for one generation will probably not be so important for another generation today. Information and entertainment media have changed again for the young generations. Television has become less important because of a marked preference for digital media. Social networks occupy the space previously occupied by conventional communications media, and are considered an effective tool of influence. People are buying and selling goods and services digitally; education has spread into cyberspace; and governments can no longer function with old management models, which were vertical and highly hierarchical. Now they have to evolve in accordance with the demands of the new global environment.

In Mexico, as in other parts of the world, the Internet has led to a reshaping of the information functions of government and business, of the information industry, and of every kind of institution, including those working in culture and education. Every new Internet application clearly favors the growth of an accentuated technological convergence that encompasses the informatics industry, the collective mass media, telecommunications, domestic consumer electronics, virtual reality, robotics, and the entertainment industry, among others. The close interdependence of these industries daily becomes more evident, and in spite of the turbulent development of the so-called digital economy, the convergence is irreversible.

The Internet is seen as the effect of change or the displacement of a paradigm in industrial structures and social relations. Understanding this new paradigm is of vital importance for continued human development. Drastic changes have occurred once again in the main human activities in this digital era, and this time the changes have taken place more rapidly and profoundly than in other historic eras. The great challenge, however, lies in understanding the direction and form of this new evolution, so as to anticipate effects that might arise from the processes of change. If the revolutionary transformations caused by Internet-related digital technologies are understood in greater depth, we will be able to anticipate and control the consequences of change to adapt more easily to a new complex dynamic environment.

References

Avilés, J., (1998) "Guerra de Internet" (Internet War), *La Jornada*, 8 February, available at: www.lajornadasanluis.com/1998/02/08/mas-aviles.html (accessed 3 May 2015).

Bartolomé, F. (2001) "Templo Mayor", *Reforma*, 1 August: 22.

Conaculta (2010) "Encuesta Nacional de Hábitos, Prácticas y Consumo Culturales" (National Survey of Cultural Habits, Practices and Consumption), *Consejo Nacional para la Cultura y las Artes* (*National Council for Culture and Arts*), available at: www.conaculta.gob.mx/encuesta_nacional/#.VoxBMpOAOko (accessed 28 January 2016).

Cortés, M. (2010) "Telmex a 20 Años de su Privatización" (Telmex 20 Years After Privatization), *El Universal*, 15 December, available at: http://archivo.eluniversal.com.mx/columnas/87644.html (accessed 28 January 2016).

De la Guardia, C. (1999) "EZLN y la Guerra de Internet" (EZLN and the Internet War), *Razón y Palabra*, no. 13, year 4, January–March, available at: www.razonypalabra.org.mx/anteriores/n13/ezln13.html (accessed 28 January 2016).

De la Vega, M. (1998) "Lagunas Legislativas Restan Seguridad a Internet; Las Páginas Del Gobierno Son Invadidas Por 'Hackers'" (Legislative Omissions Lead to Insecurity on the Internet; Government Pages Attacked by Hackers), *Proceso*, 19 July, no. 1133.

Fox, V. (2001) "Presentación del Programa Nacional e-México" (Stenographic Version of Speech Given by President Vicente Fox Quesada When Launching the National E-Mexico Program and Inaugurating the First Community Centre for Informatics and Communications in Mexico in the Telecomm Centre at El Salto), *Presidency of the Republic*, 22 February, available at: http://fox.presidencia.gob.mx/actividades/?contenido=593 (accessed 6 May 2015).

Galindo, J., and González-Acosta, J. (2013) *#YoSoy132 La Primera Erupción Visible* (#YoSoy132 The First Visible Eruption), Mexico: Global Talent University Press.

Gómez Mont, C. (2000) "La Liberalización de las Telecomunicaciones en México en el Marco del TLCAN" (The Liberalisation of Telecommunications in Mexico in the NAFTA Framework), *Razón y Palabra*, no. 19, available at: http://razonypalabra.org.mx/anteriores/n19/index.html (accessed 5 February 2016).

Interactive Advertising Bureau Mexico (2015) "7a. Edición del Estudio de Consumo de Medios y Dispositivos entre Internautas Mexicanos" (Media and Devices Consumption among Mexican Internauts—Study Edition 7a), March 2015, available at: www.iabmexico.com (accessed 3 May 2015).

Islas, O., and Gutiérrez, F. (1996) "El Notable Desarrollo que Registró Internet en México Durante 1996" (The Impressive Growth of the Internet in Mexico in 1996), *Razón y Palabra*, 1(5), available at: http://razonypalabra.org.mx/anteriores/n5/datos.htm (accessed 3 May 2015).

Islas, O., and Gutiérrez, F. (2000) *Internet: El Medio Inteligente* (The internet: The Intelligent Medium), Mexico: Patria Cultural.

Islas, O., and Gutiérrez, F. (2003a) "Internet, el Medio que Cambió a la Comunicación" (Internet, the Medium that Changed Communication), *Razón y Palabra*, 1(34), available at: www.razonypalabra.org.mx/espejo/2003/septiembre.html (accessed 3 May 2015).

Islas, O., and Gutiérrez, F. (2003b) "De 'Los Amigos de Vicente Fox' a 'Los Amigos de Microsoft'" (From "the Friends of Vicente Fox" to "the Friends of Microsoft"), *Razón y Palabra*, 1(30), available at: www.razonypalabra.org.mx/anteriores/n30/oislas.html#18 (accessed 19 April 2016).

Islas, O., and Gutiérrez, F. (2004) "Internet, Utopía y Panóptico de la Sociedad de la Información" (The Internet, Utopia and Panopticon of the Information Society), *Sala de Prensa*, 2(63), available at: www.saladeprensa.org/art515.htm (accessed 6 May 2015).

McLuhan, M., and Fiore, Q. (1967) *The Medium Is the Massage: An Inventory of Effects*, Berkeley, CA: Gingko Press.

Margáin, J. C. (2001) "Sistema e-México: Convergencia Tecnológica con Equidad" (E-Mexico System: Technological Convergence with Equality), *Mercado de Valores*, May, p. 3.

Network Information Center Mexico (2011) "Nuestra Historia" (Our History), *Network Information Center*, available at: www.nic.mx/es/NicMx.Historia (accessed 5 May 2015).

Notimex (2002) "Firman Convenio Sobre Proyecto E-México" (Agreement Signed on E-Mexico Project), *El Universal*, 17 April, available at: www.eluniversal.com.mx/notas/60968.html (accessed 5 May 2015).

Organisation for Economic Co-operation and Development (2014) "Measuring the Digital Economy", *Organisation for Economic Co-operation and Development*, available at: www.oecd.org/sti/measuring-the-digital-economy-9789264221796-en.htm (accessed 23 August 2015).

Postman, N. (1998) "Five Things We Need to Know About Technological Change", *Seventh Day Christian Assembly*, available at: www.sdca.org/sermons_mp3/2012/121229_postman_5Things.pdf (accessed 28 January 2016).

Sánchez, J. (2014) "México Tiene 49 Mllones de Usuarios de Facebook" (Mexico has 49 Million Users of Facebook), *El Economista*, 20 April, available at: http://eleconomista.com.mx/tecnociencia/2014/03/20/mexico-tiene-49-millones-usuarios-facebook (accessed 19 April 2016).

United Nations Public Administration Country Studies (2005) "Global E-Government Development Report", *United Nations Public Administration Country Studies*, available at: http://unpan3.un.org/egovkb/en-us/Reports/UN-E-Government-Survey-2005 (accessed 3 May 2015).

World Internet Project, Mexico (2012) "Estudios de Hábitos y Percepciones de los Mexicanos Sobre Internet y Diversas Tecnologías Asociadas (Studies of Mexicans' Habits and Perceptions of the Internet and Associated Technologies), *World Internet Project Mexico*, available at: www.wip.mx (accessed 12 May 2015).

World Internet Project, Mexico (2013) "Estudios de Hábitos y Percepciones de los Mexicanos Sobre Internet y Diversas Tecnologías Asociadas" (Studies of Mexicans' Habits and Perceptions of the Internet and Associated Technologies), *World Internet Project Mexico*, available at: www.wip.mx (accessed 12 May 2015).

8

THE SOCIAL SHAPING OF THE BRAZILIAN INTERNET

Historicizing the Interactions Between States, Corporations, and NGOs in Information and Communication Technology Development and Diffusion

Stuart Davis, Joe Straubhaar, Martha Fuentes-Bautista, and Jeremiah Spence

Introduction

The history of Internet diffusion in Latin America can be characterized by a complicated series of negotiations between often conflicting groups of actors, including national governments, multinational corporations, international social movements, and regional non-governmental organizations (NGOs). Within this history, different actors often get compartmentalized and thus isolated from each other: the state and corporations combat each other over issues of deregulation and privatization (e.g. Noam 1998) while NGOs work with larger social movements and transnational advocacy networks (TANs) to promote international issues or causes (e.g. Keck and Sikkink 1998; Willetts 2011). Complicating these relatively narrow categorizations, we argue that the ability of NGOs in Brazil to incorporate access to, and training in how to use, information and communication technologies (ICTs) in community development projects, such as professionalization for the workforce, technology literacy, and helping create alternatives for young people to criminal activity (Sorj 2003; Jambeiro and Straubhaar 2005) is intimately linked to the national political economic environment produced through interactions between regulatory bodies, established corporations, entrepreneurs, and local activists.

Through the study of the social and economic forces at play in the push for ICT diffusion in Brazil, we propose a multi-stakeholder framework for understanding the emergence and evolution of information and telecommunications technologies in developing nations. Our central thesis is that in Brazil, ICT diffusion was largely driven by creative innovations in diffusion from below by NGOs who sought to create new forms of access to the Internet to fulfill demand by users. However, these efforts were heavily influenced by national policies regarding public access, liberalization of regulations governing the national telecommunications market, as well as attempts by private corporations vying for consumer access. In this chapter we map this knotted history through a series of cases where governmental, corporate, and activist/NGOs collaborate and collide in attempts to promote access on a wide scale.

Theoretical Approach: The Social Construction of Technology Approach to Media History

Expanding on Marshall McLuhan's adage that "technology is neither good, nor bad, nor neutral", Manuel Castells claims that information and communication technologies must be conceptualized as contingent forces that take on different political, economic, or social meanings dependent on the context in which they are developed and/or deployed (Castells 1997: 65). In its contingency, technology may be a problem-solver or problem-generator, but it is essentially malleable. Our study analyzes this malleability in action through an empirical discussion of the connections between Internet development and social, political, and economic institutions and practices in the specific context of national societies with distinct cultural, economic, and political characteristics.

In order to analyze telecommunications networks as a process of negotiation between multiple groups of actors with varying interests, we draw upon a few central concepts from the theoretical literature on the social construction and social shaping of technology (SSOT) (Callon 1987; Bijker 1994). The first concept used in SSOT analyses of technological development is "interpretative flexibility": the notion that technological developments never follow a predetermined or inevitable path, but are the result of a negotiation process between multiple actors (Callon 1987). To address this flexibility, SSOT theorists draw upon a multi-directional model in which every stage of the development of a technology is a battle between different parties with competing interests. The first stage of analysis involves designating the main social groups associated with the technology and how they interact with each other. Power relations might enter the picture at this stage, as they are linked to actors' investments in the technological object. Stabilization or closure, the next stage, consists of the steps through which "relevant social groups *see* the problem as being solved" and possible alternative pathways close. In the final stage, the SSOT analysis connects the technology to a wider social and political context (Pinch and Bijker 1987).

Media and technology historians working within this theoretical framework have critiqued the way many SSOT analyses treat stabilization as too complete and exhaustive. Specifically, scholars like Leah Lievrouw (2002, 2011) and Susan Leigh Star (1999) have argued that while stabilization makes sense when talking about inert artifacts (bicycles, refrigerators, or electric cars), the interactive nature of media technologies make stabilization impossible. The knotted history of radio's development in the early twentieth century presented in Susan Douglas's *Inventing American Broadcasting* (1987) provides an excellent illustration of how an SSOT analysis approaches media technologies. In this study, Douglas examines how the intersection of technical developments (represented by inventors like Guglielmo Marconi and Reginald Fessenden, along with networks of amateur experimenters), corporate strategies (represented by companies like AT&T and RCA), political dialogues (mainly represented by the US Navy), and coverage by media outlets worked in frictious interaction together to create a system that became known as radio broadcasting (1987: 316–318). In this account, no single group of actors holds primacy; the collisions between them drove the invention, and eventual consolidation, of the radio industry into the "Big Three" networks that controlled broadcasting for a large chunk of the mid-twentieth century. Despite its consolidation, though, Douglas maintains that the actors who controlled first the radio, then television, industries were consistently faced with the threat of new actors entering the playing field, technological innovations, or policy developments that might radically transform the configuration.[1]

Adopting this model to describe new media technologies, Lievrouw describes this process as a combination of multiple factors, including design elements (the medium specificity of the technology), the organizational network in which it is introduced (including the political economic environment), and the perceived social consequences of the system by major actors trying to promote or restrain the diffusion of the new technology or practice (Lievrouw 2011: 15). In a similar vein, Paula Chakravartty and Yuezhi Zhao (2008) argue that the often "frictious or awkward encounters" that arise among media conglomerates, national regulatory bodies, transnational and local NGOs, and other agents make it impossible to claim that one group dominates any single event or process. The "uneven and awkward links" between multiple levels of the globalization of media technologies can only be tracked through mapping the interaction between agents in the rollout process within individual situations (2008: 13).

Critically informed by SSOT, we analyze the development of the Internet in Brazil by examining the interplay of institutions engaged in a process with government, industry and non-governmental organizations (NGOs), and universities in a regulatory context characterized by liberalization policies generated due to global pressures. We specifically track divergences and historical continuities based on both infrastructure and liberalization policy, despite commonalities based in social movements that were intervening in the policy process to define policy from below and offer new access services. We then detail the contrasting histories of our two case nations. We conclude with a discussion of the major similarities and differences observed and implications for issues of access.

Historicizing the Changing Role of the State in Telecommunications Development and Diffusion: Liberalization, Privatization, and the Influence of Non-Governmental Organizations

Before investigating how individual actors participated in the ICT diffusion process in Brazil, we offer a brief overview of larger trends within telecommunications ownership. In the 1970s, the push for import substitution industrialization led to state policy monopolies over infrastructure in various areas including the burgeoning telecommunications sector (Evans 1992). Due to this intensive national investment in protecting domestic industries from foreign competition, the state was often seen as the most reliable provider and the agent with most access to financial resources and responsibility for acting in the public interest, particularly in Brazil (Straubhaar 1995). Similarly, the national government had usually been seen as the best entity for providing education and training, although in more federal, decentralized systems (including Brazil), education was often thought of as a responsibility delegated to governments operating at state or municipal levels.

The 1980s witnessed waves of privatization and liberalization of government control over telecommunications companies that began to redefine the role of the state. During this time, the central role of the national state in both making policy and delivering services declined for several interrelated reasons. One is that forces of economic globalization tended to introduce changes in state-centered policy models, pushing them to liberalize competition in, deregulate, and privatize telecommunications. We can see this ideological push in Brazil, where President Fernando Collor de Mello publicly announced the withdrawal of the state from the telecommunications sector on a set of ideological claims for efficiency through competition and streamlining through privatization (Noam and Baur 1998; Mariscol et al. 2007). The second central impetus for privatization was that many nation states in Latin America suffered a decline in their ability to supply even basic services such as education, due to debt loads and restructuring programs pressed on them by the International Monetary Fund (IMF) and other international actors (Vreeland 1993), as well as periodic financial crises. As the nation attempted to rebuild its economy after political periods characterized by despotic military governments, followed by a shaky return to democracy plagued by accusations of business collusion and bribery under Collor (Johnson 1994), it found that attempting to integrate its economy internationally entailed a substantial amount of reliance on the IMF and other extramural funding bodies. In 1998, the Brazilian government, along with its largest bank, agreed to a massive economic restructuring that cut state involvement in protecting and subsidizing industry (Malan and de Barroso 1998). These economic transformations reduced the ability of nation states, in Latin America and elsewhere, to maintain investments in telecommunications or find new sources of financing to expand telecommunications services into underserved areas, such as urban poor neighborhoods or rural areas.[2] The economic factors described above have been the exclusion of the state from investing in, or entering, many areas such as increased rural services, subsidies for public access connectivity, or opening and operating public access centers. The withdrawal of the state from these sectors has opened a space that some new groups of actors, namely NGOs, have come to fill.

The rise of NGOs as active agents in the ICT diffusion process can be linked to transformations in structures of funding and political goals during the 1980s–1990s. Unlike national programs, NGOs drew on a diverse set of donors, ranging from transnational NGOs, like the Association for Progressive Communications (APC), to international organizations such as UNESCO and the Inter-American Development Bank that tended to work more through these groups than national governments (O'Brien and Clement 1999). Combined with a relative degree of freedom from national bureaucracies, this diversity in potential revenue channels set up NGOs to act as much more flexible agents.

The Four Phases of ICT Diffusion in Brazil: An Introduction

The history of Brazilian ICT diffusion can be broken into four discrete phases. The first phase is that characterized by the development of infrastructure by state-owned telecommunications conglomerates. During this period, the military government performed an active role in protecting domestic telecommunications and brokering deals with international firms including IBM and AT&T (Tigre 1983, 1984; Trebat 1983; Evans 1989). While this period arguably illustrates state protection against the incursion of foreign actors, it also excluded the vast majority of society from Internet access and training. As a result, several counter models developed. The second phase involved the interaction between a Brazilian NGO and an international NGO to develop a national point of access to global email networks for use predominately by local and national social movements and NGOs. The third phase was initiated by a government public policy decision to liberalize the marketplace by allowing private Internet service providers to operate outside the domain of the state-run telecommunication monopolies. In this phase, a rapid commercialization of access was seen as partnerships between transnational firms and Brazilian ISPs rapidly became the dominant model for access to the increasingly global medium. In the fourth phase, NGOs once again became central actors as they began to develop alternative access models. Rather than wait for the nation state to create conditions for Internet access, NGOs begin to offer different kinds of Internet access services themselves through public Internet cafés called telecenters. Within all four phases we see a consistent interplay of amicable and contentious interactions between the nation state, private corporations, and NGOs that ultimately created the current telecommunications landscape.

Phase One: Nationalized Telecommunications Development (1920s–1980s)

The first phase began in the early part of the twentieth century (around 1923) when the international conglomerate International Telephone and Telegraph (ITT) and later the Compania Telefonica Brasileiro (CTB) developed a telecom infrastructure that created a tele-density of about 1.4 telephones per 100 hundred people, with two-thirds of the equipment and traffic concentrated in the states of São Paulo and Rio de Janeiro (Botelho *et al.* 2002). The Brazilian military, after coming to power in a 1964 coup, built upon this existing telecommunications structure for a number of strategic reasons: national security, economic development, and extension of national media reach. By the 1960s, both civilian and military leaders realized the strategic importance of a nationally centralized telecommunication system (McClain and Straubhaar 2002). In 1962, the Goulart administration issued decree 4.117 (called "Brazilian Telecommunications Code"), which permitted the federal government to operate and regulate a monopoly (Noam 1998). By the late 1970s, the military government was able to achieve a national telecommunications infrastructure, including national microwave and satellite networks. Centered on the massive public corporation Telebrás, this infrastructure emphasized national research and development which, when combined with investment funds, helped drive national technological growth both for the sake of national security and domestic/international economic growth (Botelho *et al.* 1998; Pinhero and Giambiagi 2000).

One of the most important lasting effects of this period was the development of the Rede National da Pesquisa (National Research Network) (RNP), a backbone of the networked telecommunications infrastructure used to link research communities in the federal and state university systems (Dutta-Roy and Segoshi 1996), as well as the Centro de Pesquisas e Desenvolvimento (Center for Research and Development) (CP&D), an arm of Telebrás based in several university branches that promoted a variety of forward-looking attempts at creating wired telecommunications systems between geographically separated research sites (Gracioso 1988). Throughout this period, the military government played an extremely active role in negotiating the terms for telecommunications development: the state aggressively promoted certain research projects and deals with foreign corporations while forcefully fighting others (Trepat 1983; Evans 1989). Though the US, under the Reagan administration, attempted to force the industry to open up in 1985, by this point many multinational corporations had already established partnerships with Brazilian corporations under the terms set by that national government (Tigre 1984; Evans 1989: 218). As subsequent sections explicate, the state's *entrepreneurial guidance* in telecommunications and related industries mitigated later stages of foreign investment, leaving room for TANs and international NGOs to establish relationships with local non-governmental groups who would play an active role in the diffusion process in the 1990s to the present.

Phase Two: AlterNex and International Collaboration in the Development of NGO Access Points

Into the early 1990s, the Brazilian national research network for higher education was limited strictly to use by the research universities. While university research centers worked closely with the state agencies and state-sponsored corporations, they did not attempt to integrate technological developments into widespread access of computers or training in ICT usage for the larger population. This vacuum of access and training pushed the international NGO community to ally with Brazilian NGOs in order to fill the role vacated by the state.

The most prominent of these partnerships came through the alliance between the Association for Progressive Communications (APC) and the Brazilian Institute of Social and Economic Analysis (IBASE) to form AlterNex in 1987 (AlterNex/IBASE 1992). This new entity was based, initially, on a bulletin-board system which facilitated the exchange of messages between users. AlterNex operated via a single phone line that connected to a FidoNet node in the United States. At its initial capacity, it could facilitate the exchange of e-mail messages once a day. This constituted the first system for access to the Internet in Brazil outside of the closed government research network.

In 1992, AlterNex increased its capacity by establishing a dedicated 64 kilobyte high-speed connection. With this increase, the project was able to provide connectivity to NGOs across the country to increase exchanges concerning planning and strategizing around various social movement issues (Afonso 1996). That same year, AlterNex would gain a significant amount of international exposure for its work at the United Nations Conference on Environment and Development (UNCED, more colloquially known as the "Rio Earth Summit") in Rio de Janeiro. AlterNex took full advantage of the meeting to showcase the range of communication services it could provide. With assistance from local partners like the RPC and the Rio Network (Rede Rio), AlterNex coordinated UNCED's Strategic Information Project during the meeting. The network provided by the project was used by hundreds of delegates, researchers, and NGOs from around the world for electronic exchange between the official conference delegates and those participating in the Global Forum—an alternative event designed for NGOs and others not attached to bilateral commissions who could not participate in the official event (Frederick 1992). The success of the event established IBASE/ AlterNex as the most capable and expedient technical solutions provider for NGOs working within Brazil (Afonso 1996). A substantial customer base was developed, and AlterNex became a major force in defining Brazil's Internet development process.

The growing commercial availability of the World Wide Web in the early 1990s increased the demand for AlterNex's networking services. IBASE adjusted quickly by expanding to include WWW-based content, value-added services, and Internet consulting. This shift in role, from providing communication support for activists to contracting with individual consumers, brought to the surface concerns that AlterNex was straying too far from the organization's research and social advocacy goals. Contention around these issues eventually led to the privatization of the ISP in 1996. The company, Sistema AlterNex, was owned partially by IBASE and partially by private investors. The hope was that this private entity could both continue to serve the needs of AlterNex's NGO client base and at the same time reach a larger general market, with the latter activity helping to finance the former. Unfortunately, they could not raise sufficient profits to channel back into their NGO-based projects. In 1997, IBASE sold its portion of AlterNex to private investors. AlterNex S/A exists today as a commercial enterprise with no connections to the APC or the Brazilian NGO community.

With the NGOs we can see a clearer articulation of potential social or political goals behind Internet access. While the national projects and private companies up until that point had focused largely on domestic connectivity (i.e. providing Internet access in the home), the NGOs did not display nearly as neat or uniform a purpose. At the macro level, international social movements promoted ICT use in local contexts to support a variety of causes ranging from environmental activism to improving production practices in marginalized areas (Sorj 2003; Sorj and Guedes 2006). As we will see in phase three, the model of ICT diffusion developed by AlterNex begins to fade as the growth of private ISPs accelerates with the mass diffusion of the Internet to consumers. The advocacy or issue-based agenda of the project simply could not operate in a competitive climate because of both a lack of a critical mass of users and an increased cost of infrastructure and interconnection.

Phase Three: UOL and the Rise of Private Internet Service Providers

As part of an initiative instigated by the post-dictatorship administration to liberalize key sectors of the economy (Johnson 1994; Baer 2000), the government decided in 1995 to open access to the Internet infrastructure at Telebrás as the first step towards the gradual privatization of the entire telecommunication sector (Dutta-Roy and Segoshi 1996). The opening of competition among ISPs instantly catalyzed consumer Internet usage. In the first year after liberalization, the number of users jumped by 100,000 to one million. This growth in the private sector was initially accomplished by the expansion of competing small, entrepreneurial enterprises. However, due to the high barriers of entry due to the cost of accessing national and international Internet backbones, the marketplace witnessed a rapid consolidation into a small number of ISPs with nationwide coverage. A lack of operating capital caused a subsequent integration of the national ISPs with international telecommunications corporations and content conglomerates.

One of the most prominent examples of the corporate consolidation of post-liberalization enterprises is Universo Online (UOL). Launched on the cusp of liberalization in 1996, this company is still the largest Portuguese-language web portal and ISP provider in Latin America (Valor Online 2010). Within São Paulo, the portal was instrumental in the development of the Internet market in Brazil, and continues to lead through the popularity of its products: UOL Brazil, Bol.com, and Zipnet.com. UOL International also holds popular Spanish-language sites in Argentina, Colombia, Venezuela, and Mexico. In both ICT infrastructure and content creation, UOL developed the ability to move faster than its competitors. On the technical side, the company leveraged the financial strength it gained through early entrance into the ICT market to buy out competitors (including CompuServe's Brazilian branch) with heavy research and design foci in improving access speed (UOL 1998). Even more pronounced was UOL's innovative actions in content creation. In the late 1990s the company launched Brazil's first video streaming service (TV UOL), as well as a series of projects aimed at reaching specific audience segments, including a portal dedicated to Brazilian sports (UOL Esporte) and another focusing on pedagogical activities aimed at providing informal educational aids to parents and teachers (UOL Educação). Staying on the cutting edge of research and development while promoting innovative content helped UOL expand at an accelerated speed.

In September 1999, the company leveraged the sale of 12.5 percent of its shares to a pool of international investors to reach out to neighboring nations' markets. By the early 2000s, UOL had become one of the strongest regional ISPs and content creators, with operations in Argentina, Mexico, Venezuela, Portugal, and the United States (though this would change within a few years).[3] Hand in hand with the internationalization of UOL came its "glocalization".[4] Local media companies backed up UOL operations in Argentina, Mexico, Colombia, and Venezuela, while Google shared efforts in the US, and Portugal Telecom supports operations in Portugal (Fuentes-Bautista 2002). However, developments in the NASDAQ market in the early 2000s did not favor UOL's plans for internationalization. As the company began to internationalize its holdings, it found that it could not keep financially solvent while negotiating the national commercial and regulatory scenes in all of the areas where it was attempting to glocalize.

Theorizing out from UOL, we can see how a domestic enterprise was able to develop between state organs (in this case Telebrás), international or multinational corporations (including Google and Portugal Telecom), and regional markets within Latin America. However, it still did not achieve large-scale domestic penetration. While it could provide access on a much larger scale than the APC/AlterNex/IBASE constellation and or other social movement/NGO collaborations in Brazil, it nonetheless failed to penetrate many areas of the Brazilian nation. The inability of UOL and other private providers to achieve national saturation spurred a new set of social actors, the telecenter operators, to become widespread in the late 1990s to mid-2000s. This leads us to the fourth and final phase of our institutional history.

Phase Four: The Center for the Democratization of Information (CDI), Telecenters, and Social Entrepreneurship

Even as the ISP domestic market expanded in the 2000s, the overall penetration of both telecommunications infrastructure and Internet access in Brazil has been relatively limited and concentrated in major urban areas (de Souza e Silva 2011). As a response to this dearth in coverage, another surge of NGO interventions began. While interventions during this period followed a similar pattern of local–national–international partnership, the goals of this period shifted away from facilitating communication within transnational activist networks and on to providing access in economically and geographically marginalized regions (Davis 2015b). During this period, the main form of providing access came through the establishment of public Internet cafés called telecenters.

A telecenter can be defined in the most basic terms as a shared physical space that provides public access to information technology, usually in the form of desktop computers. Most public telecenters also offer a series of training classes in the areas of distance education, computer skills training, and job preparation/professionalization (Whyte 2000; Proenza et al. 2001). During the early 2000s, NGOs within many Latin American countries (most explicitly in Brazil, Peru, and Argentina) opened telecenters to provide a vehicle for enhancing access to the Internet, particularly for low-income groups. The earliest telecenters in Brazil were developed in the state of São Paulo through the government-coordinated project Acessa São Paulo. On 16 November 2000, state governor Mário Covas inaugurated the first of over 60 "infocenters" that would be launched in greater São Paulo (as well as 60 more locations in the interior of the state). Through a public project, Acessa São Paulo developed novel strategies to recruit funders for its projects. From the planning stages onwards, one of its central strategies was to attract partnerships with companies like Microsoft, Hewlett-Packard, and Telefônica. In adopting such an aggressive approach to "selling" its vision to potential backers, Acessa São Paulo exhibited a form of *social entrepreneurship* (Bornstein 2003; McAnany 2012) that would come to characterize many subsequent projects.

The most internationally recognized Brazilian NGO engaged in telecenter development is the Comité para Democratização de Informatica (The Center for the Democratization of information) (CDI). Founded in 1995 in Rio de Janeiro by business student Rodrigo Baggio and a team of volunteers, the CDI established itself less as a service provider (through telecenters) and more of a facilitator of innovative local projects. From initial stages, the NGO would recruit partners; it would seek out community-based associations, and provide free computer equipment, software, and guidelines for the continuous training of local instructors. Through periodic visits, regional CDI coordinators monitor each local project's performance, identifying key challenges and opportunities. Ideally, local coordinators work together with coordinators to find creative ways of addressing problems and formulating solutions (Marques Oliveira 2004). Each school is an autonomous unit, self-managed and sustained through a combination of initial seed money from the NGO, small contributions from students, and public funding that regional CDI directors help groups locate (Ashoka Foundation 1996).

CDI's perceived ability to creatively and nimbly address many of the financial issues experienced by earlier NGO projects focused on digital inclusion has garnered numerous accolades. For many foundations and funding agencies, CDI exemplifies a form of social entrepreneurship built around small-scale firms or organizations that are both economically competitive within a certain market (usually local) and oriented towards integrating profits back into their environment in a pro-social manner (Ashoka Foundation 1996; McAnany 2012). CDI also utilizes another practice valorized by social entrepreneurship proponents: scaling up. Since its foundation, the organization has continued to expand its centers across Brazil and internationally.[5] As of 2014, there are 842 autonomous and self-sustaining "Information Technology and Citizens Rights" schools using CDI's methodology and model concept in South America (Chile, Colombia, and Venezuela), North America (USA and Mexico), Europe (Romania, Spain, Ireland, England, Poland, and the Czech Republic), and Australia (CDI 2015).

With telecenter-based projects like Acessa São Paulo and CDI, we can see a dramatic shift in the locus of initiation towards the local. Within the different centers that the CDI sponsors contracted, community groups and local organizations have a large degree of autonomy. Partners promote a variety of projects, ranging from courses teaching young children to use computer software for recording and producing music, to training crafts-producers to market their products to a wider audience through social media platforms (Davis forthcoming). Following the logic of social entrepreneurship, local actors responsible for running the centers became the primary agents in deciding what projects are pursued.

In this final phase, we see an ever-increasing degree of flexibility in how ICT diffusion projects adjust to community dynamics. State and city governments in Brazil have begun to offer other telecenter models in the vein of the CDI model, often soliciting the participation of local community organizations or NGOs.

Conclusion: Theoretical Implications of the Diffusion Process in Brazil

Stepping back from our history, a few strong conceptual points around the socio-cultural and political shaping of ICTs can be drawn. As a historiography of the development and shaping of a media industry, our account corroborates critiques of *stabilization* offered by Lievrouw, Douglas, and others. In each of the four stages, main actors occupied different roles. In the 1960s, the state exercised protectionist strategies in order to bolster national companies; after the end of the military rule, it forcefully attempted to deregulate political reasons. Similarly, the way NGOs defined "access" in the late 1980s (as exemplified by the AlterNex project) was significantly different from how the CDI defined it less than a decade later. For the former, providing access was seen as part of a general networking strategy for strengthening ties between geographically separated actors within transnational advocacy and social movement networks. For the latter, access and training were conceptualized as integral components of an empowerment strategy oriented at the individual level. In fact, the CDI's tendency to stress the importance of teaching vocational skills along with computer skills has caused some controversy with social movement actors who have critiqued the project's de-emphasis on civic participation and political engagement (Ferraz 2004).

Emphasizing complexity and friction in Brazilian ICT diffusion has implications that go beyond the writing of history. It also offers a rejoinder to political economic metanarratives of media globalization that view the development and evolution of an international telecommunications infrastructure through the expanding contours of transnational media ownership (and its relationship with policy-making). Analyses offered by scholars like Jill Hills (1998, 2007) and Dan Schiller (1999) that track how the concentration of ownership among a few transnational telecommunications firms has a direct impact on the way Internet diffusion operates globally might be substantiated or enriched by the type of knotty narratives presented in this chapter. To reiterate one of the central tenets of SSOT: though actors exercise a degree of self-volition within the development of a technology, their actions are always shaped to a substantial degree by ideological forces (Callon 1987). The task thus becomes finding ways to integrate locally or nationally specific historiographies like ours with more global accounts.

The second theoretical implication (more of the practitioner sort) is connected to the way *scaling up or project expansion* works within various stages of our history. In all of the four stages, we can see a tension between addressing core constituencies and expanding to serve other audiences or locales. In the last three stages especially, innovation in the diffusion process was largely accomplished through the entrepreneurial activity of a single organization (CDI; Acessa São Paulo), corporation (UOL), or collaborative project (APC/IBASE). From a commercial perspective, histories of companies like UOL illustrate how bold decision making in technological development and creative approaches to diversifying content can rapidly expand a user base. From a social change or social justice perspective, the ability to customize projects to meet local conditions (especially in phase four) can potentially benefit communities by reducing what Heeks calls user-design gaps, or "inscribed assumptions that designers and implementers from distant locales make about local actualities" (Heeks 2002: 106).

Though innovation at the local level helped facilitate the diffusion process, the idiosyncratic and highly specific nature of many of the projects in question can be created when moving beyond the local. Problems arose when negotiating scaling up through expansion of customer base, increasing holdings, or franchising. For UOL, horizontal integration into various other types of media and national markets spread resources too thinly to continue growth. For AlterNex, expanding its consumer base irrevocably damaged the project's abilities to meet the social movement needs of its original constituency. Out of all the groups in question, CDI seems to be the only one to have addressed coordination issues related to scaling up by developing a model that is highly dependent on local partners. Nonetheless, more concrete data regarding its partnerships is needed to determine whether it is achieving the harmonious balance it claims in promotional materials or potentially is falling into the traps of organizational miscommunication or lack of accountability between local branches and parent organizations that scholars like Lamia Karim (2011) and Stuart Davis (2015a) have found in other community-development NGOs working in the Global South.

We hope that the two implications we have drawn in the history of the ICT roll-out process in Brazil speak to authors writing about other national or regional contexts. They reflect conceptual issues related to the writing of a national media industry as well as the practitioner-based issues of managing a local innovation when it starts to expand out of its locus of initiation. Though presented through a historical analysis here, these issues speak to difficulties still consistently faced by academics, activists, professionals, and policy makers.

Notes

1. The increasing number of articles, monographs, and edited collections on "post-television" evidences the lack of stabilization within the television industry. For a representative example of the new quasi-cottage industry of scholarship on the technological transformations within the television industry, please see Curtin et al. (2014).
2. While the withdrawal of the state from public spending in these areas has been widespread, it would be reductive to argue that state spending vanished completely. As Robin Mansell (1994), Noam and Baur (1998), and others have effectively argued, privatization in Latin America never entails a complete withdrawal of the state from promoting ICT diffusion. Despite the de-emphasis on economic investment in infrastructure, the Brazilian national governments developed various strategies to continue to increase access to both telephony and the Internet (see Fuentes-Bautista 2002).
3. In March 2002, UOL announced that it had 1.3–1.5 million subscribers, and 20 million users or unique visitors per month, which made it the most heavily used ISP and portal in Latin America.
4. Glocalization has been used by Robertson (1995) and others to describe the local adaptation of imported models. The term was first used to describe the Japanese business practice of importing but adapting various technologies and models.
5. In a striking testament to the group's decentralized structure, founder Baggio moved to New York City in 2008 while continuing to lead the project.

References

Afonso, C. (1996) "The Internet and the Community in Brazil: Background, Issues, and Options", *Communications Magazine, IEEE*, 34(7), 62–68.

AlterNex/IBASE (1992) "Nodo AlterNex", *The Biodiversity Network Workshop, Campinas, BR*, available at: www.bdt.fat.org.br/bin21/ws92/AlterNex.html

Ashoka Foundation (1996) *Rodrigo Baggio Barreto*, available at: http://brasil.ashoka.org/fellow/rodrigo-baggio-barreto

Baer, W. (2000) "The Privatization Experience in Brazil", in D. Parker and D. Saal (eds), *The International Handbook on Privatization*, London: Elsevier, pp. 220–247.

Bijker, W. (1994) *Of Bicycles, Bakelites, and Bulbs: Toward a Theory of Socio-technical Change*, Cambridge, MA: MIT Press.

Bornstein, D. (2003) *The Price of a Dream: The Story of the Grameen Bank*, Chicago: University of Chicago Press.

Botelho, A. J. J., Ferro, J. R., Mcknight, L., and Oliveira, A. C. M. "Telecommunications in Brazil", in Eli M. Noam (ed.), *Telecommunications in Latin America*, New York and Oxford: Oxford University Press, 1998, pp. 227–250.

Callon, M. (1987) "Society in the Making: The Study of Technology as a Tool for Sociological Analysis", in W. Bijker, T. Pinch, and J. Hughes (eds), *The Social Construction of Technological Systems*, Cambridge, MA: MIT Press, pp. 83–103.

Castells, M. (1997) *The Power of Identity*, Oxford: Wiley-Blackwell.

Center for the Democratization of Information (CDI), Home page, available at: www.cdi.org

Chakravartty, P., and Zhao, Y. (2008) *Global Communications: Towards a Transcultural Political Economy*, Lanham, MD: Rowman & Littlefield.

Curtin, M., Holt, J., and Sanson, K. (eds) (2014) *Distribution Revolution: Conversations About the Digital Future of Film and Television*, Berkeley, CA: University of California Press.

Davis, S. (2015a) "Networking the Favelas: Leveraging International Outreach to Support Digital Journalism in Rio de Janeiro's Favelas", Ph.D. thesis, Department of Radio-TV-Film, Austin, TX: University of Texas-Austin.

Davis, S. (2015b) "Citizens' Media in the Favelas: Finding a Place for Community-Based Digital Media Production in Social Change Processes", *Communication Theory*, 25(3): 230–243.

Davis, S. (forthcoming) "Relocating Development Communication: Social Entrepreneurship, International Networking, and South-South Cooperation in the Viva Rio NGO", *Journal of International Communication*.

de Souza e Silva (2011) "Mobile Phone Appropriation in the Favelas of Rio de Janeiro, Brazil", *New Media & Society*, 13(3): 411–426.

Douglas, S. (1987) *Inventing American Broadcasting, 1899–1922*, Baltimore, MD: Johns Hopkins University Press.

Dutta-Roy, A., and Segoshi, N. (1996) "Going Online with the Internet in Brazil", *Spectrum*, 33(7): 54–58.

Evans, P. (1989) *Dependent Development: The Alliance of Multinational, State, and Local Capital in Brazil*, Princeton, NJ: Princeton University Press.

Ferraz, C. (2004) "Computing for Social Inclusion in Brazil: A Study of the CDI and Other Initiatives", manuscript, University of California Berkeley School of Information.

Frederick, H. (1992) "Computer Networks and the Emergence of Global Civil Society", in L. Haraisim (ed.), *Global Networks: Computers and International Communication*, Cambridge, MA: MIT Press, pp. 283–295.

Fuentes-Bautista, M. (2002) "Universal Service in Times of Reform", in L. F. Cranor (ed.), *Communications Policy and Information Technology: Promises, Problems and Prospects*, Cambridge, MA: MIT Press, pp. 347–382.

Fuentes-Bautista, M., Straubhaar, J., and Spence, J. (2002) "Converging Print and Electronic Media in Brazil: The Rapid Rise of UOL (Universe Online) to Dominance as Both ISP and Internet Content Provider in Brazil", *International Communications Association Conference, Seoul, South Korea, 15–19 July*.

Gracioso, F. (1988) "Telemarketing: Um Milagre Brasileiro", *Estudos ESPM*, 22(179).

Heeks, R. (2002) "Failure, Success and Improvisation of Information Systems and Projects in Developing Countries", *Development Informatives Working Paper Series 11*.

Hills, J. (1998) "U.S. Rules OK? Telecommunications Since the 1940s", in J. B. Foster and E. M. Woods (eds), *Capitalism and the Information Age: The Political Economy of the Global Communication Revolution*, New York: Monthly Review Press, pp. 99–121.

Hills, J. (2007) *Telecommunications and Empire*, Champaign-Urbana, IL: University of Illinois Press.

Jambeiro, O., and Straubhaar, J. D. (eds) (2005) *Information and Communication: The Local and the Global in Austin and Salvador (Informação e Comunicação: O Local e o Global em Austin e Salvador)*, Salvador, Brazil: Edufba Press.

Johnson, R. (1994) "Regarding the Philanthropic Ogre: Cultural Policy in Brazil 1930–1945/1964–1990", in D. Levine (ed.), *Constructing Culture and Power in Latin America*, Ann Arbor, MI: University of Michigan Press, pp. 334–338.

Karim, L. (2011) *Microfinance and its Discontents: Women in Debt in Bangladesh*, Minneapolis, MN: University of Minnesota Press.

Keck, M., and Sikkink, K. (1998) *Activists Beyond Borders: Advocacy Networks in International Politics*, Ithaca, NY: Cornell University Press.

Lievrouw, L. A. (2002) "Determination and Contingency in New Media Development: Diffusion of Innovations and Social Shaping of Technology Perspectives", in L. A. Lievrouw and S. Livingstone (eds), *Handbook of New Media*, Thousand Oaks, CA: Sage, pp. 183–199.

Lievrouw, L. (2011) *Alternative and Activist New Media*, London: Polity.

McAnany, E. (2012) *Saving the World: A Brief History of Communication for Development and Social Change*, Urbana-Champaign, IL: University of Illinois Press.

McClain, S., and Straubhaar, J. (2002) "Telecommunications Liberalization and Privatization in Brazil: The Politics of Waiting for Competition", *International Studies Association Conference, New Orleans, Louisiana*.

Malan, P. S., and de Barroso, G. H. (1998) "Brazilian Letter of Intent to the International Monetary Fund", *International Monetary Fund*, available at: www.imf.org/external/np/loi/111398.htm (accessed 22 March 2012).

Mansell, R. (1994) *The New Telecommunications: A Political Economy of the Networked Environment*, Thousand Oaks, CA: Sage Publications.

Mariscol, J., Bonina, C., and Luna, J. (2007) "New Market Scenarios in Latin America", in H. Galperin and J. Mariscol (eds), *Digital Poverty: Latin American and Caribbean Perspectives*, Toronto: International Development Research Centre, pp. 55–78.

Marques Oliveira, E. (2004) "Empreendedorismo Social no Brasil: Atual Configuração, Perspectivas e Desafios—Notas Introdutórias", *Revista FAE*, 7(2): 9–18.

Noam, E. M. (1998) *Telecommunications in Latin America*, New York: Oxford University Press.

Noam, E. M., and Baur, C. (1998) "Introduction", in E. Noam (ed.), *Telecommunications in Latin America*, New York: Oxford University Press, pp. ix–xx.

O'Brien, R., and Clement, A. (1999) "The Association for Progressive Communications and the Networking of Global Civil Society: APC at the 1992 Earth Summit", *Association for Progressive Communications*, available at: www.apc.org/about/history/apc-at-1992-earth-summit

Pinch, T., and Bijker, W. (1986) "The Social Construction of Facts and Artifacts: Or How the Sociology of Science and the Sociology of Technology Might Benefit Each Other", in W. Bijker, T. Hughes, and T. Pinch (eds.), *The Social Construction of Technological Systems*, Cambridge, MA: MIT Press, pp. 11–44.

Pinheiro, A. and Giambiagi, F. (2000) *A Privitização no Brasil: O Caso de Serviços de Utilidade Publico*, Rio de Janeiro: BNDES.

Proenza, F., Bastidas-Buch, R., and Montero, G. (2001) "Telecenters for Socioeconomic and Rural Development", *Inter-American Development Bank*, available at: www.iadb.org/regions/itdev/telecenters/index.html

Robertson, R. (1995) "Glocalization: Time—Space and Homogeneity—Heterogeneity", in M. Featherstone, S. Lash, and R. Robertson (eds), *Global Modernities*, Thousand Oaks, CA: Sage, pp. 25–44.

Schiller, D. (1999) *Digital Capitalism*, Cambridge, MA: MIT Press.

Sorj, B. (2003) *Information Societies and Digital Divides*, Rio de Janeiro: Editora Polimetrica.

Sorj, B. and Guedes, E. (2006) *Internet na Favela: Quantos, Quem, Onde, Para Quê?*, Rio de Janeiro: Edelstein Center for Social Research/UFRJ.

Star, S. L. (1999) "The Ethnography of Infrastructure", *American Behavioral Scientist*, 43(3): 377–391.

Straubhaar, J. D. (1995) "From PTT to Private: Liberalization and Privatization in Eastern Europe and the Third World", in B. Mody, J. M. Bauer, and J. D. Straubhaar (eds), *Telecommunications Politics: Ownership and Control of the Information Highway in Developing Countries*, Mahwah, NJ: Lawrence Erlbaum Associates, pp. 3–30.

Tigre, P. (1983) *Technology and Competition in the Brazilian Computer Industry*, New York: St. Martin's Press.

Tigre, P. (1984) *Computadores Brasileiros: Industria, Tecnologia e Dependencia*, São Paulo: Editora Campus.

Trebat, T. (1983) *Brazil's State-Owned Enterprises: A Case Study of the State as Entrepreneur*, Cambridge: Cambridge University Press.

UOL (1998) *Universo Online absorve CompuServ Brasil*, available at: http://sobre.uol.com.br/ultnot/novidade/noticias/ult200498044.jhtm

Valor Online (2010) *Valor Economico Online*, available at: www.valor.com.br

Vreeland, J. (1993) *The International Monetary Fund and Economic Development*, Cambridge: Cambridge University Press.

Whyte, A. (2000) *Assessing Community Telecenters: Guidelines for Researchers*, Toronto: International Development Research Centre.

Willetts, P. (2011) *Non-Governmental Organizations in World Politics: The Construction of Global Governance*, London: Routledge.

9

THE HISTORY OF THE INTERNET IN ESTONIA AND POLAND

Katarzyna Kamińska-Korolczuk and Barbara Kijewska

Introduction

More than a quarter of a century ago, Estonia and Poland became democratic states again, and have since been subject to complex Europeanization processes (Mrozowska 2012: 195–213) including media and Internet markets. Broadly speaking, using cultural criteria, both countries belong to the same cultural circle, or area—namely, Central Europe. However, there are obvious differences between the two states that cannot be underestimated. Such differences result from different histories, differently shaped national and religious identities, not to mention the lack of any similarity between the respective national languages. One common thing that definitely connects the two countries is the fact that they regained independence after a period of existence in the sphere of influence of the Soviet Union (USSR)—Poland achieving independence in 1989, and Estonia in 1991.

At the end of the twentieth century, Estonians and Poles fought for independence, not for the first time. After World War I, Poland regained its independence,[1] and Estonia, for the first time in history, began existence as an independent state. The period of sovereignty did not last long, because Germany and Russia have never abandoned the desire to manage this part of Europe. As a result of a secret additional protocol of the Molotov–Ribbentrop Pact, an international agreement was struck between the Third German Reich and the USSR, defining the impact zones of both powers, with Estonia and Poland both assigned to the Russian zone of influence. Estonia was annexed to the Soviet Union in 1940, becoming one of the fifteen republics, although Estonians and some states have never recognized this annexation. During the Yalta Conference from 4 to 11 February 1945, the fate of this part of Europe was sealed (Hiden *et al.* 2008; Smith *et al.* 2002: xix–xx). As far as Poland is concerned, although after the end of World War II it did not become a part of the Soviet Union, it remained politically and economically dependent on the USSR. However, for both Estonia and Poland, this period was marked by lack of freedom of expression and the introduction of repressive and preventive censorship, the implementation of the centrally planned economic model, and comprehensive public supervision. Neither the Estonian Soviet Socialist Republic nor the Polish People's Republic was fully sovereign.

The wave of changes that led to the collapse of the USSR's guided management system in Central Eastern Europe began in Poland. On 4 June 1989, a partially free parliamentary election took place. The Solidarity Electoral Committee, opposing the Communist government, won the election, despite the fact that elections were not fully democratic. The 1989 parliamentary election and the presidential election in 1990, victorious for Lech Walesa, are the events that gave rise to the Third Republic of Poland and became benchmarks. Lech Walesa's name, and the word "Solidarity", written in a special font, symbolized the struggle for liberation from the influence of the USSR by the Eastern bloc countries. For their part, Estonians regained control of their country in 1991. For this part of Europe, the so-called "Singing Revolution" became a symbol of victory, which also helped to regain the independence of Lithuania, Latvia, and Estonia (Vogt 2005: 20–31).

Against this background, this chapter presents an analysis of how the two countries rebuilt free media—in particular, how they developed the infrastructure necessary for development of the Internet and how they have used its potential. The studies described here have a defined geographical range covering the territories of Poland and Estonia, which have been members of the European Union since 1 May 2004. Estonia is one of the smallest countries, inhabited by just over 1.3 million people. Since 1 January 2011, it has also been a member of the euro zone. It is a multinational state in which the Russian-speaking minority is the largest, and is more than 25 percent of the whole population (Statistics Estonia 2015). Poland, in turn, is a nationally homogeneous state, inhabited by over 38 million people, in which national minorities account for less than 1 percent of all citizens (Główny Urząd Statystyczny 2014). So far Poland has not adopted the common EU currency—the euro.

After regaining independence, the two countries started reforms aimed at rebuilding their ruined economies. The predatory policy of the USSR, the isolation of countries behind the Iron Curtain from modern technologies, and impoverishment of their societies adversely affected the social, economic, and political condition of these countries. As Mart Laar (2007), two-time Prime Minister of Estonia, stated: "The Soviet command economy had ruined Estonia's environment, and the infrastructure was in catastrophic shape." It seems that the countries' authorities introducing reforms after regaining independence were inspired by the idea: "When everything is destroyed, all options are open." To this day, there has been much controversy concerning the reforms (Clemens 2001; Smith 2001).

The introduced economic and social changes were not without influence on the media market, for which systemic transformation meant privatization and concentration (Dobek-Ostrowska 2011; Vihalemm 2002). Specific social division also affects the structure of the media market in Estonia (Kamińska-Korolczuk 2014: 109–140; Kamińska-Moczyło 2015: 79–101). Russian-language newspapers are prepared, and programs in Russian are broadcast for a large part of the residents of Estonia who often do not have civil rights (Vetik 2011). Broadcasts from the neighboring Russian Federation also reach the territory of Estonia. Such a split affects many problems arising in the public sphere (Kamińska-Moczyło 2014b; Lagerspetz and Vogt 2013: 58–66; Smith and Hiden 2012: 26–46).

Such relationships between the media and the world of politics were the subject of classic research by Daniel Hallin and Paolo Mancini (2004). The framework proposed in Hallin and Mancini's typology is, however, not ultimately helpful in determining the type of media model present in these countries. Polish reality is close to the model of polarized pluralism, while the Estonian one seems to be closer to democratic corporatism. These models do not exactly describe the reality, because they do not take due account of the factors that characterize this geopolitical area and specific characteristics of each country.

Although, in general, the Estonian and Polish media use global patterns, connections created during the system transformation left their permanent trace, and still influence the media market in Poland and Estonia. Political parallelism, which is one of the four dimensions of the media system according to Hallin and Mancini, occurs in each of these countries. In Estonia, however, it is incidental, because the most effective defence against the excessive influence of politics on the media is a developed principle of self-control of the media. Estonia belongs to countries with greater journalistic discipline, and standards of conduct of journalists are contained in the Code of Press Ethics introduced in 1998 (Kamińska 2007). In Poland, the nature of relations between the media and the political world still leaves much to be desired (Dobek-Ostrowska 2010, 2012).

The essential differences in the degree of the media use in the concerned countries occur mainly due to the level of newspaper readership. Estonia belongs to the countries with one of the highest levels of readership in Europe (Milosevic *et al.* 2014: 38). This results from social habits developed historically by successive authorities and the Lutheran Church, often changing on the territory of present-day Estonia. Nordic, German, and Russian influences caused the common awareness of a national Estonian identity, which only evolved at the end of the nineteenth century. Nevertheless, the need to emphasize this separateness had a stimulating influence on the development of reading skills and the development of the press market (Kamińska-Moczyło 2015). The press enjoys freedom in Estonia—in the World Press Freedom Index ranking (2015), prepared by Reporters Without Borders, Estonia ranks tenth among all countries of the world. In both Estonia and Poland, constitutions are the superior legal acts guaranteeing freedom of expression. Estonia does not have an Act concerning the press, and legal regulations that determine the framework within which the media and journalists should function are very scattered. In Poland, the Act of 26 January 1984 Press Law is in force. It covers, *inter alia*, the rights and obligations of authors and publishers, rules for the use of the information given to the media, etc. It is repeatedly emphasized, even so, that the legislation contained in the Act is not adequate to the situation with which broadcasters and recipients of the dynamically changing media have to deal every day, and many issues are not regulated at all (Sobczak 2008). In 2003, 70 percent of Estonians read paper editions of daily newspapers, which placed Estonia above Belgium or France, and placed it alongside the Federal Republic of Germany, the Netherlands and Scandinavia (Vihalemm 2006: 20). In Poland, in the same year, according to the Polish Readership Survey, 32 percent of adult Poles regularly read a daily newspaper (jz 2003). More than a decade later, the most popular way to read newspapers is online, which is done by as many as 76 percent of readers (Eurostat Database 2015). The interest in the daily press has not diminished, but the carrier has changed—Estonians willingly use electronic devices to read the press, and the Estonian Foreign Affairs Minister, in his speech in the Estonian parliament in Riigikogu, acknowledged that use of the Internet is a fundamental human right (Paet 2013).

In Poland, readership diminishes and printed press stock dwindles, but this does not translate into an increase in *online* readership. The readership traditions in Poland have never been very large, which resulted in the lack of regularity in use of the electronic press. On average, 56 percent of citizens use electronic devices for reading news posted online, but only 12 percent of users of electronic media pay for the content made available by the editors of e-editions (Centrum Badania Opinii Społecznej 2015: 12). In this respect, however, the Polish reader does not differ from other consumers of electronic press in Europe, where on average 11 percent declare that they pay for access to digital editions of the press (Milosevic *et al.* 2014: 16).

Television and radio consumption is at the same high level. Television, as a medium with the highest use rate, is watched by 83 percent of Estonians and Poles (Eurobarometer 2014: 5–12). Nonetheless, the differences in the reception of TV over the Internet are visible. Some 25 percent of Estonians and 17 percent of Poles watch TV in this way. In both countries, radio audience ratings are much higher than the average for European Union countries and amount to 93 percent for Estonia and 90 percent for Poland. The index of confidence in the media (summarized for television, radio, written press, the Internet, and social networks) is at a similar level. One-third of Estonians and Poles declare that they trust the media, especially radio (in Estonia, 69 percent, and in Poland, 61 percent) (Eurobarometer 2014: 13).

The development of the Internet in this part of Europe was hampered. Estonia and Poland, as countries belonging to the Eastern bloc, separated from Western Europe by the Iron Curtain, were subject to export controls of dual use goods and a ban on exports of sensitive technologies. Pursuant to the international agreement of the Coordinating Committee for Multilateral Export Controls (COCOM) access to, *inter alia*, modern technologies was blocked for states that were not members of this international organization (Bertsch 1981: 67–82). The Internet was one of them. In spite of this, in the 1980s, scientists attempted to develop modern forms of communication in this embargoed part of the world. In 1986, in Warsaw, a network node BBS (bulletin board system) was created. Over time, BBSs were created in various cities in Poland. The sysops, as the administrators of the system were called, were journalists, academics, or people connected with the information technology (IT) services market. It was possible to use the network thanks to the number belonging to Polish Telecom—that is, a joint-stock company of the state treasury. The company operates today as Orange Poland joint-stock company. It is the biggest Internet Service Provider in Poland. In the 1990s, and at the beginning of the twenty-first century, Polish Telecom made the HIS-NT terminal (Home Internet Solution) available to customers, which allowed constant access to the Internet on an analog telephone line or, since 2013, the FTTH (Fiber to the Home) connection for individual customers. The network allowed connecting to a computer plugged into it, in which information in text form was written (Janus 2001). Poland became a member of the American network associated with IBM, as well as the European Academic and Research Network (EARN) in April 1990, and the first technical Internet connection in Poland was established on 17 August 1990 between the Department of Physics, University of Warsaw, and Copenhagen in Denmark (Juza 2011: 8). Estonians from 1989 to 1990 also used Fidonet: residents of Tallinn, thanks to the favorable geographical location and proximity to Finland, were able to use a dial-up connection (Pakstas and Pakstiene 1993: 62). Estonian academics established the first Internet connection between Estonia and Sweden in April 1992 (Högselius 2005: 106). In the 1990s, Estonian Telecom (Eesti Telecom) became a monopolist of international and local fixed-line telephony. The process of privatization led to licensed mobile operators. Now Estonia is one of the countries with the highest rates of mobile telephony penetration.

Generally, in the last decade of the twentieth century, in the majority of European countries there was a telecommunications monopoly. Phone calls were expensive, and the liberalization of the services offered by this sector was introduced gradually (Piątek 2010: 165). Networks established in various academic centres, such as EARN, or JANET (Joint Academic Network) created by British scientists, as well as crucial for the development of Internet service EUnet (European Unix Network), which initially united several states located in the northern part of Europe, and which was later acceded by Estonia, became the cornerstone of the global network of transferring information.

Initially, the demand for network services was not big. Apart from academic circles, the communication capabilities of the new technologies were underestimated. At the beginning of 1991, when networking was established in Poland by means of an Internet connection, using the TCP/IP standard (Transmission Control Protocol/Internet Protocol), it did not arouse interest. The research among Polish Internet pioneers conducted by Juza (2011: 13–19) indicated that there was a large need among scientists to move this modern technology beyond university circles. The pioneers tried to get a broader audience interested in new communication capabilities. Striving for the maximum simplification of the language, in which the user could communicate with the server, the reduction of communication costs resulted in rapid development of the Internet technology also in Estonia and Poland. In the early 1990s, along with the provision of new tools, such as IP, webpages, browsers, and e-mail, the Internet evolved from the primary function of the electronic mail exchange among scientists and specialists to a mass communication platform and means also in this part of the world. Government policies have supported the creation of start-ups and the development of the IT sector. It is worth mentioning that Estonians have achieved many successes in the development of IT services, and Skype is arguably one of the best-known instant messengers. Skype was founded as one of the products developed by an Estonian start-up company of programmers from Sweden and Denmark. Skype was created by Niklas Zennstrom from Sweden and Janus Friis from Denmark in cooperation with Estonians Ahti Heinle, Priit Kasesalu, and Jaan Tallinn (Thomann 2006).

One of the most famous Estonian information technology scientists, Linnar Viik, former advisor to the Prime Minister of Estonia on ICT, innovation, research and development, and civic society issues, and now a lecturer and member of the board of the Estonian IT College (*The Economist* n.d.) notes: "For other countries, the Internet is just another service, like tap water, or clean streets. But for young Estonians, the Internet is a manifestation of something more than a service—it's a symbol of democracy and freedom" (Kingsley 2012).

He adds that the Internet gave Estonians a chance to return to the Western world, and the boom in the IT market resulted from the necessity—the state, and people, did not have money to buy new technologies. Therefore, they themselves have become entrepreneurs from whom the world will buy new technologies (Kingsley 2012).

Skype was sold to eBay in 2005, for $2.6 billion. Jaan Tallinn, one of the founders of Skype, stresses that start-ups allowed the creation of a new class of Estonian investors. They have been giving their experience and knowledge to develop the idea of country innovative-ness (Tegmark 2015). Income from the sale facilitated the development of new projects.

The history of the Web in Estonia began in the early 1990s. Estonians did not benefit from the Finnish offer of using their old telephone lines. They decided to rely on new technologies. And though now the most popular browser in Estonia is Google, at the beginning Estonians had their own browser—Mozaika. Internet portals in Estonia started their operation in the late 1990s. Today, the most influential is the news portal Delfi, established in 1999. The portal publishes information not only in Estonian, but also in the Latvian, Lithuanian, English, Russian, Polish, and Ukrainian languages. The reviews posted directly under some articles on the Delfi portal often cause disputes, which are widely commented on by the public, and have even led to court proceedings (Balcytiene 2005; Golubeva 2005). In Poland, commercial portals have been created since the late 1990s. The first was, operating until now, Wirtualna Polska, established in 1995, and Onet.pl, which was created two years later. Leading Polish Internet portals publish information only in Polish, because, as already mentioned, Polish society is rather homogeneous. Electronic versions of printed newspapers have appeared since 1997; the first was the electronic issue of *Gazeta Wyborcza*.

A quarter of a century has passed since the countries under discussion gained independence, and at the same time, started to implement Internet technologies. Although the development of the Internet in Estonia and Poland falls in the same period, differences in widespread use have persisted for years (Figure 9.1). In terms of Internet use by the public in 2014, Estonia was in tenth position among 28 countries of the European Union. The average for the EU countries was 84 percent, and in Estonia, 88 percent. In Poland, in turn, the percentage of Internet users was 77 percent and this placed it in 21st place (Figure 9.1).

The comparison of online activity shows that Estonians are more active than Poles in each of the activities (Table 9.1). According to Eurostat Database (2015), the differences range from 4 to as many as 29 percentage points. In both countries, Internet users most often use the Internet to search for information, use e-mail, and read free news sites, newspapers, and news magazines. For young users (16 to 19 years of age), the most popular activity is participating in social networks; it concerns, respectively, 95 percent of Estonians and 86 percent of Poles. Young people also twice as often publish entries on social networks and play games online.

Activity on the Web for Estonian and Polish Internet users does not differ from global Internet consumption patterns. According to the Alexa ranking (2016), the most popular website is the Google search engine, followed by global social network sites (SNS) like Facebook and YouTube. The following places are taken by national infotainment portals and service portals—sales and classified advertising services. In the case of Estonia, these are Delfi.ee, Postimees.ee, and cv.ee, while in Poland, these are allegro.pl, onet.pl, and wp.pl.

Twitter (a micro-blogging platform) has become an increasingly important element of the architecture of the new media in this part of Europe, especially as a tool for political and marketing communication. Currently, in Poland, Twitter has a share of internauts of over 16 percent (Wirtual Nemedia 2016), which represents four million users. Before the advent of the US social media (Facebook, Snapchat, Instagram, YouTube) and micro-blogs (Twitter),

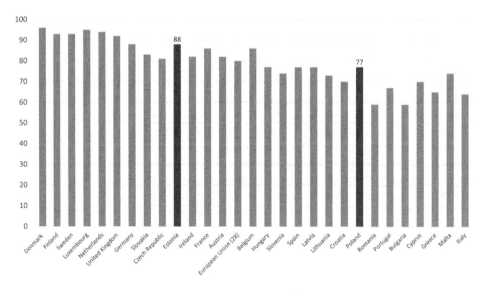

Figure 9.1 Individuals: Internet use in the EU in 2014 in percent

Source: Adapted from Eurostat Database (isoc_ci_ifp_iu).

Table 9.1 Internet activities in Estonia and Poland in 2014 in percent

Internet activities	Estonia		Poland	
	All	16–19	All	16–19
Creating websites or blogs	17	12	2	8
Finding information about goods and services	76	92	50	63
Listening to web radio	29	88	19	59
Making an appointment with a practitioner via a website	8	17	5	1
Participating in social networks (creating user profile, posting messages or other contributions to Facebook, Twitter, etc.)	51	95	37	86
Playing networked games with other persons	9	40	7	32
Playing/downloading games, images, films, or music	41	81	28	72
Posting messages to social media sites or instant messaging*	43	87	42	91
Reading online news sites/newspapers/news magazines	76	88	47	59
Reading/downloading online newspapers/news	71	78	36	46
Sending/receiving e-mails	72	90	53	83
Telephoning or video calls	43	61	28	57
Uploading self-created content to any website to be shared	26	60	12	40

* Data from 2012.

Source: Own study on the basis of Eurostat Database (2015).

indigenous projects had high popularity in Poland. However, when faced with global competition, they lost their significance. For example, in the case of SNS NaszaKlasa, launched in 2006, the number of individual users fell from 11 million in 2008 to below one million now. An equivalent of a US micro-blog was Polish social site BLIP (Bardzo Lubię Informowac Przyjaciół), which was established in 2007 and closed in 2013. The first Polish social instant messenger was a text messenger created in 2000 called Gadu-Gadu, which in record time had more than ten million users, but after a change in ownership it has experienced a steady decline in messenger users.

Currently, Estonia is often referred to as "E-stonia" due to the level of computerization of public life in the country. Thanks to the extensive educational campaign, computerization of society has progressed quickly, and has been effective. Since 1996, a government program called "tiger jump" has been implemented in Estonia (Krull and Trasberg 2006: 14). Its purpose was to provide all schools with an Internet connection, as well as a widely understood IT education of society. The country is conducive to the development of innovation. The rules for the operation of private enterprises were simplified, a transparent tax system was introduced, and communication with the authorities was improved, which has resulted in the expansion of the start-up network. The range of activity of these start-ups by definition was not limited to Estonia. World-known applications are, for example, Transferwise, which enables crowd-sourced international money transfers, or VitalFields, a tool which helps manage a farm. In Estonia, a new group of investors has developed, aimed at sharing experience and increasing innovation. Currently, the center for the technology industry is Garage48 (n.d.), established in the Science Park Tehnopol in Tallinn (Tehnopol n.d.). Tallinn has the largest number of start-ups per capita worldwide.

In Estonia, there is no room for social exclusion due to lack of access to the network or lack of skill to use the Internet. The whole territory of Estonia is within range of wireless Internet; in the capital, a free Wi-Fi network can be easily accessed. Security of information has been a state priority since 2005, and the government started introducing various programs dealing with the development of IT. One example is the program from 2007, which establishes the development of the IT society. In 2014, work on the effective implementation of the guidelines of the Estonian Research and Development and Innovation Strategy 2014–2020 started. The main purpose of the strategy is to use available information communication technology resources and other advanced technologies to create favorable conditions for securing the competitiveness of the economy, supporting the effectiveness of public administration, and improving the availability of information and other resources offered by the state for citizens and expats living in Estonia. The objectives are to be achieved by building: "A base for the ultra-fast Internet network, allowing at least 60 percent of all Estonians to use the Internet every day, strengthening of capabilities of cross-border e-services and so on" (Estonian Research and Development and Innovation Strategy 2014–2020 n.d.).

On the initiative of the Ministry of Economic Affairs and Communications (2014), the program Digital Agenda 2020 for Estonia is currently being implemented, which fits into the European Commission's Europe 2020 Strategy (European Commission 2010). The Estonian strategy describes what technological and organizational conditions will be developed so that citizens have the opportunity to find out, and are able to decide when, by whom, and for what purposes, data collected about them are used (Ministry of Economic Affairs and Communications 2014). The Polish National Broadband Plan, implemented by the Ministry of Administration and Digitization of Poland, fits into the same European Strategy (2014). The plan, called in short Digital Poland, focuses mainly on the development of infrastructure. Newly built fiber-optic networks are supposed to help in the expansion of access to the Internet and the development of services, including e-administration (Halicki 2015). The development of e-government is an essential task for member states of the European Union. The application of information technologies aims at improving access to services, which in turn should result in financial savings for the state management, and the involvement of citizens in the process of shared responsibility for functioning of the state.

In Estonia, the developed technological base allows for continuous improvement of policy related to citizens' right to access public information. The basic legal acts governing access to public information are the Constitution of the Republic of Estonia (1992), and citizens' rights included in its Article 44, as well as the Public Information Act (2000). In accordance with §29 of the Act, the holder of public information is required to publish the data on their websites, using radio, television, or printed press. The Act obliges the most important public institutions, such as the offices of the Riigikogu, the President, and the Office of the Ombudsman or government agencies to maintain websites to disseminate information. Similar guidelines also apply to local government bodies. Websites have to provide information about the activities of state administration and disseminate information in its possession. Institutions' websites cannot contain outdated, false, or misleading information. As with all regulations, in terms of access to information, certain restrictions are in force. They pertain to making classified information related to state secrets accessible. In Estonia, citizens have at their disposal the official portal eesti.ee. In addition to the information published by national authorities, it contains a bookmark with forms allowing users to send a digitally signed document (Chlewicki *et al.* 2010). Residents of Estonia use the identity card with a chip. That card in Estonia is more than a proof of identity. Thanks to it, citizens and representatives of national minorities living in Estonia have access to all the information that the state has gathered about them. Such an ID is also a patient card or a card to the bank account.

The introduction of the e-government principles in Poland started at a similar time as Estonia. In 2001, the Sejm (the lower chamber of the Polish Parliament) passed the Public Information Act (2001). The Act states that: "Any information about public affairs is public information within the meaning of the Act and is subject to availability and reuse in accordance with the principles and procedures laid down in this Act." Everybody has the right to access public information. It is, however, as in other countries, subject to restriction in the interest of the state. One of the activities that was to serve the idea of improving the functioning of e-government in Poland was the launch of the Public Information Bulletin (BIP) in 2003, which consists of web pages on which public authorities and other entities performing public tasks publish information free of charge. Moreover, since 2005, the Act on the computerization of the operation of bodies fulfilling public tasks has been in force, under the terms of which a citizen can electronically contact public institutions, and this electronic correspondence is treated on a par with the traditional one. The project, named e-Poland, being part of the European development plan e-Europe, has not achieved complete success in Poland yet. Polish citizens, compared to Estonians, use the Internet much less often for contacting public institutions (Figure 9.2). The main reason is the small amount of available e-services useful to citizens and mental resistance to digital (intangible) documents. This resistance occurs both at the level of administration as well as of the supplicant. It is particularly evident in small towns. In the ranking eGovernment Benchmark (European Commission 2014), Poland achieved the rate of 76 percent in terms of online availability of useful public

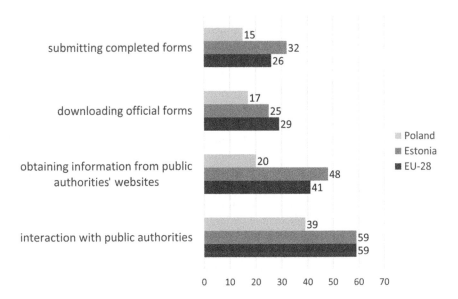

Figure 9.2 E-government activities of individuals via websites (last 12 months) in the EU, Estonia, and Poland in 2014 in percent

Source: Adapted from Eurostat Database (isoc_ciegi_ac).

services (including the establishment of own business, loss and finding a job, change of residence), while Estonia had an 87 percent rate, with the average for the whole European Union of 72 percent.

As we can see, citizens of Estonia are ahead of Poland in all activities in which services available online are used. A particularly large disproportion between the countries is evident in obtaining information from public authorities' websites. Nearly half of Estonians use this form of access to information, and almost two-thirds come into interaction with public authorities by means of the Internet. Involvement in the process of co-management of the state is also reflected in the high percentage of voter participation in elections (60 percent). Even so, this does not mean that Estonians engage themselves in the operation in the framework of organized structures of the social organization type (18 percent) (Kamińska-Moczyło 2014a).

Estonia became the first country in the world to introduce i-voting. By 2015, eight different elections took place using this method of voting. It was possible to use i-voting for the first time in the local election in 2005, and two years later in the parliamentary election. In 2009, i-voting proved useful in the election to the European Parliament. I-voting can be accessed by anyone who has a computer modem and is able to confirm his or her identity with an ID card. In the first local election in which it was possible to vote using the Internet connection, 1.9 percent of voters used this method. In the next local election in 2009, it was already 15.9 percent, and reached 21.2 percent in 2013. The number of users of i-voting in the parliamentary elections increased in a similarly dynamic way: 5.5 percent in 2009, 24.3 percent in 2011 and as many as 30.5 percent of all citizens voting in 2015 used the Internet while marking their ballot. The turnout in the elections to the European Parliament is the lowest among all achieved in the elections carried out in Estonia. In 2014, it amounted to 36.5 percent. Nevertheless, among those who cast their votes, as many as 31.3 percent did so online (Vabariigi Valimiskomisjon (VV) n.d.). Interestingly, as is apparent from the statistics provided by the Estonian National Electoral Commission (VV), Internet voters in Estonia represent every age group. In the last election held in Estonia, the parliamentary election in 2015, both in the age group 25–34 and 55 and over, 25 percent of people used i-voting, 24 percent of people were aged 35–44, and 19 percent were 45–55 years old. People aged 18–24 cast votes least often in this way. The data show that, when voting via the Internet was enabled, men were more active when the proportions of both sexes were comparable, and in 2015, 53 percent of online voters were women and 47 percent were men (VV). In Poland the possibility of voting via the Internet has not been introduced yet.

In spite of such a high voter turnout in Estonia, when compared with other states in this part of Europe, it is difficult to get the impression that the country is generally the leader of all citizens' initiatives. Even though it is a leader among the countries implementing new forms of communication in axis society-state, in the public sphere Estonians' activity remains low. It seems that reasons for the lack of Estonians' engagement in organized social life is distrust for actions in the public sphere inherited from the previous regime, perceived as forced actions, and, perhaps, focusing primarily on own development. It should be remembered that during the Soviet domination in the area, the structures of social life and activities in which citizens had to participate were imposed on them. These kinds of activities lacked the basic asset of social action—spontaneity. Probably currently it is not the only motivation, because we can see that—just as in Poland—Estonian society is still a work in progress (Kamińska-Moczyło 2014a).

The research carried out on the telecommunication service market in Estonia shows that Estonia has the highest broadband penetration rate among all countries of Eastern Europe

(Budde 2014). Slightly more than 84 percent of Estonians had access to broadband Internet in 2014 (Eurostat 2015) (Figure 9.3), which in Estonia reaches a speed of up to 30.23 Mbps, which places it in the 36th place out of 199 countries in the world (Budde 2014). In 2014 in Poland, broadband reached speeds lower than the average in Europe (Halicki 2015), and 76 percent of households had access to it (Eurostat 2015). Currently, the fastest growing segment of telecommunication services is, in turn, wireless data transmission (Kolenda 2014). Various companies offering telecommunication services compete in the Polish market. The most frequently chosen Polish telecommunication suppliers are Orange Poland—24.5 percent, Plus—11.9 percent, Netia—8.9 percent, Play—7.9 percent, and UPC—6.4 percent (Swiostek 2015). In Poland, there are also many companies that offer access to mobile Internet. By far the most popular suppliers are Blueconnect, iPlus, Orange, and Play. Netia is also one of the longest operating Internet providers in Poland. Other companies such as Dialog and Multimedia Poland, initially buying local companies, are building their own network, and offer access to the Internet with different bandwidths. UPC competed on the market as a television network which also offered Internet services (Maludziński 2012). The leading supplier of telecom services in Estonia is TeliaSonera, the majority shareholder in the mobile operator EMT—the leading mobile operator in Estonia. EMT and the fixed network operator Elion are both leaders in their respective markets.

Technological development is followed not only by favorable conditions for social development, but also by all kinds of threats. In 2007, the matter of the transfer of the Bronze Soldier monument located in Tallinn by the Estonian authorities had wide repercussions (Ehala 2009). The monument was moved from the park in the center to the cemetery for Soviet Army soldiers. The consequence was the "first war in cyberspace"—a month-long paralysis of the state, carried out with the help of Internet connections. Servers of the most important public administration institutions and banks were blocked by the data sent by hackers, which made the smooth functioning of the state impossible. It was possible to observe for the first time how the state—so dependent on computer connections—could cope with attacks on

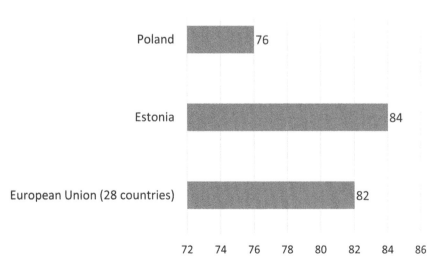

Figure 9.3 Households with broadband access in the EU, Estonia, and Poland in 2014 in percent

Source: Adapted from Eurostat Database (isoc_pibi_hba).

its institutions. In 2007, various countries, not only European ones, declared assistance in the fight against hackers. International cooperation in the fight against crime in cyberspace will probably be crucial in upcoming decades. So far, it has not been established who has been responsible for the state paralysis of 2007.

A significant problem in the face of rapidly evolving technology is the protection of children and young people from inappropriate content that may be found on the Web. Estonia, in which the right to freedom of expression is regarded as one of the most important values of a democratic state, decided to censor certain content available on the Internet. In 2010, the websites that make it possible to take part in gambling were blocked (Kaas 2010). The recently introduced Gambling Act (2008: 1) contains a provision saying that websites proposing gambling services have to be on servers registered in Estonia. An equally important issue is the fight against cybercrime, particularly with regard to the data provided by users of the network. It pertains not only to sensitive official information, but also to private photographs, movies, or statements posted on social networks. Freedom of expression, which in democratic states is constitutionally guaranteed, becomes a real threat when unauthorized persons start abusing it (Kasprzyk *et al.* 2015: 527; Tołpa *et al.* 2015: 542). The Internet becomes for many a synonym of addiction, although that is material for a separate study.

Conclusion

Even two decades ago, the Internet was a technological novelty, available to a small group of enthusiasts. Currently, the most widespread access to it determines the level of modernity of the state. Both in Estonia and in Poland, an increase in the number of network users has been noticed, although Estonia is consistently ahead of Poland in this respect (Figure 9.4). It seems, however, that this gap will be reduced, which can be inferred from the data

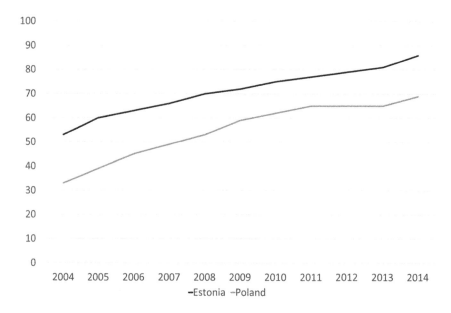

Figure 9.4 Individuals: Internet use in Estonia and Poland in 2004–2014 in percent

Source: Adapted from Eurostat Database (isoc_ci_ifp_iu).

characterizing the youngest Internet users. In the age group 16 to 19 years of age, 100 percent of Estonians and 99 percent of Poles use the Internet (Eurostat Database 2015).

Both in Estonia and in Poland, pioneering attempts to use technological capabilities to transfer data appeared at a similar time. Legal regulations, which govern the functioning of the Internet service market, are similar in both countries because the provisions contained in the documents common to all European Union countries determine the standards. Yet there is a difference in the saturation and frequency of use of Internet technology in the general population between the countries concerned. It seems, however, that the equalization of the number of users of this medium is only a matter of time. Today, young generations are rooted in the network that they use in their private, social, and professional lives. Nevertheless, it is difficult to predict whether an increase in the number of users will translate into an increase in trust in the use of the Internet in the process of the strengthening of civil society, which is a problem, according to this analysis, mainly in Poland.

Naturally, it would be easy to conclude that such widespread inclusion of society in making use of the services available via the Web was easier in Estonia than in Poland because of the small number of people who had to be convinced about modern technologies. And perhaps this statement is quite right, but what has happened and is happening in Estonia cannot be reduced to such a generalization. Estonians saw in the development of innovative technologies the chance to strengthen their sovereignty. One of the priorities was independence from a powerful neighbor who was not willing to completely give up its influence in this part of the world. The development of civil society, which was also influenced by the Internet, has been the best investment and safeguard against possible unwanted interference in the internal affairs of Estonia. Poland, the sixth state in terms of population in the European Union, still has a lot to do to modernize communications between the state and the citizen. Examples of EU countries such as the United Kingdom, Germany, and France show that even where the population is very large, beneficial results in the process of the computerization of social life can be achieved.

The Internet is called the all-medium, comparing it to a cobweb girding everyone and everything (people, things, and services). It is a cobweb that provides information, allows for better communication, expands the provision of services—but also, gradually, becomes a threat to unwary users. The future will show if this cobweb will continue helping societies to develop further or will become a double-edged sword. It will depend on the wisdom of users and authorities managing this human activity zone, which, in principle, is closely connected to freedom of expression.

Note

1. In 1772, the first partition took place, and in 1795, the third, total partition of Poland took place. Against the will of the authorities and the people, the land of the Polish state was taken over by three powers: Russia, Austria, and Prussia. Poland regained its independence only on 11 November 1918.

References

Alexa (2016) "The Top 500 Sites on the Web", *Alexa*, available at: www.alexa.com/topsites (accessed 3 February 2016).

Balcytiene, A. (2005) "Media Modernisation and Journalism Cultures in the Baltic States and Norway", in R. Bærug (ed.), *The Baltic Media World*, Riga: Flera Printing-house, pp. 169–185, available at: http://providus.lv/article_files/2151/original/Baltic_Media_World_novaks.pdf?1343297033 (accessed 23 July 2015).

Bertsch, G. K. (1981) "U.S. Export Controls: The 1970's and Beyond", *Journal of World Trade*, 1: 67–82.

Budde (2014) "Estonia—Fixed Broadband, Digital Economy and Digital Media—Statistics and Analyses", *Budde*, available at: www.budde.com.au/Research/Estonia-Digital-Economy-and-Broadband-Market-Insights-Statistics-and-Analysis.html#sthash.aTx6jZWO.dpuf (accessed 22 July 2015).

Centrum Badania Opinii Społecznej (2015) *Raport: Internauci 2015*, Warsaw: Centrum Badania Opinii Społecznej.

Chlewicki, M., Kędzierska, A., and Oranowski M. (2010) *Elektroniczna administracja w Estonii*, available at: www.repozy torium.uni.wroc.pl/dlibra/docmetadata?id=oai:www.repozytorium.uni.wroc.pl:34511 (accessed 22 July 2015).

Clemens, W. C. (2001) *The Baltic Transformed: Complexity Theory and European Security*, Lanham, MD: Rowman & Littlefield Publishers.

Constitution of the Republic of Estonia (1992) "Constitution of the Republic of Estonia", *Office of the President*, available at: www.president.ee/en/republic-of-estonia/the-constitution/index.html (accessed 27 July 2015).

Dobek-Ostrowska, B. (2010) "System partyjny a media w Polsce—zależnosci i relacje", *Media Studies*, 2(41), available at: http://sm.id.uw.edu.pl/article.php?date=2010_2_41&content=dobek&lang= pl (accessed 28 July 2015).

Dobek-Ostrowska, B. (2011) *Polski system medialny na rozdrożu: Media w polityce, polityka w mediach*, Wroclaw: Wyd. UWr.

Dobek-Ostrowska, B. (2012) "Italianization (Or Mediterraneanization) of the Polish Media System? Reality and Perspective", in D. C. Hallin and P. Mancini (eds), *Comparing Media Systems Beyond the Western World*, Cambridge: Cambridge University Press, pp. 69–108.

The Economist (n.d.), "About Linnar Viik: Estonian Internet Guru", *The Economist*, available at: www.economist insights.com/speaker/2978 (accessed 28 January 2016).

Ehala, M. (2009) "The Bronze Soldier: Identity Threat and Maintenance in Estonia", *Journal of Baltic Studies*, 40(1): 139–158.

Estonian Research and Development and Innovation Strategy 2014–2020 (n.d.) *Knowledge-Based Estonia*, available at: www.hm.ee/sites/default/files/estonian_rdi_strategy_2014–2020_en.doc (accessed 23 March 2016).

Eurobarometer (2014) "Media Use in the European Union", *Eurobarometer*, available at: http://ec.europa.eu/ public_opinion/archives/eb/eb82/eb82_media_en.pdf (accessed 23 July 2015).

European Commission (2010) "Europe 2020: A Strategy for Smart, Sustainable and Inclusive Growth", *European Commission*, available at: http://ec.europa.eu/europe2020/index_en.htm (accessed 22 July 2015).

European Commission (2014) "EU eGovernment Report 2014—Country Factsheets E-Government", *European Commission: Digital Economy & Society*, 22 May, available at: https://ec.europa.eu/digital-agenda/en/news/ scoreboard-2014-country-factsheets-e-government (accessed 21 July 2015).

Eurostat Database (2015), *Eurostat Database*, available at: http://ec.europa.eu/eurostat/data/database (accessed 15 July 2015).

Gambling Act (2008), "Gambling Act", *Riigikogu*, available at: www.riigiteataja.ee/en/tolge/pdf/530102013030 (accessed 5 August 2015).

Garage48 (n.d.) "Estonian Tech Startups", *Garage48*, available at: http://hub.garage48.org/estonian-startups

Główny Urząd Statystyczny (2014) "Ludnosc. Stan i Struktura Ludnosci Oraz Ruch Naturalny w Przekroju Terytorialnym", *Główny Urząd Statystyczny*, available at: http://stat.gov.pl/obszary-tematyczne/ludnosc/ ludnosc/ludnosc-stan-i-struktura-ludnosci-oraz-ruch-naturalny-w-przekroju-terytorialnym-stan-w-dniu-31-xii-2014-r-,6,17.html# (accessed 18 July 2015).

Golubeva, M. (2005) "EU Accession Debate on the Internet in the Baltic States: Own Heterogeneous Messages?", in R. Bærug (ed.), *The Baltic Media World*, Riga: Flera Printing-house, pp. 158–168, available at: http:// providus.lv/article_files/2151/original/Baltic_Media_World_novaks.pdf?1343297033 (accessed 23 July 2015).

Halicki, A. (2015) "Do 2020 Roku Każdy Polak z Dostępem Do Szerokopasmowego Internetu o Szybkosci co Najmniej 30 Mb/s", *Newseria Biznes*, 17 March, available at: www.biznes.newseria.pl/news/a_halicki_do_ 2020_roku,p560091228 (accessed 25 July 2015).

Hallin, D. C., and Mancini, P. (2004) *Comparing Media Systems: Three Models of Media and Politics*, Cambridge: Cambridge University Press.

Hiden, J., Made, W., and Smith, D. J. (eds) (2008) *The Baltic Question during the Cold War*, New York: Routledge.

Högselius, P. (2005) *The Dynamics of Innovation in Eastern Europe: Lessons from Estonia*, Cheltenham: Edward Elgar Publishing.

Janus, R. (2001) "10 Lat Internetu w Polsce", *PC World*, 17 August, available at: www.pcworld.pl/news/ 31762/10.lat.Internetu.w.Polsce.html (accessed 22 July 2015).

Juza, M. (2011) "Społecznosc Polskich Pionierów Internetu I Jej Dokonania. 20 Lat Internetu W Polsce", *Studia Socjologiczne*, 3(202): 7–28.

jz (2003) *PAP information*, available at: http://czytelnia.onet.pl/0,838260,wiadomosci.html (accessed 5 December 2003).

Kaas, M. (2010) "Maksuamet Asub Blokeerima Välismaiseid Netikasiinosid", *Postimees*, 1 March, available at: http://majandus24.postimees.ee/231006/maksuamet-asub-blokeerima-valismaiseid-netikasiinosid (accessed 22 July 2015).

Kamińska, K. (2007) "Obiektywizm I Samokontrola W Wypowiedziach Estońskiej Prasy Codziennej Na Początku XXI W", in L. Pokrzycka and W. Mich (eds), *Media a Demokracja*, Lublin: Wydawnictwo Uniwersytetu Marii Curie-Skłodowskiej, pp. 283–292.

Kamińska-Korolczuk, K. (2014) "Estonia", in. A. Matykiewicz-Włodarska and M. Slufińska (eds), *Systemy Medialne Państw Unii Europejskiej: Nowe Kraje Ckowskie*, Torun: Wydawnictwo Adam Marszałek, pp. 109–140.

Kamińska-Moczyło, K. (2014a) "Aktywnosc Społeczna W Estonii I Na Łotwie W: Aktywizacja Społeczeństwa Obywatelskiego", in A. Wojtaszak (ed.), *Wydarzenia na Kijowskim Euromajdanie*, Szczecin: Volumina.pl Daniel Krzanowski, pp. 163–177.

Kamińska-Moczyło, K. (2014b) "Edukacja I Imigracja W Nowych I Starych Państwach Unii Europejskiej. Przykład RFN I Łotwy", in M. Boryń, B. Duraj, and S. Mrozowska (eds), *Polityka Młodzieżowa Unii Europejskiej*, Torun: Adam Marszałek, pp. 83–101.

Kamińska-Moczyło, K. (2015) "Die Entwicklung der Medienmärkte von Estland und Lettland", in M. Łosiewicz and A. Ryłko-Kurpiewska (eds), *Media. Business. Culture. Social and Political Role of the Media*, vol. 2, Media, Business, Culture, Gdynia: Kinvara Co. Galway, pp. 79–101.

Kasprzyk, R., Maj, M., and Tarapata, Z. (2015) "Przestępstwa W Cyberprzestrzeni. Aspekty Technologiczne I Prawne", in E. W. Pływaczewski, W. Filipkowski, and Z. Rau (eds), *Przestępczosc W XXI Wieku. Zapobieganie I Zwalczanie. Problemy Technologiczno-Informatyczne*, Warsaw: Wolters Kluwer, pp. 527–599.

Kingsley, P. (2012) "Battle for the Internet: How Tiny Estonia Stepped out of USSR's Shadow to Become an Internet Titan", *The Guardian*, 15 April, available at: www.theguardian.com/technology/2012/apr/15/estonia-ussr-shadow-internet-titan (accessed 29 January 2016).

Kolenda, P. (ed.) (2014) "Raport: Perspektywy rozwojowe. Mobilne online w Polsce—IAB Polska", *Interactive Advertising Bureau Polska*, available at: http://iab.org.pl/wp-content/uploads/2014/09/raport_iab_polska_mobile.pdf (accessed 22 May 2015).

Krull, E., and Trasberg, K. (2006) "Changes in Estonian General Education from the Collapse of the Soviet Union to EU Entry", *ERIC: Institute for Education Sciences*, available at: http://eric.ed.gov/?id=ED495353 (accessed 24 July 2015).

Laar, M. (2007) "The Estonian Economic Miracle", *The Heritage Foundation*, available at: www.heritage.org/research/reports/2007/08/the-estonian-economic-miracle#_ftn2 (accessed 22 July 2015).

Lagerspetz, M., and Vogt, H. (2013) "Estonia", in S. Berglund, J. Ekman, K. Deegan-Krause, and T. Knutsen (eds), *The Handbook of Political Change in Eastern Europe*, 3rd edn, Cheltenham: Edward Elgar Publishing, pp. 51–84.

Maludziński, M. (2012) "Dostawcy Internetu w Polsce—Plusy I Minusy Ich Usług", *PC World*, 11 September, available at: www.pcworld.pl/news/385333/Dostawcy.Internetu.w.Polsce.plusy.i.minusy.ich.uslug.html?test=yesinfo_idg.html.html.html (accessed 28 January 2016).

Milosevic, M., Chishlom, J., Kilman, L., and Henriksson, T. (2014) *World Press Trends 2014*, WAN-IFRA, available at: www.arpp.ru/images/123/51253_WAN-IFRA_WPT_2014.pdf (accessed 28 July 2015).

Ministry of Economic Affairs and Communications (2014) "Digital Agenda 2020 for Estonia", *Ministry of Economic Affairs and Communications*, available at: www.riso.ee/en/information-society (accessed 20 July 2015).

Mrozowska, S. (2012) "Europeanization of Middle-Eastern Europe as a Subject of the Studies of Political Science", in M. Baranowska-Szczepańska and M. Gołaszewski (eds), *Modern Research Trends of Young Scientists: Current Status, Problems and Prospects*, Poznań: Wydawnictwo Naukowe Wyższej Szkoły Handlu i Usług, pp. 195–213.

Paet, U. (2013) "Paet in Riigikogu: Human Rights are Constant Theme in All Areas of Foreign Policy", *Postimees: Estonian News*, available at: http://news.postimees.ee/1146570/paet-in-riigikogu-human-rights-are-constant-theme-in-all-areas-of-foreign-policy (accessed 12 July 2015).

Pakstas, A., and Pakstiene, S. (1993) "Computer Networks in Estonia, Latvia, and Lithuania", *Computer*, 26(9): 53–64.

Piątek, S. (2010) "Polityka Komunikacji Elektronicznej Unii Europejskiej", in A. Jurkowska and T. Skoczny (eds), *Polityki Unii Europejskiej: Polityki Sektorów Infrastrukturalnych. Aspekty Prawne*, Warsaw: Instytut Wydawniczy EuroPrawo, pp. 165–189.

Public Information Act (2000) "Public Information Act", *Legal Text*, available at: www.riigiteataja.ee/en/eli/514112013001/consolide (accessed 24 March 2016).

Public Information Act (2001) "Ustawa Z Dnia 6 Wrzesnia 2001 R. O Dostępie Do Informacji Publicznej", *Internetowy System Aktów Prawnych*, available at: http://isap.sejm.gov.pl/DetailsServlet?id=WDU20011121198? (accessed 22 July 2015).

Smith, D. J. (2001) *Estonia: Independence and European Integration*, London: Routledge.

Smith, D. J., and Hiden, J. (2012) *Ethnic Diversity and the Nation State: National Cultural Autonomy Revisited*, New York: Routledge.

Smith, D. J., Pabriks, A., Purs, A., and Lane, T. (2002) *The Baltic States: Estonia, Latvia and Lithuania*, London: Routledge.

Sobczak, J. (2008) *Prawo Prasowe: Komentarz*, Warsaw: Wolters Kluwer.

Statistics Estonia (2015) "Population by Ethnic Nationality", *Statistics Estonia*, available at: www.stat.ee/34278/? highlight=Russians (accessed 12 May 2015).

Swiostek, A. (2015) "Ranking Polskich Miast I Dostawców Internet", *Komputer Swiat*, available at: www. komputerswiat.pl/artykuly/redakcyjne/2015/06/ranking-polskich-miast-i-dostawcow-internetu.aspx (accessed 29 June 2015).

Tegmark, M. (2015) "Existential Risk: A Conversation with Jaan Tallinn", *Edge*, 16 April, available at: https://edge.org/conversation/jaan_tallinn-existential-risk (accessed 28 January 2016).

Tehnopol (n.d.) "Tallinn Science Park", *Tehnopol*, available at: www.tehnopol.ee/?lang=en

Thomann, A. (2006) "Skype—A Baltic Success Story", *Credit Suisse*, available at: www.credit-suisse.com/pl/en/news-and-expertise/economy/articles/news-and-expertise/2006/09/en/skype-a-baltic-success-story.html (accessed 28 January 2016).

Tołpa, T., Protasiewicz, J., Kozłowski, M., and Bułkszas, B. (2015) "Zagrożenia, Nadużycia I Bezpieczeństwo W Systemach Informatycznych A Granice Ochrony Praw Podstawowych", in E. W. Pływaczewski, W. Filipkowski, and Z. Rau (eds), *Przestępczosc W XXI Wieku. Zapobieganie I Zwalczanie. Problemy Technologiczno-Informatyczne*, Warsaw: Wolters Kluwer, pp. 540–554.

Vabariigi Valimiskomisjon (n.d.), "Statistics about Internet Voting in Estonia", *Vabariigi Valimiskomisjon*, available at: http://vvk.ee/voting-methods-in-estonia/engindex/statistics/

Vetik, R. (2011) "Statelessness, Citizenship and Belonging in Estonia", in B. K. Blitz and M. Lynch (eds), *Statelessness and Citizenship: A Comparative Study on the Benefits of Nationality*, Cheltenham: Edward Elgar Publishing, pp. 160–172.

Vihalemm, P. (ed.) (2002) *Baltic Media in Transition*, Tartu: Tartu University Press, pp. 17–64.

Vihalemm, P. (2006) "Media Use in Estonia: Trends and Patterns", *Nordicom Review*, 27(1): 17–29.

Vogt, H. (2005) *Between Utopia and Disillusionment: A Narrative of the Political Transformation in Eastern Europe*, New York: Berghahn.

Wirtual Nemedia (2016) "Twitter Z 4 Mln Polskich Użytkowników", *Wirtual Nemedia*, 27 January, available at: www.wirtualnemedia.pl/artykul/twitter-z-4-mln-polskich-uzytkownikow-coraz-wiecej-starszych-dobrze-wyksztal conych-i-z-miast (accessed 3 February 2016).

World Press Freedom Index (2015) "Details About Estonia", *World Press Freedom Index*, available at: https://index.rsf.org/#!/index-details/EST (accessed 28 July 2015).

Part 3

EARLY COMPUTER NETWORKS, TECHNOLOGY, AND CULTURE

10

MAPPING A FRENCH INTERNET EXPERIENCE

A Decade of Unix Networks Cooperation (1983–1993)

Camille Paloque-Berges

Introduction

France's developments in computer communication networks were largely determined by a governmental choice in 1978 to back Transpac, a telecom virtual circuit model, to the detriment of Cyclades, a datagram-based research model, in order to stimulate French telecommunication engineering at an international and competitive level (Schafer 2012; Vedel 1984). After a decade-long institutional battle between the national and monopolistic company France Telecom and the National Institute for Research in Computer Science and Control (INRIA), Transpac was launched and set up to host Minitel online services a few years later. While Cyclades's chief researcher Louis Pouzin was exporting across the Atlantic his datagrams technology to the Arpanet (then to become Internet) team, French computer researchers and engineers were at home, deploying an alternative network based on the Unix operating system. From 1983 on, they developed Fnet, an informal infrastructure used as the local branch of EUNet, the European Unix-based data network run from the Netherlands. Doing so, they "created a computer network social environment [. . .] with the same ingredients that would make the Internet successful later" (Bloch 2013).[1] Open, decentralized, collaborative, heterogeneous, and worldwide: its qualities appealed to the community of computer research and engineering in academic and private labs. Fnet became their unofficial Internet network provider, until the success of the Web brought along commercial and official governmental-promoted new solutions, such as Renater from 1993 on (Schafer and Tuy 2013).

The history of Unixians's computer networking collaboration may have similarities to the Arpanet's "ideal scientific community" (Flichy [2001] 2007), but if we look at Usenet, ancestor to computerized social network initiated on Unix networks, we might think differently. In France, starting and running the infrastructure was done in less than ideal conditions. I intend to show, beyond shedding light on a lesser known part of computer networks history, that Fnet was a "shadow infrastructure": an informal, experimental, and unacknowledged network of machines annexed to the existing telecom network, as well as a network of peers using and rerouting public telecom resources from the academic world. I thus look into how Fnet was managed in terms of technical and administrative infrastructure, a difficult question given that it had no official existence. This can be read as a series of "tactical" practices (de Certeau [1990] 2011), as well as processes of negotiation, in a science and technology studies perspective, both of which provide a basis for actor-network theory-type of mapping method (Latour 1987)—which I use as an analytic metaphor, but will not apply literally. Although the networking side of Unix's history is documented (Kelty 2008; Salus 1994), its local role in paving the way for the Internet internationally, as in France, remains just a hint, although vivid in protagonists' memory (Griset and Schafer 2012; Huitema 1995). Original sources in this chapter comprise archives from the Computer Lab at Cnam,[2] which hosted Fnet's administration from 1983 to 1986, as well as Usenet mail archives and oral interviews with the protagonists who supported and promoted Fnet up until 1993, when its missions shifted with the rise of the commercial Internet.

The Unixian Community and its French Members: Open Cooperation in the Margins

The Conservatoire national des arts et métiers (National Conservatory of Arts and Crafts, known as "Cnam") is a higher education establishment based in Paris. It was created in the wake of the French Revolution in 1794 to stimulate industrial innovation, and has been since a privileged public institution for applied research and continuous education in the technological field. A computing center, called Laboratoire d'Informatique (Computer Lab), was created in the 1960s with support from the Department of Applied Mathematics and Computing.[3] Its purpose was to support and manage the needs in computing resources for the teaching department, as well as general IT support for the administration. In the late 1970s and early 1980s, there was no official computer science research activity at Cnam, but a small, informal team of about four researchers, calling themselves the "Systems lab", implemented and experimented with the Unix system within the laboratory. Led by Claude Kaiser, a professor at Cnam since 1974 with a research background from INRIA,[4] and Gérard Florin, head of the Computing Lab, who had defended a thesis in computer networking in 1975, they "played a major part in the implementation of Unix, but also similar experiments with Ethernet, VAX-VMS, Unix-BSD, UUCP and then TCP/IP".[5] This early interest in versions of Unix operating systems (Unix-BSD), Unix compatible machines (VAX), and network protocols (Unix's UUCP and the Internet's TCP/IP) set the stage for the deployment of Internet networks in France.

A Unixian Case for Collaboration: Standardization and Negotiation

Unix was then a paradigm for operating systems, chosen by a myriad of academic and private computer departments and research laboratories internationally (Kelty 2008). Ken Thompson designed, at his own initiative, the system in 1969 along with Denis Ritchie at Bell Labs, the research and development department of American telecommunications company AT&T, to foster the reuse of software on incompatible machines. AT&T was forbidden to sell the operating system by a 1956 anti-trust decree restricting the company to exploit anything other than telecommunications equipment. From 1975 on, it was thus distributed to universities for a small licensing fee, along with its full source code, and was largely adopted by academia as a predecessor of the free software movement (Kelty 2008; Paloque-Berges and Masutti 2013).

Unix's success is firstly rooted in then-emerging hacker ethics: a combination of informal cooperation, autonomy from traditional hierarchies placed under the banner of computer hardware, and software experimentalism. Victor A. Vyssotsky, then a Bell Labs computer engineer, sums it up:

> When Unix evolved within Bell Laboratories, it was not a result of some deliberate management initiative. It spread through channels of technical need and technical contact. This was typical of the way Unix spread around Bell Laboratories. [. . .] it was used, modified, and tinkered up in a whole variety of organizations.
>
> (Vyssotsky in Hauben and Hauben 1997: 89)[6]

Yves Devillers[7] recalls how Unix traveled to France in a similar fashion: "It was driven by demand. If technology allowed to do it, then it was done. Everything that was doable or appropriable was." At a time when the governmental Plan Calcul (Planning for Computing, 1966–1975) was still influential, requiring public institutions to use domestic technological equipment (Mounier-Khun 2010a, 2010b; Schafer 2012; Schafer and Tuy 2013), Unix was an alternative system for hands-on experiments in software, and in accessing remote computers (Cornwall 1985). Moreover, Unix offered solutions in software portability and system standardizations to the 1970s computer industry's problems (Campbell-Kelly and Aspray 1996). Doing so, it gave a sense of community beyond "user clubs", traditionally restricted to proprietary computer systems (Mounier-Kuhn 2010a, 2010b). It thus changed the face of software development, giving hacking culture a leading role in software cooperation for establishing norms and standards (Raymond 2000). At Cnam, Kaiser was one of the main advocates for Unix as an international normative system:[8] "From the point of view of software, we must avoid anarchy and incommunicability; an effort towards standardization must be made. [Unix is] a norm [. . .] being established currently, and a lot of micro constructors offer or announce it."

Resort to Unix systems in France was complicated by the end of Plan Calcul policy, fueled by two decades of a strong-willed reorganization of technological research and development, as well as a significant drop in credit for technology equipment in the science field, and political and economic problems within Cnam: all this made the acquisition of Unix-compatible machines from American constructors difficult. Another factor was an American embargo in 1979, preventing French computer users from buying American equipment for fear it would be used to build nuclear weapons. However, the Computer Lab needed to renew its computer park—having relied for a decade on the IBM 360 (Florin 2016). The research team had been familiarized with Unix machines thanks to a visiting engineer from the Netherlands, and was looking to acquire a mini-computer compatible with the system that would meet their budget and power needs (no French machine would be eligible, as testified by Florin 2016). They acquired a DEC PDP 11/70 machine in 1979, and in 1980 a DEC VAX 11/780, PDP's successor, both "workhorse machines of the early Unix culture" (Raymond 2000), but this occurred only through a lengthy negotiation with Cnam's administration (requiring the computer be used for administration and accounting needs) and a formal and legally signed declaration that the computer would only be used for research and education purposes. Unix was implemented in the summer of 1980, running "outside of working hours".[9] Eventually, a third Unix-compatible machine was acquired with another bypass method. Indeed, a VAX 11/780 clone was produced by a British manufacturer specially to sell to countries under embargo, like France and South Africa: entitled Systime-8750, it was bought in 1981 and constructed by the Computer Lab one VAX rack at a time, "importing it piece by piece" under the radar (Florin 2016). This was the machine on which the Unix network was implemented, and coincidentally the only historic computer used by Cnam preserved by the Museum of Arts and Crafts in its reserves (Cnam's Musée des arts et métiers, the French national museum of science and technology).

Protocols for Machine and Human Communication

At first, Unix was dedicated to sharing resources on time-sharing mini-computers. At Bell Labs, Mike Lesk and David Nowitz had developed in 1976 a file transmission command into a distant machine communication protocol (Hauben and Hauben 1997: 206). Called UUCP (Unix-to-Unix Copy Protocol), it copied a file from one terminal to the other, or to a printer, but was soon appropriated to send messages between user accounts, a makeshift tactic similar to the birth of email a few years before (Hafner and Lyons 1996). Implemented into a distant Unix machines network under a "store and forward" model, this point-to-point technique sent messages to a series of connected machines so as to reach its destination. It first ran on dial-up connectivity, thus needing a telecommunication network to dial into.

The UUCP protocol was encompassed with a hacker aura and do-it-yourself technical practice: "low-speed and unreliable, but cheap [. . .] over ordinary phone lines" (Raymond 2000). Like the Arpanet, and the subsequent TCP/IP protocol that led to the Internet in 1983, UUCP was an open system running on an end-to-end model, meaning that a machine administrator could make a liaison without any authorization from a central authority. This determined the ease with which UUCP liaisons were created and spread all over the Unixian international community.

UUCP networks first entered continental Europe thanks to cooperation between an academic lab and a corporate lab. The Centrum Wiskunde & Informatica (CWI)[10] of Amsterdam University had a partnership with Armando P. Strettner from the DEC Lab at Maynard (Massachusetts, USA), a founding member of DEC Unix Engineering Group who played a major role in creating UUCPnet in the US as well as in Europe and Asia. As DEC machines were Unix-compatible, a transatlantic connection was extended between DEC Labs in Maynard and their counterparts in the computing center of CWI Amsterdam, at the instigation of Teus Hagen and Piet Berteema, a computer science researcher and an engineer.

UUCP experiments appeared at Cnam in 1982, with, in the works, the implementation of an Ethernet local network with extensions to institutional partners. While Unix network experiments were not qualified as research per se, they did fall under the category of distributed networks, process and data communication research.[11] Opening communication routes was aimed at (1) finding standards for computer networking, (2) experimenting critically with "file transfer software between connected systems on a permanent line or virtual circuit" and "certain distant commands, among which the 'Mail' command for electronic mail", and, last but not least, (3) building a network between French and American research centers.[12]

International Cooperation: A Social Network of Peers

The spreading of Unix relied on a socio-professional network of peers, supported mainly by non-profit associations due to the non-commercial nature of Unix. Indeed, the Computer Lab was strongly involved with the world of computer research[13] and user organizations, such as the US-based Unix user group Usenix, or its European and French counterparts, the European Unix Users Group (EEUG), or the French Association for Unix Users (AFUU)—

the latter born in 1982. Thus, communication between distant peers was crucial in a small international community in which everyone knew everyone (Bloch 2013), fostered by events like the 11th European Unix Systems User Group OPEN Meeting held at Cnam in April 1982 and supported by EEUG.[14] Organized by Humberto Lucas and Bernard Martin, two engineers from the Computing Lab active in the "Systems lab", it was nicknamed "Spring in Paris". The focus of the meeting was the use of Unix for the purposes of telecommunications and computer networks, with several presenting applications for Unix networking protocols (UUCP) and software (among which was the news software called Usenet).[15] At this occasion, Hagen and Berteema from CWI showcased their new UUCPnet node implemented in Amsterdam, and announced they had created an organization for supporting the spread of Unix networks in Europe, called EUnet, for the European UNIX Network. Hagen also presented and distributed software for group discussions (then called "electronic conferences") on UUCP networks, a system called Usenet that he brought back to Europe on a tape from a Usenix conference in San Francisco. This stimulated the creation of local branches in several countries in Europe, among which was Fnet a year later, with the Computer Lab at Cnam used as server backbone and administrative support. As Unixians from other establishments or organizations flocked to connect to the Cnam UUCP hub or open their own, a "hive phenomenon" was triggered by the circulation of computer engineers and scientists in France and abroad: "Everyone leaving a workplace for another wanted to connect their new workplace so as to maintain the means of communication" (Devillers 2012).

The Unixians' Internet Experience amid Other Technical and Social Networks

Unix networks emerged in cooperation but also in competition with other networks of computers. In the 1970s, they were mostly centralized and proprietary. While IBM's BITNET (EARN in Europe), UUCPnet's main rival, used a similar point and forward technique, and was widely used and tinkered with within academia, it was not born as a heterogeneous network, but relied on IBM machines only, contrary to UUCPnet, compatible with any machines with the Unix system installed. Nor was DECnet a heterogeneous network, relying solely on DEC's PDP machines, although Unix could be installed on PDPs, thus allowing UUCP connection. Unix networks were based on an open, distributed, and collaborative model, keen on including new users from many professional backgrounds. This principle materialized through the implementation of UUCP-based Usenet software, the open electronic conference system it hosted effectively supporting "global conversations" from people beyond the computer science world up to the 1990s (Rheingold 1993). Accordingly, at this point I will look more closely at the technical, but also social, constraints that accompanied the deployment of Unix networks.

Opposition and Compromise: Negotiating with "Authoritarian" Norms

The loose, informal structure of the Unixian community is key to understanding the spread of a technical network based on the social values of openness and cooperation. In a January 1984 AFUU meeting report, Humberto Lucas[16] recalls the initial project: to establish an "informal network of Unix systems with the UUCP/UUCICO protocols".[17] This informality was also political: the Unix community worked in the margins of government science and technology policies, "far from the decisions made in Brussels" (Schafer and Tuy 2013).

Devillers (2012) stresses the importance of the human factor: "one person only in the hierarchy was needed to add a node to the network", contrary to a complex vertical process of decision making imposed by institutional hierarchy. Resorting to other systems and network standards such as Unix and UUCP was thus considered as against the general technological policies in France: "In France, this spirit doesn't exist, at least for now", underlines Lucas in the report, in regard to using foreign hardware equipment or software standards. This oppositional stance doesn't mention, however, that the problem with acquiring Unix-compatible machines relied on a US government embargo on shipping computer equipment to certain countries (as decided in 1979), nor that the deployment of UUCP would need to run on protocol layer in theory rejected by Unixians, the X25 protocol. Indeed, X25 was the official protocol used on European networks like Transpac, under the umbrella of the Open Systems Interconnection (OSI) normative model recommended by the International Telecommunication Union[18] after many negotiations and compromise (Schafer 2012). Compromise in technological negotiations is thus an important notion that is often shadowed by protagonists, amid their strong emphasis on resisting and bypassing institutional constraints.

The ease of installation for UUCPnet was apparent only. One of the first obstacles was an auto-dialing modem necessary to "call" a peer's number and create a new node in the network: it was strictly limited by European telecom standards, and forbidden by national telecom companies. Such modems were distributed by Hagen, initiator of EUnet at CWI in Amsterdam, at the occasion of "Spring in Paris" in 1982 to participants who took them home to their lab upon their return, allowing several places in Europe to connect to UUCPnet (Hauben and Hauben 1997: 128–130), but a step behind than in the United States, as underlined by Lucas in the 1984 AFUU reunion report.

Following the makeshift spirit of the Unixians, the deployment of a UUCP network was to rely at first on the existing infrastructure of telephone lines, in an act of derouting considered as a misappropriation, just as a few years before at the Bell Labs (Hauben and Hauben 1997: 128). As a result, much of Usenet's news distribution was implemented without explicit approval wherever a UUCP site was born, and was mostly invisible to the organizations' authorities and accounting. French Unixians justified their derouting with a criticism of the archetypal model of hierarchical and central authority implemented in France's technological policy (and especially in the new field of computer-based telecom networks). According to Devillers and Bloch, Transpac was a "bureaucratic creation" based on a principle of "descending pyramid", which Unixians fought against. By derouting the national telecoms network, they also challenged post-war engineering work models, which applied new management and marketing techniques to shape the social (Vedel 1984) and the user itself with appropriate and closed technologies—the Transpac-based Minitel was an archetype in that regard (Thierry 2012). By contrast, Unixians defended an open model where users could shape back the technology they appropriated, and were doing so themselves by replacing Minitel terminals with computers.

Moreover, an effort was made to make EUnet and Fnet compatible with other norms and not a stand-alone network, as testified by memos from the Computer Lab. This challenge would prove acute for running messaging applications, one of the main uses of the UUCP networks. Transpac's use of the official mail protocol X400, supported by the European OSI norm, was mocked as too normative by Unixians, but was necessary nonetheless to allow dialog between different servers to establish the international mail transfer protocol SMTP.[19] The distributed nature of UUCP networks allowed the different terminals to connect to different types of liaisons, but international liaisons could only be made through the EUnet backbone in Amsterdam. Thus, one of the main challenges in the following years would be to maintain the use of the UUCP protocols while at the same time complying with French and European norms.

Openness and Exclusiveness: The Intricate Relationship between Unix and the Internet

The term "Internet" was officially released in 1982 to name the state of computer networks interconnection made possible by the TCP/IP protocol (implemented on the Arpanet in January 1983). The convergence between Usenet and the Internet takes root within a common technical ethics involving autonomy to install software from the hardware infrastructure, and "no global control at the operations level" (Leiner *et al.* 1997: 104). The Arpanet and Unix appeared complementary for the spread of computer internetworking technologies throughout the 1980s, because the system was compatible with many machines present on the international network. Internet protocols were integrated in the Berkeley version of Unix (BSD) in 1976: this gave a running start to computer network technologies in the Unixian world, "a key element in the Internet's successful widespread adoption" (Leiner et al. 1997: 105). As a result, an estimated 98 percent of US computer science departments had adopted the code in the early 1990s (Kelty 2008).

Despite bridges to the Internet created from the EUnet node, allowing French Unix users to retrieve Internet-run STMP mail on Fnet, the first direct liaison from a French computer to the Internet waited until 1988. It was set up at INRIA, where the Fnet administration had migrated in 1986, through a partnership with the American National Science Foundation Network, the main Internet backbone from that year until the mid-1990s. One of the first non-US countries to benefit from a direct liaison, France's access was made possible in big part thanks to the reputation that INRIA's Cyclades had acquired with the datagram model a decade earlier (Renard 2013). INRIA financed the transatlantic liaison for the profit of public research centers in France. Every public organism benefiting from the liaison had to be certified to NSF, while private clients had to continue using the Fnet network through the EUnet backbone in Amsterdam (Huitema 1994).

There was nonetheless a running rivalry between the Arpanet/Internet social world, considered the high-class of computer network research, and UUCP/Usenet's, described by its protagonists as the "Poor Man's Arpanet" for the "commonfolk of the computer community" (Hafner and Lyons 1996; Hauben and Hauben 1997: 122–124). Hacker folklore likes to describe it as a network for "upstarts" with "primitive tools" (Raymond 2000) keen to perform hacker exploits (Cornwall 1985). There was only a faint echo of this rivalry during our interviews, alluding to the fact that great French researchers in network computing, such as Cyclades's Louis Pouzin and Gilles Khan, were more interested in theoretical network models and the Internet than in using UUCP/Usenet. Nonetheless, a parallel can be drawn between American Unix users' defiance towards the Arpanet/Internet and Fnet users' criticism of Transpac: while UUCP networks were completely decentralized and self-regulated at the servers' level, Arpanet answered to the US Defense Communications Agency; in turn, French Unixians were critical of Transpac's agreements with the French Defense Department, creating a fear of general network surveillance (Devillers 2012), a decade after the SAFARI affair.[20]

The network class struggle postulated by the first generation of Usenet users was also a way to create an identity based on social and technical differentiation towards other computer networks, in particular, to rethink the limits of the computer networks research and engineering to be more inclusive of general computer users outside the Unix-oriented computer science community. Usenet was aimed first at Unix toolbuilders, a social network "for and by the users" (Rheingold 1993: 105, 126). The focus on "users" shows an acute and early understanding of what computer networks were bound to become, a communication media reinvented by users who are less and less specialized in computer technologies, and looking to expand applications and uses outside the computer-centric world (Abbate 1999). As such, from the start Usenet prided itself on openness and inclusivity, as claimed by the first Usenet manual, "Invitation to a General Access UNIX Network", distributed as a handout to Usenix conference participants in 1979, and circulating further into the many Unixian meetings (Hauben and Hauben 1997). The Usenet software itself was an exception to other "electronic conference" systems, usually closed and limiting the number of participants (Quarterman 1990). The network thus comprised diverse participants, mostly academic but also business-oriented, connecting from within their organization or, with the advances of micro-computers in the 1980s, from outside, as users could dial in the Usenet server at a distance.

French "Administratrivia" Networks: Beyond the Ideal "Commonfolk of the Computer Community"

Principles of openness did not provide actual solutions to manage UUCP networks locally between academia and the corporate world. The history of Fnet as an informal organization shows the practical complexities of a human network running a technical network without formal support, and in a social environment where the organizational side of managing a network could be regarded as "administratrivia"—a pun made by Devillers when reporting management problems on the Usenet Fnet group in the early 1990s.

The Computer Lab at Cnam handled Fnet from 1983 to 1986, with Humberto Lucas presiding over the ad hoc loose organization, running the backbone and managing subscriptions with the help of fellow engineer Daniel Lippman. Distributing different volumes of data to members and billing them was the main issue. Because of the UUCPnet decentralized model, some sites were bigger as they were servers rerouting data from the European EUnet hub in Amsterdam to end-user terminals (Fnet members). Unix machines at Cnam played that role; soon, Usenet data in particular became a burden, as the social computer network was expanding rapidly and internationally, adding many newsgroups each year. The Computer Lab had to cover the cost of high-capacity servers and transmission lines on a tight budget, and kept Usenet group subscriptions to a minimum (restricted to groups in the comp.* and sci.* hierarchies, hosting discussions about computers and sciences). Moreover, because of administrative constraints, it could not bill Fnet members outside of a fixed rate rigid template. Lucas issued, as early as 1984, a call for participation (a financial supplement to cover the rise in traffic data), especially directed towards member organizations with looser accounting rules (industrial labs), but to no avail. This was a source of discord among the Fnet community—similar to the high bills problem produced by UUCP connections at the Bell Labs a decade earlier (Hauben and Hauben 1997: 128). This, as well as the lack of assistance and acknowledgment the Computer Lab and their employees received from within the establishment, drove Lucas to resign and leave the public sector. Fnet's administration was then transferred at INRIA, handled by Devillers's team, with about 40 machines in about 27 organizations connected to the network.[21] This is far more than the alleged 15 connections initially described in the official history of INRIA, which also disregards the contribution of Cnam's team prior to 1986 (Beltran and Griset 2007).

The resource and billing management problems continued after 1986, despite the INRIA team's choice to bill Fnet members according to their actual use. The high rise in subscription demands, yet scant effort shown by the members to participate in the technical management of Usenet, accentuated during the late 1980s and constituted a new administration problem. In 1985, the UUCP American network was requalified as a "commercial network" (like Transpac), while a new dedicated Usenet and mail service was opened to offer access to users outside academia (Quarterman 1990; Salus 1994). This seems to have changed users' perceptions of the network, less as a collaborative project and more like a service for users. Fnet itself had become the first semi-commercial, although non-lucrative, provider for French academia and beyond, and its managers were disappointed to see Fnet members turning into clients. Recursively, members, considering the cost of subscription was high, were expecting better service without connection delays of bugs. Usenet's primary ethics of "open participation" was at stake: it was born as a toolbox, an unfinished code full of bugs tackled by users (Pfaffenberg 2003: 24), with a focus on informal use and tinkering rather than formal committees and arguments (Hauben and Hauben 1997). But the more the user base grew, the less participation was offered, which proved an acute problem as Fnet remained informal and experimental. Between 1986 and 1993, Fnet was administered by the small team of "Research and Development Expertise Committee"[22] at the INRIA headquarters, in addition to taking care of new functions since 1988: Internet's IP addressing, routing, and domain name systems. Moreover, supporting organizations like AFUU started to focus on developing services for commercial users, and moving away from Fnet.[23] Eventually, with the growing success of the Internet and the general professional and popular turn towards TCP/IP Internet networks, UUCP networks were used less and less into the 1990s. Fnet's difficult management, with IT overload and high bills, was considered an abusive provider, having taken advantage of their virtual monopoly in the pre-Web era (traces of these discussions and conflicts can be found in the fnet.* newsgroups on Usenet). This reputation increased as new providers (commercial, such as Oléane, or non-profit, such as FDN—French Data Network) started to emerge in the early 1990s.[24] When the newly created RIPE organization (Europeans IP Networks) relieved the Fnet team of their IP attribution and routing functions in 1992, Fnet had just become a legal non-profit organization ("association loi 1901"). When INRIA decided to officially back another, IP-based, academia network called Renater in 1993 (Schafer and Tuy 2013), and after "five years of lengthy discussions" with the Fnet team (Renard 2013), Unixians's "Internet experience" had started a steep decline.

Mapping Unix Networks: Several Electronic Frontiers

The ethics of participative effort put forward by Unixians as a social and technical identity giving reason to the spread of their networks is in relative accordance to what will be formulated in the mid-1990s as the "electronic frontier", built by "pioneers": "the few hardy technologists who can tolerate the austerity of its savage computer interfaces, incompatible communication protocols, proprietary barricades, cultural and legal ambiguities, and general lack of useful maps or metaphors" (Kapor and Barlow 1990).

While the autonomous, anti-institutional cyberspace utopia has been reviewed critically by Internet studies researchers, it might be useful to analyze how aspects of the so-called "electronic frontiers" actually did serve as "useful maps or metaphors" for organizing com-munication networks and pushing them towards institutional forms. To sum up, how did the shadow infrastructure of Fnet and Unix networks in France produce elements useful for mapping and reflecting on the new computerized communication networks outside of the state telecoms monopoly?

Early Usenet Maps: Keeping Up a Public Network Directory

The Google archive of Usenet, going back to 1981,[25] reveals how Unix networks were spread in the United States and Europe through a network of Unix machines, a spread documented in the form of UUCP and Usenet logical maps (the network represented as links between machines) featured in a special "20 Year Usenet Timeline" compiled by Google at the moment of the archive release on the Web in 2001.[26]

The first logical maps were sent to Usenet users via the group net.general and net.news (general news about Usenet) as a way to track the progression of the network, and then through a dedicated group called net.news.map from January 1982 to January 1985 (net.news.map 1982–1985). They functioned as a utility tool, a directory to map out Usenet links for sites wishing to be grafted to the network, but they also reinforced Usenet as a public network: "Public at all times, and so any site which is on Usenet is expected to make public the fact that they are on Usenet, their Usenet connection and their name, phone number and electronic address of the contact for that site for the Usenet directory" (Hauben and Hauben 1997: 125).

The first Usenet map was produced and released by Bill and Karen Shannon from the Department of Zoology at the University of Toronto in 1982:[27] "this is a USENET map, NOT a UUCP map. It shows only NEWS connections AS WE EXPECT THEM TO BE ON FEB. 1" (Shannon and Shannon 1982). In July that year, an update was provided by Mark Horton, offering the same reminder with instructions for reading the maps and using them as a probe to contact Usenet sites unsure of their status:

> Remember, USENET is defined as all sites getting net.all. If you are reading this, the machine you are reading it on should probably be on the map. But sites that only speak uucp for mail (not news) or that only get local groups or a select set of groups from net.all are not on the map.

The Shannons' and Horton's clarifications reveal how intricate the network can be as a pile of protocols with common functionalities while operating through different systems and applications. The Usenet map message was used as a tool to verify if the logical map covered the territory of effective Usenet sites and users. Thus, it was not only referential, but also pragmatically recursive, through recurrence and expansion every time the message was posted in the newsgroup.

The first European Usenet address appeared in a 1982 September update, a site called "ukc" for the University of Kent at Canterbury in England. In late December, the first official "USENET map for Europe" was sent, showing twelve nodes: one in the UK (Kent), one in Denmark (Copenhagen), and the other ten distributed all around the Netherlands, as CWI Amsterdam was becoming the central Usenet European backbone for EUnet. The February 1983 map showed a new site at the University of Edinburgh, a partner of the Computing Lab. Thanks to these maps, it is possible to identify exactly when the French UUCP–Usenet nodes were opened at Cnam in March 1983, at a moment when the European penetration of Usenet accelerated with 41 Usenet sites, featuring among them a cluster of five Unix machines at Cnam (Berteema 1983). Figure 10.1 shows the Usenet post announcing on 10 March the surge in European Usenet sites (we extracted the very first lines, with the

```
Message-ID: <bnews.mcvax.2402>
Newsgroups: net.news.map
Path: utzoo!decvax!harpo!npoiv!hou5f!ariel!vax135!floyd!cmcl2!philabs!mcvax!piet
X-Path: utzoo!decvax!harpo!npoiv!hou5f!ariel!vax135!floyd!cmcl2!philabs!mcvax!piet
From: mcvax!piet
Date: Fri Mar 18 01:03:20 1983
Subject: Europe map
Posted: Thu Mar 10 15:30:55 1983
Received: Fri Mar 18 01:03:20 1983

The eunet (European Usenet) is expanding rapidly now.
Therefore the last version of the eunet map, that Mark Horton
put on the net is already far out-of-date. So here's the latest
one, as it is per March 10:

-------------------------------------------------------------------------------

Comments: Phone numbers are in CCITT format: +country-code area-code number

Comments: Newsnet sites are those with whom news (at least eunet) is
          exchanged, Mailnet sites are those with whom mail is exchanged.

Name: mcvax
Organization: Mathematical Centre
Contact: Teus Hagen, Piet Beertema
Phone: +31 20 5924127
Postal-Address: Kruislaan 413, NL-1098 SJ Amsterdam, Netherlands
Electronic-Address: mcvax!teus  mcvax!piet
Newsnet: diku dutesta edcaad mcpdp34 mcpdp45 philabs philmds sara70
         ukc uvapsy vu44 vub ztil
Mailnet: cern45 decvax diku dutesta edcaad ikogsmb IM60 kunivvl mcpdp34
         mcpdp45 nlgvax philabs philmds riv02 sara70 ukc uvapsy vmucnam
         vu44 vub ztil
Comments: mcvax is the gateway to EUNET, the European Usenet.


Name: vmucnam
Organization: CNAM - Laboratoire d'Informatique
Contact: Humberto Caria Lucas
Phone: +33 1 2712414 ext 438
Postal-Address: 292 Rue Saint Martin, F-75141 Paris CEDEX 03, France
Electronic-Address: mcvax!vmucnam!humberto
Newsnet: mcvax
Mailnet: mcvax

Name: sol1
Organization: CNAM - Laboratoire d'Informatique
Contact: Humberto Caria Lucas
Phone: +33 1 2712414 ext 438
Postal-Address: 292 Rue Saint Martin, F-75141 Paris CEDEX 03, France
Electronic-Address: mcvax!vmucnam!sol1!fmartin
Newsnet:
Mailnet: vmucnam

Name: lsicnam
Organization: CNAM - Laboratoire d'Informatique
Contact: Humberto Caria Lucas
Phone: +33 1 2712414 ext 438
Postal-Address: 292 Rue Saint Martin, F-75141 Paris CEDEX 03, France
Electronic-Address: mcvax!vmucnam!humberto
Newsnet:
Mailnet: vmucnam

Name: iiecnam
Organization: CNAM - Laboratoire d'Informatique
Contact: Humberto Caria Lucas
Phone: +33 1 2712414 ext 438
Postal-Address: 292 Rue Saint Martin, F-75141 Paris CEDEX 03, France
Electronic-Address: mcvax!vmucnam!humberto
Newsnet:
Mailnet: vmucnam

Name: sm0cnam
Organization: CNAM - Laboratoire d'Informatique
Contact: Humberto Caria Lucas
Phone: +33 1 2712414 ext 438
Postal-Address: 292 Rue Saint Martin, F-75141 Paris CEDEX 03, France
Electronic-Address: mcvax!vmucnam!humberto
Newsnet:
Mailnet: vmucnam
```

Figure 10.1 Two extracts of an 18 March 1983 Usenet message, entitled "Europe map"

announcement and confirmation of CWI Amsterdam as the EUnet backbone, and the very last lines, showing the entrance of Cnam into the network).

The map details the coordinates of the networked sites. The first coordinate is the name of the node through which point-to-point connection will go. From here on are displayed the connection links for two different services of communication to the other machines on the network: UUCP-supported Usenet services (newsnet), and SMTP-supported email services (Mailnet), the first protocol bridge opened by the UUCP networks. The names of the nodes often include an abbreviation of the organization hosting the site ("mc" for Mathematical Center at CWI) that can be followed by the machine hardware type ("vax" for the Unix-compatible VAX 11), but variants also apply when there are several users from the same organization and the same machines. The now five Cnam machines (vmuCnam, sol11, lsiCnam, iieCnam, and sm0Cnam) connect to both newsnet (via mcvax) and Mailnet (via mcvax in Amsterdam or their own local node at Cnam, vmuCnam).

There were only a handful of machines on Usenet addresses, among which was one named after Francis Martin,[28] a collaborator from INRIA, and located on a machine at the Computer Lab. This shows the intricacy of Usenet accounts that are shared and rerouted though the UUCP network, and another one testifying about a node at IRCAM (the French Institute for Research and Coordination Accoustic/Music). Martin, along with Devillers at INRIA, Patrick Sinz of IRCAM, Pascal Levasseur, and Sylvain Langlois at their respective computer technology companies Métrologie and Bull, were the initiators of the expansion of Usenet through Fnet, as accounted in AFUU's reports that compile the same information as in the logical maps. A year later, in 1984, Usenet French sites had effectively sprung from public organizations (CNET Issy Moulineau, for instance) as well as corporate (CGE, Bull, Métrologie, for instance). It is possible, though, to speculate that far more UUCP users would access Usenet data through bulk transfer from the main sites.

A Territory of Confusing Routes

In the early 1990s, just before the Web started to attract a mass of new users from outside the computer science and engineering world, mapping UUCP and Usenet networks was still a current practice—for example, in the Usenet group comp.mail.maps, coordinated by the University of Rutgers, which listed the UUCP maps by country (UUCP Mapping Project) (comp.mail.maps n.d.). A search for Fnet maps yields long lists of French Usenet and UUCP subdomains with an international link outside Europe, but also bridges to other French computer networks, like EARN, running on IBM's native protocol as well as X25. Since Usenet had a new protocol replacing UUCP with the Internet-friendly NNTP, and since France was directly connected to the Internet in 1988, mapping Unix network routes could be done via following the IP addresses as well. Celebrating a "routing folklore", users would analyze electronic messages routing metadata generated (a "traceroute" automatically inscribed in the message header) in which IP addresses could be read. Some cases of twisted routes were considered an absurd logic that users liked to qualify as a "routing game": messages emitted from France to France would take a detour through foreign countries via so called "exotic routes"; some were stuck in a loop between two IP addresses, thus entering a "ping pong game" (see the discussions on the topic of routing in Michot 1992). Michel Fingerhut, a pioneer Fnet user at IRCAM, started to track in 1994 such traceroute absurdities[29] when he observed between other oddities that one message he sent to Ministère de la Culture would go out to the US, back to the Netherlands, and then to France. He jokingly qualified this routing with the code name "22 à Asnières", derived from a famous comical skit describing the intricate administrative and technical complexities of the old French telephone commuted system (Raynaud 1966).

The absurd routing games revealed a major issue of the computer network landscape. Indeed, public organizations did not have a common Internet provider: for instance, INRIA was provided by Renater (from 1993), while Ministère de la Culture was provided by Fnet. Recourse to a simplification of Internet routage through a Commercial Internet Exchange hub (CIX), a precursor for internetwork connection architecture and business models for Internet providers already in use in the USA, was difficult and always delayed by the fear of a "cultural choc"[30] between the French national and centralized model, and the American commercial and decentralized model. The years 1993–1994 saw active cooperation for a French CIX and the release of a first draft under the name "F-GIX", thanks to a formal agreement between Oléane and Renater,[31] but this was not immediately implemented. In 1993, early French Fnet and Internet adopters had an insight view of the difficult construction of "the wonderful information highway that is bound to lead us towards a Radiant Future",[32] as France was entering its own Information Highways decade.[33] But Fnet administrators themselves were lagging behind in terms of infrastructure building. At the same time, Usenet was going through an international crisis, known as the "Eternal September", which symbolized the popularization of the Internet being considered a risk for users of the pre-Web computer networks golden age (Schafer *et al.* 2015).

Epilogue: The Electronic Frontier as a Political Metaphor

From the start, Unixians were part of the self-perceived digital avant-garde willing to create new institutions supported by an "electronic democracy" (Huitema 1995; Lévy 1997). Expanding the computer network by means of human and technical skills became synonymous with progress in a globalized world. Usenet aficionados defended a "netizen" identity (Hauben and Hauben 1997), considering the social network a "network nation" on its own (Raymond 2000), or even more radically a "worldnet" for "a society that hopes to progress" through general access to technological tools and cooperation helping to best wield these tools (Hauben and Hauben 1997: 133). Similar to the probing function of messages showing logical maps described earlier, Usenet news were thought of as a means to see how far and wide, and to whom, the network reached. A student experiment recounted by the Haubens shows how this probing function was accompanied by a postulate: the more difficult that electronic messages were to reach a destination, the less democratic the country was. Thus, Usenet and the Internet were seen as an enlightenment process for parts of the world still under undemocratic darkness—a rationale vivid in the last years of the Soviet bloc, during which this experimentation was conducted. Within this experiment, a French perspective was given:

> A response from a French user explained how the government charged a lot of money for an Internet connection in France and thus discouraged usage: "It's cheaper to send a 'hello' to someone in the US than to someone 5 kilometers from my desk!," the French user wrote. "If you have a 'stupidity chapter' in your paper, this could fill a few lines".
>
> (Hauben and Hauben 1997: 38)

This government charge, stemming from Transpac's unwilling support of Fnet and the Internet, is one of the reasons for the "routing game" evoked earlier, and was a flaming topic of discussion on the Fnet Usenet groups. According to Christian Huitema, one of the instigators of the first TCP/IP connection within the Fnet network, France's access to the Internet was twice as low as Germany's, three times as low as the UK's, and twenty times as low as the USA's: "It's a shame. To be honest, I think this is proof of an underdevelopment, even of a reluctance against the modernization of the world and the huge openness provided by computers" (Huitema 1995).

This techno-enlightenment ideology is present and diffused all through the Unixian networks. But it doesn't take into account "internal borders" recreated by Unixians and their peers on Usenet that have to do with actual inequality in terms of access, participation in arguments, and decision-taking (Healy 1996; Johnson and Post 2001). If Usenet was considered a virtual agora that would allow the Internet to open an electronic public sphere, its culture of flaming polemical debates makes the "electronic conference" network unreducible to a rationalistic, procedure-driven public discourse. Among "net.wars", the power dominance of the servers' administrator was strengthened, and old users were using experience and technical skills to ward off new users (Grossman 1998). In our interviews, genuine interest for the non-specialist user proved scarce, indeed; the UUCP/TCP/IP networks were seen first and foremost as a liberating tool from the constraints of the French institutional powers, to the benefit of the computer science (and computer businesses) community. Finally, following Fred Turner's study of the evolution of computer libertarian hobbyists and hackers, and his analysis of their participation in the rise of a new "virtual class" (Turner 2006a, 2006b), it would be important to follow the trajectories of Unixians to understand how the ideals of progress through the electronic frontier evolved in the Internet economy of the 1990s and 2000s.

Conclusion

It is notable that the user figure has so much importance in Unix's own worldview on human–computer interaction and was a principle for founding Usenet, the biggest pre-Web computerized social network. Meanwhile, the Arpanet development processes were much more hesitant towards integrating inventions stemming from the user point of view, despite the great part it actually played in the success of its innovations (Abbate 1999; King et al. 1997). This is one of the main reasons why Unix networks were at the avant-garde of the Internet experience that we all share today. But the example of French Unix users connecting their community to an international communication computer network reveals how the idea of using the network remains a specialist perspective, relying on active participation and to the benefit of a professional community. However, this definition of network user engagement was political. Striving for autonomy and independence from national and local technological policies while engaging in smart tinkering and negotiation with hardware and software norms meant believing in bottom-up user innovation instead of relying on top-down planning.

The remapping of France with UUCP networks is one of these useful metaphors that show the empowerment of new technological expertise, original because they did not start from a power standpoint. Unixians themselves didn't "take power" as the Internet "founding fathers" did, if we believe the power positions held currently by key figure Vinton Cerf, Vice President and Chief Internet Evangelist at Google. But they did, by diverting institutional authorities, contribute to creating a new place for new power centralities. From "Science: The Endless Frontier" (which, in 1945, gave a running start to the development of techno-science, including global communication networks)[34] to the Information Highways plan of the 1990s, do computer networks give technological progress a new meaning, supported by an "endless electronic frontier"? Previous logics of domination (social, economic, political) did not disappear, but a space was open for information organization to thrive on a supranational level, leading to the rise of organizations for Internet standards (such as RIPE, ICANN, and IETF), which independence from established institutional power is still being questioned. If it is tempting to call these organizations, or proto-institutions, a ground for technical democracy, we see them through the prism of Unixians' networked organizations as ad hocracies far from being independent from power relationships.

Notes

1. Interview with Laurent Bloch (2013), a computer engineer actively involved in Unix networks and the Fnet organization, of which he was vice president between 1991 and 1992. Bloch coined the idea of Unix networks as a "first French Internet experience", arguing that they predated the Internet in France and had similar purposes

(email and online discussion groups) despite their technical differences—a feeling confirmed by all the other interviewees. All quotes and extracts translated from French to English by the author.

2. Administrative archives of "Laboratoire d'Informatique", 1981–1986 (34–02.11 B11–B12) and "Fonds Lippman" (34–02.03 1), donated by Daniel Lippman, engineer at the "Laboratoire d'Informatique" during the 1980s and 1990s. Accessible at the archives department of the Conservatoire national des arts et métiers, Paris, France.

3. First called "Computing Center", then "Computing Lab" and "Computer Lab", it evolved into an IT department in the 1990s, still active today.

4. Kaiser was to become "Chair of Computing and Programming" in 1984, in line with predecessor François-Henri Raymond, an inventor and industrialist close to the research world who started the first French computer manufacturer. The informal "Systems lab" became official in 1988 with the creation of CEDRIC laboratory, still active today.

5. According to an unpublished and undated article by Florin entitled "La première installation d'UNIX au Conservatoire National des Arts et Métiers", sent to the author by Kaiser. Florin also mentions the help brought by Kyrian O'Donnell, from INRIA, that would start a long Unixian collaboration between the two establishments.

6. Vyssotsky developed Multics, an operating system instigator to Unix; he went on to become a Director of Research at the Bell Labs.

7. Interview with Yves Devillers (2012), a computer science researcher working at INRIA in the 1980s and the early 1990s in close partnership with the Unixians at Cnam and becoming Fnet's president between 1986 and 1993, when it was hosted at INRIA.

8. "Politique d'équipement et d'investissement pour le labo d'informatique", lab memo redacted in May 1981 ("Computer Lab's equipment and investment policy").

9. Gérard Florin ("La première installation d'UNIX au Conservatoire National des Arts et Métiers"). Stéphane Natkin, currently Chair Professor of Multimedia Systems at Cnam, testified in an informal discussion with the author: "it happened one summer at a moment when there was a grey area of law".

10. It was originally called, from its creation in 1945, the Mathematische Centrum (Mathematics Center). Despite the fact that computer science research was active early on, it was only in 1997 that it was renamed Centrum Wiskunde & Informatica ("National Research Institute for Mathematics and Computer Science").

11. "Rapport scientifique du laboratoire" (Computer Lab's scientific report), July 1982 (CL archives). Kaiser's papers testify to this theoretical aspect—for instance, Kaiser 1979.

12. (1) One recurring reference is the seminal AT&T article "A Dial-up Network of UNIX Systems" (Nowitz and Lesk 1979), asserting the need to find a "conventional mechanism" for local networks. (2) From a letter dated 20 September 1982 from Kaiser to Professor Maurice Nivat of Université Paris 7 (Mathematics Department) underlining the importance of UUCP software in a collaborative project in which the two establishments are involved called "C3: Coopération, Concurrence et Communication". (3) Lab memo: "Liaison Cnam—LERS", 5 November 1981.

13. In a letter dated 27 April 1981 to Ken Harrenstien at SRI International, Kaiser writes: "You ask to be informed about people that receives [sic] the package [of Unix software]. I expect to use your package and I am going to pass it along to: Mr. R.A. Mason, Dpt Computer Engineering, Heriot-Watt University, Edinburgh."

14. At this occasion, Kaiser defended the showcasing mission of the meeting to the then-director of Cnam, outlining its international reputation and its importance in domestic research collaborations like the SOL project with INRIA, a French Unix version in the Pascal programming language.

15. Notable presentations included: "Unix Telecommunications Applications and Evolution" by Ian Johnston (Bell Labs, New Jersey, USA), "Attaching Unix to the Edinburgh Computer Network" by Jim McKie (Edinburgh Regional Computer Network, Scotland) and "The Netherlands UUCP Network" by Teus Hagen (CWI Amsterdam, the Netherlands).

16. "Groupe de travail réseaux de l'association française des utilisateurs UNIX (AFUU)", January 1984. Lucas was part of the informal "Systems lab" research team.

17. The UUCICO program runs the telephone call that will send a list of files to transfer when the connection is established with a remote Unix computer (Garfinkel and Spafford 1996).

18. Defined by the United Nations-supervised Comité Consultatif International Téléphonique et Télégraphique (CCITT), which went on to become the International Telecommunication Union in 1992, it was adopted from 1975 and used by several countries for their respective national packet-commutated networks: France's Transpac, Great Britain's EPSS, Canada's DCS, and the USA's Telenet.

19. Interview with Annie Renard (2013), an engineer at INRIA in the late 1980s who took part in the Fnet team and was particularly in charge of Domain Name System addressing after 1988.

20. SAFARI (Système Automatisé pour les fichiers administratifs et le repertoire des individus) was a project released in 1974 by the French government, but abandoned after much criticism for creating interconnecting indexes of nominative files for French citizens. The SAFARI affair prompted the creation of the Commission nationale informatique et libertés (Cnil) in 1978.

21. A 1986 logical Fnet map shows 27 organizations connecting to Fnet—many of them having multiple connections in different labs or services, making the number of direct connections to Fnet higher—and not counting the bridged connections from other networks like EARN. Fourteen public sector research and education organisms: Centre d'Etudes et de Recherches de Toulouse (Deri—Département d'Etudes et de Recherches Informatique); CNET (Centre Structures et Logiciels pour la Commutation—Centre de Lannion, division Télématique Informatique Mathématique (TIM); Dpt. ATL Assistance Technique et Logicielle—Division Outils de gestion de l'exploitation OGE, Départements Systèmes Microprocesseurs et Logiciels); CNRS (LASS—Laboratoire d'Automatique et d'Analyse des Systèmes); Ecole nationale supérieure des mines de Paris (Centre de Mathématiques Appliquées); Ecole des mines de Saint Etienne; Ecole nationale supérieure des télécommunications; IMAG (Institut IMAG, LIFTIA—Lab. d'Informatique Fondamentale et d'Intelligence Artificielle; TIM3; INPG Architecture Group); INRIA (IRISA—Institut de Recherche en Informatique et Systèmes aléatoires; Centre de Rocquencourt; Centre de Sophia-Antipolis); IRCAM; Supelec; Université de Nancy 1 (Lab. CRIN); Université de Paris (LITP—Lab. d'Informatique Théorétique et Pratique); Université de Paris 6 (Centre de calcul et de recherche); Université Paris Sud (LRI—Lab. de Recherche en Informatique). Four public sector enterprises: Agence de l'informatique; EDF (Direction des études et recherches); Compagnie Générale d'Electricité (Centre de recherches, division Informatique); Caisse nationale du Crédit Agricole. Seven private sector businesses: ALCATEL (TELIC Unité de recherche: La téléphonie industrielle et commerciale); Axis Digital; Bull (SEMS); CAP Sogeti Innovation; CERCI; METROLOGIE; TRT (Service Central Logiciel). Two non-profit organizations: Association pour la Création et la Recherche sur les Outils d'Expression; Centre Mondial de l'Informatique.

22. Cellule Expertise Recherche et Développement, comprising Yves Devillers and Annie Renard as well as five other computer engineers and technicians.

23. AFUU's website, from 1996 to 2002, does not mention Fnet as an UUCP or Internet provider, but as a competitor; it does not offer information on AFUU's activities in the 1980s.

24. Interview with Stéphane Bortzmeyer (2012), an Unixian working at Cnam in the early 1990s, and who actively participated in the promotion of Web technologies in the old and new Internet user communities.

25. It was gathered thanks to the previous Usenet archival initiative, Giganews, in 1995 (which Google bought in 2001) and institutional as well as individual donors. We studied how this archive was received and discussed by Internet hobbyists as an ambivalent heritage, between community experiential memories, historical sources for the Internet, and communication strategy by Google (Paloque-Berges 2017).

26 Recently renamed as "Memorable Usenet moments", it is now accessible at: https://support.google.com/groups/answer/6003482?hl

27 The same department went on to gather the biggest collection of Usenet posts, donated to Google in 2001 (and making up most of the first decade of their Usenet archive) as well as Internet archive, in a zip file known as the "UTZOO Usenet archives", available at: http://archive.org/details/utzoo-wiseman-usenet-archive

28. Not to be confused with Bernard Martin, Humberto Lucas's Unixian associate within Cnam's Computer Lab.

29. Cf. a 1994 conversation on fnet.general started by Michel Fingerhut in 1994, and comprising discussions with the subjects "Routage en France" (18 April 1994), "Le 22 Asnieres derechef en reseaux" (13 August 1994), "Le 22 Asnieres (suite)" (18 August 1994), "Plus de liaison . . . ." (18 October 1994), "Voila ce qui en coute de passer par les US" (29 October 1994), available at: https://groups.google.com/forum/?hl=fr&fromgroups=#!searchin/fr.network.divers/michel$20fingerhut.

30. According to Stéphane Bortzmeyer, one of Fnet's administrators in 1993, in the previously mentioned Usenet discussion "Routage en France".

31. News posted by Jean-Michel Planche from Oléane in an FAQ for Internet, Usenet, and UUCP access in France, available at: https://groups.google.com/forum/?hl=fr&fromgroups=#!topic/fr.network.divers/01NZh2WTIBI

32. See the recurrent and much discussed topic on "Autoroutes de l'information" between 3 November and 7 December 1994 in the fr.comp.infosystemes group, available at: https://groups.google.com/forum/?hl=fr#!forum/fr.comp.infosystemes

33. The year 1993 is a turning point, with the release of the WWW software and protocol suite, the creation of the W3C, but also the launch of the "Information Highways" programs plan by US Secretary of State Al Gore, "Information Society" by the European Commission, and a year later in France, the "Rapport Théry", homologous to Al Gore's seminal plan.

34. "Science: The Endless Frontier. A Report to the President by Vannevar Bush, Director of the Office of Scientific Research and Development", July 1945 (United States Government Printing Office, Washington: 1945), hosted on the American National Science Foundation website, available at: www.nsf.gov/od/lpa/nsf50/vbush1945.htm

References

Abbate, J. (1999) *Inventing the Internet*, Cambridge, MA: MIT Press.

Beltran, A., and Griset, P. (2007) *Histoire d'un Pionnier de l'informatique: 40 ans de Recherche à l'Inria*, Les Ulis: EDP Sciences.

Berteema, P. (1983) "Europe Map", net.news.map, Usenet, 18 March, available at: https://groups.google.com/forum/?hl=fr#!topic/net.news.map/g0GcluHULRg

Bloch, L. (2013) interview, 6 June.

Bortzmeyer, S. (2012) interview, 25 October.

Campbell-Kelly, M., and Aspray, W. (1996) *Computer: A History of the Information Machine*, New York: Basic Books.

comp.mail.maps (n.d.) Google Groups, available at: https://groups.google.com/forum/#!forum/comp.mail.maps

Cornwall, H. (1985) *The Hacker's Handbook*, London: Century Communications.

de Certeau, M. ([1990] 2011) *The Practice of Everyday Life*, Berkeley, CA: University of California Press.

Devillers, Y. (2012) interview, 12 December.

Flichy, P. ([2001] 2007) *The Internet Imaginaire*, Cambridge, MA: MIT Press.

Florin, G. (2016) interview, 7 April.

Garfinkel, S., and Spafford, G. (1996) *Practical Unix and Computer Security*, 2nd edn, Sebastopol, CA: O'Reilly.

Griset, P., and Schafer, V. (2012) "'Make the Pig Fly!' l'Inria, ses Chercheurs et Internet des Années 1970 aux Années 1990", *Le Temps des Médias*, 18: 41–53.

Grossman, W. (1998) *net.wars*, New York: NYU Press, available at: http://nyupress.org/netwars/.

Hafner, K., and Lyons, M. (1996) *Where Wizards Stay Up Late,* New York: Simon & Schuster.

Hauben, M., and Hauben R. (1997) *Netizens: On the History and Impact of Usenet and the Internet*, Hoboken: Wiley-IEEE Computer Society Press.

Healy, D. (1996) "Cyberspace and Place: Middle Landscape on the Electronic Frontier", in D. Porter (ed.), *Internet Culture*, New York: Routledge, pp. 55–68.

Huitema, C. (1994) "Qui Etaient les Premiers? (Re: Au Sujet du Forum Internet . . .)", fnet.general, Usenet, 20 November, available at: https://groups.google.com/forum/#!topic/fr.network.divers/jJBTIR8OeDY

Huitema, C. (1995) *Et Dieu créa l'Internet*, Paris: Eyrolles.

Johnson, D. R., and Post, D. G. (2001) "Law and Borders: The Rise of Law in Cyberspace", in P. Ludlow (ed.), *Crypto Anarchy, Cyberstates, and Pirate Utopias*, Cambridge, MA: MIT Press, pp. 169–182.

Kaiser, C. (1979) "A Critical Study of Different Flow Control Methods in Computer Networks", *Computer Communication Review*, 9(3).

Kapor, M., and Barlow, J. P. (1990) "Across the Electronic Frontier", *Electronic Frontier Foundation*, 10 July, available at: http://w2.eff.org/Misc/Publications/John_Perry_Barlow/HTML/eff.html

Kelty, C. (2008) *Two Bits: The Cultural Significance of Free Software*, Durham, NC: Duke University Press.

King, J., Grinter, R. E., and Pickering, J. (1997) "The Rise and Fall of Netville: The Saga of a Cyberspace Construction Boomtown in the Great Divide", in S. Kielser (ed.), *Culture of the Internet*, Mahwah, NJ: Lawrence Erlbaum Associates, pp. 3–34.

Latour, B. (1987) *Science in Action: How to Follow Scientists and Engineers Through Society*, Milton Keynes: Open University Press.

Leiner, B., Cerf, V. G, Clark, D. D., Kahn, R. E., Kleinrock, L., Lynch, D. C., Postel, J., Roberts, L. G., and Wolff, S. S. (1997) "The Past and Future History of the Internet", *Communications of the ACM*, 40(2): 102–108.

Levy, P. (1997) *Collective Intelligence: Mankind's Emerging World in Cyberspace*, trans. R. Bononno, Cambridge, MA: Perseus.

Michot, J-C. (1992) "UUCP Map", *fnet.general*, 9 April, available at: https://groups.google.com/forum/#!searchin/fnet.general/routage/fnet.general/rTPMorwqRm8/xjn1Euq1zW8J

Mounier-Kuhn, P. E. (2010a) "Les Clubs d'Utilisateurs: Entre Syndicats de Clients, Outils Marketing et 'Logiciel Libre' Avant la Lettre", *Entreprises et Histoire*, 3(60): 158–169.

Mounier-Kuhn, P. E. (2010b) *L'Informatique en France de la Seconde Guerre Mondiale au Plan Calcul: L'émergence d'une Science*, Paris: Presses de l'Université Paris-Sorbonne.

net.news.map (1982–1985) *Usenet*, available at: https://groups.google.com/forum/?hl=fr#!forum/net.news.map

Nowitz, D. A., and Lesk, M. E. (1979) "A Dial-up Network of UNIX Systems", in *Unix Programmers Manual*, New Jersey: Bell Labs.

Paloque-Berges, C. (2017) "Usenet as a Web Archive: Multi-layered Archives of Computer-Mediated Communication", in N. Brügger (ed.), *Web25: Histories from the First 25 Years of the World Wide Web*, Bern: Peter Lang.

Paloque-Berges, C., and Masutti, C. (2013) *Histoires et Cultures du Libre: Des Logiciels Partagés aux Licences Échangées*, Strasbourg: Framasoft.

Pfaffenberg, B. (2003) "A Standing Wave in the Web of Our Communications: Usenet and the Socio-Technical Construction of Cyberspace Values", in C. Lueg and D. Fisher (eds), *From Usenet to CoWebs: Interacting with Social Information Spaces*, New York: Springer, pp. 21–40.

Quarterman, J. (1990) *The Matrix: Computer Networks and Conferencing Systems Worldwide*, Upper Saddle River, NJ: Prentice Hall.

Raymond, E. S. (2000) *A Brief History of Hackerdom*, version 1.24, Thyrsus Enterprises, available at: http://reg. dorogaved.ru/old/bigfish/unix/catb/hacker-history/index.html

Raynaud, F. (1966) "Fernand Raynaud 'Le 22 à Asnières'", *Institut National de l'Audiovisuel*, 10 February, available at: www.ina.fr/video/I06268515/fernand-raynaud-le-22-a-asnieres-video.html

Renard, A. (2013) interview, 7 July.

Rheingold, H. (1993) *The Virtual Community: Homesteading on the Electronic Frontier*, Cambridge, MA: MIT Press.

Salus, P. H. (1994) *A Quarter Century of Unix*, London: Addison-Wesley.

Schafer, V. (2012) *La France en Réseaux (Tome 1) La Rencontre des Télécommunications et de l'Informatique (1960–1980)*, Paris: Nuvis.

Schafer, V. and Tuy, B. (2013) *Dans les Coulisses de l'Internet: RENATER, 20 Ans de Technologie, d'Enseignement et de Recherche*, Paris: Armand Colin.

Schafer, V., Paloque-Berges, C., and Georges, F. (2015), "La Culture Internet au Risque du Web", *CIRCAV*, 24: 20–32.

Shannon, B. and Shannon, K. (1982) "Usenet Logical Map", *net.news.map*, 24 January, available at: https://groups. google.com/forum/?hl=fr#!msg/net.news.map/p9_zR8fF7eE/SiTc_TnFIt0J

Thierry, B. (2012) "'Révolution 0.1'. Utilisateurs et Communautés d'Utilisateurs au Premier Age de l'Informatique Personnelle et des Réseaux Grand Public (1978–1990)", *Le Temps des Médias*, 18(1): 54–65.

Turner, F. (2006a) *From Counterculture to Cyberculture: Stewart Brand, the Whole Earth Network, and the Rise of Digital Utopianism*, Chicago: University of Chicago Press.

Turner, F. (2006b) "How Digital Technology Found Utopian Ideology: Lessons from the First Hackers' Conference", in D. Silver and A. Massanari (eds), *Critical Cyberculture Studies: Current Terrains, Future Directions*, New York: New York University Press, pp. 257–269.

Vedel, T. (1984) "Les Ingénieurs des Telecommunications: Formation d'un Grand Corps", *Culture Technique*, 12: 63–75.

11

EARLY COMPUTER NETWORKS IN JAPAN, 1984–1994

Mark McLelland

Introduction

Teaching Internet histories to a cohort of today's students, the large majority of whom constitute "digital natives"—that is, young people who have grown up with a close familiarity with computer-meditated communication (CMC), can prove challenging. To students who complain about broken links on course outlines, or corrupted files among the e-readings, I sometimes recount the trials of my own undergraduate career, where a bicycle was a necessary prerequisite for the successful completion of any assignment. This was because I studied at a university where the central campus library was some way out of town, and if a copy of the required book or article was unavailable there, the only option was to cycle round the different college and faculty libraries scattered around, in the hope that a copy could be tracked down elsewhere. Of course, it was impossible to find out in advance whether the library held the relevant text or not—or even if a copy was available—without searching through a card catalogue and then checking the shelves. It could take an entire morning to track down a reading. All this cycling about kept me fit, but also led to some pretty close deadlines. However, when I recount this, my students just look at me blankly, rather as I might regard a medieval monk who would no doubt complain that in his day if you wanted a copy of a book you had to write it out by hand.

I mention the above as an illustration of how quickly new technological developments are assimilated, and how rapidly they can transform a given environment. These days I find myself as impatient as my students if I can't find a journal article immediately. What differentiates more senior researchers from today's students is the fact that we do remember a time before communication became computerized, and are hence aware that the Internet does in fact have a history—one that can be measured by more than periodic increases in download speeds or the invention of new apps. The histories that we remember are, however, always perspectival. A computer hobbyist in the west coast of the United States, active since the late 1970s, will have a very different appreciation of CMC from someone who first came across the fully formed Internet in 1993 via a high school computer class. What makes my own sense of Internet history unusual, perhaps, is that I first became aware of computer-mediated communication while living in Japan in the late 1980s and early 1990s, and went on to first use the Internet *in Japanese* while undertaking a Ph.D. in Japanese studies later in the 1990s. It is due to this personal background that I have always been interested in the social and cultural dimensions of Internet uptake in Japan and elsewhere (see Goggin and McLelland

2009; Gottlieb and McLelland 2003), and have been keen to investigate Internet histories from a non-anglophone perspective.

Despite the key role that the Internet has come to play in contemporary society, we know surprisingly little about the early years of CMC in countries outside North America and Europe. Likewise, dominant notions of the Internet, like those of media or culture generally, are still modeled on a limited range of experiences and conceptions, largely based on the perspectives of anglophone users and researchers, especially North Americans, who featured prominently among early pioneers. The cultural, linguistic, and social values of such anglophone users have had a strong influence—from the ubiquity of the QWERTY keyboard to the level of technical protocols, as evident in the centrality of English to computer code or to domain names.

This is perhaps unavoidable given the key role played by the United States in the development of CMC, where massive investment from the 1960s onward was driven by the military. Also, the use of computers in communication was in many ways just an extension of the kinds of office automation that had taken place a century earlier with the development of the typewriter and the roll-out of telegraph and telephone networks. It is no surprise that the QWERTY keyboard, carried over from the typewriter, has remained the main human–computer interface, even in countries like Japan where Roman script is not used for daily communication.

Albeit initially pioneered for military use in the United States in the 1960s, during the 1970s US computer hobbyists were already exploring the potential of computerized communication via dial-up technology offered by companies such as CompuServe. These early adopters were interested in discussing computer coding issues and exchanging software files over the phone lines (Banks 2012: 20–24). By the early 1980s, an Internet infrastructure was rapidly taking shape. First accessible to researchers in universities and private institutes, it became available to the general public later in the decade. US companies were world leaders at the time in developing computer technologies, consoles, and applications for sale to the public, allowing them to make use of the new communications potential offered by the Internet.

In Japan, however, despite the specialization in light-industrial manufacturing and electronics that had developed in the post-war period, there was a very different socio-cultural environment impacting on research and development into computer communications. Working without military or government support, researchers had to make incredible efforts to obtain financial and institutional backing for research into CMC as well as navigate a top-heavy bureaucratic environment that actually stifled creativity. In the early 1980s, because of the way that telecommunications law was framed, early experiments in computer communication over telephone lines were technically illegal (Matsuoka 2005: 7). Given the complexities of Japanese orthography, there were also considerable character input, coding, and display challenges that needed to be overcome in order to create programs that could handle Japanese text (Matsuoka 2005: 49). In this chapter, I revisit the earliest days of commercial CMC in Japan, and point out some of the challenges faced by researchers and developers in opening up computer networks to the Japanese public. I focus on the period between 1984, when the first computer networks were established, to 1994, Japan's "Internet year one" (Kumon 1995), when the number of regular Internet users shot up exponentially. Compared with the large discussion in English of Japan's early years of mobile Internet commencing in 1999 (see, for example, Natsuno 2003), relatively little has been written about this first decade of CMC in Japan, which the English-language literature, at least, tends to frame as a decade of "catch up". This emphasis on stressing what steps Japan needed to take in order to catch up with the more widespread use of CMC in the United States tends to overlook the important developments that needed to take place before computerized communication could appeal to the general public.

The Development of Personal Computing in Japan

My introduction to CMC came in Japan in the late 1980s, while studying as a postgraduate at Tokyo University. The first computer I bought in 1988 was a portable Toshiba "RUPO" model. Known as a *wāpuro senyōki* (single-purpose word processor), it was more of a glorified typewriter than a computer, as it displayed only a single line of text, but it did liberate me from having to write Japanese by hand, and thus submitting assignments looking as if they had been penned by a five-year-old. The Japanese writing system is complex, involving two syllabic scripts: *katakana* for foreign loanwords and *hiragana* for native terms and grammatical indicators, some limited use of Roman alphabet and Arabic numerals, as well as around 2,000 *kanji*—that is, ideographs originally deriving from China. Because of this complexity, Japan had never developed a mechanical typewriter for home use, and most people were unfamiliar with the QWERTY keyboard that had been a standard means of creating text in Europe and America for over a century. There had been (and to a much lesser extent still remains) a cultural predilection for the sharing of certain kinds of information in hand-written form, and a high appreciation of penmanship. Some older people complained that printed characters were "'cold' and lacked individuality" (Gottlieb 2000: 136–137). There were Japanese typewriters, but given the number of characters involved, even the smallest were the size of suitcases and could only be used by trained professionals. Their use was further limited by the fact that there was no standard keyboard layout (Gottlieb 2000: 18). Furthermore, although there had been some use of computers for routine office tasks, these were not general use PCs but specific-purpose machines such as accounting computers and word processors (Mori and Phoha 2002: 42).

However, beginning in the late 1970s, companies such as NEC had begun to develop personal computers that experimented with the more compact QWERTY keyboard as a means of inputting Japanese text. Whereas there are only 256 combinations necessary for Roman script included in the one-byte American Standard Code for Information Interchange (ASCII), the hybrid Japanese writing system required over 7,000 (Shapard 1993: 255). Given this complexity, and the lack of familiarity with using Roman text to input Japanese phonemes, early products were directed more at computer hobbyists than the general public. In 1979, a two-byte system that could handle all aspects of Japanese text was developed. This involved typing words phonetically, using the QWERTY keyboard, and then hitting a "conversion key" which displayed various *kanji* and *kana* options on screen. *Kana*-based keyboards were also available, but according to Ken Lunde, "over 70 percent of Japanese computer users prefer[red] transliterated Japanese input" (1999: 12). Early versions involving transliteration could only convert one word at a time, but software that was able to handle short chunks of text was soon developed (Gottlieb 2000: 67–68; Nakayama 2002: 240). The conversion process was not entirely straightforward since Japanese is full of homophones— that is, words that sound the same but are written with different characters. There could be ten or more different options listed on screen, and the appropriate one could be inserted in the text by selecting a number in a list. As programs became more refined, they were able to remember a user's preferred character combinations, and those most frequently used would appear at the beginning of the list. A problem with these early computers was that different companies had developed "vertically integrated networks that produced incompatible products" (Seo 2013: 186), meaning that files written on a Toshiba console could not be read on an NEC model and vice versa.

The different *kanji* and *kana* conversion systems meant that, unlike in the United States, where standard protocols were in place for the exchange of text and other data over computer networks, it was initially difficult for consumers in Japan to exchange files over the phone lines with users connected to a different network. The two earliest and most famous networks were NEC's PC-Van and Fujitsu's Nifty-Serve. Both were computer companies that had established networks utilizing the telephone line and modems by the late 1980s, and ushered in the era of what is known in Japanese as *pasokon tsūshin* or "personal computer communication"—initially a bulletin board system (BBS) that enabled users to seek out information from various news feeds, as well as participate in online discussions and send email to other users—but in the early years at least, only with those on the same system.

I witnessed the developments described above unfold first-hand, as I was living in Japan at the time, so saw the space given over to personal electronics in local stores that were expanding rapidly during the late 1980s and early 1990s, and enjoyed talking with Japanese friends and colleagues about their new devices and the new communication possibilities these facilitated. Both the PC-Van and Nifty-Serve networks were almost entirely Japanese-speaking. Navigation and instructions were in Japanese, and although there were some English-language boards, they were primarily used by people studying English language—and as neither network was initially accessible from overseas, there were relatively few non-Japanese communicating via these systems. Despite the fact that these different networks were not interoperative, they had the cumulative effect of introducing large numbers of Japanese people to computerized communication, resulting in the normalization of text creation via the Roman script keyboard. Surveys made at the time on changing writing patterns found that the new *wāpuro ningen* (word-processer person) was likely to write more, and to write more often, and that many felt liberated from their "handwriting complex" by the new technology (Gottlieb 2000:141, 147–148).

It was not until researching this chapter, however, that I became aware of the fact that there existed at this time an English-language BBS in Japan, the product of American–Japanese collaboration, which had been in existence since 1984. Known as Two Way Information Communication System (TWICS), this was among the first BBS-style networks founded in Japan, and in 1993 became the very first public-access Internet provider. Yet, despite its pioneering activities, TWICS has largely been overlooked by histories of the Internet written in Japanese. Although Shumpei Kumon's path-breaking 1988 book *Nettowāku Shakai* (The Network Society), one of the first to map out Japan's developing Internet culture, makes several mentions of TWICS, it says nothing about its founding philosophy, or the distinct contribution made by early TWICS members to other Japanese networks. Given that TWICS was such a key early player, it is worth recording these contributions, and recognizing TWICS's role in the early years of Japanese CMC.

Early Computer Networking Systems in Japan

As discussed above, the difficulty of inputting Japanese text, and the lack of familiarity with computing technology among the general public, meant that computer literacy was very low in Japan in the early 1980s. There were also industry and policy factors that slowed the development even of a hobbyist cohort of computer pioneers. Prior to 1985, those hobbyists who wanted to access computer networks had to do so via overseas systems such as CompuServe in the United States, requiring expensive international dial-up fees and some fluency in English (Shapard 1993: 260).

The year 1985 is a significant date, since prior to this point the Japan Telegraph and Telephone Corporation (currently NTT) had a monopoly on all domestic phone lines, whereas a separate company, the International Telegraph and Telephone Company (currently KDDI), controlled international telephone communication. During this time, it was technically illegal for any other person or company to use the telephone network for purposes other than making calls or sending faxes, and modems were not commercially available to the general public. There were some small groups of entrepreneurs, such as the researchers working with Jun Murai at Keio University, who were experimenting with CMC, mostly as a local area network—but their activities were borderline illegal, and they faced considerable restrictions imposed upon them by Japan's top-heavy bureaucracy (Matsuoka 2005: 7). These early experiments in CMC involved linking computers in Japan via dial-up to overseas networks.

However, the high cost of international phone charges, plus the fact that communication was limited to Roman text, meant that little headway was made in developing a local system. In 1985, this situation began to change, with the introduction of the Telecommunications Business Law that broke up the monopoly over Japan's domestic and international phone lines, and opened up the field to new and innovative players. Later that year, Japan's first major local network, Computer Communication of Oita Amateur Research Association (COARA), was established in Oita province of Japan's south-western island of Kyushu (considered by Tokyoites to be something of a backwater). COARA was a public–private enterprise initially aimed at networking local businesses in order to encourage regional revitalization. That same year, Murai's JUNET (Japan UNIX Network) established links between one private and two public universities.

Yet, as well as overregulation, a host of other factors continued to limit the development of local computer networking communities, which in the United States were already over a decade old by this time. Japan's overpriced leased lines and expensive metered call charges made it difficult for early adopters to engage in CMC networks. For instance, one of the founders of COARA mentioned that it cost 8,000 yen ($80) per hour to connect to a hosting service in Tokyo, but only 4,000 yen for an hour's connection via a US-based server (Ono 1994: 34). There was also a dominance of centralized mainframe computing services, a lack of local area networks, and, as mentioned, no standardized protocols for the input and display of Japanese text.

At the time, the common bureaucratic position in Japan on the potential of CMC was that it would provide an extension of existing one-to-many information exchanges (Izumi 1996: 5). Yet the experience of the early networks showed that people were not that interested in simply looking up information. COARA is significant in this regard, since its initial impetus was to serve as an information hub for local businesses, but there was little demand for this kind of one-way communication. What kick-started the community-building activity on the service was the diary of a high school student who posted daily updates about his experiences with the Japanese education system, and received many replies from other users offering him advice and support in his struggles (Ono 1994: 55–58). After graduation, he wrote to thank the members of COARA who had emailed him with feedback on his posts and treated him like a "real person" (Ono 1994: 108–110). The realization that CMC offered the potential for a wide range of people with divergent experiences to come together online in "people-to-people, two-way communication" encouraged the site's administrators to shift the project's direction, and COARA became a "network community" in 1987 (Izumi 1996: 5; Rheingold 1993: 205–206).

Unlike COARA, which started as a business information site, the philosophy behind TWICS, which had been founded a year prior in 1984, was much closer to person-to-person communication from its inception. TWICS grew out of a collaboration between Sakako Co. Ltd (a shrimp import and seafood sales company) and the Tokyo-based International Education Center (IEC), a non-profit educational organization specializing in language education and cultural exchange. Sakako provided the financing for IEC staff to develop computer networking infrastructure from scratch. The first trial system went online in 1984, with its first 30 or so users recruited from a local telecom enthusiast society known as TokyoNet (Shapard 1986: 2). Supported by a single telephone, and only a 300-baud modem, exchanges were restricted to emails and a limited number of bulletin boards. This initial system was referred to as the BeeLINE, playing on a metaphor of cross-pollination. In 1985, the system was revamped, and had its first full-time administrator, Jeff Shapard, an American teaching in Japan, who was financed by the IEC to work in this role. The new system was supported by six dial-up modems, and allowed real-time messaging as well as email and access to more bulletin boards. As Shapard noted of these early exchanges, "we were oriented more toward people and communication rather than data and information" (cited in Rheingold 1993: 215). By 1986, the number of users had increased to around 350, and a real sense of community was beginning to develop around various discussion boards. Since most users at this time were still based in the Tokyo area, online connections often led to offline meetings and friendships.

Unlike the main *pasokon* networks that were supported by specific computer manufacturers, TWICS was designed to be accessed via almost any kind of computer with either a text-based or graphical interface. However, the original custom-made system was error prone and struggled to keep pace with the increase in users, so in April 1986 a decision to convert to an existing commercial system was made. The third iteration of the BeeLINE used the Participate Conferencing System software, originally developed in the United States in 1979. This made it much easier for users to search information and engage in short discussions. In 1987, it became possible for members to send and receive email internationally via a DASnet link. This option proved popular, and by 1990 there were around 700 users, including 200 or so living overseas. Membership was evenly split between Japanese and foreign nationals. Shapard described TWICS at this time as a metaphorical electronic island Beejima (Bee Island), "a friendly little island community in the electronic seas of Japan, close to Tokyo but accessible from anywhere" (cited in Rheingold 1993: 216). Although the majority of the communication was taking place in English, the different online community spaces were all modeled on familiar Japanese terms. These included an online market, or *ichiba*, a high-tech discussion board named after the famous electronics district of Tokyo, Akihabara, as well as a *yabu*, or wooded bush area, for private discussions (Shapard 1986: 3).

As an American with a background in computing, Shapard was well placed to understand the exciting potential offered by CMC networks. In 1988, he had teamed up with US-educated Japanese national Jōichi (Joi) Ito (now a lead researcher at MIT) to attend the Electronic Networking Association Conference in Philadelphia, where they became aware of the full scale of developments in CMC that were taking place across the United States. Shapard records his impressions after this event, noting that:

> I felt like we had been living in some electronic version of the Middle Ages, building little villages off in remote regions, trying to figure out ways for people to get to us and for us to have routes to our neighbors, thinking we were really doing

something new and hot, and then discovering China, with a vast, complex, and ancient civilization.

(Cited in Rheingold 1993: 215)

In comparison with the rapid advancements sweeping America at this time, especially across university campuses, Japan was somewhat slow in capitalizing on the benefits of CMC. For instance, although Japan joined the US-based National Science Foundation Network that provided Internet links to universities worldwide at the same time as Australia, in 1989, by 1993 the amount of outbound NSFNet traffic from Japan was about the same as Taiwan, and only half that from Australia, despite Australia's much smaller population and limited number of tertiary institutions (Johnstone 1994).

It was not until 1993 that consumers in Japan had access to the Internet, and TWICS was a lead player in making this service available. This came about when representatives of InterCon International (IIKK), a subsidiary of the US-based InterCon Systems Corp., arrived in Tokyo, looking to set up business operations in what was then an open market. IIKK faced many problems, however, as a new and unknown foreign venture—it proved difficult to find a sponsor to stand surety on business accommodations, hence they originally set up in a loaned space in an abandoned karaoke bar. When this didn't work out, Ito allowed the company to move its server to an unused bathroom in an apartment he was renting, and from there they obtained a space in an office in the neighboring building (Ito 2002).

Despite this inauspicious start, IIKK was able to gain a license to offer overseas online access, and the first commercial Internet exchange from Japan took place on 17 September 1993, "sent by American engineers" (Johnstone 1994) working for the company. TWICS became IIKK's first customer, leasing a line that allowed it to offer full Internet access to its subscribers in October 1993 as a secondary service provider (*Intānetto magajin* 1995: 55). For the next six months, it was the only provider in Japan that offered the general public access to the Internet via dial-up accounts (Auckerman 1994).

In contrast to IIKK's success, Murai and his students at Keio University were constantly battling with bureaucratic restrictions. By 1987, the JUNET had been expanded to include the Widely Interconnected Distributed Environment (WIDE) research project that connected local area networks via leased lines. Technically, participation on the network was only available to universities and companies for the purpose of research, but it was difficult to always draw a line between research and commerce applications. Hence in 1992, Murai formed the Internet Initiative Japan (IIJ) and attempted to obtain an operating license from the Ministry of Posts and Telecommunications to offer a commercial Internet provider. The application was refused due to a number of concerns. These included Murai's role—whether he could be both a publicly funded academic and director of a commercial Internet provider (Johnstone 1994), and the fact that the government had already backed a slower competitor system being developed by the National Center for Science Information Systems (Coates 2000: 73). These early conflicts between Japanese Internet pioneers and the Japanese bureaucracy were well reported in the English-language communications press at the time, and were generally represented as a culture clash between "the freewheeling, democratic style of the Internet" and authoritarian "traditional Japan" (Johnstone 1994).

Hence, in the early 1990s, there were a number of distinct communities of use around CMC in Japan. There was JUNET/WIDE, the Japanese academic and research network, initially conducting most of its traffic in English or Romanized Japanese that was linked with overseas institutions, and that necessarily used international standard protocols. By 1993, there were over 800 institutions in Japan and overseas linked to the network (Suzuki 1993: 1). There were regional networks, the earliest of which was COARA, which had become connected to the Internet in 1994. TWICS was a much smaller network in terms of users, and although it offered Internet connection and had members from across the nation and overseas, it was primarily identified with the Tokyo area. In addition, there were the national *pasokon* networks using a variety of different standards that were largely incompatible with international protocols (Shapard 1993: 259), meaning that a large proportion of those in Japan who were wired for CMC were not yet on the Internet.

It was not until 1993, when the Microsoft DOS/V system was introduced, that Japanese language software could be run on any hardware. This system allowed for commands in either Japanese or English, and facilitated users' connections to overseas sites via the Internet. Yet, despite in their early years serving as a kind of national "intranet", the *pasokon* networks were extremely important in familiarizing the general public with the uses and styles of CMC. Prior to the widespread promotion of these BBS networks in the early 1990s, practically all communication across computer networks had necessarily been in English, due both to protocol issues and the general lack of content in Japanese. So, as Shapard notes: "The first domestic applications of *pasocom tsuushin* [*sic*] in Japan were to provide locally that which had only been available overseas . . . and having this locally meant having it in Japanese" (1993: 263).

Hence, 1994 has been described as Japan's "Internet year one", and there was a growing awareness in the media that a game of catch up needed to be played. For instance, in October 1994, Japan had only 82,000 host computers, similar to the level the United States had achieved in 1989 (Kumon 1995: 90). Yet, despite the fact that many of the technological issues, such as standard protocols for the input of Japanese text, had been resolved by this time, the general public in Japan still needed to adjust to this new mode of inputting and communicating the Japanese language. A 1997 survey found that, in a comparison with Americans and Koreans, the Japanese had the lowest level of computer literacy, only 23.7 percent of Japanese indicating that they could "type fast", compared to 31.6 percent of Koreans and 54.4 percent of Americans. In Japan, 50.8 percent of respondents indicated they had never used a computer, in comparison to 21.8 percent of American respondents (Fouser 2001: 274).

While attitudes to the use of computers for communication were changing, however, there were still serious infrastructure barriers to increased Internet adoption rates, not least expensive connection fees. Despite the fact that telephone service providers had been deregulated in the 1985 Telecommunications Business Law, NTT still had ownership of the telephone line infrastructure, and resisted offering flat rates for local calls as was common in the United States. Internet users were thus being charged in three-minute increments for time spent browsing. As a response to government pressure, in 1995 NTT finally offered a flat rate for Internet use, but only between 11.00pm and 8.00am. (Abate 1996: 37). It comes as no surprise, then, that pricing was one advantage that encouraged consumers to move onto the mobile Internet when services began to be rolled out in 1999—since the *i-mode* system charged only for downloads, and not for time spent browsing the system.

Conclusion

In their histories of Japan's early computer network systems, Japanese researchers have tended to focus on the importance of Jun Murai and his pioneering efforts to establish the JUNET/WIDE networks. There have also been a number of personal accounts, as well as academic studies of community building on the early *pasokon* networks. However, I have not been able to track down a substantial discussion of TWICS in the Japanese literature, despite the fact that its existence is footnoted and there has been media recognition of the pioneering role it played as Japan's first commercial Internet provider (see, for example, *Nihon Keizai Shimbun* 2005). This lack of interest can partially be explained in terms of membership. Despite the early success of TWICS in establishing international Internet connectivity, its membership did not grow exponentially, as happened with other early 1990s BBS systems such as Nifty-Serve and PC-Van. In August 1993, these companies had about 540,000 and 578,000 members respectively. This is partly because TWICS's early Japanese membership had been recruited from the computer hobbyist community, which was already outward looking, and interested in developments overseas, especially in the United States. These Japanese members were happy to communicate in English, to the extent that English had developed as the international language for computing technology discussion. Hence, attempts to increase the use of Japanese in public areas of the TWICS network "largely failed" (Shapard 1993: 264). Despite the fact that about half of TWICS membership was Japanese, the use of English as a lingua franca led to the perception in the Japanese media that it provided a service "for foreigners . . . who have a strong need to connect to the overseas' Net" (*Nihon Keizai Shimbun* 1987).

Another reason that TWICS's membership did not take off is that unlike the *pasokon* networks that were backed by major computer manufacturers, who were in competition with each other and thus had an incentive to constantly innovate and roll out new products and applications, as well as fund advertising campaigns in the mainstream press, TWICS did not have access to these income streams. Also, while Nifty, in particular, backed by its parent company, was able to archive and thus preserve for future research some of the content of its early network, no archiving of early TWICS material has taken place. The only access we now have to the early years of this network is via the few recollections written in English by some of its key members, and journalistic accounts in anglophone computing magazines of the early 1990s.

Although the early history of communication via the TWICS network is probably now lost, much more is known about the kinds of communities and communication that developed around the Japanese *pasokon* networks. A number of books were written at the time by users based on some of the material developed in various discussion groups (see, for example, Nifty Network Community 1997; Ono 1994; Yamane 1996), and academic researchers had much to say about the significance of these early networks (see, for instance, Kawakami 1993). Early *pasokon* communities were significant in a number of ways. They were the first public fora where Japanese from all walks of life used computers to communicate with each other, impacting on writing styles and changing people's perceptions of what constituted personal communication. The networks were important steps, too, in challenging the bureaucratic assumption that CMC was simply about linking people to information. As Ono points out in his 1994 book *The "COARA" Electric Nation: How Computer Communication Makes the Regional Global*, from the outset these communities were oriented around communication, arguing that "knowledge" is not simply about information exchange, but develops from human interaction (1994: 62).

It is probably the spectacular success of Japanese mobile Internet applications, initially pioneered by NTT's *i-mode* in 1999, and becoming ubiquitous soon after, that have distracted historians and Internet researchers more generally from exploring Japan's early computer network communities. There is still a dearth of information in English about this important period. What English-language commentary from the period exists was mainly concerned with pointing out the limitations of existing Japanese cultural, technical, and bureaucratic characteristics that had slowed down Internet uptake and computer-mediated communication more generally, vis-à-vis the United States. Hardly any attention was paid to what the developing Japanese networks were in fact doing—and this bias remains today, with so few accounts in English of this important period. These accounts do, however, exist in Japanese, and it is to be hoped that as Internet histories develops as a discipline, more will be written about Japan's first decade of computerized communication.

Acknowledgements

The author would like to thank Dr Takanori Tamura for comments on an earlier draft.

References

Abate, T. (1996) "The Midnight Hour: Japan Ventures onto the Net in the Dark of Night", *Scientific American*, January.

Auckerman, W. (1994) "Building On-Ramps to the Information Super Highway", *Computing Japan*, June, available at: www.japaninc.com/cpj/magazine/issues/1994/jun94/06infohi.html (accessed 3 March 2015).

Banks, M. (2012) *On the Way to the Web: The Secret History of the Internet and its Founders*, New York: Springer.

Coates, K. (2000) "Back in the Race: Japan and the Internet", in P. Bowles and L. T. Woods (eds), *Japan After the Economic Miracle: In Search of New Directions*, Dordrecht: Kluwer, pp. 71–84.

Fouser, R. (2001) "'Culture', Computer Literacy and the Media in Creating Public Attitudes to CMC in Japan and Korea", in C. Ess (ed.), *Culture, Technology, Communication: Towards an Intercultural Global Village*, Albany, NY: SUNY Press, pp. 261–278.

Goggin, G. and McLelland, M. (2009) *Internationalizing Internet Studies*, Oxford: Routledge.

Gottlieb, N. (2000) *Word Processing Technology in Japan: Kanji and the Keyboard*, Richmond: Curzon.

Gottlieb, N. and McLelland, M. (2003) *Japanese Cybercultures*, Oxford: Routledge.

Intānetto Magajin (Internet Magazine) (1995) "TWICS", June: 55.

Ito, J. (2002) *Picture of PSINet Japan POP 1994*, available at: http://joi.ito.com/weblog/2002/10/14/picture-of-psin.html (accessed 4 March 2015).

Izumi, A. (1996) *Emergence of Netizens in Japan and its Cultural Implications for the Net Society*, available at: www.ais.org/~jrh/acn/text/acn12–2.articles/acn12–2.a04.txt (accessed 3 March 2015).

Johnstone, B. (1994) "Wiring Japan: A Bitter Cultural Clash Has Reduced Japan to a Third-Rate Power in Networking", *Wired*, 2 January, available at: http://archive.wired.com/wired/archive/2.02/wiring.japan_pr.html (accessed 3 March 2015).

Kawakami, Y. (1993) *Denshi Nettowākingu no Shakai Shinri: Konpyūta Komyunikēshon e no Pasupōto* (The Social Psychology of Electronic Networking: A Passport for Computer Communication), Tokyo: Seishin Shobō.

Kumon, S. (1988) *Nettowāku Shakai* (The Network Society), Tokyo: Chūōkōronsha.

Kumon, S. (1995) "Japan's Internet Year One", *Japan Echo*, 22(1): 90.

Lunde, K. (1999) *CJKV Information Processing*, Sebastapol, CA: O'Reilly & Associates.

Matsuoka, M. (2005) *Nippon no Chōsen: Intānetto no Yoake* (Challenge of Japan: Dawn of the Internet), Tokyo: RBB Press.

Mori, Y., and Phoha, V. V. (2002) "The Internet in Japan", in S. Rao and B. C. Klopfenstein (eds), *Cyberpath to Development in Asia: Issues and Challenges*, Westport, CT: Praeger, pp. 37–62.

Nakayama, S. (2002) "From PC to Mobile Internet—Overcoming the Digital Divide in Japan", *Asian Journal of Social Science*, 30(2): 239–247.

Natsuno, T. (2003) *The I-Mode Wireless Ecosystem*, Chichester: Wiley & Sons.

Nifty Network Community (Nifty Nettowāku Komyuniti Kenkyūkai) (1997) *Denen Kōkyōshugi Nettowāku: Komyuniti no Shutsugen* (A Digital Network Symphony: The Arrival of Networking Communities), Tokyo: NTT Shuppan.

Nihon Keizai Shimbun (1987) "TWICS, Oobei Netto ni Denshi Yūbinhasshin" (TWICS, Sending Electronic Mail to the Euro-American Net), 23 October, p. 9.

Nihon Keizai Shimbun (2005) "Nihon no IT Sasaeru Gaikokujin: Igai ni Ooi NZ Shusshin Keieisha" (Foreigners Who Have Supported Japanese IT: The Surprising Number of New Zealand Managers), 18 July, p. 17.

Ono, T. (1994) *Denshi no Kuni "COARA" Pasokon Tsūshin ga Tsukuru Gurōbaru na Chihō* (The "COARA" Electric Nation: How Computer Communication Makes the Regional Global), Tokyo: AI Shuppan.

Rheingold, H. (1993) *The Virtual Community: Homesteading on the Electronic Frontier*, Reading, MA: Addison-Wesley.

Seo, D. (2013) *Evolution and Standardization of Mobile Communications Technology*, Hershey, PA: Information Science Reference.

Shapard, J. (1986) "TWICS BeeLine: From BBS to 'Bee Jima'", *Netweaver*, available at: http://groupjazz.com/netweaver/archive/nw86–64.html (accessed 3 March 2015).

Shapard, J. (1993) "Islands in the (Data)Stream: Language, Character Codes, and Electronic Isolation in Japan", in L. M. Harasim (ed.), *Global Networks: Computers and International Communication*, Cambridge, MA: MIT Press, pp. 255–270.

Suzuki, T. (1993) "Wide Area Networks in Japan", *Information Management Report: An International Newsletter for Information Professionals and Librarians*, 3(5): 1–4.

Yamane, K. (1996) *Nettowāku Kyōwakoku Sengen: Pasokon Tsūshin no Ima, Korekara* (Declaration of a Network Republic: Personal Computer Communication Now and in the Future), Tokyo: Chikuma Shobō.

12

A BRIEF HISTORY OF THE TAIWENESE INTERNET

The BBS Culture

Li Shao Liang, Lin Yi-Ren, and Arthur Hou-ming Huang[1]

Introduction

In this chapter, the history of Taiwanese Internet development will be discussed surrounding its distinctive BBS (bulletin board system) culture, which witnessed the founding of Taiwanese Internet networks in the 1980s and 1990s, accompanied its growth in the 2000s, and played significant roles in the recent social movements in Taiwan (roughly after 2008).

At first glance, it may be surprising that while in other countries the text- and telnet-based BBS sites have been replaced by Web-based online forums, the seemingly outdated BBS platform still enjoys high popularity in Taiwan, at the same time achieving greater and greater offline influence. By tracing the brief history of Taiwanese Internet development, this chapter shows how the current popularity of BBSs can be seen as the consequence of the early spread of Internet use via university academic networks, thanks to the introduction of the telnet system and its localization into Chinese language, and how the continuing technical innovations result from the internal dynamics among university student communities, be it collaboration or competition. Moreover, the current dominant BBS site in Taiwan, PTT (批踢踢實業坊), is also running under the umbrella of a university-based academic network, and this helps explain its relative autonomy against outside political and economic pressure, and its role of taking initiatives in social movements. In short, this chapter argues that the history and the current landscape of the Taiwanese BBS environment are substantially shaped by the technological innovations in the local context, as well as the free culture nurtured in universities and student communities.

Prehistory of Taiwanese Internet: Dial-up BBS

To begin with, it is important to point out that the currently prevailing BBS in Taiwan is different from the ones used in the 1980s in many countries. The BBS that people are normally more familiar with can be called dial-up BBS, which can only accommodate a very limited number of users, for it relies on telephone lines to connect users to the system (thus the name "dial-up"), and the number of users depends on the number of telephone lines that the system is equipped with. On the other hand, the BBS that has gained popularity in Taiwan for the past 20 years can be termed as Telnet BBS.[2] Telnet BBS connects the users through the telnet command using TCP/IP protocol, whereby the BBS sites can serve many more users at the same time. For example, on the current largest Taiwanese BBS site PTT, there are constantly over 100,000 users simultaneously online. This sheer difference in the number of participants can greatly change the nature of BBS interactions, as it enables tens of thousands of users to simultaneously interact with each other in real time, creating social psychological traits similar to those of a huge (but mobile) *mob* or *crowd*. As this is very different from the relatively less dynamic image of early *virtual communities*,[3] it is important that the distinction between dial-up BBS and Telnet BBS be recognized.

Despite this later technical advance, the history of Taiwanese Internet development (or rather, "prehistory", as the TCP/IP model had not been adopted) still dates back to the introduction of dial-up BBS among local hobbyist communities. As we know, the first BBS, which was named CBBS (Computerized Bulletin Board System), was created by Ward Christensen and Randy Suess in 1978 (Christensen and Suess 1989), followed by Tom Jennings's Fidonet, launched in 1984 (Jennings 1985). Whereas with CBBS the BBS sites were isolated from each other, with Fidonet, different sites could actually be connected and thus form a network, not just nationally but also beyond country borders. In May 1988, several Taiwanese local hobbyist BBS sites first connected with each other, then, with help from Hong Kong, Australia, and the United States, Taiwanese sites officially connected to the worldwide network of Fidonet.

It is important to note that, during this period, the promoters of BBS were mainly amateur hobbyists, not the government. Among the key figures were Honlin Lue (呂陳蒼林) and Jim Lin (林啟清), who established the "ROC Association for Amateur Computer Communication Network Development" (「中華民國業餘電腦通訊網路發展協會」), and claimed it to be "a group entirely developed by users from the bottom up" (Lue 1991a: 113, 1991b, 1991c). However, due to the technical limitations of dial-up BBS, at this time the BBS developer/user community size was quite small, and the BBS sites lacked the ability to gather a larger number of people. This was because the connections to the system still relied on telephone cables, so the concurrent user number was very limited, and the BBS sites in this period were still using English interface, which kept away potential local users. Further developments would have to wait until the introduction of Telnet BBS.

Telnet BBS and Official University BBS Sites

As mentioned previously, in Taiwan the Internet originally started to spread via the academic network, making the universities important sites for the promotion of Internet use. If we consider TCP/IP to be the criteria of whether a network can be properly called part of the "Internet", the establishment of TANet (Taiwan Academic Network) certainly marked the beginning of Taiwanese Internet development.

TANet and the Birth of Telnet BBS in Chinese Language

In 1990, under the support of MOECC (Computer Center, Ministry of Education, Taiwan), TANet was established along with three regional Internet centers under TANet, all of which were based in national universities: National Taiwan University (northern Taiwan), National Chiao Tung University (middle part of Taiwan), and National Sun Yat-Sen University

Table 12.1 Development of TANet (Taiwan Academic Network) and TANet BBS in Taiwan

Time	Event
25 April– 7 September 1986	Approval of MOECC's "Project of Improving University Professors' Research and Service" by Executive Yuan.[4] On 7 September, **terminal workstations were set up in 8 national universities, connecting to the MOECC machine IBM4341** (donated by IBM). This is the embryo of the Taiwanese academic Internet network.
14 August 1987	**Connection to the international academic network BITNET** (9.6 kbps) via Japan (to the US). This is the first network in Taiwan that provided functions such as email, FTP, and newsgroups, etc.
July 1990	**Planning of the academic network TANet with TCP/IP platform**, under MOECC's "Project of National Academic Computer Information Service and Expansion of University Computer Networks and Computer Systems" approved by Executive Yuan.
3 December 1991	TANet connects to JvNCnet of Princeton University (64kbps), marking the first day that **Taiwan connects to global TCP/IP Internet.**
5 April 1992	**Launch of National Chiao Tung University's[5] Dormitory Network Service**, serving over 1,000 dorm rooms. Early Internet applications, such as BBS, Gopher, news, and FTP, grew rapidly in the university. "Campus Computer Communication Association" (CCCA) was also founded, in order to manage and promote the dormitory network service and to mediate between the university computer center administration and the students.
October 1992	Prof. Nien-Hsing Chen (陳年興) from National Sun Yat-sen University introduced BBS to TANet and established the **first Telnet BBS site with Chinese interface**, for the purpose of serving as a platform of communication between universities, professors, and students.

Source: Chen and Wang 2006; Huang, Hui-Ying 1997; Sun 1998

(southern Taiwan). For the purpose of promoting Internet use, as the fees for accessing the Internet via TANet were largely subsidized by the government, university teachers and students could use the Internet almost for free. When there were few private ISPs and the charge was relatively costly due to lack of scale and competition, this policy certainly lowered the barrier for university users to access the Internet. As a result, the three university-based regional centers all played an important role in the development of BBS culture.

With the setting up of an Internet infrastructure via academic networks, the technical advance of BBS was also realized by university users. Here, two innovations were key to boosting the BBS user base in Taiwan, and they came into reality at the same time: one is the introduction of telnet-based BBS, the other is the Chinese language localization of BBS interface.

As mentioned, compared with the earlier dial-up BBS and the Web-based BBS later on (such as 2ch in Japan), in Taiwan the prevailing system was another type that we call Telnet BBS; the latter uses telnet protocol (which is also TCP/IP-based) to connect users to the system. The first BBS site in Taiwan to use telnet protocol was created in 1992 by Prof. Nien-Hsing Chen from National Sun Yat-Sen University, and the site was named NSYSU Formosa (「中山大學美麗之島」).[6] The introduction of Telnet BBS frees the system from the limitations of telephone cable numbers, enabling it to accommodate many more concurrent users. This would increase user numbers and is an important technical precondition for Taiwanese BBS sites to become gigantic in scale later on in the 2000s.

Still, what contributed more to the expansion of BBS from a small hobbyist community to a larger user base was the localization of BBS into a Chinese interface. Being the first Chinese BBS in Taiwan (we believe it is also the first in the world), NSYSU Formosa gained much popularity from the outset, as it was overloaded just two days after the site was launched.[7] But the localization was never an easy job. A "basic Chinese system environment" requires that the interface be comprehensible in Chinese (the text, the list of options, and the instructions, etc.), and that the system incorporate existing Chinese input methods so that the users can type in Chinese (Shen Chuan-Hsing 2001). As this is quite difficult work, in the early 1990s there were few online services that provided a relatively complete Chinese environment. For example, it was also in 1992 that TANet introduced *Usenet News* to Taiwan, but as there were not many discussion topics in Chinese, few local users participated in discussions. As a result, once there is a relatively complete Chinese system in which more people are participating, such was the case of NSYSU Formosa (and subsequent BBS sites in Chinese), not only users, but developers, would be attracted. The developers abandoned the idea of localizing an individual online service into Chinese, but instead started to incorporate other services into the already localized Chinese BBS. By this logic, for example, Usenet Newsgroup was later incorporated with existing Telnet BBS services and became what was known as tw.bbs, a subset of the Usenet Newsgroup (Huang Hui-Ying 1999; Huang *et al.* 1995). As a result, BBS in Taiwan gradually became an all-inclusive environment, fulfilling all kinds of user needs such as information seeking, social interactions, and playing online games. As such, Chinese localization is an important factor leading Taiwanese BBS to develop in its own way.

Here, what made possible the introduction of Telnet BBS and Chinese language localization was the open sourcing environment of BBS development. In order to develop the Formosa system, Prof. Chen used codes from Pirate BBS sites, then sent his modified codes back to the original developers of Pirate BBSs; these developers in turn reorganized the codes and renamed it as Eagle BBS. As the BBS sites using Unix mostly participated in the open source project, the codes of Eagle BBS were released and open for free use. As a result, another regional computer center in Taiwan, National Chiao Tung University, used the Eagle BBS codes to improve the Telnet BBS, and the previous command-style interface was modified into list-style interface, enabling users to use only the arrow keys to perform operations such as switching between boards and reading posts. This more user-friendly system was called Phoenix BBS, named after the official university BBS site of National Chiao Tung University, Phoenix City Information Station (「交大資工鳳凰城資訊站」). Phoenix BBS is the predecessor of the later two major branches of Telnet BBS versions that were further developed by other programmers. One was the Firebird BBS, which was later adopted by most Mainland Chinese BBS sites; the other was the Maple BBS, which became the prototype for most Taiwanese BBS sites established later. The currently dominating BBS site, PTT, also descends from the Maple system (Chen Tzu-Wen 2000).

We also have to note that university computer centers themselves also played significant roles in advancing the Telnet BBS system. In fact, not only did each of the three regional computer centers set up their own official university BBS sites, but many of the other universities in the academic network also had their own official sites. In the early 1990s, official BBS sites were regarded by university administrations as an important means to "communicate" with students, and to make official announcements online (perhaps in a way similar to how official Facebook or Twitter accounts are used nowadays).

Internal Tension of University BBSs: Ownership vs. Technical Staff and Users

However, there were internal structural tensions within the official university BBS sites. On one hand, there was the practical logic from the viewpoint of the university, treating the university BBS sites as a tool of administration; the BBS site for them was little more than just "bulletin boards". However, from the perspective of users and technical staff, BBS was an important platform for *social interactions*. By posting public articles or sending private messages, the users could interact with other BBS users, be them friends or strangers. As the BBS was a new form of communication for most people, the university administration did not have the experience or technical skills to manage the BBS sites. On the other hand, the technical staff actually in charge of running the university official sites were mostly students working at computer centers as part-time employees. In other words, the university owned the BBS site, but did not really understand how it worked; the students ran the site, but didn't have the right to make decisions. As a result, technical innovations were impeded, and the user experience was not valued properly. When the technical staff came up with new ideas or wanted to add new functions to respond to users' needs, the university did not always support the idea, as these developments may have caused "unnecessary troubles" for the school. As Peng I-Hua, the technical administrator of the National Taiwan University official BBS *Coconut Trees*, pointed out:

> After all, the machines and other stuff are provided by the university, so they are like our big boss, and things are not so flexible. For example, there are some things that we think are feasible, but the computer center would hesitate, as they have to face pressures from the university board, the principal, even the Parliament and the Ministry of Education . . . If the site was private, the administrators can do whatever they want to do, as they own the machine, the codes, and the staff, etc. But with the university site we just cannot do it.
>
> (Peng 2000)

Unfortunately, the "user needs" were not always justifiable for the university sites. In 2000, an incident concerning the function of the "Nickname" marked the beginning of decline for university official sites. Nickname is an alternative name that people can use on the BBS site other than the login user ID. While the login user ID consists only of Latin alphabet, along with some punctuation marks, the Nickname allows the use of Chinese characters, so Taiwanese BBS users use Nickname to add extra information about themselves as a means of self-representation. Moreover, as the Nickname is changeable (unlike the login user ID), people also use this function to express their current feelings, as well as showing all kinds of information about their current status, in a way similar to Facebook's "What are you doing?" function. As numerous cases have shown, users' creativity always goes beyond the intention of the design. Quite different from the original design of "Nickname", some users started to use it as a tool for looking for sex partners, by putting inviting messages in their Nicknames. This situation was rampant in the two largest university sites in the late 1990s: National Taiwan University (NTU) *Coconut Trees* (台大椰林風情) and Tamkang University Eggroll Square (淡江大學蛋捲廣場). As this type of use obviously violates the purpose of university BBS sites, and as NTU is the most prestigious national university in Taiwan, the university decided to remove the function of "Nickname" from its official BBS site (Li Wei-Ping 2001: 67). In fact, there were many other cases that embodied this tension between university BBS users and the school administration, such as strict verification of user identity, or the establishment of university-organized committees for regulating the official sites. As a result, the users gradually lost interest in using official university sites. After the year 2000, the user numbers of university sites substantially decreased, and the users gradually moved to another type of BBS sites: the private Telnet BBS.

Rise of Private Telnet BBSs and PTT

Private site (「私站」) is the term commonly used in local communities to designate Telnet BBS sites other than the official university BBSs. Many of the private sites were set up by students, and even though they are called "private" sites, most of them were not-for-profit. Although the rise of private sites started roughly around the year 2000, they had been developing much earlier, but only became dominant after the university sites declined. The story of private Telnet BBSs began with the dormitory networks and their open, sharing culture.

Dormitory Sites and Open Source Culture

On 5 April 1992 (the same year as the launch of the aforementioned NSYSU official BBS Formosa), National Chiao Tung University (NCTU) launched the first optical fiber dormitory Internet network. This introduction of optical fiber to dorms was two years ahead of Massachusetts Institute of Technology, and as one of the top natural science and engineering universities in Taiwan, NCTU students created many innovative services on the dormitory network, including the largest file database (an FTP service) in Asia at that time: NCTUCCCA.edu.tw (Ger 2004; He *et al.* 1995: 28).

On the other hand, the advanced infrastructure and students' innovative use of the dorm network created many administrative difficulties for the university, as the university computer center was not capable of managing the over 1,000 computers in the dorms and the ceaseless technical innovations by the students. As a result, students of NCTU decided to make rules themselves, and established an autonomous body called NCTU Campus Computer Communication Association (CCCA, 「交大校園網路策進會」) (CCCA 1996; He *et al.* 1995; Liang 1993). In this open atmosphere of dormitory network, university students started to try setting up their own BBS sites, by using the free Internet resources provided by the dorm network. In March 1996, a popular student Telnet BBS, Sun of Beach (SOB), was set up in Room 420, 7th Male Dorm of National Taiwan University (NTU). The site founder, Chen Hung-Wei, describes the founding process:

> Before March 1996, there was no Internet access in NTU dormitories, and there were only two larger BBS sites: the university site *Coconut Trees* and the Electronic Engineering Department's [official site] Maxwell. After the launch of the dormitory network in the spring semester of 1996, several dorm roommates and I started trying to set up a BBS site. The dorm network provided a fixed IP address and could access the academic network, and it was a very precious resource . . . We acquired and revised codes from NCTU, and finally succeeded in setting up the site. Since this was the first non-official BBS site in NTU, there were no unnecessary regulations and the site soon became popular among students.
>
> (Chen Hung-Wei 2010)

Later, the second site administrator, *woju* of SOB, developed an easy BBS installation package called "Plug & Play". By following instructions, decompressing the files and changing the site name, anyone could easily set up their own BBS site (Chen Tzu-Wen 2000). As a result, from 1996 to 2000, there was a craze among college students to set up a BBS of one's own, and the number of Telnet BBS sites grew very quickly on university campuses; in its prime time there were about 300–400 large Telnet BBS sites in Taiwan.[8]

Technically, back then it was also much easier to set up a BBS site than to establish a web forum. While setting up web forums requires the installation of web servers like Apache, as well as other database management systems, to set up a BBS site you just need a 486 PC with FreeBSD/Linux system (Fireium 2007). Moreover, the infrastructure of dormitory networks further lowered the barrier to having one's own BBS site. Compared with dial-up BBSs with telephone fees, the dorm network provided 24-hour Internet access and was totally free of telecom fees.

Here we might be able to see the reason why BBS use is more popular, and its technical level is more advanced, in Taiwan than in most other countries. This is path-dependent of Taiwan's Internet development strategy via academic networks and university dormitories, and also the consequence of proliferation of Telnet BBS sites. On one hand, from the users' point of view, in the mid- to late 1990s the WWW sites had less information, were mostly static, and not as interactive as the Telnet BBS sites. Besides, the WWW sites were not as close to the student communities as the university or dormitory BBSs were, for the latter themselves were rooted in the campus and could respond to student needs very quickly. On the other hand, from the programmers' or developers' perspective, due to the low entry barrier and the flexible, dynamic interface of Telnet BBS, the sense of achievement in setting up one's own BBS site was much higher than writing a static website. As the famous Internet security expert XDite points out:

> Back in the old days, when other countries were crazy for Web sites, for several years college students in the whole of Taiwan were mad about developing and improving BBS systems. Due to technical limitations, the Web sites were mostly static; even though there were some dynamic sites, the technical barrier was quite high. On the contrary, BBS was written in C [language], and if you followed the instructions, anyone with Linux/FreeBSD skills could easily create a real-time interactive community site (for the same speed [of user experience], it would have to wait for another 7 or 8 years for Ajax to come along). This undoubtedly best satisfied college students' vanity and desire to explore new techniques. Frequent sharing of release packages and function patches by several core teams further triggered the nationwide craze to improve codes.
>
> (XDite 2007)

This new development, combined with the decline of university official sites (due to more and more regulations), gives us a better idea of why the private Telnet BBS sites born in university dorms were able to take over the leading place of the official sites. In fact, one of the private dormitory sites born in this period, PTT from National Taiwan University, became so successful that it achieved a monopoly, after severe competition with other sites, and turned into the only dominant BBS today in Taiwan.

PTT: From Birth to Monopoly

PTT was founded on 14 September 1995 by NTU Computer Science Department student Tu Yi-Chin (杜奕瑾)[9] in his dorm room in the 8th Male Dorm of NTU (Tu 2005). Initially just a personal experiment, it soon became one of the larger BBS sites in the university. Born in the age when private Telnet BBS sites grew very fast, it was the first private site to achieve

1,000 users simultaneously online (in November 1998), a number similar to the NTU official site *Coconut Trees* at that time. In the early to mid-2000s, PTT further achieved the status of monopoly, defeating all the other Telnet BBS competitors, such as *Coconut Trees*, SOB, and Zoo (another NTU dorm site). It is also important to note that PTT has never been a commercial site; rather, it receives donations from users and from the staff themselves. So we could not help asking: without the economic drive to pursue growth, how does PTT achieve such a large scale, and what makes it more successful than other private sites?

Again, the secret of PTT's success lies in its management and recruitment strategy through the university communities. This can be discussed in three aspects. First, the PTT managing staff is recruited from university students, especially from NTU Department of Computer Science & Information Engineering. This ensure the "supply" of succeeding staff, as well as the technical ability required for site maintenance. In the early 2000s, many of the private dorm BBS sites faced the crisis of decline, largely due to lack of succeeding administrative staff. As the first wave of setting up private sites started around 1996, it could be expected that after the founding members graduated from university around 2000, they could no longer use dormitory networks for site operation. Nor would they have as much time for running the site, which would result in immediate problems for site maintenance. In fact, PTT also experienced such difficulties around 2000, but soon adapted its strategy by establishing a tradition of "passing on". Through a system similar to university student club activities, each class year takes the responsibility of maintenance from the preceding students, then hands it over to succeeding ones. This strategy also ensures that the BBS can always enjoy the benefits of using an academic network. As a result, while other private dorm sites withered away in the early 2000s, the operating and maintenance of PTT became stabilized, and the technical staff could focus on the improvement of site functions.

The second issue is the engineer mindset of the technical staff, which could explain their continuing drive for site improvement and innovation. First, since the technical staff is mostly made up of college students from the Department of Computer Science, PTT provides a golden opportunity for the students to practice their technical skills. After all, not everyone has the chance to manage a real-time interacting system with thousands or tens of thousands of concurrent users online. Second, as the top Computer Science program in Taiwan, the technical staff just could not accept that any other site should surpass PTT in terms of scale or new functions. Indeed, there was an interesting competition between PTT and Zoo, a site run by students from the neighboring Department of Electronic Engineering. As mentioned, in 1998, PTT became the first private BBS site to reach 1,000 concurrent users online, but in 2000, when PTT was struggling with the problem of finding succeeding administration staff, Zoo surpassed PTT and reached 2,000 concurrent users online first. After the second PTT site administrator (「站長」, or chief of staff) in2[10] took over PTT, the two sites started a keen competition with each other. As in2 explains:

> Back then our main competitor was Zoo. They are from electronic engineering and we are from computer science, and it's really difficult to describe that kind of feelings (laugh). At that time Zoo's advantage was that their RAM was 250 MB more than ours (theirs was 2.25GB and ours was 2GB). As there was not much difference in terms of quality of codes, that 250 MB just can give you several hundreds of users more . . . Basically computer science is doing software, and electronic engineering is doing hardware, and it's not acceptable that they should make something larger than us! No way! Our codes are supposed to be superior . . . it's completely a battle out of pride!

> (in2 2011)

Here we can see how the technical staff was engaged in "serious play", and how the growth of the BBS site itself could be regarded as recognition of the technical ability of the staff. Third, the staff was playing a double role of "user-engineer". As BBS was born in the university, using BBS has become a shared experience for Taiwanese college students for the past 20 years or so, and many of the BBS technical staff were themselves heavy users too. As a result, their drive of improving the site comes not just from responding to other users' needs, but also (if not mainly) to their own needs. As in2 points out:

> There is an idea in the community of open source, which I usually describe as: "I'm doing this because it benefits myself; after I do it, it will benefit other people too." It's like I'm decorating my garden for myself, not for other people. If my garden can make somebody else happy when they see it, it's their business, not mine . . . So it's more driven by self-interest. For example, the design of up-voting (推文) was at first just to solve our [the staff] own problem of evaluating and selecting articles; we did not think too much about other users.
>
> (in2 2011)

This helps to explain the reason why, after defeating all the other BBS sites, PTT kept improving its functions, without any commercial incentives. The staff was improving PTT for their own needs, be it for acquiring recognition of technical ability, or some other more practical needs, such as making the management of the site easier.

The last secret of PTT's success was its devolved managing structure, or refined division of labor among the staff. As the site grew bigger and bigger, the original functions among the administrative staff in many cases needed adjustment, otherwise it would not be able to respond to the increasing needs that came with the growing number of users. Since its founding stage, PTT separated its technical division and the managing division, as the technical staff often care only about technical issues, and they would be very happy if somebody else could take care of other issues. Also, the administrative staff includes students outside the Computer Science Department, even outside the university. For example, with the increasing disputes among site users, PTT created a law division; in order to raise funds for hardware purchase, PTT also set up divisions for holding events and dealing with public relations. In this way, more and more functions were created, and with the university students' support, there is a continuing supply of staff members, with different specialized knowledge and skills.

In this way, as other larger sites all faced different problems and declined in the early 2000s (Zoo also went down because of no succeeding staff), PTT became the only site that grew steadily, and finally achieved the status of monopoly roughly in the mid-2000s.[11] As there were no powerful competitors any longer, PTT almost took over the whole BBS users' population in Taiwan, and the user number skyrocketed in a very short time. In 2005, the number of concurrent online users on PTT reached 50,000, and that number was soon pushed to 100,000 in 2007. Aside from the technological innovations of PTT itself and the fading of competing BBS sites, this rapid growth of membership of PTT is also partly thanks to some online incidents that made it to the national news around 2005 (discussed below), so the user base of the site gradually expanded from university students to the general public.

At this point, as PTT has become large enough, and as many elite university students in Taiwan have the experience of using PTT and still keep the habit after starting their career in different professional fields, PTT gradually became a kind of quasi-mass media, and started to have influence on the larger society. This will be discussed in the following sections.

Online and Offline Influences of PTT

On 2 March 2005, PTT made it to the front page of *The China Times*, a major national newspaper in Taiwan. The title of the news post was "Cheating Affair in Tunghai University Flames the Internet", and it related how a college couple's alleged cheating affair provoked an episode of Internet flaming on PTT (Chen Lo-Wei 2005). The content of the news itself was trivial, but the fact that this banal online incident could make it to the national paper's front page marked the beginning of the mainstream media casting their eyes on PTT. From this day on, PTT user activities have frequently been the topic of news posts, except that it is often about such trivial issues. On the other hand, PTT users also actively seek to express alternative opinions to the mainstream media on all kinds of issues, challenging their interpretations of society, especially on political topics. The main battlefield on PTT is its largest bulletin board, *Gossiping*.

PTT Gossiping: An Emotional News Commenting Board

Since 2006, *Gossiping* has been the largest board on PTT, with constantly over 10,000 concurrent users online, which is roughly a tenth of the total user number on the BBS site. With so many users, it is like a gigantic chat room, in which everyone can have real-time interactions with thousands of other people. More importantly, it is Taiwan's largest online news discussion board, with about 2,000 posts every day, not including the (sometimes hundreds of) up-/down-voting comments attached to each post.

The way that *Gossiping* users comment on news is through a practice called "news pasting". As the term itself suggests, users copy news content from mainstream media sites, and paste it to *Gossiping* for other users to comment on. While this practice runs the risk of infringing upon the intellectual property rights of the media, the media professionals themselves also developed the habit of obtaining news materials from *Gossiping*, and some of them are even keen to cover the feedback from BBS users to their own news posts. As such, the relationship between the mainstream media and the BBS is at once competitive and mutually beneficial, and the practice of pasting news can therefore survive in the grey area. *Gossiping* users enjoy the right to comment on news contents, and once a comment is posted, it will immediately have tens of thousands of readers. This is why we can consider PTT *Gossiping* as a quasi-mass media, as it owns its own channels to speak to the public, and to provide alternative opinions to those expressed by the mainstream news media.

Here, it is important to note that, far from the expectation of online news forums being part of the Habermasian rational "public sphere", PTT *Gossping* actually demonstrates very emotional characteristics in terms of communication style. This is despite the fact that the users are relatively elite social members, and many of them are students or graduates from top universities in Taiwan. This situation can be explained both by the larger social context in Taiwan, and by the technical characteristic of Telnet BBS itself.

On one hand, since 2000, when the more China-friendly and long-time ruling party KMT (國民黨) stepped down from power after their half-century long domination, being replaced by the more localist party DPP (民進黨), the political atmosphere in Taiwan has become bipolarized—and there has been a clear split between people supporting the two parties. The same can be said of the mainstream media; many of the major newspapers or TV news channels can be classified as either pro-KMT (the Pan Blue Camp) or pro-DPP (the Pan Green Camp). As for the BBS users, generally speaking they are more critical of the ruling party and the media that support the government. However, the same division between the Blue and the

Green can be clearly observed too. This inevitably provokes quarrels and disputes when the discussions touch upon politically sensitive topics.

On the other hand, it also has much to do with the medium of the Telnet BBS itself. With the technical advance mentioned in previous sections, PTT can accommodate a large number of participants engaging in real-time interactions with each other. Therefore, rather than a rational debating space, it might be better to imagine PTT *Gossiping* as a noisy stadium, or a carnival square or marketplace, where a crowd of 100,000 people gather together to express their collective will and opinions.

In fact, this idea of being (virtually) together with such a large crowd also created a social psychological effect echoing the phenomenon that French sociologist Emile Durkheim (1995 [1912]) described: "Because he is in moral harmony with his neighbor, he gains new confidence, courage, and boldness in *action*" (1995: 213, our italics). This crowd mindset helps to explain why, in recent years, PTT has become an "arsenal", or platform of mobilization, for collective actions and social movements in Taiwan.

PTT and Offline Collective Actions

The first notable case of PTT-supported social movement might be the Wild Strawberry Movement in 2008, which urged for the amendment of the Assembly and Parade Law (「集會遊行法」). In Taiwan, too, the Internet users have long been criticized for clicktivism, meaning that Internet users would just talk online without any physical presence when needed. However, in the 2008 Wild Strawberry Movement, PTT started to show its ability to mobilize people. Professor Ming-Tsung Lee from the Department of Sociology, National Taiwan University, used PTT2 (a sister-site of PTT) to call for a sit-down demonstration in front of government offices (Huang Hou-ming 2008). On 6 November 2008, several hundred college students gathered and sat in front of the Executive Yuan (the administrative branch of the government) to support the movement (Ho and Liu 2008). Although the number is not large, it showed how social movements can recruit participants, especially university students, by using PTT as the mobilizing platform.

Since the Wild Strawberry Movement, many other events have been using PTT to gather resources, including human power and other physical things. For example, in 2009, one of the most devastating typhoons that Taiwan has ever faced, Typhoon Morakot, struck the island and took hundreds of lives in several mountainous areas, leaving many rescue and recovery tasks to the surviving residents. On the first few days of the disaster, information was still very limited, and government rescue teams were not able to cover every affected area. Seeing this situation, the users on PTT soon opened a new board called *Emergency*, in order to gather disaster information and to collect and distribute resources to those who were in need. This case further strengthened the confidence and sense of social responsibility of PTT users, and helped improve their public image.

In several other similar cases, the PTT users and administrative staff gained much experience when it comes to mobilization through the BBS site, and this prepared PTT for playing important roles in the two major social movements in Taiwan. The first one was the 2013 Hung Chung-chiu Incident (「洪仲丘事件」, or the All-Whites Movement, 「白衫軍運動」), which resulted from the death of an Army Corporal due to physical abuse by military officers. Out of anger towards the act of omission by government officers, the movement mobilized 250,000 citizens to demonstrate in front of the Presidential Office Building (Lo 2013). What is worth noting here is that the organizers of this movement, Citizens 1985 (「公民1985行動聯盟」), were a group of PTT users who established connections through

PTT *Gossiping* (Lo 2013). The name of their Facebook fan page, *pttcitizen1985*, is itself quite telling. In another major movement, the 2014 March 18th Movement (「318運動」, or the Sunflower Movement, 「太陽花運動」), Citizen 1985 collaborated with other citizen groups and had much influence.

Conclusion

In this chapter, we have traced the short history of Internet development in Taiwan, focusing on its distinctive BBS culture. Specifically, we have seen how the path-dependent effect has shaped the landscape of Taiwanese BBS environment, and the story developed surrounding the university communities. Starting from the setting up of Internet infrastructure, the introduction of Telnet BBS and the localization of the BBS system in the Chinese language established the foundation of Taiwanese BBS development. The academic TANet and the university dormitory networks also provided university users with a free and encouraging environment, which made possible the birth and spread of the Telnet BBS. Second, the strategy of recruiting administrative staff from university student communities proved to be key not only to PTT's survival, but also to its steady growth into a giant, dominating site. Also, the "serious play" mindset of the technical staff provided the continuing drive for pursuing site growth and further technical innovations. Last, when the scale of PTT grew large enough to have influence on society, the fact that it is rooted in the university campus also created advantages of mobilization, as students have always been important participants in social movements in Taiwan. In short, the BBS culture in Taiwan cannot be considered separately from the local contexts, and is contingent on several key decisions or incidents in different stages of development of the local Telnet BBS environment.

Finally, there are some issues that can be further explored. For one, it would be interesting to compare Taiwanese BBS developments with those in China and Japan. For example, according to Yang's chapter in this volume, in China roughly since the late 1990s, BBS no longer played significant roles in Chinese fan culture and the users turned to Web-based services, such as Netease personal sites, which better satisfied their needs. In contrast to this, although in Taiwan the Web also started to prevail in the same period, BBS continued to evolve and innovate, especially when university sites went down due to regulations from the authorities; BBS culture was able to continue with private sites,[12] finally resulting in the monopoly of the quasi-mass media PTT. In China, on the other hand, where BBS is also localized in the Chinese language, and where Internet innovations have been at full speed, why do we not see a similar development as in Taiwan? This might be a puzzle to be explored in future studies.

In Japan's case, there are also several interesting points to discuss. First, it has to be noted that, although often referred to as "BBS", the famous 2ch is actually a Web-based service, which can be regarded as a website and is therefore very different from Taiwan's telnet-based BBS: a Telnet BBS uses a keyboard to perform all the operations, and its users need to download specific programs (e.g. NetTerm), locally developed browsers that integrate http and telnet protocols, or mobile phone apps to gain access to the site. Second, despite such difference, both 2ch and PTT play the role of gathering and forming online public opinions, which often take alternative positions to those of the mainstream media. However, this again is what makes them different: in Japan 2ch seems to suffer much from stigmatization, often referred to as politically extreme, while PTT used to have quite a negative reputation too, but that is changing due to PTT's role in recent major social movements. As a result, we may suppose that the two "BBS" sites have different degrees of influence on public opinion (represented by mainstream media). Of course, this too requires further study.

Finally, the mobilizing ability of online services for offline collective actions, such as social movements, may be an intriguing topic. In fact, although currently the BBS culture in Mainland China seems to have declined, there are many other services, such as Weibo, that can gather a large number of people in a short time. What can be said to be common or different between the BBS sites and SNSs such as Facebook or Weibo in terms of the ability to mobilize users? Also, under what conditions can online discussions be transformed into real world (offline) actions? These questions all require further empirical and theoretical investigations.[13]

Notes

1. This chapter is mainly revised and translated from Li Shao Liang's previous work, including his Master's thesis: "How is a 150,000 users' BBS possible: the study of PTT's technological change (1995–2008)" (see Li Shao Liang 2012, originally published in Chinese) and Chapter 3 of *Hello! Netizens: Evolutional History of PTT for the Awaken Villagers* (see Li Shao Liang, 2016; the book is edited by Arthur Hou-ming Huang and was published in 2016 in Chinese by the publisher Socio, Taipei, Taiwan). The actual revision and translation of Li's work, as well as the sections concerning PTT *Gossiping* and offline participation of BBS users, are credited to Lin Yi-Ren. Li's thesis is supervised by Arthur Hou-ming Huang, and is an extension of Huang's National Science Council (Taiwan) research project (2011–2013): "The history and culture of PTT BBS: from the viewpoint of mob-ility".
2. In this chapter, we use upper case "Telnet BBS" as a proper name for the specific type of BBS, and use lower case "telnet" in other situations.
3. For more detailed discussions on the new characteristics of the "online crowds", or what we term "mob-ility", see Huang and Lin (2013).
4. The executive branch of the Taiwanese government.
5. One of the top Taiwanese universities in the field of natural sciences and engineering.
6. The name is allegedly what Portuguese sailors called the island of Taiwan ("Ilha Formosa") during the Age of Discovery (around the sixteenth century). By coincidence, it is also the name of a major anti-authoritarianism demonstration which occurred in 1987, known as the "Formosa Incident" (「美麗島事件」).
7. Professor Chen used the then prevailing Big5 code, not Unicode, to localize the Telnet BBS into Chinese. Due to the path-dependent effect, the BBS language coding system nowadays in Taiwan still remains Big5 (electronic_blue, 2009). This caused some problems for typing and reading Japanese characters.
8. The population of Taiwan in 1995 was around 21 million people.
9. Also known as Panda Tu, thus the name PTT—P(anda) T(u) with an extra T to make it sound smoother.
10. PTT user ID of the person.
11. It even annexed some other BBS sites, including the aforementioned SOB (annexation in 2004).
12. In the same period, there are also some commercial sites outside the university. For related discussions, see Li Shao Liang (2012).
13. For related discussion of some of the issues mentioned in the conclusion, see Cader and Lin (2016).

References

References in English

Cader, Joshua and Lin Yi-Ren. 2016. "Masculinity, Transgressive Play, and Offline Action on Discussion Boards in the US, Taiwan, and Japan." Presented at the 66th ICA (International Communication Association) Annual Conference. 9th–13th June 2016 in Fukuoka, Japan.

Christensen, W., and Suess, R. (1989) *The Birth of the BBS*, available at: www.chinet.com/html/cbbs.php (accessed 16 October 2015).

Durkheim, E. (1995 [1912]) *The Elementary Forms of Religious Life*, trans. K.E. Fields, New York: Free Press.

Huang, S. K., Chen, M.F., Yang, J. J., Chen, C. S., and Liu, T. C. (1995) "Design and Application of Gateways between Internet BBS and Netnews", *Taiwan Academic Network Conference*, 23–24 October, pp. F46–F51.

Jennings, T. (1985) *FidoNet History and Operation (Part 2)*, available at: www.worldpowersystems.com/FidoNet/fidohist2.txt (accessed 16 October 2015).

References in Chinese: Titles Translated into English

CCCA (Campus Computer Communication Association, National Chiao Tung University) (1996) *Internet—Infinite Expansion of Your Vision*, Taipei: Sung Gang.

Chen, Hung-Wei (2010) interview by Li S. L., 8 November.

Chen, Lo-Wei (2005) "Cheating Affair in Tunghai University Flames the Internet", *China Times*, 2 March, p. A1.

Chen, Tzu-Wen (2000), *Short History of BBS Development in Taiwan*, available at: https://market.cloud.edu.tw/content/senior/computer/ks_ks/comsense/bbs.htm (accessed 16 October 2015).

Chen, Wen-Sheng, and Wang, San-Chi (2006) "On the Development of Taiwanese Internet", *Taiwan Academy for Information Society Annual Conference*, Yuan Ze University, Tao Yuan County, Taiwan.

electronic_blue (2009) *Screen + Unicode-At-On*, available at: http://electronic-blue.wikidot.com/doc:screen-uao (accessed 23 November 2015).

Fireium (2007) *Prospect of the Telnet-Based BBS*, available at: https://bbs.sjtu.edu.cn/bbsanc,path,%2Fgroups%2FGROUP_0%2FAdvice%2FReferences%2FArticles%2FD70D77DE4%2FM.1177068159.A.html (accessed 20 November 2015).

Ger, Huang-bin (2004) "Rebel Code or National Code?—The Development and Challenge of the Free Software Movement in Taiwan (1991–2004)", Master's thesis, National Tsing Hua University, Taiwan.

He, Yuan *et al.* (1995) *My Computer Exploration*, Taipei: Infopro.

Ho, Hsing-Pang, and Liu, Shang-Yun (2008) "Student Movement Coming Back with Sit-In Protest Against the Assembly and Parade Act", *China Times*, 8 November.

Huang, Hou-ming (2008) *An Open Letter to Students in the Wild Strawberry Movement*, available at: http://blog.yam.com/retribalize/article/18111070 (accessed 17 October 2015).

Huang, Hou-ming, and Yi-Ren, Lin (2013) "Mob-ility: Re-exploring the Community Question of Virtual Community", *Mass Communication Research (Taiwan)*, 115: 1–50.

Huang, Hui-Ying (1997) "On the 'Dissenting BBS' Spilling Out of the Virtual Space: The Context of the TANet BBS Development", *2nd Conference of the Information Technology and the Social Transformation*, Preparatory Office of the Institute of Sociology, Academia Sinica.

Huang, Hui-Ying (1999) "The Internet Movement in Taiwan from the Perspective of Political Economy (1979–1999)", Master's thesis, National Chengchi University.

in2 (2011) interview by Li S. L., 28 December.

Li, Shao Liang (2012) "How is a 150,000 Users' BBS Possible: The Study of PTT's Technological Change (1995–2008)", Master's thesis, National Chengchi University, Taipei, Taiwan.

Li, Shao Liang (2016) "Spring of a Technical Living Fossil: History of Monopoly of a Platform", in Arthur Hou-ming Huang (ed.) *Hello! Netizens: Evolutional History of PTT for the Awaken Villagers*, pp. 75-116. Taipei, Taiwan: Socio.

Li, Wei-Ping (2001) "In Search of the Normalizing Force of the TANet BBS Sites", Master's thesis, National Chengchi University.

Liang, Po-Sung (1993) "Practices of Campus Internet Management Assisted by Student Associations—Anniversary of CCCA", *Information Letter of the Ministry of Education Computer Center*, pp. 30–40.

Lo, Fan-Yung (2013) "Attacking Internet Villagers: Association 'Pttcitizen1985' Mobilizes 250,000 Citizens", *Apple Daily*, 4 August, available at: www.appledaily.com.tw/realtimenews/article/new/20130804/236718 (accessed 17 October 2015).

Lue, Honlin (1991a) *The Internet World of the BBS*, Taipei: Information and Computer Magazine.

Lue, Honlin (1991b) "The Significance of Promoting BBS Communication Network", *The Third Wave*, 106.

Lue, Honlin (1991c) "Learning to Access Information for Using and Hosting BBS", *The Third Wave*, 101.

Peng, I-Hua (2000) interview, quoted from Li (2001: 68–69), 26 February.

Shen, Chuan-Hsing (2001) *FreeBSD Chinese HOWTO*, available at: www.kaiyuanba.cn/content/linux/FreeBSD/FreeBSD_HOWTO.pdf (accessed 24 November 2015).

Sun, Hsiu-Hui (1998) "Exploring the Development and Problems of Taiwanese Internet", *Journal of Radio and Television Studies*, 3(4): 1–20.

Tu, Yi-Chin (2005) "Founding Date of PTT", *PTT, "PttHistory" Board (Selected Articles (z) -> 7. Site History and Group (Board) History)*.

XDite (2007) *Introduction to BBS and Blog (3)*, available at: http://blog.xdite.net/?p=276 (accessed 25 November 2015).

References in Chinese: Original Chinese Titles

CCCA [交大校園網路策進會] (1996) 《Internet 無限拓展你的視野》。台北: 松崗。

Chen, Hung-Wei [陳鴻偉] (2010) 〈2010年11月8日陽光沙灘創站站長書面訪談稿〉。（訪談: 李紹良）

Chen, Lo-Wei [陳洛薇] (2005) 東海大學 劈腿事件喧騰網路〉。2005年3月 2日，《中國時報》A1版，要聞。

Chen, Tzu-Wen [陳子文] (2000) 〈台灣BBS發展簡史〉。網址: https://market.cloud.edu.tw/content/senior/computer/ks_ks/comsense/bbs.htm (擷取於 2015.10.16)

Chen, Wen-Sheng, and Wang, San-Chi [陳文生、王三吉] (2006) 〈台灣網際網路發展歷程之研究〉。發表於 2006 年台灣資訊社會研究學會年會。

Fireium (2007) 〈乱弾 telnet-based BBS〉。網址: https://bbs.sjtu.edu.cn/bbsanc,path,%2Fgroups%2FGROUP_0%2FAdvice%2FReferences%2FArticles%2FD70D77DE4%2FM.1177068159.A.html (擷取於2015.11.20)

Ger, Huang-bin [葛皇濱] (2004) 《叛碼或國碼? 台灣自由軟體運動的發展與挑戰 1991–2004 》。清華大學歷史研究所碩士論文。

He, Yuan et al. [賀元等著] (1995) 《我的電腦探索》。台北: 資訊人文化。

Ho, Hsing-Pang, and Liu, Shang-Yun [何醒邦、劉尚昀] (2008) 學生靜坐抗議 集遊法 再掀學運〉。2008年11月8日，《中國時報》。

Huang, Hou-ming [黃厚銘] (2008) 〈給野草莓學運同學們的公開信〉。《再部落化》部落格。網址: http://blog.yam.com/retribalize/article/18111070擷取於 2015.10.17

Huang, Hou-ming, and Yi-Ren, Lin [黃厚銘、林意仁] (2013) 〈流動的群聚 (mob-ility 網路起鬨的社會心理基礎〉。《新聞學研究》105: 1–50.

Huang, Hui-Ying. [黃慧櫻] (1997) 從TANet BBS 發展脈絡 探討跨出虛擬空 間的「異議 BBS 」〉。中央研究院社會學研究所籌備處《第二屆資訊科技 與社會轉型研討會會議論文》。

Huang, Hui-Ying [黃慧櫻] (1999) 《尋找台灣學術網路BBS站的規範力量》。國立政治大學新聞學研究所碩士論文。

in2. (2011) 2011年12月28日訪談稿。(訪談: 李紹良)

Li, Shao Liang [李紹良] (2012)，《十五萬人的BBS是如何煉成的: 批踢踢實業坊技術演變歷程之研究1995–2008》。國立政治大學新聞學研究所碩士論文。

Li, Shao Liang [李紹良] (2016) 〈第三章 技術活化石的春天: 一段BBS站獨大的歷史〉，黃厚銘(編)，《婉君妳好嗎? : 給覺醒鄉民的PTT進化史》。台北:群學。

Li, Wei-Ping [李惟平] (2001) 《尋找台灣學術網路BBS站的規範力量》。國立政治大學新聞學研究所碩士論文。

Liang, Po-Sung [梁柏嵩] (1993) 〈學生社團協助管理校園網路實務 足跡...寫於CCCA週年〉。《教育部電子計算機中心簡訊》，民國82年12月:30–40.

Lo, Fan-Yung [羅凡勇] (2013) 〈進擊的鄉民 1985聯盟竟串聯25萬公民〉。2013年8月4日，《蘋果日報》。網址: www.appledaily.com.tw/realtimenews/article/new/20130804/236718 (擷取於2015.10.17)

Lue Honlin [呂陳蒼林] (1991a) 《BBS網路世界》。台北: 資訊與電腦雜誌社。

Lue Honlin [呂陳蒼林] (1991b) 〈BBS通訊網路推廣的意義〉。《第三波》,106: 65

Lue Honlin [呂陳蒼林] (1991c) 〈學習BBS使用與設站資訊的取得管道〉。《第三波》,101: 43

Peng, I-Hua [彭怡華] (2000) 2000 年2月26日訪談。轉引自李惟平 (Li, 2001, pp. 68–69).

Shen, Chuan-Hsing (2001) FreeBSD Chinese HOWTO, available at: www.kaiyuanba.cn/content/linux/FreeBSD/FreeBSD_HOWTO.pdf (accessed 24 November 2015).

Sun, Hsiu-Hui [孫秀蕙] (1998) 〈台灣網際網路發展與問題初探〉。《廣播與電視》,3(4): 1–20.

Tu, Yi-Chin [杜奕瑾] (2005) 〈Ptt 開站日期〉。PTT -> PttHistor看板精華區 -> 7. 站史, 各群組(板)史。(擷取於 2015.10.16)

XDite (2007) 〈淺談BBS與Blog (3)〉。網址: http://blog.xdite.net/?p=276 (擷取於 2011.11.25)

13

H-MAIL AND THE EARLY CONFIGURATION OF ONLINE USER CULTURE IN KOREA

Dongwon Jo

Introduction

When did the Internet start in Korea?[1] This basic question is not clearly answered yet, as the early history of the Internet itself in other countries, including the United States, has been controversial (see, for example, Campbell-Kelly and Garcia-Swartz 2013; Russell and Schafer 2014). One may claim that in Korea the Internet began in 1982, when a research-oriented network called System Development Network (SDN) was established with the adoption of TCP/IP as its essential protocol (An 2014; Chon *et al.* 2013); on the other hand, it is more commonly argued to have unfolded in 1994, when commercial Internet services were launched, after which it gradually became a mass network (Kim and Na 2008; Koo 2008; Woo 2005; Yoon 2011). Challenging such common approaches, a few studies maintain that Internet users and their culture emerged prior to the popularization of the Internet in 1994. These studies usually base the origin of the netizens' activities and their online communities not on the Internet itself, but on personal computer (PC) communications (Hauben *et al.* 2007: 55–58; Jo 2013; Kang 2007; Yoo 2008).

In this chapter, I advance this argument further, suggesting that a popular culture of Internet use had already emerged following the first public email service, H-mail, launched in 1987. H-mail contained the major features of Korean Internet culture we see today, as Seunghyun Yoo (2008) has identified, such as a well-organized Internet café (meaning online community forum), proliferating *Pernarugi* ("scooping" or content transfer between different user communities) or user-generated content, and active commenting practices. However, very little attention has been paid to H-mail as an origin of online user culture today. Therefore, this chapter aims to investigate the ways that the culture of early online users based on H-mail developed, with these main questions in mind: How did ordinary online users emerge? How did they begin to form online communities of their own? And how did these developments influence today's Internet culture?

H-mail was the first public email service in Korea provided in 1987 by the Data Communication Corporation of Korea (DACOM), in which the first community of online users was formed. Thus, it is worth paying attention to how the system anticipated and imagined its potential users in its design and initial set-up. Bearing this in mind, "configuring the user" (Woolgar 1991) is a useful perspective when looking into how the technology shapes its user, while on the contrary, it is important to also remember that the user does not necessarily use the technology as given. Indeed, the technology can be reconfigured and repurposed by the user. In this regard, I draw on the concept of "reconfiguration" (Lievrouw 2011) to address the user's agency in reshaping the technology. The main data for the study is provided by in-depth interviews and a literature review.[2] The in-depth interviews with four former H-mail users were conducted as unstructured, but focused, conversations in 2011 and 2013. Primary source materials in Korean include computer magazines as well as general newspapers, in which my focus is mainly on the period of the late 1980s.

After the section about the local historical context of computing, networking, and particularly data communications services in the 1980s, I examine the two-way configurations between H-mail and its users from three perspectives. First, I look at how users used the system, in particular user's reconfiguration of H-mail as a horizontal many-to-many form of communication in contrast to DACOM's original configuration of the user in terms of broadcast-like one-to-many communication. Second, I consider the relationship between the users' hacking activities and DACOM's continuous security enhancement to control it. The last aspect involves the configuration at the macro level between the affluence of online user communities based on the electronic bulletin board systems (BBS) and national security issues that served as a boundary to restrict them. Encompassing all three aspects, I conclude by discussing H-mail and its users' contributions to prefiguring today's Internet culture in Korea.

A Very Brief History of Computing, Networking, and Hangulizing[3]

Computers were first introduced to Korea as electronic data-processing machines in the late 1960s. They were leased or purchased from the United States and Japan by the Economic Planning Board, the Korea Productivity Center, and the Korea Institute of Science and Technology (KIST) for the purposes of census and social control, the management of productivity and labor, and use in advanced science and technology for economic development (Jo 2015: 187–197). The first electronic data communication, among other early developments, was conducted between computers in the Economic Planning Board and KIST in June 1970 (Seo 1997: 50).

It was, however, not until the early 1980s that the fully fledged development of information industries and computer networks was initiated by the government, accompanying the popularization of computers as personal communication media and the networking of information systems, including the establishment of the National Basic Information System (NBIS) as the largest ever national project. In general, new economic development projects for the information society in Korea were launched in the early 1980s by the government of the military dictatorship. Such projects took shape in relation to global economic structural adjustments begun in the 1970s, as well as the Cold War geopolitical milieu, with a focus on the consolidation of the national administrative system and the expansion of Jaebeol[4] business structure to the information industries.

As computers were popularized and popular digital culture emerged in this period, micro-computers were not just manufactured and distributed from the top by the government and big corporations for educational and office purposes, but were also assembled, reproduced, and distributed from below, such as at electronics shops in the Seoul neighborhood of Cheonggycheon, and even by early active users of game-playing and human online communication. Popular computer networks emerged along with BBS and PC communications in the late 1980s (Jo 2013).

In the course of the history of the development of computing and networking, one crucial issue has been the Hangulization or digitalization of Korean letters—competing methods and arguments for the implementation of a Korean character code and its standardization. The first system implemented was the Hangul-printing line printer developed at KIST in 1972 (Seo 1997: 44–45). In the late 1970s, and throughout the 1980s, a variety of Hangul word processors and Hangul editing software programs were researched and developed. For imported and reproduced micro-computers in particular, there were a number of vying Hangul graphic cards and dedicated software programs, including those developed by individual tech-savvy users.

As was the case for Japanese scripts at this time (see Chapter 11 in this volume), many different and incompatible technologies for implementing a Korean character code were in use without successful standardization. Several attempts at standardization by the government in 1974, 1982, and 1987 repeatedly failed. It was not until 1987, in response to the establishment of the NBIS, that the KS C 5601 character set was controversially settled on as the national standard. It comprised a two-byte long pre-combination type for each character, including Hangul, Hanja (Chinese ideographic characters), graphic and foreign characters, etc. Disputes around the 1987 national standard were not finally solved until EUC-KR or UNICODE appeared in 1995 as a desirable standard.

Although a focused and detailed investigation of this process has not yet been conducted, and is beyond the scope of this chapter, each historical effort made for Hangulization, not only by governmental institutions but by a variety of actors, including individual users, is well worth examining further. This is because the effective implementation of a Korean character code and the search for an optimal standard were key factors necessary before new information and communication technologies could become part of popular and mass culture in Korea. With this in mind, a number of titles for development projects and software programs have used the prefixes Han or 'H', which stands for Hangul, or sometimes Hanguk (Korea) or Hangyeore (Korean race). H-mail was one of these, signifying the first Hangul-based public email system.

As mentioned, in the early to mid-1980s, the government and corporations moved forward with computer networks such as the NBIS and the data communication services for the purposes of high-speed information processing and transmission in the fields of administration, national security, research and education, and business. Accordingly, DACOM was established in 1982 with the government's financial support and its intention to control the development of a variety of value-added and information services, which began with DACOM-Net Service (DACOM-Net). DACOM-Net was officially inaugurated in July of 1984 and conceived of as "a highway of information circulation" (DACOM 1993: 230). It became "the nation's main artery for data communications flow" (Larson 1995: 73).

The early computer networks delivered from the top down in the early 1980s began to be established in a manner not unlike one-way mass media, despite their bidirectional nature. In their initial design, most were far from what we enjoy today as bidirectional human communications on the Internet. Instead, one can say that they were designed as a broadcast model. It was in such a situation that the first generation of online users was formed in Korea.

Informative Online Services Versus Communicative Users

Based on participant observation during the process of testing a new range of micro-computers, Woolgar (1991: 69) suggested that the design and production of technologies involve a process of configuring the user, by which he means "to define, enable and constrain the user". The user is rhetorically constructed and imagined by designers in the process of technology design (Mackay *et al.* 2000: 741). In the context of the initial development of data communications systems in Korea, the online user was first configured as the consumer of informational commodities provided in DACOM's data bank services.

How DACOM configured its users as informational consumers was well illustrated by Chollian, which was the videotex service launched in May 1986 as a prominent data communications service among DACOM-Net, especially for the general public.[5] Chollian was not widely successful, however, since it was only set up in such special zones as airports, hotels, and at big events like the Seoul Asian Games in 1986 and the Olympic Games in 1988 (Lee 1997: 154). It was renamed Chollian I after it was upgraded and relaunched under the name Chollian II in May 1988, providing online services which included databases, information retrieval, and home shopping. There were about a thousand paid subscribers, yet it was still not actively taken up by the general public. Both Chollian I and Chollian II were designed and deployed in a similar manner to mass media, since the corporation configured the users as consumers of commercial online services. That was a reason why Chollian, albeit targeting the ordinary user, paradoxically attracted few takers.

Contrarily, the first popular and dynamic online culture emerged around the first Hangul email system. The first email service open to the public was also an ancillary part of the DACOM-Net, but available only in English. In 1984, an international email service was launched to be connected to DIALCOM and NOTICE in the United States. The number of initial subscribers was 13 in the first year, which increased to 328 in 1991 (Lee 1997: 154). While most subscribers were research institutes and big corporations, individual users who could access it in the early days were limited to the members of Han River Sarangbang.

Han River Sarangbang was the very first online user group organized by DACOM, offered to approximately 30 influential figures such as professors, lawyers, and so on.[6] It was part of a campaign for an "expansion of online user population" and "diffusion of computer communications" that had started in 1986. Hence, those influential figures could be understood as DACOM's desirably configured users who were expected to show individual competence and a new informational subjectivity in the professional utilization of electronic data as part of the upcoming new era, referred to as the information society. In reality, they failed to satisfy these expectations and did not actively make use of the international email service, in part because it required reading and writing messages in English. They were instead more interested in using the Hangul email service known as H-mail.

H-mail was originally developed for office automation in 1984 and only used among DACOM employees (DACOM 1993: 136–137).[7] At the time, it was the first domestic value-added service connected to the DACOM-Net, mainly for its corporate customers (Larson 1995: 73). DACOM also began offering H-mail to Han River Sarangbang members as a pilot project (Yoo n.d.). Finally, due to great demand, it was offered more widely to the general public in April 1987. By 1988, the number of ordinary users of H-mail increased to about 100 (Kang 2007: 499). Thanks to H-mail (and Chollian II), the users of DACOM-Net were not limited to research institutes and big corporations, but extended to PC-based individual users (DACOM 1993: 236).

There was, however, a low rate of personal computer penetration in the late 1980s—the diffusion of personal computers was estimated at approximately 1,005,000, which was only 11 percent of households in 1990 (Information Culture Center of Korea 1998: 11; Liu 1993: 25;). Furthermore, ordinary users who wanted to access and use H-mail needed to be able to afford such expensive devices as modems (1200bps), client programs, and 16-bit IBM PC/XT, all of which cost up to $3,000, according to *Computer Study* magazine (1988: 123).

Consequently, individual users of DACOM-Net were restricted to only a very tiny portion of the population at that time.

Nevertheless, the active utilization and appropriation of H-mail by these early users had a huge impact on the newly developing online culture. As a then-active user, Park (1988) acknowledged that the main features of H-mail were a convergence of both print and broadcasting media.

> This medium has a characteristic of mass media in that my message can be sent to many receivers as a group when using group email. Also, the same message in the message board can be sent in either a simultaneous or delayed manner of delivery to anonymous users. So, this medium has advantages not only in its speed as electronic media, but in its storage as print media. What a flexible and fluid medium!

Interestingly, unlike newspaper or broadcast media, this new medium was conspicuously salient, especially when the early ordinary users of H-mail utilized it for horizontal and bidirectional communications among themselves—they were even more interested in such collective communicative features as message boards and chat-like electronic conferencing than in private email exchange.

Jang (2011) remembered that "there was a group email. Total users were just several hundred so that, when we sent a message, we usually sent it to all, that is, reply to all." Hyeon-Sang Muk (2013) highlighted the multi-chat feature, among others: "it was like being struck by lightning simply because it was amazing. With it, 7 or 8 users among 30 or so could simultaneously chat with one another." As such, one-to-many or many-to-many as well as one-to-one communications were widely welcomed and accepted by the users.[8] As a consequence, it was out of the H-mail of DACOM-Net that a different way of information production emerged in which users themselves not only consumed but also produced its content, unlike the broadcasting system:

> [In H-mail,] there was almost no content serviced by professional providers, but just messages exchanged among users. The early users were like pioneers, making use of it creatively. It is OK to say that these users actually created the service. For example, Park tried to post a serial travel journal while traveling all around the country. An episode was about what he did when he visited Chuncheon city and met someone whose ID was XXX. People enjoyed it and waited for the next episodes. Yeom, who later became the first president of Yahoo Korea, posted essays about his daily life in the US, which interested many users as well. Those user-based online content and communications were not that different from what we do today with a blog or Twitter.
>
> (Jang 2011)

With these new affordances of information technology in relation to both consumption and production, it was natural that users created and communicated with the abbreviated jargon: they typed ROM (originally meaning Read Only Memory) when referring to the users who mainly lurk (Read Only Men) in contrast to RAM (originally meaning Random Access Memory) for those who read and write; they also used "Hi" to signify smile, as in the ham radio tradition (*Computer Study* 1988: 122).

As the number of ordinary users increased, these online communities began to organize themselves. According to a magazine article reporting about the new phenomenon of online user culture (*Computer Study* 1988: 121), it was the "open mailbox" feature which encouraged users to make publicly available even a mail exchanged just between two persons that naturally led to the formation of a community based on a sense of connectedness and intimacy. Empal, meaning "Electronic Mail Pal", was one prominent online community, which will be discussed later.

Thus, through the above innovations, the users could be argued to have reconfigured H-mail in contrast to DACOM's configuring them. According to Leah Lievrouw (2011: 216), reconfiguration signifies "the ongoing process by which people adapt, reinvent, reorganize, or rebuild media technologies as needed to suit their various purposes or interests". That is what some H-mail users had done. In spite of its initial top-down configuration, the users actively sought communicative features in accordance with their needs and interests, which naturally led to the promotion of friendship and socialization online. Therefore, it was the early users rather than the technology alone that urged the computer networks to begin functioning as horizontally communicative online media, as demonstrated further below.

User Hacking Versus Corporate Security

The UNIX system of DACOM's intra-net, on which H-mail was based, had run without any particular security at that time, except the log-in procedure involving each user's ID and password (Muk 2013). Even after H-mail became a public service and expanded its user base, it operated without any security configuration for different access authorities, which seems unimaginable from today's security perspective (PC World Chulpanbu 1994: 87). DACOM's developers and administrators did not seem to have imagined anything like hacking, so they did not configure the user in terms of access restriction.

Such hacking activities were not necessarily destructive. For instance, some users gained free access to the computer system and obtained an opportunity to learn and even improve it (Jo 2013: 208–209). The features of H-mail were very poor and weak since it did not provide, for example, the feature of the binary file transfer which allows the user to attach a file to a message as the email system provides today. Some technology-savvy users, or "good-will hacker (?)" [*sic*], found that the Kermit protocol for the binary file transfer had just been deactivated, even if it was installed in the system (PC World Chulpanbu 1994: 87). They tried to hack into the system, and activated it as was necessary for their convenience.

Only then did DACOM take a measure to restrict users' access, allegedly for security reasons. The Kermit protocol was disabled again with the announcement of ostensible reasons such as traffic increment and the possibility of illegal file sharing of proprietary games and utility programs (Muk 2013). DACOM's countermeasure discouraged and annoyed the users, as they felt controlled by a powerful authority even in this "newly opened world". Jang (2011) recalled: "we asked DACOM to let us keep using it, but they refused to do so because they did not want to get in trouble." Most users who enjoyed its convenience and usability strongly protested against that countermeasure and finally won in getting it reactivated. In addition, such a conflict also triggered users to develop their own online communication systems, like Revolt of Empal, as discussed later.

Woolgar (1991: 89) has interestingly argued that "user configuration involves boundary work". Configuring the user means to establish the boundary of the user's relationship with the company (the owner of the machine) through the specific design of the machine (Woolgar 1991: 77–80). Thus, it is through boundary work that the design of technology fundamentally involves exclusion of the user from participation in its design process. It did not take long for users' activities to be followed by further boundary work.

For DACOM, there was a stronger impetus indicating the necessity of security enhancement when another kind of system hacking came from one of its users. Jang (2011), who was then an undergraduate student and H-mail user, had often visited the DACOM office to ask questions and learn how to use the system, which gradually led to him having an acquaintance with the staff members. It was not difficult for him to obtain knowledge of the staff's passwords, which were explicitly written in memos attached to a corner of their computer monitors and with which he could easily enter other parts of the system than H-mail. As he tells it:

> I accessed H-mail via a modem, though I was supposed to play inside H-mail; I got out of it to the rest of the system. If you knew the UNIX system, it wouldn't be that difficult to get around the system. At that time, it was never imagined that anyone could gain unauthorized access to the system and obtain internally sensitive information. I still remember that I could know the monthly lunch menu of the staff cafeteria, commuting times of all of the staff, and so on. One day, I came across a certain sort of documents in which Pyongyang and Sinuiju were written in English with military-related data which looked like calculated figures of missile trajectories. I was scared to see them . . . After that, I thought of becoming a computer security expert. What I thought was at least four or five years ahead of its time because the concept of computer security didn't exist then.

Before he happened to gain access to the military-related information, he often bragged by posting some internal information to the H-mail message board. He was also known for playing a trick on the system administrator of DACOM, as another user recalled:

> As a joke, he often posted with the title of "Do you want to know the lunch menu of DACOM's staff cafeteria for the next week?" or "Want to know the schedule of DACOM's president?" Once he accessed the system as a root, he played aroundwith the H-mail Sysop, who then got in trouble with Empal, by changing his Sysop level.
>
> (Park 2011)

It was natural that the corporation should respond to this and try to further configure the user with increasingly strong boundary work. In one of the regular meetings of Han River Sarangbang, a presentation by Park on the hacker culture that included Jang's "joke" and "play" as concrete examples, embarrassed president Yong-Tae Lee and a research board member, Kyung-Hee Yoo, among others in attendance, and forced them to take immediate action. Additionally, as Muk (2013) recalled, DACOM managed to identify unexpected access from outside in its regular review of the log files. DACOM's awareness of its users' trespass in the system directly resulted in the enhancement of the system security along with an announcement warning all H-mail users not to attempt unauthorized access.

All this led to a strengthened restriction of users' access and the possibility of their participation in a system reconfiguration. In this way, security enhancement began being applied and operated in the public computer networks as a form of boundary work, which controlled users' specific transgressive behaviors. In other words, the computer security of the public network was raised by the necessity of controlling the users' active involvement in reconfiguration of the technology, in addition to the increase of apparent computer crimes.

To sum up, some users, complaining about the poor features of H-mail, came forward with an intervention in the technical design to implement more diverse and desired functions, instead of using it in the way that DACOM's developers and administrators had configured it. On the other hand, coping with the users' intervention in the system, DACOM took action to reinforce the boundary to restrict them. It was through these contentious bilateral configurations, including interactions between the users' hacking activities and DACOM's security enhancement, that the newly found online territory was shaped.

Online User Community Versus National Security, and the BBS Boom

Users, too, sought new ways to reconfigure computer network technologies while confronting the control the corporation exercised through security enhancement. One of the most prominent examples was when some Empal users developed their own client and hosting programs to build their own computer network based on a bulletin board system (BBS) independent of the DACOM service (for a more detailed analysis, see Jo 2013).

The price for a commercial client program to connect to the H-mail host computer, such as Mirror, was approximately $300 at that time (Park 1989a: 22). The client program provided by DACOM was also very poor quality (Muk 2013). For reasons like this, in addition to corporate control of the network, Revolt of Empal, a client program, was developed by an H-mail user and member of Empal, Muk. With much better quality and outstanding features, it was freely distributed and used, and its source code was also made available (*The Hankyoreh*, 1988).[9] Since 16-bit IBM PC/XT was then typical for PC communications and cost approximately $2,000, some other Empal users developed the client program called Wordcomm, for example, to enable 8-bit Apple computer users to connect to H-mail, Empal BBS, and other BBSs. Some other Empal users also developed and shared anti-virus programs for peers with infected PCs (*Computer Study* 1988: 123; Park 1989b: 184–196).

In contrast to the present technological circumstance where anyone can easily get and use all online communicative tools such as email, message boards, chatting, etc. "in a box" right after signing up to any portal services, users in those days had to raise funds to establish the systems, modify or even develop their own programs in case pre-existing ones were not sufficiently good or affordable, and create their own ways to connect to each other online, as demonstrated by Empal.

Again, it was not easy for users to set up, host, and manage their own computer networks on the BBS. It did not operate without further configuration of the user who was trying to transgress the boundary. In fact, the computer network that was open to the public had been politically controlled for national security reasons, particularly regarding North Korea, in the Cold War atmosphere (Chon 2005; Park 2011). The telephone line in connection to the Empal BBS was abruptly cut, for instance, because it was defined as illegal according to the Telecommunications Act that was enacted at that time (Muk 2013; Park 2011;). Private usage of a modem, and unauthorized communications systems like the BBS, were regarded as potential threats to national security. They were also perceived by the general public as activities of espionage or of intelligence agents from North or South Korea. Consequently, another serious anecdote followed: when the Empal BBS began to operate, one of their neighbors suspected that the telephone system connected to the computer equipment might wiretap their telephone communications, and reported it to the police (Lee 1992: 331).

These anecdotes imply that there was a process of configuring the user at the macro level, responding to the emergence of new online communications and an active user culture. Configuring the user, in other words, takes place not only in the design process of specific technological systems but also in the broader socio-cultural context in which they are used. This constitutes the two-way configuration of online user culture when it was first formed.

Nevertheless, all of the early online users' activities, including Empal, led to the spawning of more independent BBSs. The technology of the BBS was introduced among early PC user groups through Cheonggyecheon electronics shops in Seoul and computer magazines around the mid-1980s (Jang 2011; Jo 2013: 205). The first BBS appeared in March 1988, was called "the first", and was experimentally managed at home by a university student who was also a member of Empal. BYTE-NET BBS was funded by a small electronics company called Byte electronics but was managed by its many users. Subsequently, teenagers' and college students' spontaneous online communities based on their own BBS grew. Empal BBS was one of those early BBSs when it began to operate in May 1988. While Empal BBS was well organized by a relatively large number of members, other BBSs were small-scale ones operated by an individual or small group with only several dozen members. Most Sysops (SYStem Operators) were college students, operating them not for profit, and setting them up in their homes through the home telephone that all family members used, so operating times had to be evening or late at night. In spite of poor conditions such as single-node access and a lack of content, there was a very strong sense of community and fellowship among members (PC World Chulpanbu 1994: 25–26, 235, 361).

In fact, the BBS was equipped with primitive but basic online communicative features, such as email, a forum, chatting, file archives, and so on, which offered socio-cultural affordances for the users to organize online communities based on their own interests and needs like computer, game, graphic, music, pet, journalism, and so on. In short, BBS was the first popular computer network set up for ordinary users and, more importantly, set up from the bottom up. Therefore, the transformation of the characteristics of data communications into collective and horizontal communication media, catalyzed by the early users of H-mail, had been fully realized and recognized when it came to the BBS boom.

As BBSs became popular, online community was no longer restricted to early tech-savvy users, but expanded among general users based on a variety of concerns and interests. At the moment, large-scale BBS or commercial BBS,[10] better known as PC Tongsin (PC communications), had acted as a catalyst to give birth to (PC) Tongsin Donghohoe or just Donghohoe (friendship association) as the most familiar form of online community in Korea. As data communications increased, friendship promotion and socialization gradually became much more important in the central activities of the online community (Donghohoe) rather than professional information retrieval. In other words, the ordinary user culture of PC Tongsin was inclined not so much toward information seeking as to friend making or social networking, which is similar to social media today. It is indeed in the first generation of online users from H-mail, and grassroots computer networks on the BBS, where Donghohoe was born and bred.

From this perspective, it is evident that user-oriented H-mail, BBS, and subsequent Donghohoe in PC Tongsin, led to the mass Internet culture of today—that is because "Community" or "Internet Café", as the present dominant form of online communities in Korea provided by several commercial portal services since they launched such services in the late 1990s, are simply imitating Donghohoe style from the PC Tongsin (Yoon 2011: 83).

Conclusion

This chapter has investigated the early public email service, H-mail, in Korea, analyzed how it evolved as the first popular computer network, and discussed how the early online user culture developed through contentious and continuous bilateral configurations. When H-mail was introduced as a broadcast-like data communications service, early users actually appropriated the primitive email system to utilize and facilitate not only one-to-one message exchanges but also horizontal one-to-many or many-to-many collective online communications. However, the two-way configurations, shaping the newly found territory that the early online users explored, were contentious in terms of the interactions between the users' hacking activities and DACOM's security enhancement, and also between the users' self-organization of online communities based on the BBS and national security to restrict user-driven new online communications. To put it another way, what gave birth to the dynamic Internet culture can be understood to be the contentious and continuous bilateral configurations between the corporation's configuring of the user and the users' reconfiguration of the technology at both the micro and macro levels.

It was the early users themselves rather than the technology alone that catalyzed the computer networks to begin functioning and be accepted in earnest as horizontal communicative online media. Above all, the dynamic interactions between the technology of early data communication networks such as DACOM-Net, H-mail, BBS, and PC communication online services and their users have configured Korea's specific online user culture, prefiguring the Internet culture in terms of active user agency and online communities, albeit developed under the authorities' control and restriction.

Acknowledgements

The author would like to thank Prof. Pyung-Ho Kim for his reading of, and suggestions regarding several drafts of this chapter, and Dr Valérie Schafer for her helpful comments. He would also like to acknowledge the support from the research team of Internet History in Australia and the Asia-Pacific.

Notes

1. In this chapter, Korea refers to South Korea (Republic of), if not specifically mentioned.
2. All quotations from the interviews and literature that were originally in Korean have been translated into English by the author. The identity of the interviewees has been concealed to protect any sensitive information.
3. Hangul is Korean script and Hangulizing or Hangulization means Korean localization, translating a computer-related product into Hangul.
4. Korean-style family-owned multinationals such as Samsung and LG.
5. Chollian literally means 'Thousand Li View' or 'Eye'. The li is a traditional Chinese unit of distance; 1 li is the standardized length of about half of a kilometer.
6. Sarangbang traditionally refers to the reception room in a house for male guests. They picked the Han River for their title since the DACOM building at that time was located next to it. The formal title named later for the media coverage was "Sarangbang for the deliberation of the information society".
7. DACOM undertook the project of Hangul electronic mail system development beginning in May 1983, as part of "a study on the development of office automation systems" conducted by KIET (Korea Institute of Electronics Technology, established in 1976 as a branch of KIST), and succeeded in developing it in February 1984 (DACOM 1993: 123–124, 136).
8. The content of electronic mail exchanged among users of H-mail can be partially found in Lee (1988, 203–210).
9. It was just released as public domain software without opening its source code until version 1.0, since, according to him, some corporate software companies appropriated and resold it as a proprietary one. However, he released it as an open source afterwards (Muk 2013).
10. With the advent of large-scale commercial BBSs, pre-existing independent BBSs were more obviously renamed "private BBS", and became gradually more marginalized.

References

An, J., under the supervision of Kang, K. (2014) *Hangug Inteones-ui Yeogsa—Doedol-Aboneun 20segi* (Internet History in Korea: A Retrospect of the 20th Century), Bloter & Media.

Campbell-Kelly, M., and Garcia-Swartz, D. D. (2013) "The History of the Internet: The Missing Narratives", *Journal of Information Technology*, 28(1): 18–33.

Chon, K. (2005) *Inteones Yeogsaleul Dol-Abonda—KAIST Jeonjajeonsanhaggwa Jeongilnam Gyosu* (Looking Back upon Internet History: KAIST Computer Science Professor Chon Kilnam), available at: http://networker.jinbo.net/zine/view.php?board=networker_4&id=1030 (accessed 19 February 2013).

Chon, K., Park, H. J., Hur, J. H., and Kang, K. (2013) "A History of Computer Networking and the Internet in Korea", *IEEE Communications Magazine*, 51(2): 10–15.

Computer Study (1988) "EMPAL: PCleul Tonghae Tongsin-ui Jeulgeoum-eul Nanuda" (EMPAL: Enjoying the Pleasure of Communicating with Your PC), *Computer Study*, December.

DACOM (1993) *Segyeleul Gakkabge, Milaeleul Gakkabge: Deikom10nyeonsa* (Close to the World, Close to the Future: 10 Years History of Dacom), Seoul: Dacom.

The Hankyoreh (1988) "Jeonjasaseoham Gyeolham Bowan, Saepeulogeulaem Gaebal" (Fixing the Flaws of Electronic Mailbox), The Hankyoreh, 24 July.

Hauben, R., Hauben, J., Zorn, W., Chon, K., and Ekeland, A. (2007) "The Origin and Early Development of the Internet and of the Netizen: Their Impact on Science and Society", in W. Shrum, K. R. Benson, W. E. Bijker, and K. Brunnstein (eds), *Past, Present and Future of Research in the Information Society*, New York: Springer, pp. 47–62.

Information Culture Center of Korea (1998) *Jeongbosahoe Tong-Gyejosa 10nyeon Jalyojib* (A Source Book of 10 Year Statistical Survey of Information Society), Information Culture Center of Korea.

Jang, M. G. (2011) personal communication, 9 September.

Jo, D. (2013) "Neungdongjeog Iyongjawa Jeongbogisul-Ui Sanghoguseong: Jeonjagesipan Iyongjaleul Jungsim-Eulo" (Co-Construction of Active User and Information Technology: A Case of BBS Users), *Media and Society*, 21(1): 184–237.

Jo, D. (2015) "Hangug-ui Dijiteol Munhwasa—Keompyuteoui Doibgwa Daejunghwaleul Jungsim-eulo" (A History of Digital Culture—The Introduction and Popularization of Computer in Korea), *Society and History*, 106: 183–216.

Kang, M. (2007) "Inteones-Ui Sahoemunhwasa" (Socio-Cultural History of the Internet), in S. Y. Yoo *et al.* (eds), *Hangug-Ui Midieo Sahoemunhwasa* (Socio-Cultural History of Media in Korea), Seoul: Korea Press Foundation.

Kim, E. M. and Na, E. K. (2008) "Keomyunikeisyeonhag Bun-Yaui Inteones Gwanlyeon Yeongu 10nyeon—PCtongsin-Eseo Web2.0kkaji" (A Meta-Analysis of Internet-Related Research in Scholarly Journals in Communication), *Journal of Cybercommunication Academic Society*, 25(1): 243–288.

Koo, J. S. (2008) "Saibeogong-Gan-E Daehan Hangug Sahoehag-Ui Yeongu Donghyang" (Recent Research Trends in the Korean Sociology of Cyberspace: 1997–2007), *Journal of Cybercommunication Academic Society*, 25(1): 197–242.

Larson, J. F. (1995) *The Telecommunications Revolution in Korea*, Oxford: Oxford University Press.

Lee, J. R. (1997) "Hangug Keompyuteo Tongsin San-Eob-Ui Hyeongseong Mich Seongjang-e Gwanhan Yeongu: Keompyuteo Maegae Keomyunikeisyeon (CMC) Gieob-Eul Jungsim-Eulo" (The Study on the Formation and Growing Process of the Korean Computer Mediated Communication Industry (KCMCI)—Focused on the Computer Mediated Communication (CMC) Companies), Ph.D. thesis, Graduate Studies in Journalism and Communication, Kyunghee University.

Lee, K. (1988) *Jeonjachulpan: Sinmungwa Chulpan-Eseo Keompyuteoui Iyong* (Electronic Publishing: Use of Computers in Newspaper and Publishing), Seoul: Youngjin Publisher.

Lee, K. (1992) *(Soseol) Keompyuteo: Soseollo Baeuneun Keompyuteo Tongsin* ((Novel) Computer: Learning Computer Communications by a Novel) Seoul: Seong-An Dang.

Lievrouw, L. (2011) *Alternative and Activist New Media*, 1st edn, Malden, MA: Polity.

Liu, C. R. (1993) "Jeongbotongsinseobiseu Suyong Mich Hwagsan-e Gwanhan Yeongu—PCtongsin-Eul Jungsim-Eulo" (Telecommunications Services Study on Acceptance and Proliferation—Focused on the PC Communication (A Study on the Adoption and Diffusion of Advanced Telecommunications Services)), MA thesis, Graduate School of International Management, Chung-Ang University.

Mackay, H., Carne, C., Beynon-Davies, P., and Tudhope, D. (2000) "Reconfiguring the User: Using Rapid Application Development", *Social Studies of Science*, 30(5): 737–757.

Muk, H. S. (2013) personal communication, 2 July.

Park, S. (1988) "Han-Meil (H-Mail) Eul Beosginda" (Let's Disclose H-Mail), *Data Communication—Dacom's monthly magazine*, July, DACOM.

Park, S. (1989a) *Jeongbohwa Sahoeleul Balabomyeo* (Looking Into the Informatiztion Society), Seoul: Heesung Publisher.

Park, S. (1989b) *PCmunhwalon* (On PC Culture), Seoul: Heesung Publisher.

Park, S-P. (2011) personal communication, 6 September.

PC World Chulpanbu (1994) *(Gaejeongpan) PCtongsin Hana-Eseo Yeolkkaji* ((Revision) PC Communication One to Ten), Seoul: Hi-tech Information.

Russell, A. L., and Schafer, V. (2014) "In the Shadow of ARPANET and Internet: Louis Pouzin and the Cyclades Network in the 1970s", *Technology and Culture*, 55(4): 880–907.

Seo, H. (1997) *Cheoeumsseuneun Hangugkeompyuteosa* (The First Written History of Computing in Korea), Seoul: The Electronic Times.

Woo, H. J. (2005) "Gugnae Inteones Yeonguui Baljeonjeog Mosaeg—1995–2005 Nyeonkkaji Keomyunikeisyeon Hagsuljie Gejaedoen Inteones Yeongue Daehan Meta Bunseog" (A Productive Investigation of Korean Internet Studies: A Meta-Analysis of Internet Studies in Korean Communication Journals during 1995–2005), *Communication Theories*, 1(1): 332–366.

Woolgar, S. (1991) "Configuring the User: The Case of Usability Trials", in J. Law (ed.), *A Sociology of Monsters: Essays on Power, Technology and Domination*, London: Routledge, pp. 57–99.

Yoo, K. H. (n.d.) *Salangbang Iyagiwa H-Mail Dwis-Iyagi* (Sarangbang Story and Behind Story of H-mail), available at: www.mediamob.co.kr/infoland/frmView.aspx?id=12425 (accessed 24 October 2011).

Yoo, S. (2008) "Internet, Internet Culture, and Internet Communities of Korea: Overview and Research Directions", in G. Goggin, and M. McLelland (eds), *Internationalizing Internet Studies: Beyond Anglophone Paradigms*, New York: Routledge, pp. 217–236.

Yoon, H. Y. (2011) "Hangug Inteones-Ui Teugjing: Sotong-Giban Jeongbochugjeog Mich Yutong Munhwa" (South Korea's Specificity of Internet Culture: Dominance of Communicative Activity in Information Accumulation and Distribution), *Korean Journal of Sociology*, 45(5): 61–104.

14

HI! TURKIYE AND TURKISH BBS AND DIGITAL CULTURES

Ivo Furman

In USA
They have a president . . . Bill Clinton
They have Stevie Wonder
They have Bob Hope
They have Johnny Cash
In Türkiye [Turkey]
We have a president . . . Süleyman Demirel
NO WONDER
NO HOPE
And . . .
NO CASH :)))))

(Arıcı 1995)

Introduction

Between 1992 and 1996, Turkey was host to a vibrant bulletin board system (BBS) ecology centered around the *Hi! Türkiye* Network (known colloquially as Hitnet). National in scale, and based on Fidonet network protocols, Hitnet connected local BBSs in the urban centers of Turkey with one another. Although BBS communication networks rapidly disappeared with the arrival of the Internet, early BBS users were the first in Turkey to engage in networked publications and experienced long-distance collaboration via electronic communication. Due to the constraints imposed by the networking technologies of the era, the communities hosted by BBSs tended to be quite local in scale. In Turkey, the networks of most BBSs were either on the scale of a neighborhood or on the scale of a town or small city. As a result, these networks tended to host communities that were relatively small and intimate. These pre-Internet networks proved to be ideal spaces to host small and disconnected local subcultures. Looking at the documentation on Hitnet correspondence logs, it seems one subculture that extensively utilized the spaces afforded by BBS networks was computer enthusiasts. Not only did Hitnet afford a space for hobbyist computing enthusiasts scattered throughout Turkey to socialize and network, it was also a valuable resource to access and share the knowledge needed to pioneer the communication culture of local networks. As a result, coders active within their respective communities began to take on organizational roles in maintaining the physical network, and producing software that would benefit the community.

As BBS network usage began to grow in Turkey during the mid-1990s, coders active within their local communities began to use the network to organize collectives dedicated to producing commercial software. Between 1995 and 2000, many of these collectives were highly successful and attracted the attention of both national and multinational companies. Seizing the opportunity to go abroad, many Turkish coders left the country for a short period of time, only to return with the popularization of the Internet in Turkey during the early 2000s. Many coders, upon their return to Turkey, used the opportunity presented by the growing number of Internet users to become pioneers in a number of different, Internet-based industries.

The first part of the study provides a brief history of BBS networks worldwide and of pre-Internet communication networks in Turkey. In the second part, using a sample from a privately owned archive of correspondences from Hitnet, the study will detail the communication culture of the Hitnet community and elaborate on coder subcultures active on the network. The final part of the chapter is a case study which presents compelling evidence of how the pioneers of computer-mediated communication (CMC) on BBS networks also played a key role in shaping local Internet communication ecologies in Turkey.

Bulletin Board Systems: Online Communities from the Pre-Internet Era

Looking at how fast Internet usage has spread in the past decade, and at the diverse array of social media tools currently at our disposal, one might be tempted to assume that the mediation of our social lives through computers is a recent phenomenon. This is simply not true. Contrary to popular belief, the process of CMC entering our social lives is a phenomenon that can be traced to the BBSs started in North America during the winter of 1978.

Bulletin board systems were small-scale networks of computers linked together using primitive modem technologies and regular telephone lines. At the same time, they were the first commercially available civilian networks that allowed humans to communicate with each other through computers on a global scale. To set up a BBS, one needed computers, a modem, and a phone line. In 1963, Bell Systems had introduced Bell 103, the first commercially available modem. The modem offered the possibility of modulating an electrical signal from a computer into a phone line and then demodulating it into data on the other end (see Figures 14.1 and 14.2). In 1974, the first commercially available micro-computer, the Altair 8800, became available (see Figure 14.2). By 1977, modems running inside computers began to be commercially available, and in the same year, XMODEM, a program and protocol for trans-ferring files via modem, was written by IBM employee Ward Christensen. The next year, on 16 February 1978, Christensen worked together with his partner Randy Suess to bring online CBBS, the first BBS. Soon afterwards, the duo wrote an article for *Byte* magazine to introduce their invention, and they began to distribute free copies of the software needed to run a BBS. Soon afterwards, the BBS craze took off in North America, and for nearly the next 20 years, dial-up BBSs were the primary way for computer users to get online.

In terms of infrastructure, BBSs were relatively simple to maintain. There would be one mainframe computer in the local network to which other computers would connect and access the data uploaded by the system operator (a "sysop") of the BBS (see Figure 14.3). The main technological impediment of early BBSs was caused by the slow connection speed of modems: the first modems had connection speeds of around 300 Baud, which was roughly equal to reading speed of about 30 characters per second. Slow connection speeds made exchanging data through terminal programs a long and arduous process. Terminal programs were software with functional graphic interfaces designed to exchange small data packets between the mainframe computer by directing the modem to call a local telephone number.[1] On the other end of the line, there would be a dedicated mainframe computer which would answer the modem to circulate the flow of data between the two computers. The key factor in running a successful BBS was the enthusiasm of sysops. Besides having the technical skills to maintain the mainframe computer needed for the local network, sysops would also be in charge of circulating mail traffic and uploading new software and multiplayer door games.[2] After the development of Fidonet in 1982, a software that allowed BBSs to network between each other, sysops were also in charge of maintaining the list of telephone numbers (the "node-list") needed to connect with other nodes in the Fidonet system (see Figure 14.4). As becoming a sysop was a voluntary position, the upkeep of the system and the circulation of data on BBSs depended greatly on the technical skills of the person assuming this position.

Regular telephone lines and slow modem speeds meant that only a limited number of users were able to simultaneously connect onto a BBS; users often had to take turns to access the mainframe computer, and only had limited connection time. Furthermore, long-distance calls

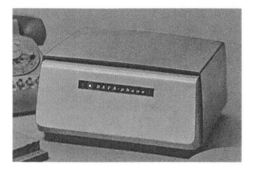

Figure 14.1 Bell modem 103 from time.com

Figure 14.2 An Altair 8800

Figure 14.3 A BBS terminal system that combines a Commodore 64 with a compatible acoustic coupler to connect to a BBS

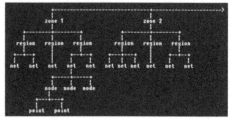

Figure 14.4 Global organization of Fidonet. The "points" are terminal access points while "nodes" are BBS mainframes which are networked with nodes from other regions. These regions are then networked with each other through nodes in other zones.

to non-local telephone numbers were prohibitively expensive during this period, often leading to inflated phone bills for BBS enthusiasts. Users also needed to know the actual telephone number of a BBS in order to be able to connect to the mainframe. These technical constraints meant that BBSs could not really scale up as networks, and as a result almost all BBSs were local phenomena. The only way for sysops to scale up their BBSs in size was through becoming commercial "super" BBSs that would offer services to users in exchange for a monthly membership fee.[3] Despite the limitations in scale, BBSs offered the possibility for users to socialize with each other through forum-like mailing lists as well as simple games accessible through the mainframe computer. Looking back, one can argue that the contents of these data packages, each perhaps the size of a few kilobytes, constitute the first bits of digitalized social life. However, due to technical limitations, the social life created on BBS networks was geographically confined to North America. It was only after the development of Fidonet during the mid-1980s that BBSs evolved into a global network and expanded beyond North America. A store-and-forward system allowed the messages to be passed along the nodes in Fidonet without incurring high costs for long-distance or international calls. This made Fidonet the first global communications network for the general public to send electronic messages through computers.[4] The scope of the Fido Network would only be surpassed after the popularization of the Internet as a communication technology. The history of online communities in Turkey can be said to begin with the expansion of Fidonet as a global network.

Hi! Turkiye Net: A Pre-Internet Digital Communication Network

In comparison to North America and Europe, Turkey can be considered a late adopter of BBS communication technologies. While the potential of the Internet for CMC remained mostly unharnessed in Turkey during the mid- to late 1990s, conventional telephone lines were hosting a vibrant ecology of BBS communities scattered throughout the country. These communities were connected with one another through a Fidonet-style network called Hitnet (Hi! Türkiye Network).

Hitnet was founded on 12 December 1992 at the home of Can Doğancan in Ankara by a group of nine coders active on ADABBS. After examining the Fidonet network protocols, this group of enthusiasts decided to form a Fidonet-style network called Hi! Türkiye Network, which linked local BBS networks through an echo-mail system that allowed messages to be exchanged on a national scale. ADABBS, their own BBS, became the first node in this emerging national network. Despite the technological constraints imposed by primitive modem technology and unspecialized telephone lines, Hitnet quickly grew from a local BBS network into a larger, nationwide network. It connected with the local BBSs that were spawning in different urban centers throughout Turkey via echo-net mail nodes, and in this way formed a wider Hitnet network. At predetermined times during the day ("event hours"), sysops would connect with one another to exchange message logs that had accumulated within their local networks.

Technical constraints on the level of access and hardware meant that exchanges through BBSs networks were not really integrated into daily life; users would have to go online either early in the morning or late at night to avoid paying peak charges for telephone lines. Furthermore, limits on the number of phone lines able to simultaneously connect to a BBS meant that users often needed to take turns to connect to the mainframe. When connected, the slow data exchange speeds of modems meant that only limited information could be exchanged between the mainframe and the user. The asynchronous nature of communication on BBSs meant that users had to use terminal programs similar to email clients to log on to the mainframe and download the most recent circulation of messages. After reading the messages, users would then use the same programs, called offline mail readers (OMRs), to compose replies which would be exchanged with the mainframe computer in the next round of CMC.

The earliest and most popular OMR during the 1990s was a program called Bluewave which was an American software product designed for Fidonet systems in the US. One of the major issues with Bluewave as an OMR was that it was designed for English, and hence did not allow users to write using Turkish characters. In contrast with Hangulization (see Chapter 13 in this volume), as well as the transcription of Japanese characters (see Chapter 11 in this volume), which were both the results of a gradual standardization process involving the adaptation of non-Latin languages to word processing, Turkish-language support for word processing remained unstandardized until the end of 1996. As a result, all Turkish BBS users had to use a "low-end ASCII" character set that included English upper and lower case letters and numerals, some commonly used mathematical and punctuation symbols (e.g., "$," "%", "()", "+", etc.) and no umlauts and other European characters. Faced with a constraint which forced both the sender and receiver to rely on a narrow set of predetermined symbols with which they endeavor to create and share meaning, Hitnet users appropriated substituted missing Turkish characters with the characters available on the Bluewave OMR. What emerged from using the combination of English language characters to communicate in Turkish is a complex code of transliteration in which Turkish phonetics are transcribed using English characters (Furman 2015). As a result, participants had to resort to a peculiar orthographic format wherein Turkish phonetics were transcribed using English characters.

The most renowned local BBSs during the early 1990s in Turkey were Ada bbs, buces, and heaven in Ankara; ess, eebbs, and kedi bbs in Eskişehir; bizim bbs, istanbul bbs, and sentinel bbs in İstanbul; and abaza bbs, bbsturk, ege bbs, and iris bbs in İzmir. There were also a large number of pirate BBSs operating in Turkey between 1994 and 1996. These pirate BBSs, too numerous and transient to have actual names, were temporary BBS boards set up to illegally share files or software within a small online community.

As the software of Hitnet was an adaptation of Fidonet protocols, the network evolved to be connected with the global Fidonet network. Hitnet was located on Fidonet zone 8, a zone for "othernets" that used Fido-compatible software, but were not Fidonet BBSs per se. This system of organization created a steady circulation of data wherein a local BBS could communicate with another BBS on the other side of the world through Fidonet. The interactions created from these data exchanges can perhaps be seen as the first attempts by Turkish speakers to communicate and socialize on a wider, global CMC network.

As the network began to expand and link local BBS networks that were emerging throughout the country, the founders of the network held a number of meetings throughout 1995 to decide on the future of the Hitnet. One of the decisions taken during these meetings was to turn Hitnet into a paid, members-only service. Trying to capitalize on the popularity of Hitnet, the founders of the network set out a number of new rules in the autumn of 1995 to standardize the quality of access for users throughout Turkey. Local BBS sysops would now either have to adhere to these rules or risk having their mainframe excluded from the wider network of Hitnet. The most important (and controversial) of these new rules was with regard to providing 24-hour access to local users and membership fees. Any local BBS network on Hitnet would now need to provide mandatory, round-the-clock access to its mainframe. At the same time, any local network on Hitnet would need to pay an annual membership fee to remain in the national network. In order to keep up with both membership fees and costs incurred with providing a 24-hour service, many local sysops started to charge membership fees to local users. These new measures, while transforming the network into a paid service, also marked the beginning of Hitnet's decline. Tired of paying membership fees to become a node on Hitnet, many local BBS sysops began to form alternative, free-of-charge networks. This caused a decline in both the number of Hitnet users and in the number of BBS nodes on the network. Some of the Fidonet-style networks founded during this period were Sciencenet (55:100/100), Turknet (35:101/104), and Peacenet (33:500/134). In comparison with Hitnet, these networks were much smaller in scale and offered free-of-charge access to national BBS networks (Varol 1996). As the national BBS network in Turkey was fragmenting into smaller, more sustainable, free-of-charge networks, the commercial Internet first became available to the general public in 1996. Being a more affordable and stable communications backbone, the Internet hastened the demise of BBS networks in Turkey. Following the global trend, BBS users began to migrate to the Internet from 1996 onwards. As a result, some commercial BBSs went bankrupt, while others evolved into Internet service providers (ISPs).[5] By the end of the millennium, BBSs were already a forgotten networking technology.[6]

Pre-Internet Computer-Mediated Communication Cultures in Turkey

Despite their rapid disappearance with the arrival of the Internet in Turkey, BBSs were the first civilian (and, to an extent, commercial) computer-to-computer network that facilitated the formation of online communities in Turkey. As has been argued elsewhere, part of the allure of joining online communities in patriarchal and conservative societies is the possibility to socialize in a safe environment (Slama 2010). This observation certainly applies to Turkey where the triad of Mediterranean cultural codes of honor and shame, Islam, and secular nationalist ideology form the basis of a society with conservative cultural values (Müftüler-Bac 1999). In this context, CMC technologies afford the possibility of circumnavigating around some of the more restrictive codes of public life in Turkish society. They also allow individuals to join online communities and socialize with people sharing similar cultural values and ideologies.

Online or virtual communities can be defined as groups of people with shared interests or goals for whom computer-mediated communication is a primary form of interaction (Dennis et al. 1998). Computer-mediated communication allows people to find and socialize with others who share similar interests, thereby forming and sustaining virtual communities (Hiltz and Wellman 1997) on the basis of social homophily. Much as social relations in the offline world, homophily, or the tendency of social actors to form ties with similar others, is the driving force behind the formation of larger social aggregates such as communities or social networks (McPherson et al. 2001). Perceived affinity between social actors creates the preconditions necessary for the aggregation of collective identities, communities, or neighborhoods online. Sustaining interaction is the other vital component for the emergence of online aggregates: "Social aggregations [. . .] emerge from the Net when enough people carry on those public discussions long enough, with sufficient human feeling, to form webs of personal relationships in cyberspace" (Rheingold 1994: 5).

Drawing from this, one can define online or virtual communities as: "Groups of people with common interests and practices that communicate regularly and for some duration in an organized way over the Internet through a common location or mechanism" (Ridings et al. 2002).

When looking at the messages posted on the correspondence logs of local BBS communities, one notices that a significant portion of the discussions on Hitnet were devoted to subjects that would be considered potentially taboo in Turkish society. Historically speaking, one can argue that the dominance of conservative cultural values in public space has made the discussion of certain subjects an avoided conversation subject for most. Nevertheless, the concerns regarding these sensitive subjects do exist and, as a result, often find their way into discussions in online communicative spaces such as Hitnet. For instance, one encounters a lot of conversations on adult-related subject matter like sexuality:

Q: How can we be sure whether a male is a virgin or not?

A: I'm not sure. But you can probably figure it from how they speak about the topic or from their attitudes regarding virginity.

Q: Would you prefer if the man you married was a virgin? (Don't laugh.)

A: :-)) I think the appropriate reply for this question is 'oh dear'.

(Saray 1996)

This conversation, which involves a male user asking a female community member about her opinions on virginity, demonstrates how Hitnet afforded a space for the discussion of subjects that normally would be avoided during conversations in regular life. Furthermore, one important aspect to these conversations and all others on Hitnet is the usage of real names for signing off messages. One can argue that the usage of real names adds both an additional dimension of authenticity to these conservations, effectively making them public conversations between two strangers. As a result, regardless of how sensitive the subject matter might be, there is always a certain degree of civility present in these discussions. Profanity is often avoided as well as any sort of discriminatory, inflammatory, or simply vulgar language.

Although the language used in Hitnet conversations tends to be civil most of the time, the subject matter is invariably determined and, to a certain degree, dominated by males. When looking at the gender composition of the communities active on Hitnet, one notices that, regardless of the local BBS network, the majority of participants are male. One of the effects of the disproportionality in the female to male ratio is that the posts of female participants tend to receive numerous replies. While the language remains civil, the register of these replies can at times veer on the edge of adolescent (and misogynistic) admiration.

While males constitute the dominant gender, another characteristic in Hitnet communities is the secular cultural values of their participants. Usually, one does not encounter discussion of religion-related topics on Hitnet correspondence logs. Conversations about religion are often in the form of joke exchanges, most of which also double up as critical commentary on the subject. As Fatma Müge Göçek (1998) has pointed out, humor in Turkish culture is often both a site of resistance against social hegemony and a vehicle for social critique. As such, making jokes about religion is an assertion of secularity:

Q: One day, a man finds a note on the street. Upon reading it, he immediately commits suicide. What was written on the note?

A: That there was only one more place left in heaven.

(Fezizoğlu 1996)

215

The last aspect of communal culture on Hitnet worthy of mention is the educational level of its participants. As has been studied elsewhere, abbreviations and acronyms are abundantly used in conversations on the network (Furman 2015). Both abbreviations and acronyms tend to use English and Turkish words in a mash-up manner that resembles "bricolage" (Hebdige 1991) to form a community lingo, which at times can be extremely difficult for outsiders to understand. What the linguistic bricolage of Turkish and English suggests is that participants needed to have an adequate grasp of both languages in order to be able to participate in the community culture of Hitnet. One rarely encounters situations wherein participants without a sufficient grasp of English post requests for help on the language used in conversations. What this suggests is that knowledge of the English language seems to be relatively widespread within the local BBS communities. As has been studied elsewhere, having fluent knowledge of English in Turkey has "become the *sine qua non* for a successful career in virtually any field and parents struggle[d] to have their children acquire a working knowledge of the language" (Doğançay-Aktuna 1998). Given the prevailing attitude that English-language education provided several instrumental benefits in the form of better job prospects, financial, and academic rewards (Kırkgöz 2008), having knowledge of English needs to be considered as a form of cultural capital and educational achievement in Turkey.

Due to the constraints imposed by the networking technologies of the era, the communities hosted by bulletin board systems tended to be quite local in scale. In Turkey, the networks of most BBSs were either on the scale of a neighborhood or on the scale of a town or small city. As a result, these networks tended to host communities that were relatively small and intimate. As such, these pre-Internet networks proved to be ideal spaces to host small and disconnected local subcultures. Looking at the documentation on local BBS correspondence logs, it seems that one subculture that utilized extensively the spaces afforded by BBS networks were computer enthusiasts.

Hobbyist subcultures based around computers and computing have a rich history in Turkey that can be traced to the Demoscene, an international community that created digital art with home computers. The origins of the international Demoscene can be traced to the late 1970s, when home computers began to appear on the consumer market for the masses (Polgár 2008). The availability of affordable home computers led to the blossoming of software piracy and the emergence of cracking as a practice. Cracking is a term commonly used to refer to the practice of removing copy protections in commercial software. Cracked copies of commercial software would either be swapped and freely shared, or would be sold off to computer shops and generate revenue needed to acquire commercial software and begin a new cracking exploit. The Demoscene began with crackers preparing elaborate introductions to commercial software that would detail their exploit with non-interactive audiovisual presentations that ran each time the cracked software was accessed. As a form of self-branding, these collectives would use graphics and sounds to "tag" the introductions of the cracked software. Coders, musicians, and visual artists formed groups and created introductions for cracked software while also trading programs, games, cracks, and demos locally and internationally. The artistic activity of the Demoscene has been likened to "art of the real-time" (Tasajärvi et al. 2004), or promoted as an emerging digital art form (Shor and Eyal 2002). On one hand, as a way of life, the subculture must be studied as a gendered youth culture (Borzyskowski 2000) or multimedia hacking culture (Carlsson 2009).

The first personal computer for the Turkish Demoscene was the Commodore 64, introduced to the domestic market around 1984–1985, featuring advanced graphics and sound for its time. The Commodore 64 brought digital games into Turkish households at a time when the only government-operated black-and-white TV channel TRT was broadcasting in limited hours. During these years, those with access to home computers in Turkey began to form collectives to crack and distribute commercial software via underground channels. Once bulletin board systems became available to the wider public, the underground disc-swapping, file-sharing activity moved online onto these networks. The earliest known demo group is Zombie Boys which started in 1988, and then grew into an international group called Bronx in 1991. Some of the internationally known Turkish Demoscene collectives of the period were Clique, Script, Bronx, Remix, Kris, Turbo, Detay, Walking Stres, Smile, Scotch, Metallic, Accuracy, Rastan, Kadem, and Barbie (see Figures 14.5, 14.6, 14.7 and 14.8 for artwork from the Turkish Demoscene). Some of these groups are still active.

The introduction of the Commodore Amiga, and then the personal computer (PC), to the domestic market during the late 1980s meant that Turkish coders had increasingly sophisticated machines at their disposal. As a result, the focus of their activities began to shift from cracking commercial software to activities that had been hitherto off-limits due to limitations in processing power. These activities were not just related to software but encompassed any other activity needing coding skills. Assembler optimizations or video compression algorithms were just a few of the new activities that coders could do with the newer, more powerful home computers available. As a result, coders evolved into a subculture that was distinct from the Demoscene, yet interrelated. One participant in Hitnet uses the following words to describe himself as a coder: "The name *coder* holds the same meaning as it would in the demoscene. However, the term also refers to programmers who take pleasure from trying to accomplish tasks on a computer that seem very difficult or even impossible to the outsider" (ssg 1999).

Figure 14.5 Artwork from the Turkish Demoscene

Figure 14.6 Artwork from the Turkish Demoscene

Figure 14.7 Artwork from the Turkish Demoscene

Figure 14.8 Artwork from the Turkish Demoscene

As BBS network usage began to gain traction throughout Turkey during the mid-1990s, the coders who were active in the Demoscene began to form their own collectives. Looking at the Hitnet archives, it seems that each local BBS community had a group of active coders. These coders utilized their community spaces to network with one another, forming programming collectives within their local environments. At the same time, coders enjoyed high levels of engagement within their respective communities, often contributing to both running the physical network as sysops and producing software that would be for the benefit of the community. As is evident from correspondence logs, these local communities of coders were linked to one another through Hitnet. Many of these coder collectives evolved into small, start-up companies producing proprietary software. Between 1995 and 2000, many of these small start-ups were highly successful and had many clients throughout Turkey. As a result, the most successful start-ups were bought up by the Turkish distributors of multinational software houses such as McAfee or Microsoft. Seizing the opportunity to go abroad, many Turkish coders left the country for a short period of time, only to return with the popularization of the Internet in Turkey during the early 2000s.[7] Many coders, upon their return to Turkey, used the opportunity presented by the growing number of Internet users to beome pioneers in a number of different, Internet-based industries. One can argue that the contacts that coders cultivated through BBS communities, as well as their technical prowess in computing, proved to be key factors in this process. The coder community organized around the Eskişehir-based ESS BBS demonstrates a valid example of how coders active within the community went on to become pioneers of digital culture and the ecology of the Internet in Turkey.

Methodology Note

The archival sample used for this study is publicly accessible and has been uploaded to the Internet by a former BBS enthusiast. However, a number of technical steps had to be taken in order to be able to access it. DosBox, a free emulator software that simulates an IBM PC computer running on MS-DOS (one of the earliest operating systems) was used to run Wolverine, an OMR with Turkish-language support.[8] Without an emulator, running Wolverine would have been impossible because of incompatibilities between older MS-DOS software and modern operating systems. The next step was to use Wolverine to access the files within the archive. Each file contained a batch of message logs which were ranked according to size, date, and the total number of messages. The message logs were primarily from three local BBS networks: ADABBS, BBS_BLUE and ESS. Of the total of 160 files that were accessible as an archive, 35 belonged to ADABBS, 6 to BBS_BLUE, and 119 to ESS. Technically speaking, Hitnet was more of a communications network linking local BBSs with each other. The Hitnet network provided the possibility of message circulation between islands of local networks, such as ADABBS (Ankara) or ESS (Eskişehir), and did not have centralized control over the localized configurations of these networks. Therefore, despite the existence of a larger Hitnet community, the archive itself is made up of message logs from local networks and not of Hitnet as a BBS. Messages belonging to the 119 ESS correspondence logs were used for the following case study.

ESS BBS and the Turkish Hitchhiker's Guide to the Galaxy

ESS BBS was founded in 1994 by Bloody (Mehmet Öztürk), a coder and graphic artist who had been active in the Turkish Demoscene (see Figure 14.9). The network ran on a 386dx-40 PC, a 14.4 bps modem, and one telephone line. According to Bloody, who was the sysop

Figure 14.9 Welcome page for ESS BBS

of the network, the original aim behind starting up a local BBS network was to save the local residents of Eskişehir from calling intercity to connect with BBS networks in larger cities like Istanbul or Ankara (ssg 2012). ESS BBS was connected to other BBSs throughout Turkey by being a member of first Hitnet and then Turknet. The assistant sysop (cosysop) of ESS BBS was Sedat Kapanoğlu (ssg), a young coder who had befriended the older Mehmet Öztürk when working at Dim-Soft, a computer shop located in a local shopping mall.[9] Upon becoming friends, Mehmet Öztürk invited Sedat Kapanoğlu to become the cosysop for his BBS network.[10]

In order to attract new community members to the newly established ESS BBS, ssg designed a BBS door game called Yogurt, which proved to be one of his earliest successful ventures. The game was based around the player trying to retype the sentences on the screen as fast as possible. Community members able to type fast would be ranked as high scorers. Yogurt proved to be so popular that ESS BBS soon began to attract community members from other cities throughout Turkey. After releasing the game as shareware on Hitnet, Yogurt became a staple offering in many local BBS networks. At the same time, the game staked out the reputation of ssg as a talented coder.

The work of ssg on ESS BBS had caught the attention of coder Meriç Şentunalı (Fatalica), who at the time was a student of computer engineering at the local university. Although Sedat Kapanoğlu had previously met Meriç through Meriç's older brother, who had also worked as a technician at Dim-Soft, the two became close friends through communicating on ESS BBS. Looking at the archives of the network, one encounters private messages between the two as well as public ones addressed to the wider community. In the private messages, the two would have long and detailed conversations about different aspects of coding and software.

Eventually, the duo decided to recruit a few other coders active within the ESS BBS community and start a company named Gensys. Starting out in a small space in a large office building, the first products of the group were Fatalvision, a library for designing graphic user interfaces (GUI), and Extidx, a Pascal-based database management system. Using both Fatalvision and Extidx, the group then prepared a number of resource management programs such as Genjin and Gendis. Both programs were geared towards the healthcare industry and were designed to help doctors keep track of their appointments and patient histories. These programs proved to be very popular, and the company received an offer from Issos Enterprises, which was the sole distributor of McAfee software in Turkey. Agreeing to be bought out by Issos Enterprises, the offices of Gensys were relocated to Ankara in 1995 and the group of coders began a series of new projects. During this period, ssg designed a program named Baston, which was a DOS-based file manager that had a GUI based on the Fatalvision library. Baston won him the first prize for the Golden Floppy Disc 95 competition that was jointly run by PC World and Microsoft. Resigning from Gensys, ssg returned to Eskişehir and developed a number of new services for BBS networks.

The first of the new services was Hitbase, a virtual telephone book for Hitnet users that aimed to fill the gap of having no central database to query for user information such as their interests or where they live. Cybershop was an e-commerce service designed to list advertisements put up by community members. Es Wall was an application that allowed community members to leave grafitti messages for one another. *Bitmeyen Savaş* (Forever War) was a multiplayer BBS door game created exclusively for ESS BBS that was played in teams. The other service, Wolverine, was the first OMR with Turkish-language support. After the arrival of the Internet in Turkey, ssg quit working for the BBS industry and started working for Internet infrastructure companies in Istanbul. Upon arriving in Istanbul, ssg came into contact with fellow Hitnet veteran Hasan Yalçınkaya, who had recently become a technology entrepreneur. After working as a technology journalist for a few years, Hasan founded Pilli with Cem Baspinar in 1999. His first successful project was the pillinetwork, a network of 11 blogs with more than 300,000 community-produced articles.

On his arrival in Istanbul, Sedat Kapanoğlu founded Sourtimes.org on 15 February 1999. The website was intended to be the entertainment portal for his envisioned business venture, Sedat Software Group (SSG). The name of the website—Sour Times—which he founded with his girlfriend and co-editor at the time (*kler*), is a reference to the Portishead song from the 1994 *Dummy* album. In the meantime, Sedat Kapanoğlu began working on building a collaborative, hyperlink-based urban dictionary called *Ekşisözlük*, which was intended as a new yet minor feature of his entertainment portal. According to Kapanoğlu, Douglas Adams's *Hitchhiker's Guide to the Galaxy* was the inspiration behind the concept of *Ekşisözlük*. According to an apocryphal account, after reading the book, Sedat Kapanoğlu began creating a platform that would channel the creative energies of participants into constructing an informational resource similar to the *Hitchhiker's Guide* (the "standard repository for all knowledge and wisdom"). He envisioned that the roles of the participants would resemble the non-professional field researchers who made the contributions to the *Hitchhiker's Guide*. In the same interview, Kapanoğlu states that after the transition to the Internet, he longed for the civil yet intimate community environment of Hitnet and had wanted to develop a website that could reproduce the communication culture of the BBS network (ssakyuz 2010).

Soon, the popularity of *Ekşisözlük* outpaced all the other applications he had designed for Sour Times Entertainment.[11] Once ssg began to notice that the number of visitors using the *Ekşisözlük* application far exceeded the number of visitors using other applications on the website, he decided to jettison the other content on Sour Times and focus on developing *Ekşisözlük*. A few years after the founding of Sour Times, ssg would write the following definition under the subject-header "*Ekşisözlük*":

> A masterpiece that can make up for the loneliness caused by time zones. [. . .] since going online [link to 15 February 1999] until today [link to 2001], more than 1,000 writers who helped develop this small and simple program, which has managed to form its own subculture, challenge the very definitions of what is "true" and demonstrated how knowledge has so many different angles. The seeds of this program were sown years back [link to Hitnet notes] and has now become a gigantic knowledge treasure thanks to technology [link to Internet] [. . .]
>
> (ssg 1999)

Despite the dazzling market penetration enjoyed by social networking platforms such as Facebook, Foursquare, Linkedin, and Instagram (Turkey is the country with the fifth most Facebook members and the 11th most Twitter users), *Ekşisözlük* has managed consistently to retain its popularity with the Turkish-speaking online audience. There are more than 69 different copycat versions of *Ekşisözlük* currently active, and the website itself has more than 355,000 registered community members. Much like Wikipedia (Niederer and van Dijck 2010), knowledge production on *Ekşisözlük* is highly regulated, and complex membership hierachies do exist. While Wikipedia-like sites tend to espouse a neutral point of view to knowledge production, *Ekşisözlük* is not necessarily concerned with producing knowledge that is based on facts. Instead, the archive of the websites is a dictionary that reflects what certain terms or phrases mean for a the *Ekşisözlük* community. As such, one can argue that sözlüks carry a post-structuralist ethos wherein meaning can be freely (and creatively) assigned to the linguistic components such as words, sentences, or phrases. A post-structural ethos to the creation of meaning and, as a result, knowledge makes sözlüks ideal sites for the expression of self-expression and creativity. At the same time, user-generated content on the site doubles up as an inform-ational guide to daily life and popular culture in Turkey. As one sözlük user suggests, the uniqueness of *Ekşisözlük* comes from "the possibility of encountering a topic [on the dictionary] that can be thought individually, but cannot be shared with anyone else" (Akca 2010).

The success of *Ekşisözlük* made Sedat Kapanoğlu one of the most desired and popular coders in Turkey. As a result, he was eventually recruited by Microsoft in 2004, and spent four years working in Seattle as a software design engineer. In the meantime, using his experience in e-commerce, he decided to introduce advertising on *Ekşisözlük*. Harnessing the potential posed by the consistently high volumes of visitor traffic on *Ekşisözlük*, he turned the website into an immensely profitable platform. Upon returning to Istanbul, he used the capital accumulated from *Ekşisözlük* to co-found a social media agency called Social IQ. The services of the agency focus on providing public relations on *Ekşisözlük* for celebrities and companies. One of the partners in this new venture was his old friend Meriç Şentunalı. Choosing to stay on at Gensys for a few more years, Meriç had been recruited by IBM and ended up moving to the USA. After a long stint working for IBM in the USA, he moved back to Turkey to become business partners with Sedat Kapanoğlu in 2011.

Conclusions

By connecting local online communities with one another throughout Turkey, Hitnet opened a space for people who had never met one another in real life to communicate in an asynchronous manner. Early BBS users were the first in Turkey to engage in networked publications and experienced long-distance collaboration via electronic communication. As evidenced by the leading Turkish blog network Pilli and the collaborative wiki-like dictionary *Ekşisözlük*, those individuals who pioneered networked CMC in the early days of BBS later became leading actors in shaping digital culture and how the technological potential of the Internet would be realized in Turkey.

Although there is a steady and growing literature on the digital culture of Turkish speakers on the Internet (see Binark and Bardaktutan-Sütçü 2008; Binark *et al.* 2009; Can and Can 2010; Ogan 2006; Sevdik and Akman 2002; Tahiroğlu *et al.* 2008), no comprehensive academic survey exists on the organization of pre-Internet online communities or pre-Internet CMC cultures in Turkey. One might argue that there are a number of reasons why pre-Internet digital culture in Turkey remains an under-researched topic. A possible explanation why the academic establishment in Turkey has overlooked both subjects can be linked to the lack of archival material. Unfortunately, most privately owned BBS networks were simply taken offline after falling into disuse from late 1996 onwards. As a result, much of the information stored by BBS administrators has remained in private hands. Furthermore, most of these private archives have been lost due to the lack of standardized and secure procedures for data storage.

Within the wider field of Internet studies, the critical contribution of this chapter is that it disputes conventional historical accounts of digital culture, which tend to be narrated from the vantage point of the North American, anglophone socio-cultural context. Much of the technological infrastructure of the Internet as a distributed communication network was gradually developed in North America over the course of the past two decades. The heart of the networked information economy is based in Silicon Valley and throughout greater California. As a result, most conventional narratives, both academic and popular, tend to frame digital culture as a North American phenomenon (see Hafner and Lyon 2006; Ryan 2010; Turner 2006). Reading these accounts and studies of early digital culture can be misleading in that one might be led to assume that the origin of digital culture was a primarily North American (and English-speaking) phenomenon. As Gerard Goggin and Mark McLelland (2009: 8) note: "The United States is all too often taken as 'the supposed vanguard of the information society,' and there has been little attempt to generate a discussion between scholars working on different language cultures or to develop modes of analysis that do not take anglophone models as their starting point."

While it is certainly important to acknowledge the strong influence of the North American socio-cultural context in the shaping of both Internet ecologies and digital culture worldwide, the evidence put forth in this chapter demonstrates that this influence is certainly not an over-determining one. Within the context of a similar argument, Mizuko Itō has pointed out that technologies are not universal; rather, it is necessary to attend to "the heterogeneous co-constitution of technology across a transnational stage" (Itō *et al.*). Such a theoretical framework, which takes into account the growing recognition that local cultures and practices have played an important role in domesticating global communications technologies, has been used within the context of Internet studies to examine how different cultures have appropriated computer-mediated communication technologies into their local contexts (Murphy 2008). In prioritizing local culture, and how pre-existing social formations have appropriated Internet-based communication technologies, studies sharing a similar point of view to the one espoused in this chapter look into how Internet users and communities "claim" online socialization spaces such as Second Life (Boellstorff 2008), Facebook (Miller 2011), or "polymedia" (Madianou and Miller 2011) to create forms of narrations and selves specific to different cultural milieus. The evidence provided in this chapter clearly demonstrates that rather than only appropriating affordances provided by the Internet, local socio-cultural milieus of relatively peripheral countries such as Turkey have played an active role in shaping the potential of the Internet as a networked communications technology.

As a conclusion, this chapter would like to argue that the need to document the origins of digital culture in social milieus other than North America is particularly pertinent, given the status of the Internet as a global communications network. Within the course of the past decade, the Internet has entered into social milieus other than North America or Western Europe. And as of 2015, North Americans constituted only 9.8 percent of Internet users around the world (Internet World Stats 2015). Not only does a chapter on how BBS pioneers played a key role in shaping the Internet ecology in Turkey demonstrate the contribution that local socio-cultural dynamics have made to the shaping of the Internet, it also serves as a call for other studies in peripheral countries that will take into account pioneer cultures and their "very local histories and cultures of use" (Goggin and McLelland 2007: 17).

Notes

1. Graphic interfaces were developed only after the popularization of BBSs in North America. The first BBS boards functioned without a screen, and instead used printers to send or receive data.
2. Trade Wars and Legend of the Red Dragon were some BBS games which were popular in North America during this period. These games relied on a door system that allowed users on BBSs to connect to external

programs located on either the hard drive of the mainframe computer or on a floppy disk. Users were allotted a specific amount of time to play these online games due to infrastructural constraints.

3. By the early 1990s, the commercial BBS industry had become a reality with many companies offering different sorts of paid services, including software, warez, and porn. There was even a magazine called *Boardwatch* dedicated to the BBS industry.

4. A system of "regions" and "nets" was developed to organize Fidonet nodes located around the world into one network. The stability of Fidonet technology caused the network to rapidly grow and last for more than 20 years. In 1984, there were only 132 nodes on Fidonet. By 1995, there were over 35,787 nodes on thenetwork.

5. Based in Ankara, ADABBS is one example of a BBS service that evolved into an Internet service provider in Turkey.

6. Although the actual community of Hitnet migrated to the Internet around the early 2000s and formed a mailing group to communicate among themselves, the mailing group soon lost popularity. Then community members started an online forum under the name of hitnet.bbs.tr around 2008. Once again, the online forum proved to be unsuccessful in terms of promoting the level of social relationships found on BBS networks and was finally closed down in 2010.

7. Although the Internet had arrived in Turkey in 1996, it did not immediately prove to be a popular communication technology. By the end of 1997, the number of computers connected to the Internet in Turkey was 30,000, and the estimated user base was only around 250,000 out of a total population of 63.5 million. The popularity of the Internet began after 2006, when there was a massive adoption of the medium by the Turkish population. Between 2006 and 2008, Internet users in Turkey increased twofold, turning the country into an important market for Internet-based services. Today, more than 35 million users go online daily, making Turkey the 17th largest country in terms of the number of Internet users.

8. OMRs were graphic interface terminal programs designed specifically for BBS networks that allowed users to send or receive messages to the mainframe computer.

9. Dim-Soft was an important location within the context of the local Demoscene as it was a space for older Demosceners to meet with both high school and university students who were interested in buying hardware or pirated games. These encounters led to the establishment of ESS BBS.

10. Sedat Kapanoğlu is an interesting character to note in that he never completed a university degree. Although he eventually managed to achieve widespread success, he had quite a few failed business ventures, including one venture which involved selling software for optimizing elevator schedules in tall buildings. Essentially put, the character portrait of Kapanoğlu is of a typical generation Xer, full of personality and intelligent ideas, but having a slightly slacker attitude to life.

11. It is quite humorous to note that a national lottery number predictor was among the less successful applications that ssg designed for his entertainment portal.

References

Akca, H. (2010) "The Internet as a Participatory Medium: An Analysis of the Eksi Sozluk Website as a Public Sphere", Master's thesis, University of South Carolina, available at: http://scholarcommons.sc.edu/etd/304

Arıcı, S. (1995) HR.TR.MIZAH, *ESS 161*, 16 June.

Binark, M., and Bardaktutan-Sütçü, G. (2008) "Türkiye'de İnternet Kafeler: İnternet Kafeler Üzerine Üretilen Söylemler ve Mekan-Kullanıcı İlişkisi", *Amme İdaresi Dergisi*, 41(1): 113–148.

Binark, M., Bayraktutan Sütcü, G., and Buçakçı, F. (2009) "How Turkish Young People Utilize Internet Cafes: The Results of Ethnographic Research in Ankara", *Observatorio*, 9: 286–310.

Boellstorff, T. (2008) *Coming of Age in Second Life: An Anthropologist Explores the Virtually Human*, Princeton, NJ: Princeton University Press.

Borzyskowski, G. (2000) "The Hacker Demo Scene and its Cultural Artifacts", *Scheib*, available at: www.scheib. net/play/demos/what/borzyskowski/

Can, H., and Can, N. (2010) "The Inner Self Desires a Friendly Chat: Chat Metaphors in Turkish and English", *Metaphor and Symbol*, 25(1): 34–55.

Carlsson, A. (2009) "The Forgotten Pioneers of Creative Hacking and Social Networking—Introducing the Demoscene", *Re: Live Media Histories Conference Proceedings, Melbourne*, Australia: University of Melbourne & Victorian College for the Arts and Music.

Dennis, A. R., Pootheri, S. K., and Natarajan, V. L. (1998) "Lessons from the Early Adopters of Web Groupware", *Journal of Management Information Systems* 14(2): 65–86.

Doğançay-Aktuna, S. (1998) "The Spread of English in Turkey and its Current Sociolinguistic Profile", *Journal of Multilingual and Multicultural Development*, 19(1): 24–39.

Fezizoğlu, N. (1996) HR.TR.MIZAH, *ESS*, 6 June.

Furman, I. (2015) "Alternatif Medya olarak Akranlararası Kolektif Üretim: 2013 Gezi Parkı Eylemleri'nde Ekşisözlük'ün rölüne dair bir inceleme", in B. Çoban and B. Ataman (eds), *Türkiye'de Alternatif Medya: Direniş Çağında, Kafka Yayınları*, Istanbul: Epsilon, pp. 199–223.

Göçek, F. M. (ed.) (1998) *Political Cartoons in the Middle East*, Princeton, NJ: Markus Wiener.

Goggin, G., and McLelland, M. (2009) "Internationalizing Internet Studies: Beyond Anglophone Paradigms", in G. Goggin and M. McLelland (eds), *Internationalizing Internet Studies: Beyond Anglophone Paradigms*, New York: Routledge, pp. 3–18.

Hafner, K., and Lyon, M. (2006) *Where Wizards Stay Up Late: The Origins of the Internet*, New York: Simon & Schuster.

Hebdige, D. (1991) *Subculture: The Meaning of Style*, London: Routledge.

Hiltz, S. R., and Wellman, B. (1997) "Asynchronous Learning Networks as a Virtual Classroom", *Communications of the ACM*, 40(9): 44–49.

Internet World Stats (2015) "Internet Users in North America November 15, 2015", *Internet World Stats: Usage and Population Statistics*, available at: www.internetworldstats.com/stats14.htm

Itō, M., Okabe, D., and Matsuda, M. (eds) (2006) "Introduction", in *Personal, Portable, Pedestrian: Mobile Phones in Japanese Life*, Cambridge, MA: MIT Press.

Kırkgöz, Y. (2008) "A Case Study of Teachers' Implementation of Curriculum Innovation in English Language Teaching in Turkish Primary Education", *Teaching and Teacher Education*, 24(7): 1859–1875.

McPherson, M., Smith-Lovin, L., and Cook, J. M. (2001) "Birds of a Feather: Homophily in Social Networks", *Annual Review of Sociology*, 27(1): 415–444.

Madianou, M., and Miller, D. (2011) "Mobile Phone Parenting: Reconfiguring Relationships between Filipina Migrant Mothers and Their Left-behind Children", *New Media & Society*, 13(3): 457–470.

Miller, D. (2011) *Tales from Facebook*, Cambridge: Polity Press.

Müftüler-Bac, M. (1999) "Turkish Women's Predicament", *Women's Studies International Forum*, 22(3): 303–315.

Murphy, P. D. (2008) "Writing Media Culture: Representation and Experience in Media Ethnography", *Communication, Culture & Critique*, 1(3): 268–286.

Niederer, S., and van Dijck, J. (2010) "Wisdom of the Crowd or Technicity of Content? Wikipedia as a Sociotechnical System", *New Media & Society*, 12(8): 1368–1387.

Ogan, C. L. (2006) "Confession, Revelation and Storytelling: Patterns of Use on a Popular Turkish Website", *New Media & Society*, 8(5): 801–823.

Polgár, T. (2008) *Freax: The Brief History of the Computer Demoscene. Vol. 1: [. . .]*, 2nd edn, Winnenden: CSW-Verl.

Rheingold, H. (1994) *The Virtual Community: Finding Connection in a Computerized World*, London: Secker & Warburg.

Ridings, C. M., Gefen, D., and Arinze, B. (2002) "Some Antecedents and Effects of Trust in Virtual Communities", *The Journal of Strategic Information Systems*, 11(3–4): 271–295.

Ryan, J. (2010) *A History of the Internet and the Digital Future*, London: Reaktion Books.

Saray, A. (1996) *ESS. 188. HR. TR. YETISKIN*, 27 February, 10.45am.

Sevdik, A., and Akman, V. (2002) "Internet in the Lives of Turkish Women", *First Monday*, 7(3), available at: http://firstmonday.org/ojs/index.php/fm/article/view/937/859

Shor, S., and Eyal, A. (2002) "DEMOing: A New Emerging Art Form or Just Another Digital Craft?", *Rhizome*, 25 April, available at: http://rhizome.org/community/26160/ (accessed 15 April 2007).

Slama, M. (2010) "The Agency of the Heart: Internet Chatting as Youth Culture in Indonesia", *Social Anthropology*, 18(3): 316–330.

ssakyuz (2010) "Ekşi Sözlük Kurucusunun Konuşması—2. Bölüm", *YouTube*, 2 March, available at: www.youtube.com/watch?v=eDjmrn68s1I

ssg (1999) "Ekşi Sözlük", *Ekşi Sözlük*, 19 February, available at: https://eksisozluk.com/entry/452

ssg (2012) "es bbs", *Ekşi Sözlük*, 31 March, available at: https://eksisozluk.com/entry/409

Tahiroğlu, A. Y., Celik, G. G., Uzel, M., Ozcan, N., and Avci, A. (2008) "Internet Use Among Turkish Adolescents", *CyberPsychology and Behavior*, 11(5): 537–543.

Tasajärvi, L., Schustin, M., Stamnes, B., and Tolonen, A. (2004) *Demoscene: The Art of Real-Time*, Helsinki: Uudenmaankatu 33 a 2, Even Lake Studios.

Turner, F. (2006) *From Counterculture to Cyberculture: Stewart Brand, the Whole Earth Network, and the Rise of Digital Utopianism*, Chicago: University of Chicago Press.

Varol, O. (1996) *HR.TR.YETİŞKİN, ESS*, 8 March.

Part 4

IMAGINING COMMUNITY VIA THE INTERNET

15

RETHINKING ARABIC LINGUISTICS

The History of the Internet in the Arabic-Speaking Region and the Rise of e-Arabic

Anissa Daoudi

Introduction

In December 2010, a week before the Tunisian Revolution, along with the prominent Tunisian scholar Professor Temimi, I organized an international conference on "The Internet and its impact on Arabic in the MENA region", in Tunis.[1] Most of the debate centered on the issue of language and identity. Examples of papers read were: "Who is Afraid of the Internet: e-Arabic as a Language of Dissent?", "Tweet like an Egyptian: Sociolinguistic Aspects of Microblogging in Egypt", and "Arabic in a Computer-mediated Communication Context". The customary debate about the dichotomy of Standard Arabic, known as *fusha*,[2] and regional dialects, known as *ammiya*, was present, but what was uncommon were the reactions and reflections of the Director of the Arab Academy, as well as of other conservative scholars, who admitted that the archaic debate over the status of Standard Arabic and vernaculars was no longer valid, and in fact needed rethinking. Furthermore, there was a consensus that the Arabic language is changing, and a new variety is emerging. Under the impact of the Internet, the present chapter will give a historical overview of the Internet in the Arabic-speaking region, outlining its beginnings and its development across more than two decades. It will also highlight a new phenomenon, which I call e-Arabic (see definition below), emerging as a direct result of information and communication technologies (ICT) use in the Arab world. This original research challenges the "archaic" dichotomy in Arabic linguistics, and places this new variety (e-Arabic) in the heart of the equation. The research also claims that the linguistic revolution in the Arab world preceded the Arab Revolutions, based on studying Arabic use in cyberspace (Daoudi 2010, 2011). To put the study into perspective, some research context is given on computer-mediated communication (CMC) in Arabic as well as framing it within the global development of CMC. Furthermore, examples are provided using data gathered from corpora made up of 150 million Internet-based words; 150 Arabic Wikipedia corpora (containing 150 million words); an Arabic legal corpus (of 12 million words); and an Arabic computer science corpus (containing five million words).[3] Data was also collected from semi-structured interviews and observations. Publications about the linguistic changes and the institutionalization of e-Arabic are published in other papers (see Daoudi 2011; Daoudi and Murphy 2011; and Daoudi 2014).

However, before embarking on the issue of the Internet and its impact on the Arab world, including Arabic, brief descriptions of the geographical spread of the Arabic-speaking world and the differences between the varieties of Arabic are needed. In addition, historical background information about the Internet in the Arab world will be discussed to give a context to the new variety of Arabic (e-Arabic) argued in this chapter.

When the word 'Arabic' is mentioned, one is confronted with a variety of 'Arabic(s)'. Is it the Standard Arabic used formally at schools and in newspapers? Is it the Classical Arabic of the Qur'an? The Gulf Arabic, the Egyptian Arabic, the Levant Arabic, or the North African Arabic? The list goes further to include varieties in each country. For example, coming from the southern part of Algeria makes my Arabic different from another Algerian from northern Algeria. As Bassiouney (2009: 1) states: "There are at least three different varieties of Arabic in each Arab country, and some linguists even claim that there are at least five different levels of Arabic in each country, not counting the different dialects of each country." The answer to the questions above is that the 23 countries in which Arabic is the official language have been described as diglossic speech communities. In other words, it is about "communities in which two varieties of a single language exist side by side" (Bassiouney 2009: 1).

Diglossia in the Arabic-speaking World

The phenomenon of separating Standard Arabic (*fusha*), which is associated with the written form, from the colloquial Arabic (*'ammiyya*) used in the oral/spoken form has been the focus of debates for decades in academic and non-academic circles. It is what is referred to as diglossia, a linguistic situation where two varieties of the same language exist to fulfill different social functions and are used in the same speech community. This is different from the use of two languages in similar situations which is called bilingualism. Ferguson (1959: 336) defines

> [d]iglossia as a relatively stable language situation in which, in addition to the primary dialects of the language (which may include a standard or regional standard), there is a very divergent highly codified (often grammatically more complex) superposed variety, the vehicle of a large and respected body of written literature, either of an earlier period or of another speech community, which is learned largely by formal education and is used for most written and formal spoken purposes, but is not used by any sector of the community for ordinary conversation.

According to Ferguson, diglossia is not only about having different dialects in the same speech community; it is also about the status of each variety. In diglossic communities there is high valued H (high) variety, which is learned in school and is not used in ordinary conversation. That is to say, no one speaks the H variety in everyday communications. The L (low) variety is the one used in conversation.[4]

Bourdieu (1991) argues that linguistic behavior is profit- and status seeking-driven, noting that language is to be viewed not only as a means of communication, but also as a means of exercising power, according to the individual's own interests and as a crucial element in the construction of social reality. In the case of Arabic, the Standard Arabic (SA) gets its high status from its association with Islam and the pre-Islamic period (Eid 2002), which is a form of symbolic capital (Bourdieu 1991). As far as dialects are concerned, the case is more complicated, as there is no single dialect; rather, there are many variations depending on geographical regions—for example, Algerian Arabic, Tunisian Arabic, Gulf Arabic, and so forth. Moreover, within the same category—for example, in Algerian Arabic—one finds other variations, such as the difference between the language spoken in the north vs. the south, the language used by old vs. younger generations, the language spoken by francophone vs. arabophone-educated[5] Algerians, and Algerian Arabic of the Arabs vs. that of the Berbers.[6] Bassiouney argues that by favoring one code over the other—for example, SA—one excludes other groups, and this may also be used as a justification for political elitism (Bassiouney 2014). Since resources and access have always been closely related to politics and ideologies, those who have access to resources would position themselves as legitimate, powerful or both (Bassiouney 2014). In practical terms, the use of SA in most of the Arabic-speaking region is an "exclusive code mastered by only few intellectuals and not by the mass populations". This is because it is not the spoken language and is different from the dialects (colloquials) (Bassiouney 2014: 3).

History of the Internet in the Arabic-speaking Region

One needs first to clarify that while the Internet has seen increasing developments in English-speaking countries in the 1980s, it is only in the 1990s that Tunisia was the first Arab country to introduce the Internet with very limited access in 1991, followed by Kuwait in 1992 as part of its reconstruction after the Iraqi invasion, Egypt and the United Arab Emirates in 1993, Qatar and so on. For Saudi Arabia, it is not until the late 1990s that public access was allowed with restrictions. In Syria, it was with the arrival of Bashar Al Assad that the Internet was introduced, and prior to that, many Syrians obtained Internet access via long-distance phone calls to Internet service providers (ISP) in Lebanon and Jordan. Similar practices of long-distance remote access to the Internet were also common in Saudi Arabia via Bahrain, before the state made access to the Internet available through locally licensed ISPs (Wheeler 2004). This is to say that the Arab countries lagged behind most of the world. Internet accessibility between the center (developed countries) and the periphery (underdeveloped countries) in the world is a phenomenon that still exists but to a lesser extent now. It is what is referred to as "digital divide".

During my last visit to Algeria in summer 2015, precisely to the southern part, I could not withdraw cash from the bank, simply because the Internet was cut off from the central network in Algiers, the capital. This is common in many cities in Algeria, despite the Internet expansion that the Algerian government has invested in. This is to say that the digital divide is not only in the number of Internet users, but also in the quality and speed of connectivity services. This digital divide can also be assessed on the macro-level of what Abdulla (2007: 63) calls the have and have nots of people in the same country. She refers to race, education, socio-economic status, or a combination of all the mentioned factors. One factor for the late expansion of the Internet in the Arab world is due to the fact that, until the late 1990s, the technical difficulty of using Arabic on the Internet meant that it was restricted to those who could use English or French. Most Internet content with texts in Arabic had to be rendered as graphics, making it extremely slow to load pages.

Over the past several years, both Microsoft and Sakhr[7] Software have been working to remedy this problem. The May release of Arabic Office 97 by Microsoft and the continuing development of the Sindbad browser by Sakhr, have made surfing the net in Arabic a reality.

(Tucker *et al.* 2002)

Another factor was the high cost of connections, which hindered countries such as Egypt, as well as issues of access and restrictions, which other countries like Saudi Arabia had to find a solution to. However, once Internet access was made officially available in Saudi Arabia, the kingdom witnessed the largest and fastest growth in Internet user population of any Arab country.

According to a study by the Mohammed bin Rashid School of Government (2014):

There are more than 135 million individuals using the Internet in the 22 Arab countries. This is coupled with a mobile penetration rate of around 110 percent on a regional level; and more than 71 million active users of social networking technologies.

During recent years, a few Arab countries have invested heavily in IT. For example, Saudi Arabia has made efforts, albeit monitored, to increase connectivity. It has invested in King AbdelAziz City for Sciences (KACST). In addition, Tunisia also invested in very interesting projects like "Internet Caravans", which were buses, assisted by the Internet, that travelled the entire country. In 2005, Tunisia hosted the World Summit of Information Society (WSIS). In the section below, I refer to the socio-political aspects of the Internet's impact on Tunisia and on the claims about the Tunisian Revolution as being called "Facebook/Internet revolution". This rapid development has had different impacts on the Arab world, including on the language. In the following section, the changes that occurred on the linguistic level are illustrated.

The Linguistic Revolution in the Arabic-speaking Region

Arabic, like other languages, is undergoing a revolution in the speed of its diffusion as well as innovation in both verbal and written communication. This revolution, which comes as one of the effects resulting from information technology (IT), including the Internet revolution, is redefining the way people interconnect, how they use the language, and how they express their identities. This new form of writing has been the subject of both positive and negative reactions, depending on the age group, social class, and many other factors related to identity, ideology, and so forth. As an example, it would be difficult to imagine that my late father, who was educated in French during the French colonial period in Algeria, would have thought that there would be a time when he could actually convey a message in Arabic using Roman script—for example, *ahla beek* (Hi). In addition, he would not have made any "distortion" to the French language by using the abbreviations common nowadays in instant messaging, such as *Slt, cmt ca va?* (Hi, how are you?). Adopting Roman script would have possibly made his struggle with learning to write in Arabic easier. Yet, his attitude to language change would not have been so different from Labov's argument about people's widespread attitudes towards language change:

[C]ommunities differ in the extent to which they stigmatise the newer forms of language, but I have never yet met anyone who greeted them with applause. Some older citizens welcome new music and dance, the new electronic devices and computers. But no one has ever been heard to say "it is much better than the way we talked when I was a kid".

(Labov in Greiffenstern 2010: 80)

Labov's reference to what is widely known as the Golden Age Principle can explain some of the negative attitudes and the resistance to change felt globally, not just in the Arabic-speaking region. The study engages with some language theories, including Labov's Apparent Time Construct (1963, 1966). His distinction between apparent-time and real-time changes is helpful. The underlying conception of the apparent-time change is that age stratification of linguistic variables do not only reflect change in the individual as he or she moves through life (age grading), but also historical changes in the speech community as it moves through time. In other words, some of the variables used by one age group, usually young people, may spread through the entire population and consequently slowly change the language. We should bear in mind that the rate of change, as far as human communication occurring through the use of electronic devices is concerned, is rapid, and is neither systematic nor stable. This idea will help in positioning e-Arabic as a language variety when discussing language change. However, before elaborating any further, a detailed definition of e-Arabic is needed.

e-Arabic is the medium used on the Internet and in mobile telephony. It is a variety among others; its basis is both Modern Standard Arabic (MSA) and Arabic dialects. It borrows and adapts words from various languages (for example, English and French); it allows code switching and code mixing, and uses numbers to substitute for missing sounds in Arabic. Additionally, it permits the use of Romanized Arabic. Furthermore, e-Arabic is not bound by the traditional syntactic, semantic, and lexical rules. One of its characteristics is language distortion in order to create impact, aiming to engage not only with the globalized discourse as such, but also to highlight the specific ways in which the local interacts and frames the global (Daoudi 2011; Daoudi and Murphy 2011). Studying e-Arabic is not only to highlight the phenomenon at this stage but more importantly to rethink the linguistic dichotomy of *fusha* as opposed to *ammiya* by adding this new language variety to the equation, recognizing the local nature of the phenomenon, but also framing it within the global situation of CMC. The existence of this new variety—that is, e-Arabic—is undeniable and at the same time inevitable, as it is part of an organic reaction as a result of language contact. Most importantly, it affects most languages to differing degrees.

As far as CMC is concerned, my argument is that one only needs to look at the Arabic cyberspace[8] to realize that there are actually two distinctive levels of interaction: online and offline. The two levels have two distinctive dynamics and are not necessarily in harmony. One good reason for that could be the nature of the online sphere, which protects the anonymity of the user, freeing him or her to communicate ideas in a more open way. By this, I mean that the innovative ways of writing online in Arabic, the themes and discussions around and about linguistic issues such as mother tongue, religion, and politics, are not necessarily followed up in the same ways as offline. An example of this is a Facebook page known as /lu:ghti alu:m altunnsi/ (My mother tongue is Tunisian Arabic). It is written in Tunisian dialect, a practice that was once not allowed for political reasons due to the ideology of Arab nationalism, which called for the entire Arab nation to unite under one language, Standard Arabic, and banned any voices that prevented it from achieving that unity. Another example is a well-known blog, 7ibir (ink), which has chosen deliberately the use of e-Arabic. Similar websites, Facebook pages, and blogs have mushroomed in the last decade. Therefore, two codes (Standard Arabic as well as e-Arabic) as writing codes coexist, and have even made it to the offline sphere. For example, what once used to be banned in Syria by the Ba'ath

Party in the 1980s, such as writing in Roman script on shop signs, in the name of Arab nationalism and purism (Palfreyman and Al Khalil 2007: 45) is now allowed, and found in most Arab capitals and cities. Therefore, the Arabic cyberspace demonstrates what Grivelet (2001) calls in socio-linguistics "synchronic digraphia" (the coexistence of two or more writing systems for the same language), with the exception that the e-Arabic writing system is not officially recognized, despite its widespread use. In explaining digraphia, Palfreyman and Al Khalil (2007) mention the example of the alphabet revolution in the new Turkish Republic, which converted from Arabic to Roman script, showing not the coexistence of two languages, as is the case with the synchronic digraphia, but a replacement of one system with another.

e-Arabic: A Challenging New Variety

Rethinking Arabic linguistics entails questioning the simplified definition that restricts a language spoken by more than 250 million people into dichotomies between *fusha* and *'ammiya* which remain unchangeable over time. Moving away from the dichotomies was also attempted by Terence Mitchell (1956: 9), who introduced the new idea of Educated Spoken Arabic (ESA), which "is not a separate variety but is 'created' and 'maintained' by interaction between the written language and the vernacular" (Bassiouney 2009: 16). The linguistic variety I am introducing in this chapter is different from ESA. Unlike ESA, e-Arabic is a new variety "created" and "maintained" by Arab Internet users. Linguistically speaking, groups of Internet and IT users in the various Arabic-speaking regions created what John Swales calls a "discourse community", which is formed by analogy with the socio-linguistic term "speech community". The former identifies regional groups that share linguistic norms and/or typical phonological, lexical, morphological, and syntactic patterns. Swales describes it as "groups that have goals or purposes, and use communication to achieve these goals". In fact, CMC in Arabic allows distinguishing between "discourse community", which uses e-Arabic, and "speech community". The concept of "speech community" (SC) was introduced by Labov (1963, 1966, 2000) referring to the most often cited and critiqued definition:

> [t]he speech community is not defined by any marked agreement in the use of language elements, so much as by participation in a set of shared norms; these norms may be observed in overt types of evaluative behaviour, and by the uniformity of abstract patterns of variation which are invariant in respect to particular levels of usage.
>
> (Labov 1972: 120–121)

Significant here is the idea that members of an SC do not *necessarily* have to speak the same way—they must simply share a set of evaluations about the speech of that community. A good example is the SC shared by IT users from North Africa, who might mix Arabic with French, and the SC shared by IT users from the Middle East, where there might be a mixing of Arabic with English. This is to say that they both share the sets of evaluations about the speech, but in practice they use different words. For example, in North Africa, the verb "to save" is referred to as /ansuvgardi/ (sauvegarder), whereas in the Middle East, the same verb is known as /ansaivi/. Another example is the use of the verb *dégage* in French, which started off as a speech community used by Tunisians—French is commonly used in Tunisia—and later traveled to Egypt to be used in the Egyptian Revolution, and to Yemen as part of the "discourse community".

Social network (SN) is another concept based not on shared language use or shared evaluations, but on the social ties in which people engage, such as with close friends, relatives, colleagues, and neighbors. Here, members of the community are known to each other. SC approaches, however, do not insist that members actually know each other or interact regularly. The notion of *community* is introduced and applied to socio-linguistic investigations by Eckert (Eckert and McConnell-Ginet 1992a, 1992b, 1999; Eckert 2000) who refers to a Community of Practice (CofP), which is "groups whose *joint engagement* in some activity or enterprise is sufficiently intensive to give rise over time to *repertoires of shared practices*" (Eckert and McConnell-Ginet 1999: 185). "Joint engagement" indicates that members of a CofP must be engaged with one another and not simply share a certain characteristic (Moore 2003: 19). As highlighted earlier, members of an SC do not necessarily know each other, whereas members of an SN are likely to do so. What distinguishes CofP is the fact that it is concerned only with what a person does. The other criterion of a CofP "enterprise" refer to "the purpose around which mutual engagement is structured" (Moore 2003: 19). In addition, CofP "repertoires of shared practices" refer to a set of resources that "are a cumulative result of internal negotiations" (Meyerhoff 2002: 528). Clarifying the criteria for each definition will be of particular help when discussing the phenomenon in order to position e-Arabic in the global context. It will also help in deciding whether the approach is top-bottom or bottom-up when analyzing the data. To put things into perspective, I add to my definition of e-Arabic the following:

> From the definition, e-Arabic is an established language variety utilized by IT users, a means of communication using a created jargon to exclude, and at the same time, include, members into its community. This shared language has created an SN and a CofP allowing its members to have subjective perceptions.

Another striking characteristic of the e-Arabic definition given above is the use of Roman script to render spoken into written Arabic and substituting the missing sounds in Western languages with numbers. The digits are [2, 3, 5, 7, 8, and 9] with [3, 9, and 7] as the most used digits.

The mixing of languages does not stop at Romanizing Arabic, but extends to mixing languages with dialects or registers, as is the case in the following examples given by El Essawi (2011: 254):

a. "*Happy birthday 3oba 1000000 sana*" (Happy birthday. May you live till you are 1000000 years).

b. "*sa7ini 2saa3a sab3a*" (Wake me up at seven).

While (a) is a mixture of Arabic and English, (b) is in Egyptian dialect and the numbers used are to substitute the missing sounds in English. This mixture of languages is a variety that is widespread among Arab youth, particularly from Egypt, the Gulf, and the Levant. In North Africa, the varieties are slightly different, as there will be mixtures of French, or possibly English, colloquial and SA.

Table 15.1 Romanizing Arabic with number substitution

2	3	5	7	8	9
ء	ع	خ	ح	ه	ق

c. *"Slt, c Asma. Stp, galek papa choufili tbib fi Londres"* (Hi, This is Asma. Dad (papa) says find me a doctor in London please).

d. *"mana3rafch ween fi London? N7abek ta3rfi minu l'addresse"* (I don't know where in London? I want you to know from him the address).

e. *"ISA"* (In shaa Allah, God willing).

The above examples are mixtures of languages, registers, and forms. They all create a hybrid language. In other words, they fall into the categories of my working definition of e-Arabic (mentioned above). (c) is a mixture of French and Algerian Arabic. It is also an abbreviated form of French as in the "Slt", which is in French *Salut* (Hi). Also (the letter "c", is the French abbreviation for "it is". (Londres is written in French; in English, London.) (d) is similar to (b) in terms of using Roman script for Arabic dialect. (d) is in Algerian dialect. The use of 3 is to substitute the Arabic letter and sound ع in transliteration /'/ and 7 for the ح in transliteration ḥ. Finally, (e) is an abbreviation of the Arabic religious formulae (God willing). The mixture of the written and the spoken forms is specific to CMC, including e-Arabic. It also mixes the informal and relaxed way of talking with the formal one in what Baron calls "the written talk" (Baron, cited in El Essawi 2011: 257).

As mentioned in the introduction, the study I conducted for more than three years was well before the Arab Revolutions. The Arabic cyberspace was already active and Arab users, particularly the youths in most countries—for example, Egypt—had established language to communicate between each other. Activists like Lina Ben Mhenni (2016) had a blog called *bnaya Tunsiyya* (Tunisian Girl). Other bloggers from Egypt whom I followed before, during, and after the revolutions are Hossam Al Hamalawy (2016), whose blog :3arabawy included e-Arabic (he substitutes the Arabic letter ع with the number 3); Wael Abbas (2015), whose blog was very famous for controversial statements that challenged the ousted Egyptian government of ex-president Mubarak; 7ibr (n.d.), another blog from Jordan, again using e-Arabic in the title of the blog (substitution of an Arabic letter ح with the number 7, see table above). What unites these bloggers/activists (many of whom had never met before the Arab Revolutions) is their mission to bring out the opposing opinion to their governments. This activity has not always been common in the Arab world.

Research on CMC and the Arabic Cyber Sphere

Netspeak, a term associated with the Internet language coined by Crystal (2000, 2004), has been affecting languages globally, including non-European languages such as Arabic. As far as CMC studies are concerned, there is a clear distinction between synchronous language (e-chat, instant messaging) and asynchronous language (mailing lists, newsgroups, discussion boards). New terminology has appeared, such as e-language and e-literature, referring to the language used in "computer-mediated registers" (Herring 1996, 2003). This has led to a clear emergence of unique features in this language, such as the use of emoticons, acronyms, and mixtures of spoken and written forms in the same register (Crystal 2000). Herring (2003) moved away from "the language of CMC" towards "computer-mediated discourse" (CMD), which is helpful in analyzing and subjecting to scrutiny what goes on beyond language.

As far as Arabic is concerned, research on CMC or CMD has barely begun, and the number of studies is very limited. This does not mean that communication technology is not significant. On the contrary, it has revolutionized the individual's everyday life, and radically changed the face of communication (Al-Khatib 2008). The first study conducted on Arabic concerning the issue of CMC and Romanized Arabic was by David Palfreyman and Muhamed

Al-Khalil, linguists at Zayed University in Dubai. Their research focus was on "ASCII-ized Arabic"— that is, using the Latin alphabet to replace Arabic letters and substituting the missing letters with numbers. Another study was carried out by Warschauer *et al.* (2002, 2007) on informal email messages and code switching, and in some cases code mixing, that took place between female students in the UAE. Similarly, another study was conducted by Al-Tamimi and Gorgis (2007) on "Romanised Jordanian Arabic E-messages". Other studies have used the term Arabizi to refer to Arabic in Roman script (Yaghan 2008; Muhammed *et al.* 2011; Attawa 2012). Hamzah (2004) summarizes the benefits of CMC in the field of foreign language learning. Furthermore, Bjørnsson (2010) wanted to know the extent of influence of Arabic orthography on Arabizi, or what he called "Egyptian Romanized Arabic (ERA)". In the same vein, Nasser Berjaoui (2002: 451) argued that the origin of an ERA user could be identified from his/her way of writing. According to him, this is mainly because ERA is a reproduction of the spoken dialect.

The section below presents the e-Arabic phenomenon as a new emerging language variety that has been making its way into various forms of language. It will also show the dynamics of the cyber *community* in highlighting CMC and in illustrating its expansion. The Arab uprisings are a good case for showing how e-Arabic has been used. Furthermore, the expansion of e-Arabic into Arabic literature is used to provide more evidence of the practical use of the e-Arabic phenomenon.

The Arab Uprisings: A Landmark in the Expansion of e-Arabic

The so-called "Arab Spring" is characterized by linguistic features that show a revolution in its own right for many reasons. First, as soon as the first uprising ignited in Tunisia, it was named the Jasmine Revolution,[9] bringing to life similar uses of political metaphors such as Lebanon's Cedar Revolution, Ukraine's Orange Revolution, the Iranian Green-Twitter Revolutions, the Maple Spring, and so on. Research on metaphors in rhetoric and politics has increased, particularly after Lakoff and Johnson's conceptual metaphor theory (1980), which has since been developed and elaborated. Second, the revolution in Tunisia started off with, as Jerrad (2012: 118) rightly puts it, a word that changed history, a word that broke walls of fear, silence, and self-censorship for decades in the time of dictatorship. Collectively, from all social classes and all ages, Tunisians loudly shouted to oust (*degage*) Ben Ali (ex-president). Soon, other words came to be used, such as freedom, dignity, and employment. These three words defined the Tunisian Revolution and positioned its narrative as language acts (Austin, cited by Jerrad 2012: 119). Jerrad (2013: 241) argues that language during the Tunisian Revolution was crucial in shaping the fight for democracy. She gives the following examples:

a. *Tunis hurra hurra wa Ben Ali ala barra!* (Tunis is free, free and Ben Ali is out!)
b. *Ben Ali dehor!* (Ben Ali out!)
c. *Ben Ali Assassin!* (in French, Ben Ali assassin)
d. Mafia out!
e. *Tunisie libre! Trabelsi: voleurs dehors!* (Tunis free! Trabelsi: thieves, out!)
f. Game over.
g. *Liberté*, freedom, *hurriya* (the word "freedom" in three languages).

The above examples show a great deal of multilingualism and multiculturalism. They are in French (as in examples: b, c, and e), in Tunisian Arabic (a), in English (d and f), and in a mixture of languages (e-Arabic) as in (g). Again, the examples are part of e-Arabic. This hybrid language was popular before the revolutions (see Daoudi 2011) and at that time, this project was the first to my knowledge to deal with the linguistic phenomenon in an interdisciplinary way, showing the role of language in shaping and framing discourses, at a time when social science studies were more interested in what goes on in the Arabic cyber sphere from a political, social, and economic framework. During and after the revolutions (from 2011), this linguistic phenomenon has become even more prevalent, and is now used by Arabic-speaking users as an established medium (variety of language). The slogans that were used in the revolution did not only have an impact on the masses locally, but traveled regionally. The uprising has impacted the whole world (that is, traveled globally). Expressions like /*harimna*/ used by a Tunisian old man became iconic, literally meaning that *we have grown old while fighting for this historic moment*, referring to a whole generation that has witnessed dictatorship. What is worth noting is that the word itself is not a modern one. It is in Standard Arabic and not a common word. The word also retained its interpretation. Standard Arabic was also used, which is not something common, as usually slogans are in the dialect and they follow a rhythm. The slogan /*al sha'b yurid*/ is in Standard Arabic and is from a well-known poem by the Tunisian poet Abu al Qasim Al Shabbi—"Will to Live" (literally translated as "the people want"). It was also utilized extensively, starting in Tunisia then on to Egypt and Yemen. However, this is not at all to say that there was one homogeneous corpus for the revolution. While a word like /*shibbiḥa*/—literally, "phantoms"—has been used in Syria to mean the people fighting for the dictator, in Egypt, /*baltagiya*/ was used to mean more or less the same thing. Other words like /*fulūl*/ in Egypt and /*azlām al nidhām*/ in Tunisia, meaning people who used to be part of the authoritative regime, are old words that were given a new connotation. What is worth mentioning is that the linguistic corpus of the revolution can be divided into three categories.

The first category is the one that covers Standard Arabic: for example, /*fulūl*/, /*azlām al nidhām*/, and /*shibbiḥa*/. These are words that have been given new connotations. Their meanings changed, and so did their usages. In linguistics, the phenomenon is referred to as semantic change, semantic shift, semantic progression, or semantic drift.

The second category of the revolution corpus is the dialect and SA: for example, in Egypt, /*ya jamal . . . qul la būk, shab Misr biykrahūk*/ [o, Gamal, tell your Dad, the Egyptian people hate you]. One characteristic of this category is reliance on the rhyme between words.

The third category is the hybrid or e-Arabic category, such as the French verb *dégage* and the English slogan *yes, we can* (referring to the American slogan used by President Obama in his presidential election). *Dégage* has traveled from Tunisia to Egypt, Libya, and Yemen where French is not commonly used. This shows the interconnections between the local and the global.

As far as the online sphere and CMC are concerned, the normalization and the ease of using the dialect and e-Arabic are widespread and on the rise. Nesma TV, a channel targeting viewers in North Africa, is another example of e-Arabic usages, where the medium used is a mixture of dialects, SA, and French. The news bulletin, usually formal, is now being read in the dialect in order to simplify the language for the listener or viewer (combination of registers). There are two important platforms which facilitate the rapid spread of e-Arabic. The first is related to the multilingual nature of the Arabic dialects. For example, the North African Arabic dialects allow combining words from French as well as code switching from one language to another in the same sentence. They also "Arabize" French—that is, the French word is pronounced with Arabic intonation, which sounds like Arabic. This same phenomenon is also true of the Gulf and other Arab countries in the "East", known as *al Mashreq*, except that it involves English and not French. The second point is the "democratization" of the Arabic language. By this, I mean e-Arabic is used by all social classes, including those with limited education, as they can write the spoken form using e-Arabic tools mentioned above.

The other question that has been asked concerns the role of e-Arabic, and ultimately the Internet in the struggle towards democracy (see Hofheinz 2011). It goes without saying that this is not the first technological innovation used in the past as a tool for liberation. The best example is the invention of the printing press. When used in the Arab region, particularly in Egypt and Lebanon, it created what is now known as the *Nahdha*—the Arab Renaissance— in the nineteenth century. At that time, its leaders, such as the Egyptian scholar Tahtawi, were advocating for openness to the world and the coining of new words, including the Arabization of foreign words for which there were no equivalents in SA. This was not an easy task for the linguists, as their approach was objected to by the purists, who are still resisting any foreign addition to the SA. However, the advancement of e-Arabic is going ahead despite the opposing voices.

e-Arabic and the Emergence of a Contested New Literary Genre

After spending some time working on the impact of the Internet, I extended my project to highlight the emergence of a new type of writing by young Arabs using the Internet to write about various topics, making use of e-Arabic as a medium. This new genre of writing was, and still is, controversial, not only in terms of the themes discussed which are/were considered taboo—for example, sex, politics, and religion—but also due to the language used that is not Standard Arabic, which created heated debates about certain ideologies related to language. The concept of Standard Language is present in many languages, including Arabic. As Maureen Milroy and Feng Li (2001: 535) rightly put it, "an extremely important effect of Standardization has been the development of consciousness among speakers of a 'correct', or a canonical form of language". Similarly, the notion of using Standard Arabic in writing is an institutionalized idea. Likewise, using the dialect for the spoken form is the norm, and anything that does not respect these two conventions is considered to be "incorrect" and uncanonical. This is not to say that the dialect has never been used in literature. What is innovative, however, is the sole use of dialects as well as mixing languages throughout the writing. This practice is still controversial, despite being popular in terms of readership in the Arabic-speaking region. "Language is a means and not an end" is the motto that is motivating a high number of young bloggers to write in order to be heard in countries where voices have been censored. The argument is that Standard Arabic—the supposedly "high" language—has been for a long time a stumbling block for the vast majority of Arabic native speakers, and is monopolized by a minority of the elite population. The same argument was once advocated by nationalist leftist movements, promoting the social mission of literature to narrow the gap between the elite (bourgeois) and the mass population (Azam 2007). However, what was meant then was to encourage writers to interact with the mass population by using a simple language and stepping down from ivory towers to write about what preoccupies these people. It did not mean writing in colloquial ways, as this option was non-existent.

The emergence of new publications in colloquial Arabic written by Internet users as blogs, then published in book format as novels/novellas, is shifting the emphasis from whether or not Modern Standard Arabic (MSA) should include colloquial forms, to insisting on writing in colloquial forms only. This phenomenon started in Egypt as one of the pioneering projects by Dar Al Shurouq, the Egyptian publishing house, which created a book series called

/*mudawanat al shurūk*/ and asked a young Egyptian blogger, Ghada Abdel Aal, to publish her popular blog in a book called /*Ayza Atgawiz*/ (Wanna Get Married) (2008), which was later turned into a TV series shown in Ramadhan. The theme of "being a spinster", which is a taboo, is rendered in this story as light-hearted and easy to be written about and read. Other examples include /*Ruz bi laban li shakhsain*/ (Rice Pudding for Two) (2008), /*Kahwat Al Masriyeen*/ (Egyptian Café) (2009), and many more. In Egypt, the phenomenon mushroomed. However, the first ever appearance of this new genre was with Raja' Alsanea's book *Banat al Riyadh* in 2005, which will be discussed further in the sections below.

In a special edition in *Al Majalla al Arabiyah* (2009), writers around the Arab world expressed their views about the new phenomenon which they called *The Internet Story Teller*. Their views varied between those who found this form of writing amusing and an addition to what is being written in MSA, and those who view this genre as a temporary phase which will fade out in the future, as it is not based on solid ground. The new trend of writing is not restricted to Arabic, and studies have been focusing on the effects of computer-based writing as opposed to earlier forms of written language production. Schmitz distinguishes between four levels at which CMC has affected the nature of writing.

1. *Monologic* (computer writing enabling flexible composition techniques and a less disciplined and uninhibited writing, which is one of the characteristics of young Arab writers using e-Arabic, as it frees them from centuries of institutionalized rules).
2. *Dialogic* (a new writing style emerging in sites of public, anonymous participation, a "playful anarchy" of hybrid, spoken/written patterns). A good example of this category is *Banat al Riyadh* (*Girls of Riyadh*) (2005), which will be discussed in the next section.
3. *Non-linear* (hypertext as a new principle of information structure).
4. *Interactive* (collaborative writing and the fuzzy distinction between author and reader) (Androutsopoulos 2011).

This interactive approach is adopted by Ahlem Mosteghanemi, a prominent Algerian writer, whose book mixes Arabic and English in its very title, نسيان. com (Forgetting.com), which includes a website address for readers to comment on the book, enabling both the readers and the writer to exchange ideas and interact with each other. This privilege is made available via the virtual sphere. The book is also accompanied by a CD, aiming to support and reinforce the theme of the novel, which is forgetting and moving on in life.

Girls of Riyadh

Here I am suggesting that a "new literary genre" is emerging out of blogs and emails, making full use of IT and CMC as mediums. *Banat al Riyadh* بنات الرياض (Girls of Riyadh) (2005) is a novel by a young Saudi dentist living in the USA.

Alsanea, and many authors of her generation, are making use of the Internet in order to engage with the global discourse on their chosen subject matter, and also to represent their societies in the most dynamic and spontaneous way possible. Alsanea's book *Banat al Riyadh* (Girls of Riyadh) is one of the most controversial publications in modern Arabic literature. Reactions to this novel range from literary concerns—that is, whether or not one can include this novel under the category of literature—to religious condemnation, specifically the issuing of a fatwa[10] to kill the writer as she is perceived as promoting a type of Westernized femininity which is devoid of morality. Aside from this controversy, one area which has not yet been sufficiently explored is the language used by this author and many others like her, who channel their ideas through the Internet.

Alsanea's use of e-Arabic demonstrates the creative challenges posed to the status of formal Standard Arabic by the younger generation in Arab-speaking countries. The great flexibility of e-Arabic encourages the use of simplified and hybrid written language, including colloquial Arabic, Romanized Arabic (using Roman characters to represent Arabic letters), and the mixing and switching of codes to convey these writers' ideas. The younger generation in Saudi Arabia is distinct in terms of motivation and action, even within its own culture, and in global terms, as Alsanea declares in the first chapter of her novel: "we all live in this world but do not really experience it, seeing only what we can tolerate and ignoring the rest" (Alsanea 2005: 1). Thus, a far more dynamic and contemporary language was used, far from the traditional restrictions imposed by the use of the standard form of writing used in mainstream Arabic literature. Alsanea merges Modern Standard Arabic (MSA), the official language used in the Arab world and the one traditionally used for the written form, with different vernaculars (for example, Lebanese and Saudi), Roman characters, numerals, French, and English, and she adopts English written in Arabic characters. These features are not the author's own invention, but part of the repertoire of e-Arabic. By exploiting new vernaculars, and marginal voices for the Arab world, not only does she break the rules and discard the traditional status of using MSA in the written form, but more importantly, she widens her readership, thereby reaching a far larger proportion of the population and not restricting her readership to the social elite. Her work embodies the principle that language is a means of communication and not an end in itself.

Examples from Alsanea's novel in which she directly uses e-Arabic are: ام ندح یرد كنع يام اري د ون بودي ناك لت اذ فرنس/ *ma ḥadan deri 'anik (my dear, nobody can tell the difference)*/(English: nobody can tell the difference). This section, which contains English mixed with the Saudi dialect at the beginning of the phrase ام ندح یرد كنع (Lebanese dialect, in English, "no one notices you").

Here is another example: ول فرعت الادارة، واللله يلفنشوني *law 'irfit al idāra, wallahi layfanishu:ni*/ The English (Booth 2007: 39) reads: "If the principal finds out, I'm screwed!" Here, the word يلفنشوني/*layfanishu:ni*/ is an English verb adapted to the Lebanese dialect, from /*fannash*/, deriving from English "finish". The verb is used in the future tense (Lebanese dialect). This word is very often used by expatriates in the Gulf to refer to the relationship between "employer" and "employee".

As mentioned above, at the core of my focus lies the mixture of languages used at the beginning of each chapter or email, particularly in *Banat al Riyadh* (the Arabic version). Alsanea starts each chapter using English in the email format, using the "@" sign, then Roman characters for Arabic words, and also numerals for letters that have no equivalents—for example, number 7 for /h/—numbers for the date of sending the email and part English and part Arabic phrases—for example, in the "subject" heading: Subject: عن صديقاتي بتكأس/*sa aktub 'an sadikāti/* (I Shall Write of My Friends).

Lebanese Arabic is used intentionally, and sometimes used sarcastically, as, for example, when she refers to Lebanese female TV presenters as being "pleasant", using a Lebanese Arabic term مهضومة/*mahzouma*/. The use of Lebanese Arabic in a "flirtatious" and at the same time a "stereotyping" manner is to refer to the cultural difference between the dialects (Saudi and Lebanese) and is related to "stereotyping" the Saudi dialect as being rough, and the Lebanese as being sweet and flirtatious.

To explain this phenomenon theoretically, one can say that among the characteristics of this genre is not only the use of e-Arabic as a hybrid language, but also the reliance on what

Androutsopoulos (2011) calls "conceptual orality"— that is, "all aspects reminiscent of casual spoken language in written discourse" (Androutsopoulos 2011). Naomi calls it the "general tendency for writing to become a transcription of speech" (Androutsopoulos 2011). Putting the argument about writing aside, one can see that there is a "speech community", as Labov (1963) argues, of users who do not necessarily know each other, who are using this language variety that is different from the mainstream one. Similarly, Community of Practice (CofP) refers to "groups whose *joint engagement* in some activity or enterprise is sufficiently intensive to give rise over time to *repertoires of shared practices*", and this can be applied to the writers across the Arabic-speaking region, whose engagement is to voice their arguments against the standardization and canonization of language, and other sorts of cultural production such as literature. This move for "public vernacular writing" is not unique to Arabic (see Androutsopoulos 2010). The second criterion for CofP—that is, "*the purpose around which mutual engagement is structured*"— is exemplified in the writers' determination to publish and make visible their writings. One also needs to mention the role of publishers in promoting this new literary genre and making it an unprecedented success. Success here is economic, as these publications have been reprinted at least six or seven times. This dynamic has created "*repertoires of shared practices*" (Meyerhoff 2002: 528).

Conclusion

In this chapter, I have discussed the state of CMC in Arabic, positioning it in the local linguistic arena and at the same time within the global sphere. CMC expansion and its various innovative usages made acquiring and mastering the use of this tool an urgent need. With the dramatic rise in the number of Arab Internet users, unexpected opportunities occurred. For example, in Saudi Arabic, female Internet users are taking advantage of Instagram to offer catering and other business activities from which they are excluded offline. These women use e-Arabic for their publicity and as a medium for communication. Therefore, e-Arabic is becoming a symbolic power for those who lack power offline. This is a local variation on a global phenomenon highlighted by variationist socio-linguists (for example, Labov 1972, 2000). They state that "the language variety with high social prestige, be it overt or covert prestige, is likely to show its impact upon people's language use and to be emulated by people who seek prestige" (Liwei 2008: 361).

The widespread use of CMC in the dialect as well as in e-Arabic, despite resistance to it, shows, in my opinion, a transformation that has happened in the Arab world at various levels (word, compound word, phrase, and sentence). As I have shown, this revolution did not only affect the literal language but also extended its reach to the figurative level. A further step was the use of e-Arabic in literature as a result of CMC growth. This wide range of writings in the dialect, including e-Arabic, is not only accessible and cheaper for readers, but has also made publishing easier. Young writers whose talents were hidden and in some cases obstructed because of SA, found in e-Arabic a liberating medium and a flexible mode to express ideas and concerns about their societies. Their writings are very popular in terms of readership, which is in turn affecting the discourse(s) on linguistic and literary canon. I argue that this "new" way of writing is creating a "new" literary genre. I believe the breaking of the literary and linguistic canon is directly affecting accessibility to literature, which no longer belongs exclusively to the elite. This democratization of literature in terms of readership and accessibility of writing will certainly impact language, as access is no longer restricted to the people in power. Finally, I strongly believe that we need to rethink the range of Arabic linguistics to include new varieties such as e-Arabic. Arabic socio-linguistics in particular needs to contextualize the various changes that have affected Arab societies, including the Internet revolution, to include the transformations that have taken place in the Arabic language, both in SA and in the vernaculars.

Notes

1. Papers from the conference were published in an edited volume, *Arabic Language and the Internet* (2011), Serie 6: La Recherché Scientifique en Science Humaines dans les pays Arabes No 20. Publication de la Fondation Temimi pour la Recherche Scientifique et l'Information.
2. For more information about Arabic socio-linguistics, Reem Bassiouney gives a sketch of the main research trends about Diglossia, language contact and language change, and many more issues related to Arabic socio-linguistics, which is the title of her book, *Arabic Sociolinguistics* (2009), Edinburgh: Edinburgh University Press.
3. I would like to thank Dr Latifa Al Sulaiti for her help and support with using the corpus. For more information on Leeds Corpus, see: http://smlc09.leeds.ac.uk/query-ar.html
4. "Note that this H and L labelling reflects, first, language attitudes among users and, second, the superposed nature of the H. Likewise, it is worth mentioning that sociolinguists may feel discomfort with theses labels, since clear covert prestige attaches so strongly to the L and since the L has sometimes been the target of attempts in Egypt and Lebanon, among others, to be considered the national variety" (Bassiouney 2009, 27).
5. Francophone-educated Algerians are those who were educated under the French educational system before independence in 1962 and/or before the Arabization movement in the 1970s, when French was replaced by Arabic as the official language and the medium of education.
6. Berber languages, the languages of the indigenous people in North Africa, are also called Tamazight; there are variations within the Berber language, such as Tashelhit and Taqbaylit.
7. Sakhr was founded in 1982 by Mohammed Al-Sharekh after branching out of his computer hardware company Alamiah Electronics, by producing Arabic versions of the MSX computers. After nearly three decades in the industry and more than US$100 million investments, it now leads the field in Arabic language machine translation, OCR, speech recognition, speech synthesis, search, and localization.
8. For more information on the statistics about Arabic cyberspace, see Dubai School of Government (2014).
9. For more information about the debates on use of the Jasmine Revolution metaphor, see Omri (2011).
10. A ruling on a point of Islamic law given by a recognized authority.

References

7ibr (n.d.) *7ibr*, available at: www.7iber.com/

Abbas, W. (2015) *Egyptian Awareness*, available at: http://misrdigital.blogspirit.com/

Abdel Aal, G. (2008) *Ayza atgawiz*, Cairo: Dar al-Shorouq.

Abdulla, R. (2007) *The Internet in the Arab World: Egypt and Beyond*, New York: Peter Lang, International Academic Publishers.

Al Hamalawy, H. (2016) *:3arabawy*, available at http://arabawy.org/

Al-Issa, A., and Dahan, S. (2011), *Global English and Arabic: Issues of Language, Culture, and Identity*, Oxford: Peter Lang.

Al-Khatib, M. (2008) "E-mails or Mode of Communication among Jordanian University Students: A Sociolinguistic Perspective", *International Journal of Language, Society and Culture*, 25: 1–17.

Alsanea, R. (2005) *Banat al Riyadh [Girls of Riyadh]*, London: Dar Al Saqi Publisher.

Al-Tamimi, Y., and Gorgis, D. (2007) "Romanised Jordanian Arabic E-messages", *International Journal of Language, Society and Culture*, 21: 1–12.

Androutsopoulos, J. (2010) "Localizing the Global on the Participatory Web", in N. Coupland (ed.), *The Handbook of Language and Globalization*, Chichester: Wiley-Blackwell, pp. 203–231.

Androutsopoulos, J. (2011) "Language Change and Digital Media: A Review of Conceptions and Evidence", in *Standard Languages and Language Standards in a Changing Europe*, Oslo: Novus, pp. 145–159.

Arabic Language and the Internet (2011) Serie 6: La Recherché Scientifique en Science Humaines dans les pays Arabes, no. 20, publication de la Fondation Temimi pour la Recherche Scientifique et l'Information.

Attawa, M. (2012) "Arabizi: A Writing Variety Worth Learning? An Exploratory Study of the Views of Foreign Learners of Arabic on Arabizi", MA thesis, The American University in Cairo.

Azam, M. S. (2007) "Adoption and Usage of Internet in Bangladesh", *Japanese Journal of Effects of Internal, External Factors on Internet-Based Digital Technology Use*, available at: http://jaas-web.sakura.ne.jp/doc/pdf/journal/20_1_04.pdf

Bassiouney, R. (2009) *Arabic Sociolinguistics*, Edinburgh: Edinburgh University Press.

Bassiouney, R. (2014) *Language and Identity in Modern Egypt*, Edinburgh: Edinburgh University Press.

Baron, N. S. (1984) "Computer Mediated Communication as a Force in Language Change", *Visible Language*, 18(2): 118–141.

Ben Mhenni, L. (2016) *A Tunisian Girl/Structure Tunisian*, available at: http://atunisiangirl.blogspot.co.uk/

Berjaoui, N. (2002) "Aspects of the Moroccan Arabic Orthography with Preliminary Insights from the Moroccan Computer-Mediated Communication", in M. Beißwenger, (ed.), *Chat-Kommunikation: Sprache, Interaktion, Sozialität & Identität in Synchroner Computervermittelter Kommunikation*, Stuttgart: ibidem-Verlag, pp. 431–468.

Bjørnsson, J. (2010) "Egyptian Romanized Arabic: A Study of Selected Features from Communication among Egyptian Youth on Facebook", MA thesis, University of Oslo.

Booth, M. (2007) *Girls of Riyadh*, New York: The Penguin Press.

Bourdieu, P. (1991) *Language and Symbolic Power*, Cambridge, MA: Harvard University Press.

Crystal, D. (2000) *Language Death*, Cambridge: Cambridge University Press.

Crystal, D. (2004) *A Glossary of Netspeak and Textspeak*, Edinburgh: Edinburgh University Press.

Daoudi, A. (2010) "Globalisation, e-Arabic and the Emergence of Sub-culture in the Arab World", in A. Al-Issa (ed.), *Global English: Issues of Language, Culture and Identity,* Oxford: Peter Lang.

Daoudi, A. (2011) "Globalization, Computer-Mediated Communications and the Rise of e-Arabic", *Middle East Journal of Culture and Communication*, 4: 146–163.

Daoudi, A. (2014) *e-Araby: E-Arabic, The New Linguistic Capital*, available at: http://earaby.blogspot.co.uk/

Daoudi, A., and Murphy, E. (2011) "Framing New Communicative Technologies in the Arab World", *Journal of Arab & Muslim Media Research,* 4(1): 3–22.

Dubai School of Government (2014) *Arab Social Media Report*, 6th edn, available at: www.arabsocialmediareport.com/Facebook/LineChart.aspx?&PriMenuID=18&CatID=24&mnu=Cat

Eckert, P. (2000) *Linguistic Variation as Social Practice*, Oxford: Blackwell.

Eckert, P., and McConnell-Ginet, S. (1992a) "Think Practically and Look Locally: Language and Gender as Community-based Practice", *Annual Review of Anthropology*, 21: 461–490.

Eckert, P. and McConnell-Ginet, S. (1992b) "Communities of Practice: Where Language, Gender, and Power All Live", in K. Hall, M. Bucholtz, and B. Moonwomon (eds), *Locating Power: Proceedings of the Second Berkeley Women and Language Conference*, Berkeley, CA: Berkeley Women and Language Group, pp. 89–99.

Eckert, P., and McConnell-Ginet, S. (1999) "New Generalizations and Explanations in Language and Gender Research", *Language in Society*, 28: 185–201.

Eid, M. (2002) "Language Is a Choice: Variation in Egyptian Women's Written Discourse", in A. Rouchdy (ed.), *Language Contact and Language Conflict in Arabic: Variations on a Sociolinguistic Theme*, Oxford: Routledge, pp. 260–286.

El Essawi, R. (2011) "Arabic in Latin Script: Who Is Using It and Why in the Egyptian Society", in A. Al-Issa and L. S. Dahan (eds), *Global English: Issues of Language, Culture, and Identity in the Arab World*, Oxford: Peter Lang, pp. 253–284.

Ferguson, C. A. (1959) "Diglossia", *Word*, 15(2): 325–340.

Greiffenstern, S. (2010) *The Influence of Computers, the Internet and Computer-Mediated Communication on Everyday English*, Berlin: Logos-Verlag.

Grivelet, S. (2001) "Digraphia: Writing Systems and Society", *International Journal of the Sociology of Language*, 150: 1–32.

Hamzah, M. (2004) "Facilitating Second Language Acquisition (SLA) in a Computer-Mediated Communication (CMC) Learning Environment", *Internet Journal of e-Language Learning & Teaching*, 1(1): 15–30.

Herring, S. C. (ed.) (1996) *Computer-mediated Communication*, Amsterdam: John Benjamins.

Herring, S. C. (2003) "Gender and power in online communication", in J. Holmes and M. Meyerhoff (eds), *The Handbook of Language and Gender*, Oxford: Blackwell Publishers, pp. 202–228.

Hofheinz, A. (2011) "Nextopia? Beyond Revolution 2.0", *International Journal of Communication*, 5: 1417–1434

Jerrad, N. (2012) *La Revolution Tunisienne: Des Mots qui ont Fait l'Histoire aux Enjeux des Langues*, La Tunisie du XXIe Siecle: L'Harmattan, pp. 113–135.

Jerrad, N. (2013) *The Tunisian Revolution: Words that Made History*, La Tunisie du XXIe Siecle: L'Harmattan.

Labov, W. (1963) "The Social Motivation of a Sound Change", *Word*, 19: 273–309.

Labov, W. (1966) *The Social Stratification of English in New York City*, Washington, DC: Center for Applied Linguistics.

Labov, W. (1972) *Sociolinguistic Patterns*, Oxford: Blackwell.

Labov, W. (2000) *Principles of Linguistic Change: Social Factors*, Oxford: Blackwell.

Lakoff, G., and Johnson, M. (1980) *Metaphors We Live By*, Chicago: University of Chicago Press.

Liwei, G. (2008) "Language Change in Progress: Evidence from Computer-Mediated Communication", in M. K. M. Chan and H. Kang (eds), *Proceedings of the 20th North American Conference on Chinese Linguistics (NACCL-20)*, Columbus: The Ohio State University, pp. 361–377.

Meyerhoff, M. (2002) "Communities of Practice", in J. K. Chambers, P. Trudgill, and N. Schilling-Estes (eds), *The Handbook of Language Variation and Change*, Malden: Blackwell, pp. 526–548.

Milroy, J. (2001) "Language ideologies and the consequences of standardization", *Journal of Sociolinguistics*, 5/4, 2001: 530–555.

Mitchell, T. F. (1956) *An Introduction to Egyptian Colloquial Arabic*, London: Oxford University Press.

Mohamed Bin Rashid School of Government (2014) *The Arab World Online 2014: Trends in Internet and Mobile Usage in the Arab Region*, Mohamed Bin Rashid School of Government, available at: www.mbrsg.ae/getattachment/ ff70c2c5-0fce-405d-b23f-93c198d4ca44/The-Arab-World-Online-2014-Trends-in-Internet-and.aspx (accessed 10 December 2015).

Moore, E. F. (2003) "Learning Style and Identity: A Sociolinguistic Analysis of a Bolton High School", Ph.D. thesis, University of Manchester.

Muhammed, R., Farrag, M., and Abdel-Ghaffar, N. (2011) "Arabizi or Romanization: The Dilemma of Writing Arabic Texts", *Jil Jadid Conference, University of Texas, Austin, February 18–20*.

Omri, M-S. (2011) *Tunisia: A Revolution for Dignity and Freedom that Can Not Be Colour-coded*, Transnational Institute, 29 January, available at: www.tni.org/en/article/tunisia-revolution-dignity-and-freedom-can-not-be-colour-coded

Palfreyman, D., and Al Khalil, M. (2007) "'A Funky Language of Teenz to Use': Representing Gulf Arabic in Instant Messaging", in B. Danet and S. C. Herring (eds), *The Multilingual Internet*, Oxford: Oxford University Press, pp. 43–63.

Swales, J. "The Concept of Discourse Community", in *Genre Analysis: English in Academic and Research Settings*, Cambridge: Cambridge University Press, 1990, pp. 21–32.

Tucker, A., Younis, S. F. and Shalaby, T. (2002) "Cross Cultural Perceptions of the Internet and Virtual Reality", *WWW2002: Eleventh International World Wide Web Conference, Honolulu, Hawaii, USA, 7–11 May*, available at: www2002.org/CDROM/alternate/669/ (accessed 16 November 2015).

Warschauer, M., Said, G. R. E., and Zohry, A. (2002) "Language Choice Online: Globalization and Identity in Egypt", *Journal of Computer-Mediated Communication*, 7(4).

Warschauer, M., Said, G. R. E., and Zohry, A. (2007) "Language Choice Online: Globalization and Identity", in B. Danet and S. C. Herring, *The Multilingual Internet*, Oxford: Oxford University Press, pp. 303–318.

Wheeler, D. L. (2004) *The Internet in the Arab World: Digital Divides and Cultural Connections*, Royal Institute for Inter-Faith Studies, 16 June, available at: www.riifs.org/guest/lecture_text/Internet_n_arabworld_all_txt.htm

Yaghan, M. (2008) "'Arabizi': A Contemporary Style of Arabic Slang", *Massachusetts Institute of Technology Design*, 24(2): 39–52.

16

SOCIAL IMAGINARIES OF THE INTERNET IN CHINA

Haiqing Yu

Introduction

As the world's biggest Internet, mobile phone, and smart phone market, China has 632 million Internet users, with 83.4 percent on mobile (China Internet Network Information Center 2014). The rapid growth in smartphone ownership fueled the consumption of mobile social media apps like *Weibo* (microblogging) and WeChat (a mobile text and voice messaging communication service) and explosion of the e-commerce industry. From 1986, when the first email was sent from Beijing to Germany, to 1994, when China was linked to the emerging World Wide Web through a dedicated line with the United States, to 1996, when the Chinese Internet was opened to the public nationally, and to 2014, when China overtook the United States to become the world's largest e-business market, the Chinese Internet has migrated from the labs of research institutes to the urban elites and then to the vast strata of Chinese society. This is also a migration from the "read only" era of the early Internet to the "read and write" era of Web 2.0 and 3.0 and the era of mobile, social, and immediate Internet.

The field of Chinese Internet studies is rich, diverse, and expanding. Every year exciting new books, reports, and journal articles are published to delineate the development and characteristics of the Internet in China. It is well documented that the Chinese government regards its media and communication sectors as key to China's technological and economic great leap forward in its race to catch up with the West and thrive in the global market economy—hence a "neotechnonationalism" to label China's communications policy (Suttmeier and Yao 2004). The Internet is an integral part of the effort of the Chinese government to extend its control over information management, enhance its legitimacy, and promote its soft power on the international stage (Wu 2009; Zhang 2009). The Chinese government has spared no effort or resource in making sure that its Internet is guarded against unwanted information and influence while at the same time serving its national and commercial goals.

In the meantime, China's more than half a billion Internet users have managed to have fun, engage in e-commerce, feel freer to express themselves, and search for information on the world's largest and perhaps most censored network. It is time that we looked closely at how ordinary Chinese people imagine their Internet at both personal and collective levels. It is also time that we viewed the Internet as a lived space and experience that intersects, infiltrates, absorbs, and at the same time defies boundaries between online and offline worlds, legitimate and illegitimate cultures, production and consumption, participation and carnivalesque cultures, resistance and playfulness, youth subculture and middle-class aspirations.

The Internet is an ecosystem with boundaries if it is viewed as a technological and material device, machine, or design. At the same time, the Internet does not respect any boundary, especially when it is viewed as an immaterial, abstract existence, or way of life. Hence, the concept of social imaginary is apt in capturing the largely unstructured and inarticulate understanding of the unlimited and indefinite nature of the Internet. It is a useful analytical tool for making sense of and critically assessing the multiple dimensions of communication, association, or digital life in the Internet age. Here I employ Charles Taylor's (2002) definition of the social imaginary as an open and flexible concept that incorporates a sense of normal expectations and common understanding to enable collective imagination of our digital lives. It connotes a widely shared sense of understanding of what things usually are, as well as how they should go. It is not a set of theories, but an ethos that enables ordinary people to make sense of their social surroundings. The term social imaginary describes:

> the ways in which people imagine their social existence, how they fit together with others, how things go on between them and their fellows, the expectations which are normally met, and the deeper normative notions and images which underlie these expectations.

> (Taylor 2002: 106)

It is important to note that Taylor describes social imaginary as ideas that are "carried in images, stories and legends" (2002: 106), and as an extension of the immediate personal experience in order to exercise a wider grasp of the whole picture and power structure at work—"how we stand in relation to others and to power" (2002: 109). Thus, it is the repertoire of images, metaphors, stories, and legends, which are often taken for granted, that is central to my discussion of social imaginaries of the Internet in China. The social imaginaries of the Internet in turn enable one to look backward into the future.

This chapter gives an historical overview of the different kinds of uses to which Internet technologies are put and the ways in which users imagine their relationship with these technologies. It discusses social imaginaries of the Internet in China through three interrelated metaphors that have developed over the last 20 years: the Internet as *jianghu* (rivers and lakes), as a battlefield, and as a playground. These metaphors summarize my understanding of scholarly discussions on the Internet in China and my brewing of conversations with Chinese people (aged 18–45) on what the Internet means to them during my multiple trips to China between 2009 and 2014, and also through participation in social media forums such as Tianya, Wechat, and Qzone. These people either grew up as digital natives or are seasoned Internet users who were born or grew up in the Internet age. Their imaginaries of the Internet, although scattered, incoherent, and diversified, shed light on how the ordinary Chinese understand their digitized lives in a networked society.

The Internet as *Jianghu* (Rivers and Lakes)

Chinese Internet control and censorship has been consistently in the spotlight of Western media and public discourse. To many China observers, the Internet in China resembles an "intranet", a "cage", or a "fenced-off playground with paternalistic guards" (Epstein 2013), because it is separated from the rest of the world through an increasingly sophisticated filtering system commonly known as the Great Firewall (GFW). The GFW is only part of the ever more sophisticated, decentralized, and dispersed Internet censorship and management regime, especially since 2005 when the Chinese government prioritized information management and Internet governance as its top national security policy. Since then, scholarly and journalistic focus has been on an underlining dichotomy between control and resistance on the Chinese Internet. Some invoke a moral and ideological panic by focusing on political implications of China's media and Internet control and censorship, on the socio-cultural implications of Internet addiction, stalking, and verbal violence (particularly among young people and children), and on the international impact of Chinese cyber-nationalism and cyber-cacophony (Herold 2011; King 2013; Leibold 2011; MacKinnon 2008; Wu 2007). Other analysts take a less dystopian approach to examine citizen activism online, the development of digital civil society, and uptakes in media marketization and globalization, and their democratic potentials (Hu 2014; Tai 2006; Yang 2009). They view the Internet as indicative of China's transformation. As Johan Lagerkvist (2006: 13) writes, "government control of, and social freedom on, China's Internet are growing simultaneously", and that Chinese citizen activism is "more indicative of social and generational change, building up ever more pressure against the political system—in the long term", rather than being politically subversive and resistant to the party-state (Lagerkvist 2010: 158).

To many early users of the Internet in China, however, especially in the first ten years since the Internet was made available to the public in 1996, the images of chivalry, home, and freedom characterized their understanding and imagining of this brave new world. A reading of personal accounts and diaries of early users of the Internet in China (who are now in their 40s and 50s) would find such metaphors as the public square, a marketplace, the family, and a brand new world. These images are those of freedom (public square), exchange (marketplace), solidarity (family), and adventure (new world). But most of all, the Internet was viewed as "rivers and lakes" (*jianghu*) in the Chinese martial arts tradition. As Guobin Yang (2009: 174–175) documents, the *jianghu* metaphor has been used in accounts and publications from individual Internet users, Internet companies, media, and academia. "The Internet is Rivers and Lakes" with "gusty winds and clouds", as well as heroes and villains— just like the *jianghu* of contemporary Chinese society where new orders are being established to replace the dying old ones, where little brothers and sisters must take control of their own fate and fend for themselves against social ills and injustice in a lawless world (Yang 2009).

Jianghu is an imaginative space of alternative, subaltern, and counter publics, where the knights-errant, outlaws, and figures like Robin Hood or Ned Kelly roam. The image of *jianghu* bespeaks a second world "away from the established social and political order", and "a world of adventure, freedom, transgression, and divine justice, but also a world of betrayal, intrigue, and evil" (Yang 2009: 173). The world of *jianghu* is a "marginal terrain", "an alternative socio-political system" (Hamm 2005: 17), and an activist and chivalric alternative to both the established order (*miaotang*, official temples) and the quietened self-cultivation in the Daoist or Confucian tradition (*shanlin*, hills and woods). It epitomizes what the Internet brings to the ordinary people: high mobility (virtually), low visibility (anonymity), unpredictability (in netizen whereabouts and behaviors), multiplicity and diversity (in types of communities and interests), and brotherhood (and sisterhood).

The Internet *jianghu* is the birthplace of Chinese grassroots entrepreneurship. Almost all major players in China's Internet industry, including B(aidu)A(libaba)T(encent), are early users of the computer-mediated communication (via CFido networks) and the Internet (through BBS forums) (Lin 2009). Many of the pioneers who were active figures in the 1990s have retreated to *shanlin*, while a few have continued to face the "gusty winds and clouds" of not just the Chinese, but also global Internet *jianghu*. As the next sections detail, the Internet *jianghu* is a battlefield for both veteran and new actors to create new playgrounds for testing new ideas and serving the needs of consumers.

Central to the world of *jianghu* is the image of the knight-errant (*xia*) who symbolizes the supreme code of behavior in *jianghu*, honor. The knight-errant is born out of the need to defend oneself, redress injustice, and restore social order and trust, when established institutions of the world of rivers and lakes become corrupted, incapable of helping those in need, or inefficient in carrying out their duties. As Guobin Yang (2009: 175–180) demonstrates, a plea for help in a BBS forum at Tianya.cn (China's most popular online community) by a girl to help pay for her mother's liver transplant could generate a community of compassion within hours and more than RMB100k in monetary donations within six weeks. It also gave birth to a netizen knight-errant who was able to restore people's confidence in grassroots justice, heroism, trust, and charity through his selfless and altruistic action by investigating the suspected case of charity fraud, and sharing his report with fellow netizens. Such altruism has seen more and more people volunteer in online campaigns to redress social ills, and participate in social media-mediated grassroots philanthropy to help fellow citizens in need (Yu 2015a).

The Internet *jianghu* therefore serves as a nexus of civic movements and collective actions when it comes to the socio-political uses of digital networks (Chen and Reece 2015). Despite the increasingly sophisticated state control and censorship effort, the digital *jianghu* provides individuals with an alternative space to exercise citizenship through networked collective actions, or simply skilful play of humor, music, videos, games, symbols, words, and memes. Such digital remix creates new forms of expression and association—commonly known as *e'gao*—that are intrinsically subversive of and yet at the same time conform to political and cultural tradition and establishment (for example, Meng 2011; Yang and Jiang 2015; Yu 2015b). Through posting, spoofing, culture jamming, and human flesh searching in various forums, post bars, blogs, microblogs, social networking sites and apps, and instant messaging tools, Chinese netizens form an "alternative public sphere", which "does not confront with the ruling power directly and roundly, but resists and struggles improvisationally and sinuously" (Lin 2014: 146). Such an alternative world of *jianghu* bypasses, rather than challenges and fights against, the ruling power and state-sanctioned media and communication system, often in the form of entertainment. As the last section of this chapter illustrates, digital "play" in the Internet *jianghu* has become a rite of passage for today's young people in China.

Individuals roaming in the Internet *jianghu*, who belong to different interest groups and circles (like sects, clans, and schools of the martial art world), do not share common interests and are not united in the pursuit of a common cause. Numerous Internet events have been sifted into instantaneous oblivion after instantaneous satisfaction. In the 20-year history of the Internet in China, we have witnessed increasing fragmentation of cyberspace. The *jianghu* of BBS-ers (since 1991 with computer-mediated CFido and later Internet-based BBS since 1996), hackers (since 1997), online novelists (since 1998), QQ-ers (since 1999), fansubbers (since 2001), gamers (since 2001), bloggers (since 2005), spoofers (since 2006), human flesh searchers (since 2007), microbloggers (since 2009), and WeChatters (since 2013)—to name just a few—have had their ups and downs. Legendary figures and services in the Internet *jianghu* have either retreated into memory (such as P2P sharing site BitTorrent), been forgotten (such as numerous small sites and services), been heavily sanitized (such as eMule and Sina Weibo), or remain ever popular (such as QQ). The Internet *jianghu* is indeed a treacherous battlefield (as shown in the next section). It nevertheless continues to convey people's enthusiasm and hope for new technologies, particularly the opportunities it offers for Chinese youth to seek for entertainment, communication, and wealth (as illustrated in the last section). Even though "the yearning for freedom is dampened by growing political control", as Guobin Yang (2009: 168–169) points out, "it is never lost. Instead, it manifests itself more as self-conscious struggles in a cyberworld increasingly seen as torn between the good and the evil, a world of Rivers and Lakes."

The Internet as a Battlefield

The Internet as a battlefield metaphor has been used to describe the effort by entrepreneurs, private Internet companies, and ICT starters to compete with one another to come up with the next new idea and capitalize on it to reap the maximum profit, and by average Chinese netizens to "scale the walls" to access censored websites. Although not everyone uses the word "battlefield" (*zhanchang*), the sense of urgency and desire to gain an upper hand over one's competitors or potential rivals permeates casual conversations with urban young and middle-aged netizens.

The metaphor of the Internet as a battlefield is different from the idea of the Internet as "the prime battleground in the fight over public opinion" (declared by President Xi Jinping, quoted in *The Economist* 2014), or "Internet sovereignty", which has been brought up to outline China's envisioned battle with the United States in global Internet governance and to defend China's Internet censorship (Tiezzi 2014). I do not discuss cyber nationalism (Wu 2007), cyber attacks, or cyber espionage that invokes the notion of a new Internet version of the Cold War (Mueller 2011: 189). Rather, I discuss the history of the Chinese Internet in terms of Chinese entrepreneurship. The "*corporate* rather than *state or public service* mentality" has been seen to characterize China's telecommunications market (Zhao 2000: 49). Consumer interest achieved through a competitive market has been seen as the public interest in the "market-oriented, high-end customer-centred and profit-driven development strategies" in China's telecommunications industry (Zhao 2007b: 109). Yet, Chinese entrepreneurship plus consumer interest can have unexpected twists when they are coupled with agendas of the state and government officials, as exemplified in the "1984 industry".

China's "1984 industry" (a reference to the title of a famous George Orwell novel) is a semi-underground Internet industry specializing in public sentiment analysis and monitoring. It has evolved into a 10 billion yuan business with a 1.2 million talent gap. Its services include paid Internet sentiment analysis reports, career training of Internet sentiment analysts, customer-made public sentiment management software, and "integrated solution" services including consulting, report tailoring, and crisis management (Botong 2014). There are four pillars to support the new industry: partnership of software companies with information security and public relations companies (such as Founder Group, Beijing TRS Information Technology, and Meiya Pico), surveillance platforms offered by mainstream media (such as those by people.com and Xinhua.com), university-based public opinion research institutes (such as those of Communication University of China and Renmin University), and public opinion labs established by software companies in partnership with universities (such as Nanjing University-Goonie Software and Tsinghua University-UU Watch).

The 1984 industry has made its way into serving various propaganda departments, government-owned enterprises, and administrations at different levels. Companies compete with one another to provide the most affordable, up-to-date, sophisticated, and customer-made reports of online public opinion analysis to the huge pool of desiring clients. An official from the Propaganda Department of Shandong Province and another one from the Propaganda Department of Gansu Province both indicated to the author that their departments had bought public sentiment analysis services (including public opinion management software) to keep track of online trends, especially those concerning their province, in order to deal with hot issues in time before they escalate out of control.

Ironically, as the case of the 1984 industry shows, the Chinese state's concern over Internet security and public opinion management can benefit the Chinese ICT industry. Baidu, China's biggest search engine, for example, launched a Chinese version encyclopedia (Baidu Baike) in April 2006 after Wikipedia was blocked in 2005, and benefited from Google's retreat from the Chinese market in 2010. China's Internet development has been built around broader socialist market economy principles—an efficient and state-of-the-art telecommunications and information infrastructure to facilitate China's eventual leading role in the global digital economy, and an equally efficient and state-of-the-art system to control the flow of information and assert political control. The concern over social stability, public morality, national security, and sovereignty has not tempered the growth of technology platforms, ICT entrepreneurship, or the continued input of foreign capital into the Chinese digital media economy. The Internet and ICT in general are given priority in the state's strategic planning as long as they support and maintain the status quo political structure and social cohesion. As the online gaming industry illustrates, priority is given to domestically developed, high-quality entertainment and educational products as well as nationalistic online games. Chinese companies such as Shanda have taken a pragmatic approach: help the government develop nationalistic propaganda games while licensing with Disney for online game content (Ernkvist and Ström 2008).

Getting the right partnership means a head start in providing speedy services that can be translated into real market competitiveness for commercial ISPs. It has been recorded that Chinese ISPs vied with each other to sign up with CCTV.com (China's only national television network with a monopoly over broadcasting rights of all major international sporting events) as its new media partners for the rights to video stream the Olympic Games in 2008, and BSPs mobilized netizens to contribute to the e-Olympics frenzy through blogging (Yu 2013). Video websites such as Sohu and Tudou have formed strategic partnerships with subtitle groups in the battle to show programs within 24 hours after the original release in order to gain speed advantage over their competitors (Hu 2013).

Foreign companies have been trying for years to gain access to the Chinese market, often through joint venture partnerships with local Chinese Internet operators and media companies, with mixed results. Google and Time Warner retreated from the Chinese market in 2010 and 2004 respectively, following setbacks on the political front (Weber and Jia 2007: 779), while Disney (with Sohu.com), Viacom (with Netease.com), NBA (with qq.com), and CBS (with Sohu.com) have successfully penetrated the Chinese digital market through their partnerships with leading Chinese Internet companies to provide high-quality entertainment and educational products such as cartoons, movies, TV dramas, music, and sports to young Chinese netizens. As expressed by one respondent: "This is a war minus the shooting. The one who has the right idea and right product wins."

For ordinary netizens, the battlefield is on their palm tops and laptops. Chinese netizens do not seem to be bothered by the GFW or the 1984 industry; they view "censorship and other forms of manipulation as a necessary trade-off required to obtain the right to interact online" (Marolt 2011: 58). China's more than half a billion Internet users have managed to "scale the wall", to have fun, engage in e-commerce, and feel free to express themselves. As more than one has told me, in the earlier days they took great pride in their technology savviness, but now wall scaling was such a common practice that nobody even mentioned it.

Apparently, a business to provide a "scaling the wall" (fanqiang) service has thrived. On Baidu, if one searches "fanqiang software", "proxy", "ssh", or "VPN", one will get thousands if not millions of results that teach you how to download, instal, use, and update (free or paid) software in order to access blocked websites, often with the proxy servers based in the United States, Japan, or Taiwan. One can even buy such services on Taobao (China's largest virtual bazaar, equivalent of eBay and Amazon) by searching "proxy" or "ssh". Often the US-based proxy server services are more expensive, and yet more reliable and faster than Japan- or Taiwan-based services. Many Chinese urban Internet users, especially among professionals such as academics, journalists, and lawyers, routinely scale the wall to access Facebook, YouTube, *New York Times*, VOA, CNN, BBC (Chinese), *South China Morning Post* (HK), *Zaobao Newspaper* (Singapore), and overseas Chinese websites (wenxucity.com, tigtag.com, or Vancouver.iask.ca). They access these sites to keep track of family and friends living overseas, get the latest news on international and regional affairs, practice English, and access written and video materials for research. None of them are worried about the political or legal implications of their activities. As one told me: "I access those sites to entertain and educate myself. I do not spread controversial content on Weibo or Tianya." Occasionally, people complain that they have to adopt the Martian language or coded words (homonyms) to post online. As long as they are not the so-called "Big V" (that is, opinion leaders on Weibo), they do not attract attention from censors. When they wish to share sensitive information such as BBC reports on the Hong Kong protest (accessed via VPN), they resort to screen shots of such video and written reports and share with closed-circle and member-only groups on WeChat or QQ.

The efforts by the Chinese government to reduce the digital divide by providing and lowering the cost of mobile phone and Internet services to its mobile population have allowed even the poorest and most isolated to air their grievances and yearnings online. It used to be urbanites who used the Internet to launch successful campaigns to prevent the construction of dams, polluting factories, and waste incineration projects. Now migrant workers and farmers have joined the citizen activism online (Zhao 2007a). Equipped with smart phones and computers, China's migrant factory workers and sanitation workers have joined in the emerging labor movement. For them, the battlefield is capricious. QQ is perhaps the most favorable network for Chinese labor movements because of its popularity among young people and easiness to use, but it offers no privacy or protection from government and company security agents who have been found to have infiltrated right-defense QQ groups set up by striking workers themselves (Barboza and Bradsher 2010). This has forced disgruntled workers to tap into the broader communications web by utilizing a wide range of different platforms (BBS, SNS, video-streaming sites, Weibo, and WeChat), using coded words to discuss sensitive information such as protest gatherings, and resorting to established e-platforms, such as Weibo accounts of individual students and student body @e先每日资讯 during the collective bargaining by Guangzhou's University town sanitation workers in August to September 2014 (Barboza and Bradsher 2010; Wang 2014).

The social imaginary of the Internet as a battlefield is not shared by all. For some, the Internet resembles a playground, rather than a battlefield. A popular phrase among young and old ICT entrepreneurs—"Let's play it up first" (*xian wan'r qilai*)—suggests a light-hearted daredevil spirit and Deng Xiaoping style "crossing the river by feeling the stones" in putting ideas into practice and testing them in the market. The battlefield is thus a playground as well, for resourceful and creative minds. For everyday Internet users, the Internet resembles a huge playground with limitless means and potential for entertainment. Even resistance and defiance can be like a kind of game (Wacker 2003: 72).

The Internet as a Playground

The Internet as a playground metaphor highlights "play" as a prominent and ubiquitous feature of the Chinese Internet and is central to the heteroglossia in contemporary Chinese culture. The most popular services and content that Chinese netizens access online—games, music, fan communities, BBS, blogging and microblogging, video streaming, e-literature, various social networking services, instant messaging, and e-commerce—all incorporate "play" elements to attract and retain users.

It has been pointed out that Chinese people enjoy the Internet "not because it offers a means to rebellion, but because it gives them a wide variety of social and entertainment options" (Barboza 2010). Business and entertainment are not deterred by political control of the Internet; rather they have fueled the continued growth of the Internet in China (Harwit 2008: Ch. 4). The latest Internet statistic report shows that the Chinese Internet continues to be led by students (25.1 percent) and self-employed people (21.4 percent) under 45 years old, who have led the rapid growth of mobile-phone based e-commerce and entertainment (China Internet Network Information Center 2014). The mobile wallet systems offered by Alibaba and Tencent offer one-click online transactions and bookings, which in turn have placed mobile gaming and music downloading at one's fingertips.

People of different age groups have all reported using the Internet mainly for entertainment and communication. The huge popularity of gaming and music has been discussed elsewhere (Cao and Downing 2008; Wang 2005; Yu 2014). China's gaming industry is a multi-billion-dollar business. In 2009, China became the world's largest online gaming market, contributing one-third of global revenue in this sector (Hao 2010). Its mobile gaming market is nearly as big as that in the United States and growing at a much faster rate. Online music and video downloading is equally huge. Despite international outcry at the Chinese record of intellectual property violation and the Chinese government's effort to curb the rampant piracy and intellectual property rights violations, young netizens (especially college students) routinely use university-hosted servers to download, store, and share their audiovisual collections (Priest 2006). It is common to find hundreds of singles and albums as well as numerous movies on students' smart phones and computers. Some newly released singles or albums and films from foreign markets quickly find their way into these amateur collections, even before they make their official entry onto the Chinese market.

For China's young netizens, the Internet is a playground where beauty, talent, and money form a holy trinity, and where young hormone-charged impulses release and play up. It is the space where they get their real sex education, tell their sexual stories, become popular as sexual dissidents, experiment with novel sexual practices, search for casual sexual partners, and get their ego stroked. It is not unusual to hear from a Chinese high school or university student that their sexual knowledge comes from pornographic videos and DVDs, Japanese manga, books and magazines, and most of all, the Internet. Dating and sexual behaviors are increasingly mediated by the Internet. Online dating, cybersex, virtual marriage, and in-game marriage, have become a part of young Chinese netizens' lives. They create and live out their fantasies through their avatars, they "meet" their sexual partners online, they transcend the boundary between the virtual and physical realities, and develop offline relationships including dating and sex (Wu and Wang 2011). For some young people, sexual pleasure is now more important than love, virginity, and loyalty, and they are prepared to get it in unconventional ways. In a study of "the rhetoric of sexuality of everyday social interactions" among Shanghai-based youth, James Farrer (2002: 3) characterizes young people's sexual acts as "play".

For many Chinese youth today, sexual play is like a rite of passage, where private narratives and sexual stories are shared, compared, and retold though digital communication technologies. It is also central to a hormone-charged economy that allows both men and women to live out their fantasies. People like the Super Girls and sex bloggers Mu Zimei and Furong Jiejie perform androgynous or highly sexualized personas on screen and online as an expression of their individual identity, desire, and fulfilment (Jeffreys and Yu 2015: Ch. 3). Others stretch the meanings of "romantic feeling" to encompass casual and virtual sexual encounters.

The term "virtual live broadcasting" started to be popular around 2010. They are virtual rooms hosted by grassroots talents including gamers and e-sports commentators, weirdos, and especially beauties, at barrage sites such as bilibili.com, game video streaming sites like douyutv.com, and real-time video social networking sites like YY.com, 9158.com, immomo.com, and 6.cn. They offer platforms for young male gamers to play real-time Korean e-sports games (League of Legends and DOTA), comment on real-time e-sports tournament coverage, and get lots of money from fans who interact with them through barrage comments and virtual gifts, paid with real money (Liu 2015). But most of all, they provide opportunities for young women to earn quick and easy money by simply performing singing, dancing, and sweet-talking in front of their computers and microphones to their fans who often compete with one another to lavish virtual gifts on their favorite hostesses. The girls take a portion (up to one-third) of whatever they spend. And the men's ego, self-esteem, and perceived masculinity get satisfied as they can buy their status as "kings", "dukes", or "knights", and get called "hubby" by their favorite girls (Lu 2014). As the new rich show off their wealth by splashing luxurious gifts on their favorite girls in the virtual world, young, lonely, plain-looking, and sexually active males from a humble family background (known in Chinese as "*diaosi*") also take their hard-earned money into cyberspace; and young ambitious women with heavy make-up get paid for doing nothing other than being an object of desire—a hormone economy is born out of the virtual playground.

The hormone economy combines online forum, social networking, gaming, e-commerce, video streaming, e-literature, online dating, and instant messaging to create a virtual playground with Chinese characteristics. It relies on "value co-creation" by turning consumers (for example, surplus males) into prosumers and capitalizing on user-generated content. It operates on the principle of "playing the edge ball" between what's considered as legal (entertainment) and illegal (pornography).

The playground of the Internet is a gendered and embodied space loaded with gender stereotyping that reinforces patriarchal structures. Women are still subject to heterosexual and masculine authority as objects of desire. Chinese hostesses of virtual live broadcast rooms, female sex bloggers, and cross-dressing idols have not been able to disrupt gender and sexual representations of women. The rapid rise in Internet use has also been accompanied by an increase in online pornographic content, sex tourism, mail-order bride businesses, and the trafficking of Chinese women (Leung 2008). The playground of the Internet is indeed a carnivalesque place, where the beautiful and the ugly are both on display (Herold and Marolt 2011). At the same time, the playground is also the battlefield for entrepreneurs-to-be to seek, incubate, and test new ideas and money; the world of "rivers and lakes" for knights-errant, mavericks, and rebels to defend order, justice, and trust in the second world away from and yet interlinked with the established social and political order. The discussion of social imaginaries of the Internet in China has enabled us to review how Chinese people imagine themselves and their relationship with digital technologies in their 20-year history of public Internet (1996–2016) and into the future.

Conclusion: The Internet as the Way

The Chinese Internet can be studied through images, imageries, and imaginaries that ordinary Chinese can easily relate to and identify, rather than the usual focus on access and usage (development and growth, socio-cultural and economic impact), or censorship and resistance (democratization, freedom of speech, and citizen activism). The Chinese view their Internet as the Way (*dao*) of life, a second world that bypasses, and at the same time has become one with, the real reality. The Internet has changed how people relate to one another; how they make choices about their lives, both individually and collectively; and how they imagine the past and the future.

When the Chinese are asked "What's the Internet to you?", there is a consensus that the Internet is the best present that the Chinese have ever received from the West. Almost all my informants are immensely positive about the future of their country. They believe China will become a knowledge-based, wired, and more equitable society, and the Internet is viewed as essential to such a vision. Those who are less optimistic equally trust that the Internet is key to revolutionizing Chinese society and saving China. They point out how the Internet is dissolving the geopolitical, cultural, class, gender, and other hierarchical boundaries and how it enables both the beautiful and the ugly to surface and compete at the same level. What is personal—the Internet as their "air" and "food"—is often intertwined with what is collective and national—the Internet as rivers and lakes (*jianghu*), a battlefield, and a playground.

Manuel Castells's verdict on the Internet

> The culture of the Internet is a culture made up of a technocratic belief in the progress of humans through technology, enacted by communities of hackers thriving on free and open technological creativity, embedded in virtual networks aimed at reinventing society, and materialized by money-driven entrepreneurs into the workings of the new economy
>
> (Castells 2001: 61)

is held close to the Chinese heart. The Chinese would add to Castells's comment that the Internet is the new way of the dao, which redefines the natural order of things.

Further Reading

Clark, P. (2012) *Youth Culture in China: From Red Guards to Netizens*, New York: Cambridge University Press.

Zhang, M. Y., and Stening, B. W. (2010) *China 2.0: The Transformation of an Emerging Superpower . . . and the New Opportunities*, Singapore: John Wiley & Sons.

Zhou, Y. (2006) *Historicizing Online Politics: Telegraphy, The Internet, and Political Participation in China*, Stanford, CA: Stanford University Press.

References

Barboza, D. (2010) "For Chinese, Web is the Way to Entertainment", *The New York Times*, 18 April, available at: www.nytimes.com/2010/04/19/technology/19chinaweb.html (accessed 25 August 2014).

Barboza, D., and Bradsher, K. (2010) "In China, Labour Movement Enabled by Technology", *The New York Times*, 16 June, available at: www.nytimes.com/2010/06/17/business/global/17strike.html?pagewanted=all&_r=0 (accessed 25 August 2014).

Botong (2014) "The 1984 Industry in China: Public Sentiment Analysis and Monitoring [Zhongguo de 1984 chanye: yuqing fenxi yu jiankong]", *Huxiu*, 21 August, available at: http://en.huxiu.com/article/4711789096 (accessed 1 September 2014).

Cao, Y., and Downing, J. D. H. (2008) "The Realities of Virtual Play: Video Games and Their Industry in China", *Media, Culture and Society*, 30(4): 515–529.

Castells, M. (2001) *The Internet Galaxy: Reflections on the Internet, Business, and Society*, New York: Oxford University Press.

Chen, W., and Reece, S. D. (eds) (2015) *Networked China: Global Dynamic of Digital Media and Civic Engagement: New Agendas in Communication*, London and New York: Routledge.

China Internet Network Information Center (2014) "The 34th Statistic Report on Chinese Internet Development [Di 34 Ci Zhongguo Hulianwang Fanzhan Zhuangkuang Tongji Baogao]", *China Internet Network Information Center*, July, available at: www.cnnic.cn/hlwfzyj/hlwxzbg/hlwtjbg/201407/P020140721507223212132.pdf (accessed 26 September 2014).

The Economist (2014) "The Internet: From Weibo to WeChat", 18 January, available at: www.economist.com/node/21594296 (accessed 25 February 2014).

Epstein, G. (2013) "China's Internet: A Giant Cage", *The Economist*, 4 April, available at: www.economist.com/special-report/21574628-Internet-was-expected-help-democratise-china-instead-it-has-enabled (accessed 26 April 2013).

Ernkvist, M., and Ström, P. (2008) "Enmeshed in Games with the Government: Governmental Policies and the Development of the Chinese Online Game Industry", *Games and Culture*, 3(1): 98–125.

Farrer, J. (2002) *Opening Up: Youth Sex Culture and Market Reform in Shanghai*, Chicago: University of Chicago Press.

Hamm, J. C. (2005) *Paper Swordsmen: Jin Yong and the Modern Chinese Martial Arts Novel*, Honolulu: University of Hawai'i Press.

Hao, Y. (2010) "China's Online Game Revenue Tops the World", *China Daily*, 23 June, available at: www.chinadaily.com.cn/bizchina/2010–06/23/content_10010928.htm (accessed 23 July 2010).

Harwit, E. (2008) *China's Telecommunications Revolution*, Oxford: Oxford University Press.

Herold, D. K. (2011) "Human Flesh Search Engines: Carnivalesque Riots as Components of a 'Chinese Democracy'", in D. K. Herold and P. Marolt (eds), *Online Society in China: Creating, Celebrating, and Instrumentalising the Online Carnival*, Abingdon: Routledge, pp. 127–145.

Herold, D. K., and Marolt, P. (eds) (2011) *Online Society in China: Creating, Celebrating, and Instrumentalising the Online Carnival*, Abingdon: Routledge.

Hu, K. (2013) "Competition and Collaboration: Chinese Video Websites, Subtitle Groups, State Regulation and Market", *International Journal of Cultural Studies*, 17(5): 437–451.

Hu, Y. (2014) "From Control to Participation: The Structural Transformation of China's Public Opinion", *Global Asia*, 9(2): 26–30.

Jeffreys, E., and Yu, H. (2015) *Sex in China Today*, Cambridge: Polity Press.

King, G., Pan, J., and Roberts, M. (2013) "How Censorship in China Allows Government Criticism but Silences Collective Expression", *American Political Science Review*, 107(2): 1–18.

Lagerkvist, J. (2006) *China and the Internet: Unlocking and Containing the Public Sphere*, Lund: Lund University Press.

Lagerkvist, J. (2010) *After the Internet, Before Democracy: Competing Norms in Chinese Media and Society*, Bern: Peter Lang.

Leibold, J. (2011) "Blogging Alone: China, the Internet, and the Democratic Illusion?", *The Journal of Asian Studies*, 70(4): 1023–1041.

Leung, M. W. H. (2008) "On Sale in Express Package," in K. E. Kuah-Pearce (ed.), *Chinese Women and the Cyberspace*, International Convention of Asia Scholars publication series, Amsterdam: Amsterdam University Press, pp. 223–248.

Lin, J. (2009) *Bubbling 15 Years: Chinese Internet 1995–2009 (Feiteng 15 Nian: Zhongguo Hulianwang 1995–2009]*, Beijing: China CITIC Press.

Lin, Z. (2014) "Internet, 'Rivers and Lakes': Locating Chinese Alternative Public Sphere", *Chinese Studies*, 3: 144–156.

Liu, Z. (2015) "Virtual Broadcasters in Vogue: Thousands Eyeing 'The Truman Show' [Wangluo Zhubo Zouhong Ji: Qianwan Ren Dingzhe Zhege 'Chu Men De Shijie']", *Southern Weekend*, 29 October, available at: http://mp.weixin.qq.com/s?__biz=Njk5MTE1&mid=400223361&idx=1&sn=6032e024bf3af8197bd383feae49f3f8&scene=0#wechat_redirect (accessed 9 December 2015).

Lu, R. (2014) "China's 'Hormone Economy': Monetizing Male Loneliness", *Foreign Policy*, 22 August, available at: www.foreignpolicy.com/articles/2014/08/22/cashing_in_chinas_hormone_economy_yy_online_hostesses (accessed 6 September 2014).

MacKinnon, R. (2008) "Index on Censorship", *Cyber Zone*, 37(2): 82–89.

Marolt, P. (2011) "Grassroots Agency in a Civil Society? Rethinking Internet Control in China", in D. Herold and P. Marolt (eds), *Online Society in China: Creating, Celebrating and Instrumentalising the Online Carnival*, Abingdon: Routledge, pp. 53–68.

Meng, B. (2011) "From Steamed Bun to Grass Mud Horse: E Gao as Alternative Political Discourse on the Chinese Internet", *Global Media and Communication*, 7(1): 33–51.

Mueller, M. L. (2011) "China and Global Internet Governance: A Tiger by the Tail", in R. Deibert, J. Palfrey, R. Rohozinski, and J. Zittrain (eds), *Access Contested: Security, Identity, and Resistance in Asian Cyberspace*, Cambridge, MA: MIT Press, pp. 177–194.

Priest, E. (2006) "The Future of Music and Film Piracy in China", *Berkeley Technology Law Journal*, 21: 795–871.

Suttmeier, R. P., and Yao, X. (2004) *China's Post-WTO Technology Policy: Standards, Software, and the Changing Nature of Techno-nationalism*, Special Report 7, Seattle, WA: National Bureau of Asian Research, available at: http://unpan1.un.org/intradoc/groups/public/documents/APCITY/UNPAN026775.pdf (accessed 26 September 2014).

Tai, Z. (2006) *The Internet in China: Cyberspace and the Civil Society*, London and New York: Routledge.

Taylor, C. (2002) "Modern Social Imaginaries", *Public Culture*, 14(1): 91–124.

Tiezzi, S. (2014) "China's 'Sovereign Internet'", *The Diplomat*, 24 June, available at: http://thediplomat.com/2014/06/chinas-sovereign-Internet/?allpages=yes&print=yes (accessed 5 September 2014).

Wacker, G. (2003) "The Internet and Censorship in China", in C. R. Hughes and G. Wacker (eds), *China and the Internet: Politics of the Digital Leap Forward*, London and New York: Routledge, pp. 58–82.

Wang, J. (2005) "Youth Culture, Music, and Cell Phone Branding in China", *Global Media and Communication*, 1(2): 185–201.

Wang, S. (2014) "A Recount and Analysis of the Strike and Right Defense Movement of Guangzhou University Town Sanitary Workers [Guangzhou Daxuecheng Huanwei Gongren Bagong Weiquan Shijian Shio Ji Qi Fenxi Jiedu]", *New Citizen Movement*, 10 September, available at: http://xgmyd.com/archives/7066 (accessed 25 September 2014).

Weber, I., and Jia, L. (2007) "Internet and Self-regulation in China: The Cultural Logic of Controlled Commodification", *Media, Culture & Society*, 29(5): 772–789.

Wu, G. (2009) "In the Name of Good Governance: E-government, Internet Pornography and Political Censorship in China", in X. Zhang and Y. Zheng (eds), *China's Information and Communications Technology Revolution*, London: Routledge, pp. 68–85.

Wu, W., and Wang, X. (2011) "Lost in Virtual Carnival and Masquerade: In-Game Marriage on the Chinese Internet", in D. K. Herold and P. Marolt (eds), *Online Society in China: Creating, Celebrating, and Instrumentalising the Online Carnival*, London: Routledge, pp. 106–123.

Wu, X. (2007) *Chinese Cyber Nationalism: Evolution, Characteristics, and Implications*, Lanham, MD: Lexington Books.

Yang, G. (2009) *The Power of the Internet in China: Citizen Activism Online*, New York: Columbia University Press.

Yang, G., and Jiang, M. (2015) "The Networked Practice of Online Political Satire in China: Between Ritual and Resistance", *International Communication Gazette*, 77(3): 215–231.

Yu, H. (2013) "Blogging the Beijing Olympics: The Neoliberal Logic of Chinese Web 2.0", in B. Hutchins and D. Rowe (eds), *Digital Media Sport: Technology and Power in the Network Society*, London: Routledge, pp. 186–203.

Yu, H. (2014) "Internet in Everyday Life", in A. Esarey and R. Kluver (eds), *The Internet in China*, Great Barrington, MA: Berkshire Publishing.

Yu, H. (2015a) "Micro-Media, Micro-Philanthropy, and Micro-Citizenship in China", in Q. Luo (ed.), *Global Media Worlds and China*, Beijing: Communication University of China Press, pp. 79–92.

Yu, H. (2015b) "After the 'Steamed Bun': E'gao and Its Postsocialist Politics", *Chinese Literature Today*, 5(1): 55–64.

Zhang, X. (2009) "From 'Foreign Propaganda' to 'International Communication': China's Promotion of Soft Power in the Age of Information and Communication Technologies", in X. Zhang and Y. Zheng (eds), *China's Information and Communications Technology Revolution*, London: Routledge, pp. 103–120.

Zhao, Y. (2000) "Caught in the Web: The Public Interest and the Battle for Control of China's Information Superhighway", *Info*, 2(1): 41–66.

Zhao, Y. (2007a) "After Mobile Phones, What? Re-Embedding the Social in China's 'Digital Revolution'", *International Journal of Communication*, 1(1): 92–120.

Zhao, Y. (2007b) "'Universal Service' and China's Telecommunications Miracle: Discourses, Practices and Post-WTO Challenges", *Info*, 9(2/3): 108–121.

17

"PORN SHOCK FOR DONS" (AND OTHER STORIES FROM WELSH PRE-WEB HISTORY)

Rhys James Jones

Introduction

This chapter examines the debates and discussions surrounding the Internet that were apparent in printed news media in Wales between the start of 1990 and the end of 1996. The aim is to investigate the early social imaginary of the medium: the ways in which the Internet was imagined and conceived within society's structures during an early stage in its adoption. Taylor (2004: 23) notes that the social imaginary is "often not expressed in theoretical terms, but is carried in images, stories and legends". It is reasonable to assume, therefore, that news reports and feature articles would have played a significant role in forming early ideas and predictions about the nature of online media.

In searching for early predictions about the Internet, the early 1990s appear to be a particularly fruitful era to examine. These years are seen by Janna Anderson (2005: 4) as the medium's "defining years of public acceptance", and the number of articles written about online computing increased significantly during this period, reflecting the growth of the medium itself. In investigating the Internet's social imaginary as presented in newspaper reports, the aim is to avoid undue focus on one particular aspect of the medium's development within the country. It is hoped that, instead, the result will be a wide-ranging overview of various overarching themes, common not only to Wales but to many other nations during the early stages of Internet adoption. The time period was not arbitrarily chosen; as Anderson notes, the Internet started to gain widespread publicity in the very early 1990s, but by 1996, in the public imagination, the "Internet" gave way to its dominant application, namely the "Web". Specifically, extrapolating the statistics collated by Matthew Gray (n.d.) implies that by late 1996, more than 50 percent of the traffic on the US Internet backbone was flowing to and from web servers—the Web, at a technical and, arguably, a conceptual level, dominated the American Internet from that point onwards.

Significant work has already been carried out on early imaginings about the Internet, notably by Anderson's team at Elon University, North Carolina, jointly with the Pew Internet and American Life Project, which collected more than 4,000 examples of early predictions about the Internet, published between 1990 and 1995 (Anderson 2005; Elon University 2014). This chapter both reflects and extends that work through a specific focus on a small, bilingual country in Western Europe. However, many of the uncovered discourses are internationally relevant, and reflect the findings of others who have researched similar outputs within different national and linguistic cultures.

In its focus on Wales and, to some extent, the Welsh language, the work presented here complements Daniel Cunliffe's historical overview of the Welsh-language Web (Cunliffe 2009: 96). It explores a similar time period to Hugh Mackay and Tony Powell's survey of early Welsh-interest newsgroups and discussion forums (Mackay and Powell 1998), and Wayne Parsons's (2000) exploration of online Welsh diaspora.

This chapter outlines the methodology used in the work carried out on the Internet in Wales, before discussing more generally the challenges inherent in writing histories of the early Internet. The key themes within the newspaper articles are then explored in some detail, and the chapter concludes by examining the extent to which the discourses surrounding the Internet can be said to have changed or adapted during the intervening two decades.

Methodology

The research outlined here has a specific geographical focus on Wales, one of the four constituent nations of the United Kingdom (UK). Until the mid-1800s, the Welsh language (Cymraeg) was the only language spoken by the majority of the Welsh population (Morgan 2001). Wales is a bilingual country, and in the 1991 UK census, 508,098 people in Wales, comprising 18.7 percent of its population at the time, claimed to be able to "speak, read or write Welsh" (Jones 2011: 13), a percentage that has grown slightly since. The vast majority of Welsh speakers are natively fluent in English. This bilingualism is reflected in this study, which looks at the representations of new media in both English- and Welsh-language newspapers/magazines between 1990 and 1996.

Wales has no indigenous daily newspaper that may truly be described as national in its reach: as David Barlow *et al.* (2005: 49) note, "[t]he press in Wales is essentially local". In the early to mid-1990s, the main daily morning newspapers with a specifically Welsh focus were the *Western Mail*, mostly read in south and south-west Wales, and the north Wales version of the Liverpool *Daily Post*, which, in its editorial structure, could be regarded as a Welsh edition of an English regional newspaper. The most widely read of these newspapers, the *Western Mail*, was published as a broadsheet throughout this period, and had a circulation of 60,251 from July to December 1996 (Williams and Franklin 2007: 123).

The Welsh-language press, however, can be described as having national reach. Both *Y Cymro* (a weekly newspaper, first published in 1932) and *Golwg* (a weekly magazine, established in 1988) are read by Welsh-speakers throughout Wales. *Y Cymro* claimed to have a circulation of 4,500 copies per week in 1996 (*Y Cymro* 1996b: 16) and *Golwg* a circulation of 3,275 during 1994–1995.

All 1990–1996 editions of the *Western Mail* (*WM*), *Y Cymro*, and *Golwg* were examined in detail to uncover the key trends and discourses from the time in the reporting of new media. In general, no electronic databases containing the publications from this era were available, so copies were searched manually: microfilm reels (for the *WM*) and physical paper copies (for *Golwg* and *Y Cymro*) were examined to isolate stories considered relevant to the Internet and computer technology. The exception was the *WM* from mid-1995 onwards, which was available on CD-ROM: in order to search this, Elon University's (2006) list of 36 synonyms commonly used to describe the early Internet was used to determine search keywords, and relevant stories were thus extracted. A search for articles mentioning online computing was also made in the National Library of Wales's (2014) digitized archive of Welsh journals, but no relevant content was found to have been published between 1990 and 1996.

Once searching was complete, very short items, which typically appeared in "news in brief" columns, were discarded, and the remaining material was analyzed thematically. A deductive rather than an inductive approach was primarily used, in order to reveal the utopian and dystopian discourses prevalent within the news stories, and to enable the Internet to be contextualized within the wider context of other infant media of the time.

While care has been taken to avoid bias in the selection of articles highlighted in this chapter, there are two inescapable limitations to the research. First, the primary research data used is, necessarily, subject to editorial decisions made by newspapers and magazines. In the context of this chapter, it is difficult to overstate the role of newspaper editors in gatekeeping how the Internet was to be depicted. Second, it is highly likely that many of the articles were published as a direct or indirect result of public relations activity by marketing companies. Without access to a contemporary archive of press releases, it is impossible to state with certainty how many articles would have originated in this way. It should be noted, though, that the 1990s were a time of significant growth in the UK's public relations industry, and, as it matured, its effectiveness in publicizing its clients' activities grew with it.

The Challenges of Pre-Web History

To attempt to construct a history of any medium is impossible without contextualizing that history more widely. Inevitably, media are inextricably linked with the wider contemporaneous stories of the societies in which they are situated: indeed, Jean Seaton (2004: 143) inverts this argument by stating that "you can no longer do proper history without [considering media], because they change everything". The nature of new, decentralized media, does, however, pose additional challenges. The Internet cannot be described as institutionalized to any great extent, so unlike broadcast history, applying a narrative of institutionally based developments to the Internet would at best result in an incomplete, narrowly circumscribed account, and would at worst be misleading.

Various possible approaches for the then largely undefined field of web history have been explored by Niels Brügger (2010), who also defines "Web history" as a subfield of "Internet history". He takes the former's starting point as August 1991, the month in which Tim Berners-Lee released the earliest HTTP package for free online (Connolly 2000), which, once installed on networked computers, enabled them to become Web servers. Such a definition of "Web history" allows the Web to be delineated both temporally and technically from the Internet which hosts it, but, as Brügger goes on to note:

> although the "Internet" and the "web" are not the same, the two are intertwined. In many cases, the history of the Internet must be part of historical analyses of the web because the Internet is a precondition for the web; conversely, the history of the web can also shed light on the history of the Internet.
>
> (2010: 2)

I tentatively use the term "pre-Web history" to describe the contents of this chapter. The starting point for what I describe is definitively within the pre-Web era, as the oldest publications examined date from the beginning of 1990. This date was chosen deliberately, because the earliest, widespread, public online discussions about Wales and the Welsh language appeared only a few months prior to this, through the establishment in 1989 of the Usenet group soc.culture.celtic (Jones 2010). However, it is misleading to imply, even for the more technologically developed nations of the time, that early 1990s Internet history can be perfectly cleaved into "pre-Web" and "Web" eras. The emergence of the Web as an online application helped popularize the Internet both as a supporting medium for the Web and as a new media form in its own right. As will be seen, in many reports from 1995 to 1996 in particular, the Internet and the Web are conflated, and some journalists appear to be greatly confused about the separation between one and the other.

As Brügger also notes, many of the "functionalities of the web are anticipated in media types and technologies which were invented years before the advent of the web, thus laying down the foundations of the web" (2010: 2). It is true that the Web can be historicized in many ways, and its pre-history is certainly older than that of connected computing in isolation. However, the novel, peer-to-peer, decentralized, and personalized nature of the early Internet is shared by the early Web, and there are obvious conceptual and technological connections between them. This also means that a key complicating factor of Web historiography—specifically, the need to form a narrative of a medium which has largely lacked unifying institutions or authorities—is equally relevant to histories of the online pre-Web period.

An alternative approach to chronicling Welsh Internet history has been taken by Rhodri ap Dyfrig (2014), who has attempted to build a crowd-sourced timeline of Welsh-language Internet and Web developments from 1989 to the present day. The *Hanes y We Gymraeg* (History of the Welsh-Language Web) project solicited contributions to a wikified chronology during a four-week period in early 2013, and gathered over 150 entries during that time. The timeline is still available online (ap Dyfrig and various contributors 2013), and the methods used can be replicated for many other Web spheres. This represents a significant, and intriguing, addition to a Web historian's methodological arsenal.

The Internet and New Media, 1990–1996

In their study of the conceptualization of the Internet during the late twentieth century, Dana Fisher and Larry Wright (2001) resurrect William Ogburn's previously unfashionable theory of cultural lag (Ogburn 1964), which outlines a delay between a technology's distribution across society and the resulting social adjustment. They argue that such a lag gives rise to competing, charged discourses during the early period of a technology's adoption, and correspondingly they outline the dominant "utopian and dystopian visions" surrounding the Internet at the time.

Very little material about the Internet, or connected computing in general, was found in the periodicals published up until autumn 1994. However, other complementary technologies gained widespread attention in the newspapers of the time. Even the concept of owning a home computer, let alone putting it online, was relatively novel in the UK in the early 1990s, and if we accept Ogburn's cultural lag theory, then we should expect to see polarized discussions surrounding personal computing in general during this time. The reports in the *WM*, in particular, do indeed show these extreme discourses at work, and they prefigure the discussions that were to appear, only a few months later, about the Internet.

Fears about digital pornography are apparent in the *WM* from late 1993 onwards. Under the headline "Porn hits the Playground" (Swift 1993b), the paper reported that schoolchildren in the county of Blaenau Gwent "were gaining access to computerized pornography from playground friends", and that explicit material originating on bulletin board systems was being copied onto floppy disks and circulated by pupils. The deputy head of Gwent police was quoted as raising concerns about a possible consequent increase in sex attacks, and bemoaning the lack of parental awareness of children "watching porn in their bedrooms via their computer screens".

Pessimistic visions such as the one implied by the previous story—that of a new development corrupting its users—is, of course, by no means unique to the past 25 years or, indeed, to the media in general. Claude Fischer's social history of the telephone in the USA opens with an account of the deliberations of the Knights of Columbus Adult Education Committee, who, in 1926, examined the problems of contemporary developments as diverse as the automobile and broadcasting. They "considered whether modern comforts 'softened' people, high rise living ruined character, electric lighting kept people at home, and radio's 'low grade music' undermined morality" (Fischer 1992: 1).

It is unsurprising, therefore, that fears about the lack of regulation of electronic media were not restricted to online systems, and Greg Swift's report on computerized pornography has as its coda the concern that computer games could lead to "unnaturally aggressive behavior in teenagers", which is echoed in the paper's reporting of a preview of a survey (later to be published as Griffiths and Hunt 1998), which claimed that one in five adolescents were "dependent" on computer games (Jackson 1993). Regulation of violent video games was also a well-exercised contemporary debate: in particular, the release of the fighting game *Mortal Kombat* in September 1993, which featured graphic decapitation scenes, led to an examination of whether the video games industry was facing a "moral crisis" (Swift 1993b). Computer games were also blamed by the *WM* for encouraging inactivity among children (Walford 1993), and for triggering seizures in players who had photosensitive epilepsy. None of these concerns, however, were apparent in the paper's weekly *Family Life* supplement, which at the time carried regular reviews of games console cartridges.

The arrival of direct broadcasting by satellite to UK homes also caused concerns, notably surrounding the lack of regulation over content. In 1993, the *WM* would report fears over a "continental-style hard core pornography channel" originating from Denmark (Basini 1993), highlighting its foreign otherness by depicting the UK government "[l]ike Canute struggling to turn back the tide" due to European Union harmonization regulations. Satellite technology was not, however, seen as wholly negative; its role in assisting language learning through viewing foreign news programs in the classroom (Clarke 1991), and in giving schoolchildren access to geospatial images to assist with their geography lessons, also gained significant attention in the *WM*. The tension between satellite television as an external vehicle for moral corruption and its role in constructing an idealized, multilingual, technologically aware, educated citizen, can perhaps be understood by the perception of the medium as existing outside previous norms. This metaphor of foreign otherness is also present in early reporting about the Internet. Within the technologically deterministic, charged discourses that are present during a period of cultural lag, it seems that external influences cause extreme dystopian or utopian outcomes—they are hardly ever viewed as neutrally benign.

The Pathologies of the New Media

In his encyclopedic social history of railway developments, Wolfgang Schivelbusch discusses the pathologies associated with the new transport medium as it spread through industrialized countries in the nineteenth century. These ranged from passengers being deafened by the noises caused by friction between the rails and the carriage wheels, to *maladie des mécaniciens* (Schivelbusch 1978: 114)—the "engineers' malady", a phrase used to describe the pseudo-rheumatic pains observed in railway workers.

Every medium, whether mechanical or electronic, brings its pathologies with it. During the 1990s, video games were seen as promoting sedentary lifestyles (Walford 1993) and, for the first time, carried warnings against their use by individuals prone to photosensitive epilepsy.

The Internet, too, had its pathologies, but the examined articles usually frame these in moral, rather than physiological, terms.

Much of the early reporting about the Internet focuses on the content accessible through the medium: in particular, and as seen in earlier reports about satellite television, the ease of access to pornography was highlighted as problematic. A typical account can be seen in a story entitled "Porn shock for dons", which recounts the case of a student at the University College of Wales, Swansea (now Swansea University), who used the main undergraduate mainframe computer to access pornographic material, reportedly causing the system to crash:

> The 19-year-old student dialed the hard-core computer sex line in America from the university's multi-million pound system. College staff and students got a shock when they switched on and found sex acts including a striptease game being played on the screen. But as the video filth poured onto the university's computer banks, it caused a massive overload.
>
> (*Western Mail* 1994)

Though presented in a jocular style, with an associated cartoon showing a computer smoking a (presumably post-coital) cigarette and asking its user "How was it for you?", there is an undercurrent of unease in the report, particularly in its confused coda which states that "the Computer Misuse Act of 1989 made it illegal to possess computer porn" (*Western Mail* 1994). The Act was actually passed in 1990, and the more relevant Obscene Publications Acts outlawed only specific forms of pornography, regardless of whether they were found online or offline. This, perhaps, demonstrates the challenges faced by reporters in attempting to précis this new medium to a public who were unlikely to have used it.

Misleading reporting of the Internet did not, however, always go unnoticed. In a front-page story from 1995, under the headline "Internet subverted by sick anarchists" (*Western Mail* 1995a), it was reported that an "information security expert" had found that the medium, "used by thousands of children and adults", contained information on cannibalism and murder. The pages in question had been placed online by members of a proto-hacktivist collective, Cult of the Dead Cow, and they appear to be either a provocation or, possibly, a spoof. The *WM*, though, was quick to editorialize the news, writing about the need to "regulate this new medium" (*Western Mail* 1995b), alongside satellite television, "to prevent corruption of children's minds". This response was critiqued in a reader's letter published a few days later, which took to task the earlier claim that the expert had "stumbled within seconds" upon the content, and pointed out that:

> with a rather conservative 200,000 [Usenet] messages a day, I hardly think that you could stumble across any particular message. On the contrary, as with everything on the Internet, you must be actively looking for certain areas . . . and more importantly you must nearly always know where to look.
>
> (Hopkins 1995)

Those conducting research into Internet use during this period were also subject to newspapers skewing their interventions towards the poles of the debates surrounding the medium. In late 1995, Professor Harold Thimbleby, then of Middlesex University, presented at the British Association for the Advancement of Science his analysis of one of the earliest known search engines, which had been developed by one of his students, Jonathon Fletcher (Miller 2013). His discovery—that 47 percent of the most frequently repeated searches made through the engine were for pornographic content—was the main focus of the subsequent reporting, not only by the UK press (for example, Connor 1995) but also in Welsh periodicals. As with Mark Griffiths's work on computer games, Thimbleby's call for reflection about this new medium was largely ignored in the reportage. *Y Cymro's* political commentator, Catrin Iwan, framed Thimbleby's findings in opposition to a party conference speech by the then-leader of the British Labour Party, Tony Blair, who at the time headed the UK opposition parties. Blair had stated that were he to be elected prime minister at the forthcoming general election, he would put in place an agreement, funded by the telecommunications company BT, to offer a laptop to every schoolchild. Conflating the fears over online pornography with other, unsourced, claims about child illiteracy, Iwan wrote in response:

> Had Mr Blair persuaded BT to . . . persuade schoolchildren to read more books . . .
> I'd have been far more impressed! . . . Mr Blair would have been more responsible
> had he also drawn attention to the dangers of a system which opens the doors to
> such a large amount of information. . . . It also appears that pedophiles peddle their
> perversions [online] under the guise of child welfare groups.
>
> (Iwan 1995; author's translation)

As can be seen, polarized, charged discourses are evident in the discussions that surrounded the Internet in Wales during the period in question. Those attempting to walk a middle ground between utopian and dystopian visions, such as Thimbleby and the letter-writer Gary Hopkins (1995), found themselves almost magnetically pulled towards the poles of the debate when their interventions were reported by the newspapers of the time.

Broadcasting Wales

Historians of radio and television within Wales have seen broadcasting as a key driver of the nation's self-conception. Davies's account of the BBC in Wales even claims that the country is "an artefact produced by broadcasting" (Davies 1994, cited by Johnes 2010: 1261). As Martin Johnes notes, Davies does give convincing evidence for broadcast media's role in uniting the diverse social geographies of Wales, which are sometimes simplistically seen as consisting of an English-identifying East, a patriotic, industrialized south and a rural Welsh-speaking West.

It is perhaps not surprising, therefore, that much early reporting appears to understand the Internet as a way of "broadcasting" Wales to the world. Of the articles examined in writing this chapter, the first feature piece to mention online conversations appears in *Y Cymro* in January 1993. It focuses on *WELSH-L*, an e-mail list devoted to conversations in, or about, the Welsh language, which was launched a few months previously. The article opens with a sampling of the topics discussed by its subscribers in the previous weeks: "What was the result of the rugby match between West and East Wales [two minor-league teams] over the weekend? What information is available on modern-day druids? What books are available for learning Welsh?" (Glynn 1993; author's translation). Annes Glynn then moves from the implicit framing of *WELSH-L* as an information source, and goes on to note the peer-to-peer nature of the group's communications. However, the article's subheadline, "*Cyfrifiaduron yn 'siarad' am Gymru ar draws y byd*" (Computers "talk" about Wales throughout the world) appears again to veer towards the language of broadcasting in its implication that the concept of "Wales", defined by its geography and language, is now being spread worldwide through a new medium. It could be argued that there is a similar subtext to the article's boast that the most popular discussion topic on *WELSH-L* has been the resources available to learners of the Welsh language.

In fairness to *Y Cymro*'s reporter, she was very far from being alone in failing to grasp the fundamental shift that was to occur online towards massively decentralized peer-to-peer communication. The discourse of the "information superhighway", a term first used in 1983 to describe new cables that linked major US cities, entered the public consciousness following a speech given by the then US Vice President, Al Gore, to the American Television Academy (Ibiblio 1994). Gore's speech, in which he announced a major US infrastructure investment in fiber-optic links, explicitly cited the case of an unnamed businessman who wished to buy into "new technology to avoid ending up as 'roadkill' on the information superhighway". This provided a potent metaphor that was seized upon by thousands of commentators worldwide. By 1995, many of the articles about connected computing were devoid of terms such as "Internet", or even "online": the superhighway was considered to be a convenient, universally understandable shorthand for the perceived technological revolution. Nevertheless, it should be noted that the term "superhighway" once again implies a broadcast-era metaphor —it evokes a cultural industrial complex sending its outputs to largely passive consumers via expensively constructed infrastructures.

Academic futurologists, too, were drawn towards broadcast metaphors in their attempts to understand the Internet. Nicholas Negroponte's seminal *Being Digital* (1995) is still seen as a pioneering technophilic account of the move from the material towards the informational. However, even that work still sees news sources, albeit personalized, as being directed from central sources towards consumers in the form of a "Daily Me"; Negroponte says little about the inversion of power that was later to occur when individual Internet users realized their ability to post their own updates online. As Kevin Kelly (2005) notes, when broadcasters launched their initial Web presences in the mid-1990s, they too saw the Internet merely as an extension of their existing linear channel offerings. Even the Web's founder was moved to state, during these early years in the medium's development, that "I had (and still have) a dream that the web could be less of a television channel and more of an interactive sea of shared knowledge" (Berners-Lee 1995).

The Internet was later to cause a paradigm shift in the newspaper and periodical industry by enabling such "shared knowledge" to be disseminated through instant responses to articles, but journalists showed little awareness of this in the Wales of the mid-1990s. Writing in *Golwg*, Robin Gwyn saw the Internet merely as a way of reinforcing the magazine's existing global reach, by claiming that: "Eventually, it should be possible for *Golwg*'s readers in Australia to 'receive' their copy by connecting a credit card-sized computer to a local terminal, and watch video versions of the stories" (Gwyn 1994; author's translation).

There is little or no speculation, in any report, that the Internet might eventually become a home to news-breaking, fact-checking citizen journalists. As in so many other countries at the time, writers within the "artefact produced by broadcasting" seemed keen to imagine the world of online communication as yet another broadcast medium.

We're on the Interweb!

From 1995 onwards, the articles about online computing start to explicitly mention the World Wide Web. As chronicled by Elon University (2006), the synonyms used to describe connected electronic systems multiplied in the early 1990s, and the term "Web" was often used interchangeably with other related concepts, such as the "information superhighway" (or "infobahn"), and various terms containing "cyber" as their first element.

This terminological confusion is reflected in much of the contemporary reporting, and can even be found within the newspapers' editorial content, exacerbated by the misinterpretation of some terms when they were translated into Welsh. Articles from *Y Cymro* appeared online for the first time on 1 March 1996, through a website set up by its owners, North Wales Newspapers (NWN). For much of that year, though, the paper vacillated over the best way to describe its Web presence. *Y Cymro*'s initial announcement that it was "on the Web" described the NWN website as "our email address" (*Y Cymro* 1996c: 5). The following month, the same Web address appeared on *Y Cymro*'s masthead (*Y Cymro* 1996a: 1) under an exhortation for readers to "Remember: we're on the Web". By December, the masthead also contained an email address for correspondence, correctly described as such. The NWN Web address, however, was now headlined with the term *rhyngwe*, a portmanteau which can be translated, literally, as "interweb". Though this appears to be simply due to journalistic confusion between the Web and its supporting medium, it does demonstrate some of the challenges faced in trying to coin a new terminology for a new medium in a new language. Whereas early articles (for example, Gwyn 1994) would often make no attempt at translation, and simply insert words such as "email" or "cyberspace" in the middle of a Welsh-language feature, later pieces saw the development of Welsh phrases for key concepts. Most of these followed the conceptual bases of the corresponding English terms (the commonly used *rhyngrwyd*, for example, is a direct translation of "Internet") but there was some evidence of adaptation, notably in the translation of "information superhighway" as *archdraffordd wybodaeth*, the highway being replaced in Welsh with its localized counterpart, the motorway.

"Backwards into the Future"

The extent to which new technologies should be framed in terms of the developments that preceded them forms an open, and controversial, historiographical debate. In the context of medium studies, Marshall McLuhan was adamant that:

> When faced with a totally new situation, we tend to attach ourselves to the objects, to the flavor of the most recent past. We look at the present through a rear-view mirror. We march backwards into the future.
>
> (McLuhan and Fiore 2008 [1967]: 74–75)

In a later interview with *Playboy* magazine, he expounded further on what he saw as a human tendency to conceptualize new developments in terms of what was already well understood. He said:

> Most people . . . still cling to what I call the rearview-mirror view of their world. By this I mean to say that because of the invisibility of any environment during the period of its innovation, man is only consciously aware of the environment that has preceded it; in other words, an environment becomes fully visible only when it has been superseded by a new environment; thus we are always one step behind in our view of the world.
>
> (McLuhan 1995 [1969])

Though a characteristically gnomic utterance, it is difficult not to draw parallels between McLuhan's claims and Ogburn's near-contemporaneous idea of cultural lag. It is perhaps only now that we have begun to make the Internet "fully visible". Even so, some of the tropes surrounding Welsh use of the Internet, particularly those that see Wales as having or needing an online identity defined by geography and, sometimes, language, are as ubiquitous now as they were in the early 1990s. During the writing of this chapter, the Welsh government formally launched two top-level domains for Wales. "I'm so pleased", the Welsh First Minister, Carwyn Jones, was quoted as saying, "that we will be able to register domain names in .wales and .cymru—we will . . . have a way of using our websites . . . to reflect the identity we feel in our hearts" (quoted by Williamson 2014). There is, perhaps, little to distinguish Jones's words from the earlier utopian hopes that emerged around *WELSH-L*, when for the first time "computers talk[ed] about Wales throughout the world" (Glynn 1993).

It could be argued that the societies that were first exposed to the Internet in the early to mid-1990s have now passed through the period of cultural lag. However, if it is true that the Internet, as a supporting *infrastructure*, is now often represented in a more nuanced manner than before, the same cannot often be said about newer manifestations of online *content*, particularly social network sites. As danah boyd and Nicole Ellison (2007) point out, social networking systems (SNS) first came into being in 1997, shortly after the Web began to dominate the Internet, but they reached ubiquity only as recently as the early 2010s. Cultural lag has been evident in recent UK reporting of the perceived dangers of social media; in particular, Ann Luce (2012) recounts the fears apparent in newspaper accounts of a cluster of suicides that occurred around Bridgend, South Wales, in 2008. During the first six months of that year, 20 people from the area, aged between 15 and 29, died by suicide; many of them followed each other on sites such as Facebook, Bebo, and MySpace. Despite the weakness of the ties between the individuals, newspapers were quick to claim that the use of SNS was a contributing factor in the deaths, with a widely reported agency report (cited by Cadwalladr 2009) even linking some of them to a "cyber-suicide ring". This claim was later discredited, and much of the newspaper reporting surrounding the deaths was heavily criticized by South Wales Police and community leaders. In the context of the reports previously presented in this chapter it is, perhaps, telling that the reportage of the Bridgend suicide cluster grasped for decades-old metaphors. Bebo, in particular, would have been widely used during this time by schoolchildren throughout Wales and beyond, but the "cyber" concept used in reporting the Bridgend suicides carries with it an older connotation, as outlined by John Barlow (1996)—that of an untamable, alien "home of the mind", which cannot be grasped by those who do not inhabit it. While driving through a new social media landscape, it would seem that newspapers saw only an unfamiliar cyberspace, dimly, through their rearview mirrors.

Conclusion

The work presented here has attempted to avoid a linear, institutional narrative of early Internet developments by focusing instead on how a social imaginary was constructed around the new medium. As it relies on printed reports published during a relatively early stage of the Internet's enculturation, the methodology can also be applied to the development of other nations' online spheres, provided that newspaper or periodical archives exist for the relevant periods.

Following Ogburn's cultural lag theory, it is perhaps unsurprising that euphoria and disquiet about the new medium are seen in many of the reports. The perceived advantages of near-instantaneous and cheap worldwide interpersonal communication, and the benefits of the "information superhighway" to businesses are tempered by fears over unrestricted access to inappropriate or morally questionable content.

Similar uncertainty is evident in the articles' exploration of the shape of Wales online. The ability to spread a somewhat nebulously defined Welsh culture online was welcomed in articles which, sometimes in the same paragraph, acknowledged that there would also be an opposite cultural flow. Often framed in terms of the Welsh language itself, many reports called on Welsh people to act and ensure an online presence and visibility for Wales. Cunliffe (2009) theorized such actions as "linguistic resistance" to the online spread of English. The genesis of such a movement can perhaps be seen in statements such as those by the then European Member of Parliament, Eluned Morgan, who wrote in *Golwg* that "Welsh should have a voice in setting the foundations for the use of the new technologies" (Morgan 1994; author's translation).

While this chapter has investigated various historical narratives with an attempt to avoid centralism in a history of the Internet, there are limiting factors which should be taken into consideration. Newspaper gatekeeping and the influence of public relations practitioners in some of the stories, especially when combined with the limited understanding of new media among many journalists at the time, may have the effect of reintroducing an institutional bias to the work. It is evident that a single approach to Internet history can only tell part of the story of the emergence of online spaces. However, it is believed that the methodology outlined in this chapter is a useful way to carry out geographically bound discourse analyses of the Internet's social history, and can reveal much about the way the medium was imagined in its earliest days.

Further Reading

An overview of the information "society" and "superhighway" metaphors in the European context can be found in S. R. Schulte's (2009) paper, "Self-Colonizing eEurope: The Information Society Merges onto the Information Superhighway", in Vol. 1, No. 1 of the *Journal of Transnational American Studies*. Richard Barbrook's *Imaginary Futures* (Pluto Press, 2007), provides an excellent corrective to early utopian visions surrounding online culture. Martin Johnes's *Wales Since 1939* (Manchester University Press, 2012) gives a comprehensive yet pithy account of the modern history of Wales. Accounts of the development of the Internet in Wales during the period in question can be found in Mackay and Powell (1998), Parsons (2000) and Rhys Jones (2010). Researchers wishing to carry out their own work into the time period in question here should be guided towards relevant newspaper archives, but Google's archive of the Usenet group alt.internet.media-coverage (searchable by date as well as topic) may also be of interest to researchers within specifically anglophone contexts. It is accessible via https://groups.google.com/

Acknowledgement

I am indebted to members of the Swansea University Media Studies research seminar series, notably William Merrin, Sian Rees, and Yan Wu, for their constructive comments during the preparation of this chapter. Any errors and misrepresentations remain my sole responsibility.

References

Anderson, J. Q. (2005) *Imagining the Internet: Personalities, Predictions, Perspectives*, London: Rowman & Littlefield.
ap Dyfrig, R. (2013) *Hanes y We Gymraeg*, available at: www.hanesywegymraeg.com/ (accessed June 2014).
ap Dyfrig, R. (2014) "Cydgyfeiriant Cyfranogol a'r Economi Ddigidol", Ph.D. thesis, Department of Film and Television Studies, Aberystwyth University.

Barlow, D. M., O'Malley, T., and Mitchell, P. (2005) *The Media in Wales: Voices of a Small Nation*, Cardiff: University of Wales Press.

Barlow, J. P. (1996) *A Declaration of the Independence of Cyberspace*, Electronic Frontier Foundation, available at: https://projects.eff.org/~barlow/Declaration-Final.html (accessed June 2014).

Basini, M. (1993) "Battling Against Porn Invasion", *Western Mail*, 1 September, p. 9.

Berners-Lee, T. (1995) *Hypertext and Our Collective Destiny*, World Wide Web Consortium (W3C), available at: www.w3.org/Talks/9510_Bush/Talk.html (accessed June 2014).

boyd, d. m., and Ellison, N. B. (2007) "Social Network Sites: History, Definition and Scholarship", *Journal of Computer-Mediated Communication*, 13(1): 210–230.

Brügger, N. (2010) "Web History, an Emerging Field of Study", in N. Brügger (ed.), *Web History*, New York: Peter Lang, pp. 1–25.

Cadwalladr, C. (2009) "How Bridgend Was Damned by Distortion", *The Observer*, 1 March, available at: www.theguardian.com/lifeandstyle/2009/mar/01/bridgend-wales-youth-suicide-media-ethics (accessed June 2014).

Clarke, R. (1991) "Satellite TV Boosts World of Languages", *Western Mail*, 17 October, Education Supplement, p. 1.

Connolly, D. (2000) *A Little History of the World Wide Web*, W3C, available at: www.w3.org/History.html (accessed June 2014).

Connor, S. (1995) "Pornography Most Popular Subject for Internet Searches", *The Independent*, 13 September, available at: http://goo.gl/mxpzj3 (accessed June 2014).

Cunliffe, D. (2009) "The Welsh Language on the Internet: Linguistic Resistance in the Age of the Network Society", in G. Goggin and M. McLelland (eds), *Internationalizing Internet Studies*, New York: Routledge, pp. 96–111.

Elon University (2006) *Early 90's Synonyms*, Elon University School of Communications, available at: www.elon.edu/e-web/predictions/early90s/internetsynonyms.xhtml (accessed June 2014).

Elon University (2014) *Imagining the Internet*, Elon University School of Communications, available at: www.elon.edu/e-web/imagining/ (accessed June 2014).

Fischer, C. S. (1992) *America Calling: A Social History of the Telephone to 1940*, Berkeley, CA: University of California Press.

Fisher, D. R., and Wright, L. M. (2001) "On Utopias and Dystopias: Toward an Understanding of the Discourse Surrounding the Internet", *Journal of Computer-Mediated Communication*, 6(2).

Glynn, A. (1993) "Parablwyr Brwd Welsh-L", *Y Cymro*, 27 January, p. 11.

Gray, M. (n.d.) *Web Growth Summary*, available at: www.mit.edu/people/mkgray/net/web-growth-summary.html (accessed June 2014).

Griffiths, M. D. and Hunt, N. (1998) "Dependence on Computer Game Playing by Adolescents", *Psychological Reports*, 82(2): 475–480.

Gwyn, R. (1994) "Priffordd Beryglus", *Golwg*, 17 November, pp. 8–9.

Hopkins, G. (1995) "Knowing Facts About Internet", *Western Mail*, 21 June, p. 10.

Ibiblio (1994) "Remarks Prepared for Delivery by Vice President Al Gore", *Ibiblio*, 11 January, available at: www.ibiblio.org/icky/speech2.html (accessed June 2014).

Iwan, C. (1995) "Laptop i Bawb o Bobl y Vyd", *Y Cymro*, 18 October, p. 2.

Jackson, L. (1993) "Growing Price of Computer Fun", *Western Mail*, 15 December, p. 8.

Johnes, M. (2010) "For Class and Nation: Dominant Trends in the Historiography of Twentieth-Century Wales", *History Compass*, 8(11): 1257–1274.

Jones, H. M. (2011) *A Statistical Overview of the Welsh Language*, Cardiff: Welsh Language Commissioner, available at: http://goo.gl/hmLNTi (accessed June 2014).

Jones, R. J. (2010) "Cilfachau Electronig: Geni'r Gymraeg Ar-Lein, 1989–1996", *Cyfrwng: Media Wales Journal*, 21–37, available at: http://analog.newydd.net/2013/11/01/ (accessed June 2014).

Kelly, K. (2005) "We Are the Web", *Wired*, 13(8), available at: http://archive.wired.com/wired/archive/13.08/tech.html (accessed June 2014).

Luce, A. (2012) "The Bridgend Suicides: How the Story Unfolded", *Cyfrwng*, Cardiff: University of Wales Press, 9: 41–55.

Mackay, H., and Powell, T. (1998) "Connecting Wales: The Internet and National Identity," in B. D. Loader (ed.), *Cyberspace Divide: Equality, Agency and Policy in the Informational Society*, London: Routledge, pp. 203–216.

McLuhan, M. (1995 [1969]) "The Playboy Interview", in E. McLuhan and F. Zingrone (eds), *Essential McLuhan*, New York: Basic Books, pp. 233–269, available at: www.nextnature.net/2009/12/the-playboy-interview-marshall-mcluhan/ (accessed June 2014).

McLuhan, M., and Fiore, Q. (2008 [1967]) *The Medium is the Massage*, London: Penguin.

Miller, J. (2013) *Jonathon Fletcher: Forgotten Father of the Search Engine*, BBC News, 4 September, available at: www.bbc.co.uk/news/technology-23945326 (accessed June 2014).

Morgan, E. (1994) "Her i'r Iaith", *Golwg*, 9 March, p. 10.

Morgan, G. (2001) "Welsh: A European Case of Language Maintenance", in L. Hinton and K. Hale (eds), *The Green Book of Language Revitalization in Practice*, San Diego, CA: Academic Press, pp. 107–113.

National Library of Wales (2014) *Welsh Journals Online*, National Library of Wales, available at: http://welshjournals.llgc.org.uk/ (accessed June 2014).

Negroponte, N. (1995) *Being Digital*, London: Coronet Books.

Ogburn, W. F. (1964) *On Cultural and Social Change: Selected Papers*, Chicago: University of Chicago Press.

Parsons, W. (2000) "From Beulah Land to Cyber-Cymru", in *Contemporary Wales*, Cardiff: University of Wales Press, 13: 1–26.

Schivelbusch, W. (1978) *The Railway Journey: The Industrialization of Time and Space in the 19th Century*, Leamington Spa: Berg.

Seaton, J. (2004) "Writing the History of Broadcasting", in D. Cannadine (ed.), *History and the Media*, Basingstoke: Palgrave Macmillan, pp. 141–160.

Swift, G. (1993a) "Escape into a Violent Video Fantasy Land", *Western Mail*, 15 September, p. 9.

Swift, G. (1993b) "Porn Hits the Playground", *Western Mail*, 28 October, p. 1.

Taylor, C. (2004) *Modern Social Imaginaries*, Durham, NC: Duke University Press.

Walford, J. (1993) "'Get Off Couch' Call to Lazy Young Loafers", *Western Mail*, 4 December, p. 5.

Western Mail (1994) "Porn Shock for Dons", *Western Mail*, 24 August, p. 1.

Western Mail (1995a) "Anarchists Subvert Internet", *Western Mail*, 15 June, p. 1.

Western Mail (1995b) "Time to Pull Plug", *Western Mail*, 15 June, p. 8.

Williams, A. and Franklin, B. (2007) *Turning Around the Tanker: Implementing Trinity Mirror's Online Strategy*, Cardiff: Cardiff University, available at: http://image.guardian.co.uk/sys-files/Media/documents/2007/03/13/Cardiff.Trinity.pdf (accessed June 2014).

Williamson, D. (2014) "Wales Now Has 'Natural Home' on the Internet", *Western Mail*, 24 June, p.3, available at: http://technews.tmcnet.com/news/2014/06/24/7890842.htm (accessed June 2014).

Y Cymro (1996a) "Masthead", *Y Cymro*, 10 April, p. 1.

Y Cymro (1996b) "Holi Ynglŷn â Nawdd i Gylchgronau", *Y Cymro*, 10 April, p. 16.

Y Cymro (1996c) "Taflu'r Rhwyd Yn Eang", *Y Cymro*, 6 March, p. 5.

18

GROSS NATIONAL HAPPINESS AND FACEBOOK

Bhutan Localizes the Internet

Bunty Avieson

In the past 15 years, the isolated kingdom of Bhutan has leapfrogged over centuries of media evolution to arrive at the same technological endpoint as developed countries. This small Himalayan country of just 773,000 people (National Statistics Bureau 2016) had long existed in self-imposed isolation, rejecting modern media technologies as another unwelcome foreign influence, along with Western values and materialism (Royal Government of Bhutan 2003: 5; Gyabak and Godina 2011: 2237). Bhutan's only media consisted of a little-read government gazette, *Kuensel*, short-wave radio, and word of mouth. But in 1999, the Fourth King, His Majesty Jigme Singye Wangchuck, announced the arrival of the Internet and television, telling his people that they offered a range of possibilities, both beneficial and negative, and warned them to exercise "good sense and judgement" (Ministry of Information and Communication 2003: 19). Over the next decade, the king expanded the media landscape to include independent newspapers, radio stations, and mobile telephones. His vision was for Bhutan to take its place in the world as a modern democracy, which required embracing the latest media technologies. In 2008, the people voted in government elections for the first time. Democracy and modern media arrived at the same time and are inexorably linked, creating a new political culture.

Bhutan's Ministry of Information and Communication conducted a series of detailed media impact studies, investigating the people's reactions to the introduction of each new platform (Ministry of Information and Communication 2003, 2008, 2013). Newspapers were influential among the political elite, but largely ignored by the rest of the community, while mobile telephones quickly became an indispensable multitasking tool embraced by every level of society—from government ministers to yak herders, farmers, housewives, civil servants, and monks. The Internet has also been readily adopted, wherever it has become available. The government is rolling out broadband across the country, which has the potential to empower rural people, bringing government services and the World Wide Web to each of the 205 *gewogs* (groups of villages). In the second election in 2013, online media proved to be highly effective platforms for public discourse. In Europe and elsewhere, the invention of the printing press contributed to centuries of political and social revolutions. Bhutan bypassed those centuries of change and is beginning to experience similar societal transformations via the

Internet, mobile phone, and platforms such as Facebook, blogs, and Twitter. The media revolution in Bhutan is an online revolution.

Bhutan's experience of modern media offers interesting insights because of its cultural specificity. As an oral culture, they lack the baggage of print capitalism, and are challenging existing notions of literacy as people not considered print literate engage online, via Facebook, and with apps on mobile phones. The Internet is creating a bridge to literacy that bypasses traditional trajectories, as well as providing new spaces for public discourse, national imagining, and the emergence of a political culture.

Situating Bhutan, its People and its Media

The strongest influences determining Bhutan's use of modern communications technologies are its distinctive geography, history, culture, and values. This includes its oral traditions, mountainous terrain, and Buddhist heritage, from which has evolved its holistic development philosophy of Gross National Happiness (GNH) as a more effective measure of the country's wealth than Gross Domestic Product.

Bhutan is about the size of Switzerland, situated at the eastern end of the Himalayas, covering about 46,500 square kilometers, though some borders with China remain under dispute (Kasturi 2014). It is wedged between Tibet and India, providing Bhutan with geopolitical importance that surpasses its size, population, and economy (Penjore 2004: 109). When China invaded Tibet in 1949, Bhutan chose to align with India, signing the Indo-Bhutan treaty and India continues to be its closest ally, providing funding in a series of five-year plans (Galay 2004; *Economic Times* 2014). About 80 percent of the people live in rural areas, dotted along a series of mountains and valleys, with around 100,000 living in the capital city, Thimphu (Tourism Council of Bhutan 2016). Some 60 percent of the population is below the age of 22 (Limbu 2014).

For centuries, Bhutan was isolated both by geography and by deliberate policy, preferring to look inwards and develop its own culture. In modern times, the nation has opened itself to the outside, but the attitude of wariness to outside influences is a persistent concern for this small country wedged between behemoths China and India. There is a saying in Bhutan to "take the best from the West and leave the rest" (Avieson 2015: 222).

Rural communities are often isolated and under-resourced because of the mountainous terrain (Gyabak and Godina 2011: 2237). The society is ethnically pluralist with 19 native languages, of which only one has a written form, the national language Dzongkha, which derives from Choke or Classical Tibetan script (van Driem 1994: 87–88). Bhutan is the last Mahayana Buddhist kingdom in the Himalayas, and practices an esoteric form of Buddhism in which aspects of orality are considered sacred and privileged over print (Phuntsho 2007: 23–24). In 2012, print literacy was estimated at 63 percent (National Statistics Bureau 2016), but the culture that surrounds print is underdeveloped. According to Siok-San Pek, head of the Bhutan Centre for Media and Democracy: "Reading and writing in Bhutan is still largely associated with office and school 'work' and the concept of reading as recreation is new" (Ministry of Information and Communication 2003: 15; 2013: 36). Journalist Sonam Ongmo (2009) wrote: "If you want to keep a secret, write it in a book, no-one will read it." The Ministry of Information and Communication explicitly recognizes the contemporary importance of its oral culture, putting it first in its list of the eight different media that are its responsibility—that is: "oral, television, radio, Internet, film, publishing, gaming and mobile phone" (Ministry of Information and Communication n.d.: 6). As well as an undeveloped reading culture, Bhutan has yet to develop a newspaper culture that extends beyond the political elite (Josephi and Dahal 2014). The 30-year-old *Kuensel*, which grew out of the government gazette, is the country's dominant newspaper, with an audited circulation in 2012 of just 6,350 national sales. In the same year Facebook, available only in the major cities, had more than ten times that figure, with 76,000 users (*Bhutan Observer* 2012; *The Bhutanese* 2012). By 2014, there were 12 private newspapers and all were in financial crisis (Pokhrel 2014). One had moved online to save printing and distribution costs, but that had not proved successful.

Bhutan's low engagement with newspapers reflects the lack of print culture, and is not representative of the Bhutanese approach to other new media technologies. Radio reaches the largest segment of the population with seven stations offering information, news, and entertainment. The number of radio sets in the country has decreased from 77,800 in 2008 to 49,641 in 2012, which may be the result of increased mobile phone coverage, given that most mobile phones have radio reception (Ministry of Information and Communication 2013: 28–29). The mobile telephone has overtaken the radio as the most widely owned "asset" in Bhutanese households, in both urban and rural areas (Ministry of Information and Communication 2013: 27).

Mobile telephones have been the greatest communications success since their introduction in 2003. In one decade the number of households who owned a mobile telephone reached 92.8 percent, with nearly 30 percent of them subscribing to mobile broadband (Ministry of Information and Communication 2013: 27). Mobile phones suit Bhutan, with its isolating geography, strong community networks, and oral culture. Bhutanese use it to stream radio, check Facebook, post on Twitter, and record and watch videos (Ministry of Information and Communication 2013: 31). Mobile phones are the most popular method of accessing the Internet (Ministry of Information and Communication 2014a: 13). Mobile services are competitive, with two providers—the state-owned Bhutan Telecom, and private operator TashiCell. A range of phones is available, from basic smartphones at Nu 5–10,000[1] (US$75–150), to Samsung and Apple at Nu 45,000 (US$680). A basic handset without Internet capability can be bought for less than Nu 2,000 (US$30).[2] There are dedicated phone shops in the capital and larger cities. Handsets are brought in across the border from China and India, as well as during foreign holidays to Thailand and elsewhere, and some are sold inside the country via Facebook.

Bhutan is divided into 20 *dzongkhags* (districts) and 205 *gewogs* (groups of villages). All have mobile telephone coverage (Ministry of Information and Communication 2014a: 14). Fifteen of the 20 *dzonkhags* have 3G coverage and the capital, Thimphu, has partial/limited 4G coverage (Ministry of Information and Communication 2014a: 13).

While the Internet arrived in the country in 1999, it took the explosion of Facebook around 2006 for the Internet to begin to "really take off", according to prominent blogger Passang Tshering (Avieson 2015: 216). Government figures would appear to support his claim. Internet subscribers rose in five years from just 5,548 in 2008 to 251,441 in 2013 (Ministry of Information and Communication 2014b: 9). This had risen to 349,116 Internet users in 2014 (Dorji 2015).

Access to the Internet has been mostly limited to Thimphu and other major cities, but that is changing as the government rolls out its US$11.4 million, India-funded, national broadband network into rural areas. Central to its strategy to bridge the rural–urban digital divide is the establishment of Internet-connected community centers in each of the 205 *gewogs*. A total of 185 centers were built and operational by March 2015, with the rest due to be finished by the end of 2016 (Dorji 2015). These centers provide facilities for rural people to access more than 110 government services, such as filing taxes, medical pensions, permits to

ICT/telecommunication subscribers: actual and as percentage of population

Year	Fixed line subscribers		Internet subscribers*		Mobile cellular subscribers	
	Total subscribers	% Population	Total subscribers	% Population	Total subscribers	% Population
2004	30,285	5.9	35	0.006	18,995	3.7
2005	32,709	5.1	48	0.008	37,842	5.96
2006	31,526	4.9	61	0.01	82,078	12.7
2007	30,279	4.6	4,040	0.6	148,179	22.5
2008	27,937	4.2	5,548	0.83	228,347	34.3
2009	26,348	3.8	18,542	2.7	327,052	47.9
2010	26,292	3.78	94,285	13.6	394,316	56.7
2011	27,490	3.88	139,896	19.8	484,189	68.4
2012	27,005	3.7	133,289	18.5	560,890	77.8
2013	26,485	3.6	251,441	34.3	544,337	74.3

Figure 18.1 ICT/telecommunication subscribers: actual and as percentage of population

Source: Bhutan Telecom, Tashi-Cell, BIMA as compiled by Ministry of Information and Communications, Bhutan

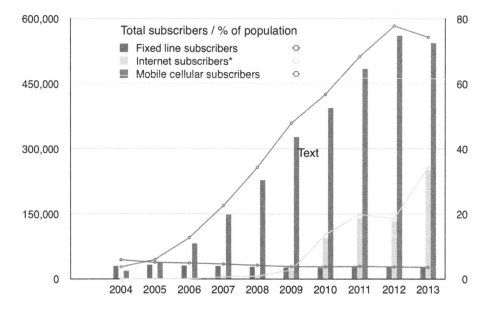

Figure 18.2 Total subscribers/percent of population (Ministry of Information and Communication 2014b: 9)

*Internet subscribers refer to the number of registered individuals, households, corporate houses and government offices connected with internet by any modem and not the actual number of people using internet from any source mentioned above or other sources.

cut timber, registering births and deaths, and completing land transactions. The centers also offer them access to a vast array of online services, such as online banking, paying telephone bills, accessing Wikipedia, BBSTV news, and other news websites, as well as YouTube and Facebook, where the Ministry of Agriculture posts videos on best farming practices. They can also join the national discussion via Bhutan's bloggersphere, where former print journalists and others are creating a lively new space (Bhutan Media Foundation 2012: 23, 64). The government aims to provide affordable broadband connections to 90 percent of the rural population by 2020 (Dorji 2014b).

The introduction of the Internet and digital communication technologies by the Fourth King are part of a longer term strategy of careful modernization that can be traced back to the Third King, His Majesty Jigme Dorji Wangchuck, who reigned from 1952 to 1972. He joined the Colombo Plan in 1962 and the United Nations in 1972. He also built a national highway that connected east to west, introduced fixed telephone lines, and created the *Bhutan Post*. His son and heir, the Fourth King, continued building communications infrastructure and cautiously opening the country to outside influences, but first he established an overarching development framework that reflected Bhutan's own cultural values and Buddhist roots— Bhutan's philosophy of Gross National Happiness.

Development Philosophy: Gross National Happiness

The Fourth King, His Majesty Jigme Singye Wangchuck, had been schooled in India and Britain, and understood life outside his own isolated country, particularly the focus on economic growth in industrialized economies. When he assumed the throne, he talked about a different path to development, based on Bhutan's own cultural values and Buddhist roots. He explained his views to a British journalist based in India:

> We must aim for contentment and happiness. Whether we take five years or 10 to raise the per capita income and increase prosperity is not going to guarantee that happiness, which includes political stability, social harmony, and the Bhutanese culture and way of life.
>
> (Elliot 1987)

The Fourth King established a framework of four pillars that he believed were significant in creating conditions that would enable happiness:

1. sustainable and equitable socio-economic development;
2. preservation and promotion of culture;
3. conservation and sustainable utilization and management of the environment;
4. good governance.

(Royal Government of Bhutan 2013: 3)

By making sustainable economic progress just one of the pillars, it became part of the process rather than the end goal. The Fourth King tasked the Center for Bhutan Studies, a scholarly institute in Thimphu, with creating metric indicators to measure the success or failure of progress under these pillars and every government policy was assessed according to these criteria. The Center for Bhutan Studies further developed the measures into the GNH index, which comprises nine domains, 33 indicators and 124 variables (Royal Government of Bhutan

2013: 32). It is according to this philosophical framework that communications technologies have been introduced and the media landscape continues to evolve.

> A critical element of GNH . . . is the empowerment of the citizen, which is, as we understand, the basis of democracy. This means giving citizens the education to make informed decisions. It means enabling citizens to have the critical wisdom to open our minds to the possibilities of enlightened living. It means, not just providing access to information but enabling the citizen to make reasoned decisions at the individual, community, and national level. In other words it means the need for an effective media. The media becomes, in Buddhist terms, the skilful means—an indispensable tool—for the achievement of the four pillars identified by the government as well as other elements in the broader interpretations of Gross National Happiness. The media is, therefore, inextricably linked to GNH.
>
> (Dorji and Pek 2005: 8)

In 2014 the government launched its "eGov Master Plan" explaining how its strategies for the development of information and communications technologies (ICT) fitted with the spirit of GNH. Prime Minister Tshering Tobgay said that building infrastructure to improve reach, quality, and affordability was a national priority. He called ICT the principal enabler for a knowledge-based society—that is, a society "that learns to learn" (Royal Government of Bhutan 2014b: 1). This reflects the prevailing view of international policy makers that knowledge is power and investment in communication systems is required to drive wealth creation in the knowledge-based economy (Mansell 2012: 44–45). Tobgay said that the government's aim was to develop "GNH-inspired policy to create an informed populace with a shared national consciousness". He identified three desired outcomes that aligned with three of the four pillars as good governance, preservation of culture and environment, and sustainable socio-economic development (Royal Government of Bhutan 2014b: 1).

Gross National Happiness emerged out of Bhutan's Buddhist heritage, which is also an influence on how citizens approach the Internet. Respected Bhutanese lama, His Eminence Dzongsar Jamyang Khyentse Rinpoche, composed a prayer for cyberspace and published it on Facebook, on its own page, explaining how to use the Internet mindfully—that is, guiding his people on how to "surf the waves of attraction and distraction" (Khyentse 2012). It states, in part:

> Bless this cyber-space with comfort, bliss and enlightenment—May it be of benefit to myself and others.

Bhutan Localizes the Internet

> Social Media through Facebook, Twitter, Blogs, online discussion forums . . . has brought in an information revolution among the growing community of educated, and young population of Bhutan.
>
> (*The Bhutanese* 2012)

> Social media (e.g. Facebook, Twitter, LinkedIn etc.) are picking up fast among the urban literate population and provides a unique platform for public discourse on governance and development issues, and the dissemination of real-time news and views.
>
> (Ministry of Information and Communication 2013: 26)

Prime Minister Tshering Tobgay was one of Bhutan's Internet pioneers, showing the way when he was the country's first opposition leader, leading an opposition of two elected members against a government of 45 elected members. In November 2008, when there were just 5,548 Internet subscribers, he launched one of the country's first blogs, sometimes updating it twice daily, with news about government matters. It became compulsive reading for the political class and by 2011, was the second most trafficked website in Bhutan, getting 10,000 hits a day, 1,000 of them unique users (Avieson 2015: 245). Traversing the country in his role as a member of parliament, Tobgay also provided running commentary via his blog, Twitter, and Facebook. He continued his domination of social media in the lead-up to the 2013 election, personally sending 3,676 tweets, while the government account sent just 615 tweets (Sithey 2013: 232). According to Lily Wangchuk, the president of minor political party *Druk Chirwang Tshogpa*:

> His [Tshering Tobgay] blog was his platform to test out ideas and see if the people supported them or not. He would share an idea and then listen to the response. He managed to create a lot of popularity through social media . . . . The younger lot and the educated lot were his followers. He was talking to a certain section of the population who had influence back in the villages. The youth and the educated would influence their parents back in rural areas.
>
> (Wangchuk 2014)

By 2013, more blogs had appeared and in the lead-up to the election in July, a controversial political blog appeared, "Bhutanomics". It was aggressively critical of the government, alleging corruption, and publishing a series of digitally altered photographs of the prime minister and other leaders. The anonymous creators, who were also active on Twitter, offered no evidence for the allegations, and on 15 March 2013, the Phuentsholing Court banned the page. The creators moved it to Facebook, where its posts were more easily circulated. "Authorities ignored the fact that as a social networking site, Facebook gets more traffic than a website" (Sithey 2013: 234). According to Sithey, even people who were against the way the site treated issues felt compelled to follow it.

It is not possible to quantify how much social media affected the outcome of the election, but it is clear it played a major role in extending discussions. Bhutanese citizens had specific issues with their first government, including youth unemployment, rural poverty, education, the currency crisis, and the tense relations with India which, in the lead-up to the election, withdrew vital fuel subsidies (Dahal 2013). The role that social media played was to create a space to examine those issues, which then spread by word of mouth throughout all levels of society:

> The battle was equally fought at campaign meetings in remote communities as well as via Facebook and Twitter in urban towns. Every statement made by candidates were scrutinized threadbare on social media; updates on Internet containing political accusations were relayed instantly to village meetings. Political parties hurled allegations and counter allegations on a daily basis on Facebook.
>
> (Sithey 2013: 230)

Another Bhutanese citizen leading the way into the world of online media is Passang Tshering, a high school teacher of computer science and a prominent blogger. He created an Internet "park" in the grounds of his rural school, using a wireless router in the school's office to connect students via Wi-Fi to the Internet. He helped the students to build small, open pavilions with electrical outlets to charge laptops and mobile phones. On weekends, many schoolchildren can be found there, completing school assignments using Khan Academy, the online non-profit educational organization, or Wikipedia, as well as connecting to Facebook and uploading their own music videos to YouTube (Avieson 2015: 216). Tshering is excited by the possibilities of Facebook and has set up a series of community pages. His Facebook "B-Bay" page has more than 40,000 local members selling goods as diverse as houses, cars, air tickets, laptops, puppies, plants, and woven cloth for *kiras*, the Bhutanese national dress for women. He set up a Facebook "Breaking the News" page to encourage villagers to report what is happening in their local areas. He also created BhutanToilet.Org as a website and Facebook page to start a national conversation about better hygiene through cleaner toilets. Followers post photos of toilets across the country, from the automatic-flushing, music-playing urinals of the new Le Meridien Hotel in Thimphu, to rural lean-tos sitting precariously atop cliffs.

Tshering likens Facebook to the Bhutanese cultural event of the *tsechu*. Local monasteries hold these annual festivals, which feature elaborate sacred dances by the lamas and monks, to tell the culturally unifying tales of Buddhist heroes. Traditionally, whole communities would gather from nearby valleys for the shared experience, thus creating what Françoise Pommaret called an early "media event" (2001: 2). Tshering considers Facebook the modern equivalent because of the huge numbers that gather. He said starting B-Bay on Facebook was like "setting up a tea stall at a *tsechu*" (2014a).

Tshering's own blog, PaSsu Diary: Journal of an Ordinary Bhutanese, is an influential forum. When two illicit Bhutanese sex videos started to appear in his Facebook feed early in 2014, he wrote about it on his blog, chastising anyone who watched the videos, reposted them, or forwarded them by phone (Tshering 2014b). His post had 25,000 hits and prompted a radio DJ to start an online petition at change.org calling for laws against the non-consensual distribution of sexual material. Four months later, the prime minister announced that the government would strengthen anti-porn laws (Zangmo 2014).

The government has also recognized the potential of modern media technologies. In March 2014, Bhutan Telecom partnered with Swedish communications company Ericsson to pilot an Internet-based education program. A well-resourced private school in Thimphu, Pelkhil High School, was connected via video conferencing to 250 ninth-grade students in five rural schools to teach subjects including mathematics, physics, chemistry, biology, English, environment, and social studies. Ericsson provided the hardware and Bhutan Telecom provided high-speed connectivity of 8Mbps to each of the schools (Press Trust of India 2014).

Some MPs have also seen the potential of the Internet for their new government roles. One prominent example is Sangay Khandu, representative for Gasa, a remote *dzongkhag* that borders China in the north, and whose population is widely dispersed. He uses his Facebook page to seek feedback on government policies, and established another page, which he calls a "Virtual Gasa", where people from his constituency can communicate with each other about community problems, such as providing assistance to struggling families, as well as keeping in touch from Thimphu or if they are studying abroad. Khandu also writes a blog where he has posted for comment his proposed draft for a Right to Information Act (Khandu 2012).

In July 2014, the National Assembly speaker Tshogpon Jigme Zangpo conducted the government's first "virtual zomdu", a meeting with constituents using video conferencing technology (Zangpo 2014). His constituents in Mongar, four days' travel away, attended their local Internet-connected community center to question him directly about tax increases, mining clearances, and vehicle import laws. Two high school students told him that their 20-year-old bus needed replacing (Dorji 2014a).

Bhutan's government is utilizing the Internet to provide government-to-citizen services, as well as communication and transparency as part of the GNH pillar of good governance. Social media and blogs are providing new spaces for public discussion about things that matter to the Bhutanese and reinforcing a sense of collective nationhood.

Facebook Creates Space for Public Discourse

Facebook, in particular, has facilitated the development of a political consciousness and is providing a culturally appropriate space for dissension. This is significant in a country which values harmony over individual agency. The controversial Tobacco Act provided a watershed moment for citizens in marrying political activism to online media, demonstrating how both could function as part of their new democracy. In January 2011, the government introduced the strictest anti-tobacco laws in the world. Smokers entering the small Himalayan country were limited to fewer than 200 cigarettes, 30 cigars, or 150 grams of chewing tobacco, and had to register their tobacco products at the border. A few weeks later Bhutanese police arrested a 23-year-old monk for possession of 480 grams of unregistered chewing tobacco worth US$2.50. He was sentenced to three years in jail. More convictions followed, including businessmen and women, housewives, expatriate Indian workers, bus drivers, army personnel, and farmers: the youngest was 16 and the oldest 81 (*The Independent* 2011; Pem 2011; Dema 2013).

International media reported the harsh penalties, while inside Bhutan there was much criticism and debate in online news forums and blogs, mostly under the cover of pseudonyms (Bhaumik 2011; *The Independent* 2011; Ongmo 2011a; 2011b; Tobgay 2011). But the most influential discussion occurred on a Facebook page set up by two Bhutanese journalists. Their "Amend the Tobacco Act" page attracted nearly 3,000 members (Wangdi 2011; Parameswaran 2012). Jurmi Chhowing, a well-known journalist and blogger, posted photos to the page each day showing himself defiantly lighting a cigarette; Cee Dee Jamtsho visited the jailed monk and posted of her anguish at seeing him in tears and handcuffed "like a serious criminal". Other members shared letters they had written to their MPs and created an online petition. Typical comments included:

> Passang Tshering: My village is populated with smokers and Tobacco chewers and sniffers . . . my [whole] village is gonna be [put in] jail . . .

> Kencho Namghyal: [The] Tobacco control act is a great tool to criminalize otherwise law-abiding citizens.

> Kinga Sithup: Bad roads took more lives than smoking.
>
> (Ongmo 2011c)

A year after the government voted in the controversial laws, they passed an urgent bill to amend them (Dema 2013).

The Facebook campaign demonstrated the possibilities of online media in a country with no experience of either mass media or activism. Social researcher Gyambo Sithey called it a "game-changer" and "historically significant" for pushing Facebook into the realm of mainstream political activity (2013: 231). Opposition leader Tshering Tobgay noted that it differed from other Bhutanese online spaces in three important ways: members used their real identities; they stayed on-topic and were not abusive; and the page became a platform for political activism (Tobgay 2011).

The prime minister at the time, Jigmi Y. Thinley, was less enthusiastic. He said he feared that citizens had been inspired by the Arab Spring uprisings that were then occurring in Tunisia, Egypt, and Libya (Ongmo 2011c). But Tobgay warned him not to ignore what people were saying in that space or the dissent might spill onto the streets. He welcomed the Facebook page as an example of peaceful citizen engagement. Tobgay wrote on his blog:

> In a healthy democracy, citizens must be able to express themselves—individually and collectively. Facebook has provided a platform to do so. We can protest, rally, picket and demonstrate online, on Facebook. But for that to work, the government must also take part, and ensure that the voices on Facebook groups are heard. The government should use Facebook, not ignore it. That's why I say: "*Rather than taking to the streets, take it to Facebook!*"
>
> (Tobgay 2011)

The ability for citizens to speak freely and criticize their government is a fundamental part of democracy, but it can only occur in a culturally relevant form and within a national, cultural context. The enthusiasm of Tobgay, Sithey, and other leaders for Facebook as a site for political dissent is a reflection of Bhutan's context. This country had lived in harmony under royal rule, where successive kings made national decisions. As a new democracy, it is experimenting with new forms of citizen engagement across all levels of society. Citizens, leaders, and institutions are trying to reconcile their new democratic powers and responsibilities with their traditional societal values, and engaging with each other in new, untested ways.

Another reason the "Amend the Tobacco Act" page was considered so significant is that it was a second attempt by citizens to publicly express their displeasure, following a protest two years earlier that had left a sour aftertaste. In 2009, seven schoolboys tragically drowned in a river, and about 100 people staged what they called "a solidarity walk" through the capital city of Thimphu. Their intention was both to show empathy for the grieving families and to protest at the government's inability to rescue the boys. The group walked silently behind a banner showing flickering butter lamps, a traditional Buddhist offering. While the march was orderly and peaceful, the sight of citizens walking together for a political purpose evoked images of the sort of violent unrest that Bhutanese expect to see on CNN and BBC World, not on their own streets. While some welcomed the group walk as a demonstration of democracy in action, many more feared it was the first step to anarchy on their streets and called it "unBhutanese" (C. Dema 2009; K. Dema 2009; *Kuensel 2009*; Tobgay 2009; Wangdi 2011; Avieson 2015: 197–201). On kuzuzangpo.com, a popular anonymous online forum that has since closed, the following comment was representative:

> I can guarantee you that the floodgates will have been opened. Many will follow and before long, they will want to indulge in strikes and sit-ins and other acts of public disobedience. For God's sake, we don't need this in our country—not now, not ever! . . . the death of the 7 unfortunate children will be remembered as an event that ushered in a movement that gave birth to the social evil known as STRIKES. Let not an event of national mourning be remembered as such a dark day! The Laggard.
>
> (Avieson 2013: 161)

Whether the march was appropriate or the beginnings of anarchy and street violence became a major topic of discussion in Thimphu, overshadowing what the marchers had been trying to achieve. The medium overwhelmed the message. By contrast, the Facebook page arguing against the Tobacco Act of 2011 had provided a public space where members could openly criticize the government, but because it was in the virtual world, it appeared less threatening to social stability. As a result, the discourse was not derailed and the desired political outcome could be achieved.

New Definitions of Literacy

The way that Bhutan, as a traditionally oral culture, is utilizing the Internet provides a fresh perspective from which to reappraise notions of literacy, which is generally understood as the ability to read and write in an unspecified language. Often media theories reflect a print bias, placing print literacy as a desirable end point on some universal evolutionary continuum. "Media history moves from oral culture, to chirographic or manuscript culture, and then to print or typographic culture, and on to electronic culture" (Grosswiler, 2001: 22). This does not reflect Bhutan's trajectory. Historically, print literacy was part of monastic life and among the educated elite, while the majority of the population operated as an oral culture, employing folk tales and stories as methods of knowledge transmission. In the first decades of the twenty-first century, at the same time that education outcomes are improving for the younger generation, modern media platforms are becoming available to non-literate members of the community.

The way that Bhutan is employing mobile phones, Facebook, and other online media suggests the application of a socio-cultural perspective to notions of literacy. Silvia Scribner and Michael Cole explained literacy as "a set of socially organized practices which make use of a symbol system and a technology for producing and disseminating it" (1981: 236). Richard Lanham said that "literacy" had extended its semantic reach from meaning "the ability to read and write" to "understand information however presented" (1995: 198).

Bhutanese people lacking print literacy are connecting to public space via a range of digital or Web-based media, exemplifying what Paul Gilster described as digital literacy being about "mastering ideas, not keystrokes" (1997: 1). In rural areas, non-print-literate farmers are proficient with mobile phones, able to utilize voice apps such as Wechat, stream radio, swap video and photos via Bluetooth—all with just an elementary knowledge of signifiers (Dema 2014). Although some may not be able to read what is written, most know how to use applications and recognize the logos. "I learn from friends, who know about it", Yangchey, a farmer, told *Kuensel* (Dema 2014).

Robin pointed to the "clever services" enabled by inexpensive mobile phones that benefited communities, particularly economically poorer citizens (Mansell 2012: 19). This is true of Bhutan as it begins to invest in mobile phone apps to meet its own cultural needs. These include one for road traffic, alerting travelers to roadfalls and blockages that occur regularly along the main highway that connects the country.

Former editor-in-chief of the *Bhutan Observer*, Needrup Zangpo, lives and works in Thimphu but keeps in touch with friends from his childhood village of Mongar, in the east, via Facebook on their mobile phones. Some of them left school after grade two or three, and speak only the local dialect of Chocha Ngacha, which has no written form. "They know one English word, 'Hi', but they communicate with me on Facebook using English script to write our language. We manage to communicate" (Zangpo 2014). It demonstrates the phenomenon described by Brenda Danet and Susan Herring that socio-linguistic norms that are acquired in a face-to-face context are not static but change over time, and online relationships are grounded in offline cultures, which are themselves defined by national and ethnic boundaries (Danet and Herring 2009: 7).

Lawrence Lessig suggested that the aim of any literacy is to empower people to choose the appropriate language for their needs, and calls digital literacy "the language of the 21st century" (Lessig 2004: 37). This is relevant to Bhutan's experience. *Bhutan Observer* journalist Jigme Wangchuk noted:

> Media literacy is literacy of the new millennium, sometimes called the 21st century literacy. Literacy today depends on understanding the multiple media that make up the high-tech reality and developing the skills to use them effectively. As Bhutan is becoming increasingly media-saturated, being just literate in the traditional sense of the term is not enough.
>
> (Wangchuk 2012)

The digital technology that is sometimes seen as a threat to literacy in developed countries may, paradoxically, result in a higher rate of print literacy and engagement for Bhutanese. In Bhutan, print literacy may be co-emergent with digital media literacy, or that twenty-first-century multimedia literacy that Wangchuk envisaged. Lessig said that new tools of writing can be "a powerful and productive conduit for learning to write (or write better) with 'the old words'". He noted that the language of digital media comes more easily to some people than others—and not necessarily to those people who excel in formal written language (Lankshear and Knobel 2008: 288). This has implications for the way that literacy continues to develop in Bhutan. According to McMahan and Chesebro:

> If a nation-state "leaps" from an oral to an electronic culture, the "leap" may ultimately promote the development of literacy. Consequently, for some nation-states, the historical and temporal formula may evolve from orality to electronic to literacy.
>
> (2003: 135)

Conclusion: The Future

There are many narratives about the Internet. Robin Mansell identified competing research traditions depicting it variously as a progressive medium contributing to economic growth, an inclusive technology and inherently democratic medium, as well as one that enforces existing inequalities, particularly in power relations (2012: 36, 45). It has been criticized, particularly in the mainstream media, for causing memory loss and changing people's cognitive abilities (Carr 2010; Sparrow *et al.* 2011: 777). Pippa Norris suggested that countries follow a normalization pattern where an initial period for adapting to the new technologies has the potential to widen social inequalities, but eventually the temporary gap should close (2001: 30). While each of these approaches has some relevance to Bhutan's experience, none adequately explains the myriad ways this small, isolated Buddhist kingdom, with its strong oral traditions, has adopted the Internet or the effects on the society of this powerful new technology, best considered as a diverse assemblage of technologies, applications, and cultural practices (Goggin and McLelland 2009: 10).

Bhutan was a relative latecomer to the Internet, connecting at the end of the last century. It was only from 2006 onwards that it started to achieve social relevance, and parts of the country are still yet to be connected. Digital inequalities caused by connectivity, geography, and access (categorized as first-level digital divide: Castells 2001; van Dijck 2005) will diminish as the government rolls out broadband to provide free Internet hubs to all 205 *gewogs* and mobile telephony networks continue to be upgraded. However, it should be noted that the costs of ongoing maintenance of such infrastructure may be a challenge for the government in the future, and it is inevitable that some areas, for reasons of topography, will remain inaccessible. Inequalities around digital skills (or second-level digital divide: van Dijck 2013) are more complicated, particularly in regard to literacy. There is a singularity about the way in which the Bhutanese are approaching the Internet that reflects their cultural traditions of orality. Print literacy and digital literacy are concomitant, occurring both independently and contributing to each other.

The arrival of the Internet in Bhutan coincided with the king devolving absolute monarchical power to a democracy, which required a politically engaged populace and a public sphere for political discourse. Online media is showing great promise to meet those needs, providing a platform for dissent that is culturally appropriate. It is also helping to collapse the communication challenges of the mountainous terrain and dispersed rural communities, allowing rural people to engage with their leaders, government services, and each other. Before television and the Internet, the Bhutanese had no experience of mass media and little sense of their fellow citizens who lived beyond their immediate proximity, perhaps meeting only at the annual *tsechu*. The Internet is contributing to the imagining of the nation, allowing citizens to see their own traditions and voices reflected back to them, and joining in discussions about what matters to them as Bhutanese. Monasteries are using the Internet to further their spiritual aims, while prominent leaders such as Khyentse and the Fourth King advocate a cautious embrace. Their underlying message is that it is a useful technology—when used wisely. The potential of the Internet is yet to be fully realized in Bhutan, but the early signs are that it is contributing to the country's development as a modern, educated, interconnected nation and twenty-first-century democracy.

Notes

1. The Bhutanese ngultrim is pegged at the Indian rupee.
2. These are the prices of phones for sale in the phone shop on Chhoten Lam, near Norzin Lam traffic roundabout, on 11 July 2014. According to the Ministry of Finance, Pay Revision 2014, a teacher at a community school would earn between nu 8,000 and 12,000 a month (US$120–180).

References

Avieson, B. (2013) Ph.D. Exegesis, Sydney: Macquarie University.

Avieson, B. (2015) *The Dragon's Voice: How Modern Media Found Bhutan*, St Lucia: University of Queensland Press.

Bhaumik, S. (2011) "Bhutan Monk Faces Jail for Anti-Smoking Law Violation", *BBC*, 1 February, available at: www.bbc.com/news/world-south-asia-12329957

Bhutan Media Foundation (2012) "Media Baseline Study", *Bhutan Media Foundation*, available at: www.bmf.bt/wp-content/uploads/2012/08/Media-Baseline-study.pdf

Bhutan Observer (2012) "Audit Shines Light on Newspaper Figures", *Bhutan Observer*, 28 December, available at: http://bhutanobserver.bt/print.aspx?artid=1260

The Bhutanese (2012) "Social Media Does Greater Good", *The Bhutanese*, 12 September, available at: www.thebhutanese.bt/social-media-does-greater-good

Carr, N. (2010) *The Shallows: What the Internet Is Doing to Our Brains*, New York: WW Norton.

Castells, M. (2001) *The Internet Galaxy: Reflections of the Internet, Business, and Society*, Oxford: Oxford University Press.

Dahal, R. (2013) "Tough Job Ahead for New Government", *Bhutan Observer*, 13 July, available at: http://bhutanobserver.bt/7416-bo-news-about-tough_job_ahead_for_new_government.aspx

Danet, B., and Herring, S. (2009) *The Multilingual Internet: Language, Culture and Communication Online*, New York: Oxford University Press.

Dema, C. (2009) "Walk for Seven Kids Still a Question", *Bhutan Today*, 14 August, p. 7.

Dema, K. (2009) "7 Schoolboys Washed Away by Wangchu (Bhutan)", *International Centre for Integrated Mountain Development*, 28 July, available at: www.icimod.org/?q=5304

Dema, K. (2013) "The Toned-Down Tobacco Control Act", *Kuensel*, 5 June, available at: http://kuenselonline.com/archive/the-toned-down-tobacco-control-act/ (accessed 23 February 2015).

Dema, T. (2014) "The Mobile Revolution (in Rural Communities)", *Kuensel*, 26 June, available at: http://kuenselonline.com/archive/the-mobile-revolution-in-rural-communties/ (accessed 8 February 2015).

Dorji, G. (2014a) "Tshogpon Takes Part in 'Virtual *Zomdu*'", *Kuensel*, 30 July, available at: http://kuenselonline.com/archive/tshogpon-takes-part-in-virtual-zomdu/

Dorji, G. (2014b) "Bhutan to Bridge Digital Divide by 2020", *Kuensel*, 23 October, available at: http://kuenselonline.com/archive/bhutan-to-bridge-digital-divide-by-2020/

Dorji, G. (2015) "BDBL to Takeover Community Centres", *Kuensel*, 3 January, available at: www.kuenselonline.com/bdbl-to-takeover-community-centres/#.VQj73EbCrvQ

Dorji, K., and Pek, S. S. (2005) "The Bhutanese Media: In the Service of the Public", Proceedings of the Second Conference on Gross National Happiness, *Genuine Progress Index Atlantic*, available at: www.gpiatlantic.org/conference/papers/pek-dorji.pdf

Economic Times (2014) "Wary of Chinese Advances, Narendra Modi Woos Neighbours", *Economic Times*, 13 June, available at: http://economictimes.indiatimes.com/news/politics-and-nation/wary-of-chinese-advances-narendra-modi-woos-neighbours/articleshow/36468025.cms

Elliot, J. (1987) "The Modern Path to Enlightenment", *Financial Times*, 2 May.

Galay, K. (2004) "International Politics of Bhutan", *Journal of Bhutan Studies*, 10: 90–107.

Gilster, P. (1997) *Digital Literacy*, New York: Wiley.

Goggin, G., and McLelland, M. J. (2009) "Internationalizing Internet Studies: Beyond Anglophone Paradigms", in G. Goggin and M. J. McLelland (eds), *Internationalizing Internet Studies*, New York: Routledge, pp. 3–17.

Grosswiler, P. (2001) "Jurgen Habermas: Media Ecologist?", *Proceedings of the Media Ecology Association*, Vol. 2.

Gyabak, K., and Godina, H. (2011) "Digital Storytelling in Bhutan: A Qualitative Examination of New Media Tools Used to Bridge the Digital Divide in a Rural Community School", *Computers and Education*, 5(4): 2236–2243.

The Independent (2011) "Be Happy, No Butts, Bhutan's Smokers Told", *The Independent*, 11 September, available at: www.independent.co.uk/life-style/health-and-families/be-happy-no-butts-bhutans-smokers-told-2352949.html

Josephi, B., and Dahal, R. (2014) "How Bhutan's Journalists Carve Out their Own Path", paper presented at *International Association Media and Communications Research Conference* in Hyderabad, 15–19 July.

Kasturi, C. (2014) "Bhutan Trip, China on Mind", *The Telegraph (India)*, 28 October, available at: www.telegraphindia.com/1141028/jsp/nation/story_18972446.jsp#.VPFHinbCrkM

Khandu, S. (2012) "Perspective on Bhutan and Right to Information: Working Towards a Vibrant Democracy [Part 1]", *sangaykhandu's blog*, 5 March, available at: https://sangaykhandu.wordpress.com/2012/03/05/perspective-on-bhutan-and-right-to-information-working-towards-a-vibrant-democracy/

Khyentse, D. J. (2012) "Prayer for Internet Practice", *Facebook*, available at: www.facebook.com/PrayerForInternetPractice/timeline (accessed 12 October 2012).

Kuensel (2009) "Cracks in the Solidarity Walk", *Kuensel*, 4 August, p. 4.

Lanham, R. A. (1995) "Digital Literacy", *Scientific American*, 273(3) 198–200.

Lankshear, C., and Knobel, M. (2008) *Digital Literacies: Concepts, Policies and Practices*, New York: Peter Lang Publishing.

Lessig, L. (2004) *Free Culture: How Big Media Uses Technology and the Law to Lock Down Culture and Control Creativity*, New York: The Penguin Press, available at: www.free-culture.cc

Limbu, T. (2014) "Bhutan's Youth Is Experiencing a Democratic Awakening", *Story South Asia*, available at: http://storysouthasia.com/bhutans-youth-is-experiencing-a-democratic-awakening/

McMahan, M. T., and Chesebro, J. W. (2003) "Media and political transformations: Revolutionary changes of the world's cultures", *Communication Quarterly*, 51: 2, 126–153.

Mansell, R. (2012) *Imagining the Internet: Communication, Innovation and Governance*, Oxford: Oxford University Press.

Ministry of Information and Communication (2003) *Media Impact Study*, Ministry of Information and Communication, Thimphu: Royal Government of Bhutan.

Ministry of Information and Communication (2008) *Media Impact Study*, Ministry of Information and Communication, Thimphu: Royal Government of Bhutan.

Ministry of Information and Communication (2013) *Bhutan Information and Media Impact Study*, final draft, Ministry of Information and Communication, Thimphu: Royal Government of Bhutan.

Ministry of Information and Communication (2014a) *Annual Report*, Ministry of Information and Communication, Thimphu: Royal Government of Bhutan.

Ministry of Information and Communication (2014b) *Annual InfoComm and Transport Statistical Bulletin: 5th Edition* Ministry of Information and Communication, Thimphu: Royal Government of Bhutan.

Ministry of Information and Communication (n.d.) *Vision for Information Society: Bhutan in the 21st Century* Ministry of Information and Communication, available at: www.moic.gov.bt

National Statistics Bureau (2016) available at: www.nsb.gov.bt (accessed 8 April 2016).

Norris, P. (2001) *Digital Divide: Civic Engagement, Information Poverty, and the Internet Worldwide*, Cambridge: Cambridge University Press.

Ongmo, S. (2009) "We Want More Bhutanese Writers", *Kuensel*, 2 May, p. 5.

Ongmo, S. (2011a) "Bhutan: Criminalizing the Use of Tobacco Stirs Outrage", *Global Voices*, 8 January, available at: http://globalvoicesonline.org/2011/01/08/bhutan-criminalizing-the-use-of-tobacco-stirs-outrage

Ongmo, S. (2011b) "Is Bhutan's GNH Going Up in Smoke?", *Dragon Tales*, 12 January, available at: www.sonamongmo7.com/2011/01/is-bhutans-gnh-going-up-in-smoke.html

Ongmo, S. (2011c) "Bhutan: Monk Becomes the First Victim of the Tobacco Act", *Global Voices*, 5 March, available at: http://globalvoicesonline.org/2011/03/05/bhutan-monk-becomes-the-first-victim-of-the-tobacco-act/

Parameswaran, G. (2012) "Bhutan Smokers Huff and Puff Over Tobacco Ban", *Aljazeera*, 28 September, available at: www.aljazeera.com/indepth/features/2012/09/201292095920757761.html (accessed 25 February 2015).

Pem, T. (2011) "Monk Gets Three Years for Smuggling Tobacco", *Bhutan Observer*, 4 March, available at: http://bhutanobserver.bt/3744-bo-news-about-monk_gets_three_years_for_smuggling_tobacco_.aspx

Penjore, D. (2004) "Security of Bhutan: Walking Between the Giants", *Journal of Bhutan Studies*, 10: 108–131.

Phuntsho, K. (2007) "The Marriage of the Media and Religion: For Better or Worse", in *Seminar on Media and Public Culture*, Thimphu: Centre for Bhutan Studies, pp. 19–30.

Pokhrel, N. (2014) "Falling Like Ninepins", *Kuensel*, 10 July, p. 3.

Pommaret, F. (2001) "Dances in Bhutan: A Traditional Medium of Information", in *Seminar on Media and Public Culture*, Thimphu: Centre for Bhutan Studies.

Press Trust of India (2014) "Ericsson Partners with Bhutan Telecom for E-Learning Project", *The Economic Times*, 29 March, available at: http://telecom.economictimes.indiatimes.com/news/3g-4g/ericsson-partners-with-bhutan-telecom-for-e-learning-project/32913197

Royal Government of Bhutan (2003) *9th Five Year Plan*, Thimphu: Royal Government of Bhutan.

Royal Government of Bhutan (2013) *11th Five Year Plan*, Thimphu: Royal Government of Bhutan.

Royal Government of Bhutan (2014a) *Bhutan Telecommunications and Broadband Policy*, Thimphu: Royal Government of Bhutan.

Royal Government of Bhutan (2014b) *Bhutan e-Gov Master Plan*, Thimphu: Royal Government of Bhutan.

Scribner, S., and Cole, M. (1981) *The Psychology of Literacy*, Cambridge MA: Harvard University Press.

Sithey, G. (2013) *Democracy in Bhutan: The First Five Years*, Thimphu: Centre for Research Initiatives.

Sparrow, B., Liu, J., and Wegner, D. (2011) "Google Effects on Memory: Cognitive Consequences of Having Information at Our Fingertips", *Science*, 333(6043): 776–778.

Tobgay, T. (2009) "Walk Talk", *Tshering Tobgay: Life and Politics in Democratic Bhutan*, 31 July, available at: www.tsheringtobgay.com/democracy/2009/walk-talk.html

Tobgay, T. (2011) "Facebook Strikes", *Tshering Tobgay: Life and Politics in Democratic Bhutan*, 2 June, available at: www.tsheringtobgay.com/?s=facebook+strikes.

Tourism Council of Bhutan (2016) *Tourism Council of Bhutan*, available at: www.tourism.gov.bt/map/thimphu

Tshering, P. (2014a) personal communication, 2 July.

Tshering, P. (2014b) "Say No to Sex on Camera", *PaSsu Diary*, 10 June, available at: www.passudiary.com/2014/06/say-no-to-sex-on-camera.html

van Dijck, J. (2005) *The Deepening Divide: Inequality in the Information Society*, London: Sage.

van Dijck, J. (2013) *The Culture of Connectivity: A Critical History of Social Media*, New York: Oxford University Press.

van Driem, G. (1994) "Language Policy in Bhutan", in M. Aris and M. Hutt (eds), *Bhutan: Aspects of Culture and Development*, Gartmore: Kiscadale Publications, pp. 87–105.

Wangchuk, J. (2012) "Separating Grain from Chaff", *Bhutan Observer*, 4 February.

Wangchuck, K. (2011) "Royal Speech of Fifth King", *Bhutan Research*, 23 August, available at: www.bhutan-research.org/the-kings-speeches/23-august-2011-royal-address-at-the-graduates%E2%80%99-orientation-program

Wangchuck, L. (2014) personal communication, 6 July.

Wangdi, K. (2011) "Do Bhutan's Anti-Smoking Laws Go Too Far?", *Time*, available at: http://content.time.com/time/world/article/0,8599,2057774,00.html

Zangmo, T. (2014) "Private 'Porn' Petition Gets PM's Consent", *Kuensel*, 10 October, available at: www.kuensel online.com/demo/private-porn-petition-gets-pms-consent/#.VRNOw0bCrkM

Zangpo, N. (2014) Personal communication, 10 July.

19

LAND OF THE DISCONNECTED

A History of the Internet in Papua New Guinea

Sarah Logan and Joseph Suwamaru

Introduction

Internet scholarship has largely focused on countries with long telecommunications histories. Rarely do such studies focus on countries which are younger than the Internet itself, although it is these which arguably experience the greatest change as a result of this technology. Papua New Guinea (PNG) is one such country: gaining independence in 1975, its population only acquired widespread access to the Internet in 2007. Prior to this, Internet penetration was close to zero, and the country had very limited national press, TV, and radio networks, and little access to international media. This means that even though Internet access is still limited, with less than 10 percent penetration, PNG has experienced a massive upheaval in its national telecommunications landscape as a result (World Bank 2015).

PNG is a country of staggering diversity, with over 800 language groups in a population of just over seven million. Located just to the north of Australia, it comprises over 600 islands. The country was formerly a colony and protectorate of Germany and Australia respectively, achieving independence in 1975. It has a Westminster system of government, with 22 provinces being the primary administrative units. Regional identities are also important culturally and politically—the four regions often jockey for political positions although they have no administrative function. Some 80 percent of PNG's population is rural, and despite a current resource-led economic boom, an estimated 40 percent of the population lives in poverty (Human Rights Watch 2014). The country suffers from declining literacy rates—60 percent in 2009, but anecdotally far less—and one of the highest rates of gender violence in the world (UNESCO 2011; ChildFund 2013).

Like many emerging democracies, PNG has struggled with issues of development and governance, and is rated the lowest of all countries outside sub-Saharan Africa on the United Nations Human Development Index. One of PNG's most persistent and visible political problems is corruption. The country is currently in the bottom 10 percent of Transparency International's corruption perceptions index (Transparency International 2014), and is marked by grand fraud by politicians and other community leaders. A recent case, for example, saw investigators allege that one of the nation's top lawyers had colluded with politicians and bureaucrats to defraud the state of over $A130 million (Fox 2013).

PNG's geography is brutal, dominated by soaring mountain ranges, deep fjords and valleys, dense rainforest, and high rainfall. There are few—if any—passable roads outside the urban centers on the country's largest land mass, and a significant proportion of the population lives on scattered smaller islands. Such geographical challenges have substantially limited PNG's development, including the development of telecommunications. This chapter provides a brief technical history of the Internet in PNG, and outlines the still emerging social and political impact of the technology.

Late and Fragmented Access

From 1975 to 1997, PNG's telecommunications systems were regulated via a series of laws inherited from Australia, PNG's former colonial administrator. In 1997, the corporatization of the Post and Telecommunications Corporation (PTC) saw the establishment of the Papua New Guinea Telecommunication Authority (PANGTEL) as an industry regulator, and Telikom, a service provider with monopoly rights dating from the colonial period (Stanley 2008). Telikom was a vertically integrated monopoly operator providing landline-based phones, lease lines, facsimile, and data services including mobile phone services to an array of customers principally in the country's two urban centers. Given that most of the country's population is rural, these services reached only a tiny minority of the population. Unsurprisingly, Telikom exhibited all the problems generally associated with state-owned monopolies— inefficient and predatory pricing combined with difficult terrain to inhibit the development of the Internet in PNG for many years.

Internet services first appeared in PNG in the early 1990s. The first users were educational institutions, accessing the Internet via dial-up to university networks in Australia. Unitech, a university in Lae, became (and remains) the registration and managing agency for the .pg domain (Haoda 2005). In 2002, as part of a broader effort to introduce competition in the provision of utilities, the Independent Consumer and Competition Commission Act 2002 established two different regulatory roles—one for the newly created Independent Consumer and Competition Commission (ICCC) and one for PANGTEL. Telecommunication licenses were to be issued by the ICCC and frequency spectrum licenses were the responsibility of PANGTEL. This dual regulatory arrangement led to confusion about regulatory responsibilities, and further inefficiencies in an already cumbersome telecommunications environment in PNG (Gulo-Vui 2010).

In 2003, Telikom established the Tiare gateway, connecting PNG to the Internet via undersea cable to Sydney, Australia. This offered Internet access to a wider user base in PNG for the first time. Users were offered 64kpbs access, with licenses issued to five Internet service providers—the first in the country. These ISPs used both wired and wireless infrastructure to serve their customers, but their services were also limited because the point of presence (POP) provided by Tiare was limited to only two towns, Port Moresby and Madang (Yandit 2015). The lack of ubiquitous POPs across PNG impeded the delivery of Internet services via landlines to many parts of the country. In any case, landline penetration was less than 2 percent nationwide, and users needed an existing copper-based landline to connect via Telikom's services. Users located outside these two towns were restricted to other modes of access, including via high-frequency radio modems, which could be used for limited, text-only email access. In response to limited and costly access via Telikom, many business users in PNG also began installing very small aperture terminals (Suwamaru 2005; Kero 2013). This allowed them to source an independent Internet link via international satellite operators, bypassing Telikom entirely.

Overall, even though PNG technically had access to the Internet in 2001, that access remained extremely limited, unreliable, slow, and expensive. In addition, regulation was cumbersome: a regulatory bottleneck meant that only Telikom could legally instal and operate such systems (Kero 2013). However, this was widely circumvented. In 2005, for example, PANGTEL reported that 48 companies had installed and operated independent data transmission networks—mainly VSAT—without receiving regulatory approval (Kero 2013). In October 2005 PANGTEL officers, with the support of police, confiscated a 2.8-meter satellite dish from one of the country's five ISPs, Daltron. The Daltron manager reported to the press that the company had installed the satellite access to try to overcome the slow and costly access they were otherwise required to buy directly from Telikom. Within a month of this incident, Telikom announced plans to upgrade its network and, as the following paragraphs show, these events presaged a liberalization in the PNG telecommunications sector (Mitchel 2008).

From 1996 to 1997, the PNG government made commitments arising from its entry into the WTO to liberalize the telecommunications sector, and in December 2005, the government finally acted on this commitment with a decision to introduce competition in mobile telephony. March 2007 was the date set for open competition in the mobile phone market. The decision also introduced a new streamlined licensing regime, general carrier licenses, public mobile licenses, and value added service licenses, which included the Internet and associated services (Gulo-Vui 2010). These licenses were to be administered and managed by a single regulator. However, in September 2006, Telikom refused to relinquish its monopoly, and the government simultaneously released a new information and communication technology policy that reneged on the December 2005 NEC decision. Despite the new policy, and continued obstruction from PANGTEL, the ICCC pressed ahead with deregulation, and Irish company Digicel launched its mobile phone service in May 2007.

Despite the best attempts by interests associated with Telikom to bar Digicel from entering the market, increased competition in the mobile sector had an almost immediate effect. Accessibility has expanded from less than 3 percent population coverage by mobile networks in 2006 to almost 80 percent in 2015 (World Bank 2015). The result was a substantial increase in mobile penetration, from 1.6 percent in 2006 to 35 percent in 2015. In 2011, 3G access was introduced by Digicel, followed soon after by B-Mobile, Telikom's mobile operator. Mobile broadband now has an estimated 9 percent penetration, up from zero in 2006 (Budde 2015). In 2014, Digicel introduced 4G to the capital city, Port Moresby, and plans to expand its 3G and 4G networks across major urban centers in 2015 to 2016. Both Digicel and B-Mobile are now concentrating their business model on expanding their data markets (Business Advantage 2013). Today, PNG citizens enjoy a range of mobile Internet products, including 4G services, as well as a greater range of fixed line Internet services such as asymmetric digital subscriber line (ADSL) and worldwide interoperable microwave access systems (WiMAX) (Yandit 2015). However, PNG still has some of the most expensive Internet access rates in the world. The cost of off-island fiber Internet is three to four times more expensive than the cost of satellite Internet bandwidth in PNG, the reverse of other countries (Business Advantage 2014).

Access problems also continue. Telikom's infrastructure—the Tiare gateway—has not been able to handle increased Internet traffic stemming from greater uptake, which is primarily driven by Digicel traffic. However, when Digicel approached the regulator for an international gateway license, its request was denied: an attempt to block Digicel's increasing dominance of the market and also sustain Telikom's legacy monopoly on data infrastructure. Digicel installed its own international satellite-based gateway but it is still limited by the regulator to buying bandwidth from Telikom for its international traffic requirements, meaning that Internet access in PNG is still slow at peak times. This means that data supply will be relatively limited in PNG for the foreseeable future, until the new infrastructure outlined below is completed. At present, 80 percent of Digicel's Internet traffic is going out over satellite, and only 20 percent is going out across fiber (Business Advantage 2014).

Prices are unlikely to drop any time soon. The inefficiency of the government operator, B-Mobile, means that Digicel dominates the market, which is now essentially a monopoly. Government policies continue to attempt to address this issue. The National Information and Communication Act 2009 was supplemented by a new national ICT policy introduced in 2008 which introduced regulatory reforms and universal service requirements. The latest stage of the ICT reform process began in 2010 with the passing of a new ICT Act, the creation of a new industry regulator (NICTA: the National Information and Communication Technology Authority), and the commencement of a new regulatory regime on 1 November 2010. The new regime was designed to remove Telikom PNG's remaining monopolies in fixed line and broadband services, and encourage greater competition, but neither the legislation nor the accompanying regulations address quality of service or regulate tariffs based on the effective cost of doing business (Suwamaru 2015b).

However, the government has taken major steps to address data speeds and costs in PNG. In 2012, NICTA launched a public enquiry into international connectivity, issuing a discussion paper which noted Telikom's absolute dominance of the country's wholesale Internet capacity. In response, in March 2013 the Ministry for Communications and Information Technology (MCIT) made wholesale Internet capacity a declared service, limiting Telikom's ability to withhold access to other operators—namely Digicel. The department also issued a revised draft National Broadband Policy on 22 April 2013 (the final version has yet to be released). This policy attempts to address competition in the sector and to introduce mandatory service provisions; noting Digicel's absolute dominance means that the company enjoys a quasi-monopoly, especially in the mobile telecommunications market. The draft policy has the following goals:

- To have in place a competitive structure for the provision of broadband in PNG.
- To support the provision of broadband services to communities with an active interest in acquiring early broadband access.
- To achieve broadband service availability of 100 percent in urban areas and 70 percent in rural areas of PNG during the next five years.
- To ensure that broadband services become and remain more affordable for everyone in PNG.
- To support all academic institutions to have access to broadband.
- To support the government in delivering its services online over broadband.

Given the constraints under which it operates, and the history of Internet access in PNG, these lofty goals are unlikely to be met within five years. However, the government has also taken steps to address the fundamental limitations of Internet infrastructure in PNG. In 2013, Telikom signed an agreement with Chinese company Huawei to build a $US313 million National Broadband Network (NBN) to be managed by PNG DataCo Limited, a new state-owned broadband wholesaler supplying bandwidth to telecommunications providers. Any service provider in PNG will be able to lease bandwidth at non-discriminatory wholesale prices from DataCo. PNG's NBN will connect to the rest of the world via the PPC1 submarine cable landing in Madang, which offers far more bandwidth than the APNG-2 cable landing near Port Moresby—the site of the old Tiare gateway. The new gateway connects to an undersea cable, which connects to the Internet via Guam. It is 100 times larger than the old cable, which is only operating at between 40 and 50 percent capacity because of the way the undersea cable was laid. Two of PNG's major centers (though not its capital) were connected to the Guam cable in mid-2012. A network of microwave transmitters will link the NBN to smaller centers and islands off the PNG coast (Business Advantage 2015).

Better Late Than Never: Economic, Political and Social Impact

The economic and social impact of the Internet and PNG is difficult to measure accurately, given the complete dearth of studies. However, its impact is easy to see. Today, where once sending an email entailed a trip to an official office and where the email was unlikely to reach its intended recipient, Papua New Guineans use the Internet to bank, run discussion groups, flirt, share Bible messages, and read the news from home and abroad. Surveys show that regular users use the Internet mainly to send and receive emails, catch up on news, watch videos, and access social media (Debeljak and Bonnell 2013). The majority of Internet users in PNG are young—between 15 and 24—and urban, as are the majority of smartphone users (Debeljak 2014: 42). They are also more highly educated than the rest of the population, and these users are unsurprisingly more likely to trust the Internet and social media as news sources than older and less educated citizens (Debeljak and Bonnell 2013; Debeljak 2014). Those who do have Internet access available in their households—overwhelmingly via phone—use it regularly. It is important to note, however, that Internet access is by no means *limited* to urban-educated users. Rural users maintain Facebook accounts and update them when signals can be accessed. One prominent blogger, for example, told of how he and his friends from their remote village walked up a nearby mountain to get coverage. This young man maintained a blog and social media accounts this way, using them to coordinate his NGO, which focused on building clean waterways for local villages. One of the administrators of PNG's largest Facebook group, PNGNews, argued that a significant percentage of the group's users appeared to be rural. He noted that users would update their profiles or participate in discussions intensely but sporadically, when visiting urban centers to trade or for schooling (Ephraim 2015).

Economic Impact

World Bank research suggests that the introduction of broadband adds an average of 1.4 percentage point increase in economic growth per 10 percentage point increase in tele-communications penetration (Qiang et al. 2009). No detailed research exists on this issue in PNG. The biggest businesses in PNG—the mining sector, for example—already had access to the Internet before market liberalization, usually via VSAT. The most visible changes in the everyday economic circumstances of Papua New Guineans have come from Internet access via mobile phone for individuals and Internet access for small and medium-sized enterprises. For example, approximately 80 percent of the PNG population is unbanked, one of the highest rates in the world (Grupe Spécial Mobile Association 2014: 30), due to the remoteness of much of the population and security issues associated with the movement of cash. The main airline, Air Niugini, refuses to carry cash after a series of violent robberies, and the lack of passable roads to much of the country prevents such cash being moved to outlying areas, which are in any case rife with security risks. PNG's largest bank, the Bank of the South

Pacific, started offering mobile banking services in 2010 and released a banking app in 2014. Other major banks soon followed suit. Now, all five major banks in PNG offer banking via mobile broadband as well as via SMS, and major utilities allow bills to be paid online. Importantly, though, literacy—including financial literacy—in PNG is extremely low. Much of the population is rural, living a low-cash existence, with limited access to mobile Internet services, which are, in many cases, simply priced beyond these populations. This means that Internet-based applications are still not ideal for the needs of many Papua New Guineans, although they are certainly useful for the needs of urban populations and small to medium-sized businesses. Although basic mobile phones have had a visible impact on smallholder agriculture market chains (Suwamaru 2015a), chat apps appear to be becoming more common for group communication. Recent anecdotal evidence, for example, indicates that fishermen use WhatsApp to communicate the prices for catches among a group when offshore, where previously they would have used simple SMS messages.

Social and Political Impact

Perhaps the most visible impact of the Internet has come in the form of social media use. PNG is an oral society, and Papua New Guineans have taken to Facebook with gusto. Bloggers marked the early days of the Internet in PNG, especially as universities gained comparatively reliable access. These blogs focused on discussions of PNG politics, seeking to address deficiencies in the print media. However, blogging in PNG has declined markedly since the introduction of mobile broadband, and especially since the advent of social media in PNG. For example, The Garamut, begun in 2008, was once PNG's leading political blog, quoted in the *New York Times* and *The Economist* among others, but has not been updated since late 2012. A similar fate has befallen other blogs, with authors migrating to Facebook and Twitter.

From April to September 2012, PNG was Facebook's fourth largest per capita market, with a growth rate in excess of 50 percent (Socialbakers 2012). Facebook provides an avenue for the sharing of news in a country which has until now been lacking any truly national news service. In the past, newspapers took days to move across the country, and with limited electricity and reception in many areas, neither radio nor TV has been truly national (Intermedia 2012). Indeed, a recent survey found that Facebook's weekly audience is significantly larger than any one news site in PNG. Some 53 percent of those surveyed who used the Internet weekly had used Facebook in the past week, in comparison to 33 percent and 32 percent who had accessed the websites of the country's two main newspapers (Intermedia 2012).

A myriad of Facebook discussion groups have flourished in PNG, covering a range of topics. These include regional discussion groups—where PNG's strong regional and local identities frame discussions around local issues—as well as groups devoted to Bible study and sports groups. However, the PNG-based Facebook discussion groups which have the most members and are most prominent are those devoted to discussions of governance and related social issues. The three largest Facebook groups in PNG are Sharp Talk, PNGNews, and Paitim Garamut (loosely translated as "beating the drum"), and these are devoted exclusively to these topics. Sharp Talk is the oldest of the three groups, with over 27,000 members. It was founded in early 2011 by a prominent member of PNG's civil society—the executive director of the Business Council of PNG, also a member of the board of Transparency International in PNG. The forum was created to "empower the voiceless majority of Papua New Guineans to voice their opinions on matters of public interest", and the forum's founder described its founding—

in the very early days of the Internet in PNG—as an experiment to bridge the gap between the print media and academic journals (Henao 2013). The forum has lately been in decline due to allegations of poor and biased administration.

PNGNews, founded in December 2012, is currently the largest group. The group was created by one individual and currently has nine administrators. Current membership is at 112,000 and still growing. PNGNews' mission is to "inform the collective PNG conscience, shape public opinion and be a catalyst for change at all levels of society". The administrators take responsibility for posting material, and undertake a quasi-investigative role, posting leaked documents and anonymously sourced news items. Founded in October 2013 by a board member of Transparency International PNG, Paitim Garamut has close to 10,000 members, and states its goal as to "Provide a credible platform for meaningful, objective and constructive discussion and debate on national issues and offering alternatives and solutions to the government and private sector; independently investigate and publish credible information on issues affecting PNG".

The history of these groups is difficult to track, but all have faced accusations from users of biased administration, although Sharp Talk more than most. Founders and administrators have fallen out on several accusations, and at least one of the groups—PNGNews—was created as a splinter group from Sharp Talk. In addition, although the groups do not currently share administrators, the pool of online civil society activists in PNG is small, and most administrators are likely to know one another offline.

Members of these discussion groups discuss a range of political and social topics, from religion, to gender relations, to the resurgence of sorcery and witchcraft-related violence in PNG. However, the bulk of discussions concern corruption and failures of governance. Such discussions regularly include photographs of concerning events or scenes, such as potholed roads or illegal immigrants, and often include photos of newspaper stories in one of the nation's two national newspapers. Neither of these newspapers have well-functioning websites, so users tend to take photographs of news articles and share them, rather than linking to the articles themselves.

Sharp Talk, the oldest of these groups, has had a long tradition of organizing offline meetings of its members, open to the general public, including meetings with politicians, and question-and-answer sessions with prominent civil society members. It has also engaged in discussions about formalizing its membership into an official association. Both PNGNews and Paitim Garamut have also engaged in offline meetings of its members, but have been less inclined to discuss formalizing their membership. On occasion, these groups have engaged in organizing and documenting political protests in PNG. The most notable, in 2012, attracted thousands of peaceful participants marching against a constitutional crisis and the delaying of elections. Such protests are unusual in PNG, and many commentators have attributed their apparent increase to the role of groups like Sharp Talk (Logan 2012). In the past, protests have been smaller, less organized, and occasionally violent. Posters offered photos from concurrent demonstrations elsewhere in PNG, and offered votes of thanks to those who participated. In the past, mass demonstrations in PNG have been rare, and have been organized by pre-established community organizations such as unions, churches, and student groups. These groups were certainly active in organizing the 2012 protests, but the discussions on Facebook showed an arguably new national sensibility (see Logan 2012). In November 2013, these three groups were part of a coalition of 24 online and offline groups which cooperated in a Social Media and Coalition Partners media conference to present a co-signed petition to the then opposition leader in protest at the government's ongoing embroilment in a corruption scandal.

This scandal and its associated entanglements boiled over into organized street protests in 2014, which were also largely organized via Facebook and exhibited similar characteristics. These protests saw the emergence of hashtag activism in PNG. Although exact figures are not available, Twitter use in PNG is far lower than Facebook use. However, some prominent individuals are active on Twitter, and were also active in organizing the protests via Facebook. These individuals chose to adopt a number of hashtags with which to organize Twitter content around the protests, the most prominent of which was #OccupyWaigani, Waigani being the location of PNG's Houses of Parliament. This hashtag—used initially on Twitter but also on Facebook—obviously referenced the broader Occupy movement, although other hashtags were also used, like #arrestPeter (Peter O'Neill is PNG's prime minister). These same individuals also began adopting the "I am the 99%" meme associated with the global Occupy movement. This meme was less successful than the associated hashtags, with fewer than 20 participants. However, its use at all is striking in PNG, a country historically isolated from global political protest movements.

The emergence of this sort of personally oriented activism amidst the broader political activism surrounding protests since 2012 suggests the emergence of personal action frames in PNG protest activity (Bennett 2012). Briefly, the literature on this topic sees personal rather than group identity politics emerging as the framing devices for protest movements, facilitated by social media. However, the fact that these modes of protest have failed to be widely adopted, and the apparently persistent role of traditional organizations in organizing protest movements in PNG suggests that technology in PNG protests does not facilitate the "personalized" mode of protest it may elsewhere.

Indeed, imagery associated with more traditional identity politics rather than "personalized" politics is arguably more widely shared on Papua New Guinean Facebook groups. For example, images associated with the American civil rights movement are posted sporadically to PNGNews, Sharp Talk, and Paitim Garamut. Here, motifs of political empowerment pepper discussions of the failings of PNG's own government and political class. Similarly, one of the most prominent international political issues discussed on these three Facebook discussion groups is the plight of West Papua. Briefly, West Papua is a province of Indonesia whose population—like Papua New Guinea's—is Melanesian. The province has a strong and harshly repressed independence movement, and shares a land border with Papua New Guinea. Although West Papuan solidarity has existed in PNG and across the Pacific since the birth of the independence movement there, social media has arguably intensified the collective Melanesian identity associated with it. Facebook has been widely used in PNG to condemn Indonesian suppression of West Papuan activism, and to share videos of atrocities and call for action. Similar uses of Facebook appear across Pacific nations which share Papua New Guinea and West Papua's Melanesian heritage. For example, in the wake of the November 2015 terrorist attacks in Paris, social media users across the Pacific, including in PNG, adapted memes which appeared elsewhere on Facebook. These memes reminded users that although Paris was a tragedy, appalling terrorist attacks had also occurred in Lebanon, for example, and Egypt. Melanesian users adapted the meme to include West Papua, and, in doing so, to question why global attention had not focused on ongoing atrocities there. Here, social media is used to facilitate collective action and discussion around a traditionally marginalized identity group: Melanesians in the context of post-colonial politics. Although in-depth studies have yet to be conducted, then, rather than engendering entirely new forms of protest, the Internet in PNG appears to have adapted to, or re-energized, pre-existing organizational forms. This judgment is corroborated by ongoing productive collaboration between Facebook discussion groups and offline community groups, such as trade unions and churches in organizing protests and other political activity.

Importantly, the PNG government moved to censor Facebook and other social media outlets in 2014, suggesting that the government, at least, sees the medium as a threat. The National Information and Communication Technology Authority (NICTA) drafted a cybercrime policy which included provisions to require all social media users in PNG to use their real names only and proposed penalties for those users who, according to the Minister for Communications, "abuse the social media to attack another individual, and make defamatory and slang statements" (Callick 2014). The policy also includes measures to store data and require SIM registration, and associated legislation was due to be tabled in August 2015.

Not all citizens see Facebook and other social media sites as an unmitigated good. Even within the online community, regular accusations of "clicktivism", damaging rumors, and gossip circulate. Similarly, community concerns about online pornography are often reflected in online discourses, and are similar to those found in discussions about the impact of mobile phones on gender and social relations (see Watson 2011; Suwamaru 2014). For example, much consternation ensued as a result of the January 2015 Google trend data, which showed that PNG had the greatest percentage of Google searches for the word "porn" anywhere in the world that month. These statistics are misleading, given the small number of Internet users in PNG and the nature of the search for "porn"—suggesting a naive rather than an experienced user. But commentary on the topic reflects community angst in this deeply Christian country, and the issue engendered a number of newspaper editorials and much discussion online, with some comment threads reaching over 400 contributions in a matter of days (Cochrane 2015). The Papua New Guinea Office of Censorship had announced in 2014 that it was planning to spend K4 million ($1.4 million) to instal a filter system to block all pornographic sites and materials which are currently accessible to PNG; this proposal was discussed widely in response to the embarrassment of the Google trend data. However, the filter is yet to be implemented, and it remains unclear whether PNG has the capacity to employ such a comprehensive filtering system. The filter will fall under a new bill that was developed in 2014 but which has yet to be tabled—the Classification of Films, Publication and Online Services Bill 2014 (PNG Technology News 2015).

Conclusion: Placing the Internet in PNG

It is important to note that narratives surrounding the Internet in PNG are both similar and different from those surrounding mobile phones. These narratives appear in mainstream media, in the limited research available, and are gleaned from the content of online discussions. Mobile phones are far more widely used than the Internet, and their use offers specific instances of Papua New Guineans adapting the technology to local needs (see Watson 2011; Suwamaru 2014). For example, local forms of practice have emerged, particularly in the context of courtship (Andersen 2013) and in the development of local SMS languages. Mobile phones occupy an important place in commercial activity as they are at the center of an ecosystem of the sale of accessories and top-up credit, and market price information systems which have engineered new forms of income and ways of interacting. Despite the fact that most Internet access occurs via mobile phones in PNG, Internet use is far more expensive and far more limited in the context of the everyday lives of Papua New Guineans. Unlike mobile phones, there is no local commercial ecosystem surrounding the Internet. There is little—if any—locally produced online content beyond social media and blogs, and no local technological innovation: the Internet in PNG is a wholly foreign technology.

Importantly, as outlined in the earlier sections of this chapter, widespread access to both mobile phones and the Internet arrived in PNG in the face of active government opposition. The technology was introduced and made accessible almost wholly by a private actor. This means that from the very beginning, the narrative surrounding both the Internet and mobile phones was anti-government and anti-state, with the state seen as a brake rather than an accelerator on development. This concurs with wider narratives around development in PNG, where the "broken-backed state" (Tinker 1967) has long been framed by citizens and development actors as absent from the lives of most Papua New Guineans. The use of mobile phones for service delivery in the face of state incapacity animates research on mobile phones in PNG (Watson 2011; Suwamaru 2014, 2015a), and engages in the "leapfrog" narrative surrounding much research on mobile phones in developing states elsewhere. Similarly, as we have seen, the failure of the state dominates discussions on Facebook, suggesting that the Internet, or at least social media, in PNG is part of a "social imaginary" of the Internet which locates it as a source of power and politics outside the state (see Taylor 2004; Mansell 2012).

Narratives surrounding the use of both mobile phones and the Internet also have a strong moral component. As described above, much consternation ensued when Google trend data from January 2015 revealed that PNG had the highest number of searches for the word "porn" per capita in the English-speaking world for that month. Similar moral panics surround the use of mobile phones, which have been widely blamed for marriage break-ups, for promiscuity, and for declining moral standards (Watson 2011; Suwamaru 2014; Logan and Spark 2015).

Both these narratives, of the Internet as a marker of the absent state, and of the dangerous moral component of the technology, place the Internet as resolutely foreign and separate to PNG. In this, the narratives arguably reference receptions of other flows of globalization in PNG as reported by detailed ethnographic studies which see Papua New Guineans framing themselves as residents of a place not yet modernized and remote from the rest of the world. This is a marginalized identity lacking in the benefits of modernity (see Foster 2002: 132). Importantly, however, these narratives of remoteness and marginality in PNG do not necessarily see this as a disadvantage. Rather, subjects may see this marginality—this separateness from the world—as disguising a sort of agency and optimism: a moral confidence. For Robert Foster, this means that in PNG globalization can be framed as an enlargement of one's own world rather than encompassment of it by someone else's world (2002: 130–136). Although the Internet is foreign, then, it is not necessarily framed in PNG as an agent of foreign *power*, simply of foreign origin. This is arguably the case even in the sense that the technology is viewed by many as facilitating the dissemination of pornography. Here, discourse about the Internet facilitates the assertion of a moral national identity against a technology of foreign origin, used by foreigners for immoral purposes but one which should—and *can*—be resisted by Papua New Guineans. Despite their usual disdain for the PNG government, then, not one of the discussions about PNG's high rate of searches for "porn" in January 2015 on the three most popular Facebook groups disagreed with the government response.

More usually, however, the Internet is enthusiastically adapted, primarily in these groups, for the task of political discussion. PNG's failures are discussed in detail and bemoaned, but never do discussants simply opt out and suggest that the task is useless. Rather, the discussion continues, endless but not hopeless. Participants take their role as provocateurs seriously: as the origin statements of the three Facebook groups outlined show, the administrators see the technology as facilitating important national endeavors, and discussions regularly turn to the government's ongoing enragement at the role of social media in uncovering corruption. The founder of Sharp Talk sees this enthusiastic discussion as the adaption of longstanding traditions and practices of political and social expression to the new technology, likening energetic discussions on Facebook to the production of tapa cloth and carvings in the pre-colonial era. He argues that "if Facebook was here 400 years ago the carvings would speak. This is the manifestation of a society that has always been very opinionated" (Henao 2013). Importantly, discussions on all three Facebook groups are punctuated by moments of national pride—celebrating Papua New Guinean sporting figures who have gone on to succeed internationally, or national pride in, for example, PNG's natural beauty and strong traditions.

Here, we see dedicated discussions of what the state *should* be, combined with a collective pride in PNG nationality. This accords with what Foster (2002: 17) sees as a perennial binary in PNG which "pits the nation against a doubly weak state—unable both to coerce citizens to enact its will and to redeem for those same citizens the promise of national development". In this reading, Facebook discussion groups serve as an outlet for discussions which have long marked PNG's evolution into an independent state. As the first truly national discursive process in PNG, the Internet—and especially Facebook—provide for an Andersonian space where national identity is configured and progressed. Narratives surrounding the Internet in PNG may frame the technology as foreign, then, but see the use to which it is put as resolutely Papua New Guinean. The technology is not reconfigured or framed as incommensurable, damaging, or colonial (Michaels 1986): it is *adopted* rather than necessarily *adapted*, although this may change as usage increases.

References

Andersen, B. (2013) "Tricks, Lies and Mobile Phones: Phone Friend Stories in PNG", *Culture, Theory and Critique*, 54(3): 318–334.

Bennett, L. (2012) "The Personalization of Politics: Political Identity, Social Media, and Changing Patterns of Participation", *The Annals of the American Academy of Political and Social Science*, 644(1): 20–39.

Budde, P. (2015) *Papua New Guinea—Telecoms, Mobile and Broadband Market Insights and Statistics*, Sydney: BuddeComm, available at: www.budde.com.au/Research/Papua-New-Guinea-Telecoms-Mobile-and-Broad band-Market-Insights-and-Statistics.html

Business Advantage (2013) "Telecommunications Price Falls Will Continue in Papua New Guinea Say Telikom and Digicel", *Business Advantage*, available at: www.businessadvantagepng.com/telecommunications-price-falls-will-continue-in-papua-new-guinea-say-telikom-and-digicel/ (accessed 1 August 2015).

Business Advantage (2014) "Digicel PNG Plans Television Network as it Expands its Mobile Network", *Business Advantage*, 14 July, available at: www.businessadvantagepng.com/digicel-plans-expansion-mobile-network-creating-television-network (accessed 1 August 2015).

Business Advantage (2015) "PNG's National Broadband Network Speeding to Completion", *Business Advantage*, available at: www.businessadvantagepng.com/papua-new-guineas-national-broadband-network-speeding-to-completion (accessed 1 August 2015).

Callick, R. (2014) "PNG Takes the Fight to Social Media Critics", *The Australian*, 12 April, available at: www.theaustralian.com.au/news/world/png-takes-the-fight-to-social-media-critics/story-e6frg6so-1226881428323 (accessed 1 May 2015).

ChildFund (2013) "Family and Sexual Violence in Papua New Guinea", *ChildFund*, Port Moresby, available at: www.childfund.org.au/sites/default/files/development/Family-and-Sexual-Violence-Papua-New-Guinea.pdf

Cochrane, L. (2015) "Papua New Guinea Tops Google Porn Searches", *Australian Broadcasting Corporation News*, 26 February, available at: www.abc.net.au/news/2015-02-25/papua-new-guinea-tops-google-porn-searches/6262 028 (accessed 1 March 2015).

Debeljack, D., and Bonnell, J. (2013) *Citizen Access to Information in Papua New Guinea*, Washington, DC: Intermedia.

Debeljak, K. (2014) *Citizen Access to Information in Papua New Guinea*, Washington, DC: Intermedia.

Ephraim, D. (2015) personal communication with S. Logan, 1 November 2015.

Foster, R. (2002) *Materializing the Nation: Commodities, Consumption and Media in Papua New Guinea*, Bloomington, IN: Indiana University Press.

Fox, L. (2013) "Investigators Allege Massive Fraud by Papua New Guinea Elite", *Australian Broadcasting Corporation News*, 25 October, available at: www.abc.net.au/news/2013-10-25/an-investigators-allege-massive-fraud-by-papua-new-guinea-elite/5047050 (accessed 1 October 2015).

Grupe Spécial Mobile Association (2014) *State of the Industry: Mobile Financial Services for the Unbanked*, Barcelona: Grupe Spécial Mobile Association, available at: www.gsma.com/mobilefordevelopment/wp-content/uploads/2015/03/SOTIR_2014.pdf

Gulo-Vui, K. (2010) "Small Islands, Small Populations: What Can Be Future Opportunities?", *Pacific Telecommunication Council*, available at: www.ptc.org/ptc10/program/images/papers/slides/Slides_Kila%20Gulo-Vui_PITA%20Wkshop.pdf (accessed 30 June 2015).

Haoda, C. (2005) "A Response to Telikom", *The National*, 3 June 2005, p. 23.

Henao, D. (2013) "Sharp Talk Founder on Using Facebook to Create PNG's Hottest Digital Conversations", *Radio Australia*, 6 August, available at: www.radioaustralia.net.au/international/radio/onairhighlights/sharp-talk-founder-on-using-Facebook-to-create-pngs-hottest-digital-conversations/1170362 (accessed 1 October 2015).

Human Rights Watch (2014) "World Report", *Human Rights Watch*, available at: www.hrw.org/sites/default/files/wr2014_web_0.pdf

Intermedia (2012) "Citizen Access to Information in Papua New Guinea", *Australian Broadcasting Corporation*, available at: www.abcinternationaldevelopment.net.au/sites/default/files/ABC%20PNG%20Report.pdf

Kero, G. (2013) "High Internet Costs Due to Small Market", *The National*, 2 May 2013, p. 21.

Logan, S. (2012) "Rausim! Digital Politics in Papua New Guinea", *State, Society and Governance in Melanesia*, Australian National University, available at: http://ips.cap.anu.edu.au/sites/default/files/2012_9.pdf

Logan, S., and Spark, C. (2015) (forthcoming) "ICTs and Moral Panic in PNG", *State, Society and Governance in Melanesia*, Australian National University.

Mansell, R. (2012) *Imagining the Internet: Communication, Innovation and Governance*, Oxford: Oxford University Press.

Michaels, E. (1986) *The Aboriginal Invention of Television in Central Australia, 1982–1985*, Canberra: Australian Institute of Aboriginal Studies: Canberra.

Mitchel, R. (2008) "Pathways to Telecommunication Reform", in B. Gomez (ed.), *Papua New Guinea Yearbook*, Port Moresby: The National and Cassoway Books, pp. 134–137.

PNG Technology News (2015) "PNG Censorship Office Plans to Filter Adult Content from the Internet", *PNG Technology News*, available at: http://tech.pngfacts.com/2015/02/png-censorship-office-plans-to-filter.html (accessed 1 July 2015).

Qiang, C., Rossotto, C., and Kimura, K. (2009) "Economic Impacts of Broadband", in *Information for Communications and Development: Extending Reach and Increasing Impact*, Washington, DC: World Bank, pp. 35–50.

Socialbakers (2012) "Papua New Guinea Facebook Statistics November 2012", *Socialbakers*, available at: www.socialbakers.com/Facebookstatistics/papua-new-guinea (accessed 1 February 2014).

Stanley, L. (2008) *Information & Communication Technology (ICT): Into the Future*, ICT Seminar, University of Papua New Guinea, Waigani.

Suwamaru, J. K. (2005) "The Status Quo and Coming Initiatives: Papua New Guinea", *ICT Technologies and Broadband Applications Conference*, Bangkok, Thailand.

Suwamaru, J. K. (2014) "Impact of Mobile Phone Usage in PNG", *State, Society and Governance in Melanesia*, Australian National University, available at: http://ips.cap.anu.edu.au/sites/default/files/IB-2014–41-Suwamaru-ONLINE.pdf

Suwamaru, J. K. (2015a) "Aspects of Mobile Phone Usage for Socioeconomic Development in Papua New Guinea", *State, Society and Governance in Melanesia*, Australian National University, available at: http://ips.cap.anu.au

Suwamaru, J. K. (2015b) "Emerging Challenges in Information and Communication Technologies for PNG", *State Society and Governance in Melanesia*, Australian National University.

Taylor, C. (2004) *Modern Social Imaginaries*, Durham, NC: Duke University Press.

Tinker, H. (1967) "Broken Backed States", *New Guinea and Australia, the Pacific and South-East Asia*, 2(3): 42–45.

Transparency International (2014) "Corruption Perceptions Index 2014", *Transparency International*, available at: www.transparency.org/cpi2014

UNESCO (2011) *PNG Literacy Rate Still a Mystery*, available at: www.unescobkk.org/news/article/png-literacy-rate-still-a-mystery-over-2-million-people-print-illiterate/ (accessed 1 October 2015).

Watson, A. (2011) "The Mobile Phone: The New Communication Drum of Papua New Guinea", Ph.D. thesis, Queensland University of Technology.

World Bank (2015) *Statistical Database*, available at: http://data.worldbank.org/ (accessed 1 July 2015).

Yandit, M. (2015) interview with J. Suwamaru, 27 May, Telikom District Office, Madang, Papua New Guinea.

20

MOBILE COMMUNICATION IN MYANMAR

Rich Ling, Chitra Panchapakesan,
Rajiv Aricat, Elisa Oreglia,
and May O. Lwin

Introduction: The Development of a "Digital Imagination"

To contextualize the development of the Internet in the Global South, it is useful to examine the adoption and use of mobile communication. Indeed, this communication form is often people's first meeting with mediated communication and digital information access. Mobile communication has affected both business processes and social life across the world. Mobile communication has reconfigured the work processes in a range of business sectors while bringing in economic benefits to the stakeholders (Cáceres *et al.* 2012; Donner and Escobari 2010; Ling *et al.* 2015). Mobile phones have helped achieve new spatio-temporalities in everyday experiences, connections, and relationships (Haddon 2013; Kraemer 2015). Mobile phones in post-colonial societies are at the nexus of the negotiation between modernity and traditional customs (Ling and Horst 2011). Mobile phones have challenged, but not replaced, the myths and folk beliefs surrounding morality, friendship, and socially acceptable relationships (Andersen 2013; Archambault 2013; Lipset 2013; Tenhunen 2008). Mobile phones have mediated gift exchanges in Papua New Guinea (Andersen 2013) and have helped arrange sexual liaisons in Jamaica (Horst and Miller 2005). Migrants have appropriated them to gain social support (Qiu 2008) and to communicate with family and loved ones in faraway homes (Madianou and Miller 2011). Indeed, the social and the professional overlap in the day-to-day use of mobile phones (Donner 2009).

Myanmar (also referred to as Burma)[1] was under military rule from 1962 to 2011, leading to low economic growth and pervasive underdevelopment.[2] Research pertaining to the changing landscape of Myanmar/Burma is limited, partly due to the decades-long closed-door policy of the country. Myanmar ranked 148 among 188 in the United Nation's Human Development Index (UNDP 2015). The mean years of schooling in the country is 4.1, and life expectancy is 65.9. About 66.9 percent of the working population makes less than US$2 a day, and half of the population is multidimensionally impoverished (UNDP 2015).

Mobile communication and digital access is quite fresh in Myanmar. This is a country that opened its doors to foreign private investment in the telecommunication sector after its transition to civilian rule in 2011. Until 2014, mobile communication was provided by the state monopoly Myanmar Post and Telecommunications. A subscription prior to 2014 could cost as much as US$1,500. The private mobile service providers Telenor and Ooredoo began to operate in 2014. This has reduced the price of a subscription to only about US$1.50.[3] Faster diffusion of mobile phones has ensued, which many commentators observed as a leapfrogging to the smartphone era (Vota 2015) and the eventual embrace of the Internet. Our field visits (August 2014 to July 2015) were timed in such a way as to capture the changes following the entry of private mobile operators to the country.

This chapter reports the findings of a year-long study in Myanmar.[4] The overall project explored the adoption of mobile phones, and in some cases, digital access among the Myanmar people. We report our observations regarding adoption and impact among a range of business sectors and social groups: trishaw operators, rag pickers and scrap handlers, brick makers, an Indian Tamil enclave, and farmers.

More broadly, we discuss how the adoption and use of mobile phones, and other forms of digital access, can be described as the development of what we call the "digital imagination" (Oreglia and Ling 2015). We see this as a process through which people came to realize both the benefits and also problems associated with the adoption of digital devices and access. The digital imagination is not necessarily based on actual experience with digital devices, but rather it is an individual's notion of the potentials and threats of digital access. We suggest this term encompasses:

- the technical, personal and social skills necessary to use the technology;
- a conceptualization of its potential benefits; and
- a recognition of the real and perceived dangers of use.

It describes the evolving expectations, fears, folk beliefs, and local knowledge about these devices. Once constructed, the digital imagination can be amended and extended as new functions are discovered, new uses are developed, and new threats are encountered. However, with the introduction of mobile communication, we begin to see how digital technology unfolds itself and encourages/demands that people develop a conceptualization of the potentials and the threats of the digital world.

In a sense, digital imagination is similar to digital literacy, but the latter notion is too narrow. Rather, our material illuminates how people discover the potentials as well as the pitfalls and problems with digital interaction, often before they have even actually used the technology. Our work shows how people developed a set of more, but sometimes less, precise mental images describing the potentials and limitations of digital media. These were initially shaped by their exposure to the technology, perhaps only via TV or imported films. Later, as their friends and family also used mobile phones, they could see the device in active use. They could speak to the mobile phone sales people to understand the costs. They could see how work colleagues started to use the mobile phone to address quotidian problems and to better organize their days. They could also begin to understand the expense, the vulnerability to scams, and the ways that the device either supported or contradicted their sense of what was culturally appropriate. They could begin to understand how the digital technology opens up access to sites that are potentially very useful, just as it opens up access to sites that are not necessarily in line with their sense of what is morally or culturally correct.

The trishaw operators, Tamils, rag pickers, tea growers, and brick makers we studied were in the throes of developing a digital imagination, regardless of whether they were adopters or rejecters. We saw how some marshaled their economic wherewithal in order to purchase and use a device. We also saw how they developed their repertoire of digital skills, and learned to exploit the potentials of the technology. We saw how they drew on intermediaries, or what Maria Bakardjieva and Richard Smith (2001) call "warm experts", to instruct them as they developed their skills. The advice they received from these sources may have been well founded, but it could also have been less reliable, second-hand, unfounded notions gathered through casual discussion. We also saw how the structure of work was changed by others' adoption of digital technology. In some cases, they could strive to join the group of users. In yet other cases, we saw that people were relegated to the remaining niches of non-users.

We have been able to witness a transition in how people conceptualize and carry out mediated communication and access online information. We have seen how people discover mobile communication as a tool that facilitates their lives, but also raises a new set of issues/threats that were not a part of their previous communication/coordination regime. We use the lens of digital imagination to describe this process and to put the spotlight on how newly minted users of mobile telephony (and more generally digital media) in the Global South learn to cope with the new technology.

Description of the Context and the Work

Mobile Communication and Social Life

Research has highlighted the ways in which mobile phones have enhanced feelings of security and better social coordination, while supporting social cohesion in the intimate sphere (Ling 2008; Ling and Yttri 2002; Matsuda 2005; Rettie 2008). Mobile phones provide opportunities for "phatic calls" (Haddon 2013), "social grooming" (Ling and Haddon 2001), and quasi-continual "connected presence" (Licoppe 2004). Matthew Smith et al. (2011) observed how mobile communication strengthened family ties, while promoting feelings of well-being. Although the benefits of using mobile phones have been uneven across socio-cultural groups and genders, underprivileged groups in Myanmar, such as low-skilled workers and small-scale enterprises, have increasingly benefited (Ling et al. 2015; Ureta 2008).

While there is rapid adoption of mobile communication in Myanmar, there are still limitations at the time of our data collection. The coverage in many semi-urban and rural areas is still weak, spotty, or unpredictable. In addition, there is no native Burmese operating system, and Burmese fonts typically need to be downloaded after the phone has been purchased. There are apps in Burmese, but more often than not people are faced with settings and apps that are in English or Chinese. This constitutes a significant barrier to use, especially for less educated users.

Mobile Communication and Small-scale Enterprises

Mobile phones have been adopted by small-scale enterprises across the world to facilitate timely price information (Jensen 2007), risk reduction, and better logistical coordination (Jagun et al. 2008; Molony 2006). Following the theory of individual addressability (Ling 2008), mobile phones facilitate micro-coordination, the flow of information (Ling and Yttri 2002), and the organization of logistics.

It follows that those without access can be on the losing side of the digital divide. Jonathan Donner and Marcela Escobari (2010: 652) observed that the benefits of using mobile phones were not uniform: "The benefits of mobile use accrue mostly (but not exclusively) to existing enterprises, in ways that amplify and accelerate material and informational flows, rather than fundamentally transforming them."

Indeed, the business structures, information flow, and day-to-day requirement of logistics vary across sectors. In our work we focused on a few trades—trishaw riders, rag pickers, brick makers, Indian Tamil communities, and farmers in Myanmar. These groups illuminate mobile phone use among low- and middle-income enterprises in the country (Ling *et al.* 2015).

Mobile Communication and Female Entrepreneurship

Millennium Development Goals emphasize an equitable access of information and communication technology (ICT) across class, caste, and gender (United Nations 2015). The "bottom of the pyramid" women entrepreneurs have benefited from the use of mobile phones, like the case of Grameen Phone in Bangladesh (Bayes 2001; Dolan 2012). ICTs have also supported women as they take up entrepreneurial tasks in developing regions (Chew *et al.* 2015). Migrant mothers have utilized mobile phones for long-distance transnational calling, which has helped them retain sustained contact with families (Madianou and Miller 2011). However, the benefits of using ICTs in entrepreneurship have been, in some cases, limited by culturally based gender barriers. Viju Mathew (2010) noted that the extended availability and usage of ICT among women in the Middle East have not been on a par with that of men, and Cara Wallis (2008) noted that despite the widespread use of mobile phones by female migrants in Beijing, the patriarchal structures have remained unaltered.

Socio-cultural norms determine the freedom that women enjoy in a society, which can be a determinant of their ICT adoption and usage. Burmese women have traditionally played active roles both in social life and in entrepreneurial tasks (Khaing 1984). However, as a culture deeply rooted in Buddhist principles, there are religious and historic justifications for Burmese women's unequal status in society and in public life (Harriden 2012).[5] In other cases, minority groups have a more patriarchal system that sets certain boundaries on women's ownership and use of mobile phones. In recent years, mobile phone operators have increasingly focused on the development needs of women (Barrie 2015). The status of women has been a particular focus of this work.

Methods

The primary method involved ethnographic interviews and participant observation in a number of townships in Myanmar. The townships upon which we focused span both urban and rural communities across the vast country. The geographical locales covered by the research team include:

*   Bago—around 80 kilometers (50 miles) north east of Yangon;
*   Chaungzon—an island-township in Lower Myanmar;
*   Kyaikto—in Lower Myanmar;
*   Mawlamyine—in Lower Myanmar;
*   Mandalay and surrounding villages;
*   Hsipaw and surrounding villages.

The researchers lived in the townships and interacted with the urban and rural population with the help of translators who were Burmese nationals. In the two phases of the study, the team interacted with several hundred persons. We formally interviewed 226 individuals from different walks of life—trishaw and motorbike drivers, women, farmers, gold traders, rag pickers, scrap handlers, fishermen, and students. Interviews were held in homes, work sites, markets on the street, or in tea shops. While interviewing a respondent, it was not uncommon for his/her co-workers or family members to gather around and add bits and pieces of information to the interview. A broader picture on the appropriation of mobile phones by Burmese society was created using the information from these supplemented interviews.

Our study respondents were asked about their adoption and use of mobile phones, as well as how ownership and/or usage of the phone played into their work and social life. About two-thirds of our respondents had some kind of access to mobile phones by the end of our study. However, we took care to interview those without mobile phones—for example, the rag pickers on the street. We were interested to know their understanding of mobile telephony, and how the transition to a mobile culture had affected them.[6]

All the interviews were transcribed, and both the transcripts and field notes were coded using an online application for qualitative data analysis (Dedoose). The major findings of the study—grouped according to livelihoods or social classes—are discussed in the following sections.

Major Findings

Trishaw (Rickshaw) Operators

The first paper from the project examined the use of mobile communication among trishaw operators (Ling *et al.* 2015). The article examined the changes brought about by the introduction of mobile telephony on this sector of the economy. In this case the focus was on the logistical and power dimensions of mobile communication.

Trishaw operators often occupy a lower position in the economic hierarchy. Their job of transporting people and goods is physically demanding. They often make as little as US$2 per day. In broad strokes, the paper found that trishaw operators faced the decision whether or not to invest in a mobile phone. For some, this represented an exciting new opportunity, since it allowed them a new way to coordinate their daily work. For others—in particular older operators—the cost of obtaining a subscription, buying a phone, and learning how to use it was seemingly beyond them.

Those who had decided to adopt mobile communication displayed a certain entrepreneurial spirit—in effect, they had embraced the digital imagination. They grasped how the device would allow them to contact eventual customers and to arrange their work. These operators had given their phone numbers to important customers, often shopkeepers who regularly needed to transport goods locally. They noted that this helped them to better coordinate their tasks since the shopkeepers could contact them as needed. In some cases, ownership and use of the mobile phone had become structured into their daily routines. An example of this approach to mobile communication is seen in the case of U Aye Kyaw, an operator from Kyaikto. He said that were his phone broken or lost he would quickly purchase a cheap replacement so his important customers could reach him. In this way, he had adopted the stance of needing to be individually addressable via the mobile phone (Ling 2008; Ling and Donner 2009) to facilitate micro-coordination (Ling and Yttri 2002).

The use of mobile telephony by these trishaw operators also meant that there were new considerations to be dealt with in their work. One issue that the operators were quick to note is that they were not reachable if they moved outside the mobile telephone coverage area. This constrained their radius in some cases, since they did not want to risk missing calls from their primary customers. These primary clients had taken on greater importance for the operators. Indeed, this is described as a patron–client relationship. While at one level there was an independence afforded by the phone, it was also the locus of newly developed dependencies within the socio-economic sphere of the operators. On one hand, the mobile phone helps the operator to realize a more balanced flow of income, while simultaneously making them vulnerable to the vagaries of the digital world. It was a source of income and the device through which power-based interactions with customers were worked out.

In other cases, trishaw operators were not able to purchase a mobile phone because of the cruelty of poverty and the weight of aging. For those operators who have not, or cannot, acquire a mobile phone, there are other considerations that arise from the diffusion of mobile communication in Myanmar. The mobile phone disrupts the established ways of finding fares that were based on the use of trishaw stations where the customers took the first rider in a queue. The mobile phone means that customers can simply call a favored rider, skipping the more egalitarian system of the trishaw queue. As the system of calling riders directly spreads, there are fewer fares left for the riders who rely on the queue system or prowling to find fares. Since the cost/mastery of mobile telephony is perhaps beyond the means of these operators, it is possible that they will see their opportunities to get fares become more limited.

The differences between these two approaches to the adoption/rejection of mobile communication point, in a broader way, to the issue of digital imagination that will be further developed below. Mobile communication is working its way into how the trishaw sector functions. Most likely, it will become taken for granted in the coming years. In the period of transition, it is possible to see the schism between those who adopted and those who did not. In both cases, there were new issues that the users needed to resolve. These come to light as we examine their situation and probe into the dimensions of this socio-technical transition.

Rag Pickers

The second paper from the project examined the position of rag pickers and scrap handlers in Myanmar. Formal systems of waste collection remain few and far between in developing countries. Recyclable scrap is a source of income for individuals who collect and integrate the items, and eventually send them for recycling. In Myanmar, this business involves individuals working at different levels with varying capital and land investments. At the bottom of the business chain is the collector who goes around the street to collect empty cans and bottles from houses and restaurants. Scrap integrators at the next level buy the items from the street collectors and stockpile the collected scrap prior to transporting it to a recycler in big cities. Knowledge of price fluctuations is key in actualizing profit in the business. Integrators also have to tread a fine line between stockpiled scrap, which represents invested capital, and the target of attaining maximum profit for the scrap items. Thus, the scrap integrators constantly update themselves on the demand for a specific item (for example, tin, aluminum, or iron, as the case may be) for a recycler to sell off the stockpiled scrap materials and to actualize higher profits.

The primary role of the mobile phone in this sector was to make available the price information on a range of scrap items to the integrators. Depending on this information, the scrap integrators instructed their employees, who go door to door to collect scrap, on whether to pick an item or not. "Every day I telephone to Sawbwagyigone,[7] even though I don't send my load there that day. I just want to know the price. Every day the rate changes . . ." (Ismail, scrap integrator).

Scrap integrators sold most of their items to recyclers in Yangon. Depending on which item had greater demand among the recyclers, the scrap integrators in smaller towns transported and sold that item at a higher price. The information on the rise or fall in demand of a scrap item is passed on to the integrators on their mobile phones. In view of this, it was incumbent on the integrators to equip their rag pickers with a mobile phone. It reduced uncertainty over which items to collect and what price to pay for it, especially in the case of unique scrap materials whose resale value and current price are not known to the street collectors. Mobile phones also helped integrators to arrange transport and other logistics.

> When the workers didn't have a mobile phone, they went around . . . and when they saw things, they could not decide whether to buy it or not. They just bought them and came here. It might be a loss for me. Now it's not like that . . . they directly call me. Then I tell them whether to buy the item or not, [and] how much to pay . . .
>
> (Venkaiah, scrap integrator)

As a consequence, those rag pickers who worked independently, without the possibilities of social connections, were further sidelined due to their non-usage of the mobile phone. They were unwilling to take a risk by collecting a rare but "costly" item such as a damaged motor, but contented themselves with regular low-margin scrap items like cans and bottles. Thus, we observed a widening divide between those who effectively used the mobile phone in their business (for example, the scrap integrator with capital investment and storage space for stockpiling the scrap), and those who remained outside the knowledge syndicate supported by mobile phones (for example, the rag pickers who collected scrap and sold it to an integrator on a daily basis, without any knowledge on the fluctuations in price). This finding thus foregrounds the broader debate on digital divide.

Brick Makers

The Myanmar brick industry employs a large number of the rural poor in the developing world, especially the landless poor who seek job prospects in the urban regions (Majumder 2015; Shah 2006). While sustainability concerns have been raised against the industry's overexploitation of land as well as ground-water resources, demands from the construction sector have led to a steady growth in the industry (Franco *et al.* 2015). As the work is seasonal, the industry has to adapt to price fluctuations in the peak—between October and April— and off-peak seasons (Aung 2014).

In Myanmar, brick-making units are divided broadly as large and small. Large brick kilns that employ 150 to 200 workers are owned by private individuals, whereas small kilns with 40 to 60 workers are usually run on land leased out by private individuals, or owned by the government.[8] In large kilns, workers are divided into teams supervised by a team leader, generally a senior male worker. Team leaders and truck drivers have been provided with mobile phones by the employer, mainly to manage work and arrange logistics related to the delivery of finished products and the collection of firewood for the kilns from distant forests.

With this top-down introduction of mobile phones in the brick-making units, the unit owners eventually achieved greater control over the work process. Inexpensive feature phones given to the team leaders and truck drivers hardly provided any entertainment opportunity for the users, but were used only as a means to update the owner regarding work-related matters, and to receive instructions from him. U Thiha Naing, a team leader in a large brick kiln who had been provided with a mobile feature phone by the employer six months earlier, recalled that the most important use of his mobile phone was to give updates. Mobile phones also had instrumental uses in times of emergency, helping the team leaders to call for assistance.

> The employer pushes me to produce as many bricks as possible. I, on my part, have to report to him if there is any problem with an employee [in my team] or with the machine.
>
> (U Thiha Naing, team leader in a brick kiln)

> There have been instances of workers falling into the burning pit. Before the advent of mobile phones, someone had to come [5km] down to my place to inform me of the accident. These delays were dangerous. Now, I get the news very fast, and I attend to the problem immediately.
>
> (Ko Hein, large brick kiln owner)

Provision of mobile phones to these workers shows how the owners rethink their operations in light of access to digital technology. They are working out the digital imagination in order to facilitate the production process.

Most of the employees in the brick kilns are rural-to-urban migrants from the same township or nearby regions. They stay at the work sites throughout the brick-making season. Hence, there is a demand for social communication among these migrant workers, who want to communicate with their families and their community back home. This demand is met by the sharing of mobile phones provided by the employer, or in rare cases, sharing of phones owned by a few workers themselves. In the latter case, the phones are used not only for making social calls, but for accessing entertainment content, games, and for social networking. Sharing of mobile phones was thus woven into a web reciprocity of the workers. As most of the workers in a team are originally from the same village, there is a greater willingness to share the device.

The privileges that helped the mobile phone users to incorporate both kinds of uses—instrumental and expressive—into their daily routines were not the same. Brick unit owners could seamlessly subscribe to the mobile phone's dual articulation of facilitating instrumental and expressive tasks. This is particularly observed in the case of a woman contractor, who managed her business while running her household from the kiln. Ma Htet Thiri, aged 30 and a mother of two, oversaw a team of 40–50 workers, ran the kiln, organized transport, and secured buyers. In addition, she used her mobile phone to coordinate her household work, even though she had to stay in the brick field for long hours. As she explained: "[My] mobile phone has improved the way I organize family matters, even when I am here in the brick field."

In contrast, at the level of workers, this dual articulation, the synergy of instrumental and expressive uses of the mobile, was often challenged by lack of resources to own a mobile phone, lack of entertainment available on shared devices, and multidimensional deprivation. The findings revealed the unequal socio-economic status of lower level workers and employers in the brick-making sector, which was also reflected in their mobile phone usage.

Tamil Enclaves

In 1824, the British started importing Indians to Myanmar as soldiers, laborers, and coolies (Kesavapany et al. 2008). After Myanmar's independence in 1948, Indians started leaving the country in rescue ships and other modes due to unsafe conditions and insecurities

(Bhattacharya 2003). Communities of those remaining Indians in Myanmar are the Telugu (from the state of Andhra Pradesh), Bengali, Bihari, Gujarati, Marwari, Oriya, Sikh, and Tamil. Tamils are the majority among people of Indian descent. The number of overseas Indians in Myanmar is estimated to be 2.9 million. The majority of the Indian population lives within Yangon Division and Bago Division (Kesavapany et al. 2008).

Another study in the project focused on Tamils in five small, exclusive Tamil villages near Bago. These villagers owned small patches of agricultural land. They produced crops ranging from rice to pulses. These were consumed locally, with the excess being sold in nearby markets. In addition, they engaged in small-scale animal husbandry. Most of the men from these villages work abroad in Malaysia or in other larger cities like Yangon and Bago. They were able to get jobs in factories, on poultry farms, or in shops. The women stay in the villages to care for parents and children. They also work in the fields of larger landowners during crop seasons for daily wages.

A major reason to own a phone is to stay in touch with the men who are working outside the village. Some are working in nearby towns and visit home once a month, whereas the ones living abroad may be away for years. If the men need to convey information or just check how their family members are, they have to make a visit, in the case of those working locally, or call. According to our informants, until recently there were few mobile phones in the villages, making communication difficult.

The informants noted that in one village there was a single landline phone in the grocery shop. Otherwise, there were fewer than five phones for 55 houses and around 200 people, including one Chinese smartphone (gifted to the family from the son working in Malaysia), and four feature phones bought locally.

In a second village, residents walked about 30 minutes to use an acquaintance's phone in a neighboring village. During the monsoon period they could not walk, but relied on boats to reach the neighboring village. This made it difficult for them to stay in touch with family members who were living and working outside the village. If the callee did not have a mobile phone, this further complicated things, since the two interlocutors needed to work out a time when both would agree to be near the landline phone. Indeed, the informants spoke of complex systems relying on children in the homes with phones coming to them to let them know that a husband or son had called and would try to call back at some specific time in the near future. At the time of our interviews, mobile phones were starting to arrive. There were around ten phones for 48 homes and 150 persons. Several of them were smartphones that could eventually facilitate Internet access. Others were feature phones that husbands and sons who were working in Malaysia had gifted to parents and wives.

Thus, the former awkward system of making and receiving calls was being superseded by access to mobile devices. Having a phone at home helped them communicate with their family. Those families with a mobile phone did not have to disturb others while asking for the favor of using their phone. Families without phones did not have to travel as far to place a call.

A challenge associated with mobile phone ownership noted by the villagers is the difficulty of charging the batteries, since there is no electric power in the villages. Our informants noted that they either depend on neighbors who have solar power or on a separate battery-charging system to charge their phones. As one might expect, in order to conserve and maximize battery usage, the mobile phones are primarily used for instrumental communication purposes such as calling family members. However, smartphone users with battery-charging capabilities were able to understand how the device could be used as an entertainment terminal—they developed a dimension of the digital imagination when they downloaded Tamil video clips and songs for entertainment.

In the villages, it is the men who are mostly in charge of the phones. The arrival of the mobile phone becomes, in some ways, a lens through which we can examine the functioning of gender roles and patriarchy in the villages. Indeed, the telephone in its time, and now the mobile phone, has been seen as contested. The landline telephone was extensively discussed in the USA in the 1930s since it allowed unchaperoned interaction between the genders (Fischer 1992: 186). The mobile phone was also seen as a mixed blessing among many groups, including the Amish (Umble 2000) and Orthodox Jews.[9] While there is an undeniable functionality in the device, it also engenders fear that it will give voice to interactions that run counter to that which is seen as culturally acceptable. Our analysis also showed how adoption of the mobile phone raises concerns regarding the position of women. For example, it is not considered good to let unmarried girls own mobile phones, as they fear it will lead to romantic affairs. The loss of parental (or paternal) control over daughters is a theme that has been seen in other contexts (Cohen *et al.* 2007). Thus, as with other research, our findings indicate that the lowered communicative threshold afforded by mobile telephony challenges the sense of control within the family. At the same time, once a woman is married, she may receive a phone from her husband. Our informants noted that married women own and use mobile phones gifted by their husbands. These provide the husbands a channel of communication/control when they are working away from their villages. Thus the device is one more way in which the women are bounded. Our analysis shows that they are not only controlled by their husbands, but also by their parents, in-laws, and other elders.

There are variations in the degree to which fathers limit mobile phone access and in the way that it is controlled. For example, a 22-year-old Tamil woman living in Bago, Ma Kali, received a smartphone from her brother. However, she could only use it on condition that she would not open a Facebook account. Thus, while interpersonal interaction afforded by voice calls was acceptable, the social world of Facebook was beyond the pale. Seen through the lens of digital imagination, the conceptualization of Facebook content obviously runs counter to that which is seen as culturally wholesome.

Patriarchy was also exercised when fathers demanded to see what was stored on the phone. Ma Azhaki, who manages her father's shoe shop, said:

> The phone shows you the world in your hands. But I don't have full freedom over my phone. I am a 29-year-old unmarried girl. If my father leaves me alone with my phone for some time, he makes sure to check the phone to monitor my activities when he is back. My father even knows my Facebook password and checks my online activities. If he finds out something in my phone that he doesn't like, there will be a fight and he may even beat me up.

American teens reported the same types of parental overview. When interviewed in 2009, they noted the practice of regularly erasing the memory of their phones to avoid conflicts with parents (Lenhart *et al.* 2010). The development of cloud-based services such as Facebook mean that simply erasing material is no longer viable.

For their part, the young women with whom we spoke noted that it is not always good to own a phone, as other men may call and disturb them. They noted that if a girl owns a phone, men may get their number and pester them with regular unwanted calls. Thus, the fears of the fathers are to some degree founded. The position of women is not necessarily being changed by the adoption of mobile communication. While it may facilitate some activities, such as staying in touch with family, it also becomes a route through which unwanted attention is channeled. Indeed, this potential was noted by Rakow and Navarro (1993) in their early work on mobile communication. By contrast, similarly aged young men use their phones freely, as it is not considered to pose any threat to them. This finding thus foregrounds the broader debate on gender bias.

Mobile Phones in the Agricultural Sector

Although statistics on occupation by sector in Myanmar are lacking, agriculture is a key sector of the economy, both in terms of contribution to the gross domestic product and in terms of employment. Farming and fishing provide livelihoods for millions of people in Myanmar, and the sector is undergoing profound changes, like the rest of the economy. Until 2014, people working in the agricultural sector could not afford mobile phones, nor was there often coverage outside urban areas. As of the fall of 2014, however, they were slowly among those who are able to participate in the country's mobile phone revolution.

Against this background, we wanted to explore whether mobiles could make a difference in farming practices at large, from seeking advice on what/how to cultivate different crops, to negotiating with traders and markets. The consequences of the diffusion of mobile phones among small-scale farmers and food producers in the Global South is the object of many studies (Fafchamps and Minten 2012; Jensen 2007; Srinivasan and Burrell 2013; World Bank 2012), and this is the literature where we situate ourselves, as we set out to explore how farmers were integrating or thinking of mobile phones in their lives. A common theme in the villages we visited was to conceptualize what they would do once they could afford a mobile phone.

Although we talked to farmers in different areas of the country, in this section we refer mostly to farmers in the area near Mandalay, the second largest city in Myanmar. The area produces rice, cotton, and pulses (Thorpe 2014). Small agricultural villages are dotted along the main roads. Many of the villagers have non-agricultural jobs in Mandalay or in nearby towns, which means increased disposable income for local families. As a consequence, mobile phones had started to appear around 2012. According to our informants, the phones are more likely to be owned by males rather than females, since the former have more disposable income, and they are not shared, even within families and among husbands and wives. The initial and key use is to coordinate transportation to workplaces outside the village. Especially during monsoon season, villagers need to know whether the road is passable by motorbike, and whether public transport is running along the main road. Mobile phones are used to coordinate shared rides with people living in other villages.

A number of farmers also use mobiles to coordinate with traders and market sellers in Mandalay. As in other sectors, the mobile phones facilitate immobility in that they can call buyers when they are ready to sell, instead of wasting time on trips. They noted that they can keep in touch with wholesale sellers about deliveries and quantities, but not about prices. Our findings echo those of other studies, underscoring the importance of mobiles in supporting the logistics of commercial relations in the marketing chain rather than creating new ones, even when the existing ties are exploitative (Aker and Mbiti 2010; Burrell and Oreglia 2013; Srinivasan and Burrell 2013). This was seen among the farmers in and around the market town of Hsipaw. Many established traders have invested in a mobile phone in spite of the cost as they are seen as a necessity.

The use of mobile telephony is spreading, albeit, as noted above, in fits and starts. There is, however, the adoption of the device. As a pineapple trader commented when we asked her whether the numbers she had written on the wall in front of the landline were the numbers of other traders: "Of course not! These are the numbers of the workers in the field, in case we need to reach them. Now everybody has a phone, even the laundry woman!" For smallhold farmers or casual field laborers, mobile phones are increasingly seen as a way to be reachable. Indeed, as more people have mobiles, those who do not are left out of the pool of casual laborers, creating a situation where they need to spend more money to maintain past levels of access (Ling *et al.* 2015).

The case of tea growers on the hills around Hsipaw is particularly interesting. This is an activity carried out in the hill villages where the Ta'ang, or Palaung, people live. It is a small-scale family business that is carried out using very traditional and mostly unmechanized methods. Now that mobile phones are becoming available, albeit with poor signal strength, the same story is repeated. Tea growers who have bought mobiles are now using them to stay in touch with the same traders they used in the past, because of habit, expertise, and old credit relationships. The phones are making it easier to coordinate logistics, but they are not being used to find out about better agricultural techniques or about fertilizers, etc. Most of the innovation efforts by more entrepreneurial farmers are focused on the mechanization of existing processes, as it can speed up the time it takes to get the tea leaves ready for sale and increase yield. Market information via the mobile phone was not mentioned in the interviews.

Ultimately, for many farmers, the importance of the mobile phone revolution is in being able to talk to other people in real time—a feat that is often taken for granted in countries with reliable landlines, but that is still novel and much appreciated in places where the telephone was a rarity. Many interviewees recounted the long waits, expenses, and complications of making phone calls on public phones, which is still a reality for many Burmese.

Development of a Digital Imagination

The lens provided by the digital imagination (Oreglia and Ling 2015) helps to tell the unfolding story of digital access in Myanmar. The country's transition to mobile communication has provided perhaps one of the last opportunities to study how people adopt and adapt to a fundamental shift in mediated communication. Our analysis has shown that it is quickly adopted by small-scale entrepreneurs because of its functionality. In addition, it also provides a channel for social contact and entertainment. Our analysis also shows that the potentials are unevenly distributed. In a broader way, the material shows how the meeting between mediated communication and traditional culture is worked out in the everyday lives of people.

The digital imagination helps us to see how the adoption process draws on a set of insights, folklores, second-hand techniques, and cultural appropriations in their imagining of digital access. Our findings concur with past literature, indicating that there are both societal and economic benefits afforded by mobile telephony and digital access. Indeed, they enable greater social and commercial connectedness. Our observations among the bricklayers, rag pickers, and trishaw riders in particular reveal how mobile communication strengthened business ties, marketing opportunities, and entrepreneurship. This is because the device facilitated coordination and the organization of logistics. At a more macro level, advantages gained by mobile users include greater access to information, and better home and community links, hence ensuring a greater sense of well-being.

There were, however, modifications to this positive description of mobile communication. Those people who were too impoverished to afford the device were not only denied these benefits, but they eventually saw others who had a phone out-competing them for various types of work. For example, the elderly trishaw operators and the independent rag pickers who had less capacity to earn may be squeezed out. Further, the benefits of mobile telephony are not evenly felt across the genders. This was seen in the situation of the Tamil women where, for example, Ma Azhaki faced being abused if her use of Facebook ran counter to the moral compass of her father. In this case, the understanding and use of digital technology was tilted in favor of males. Use of mobile phones was a tool with which to exert male dominance. In sum, we saw both benefits and also problems associated with the adoption of mobile communication, and the lens of the digital imagination helped us to frame our insights.

We have been privileged to see how people develop an understanding of digital technology and its role in their lives. We have had the privilege to see how people discover that mobile communication facilitates various dimensions of their lives. We have also had the opportunity to see how digital technology raises a new set of issues/threats that were not a part of their previous communication/coordination regime. It is for these reasons that broader Internet histories need to pay heed to cases like Burma (and indeed the Global South generally) as it comes to grips with the social consequences of digitalization.

Notes

1. Myanmar and Burma are used interchangeably in this chapter, without elaborating on the political motivations behind these names.
2. Myanmar's PPP GDP/capita for 2014 is $4,800, 170th among 230 countries. For more details, see www.cia.gov/library/publications/the-world-factbook/geos/bm.html
3. See http://qz.com/62523/this-sim-card-used-to-cost-3000-democracy-may-bring-it-down-to-zero/
4. This project has been financed by Telenor and Nanyang Technological University.
5. Fundamental to the idea of male superiority is the concept of *Hpon*, considered to be a natural and abstract quality that gives higher authority and status to men. In Theravada Buddhist societies like Myanmar, *Hpon* has a hold on social, cultural, and religious practices, suggesting an inferior status for women in comparison to men (Thein 2015).
6. It must be noted that it was not always feasible to interview the lowest persons in the economic pyramid. Issues such as the language barrier, social withdrawal, and indeed some mental conditions limited access. In such cases, we had to rely on the information provided by our translators who doubled as informants in the study.
7. Sawbwagyigone is an industrial area in Yangon where most of the respondents sent their consignments.
8. Following the reforms in 2011, the military has loosened its grip on economic holdings.
9. See http://venishmartem.com/devices/mobiles/item/kosher-smartphones

References

Aker, J. C., and Mbiti, I. M. (2010) "Mobile Phones and Economic Development in Africa", October, doi:10.2139/ssrn.1693963.

Andersen, B. (2013) "Tricks, Lies, and Mobile Phones: 'Phone Friend' Stories in Papua New Guinea", *Culture, Theory and Critique*, 54(3): 318–334.

Archambault, J. S. (2013) "Cruising through Uncertainty: Cell Phones and the Politics of Display and Disguise in Inhambane, Mozambique", *American Ethnologist*, 40(1): 88–101.

Aung, H. (2014) "Sand and Stone Industries Thrive as Brick Begins to Sink", *Myanmar Business Today*, available at: http://mmbiztoday.com/articles/sand-and-stone-industries-thrive-brick-begins-sink

Bakardjieva, M., and Smith, R. (2001) "The Internet in Everyday Life: Computer Networking from the Standpoint of the Domestic User", *New Media & Society*, 3(1): 67–83.

Barrie, G. (2015) "Connected Women: Case Study—Ooredoo Myanmar: Mobile and Maternal Health", *Grupe Spécial Mobile Association*, available at: www.gsma.com/connectedwomen/wp-content/uploads/2015/03/Ooredoo-Myanmar-Case-study-30March15-FINAL1.pdf

Bayes, A. (2001) "Infrastructure and Rural Development: Insights from a Grameen Bank Village Phone Initiative in Bangladesh", *Agricultural Economics*, 25(2–3): 261–272.

Bhattacharya, S. (2003) "Indian Diaspora in Myanmar", in Sarva Daman Singh and Mahavir Singh (eds), *Indians Abroad*, Gurgaon, Haryana: Hope India Publications, and London: Greenwich Millennium. Published for Maulana Abul Kalam Azad Institute of Asian Studies, Kolkata, pp. 172–204.

Burrell, J., and Oreglia, E. (2013) "The Myth of Market Price Information: Mobile Phones and Epistemology in ICTD." Working Paper No. 1 (NSF Grant: 1027310).

Cáceres, R., Barrantes, A. A., Cavero, M., and Huaroto, C. (2012) "The Impacts of the Use of Mobile Telephone Technology on the Productivity of Micro-and Small Enterprises: An Exploratory Study into the Carpentry and Cabinet-Making Sector in Villa El Salvador", *Information Technologies & International Development*, 8(4).

Chew, H. E., Ilavarasan, V. P., and Levy, M. R. (2015) "Mattering Matters: Agency, Empowerment, and Mobile Phone Use by Female Microentrepreneurs", *Information Technology for Development*, 21(4): 523–542.

Cohen, A., Lemish, D., and Schejter, A. M. (2007) *The Wonder Phone in the Land of Miracles: Mobile Telephony in Israel*, Cresskill: Hampton Press.

Dolan, C. (2012) "The New Face of Development: The 'Bottom of the Pyramid' Entrepreneurs", *Anthropology Today*, 28(4): 3–7.

Donner, J. (2009) "Blurring Livelihoods and Lives: The Social Uses of Mobile Phones and Socioeconomic Development", *Innovations: Technology, Governance, Globalization*, 4(1): 91–101.

Donner, J., and Escobari, M. X. (2010) "A Review of Evidence on Mobile Use by Micro and Small Enterprises in Developing Countries", *Journal of International Development*, 22: 641–658.

Fafchamps, M., and Minten, B. (2012) "The Impact of SMS-Based Agricultural Information on India", *The World Bank Economic Review*, 26(3): 383–414.

Fischer, C. (1992) *America Calling: A Social History of the Telephone to 1940*, Berkeley, CA: University of California Press.

Franco, J., Twomey, H., Ju, K. K., Vervest, P., and Kramer, T. (2015) "The Meaning of Land in Myanmar: A Primer", *Transnational Institute*, Amsterdam, available at: www.tni.org/files/publication-downloads/tni_primer-burma-digitaal.pdf

Haddon, L. (2013) "Mobile Media and Children", *Mobile Media & Communication*, 1(1): 89–95.

Harriden, J. (2012) *The Authority of Influence: Women and Power in Burmese History*, Copenhagen: NIAS Press.

Horst, H. A., and Miller, D. (2005) "From Kinship to Link-up: Cell Phones and Social Networking in Jamaica", *Current Anthropology*, 46(5): 755–778.

Jagun, A., Heeks, R., and Whalley, J. (2008) "The Impact of Mobile Telephony on Developing Country Micro-Enterprise: A Nigerian Case Study", *Information Technologies and International Development*, 4(4): 47–65.

Jensen, R. (2007) "The Digital Provide: Information (Technology), Market Performance and Welfare in the South Indian Fisheries Sector", *The Quarterly Journal of Economics*, 122(3): 879–924.

Kesavapany, K., Mani, A., and Ramasamy, P. (2008) *Rising India and Indian Communities in East Asia*, Singapore: Institute of Southeast Asian Studies.

Khaing, M. M. (1984) *The World of Burmese Women*, London: Zed.

Kraemer, D. (2015) "'Do You Have a Mobile?' Mobile Phone Practices and the Refashioning of Social Relationships in Port Vila Town", *The Australian Journal of Anthropology*, doi:10.1111/taja.12165.

Lenhart, A., Ling, R., Campbell, S., and Purcell, K. (2010) "Teens and Mobile Phones", *Pew Research Center*, available at: www.pewInternet.org/2010/04/20/teens-and-mobile-phones/

Licoppe, C. (2004) "Connected Presence: The Emergence of a New Repertoire for Managing Social Relationships in a Changing Communications Technoscape", *Environment and Planning D: Society & Space*, 22(1): 135–156.

Ling, R. (2008) *New Tech, New Ties: How Mobile Communication Is Reshaping Social Cohesion*, Cambridge, MA: MIT Press.

Ling, R., and Donner, J. (2009) *Mobile Communication: Digital Media and Society Series*, Malden: Polity Books.

Ling, R., and Haddon, L. (2001) "Mobile Telephony and the Coordination of Mobility in Everyday Life", in J. E. Katz (ed.), *Machines that Become Us: The Social Context of Personal Communication Technology*, New Brunswick, NJ: Center for Urban Policy Research Press, pp. 245–265.

Ling, R., and Horst, H. A. (2011) "Introduction, Mobile Communication in the Global South: Special Issue of New Media & Society", *New Media & Society*, 13(3): 3–6.

Ling, R., and Yttri, B. (2002) "Hyper-Coordination via Mobile Phones in Norway", in J. E. Katz and M. Aakhus (eds), *Perpetual Contact: Mobile Communication, Private Talk, Public Performance*, Cambridge: Cambridge University Press, pp. 139–169.

Ling, R., Oreglia, E., Aricat, R. G., Panchapakesan, C., and Lwin, M. (2015) "The Use of Mobile Phones Among Trishaw Operators in Myanmar", *International Journal of Communication*, 9(18): 3583–3600.

Lipset, D. (2013) "Mobail: Moral Ambivalence and the Domestication of Mobile Telephones in Peri-Urban Papua New Guinea", *Culture, Theory and Critique*, 54(3): 335–354.

Madianou, M., and Miller, D. (2011) "Mobile Phone Parenting: Reconfiguring Relationships Between Filipina Migrant Mothers and their Left-behind Children", *New Media & Society*, 13(3): 457–470.

Majumder, B. (2015) "Forced Migration of Labourers to Brick Kilns in Uttar Pradesh", *Economic & Political Weekly*, 50(26/27): 19–26.

Mathew, V. (2010) "Women Entrepreneurship in the Middle East: Understanding Barriers and Use of ICT for Entrepreneurship Development", *International Entrepreneurship and Management Journal*, 6(2): 163–181.

Matsuda, M. (2005) "Mobile Communication and Selective Sociality", in I. Mizuko, D. Okabe, and M. Matsuda (eds), *Personal, Portable, Pedestrian: Mobile Phones in Japanese Life*, Cambridge, MA: MIT Press, pp. 123–142.

Molony, T. (2006) "'I Don't Trust the Phone; It Always Lies': Trust and Information and Communication Technologies in Tanzanian Micro-and Small Enterprises", *Information Technologies & International Development*, 3(4): 67–83.

Oreglia, E., and Ling, R. (2015) "Digital Imagination", in *Proceedings of the ICTD 2015 Conference*, Singapore: ICTD.

Qiu, J. L. (2008) "Working-Class ICTs, Migrants, and Empowerment in South China", *Asian Journal of Communication*, 18(4): 333–347.

Rakow, L. F., and Navarro, V. (1993) "Remote Mothering and the Parallel Shift: Women Meet the Cellular Telephone", *Critical Studies in Mass Communication: CSMC: A Publication of the Speech Communication Association*, 10: 144–157.

Rettie, R. (2008) "Mobile Phones as Network Capital: Facilitating Connections", *Mobilities*, 3(2): 291–311.

Shah, A. (2006) "The Labour of Love: Seasonal Migration from Jharkhand to the Brick Kilns of Other States in India", *Contributions to Indian Sociology*, 40(1): 91–118.

Smith, M. L., Spence, R., and Rashid, A. T. (2011) "Mobile Phones and Expanding Human Capabilities", *Information Technologies & International Development*, 7(3): 77–88.

Srinivasan, J., and Burrell, J. (2013) "Revisiting the Fishers of Kerala, India", in *Proceedings of the Sixth International Conference on Information and Communication Technologies and Development: Full Papers—Volume 1*, available at: https://msu.edu/~steinfie/ICT4D_White_Paper_2013.pdf

Tenhunen, S. (2008) "Mobile Technology in the Village: ICTs, Culture, and Social Logistics in India", *Journal of the Royal Anthropological Institute*, 14(3): 515–534.

Thein, P. T. (2015) "Gender Equality and Cultural Norms in Myanmar", paper presented at the *1st International Conference on Burma/Myanmar Studies*, Chiang Mai, Thailand.

Thorpe, J. (2014) "Delivering Prosperity in Myanmar's Dryzone: Lessons from Mandalay and Magwe on Realizing the Economic Potential of Small-Scale Farmers", *Oxfam International*, available at: http://policy-practice.oxfam.org.uk/publications/delivering-prosperity-in-myanmars-dryzone-lessons-from-mandalay-and-magwe-on-re-325412

Umble, D. Z. (2000) *Holding the Line: The Telephone in Old Order Mennonite and Amish Life*, Baltimore, MD: Johns Hopkins University Press.

United Nations (2015) "The Millennium Development Goals Report 2015", *United Nations*, available at: www.un.org/millenniumgoals/2015_MDG_Report/pdf/MDG%202015%20rev%20(July%201).pdf

United Nations Development Programme (2015) "Human Development Report 2015", *United Nations Development Programme*, available at: http://hdr.undp.org/sites/default/files/2015_human_development_report_1.pdf

Ureta, S. (2008) "Mobilising Poverty? Mobile Phone Use and Everyday Spatial Mobility Among Low-Income Families in Santiago, Chile", *The Information Society*, 24(2): 83–92.

Vota, W. (2015) "Wow! Myanmar is Going Straight to Smartphones", *ICT Works*, 30 September, available at: www.ictworks.org/2015/09/30/wow-myanmar-is-going-straight-to-smartphones/

Wallis, C. (2008) *Technomobility in the Margins: Mobile Phones and Young Rural Women in Beijing*, Los Angeles, CA: University of Southern California.

World Bank (2012) *Information and Communications for Development 2012: Maximizing Mobile*, available at: http://siteresources.worldbank.org/EXTINFORMATIONANDCOMMUNICATIONANDTECHNOLOGIES/Resources/IC4D-2012-Report.pdf

Part 5

HISTORIES OF SOCIAL INTERNETS

21

TALKING ABOUT OURSELVES ON THE JAPANESE DIGITAL NETWORK

Takanori Tamura

Introduction

In this chapter, I provide an historical perspective on human interaction, specifically *self-narratives* (that is, talking about ourselves) via computer-mediated communication (CMC) in Japan, including in the pre-Internet era. Although during this period there were online English-language communities in Japan (such as TWICS, discussed by McLelland in Chapter 11 of this volume), I concentrate on communication taking place in the Japanese language only.

I focus on self-narratives because these have been a prominent feature of the Japanese Internet from early on. There are various other ways of using digital networks in Japan, but self-narratives help us understand how Japanese people have used digital networks, and in so doing, redefine them. Since the use of digital networks involves "a range of different histories and experiences" (Goggin and McLelland 2009: 10), we need to explore the actual uses of specific technologies to understand how they have functioned within the Japanese community, rather than relying upon understandings predicated just on English-language users.

An approach which prioritizes self-narratives as the key to understanding people and society is known as the *narrative approach*. This approach has been adopted in various fields of social science such as qualitative sociology, self-help group studies, life history studies, psychotherapy, education, and nursing science. A narrative is defined as a "meaning structure that organizes events and human actions into a whole, thereby attributing significance to individual actions and events according to their effect on the whole" (Polkinghorne 1988: 18). Jerome Bruner (1987) has claimed that people have two modes of cognitive functioning, or two modes of thought. He separates them into the *narrative mode* and the *logico-scientific mode*. Each provides us with a distinct way of ordering experience and constructing reality. Efforts to reduce one mode to the other, or to ignore one at the expense of the other, inevitably fail to capture the rich diversity of thought (Bruner 1987: 11). This claim underlies the importance of the narrative approach, but it also means that the narrative approach cannot cover all aspects of human communication. However, we can say that self-narratives are important in understanding the socio-cultural aspects of human relationships and interactions, even by means of CMC.

My research has shown that this mode of communication is prominent for Japanese digital network users, although not every Japanese user pays attention to self-narratives or self-disclosure on the Internet. This is illustrated in the results of an online survey regarding the interests of Japanese Internet users in writing and/or reading about their own or other people's experiences (presuming they could be deemed to be self-narratives; see Figure 21.1). The results showed that 65 percent of female and 61 percent of male respondents were interested in writing or reading about themselves and others. Yusa Tabuchi and Yuriko Norisada (2013) have also shown that 46 percent of male students and 65 percent of female students have disclosed personal experiences online (Tabuchi and Norisada 2013: 207–208).

Other scholars have discussed self-narratives on digital networks from various perspectives. For example, some studies have examined the medical or psychological effects of online narratives (Engqvist and Nilsson 2011; Fleischmann and Miller 2013; Heilferty 2011; O'Brien and Clark 2010). Others have studied intimate aspects of life (Chiou and Wan 2006; Lee Bee Hian *et al.* 2004; Solanilla 2008), and the development of awareness toward social issues from self-narratives (Simmons 2008).

Psychotherapeutic approaches have acknowledged CMC as a way to convey self-narratives from early on in Japan. The Japan Online Counseling Association was established in 2001, and some books dating from the early 2000s also covered online counseling (Muto and Shibuya 2002; Tamura 2003). Even though they have not dealt directly with narratives, self-disclosure via CMC has been studied mainly by socio-psychologists in Japan, especially in relation to web diaries and weblogs (Kawaura *et al.* 1999; Yamashita *et al.* 2005) and online self-help groups (Miyata 2005). These researchers analyzed the psychological effects of talking about the self and receiving counseling online through questionnaire surveys. However, due to the nature of their discipline, they focused on the motivation for, and psychological effects of, such communication, rather than on the social interaction through CMC.

Elsewhere, Norman Denzin (1989) has analyzed self-help groups on Usenet, aiming to "show how a new information technology (IT), Usenet, has created a site for the production of new emotional self-stories, stories that might not otherwise be told" (1989: 98). Some studies have presented psychological analyses of narratives on the Internet (Engqvist and Nilsson 2011; Robinson 2001). Engqvist and Nilsson have claimed, based on Katherine Robinson (2001), that online narratives tend to be more detailed than verbal narratives, because the secure feeling of being anonymous allows individuals to share their innermost thoughts and feelings, particularly in light of the stigma associated with mental illness (Engqvist and Nilsson 2011: 138; Robinson 2001: 709).

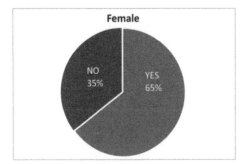
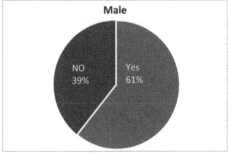

Figure 21.1 Students writing or reading about themselves on CMC[1]

These studies on English-language users clearly show that self-narratives by CMC deserve to be a target of scientific research. Nevertheless, in Japan, we can only find a few studies about self-narratives from a sociological point of view. This is a significant gap, not only for the Japanese case, but also for the international understanding of this important aspect of the history and development of the Internet in Japan. Accordingly, this chapter will examine self-narratives via CMC from three different eras: the pre-Internet era, the popularized Internet era, and the current social networking era. It will explore how Japanese people used these evolving digital networks, as well as analyze how they imagined and redefined them.

Through exploring this history of self-narratives via CMC, it can be seen how a path from the *intimate sphere* to the *public sphere* developed in Japan's digital network. If we adopt a classical division between the public sphere and the intimate sphere, then rational discussion belongs to the public sphere as proposed by Jürgen Habermas (1992). Although there are several studies that discuss the public sphere on digital networks in Japan (Hoshikawa 2001; Yoshida 2000), these have merely attempted to find proof for the existence of a classic Habermasian public sphere, and yet have not found much evidence for this. Yasuaki Narita has suggested that Japanese people were against discussion through *pasokon tsūshin* (communication via personal computers), because they have traditionally disliked public arguments, and attached greater importance to reconciliation in human relationships (Narita 1993: 84–89). On the contrary, however, there are many cases of self-narratives that can be found on Japan's digital network at this time. This tendency toward communication about the self appeared early in the pre-Internet domestic digital communication networks (that is, *pasokon tsūshin*, which will be explained in detail later).

The classic concept of the public sphere has, however, been challenged. Ken Plummer (2003) has discussed kinds of hybrid public/personal space in terms of *intimate citizenship*. He has criticized the traditional idea of the public sphere, which he deems male-dominated and exclusive of certain groups, such as women, sexual minorities, and those with little or no literacy (Plummer 2003: 52). In contrast, he suggests that the public sphere today should imply a plurality of multiple public voices and positions—that is, multiple, hierarchically layered, and contested public spheres—for example, the black public sphere, the gay public sphere, the sex-worker sphere, the evangelical Christian sphere, and so on (Plummer 2003: 15). At the same time, one cannot simply speak about an intimate sphere that is separate from the public, the social, and the political spheres. Intimate citizenship refers to all those areas of life that appear to be personal but are in effect connected to, structured by, or regulated through the public sphere (Plummer 2003: 70). Plummer claims that such an interactive public sphere has developed on the Internet (Plummer 2003: 77).

Communication on self-narratives on the pre-Internet domestic networks provided a context for later developments—on the Web, and then on social media. Such narratives, and CMC communication, helped develop this sense of intimate citizenship that later fed into, and made possible, the social movements that have emerged in the recent crises in Japan after the earthquake and nuclear power disasters in 2011.

Talking about Selves in the Pre-Internet Age

The Japanese digital network first originated in 1985 with the enactment of the Telecommunications Business Act (TBA). Until this point, Japan's electronic communication industry had been dominated by two companies that had divided telecommunications into domestic and international sectors. Domestic telecommunications could only be conducted through NTT (*Nippon denshin denwa kōsha*—Nippon Telegraph and Telephone Public

Corporation), and international communications were under the purview of KDD (*Kokusai Denshin Denwa*). Thus, before the TBA, telecommunications involving the Internet were experimental only and, although important, were not available to the general public (Matsuoka 2005). After the enactment of the TBA, the domestic network often referred to as *pasokon tsūshin* (personal-computer communication) started operating. *Pasokon tsūshin* was a CompuServe-like system where all members were connected to one host system. In the first era of Japanese Internet history, *pasokon tsūshin* played a significant role in Japanese CMC and stimulated various discussions (Kumon 1988; Okabe 1986).

The two most popular *pasokon tsūshin* networks, Nifty-serve and PC-VAN, were set up by rival computer manufacturers, and were different from the Internet because users could only communicate with other members within their own network, and could not communicate with members who belonged to other *pasokon tsūshin* networks (see Chapter 11 for a detailed history of their development). The functions of *pasokon tsūshin* included email, BBS (bulletin board systems that were often called forums or electric meeting rooms), chat rooms, and data download services.

In forums and electronic meeting rooms, there were people in charge called system operators (*shisu-ope*) in Nifty-serve and SIG (special interest group) operators (*shigu-ope*) in PC-VAN. In addition to these two major commercial providers, there were grassroots BBSs set up by individuals. In these smaller networks, system operators or SIG operators were in charge of both technical engineering and facilitation of forum discussions, much like the role of chairpersons during meetings. These roles did not involve technical engineering so much in Nifty-serve and PC-VAN because the parent companies provided technical support. Users of these services had handle names (*handoru nēmu*), or pseudonyms, which they used to communicate in forums and electronic meeting rooms. Unlike Web-based BBS in the Internet era, there was not complete anonymity, however, since service providers held personal information about members because they charged fees for participating in *pasokon tsūshin*, mainly through credit cards. Telephone line fees to connect a host were expensive in Japan, too. So, members of *pasokon tsūshin* were generally those who had a good income, social credibility, and computer literacy, the last being uncommon in Japan at that time (see Chapter 11 for a discussion of early computer literacy in Japan).

I analyzed a case of self-narratives in a forum called FLADY on the Nifty-serve network. This was a women-only forum. Men could become members of FLADY, but were not allowed to post there, except for two rooms that were open to them. However, the citation of women's messages from women-only rooms was prohibited. To register, members needed to inform the system operator of their real names and sex to gain access to the forum. These conditions were set to prevent male members from disturbing the majority female membership.

Written between March 1994 and January 1995, the posts came from a discussion room, which was a subsection of FLADY, called "society as seen by women (*onna no miru shakai*)". In order to understand and visualize the general tendencies of the text, I conducted a quantitative text analysis, known as text mining, with the KH Coder software.[2] The result of the analysis is plotted in Figure 21.2. Words that unite plural networks are called words with high "betweenness centrality". This means that they are related to multiple topics, and are thus significant. In this figure, <myself> (*jibun* in Japanese) has the highest betweenness centrality. Members talked about gender issues with words like "men" and "women", society with "human" and "discrimination", work with "work", "company", and "life", and marriage with "marriage", "couple", "children", and "name". Because feudal aspects of the Japanese family system were still problematic, they talked about their selves, "myself", using the terminologies mentioned above.

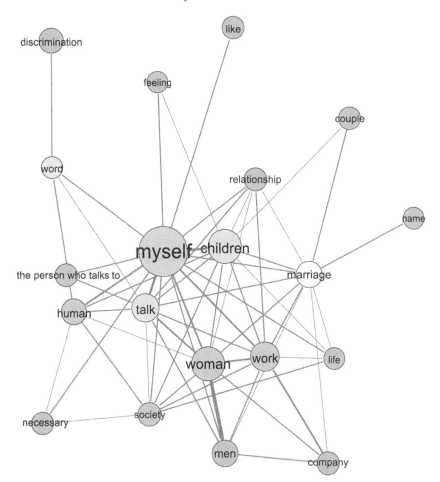

Figure 21.2 Network map of frequently concurrent words on FLADY

In brief, after talking about matters of personal concern, women found that other members had similar problems, although they originally believed that they were the only ones who had them. They became aware of the fact that their problems were not just individual in nature, but also social and political, as contended by second-wave feminism (Hanisch 2006).

One member, who for our purposes will be referred to as A, posted about her life history and confessed to her suffering. For example, she wrote about her childhood, her relationship with her mother, the divorce of her parents, and how it all influenced her. In response, another poster, B, shared her experience. A replied to B and added her interpretation of B's story. It was an exchange of sympathy. Yet another member, C, advised A that she could open her heart in the FLADY forum. C said: "Maybe I am not good enough to help you but you have many supporters in this forum." A's story turned out to be not just personal, but something general and sharable with other women.

Over the course of the conversation, A had started to change her perception of herself. The more she shared, and retold, her experience in conversation with other participants, the more objective she became about herself. As Sakurai has argued, storytelling is a device for changing past experience into something meaningful, so that it becomes understandable and acceptable. This is a framework through which human beings experience the world (Nakano and Sakurai 1995: 235). In the above example, we can see how this process started as a sympathetic intimate conversation and then expanded to encompass more general issues in society. In effect, it changed the participants' views of others and the world, and brought about possibilities to fix their damaged relationships.

This process is similar to the process of consciousness raising (CR), which was a group activity for women and minority groups that gained prominence in the 1960s in the USA. CR is a group conversation without hierarchy, where participants can talk about their experiences freely. They are encouraged to accept each other and reconsider personal problems as social ones. Barbara Kirsh divided the process of CR into four components: *opening up*, *sharing*, *analyzing*, and *abstracting* (Kirsh 1974: 344–346). It can be argued that there are two main reasons why there were similarities between posts on FLADY and CR activities. First, there is the general characteristic of digital network communication which enabled women in isolated situations to converse with others, because digital network communication gave them the ability to communicate beyond time and space (Poster 2013: 15). Fictitious names also afforded them the freedom to talk about their private, innermost concerns that they had previously not been able to discuss (cf. Engqvist and Nilsson 2011: 138).

The second reason comes from the particular conditions of *pasokon tsūshin* and FLADY. The site had a moderator who took care of members, allowing them to communicate without being disturbed by men (as men were prohibited to write in the forum). A woman was free from any judgment from men due to her opinions or her looks, because communication was based on text only. The atmosphere of the FLADY was sympathetic and therapeutic, but not very radical in terms of feminism (for instance, I found no flaming in the FLADY forum). On the other hand, one female member tried to hold a CR meeting in another forum, but she did not succeed (Nifutei Soshō wo Kangaeru Kai 2000: 254) because that particular forum was open to both women and men to discuss philosophy and general issues. During her attempt to experiment with CR, there were serious arguments and flaming which resulted in a court case (Tokyo High Court 2001). This tendency to modesty is similar to the situation of CR, as it unfolded in face-to-face communication in Japan. CR was introduced to Japan by a feminist counselor Kiyomi Kawano (1991) and became popular around 1994 and 1995 (the time when I collected data from FLADY). Since Kawano was a psychological counselor, CR was introduced as a method of feminist counseling. However, as feminist counselor Itsuko Kato argued in her subsequent review, CR in Japan was more concentrated on individual awareness but not focused on preparation for feminist social actions as emphasized in a guideline for CR by the National Organization for Women in the US (Kato 1999, 2002).

Thus, this CR-like phenomenon happened rather spontaneously, and at the same time it was the result of the interaction of technology and society. The *pasokon tsūshin* system and FLADY forum enabled CR because of its anonymity and therapeutic atmosphere, and because it took place at a time when the CR movement was being introduced to Japan. This case was an experiment in finding a method to share self-narratives via digital networks, offering a space for Japanese women to discuss their problems, providing a good illustration of the way in which talking about selves via CMC had started in the *pasokon tsūshin* era.

Narrating the Self as an Established Strategy on BBS

The Japan Network Information Center (JNIC, later renamed JPNIC), which managed Japan's domain name service (DNS), started its operations in 1991. The first commercial Internet service provider, Internet Initiative Japan (IIJ), started its services in 1992 (Matsuoka 2005: 79). In 1993, the US White House launched its website, and in 1994, the prime minister's official residence in Japan also launched its own. Windows 95, which came with the TCP/IP protocol, was released in 1995, and played a major role in expanding the use of the Internet. In 1997, there were 7,894,000 *pasokon tsūshin* (Somushō 1998: 178) and 11,550,000 Internet users in Japan (Somushō 2010: 1). However, by this time, *pasokon tsūshin* and the Internet had been linked and 43.1 percent of users had experience using *pasokon tsūshin*, and 20.1 percent of Internet users connected to the Internet via a *pasokon tsūshin* host (IAjapan 1998: 37). Despite the growth in direct connections to the Internet, Tomo'o Okada, the president of Nifty-serve, thought that *pasokon tsūshin* would be able to survive in the Internet era because they offered community services on the forums (NIFTY 1997: 275) at a time when social networking systems had not yet developed on the Internet. However, as *pasokon tsūshin* gradually lost users to the Internet, PC-VAN terminated in 2001 and Nifty-serve closed down, too, in 2006.

At the beginning of the Japanese Internet era, personal websites became popular despite the fact that websites at the time were based on static HTML and were not very interactive. Self-narratives were widely seen on personal websites in this era, more so than in other nations. For instance, Japanese Internet users uploaded more web diaries than users in Taiwan and the USA (Ishii *et al.* 2000: 25). Web diaries were not very private, but individuals nonetheless wrote about their daily experiences and thoughts on their websites (Tamura 2008). Although web diaries were significant places to talk about the self, here we will look into cases of interactive self-narratives on BBS because we can observe human interaction there. In Japan, web-based BBSs also became popular around 1996. Free CGI scripts and commercial, but free, BBS services prompted people to establish their own bulletin boards. During the *pasokon tsūshin* era, it was expensive to build individual spaces for communication and it demanded high computer skills. The popularization of web-based BBSs provided more flexible spaces for digital communication. A method that was invented in the *pasokon tsūshin* era became an established strategy for Internet users to share their self-narratives in the Internet BBS era. Users intentionally came to use the Internet in order to talk about themselves. This can be seen in the case of narratives that arose in an online community of women who had lost their children during delivery. These kinds of communities are called "grief communities" (Swartwood *et al.* 2011). In cases of other online communities, generally, people gathered because they wanted to. Such communities include the TV drama fan community analyzed by Nancy Baym (1994) and FLADY (discussed above). However, grief communities are groups of people who have experienced traumatic events in their lives and are motivated to gather together because of these traumatic events. These people have experienced an *epiphany* as described by Denzin (1989: 15). I chose this case study because an epiphany is a crucial moment that motivates people to begin constructing their self-narratives.

As noted, the self-narratives of grief community participants stem from some crisis. This is also true for communities centered on disease and illness (Josefsson 2005: 148). However, there are differences between grief communities, and disease and illness communities. The latter communities are less emotional and exchange a lot of information about medication and treatment (Haker *et al.* 2005: 475). In addition, their members can often expect treatment or remission. On the other hand, in grief communities, the members have no hope of treatment or recovery but are required to live with the ongoing suffering. When they start to deem information as useless, they produce self-narratives aimed at interpreting their situations, feelings, or fate.

Prior to introducing an analysis of the BBS cases, I will mention a book written by parents who lost their children at birth who had been involved in such an Internet grief community. Parents who had similar experiences met online, talked about their loss, and found that it was a common social problem. They published a book resulting from these discussions entitled *Tanjo Shi* (stillborn). *Tanjo shi* was a term coined by them to specify the phenomenon and attract people's attention. These were the first generation of *tanjo shi* storytellers. One of the authors wrote as follows:

> I did not have anybody to speak to about my feelings. I was lonely. My husband went back to his job as if he did not experience any sadness. It was uncomfortable for him that I kept crying over it. [. . .] I wanted to talk to anybody who had the same experience.
>
> (Oyanokai 2002: 137–138)

These parents were suffering due to their experience, but they could not talk about it with others because, although there were many books about successful births, there was no information or books about stillbirth. The phenomenon of stillbirth was an undiscussed social issue. Stillbirth was not recognized as an important issue at that time, and people treated the bereaved parents as if they did not exist. The Internet enabled discussions about stillbirth and helped raise awareness of it as a social problem. Internet users discovered the problem, named it, and shared information and experiences about it. It was a process of acknowledging stillbirth as a social problem, a process known as a "claims-making activity" by social constructivists (Spector and Kitsuse 1987: 78).

Once the phenomenon had been publicized, other people and groups who had similar experiences started to use the term *tanjo shi* and started independent BBSs to discuss their experiences. The following are analyses of two BBSs, from 2004 to 2006, which were created after the publication of the book. The text from the two BBSs was downloaded by the author and no longer exists online.

I conducted the multidimensional scaling analysis (MDS), which is a method for visualizing the level of similarity among individual cases in a dataset (see Figures 21.3 and 21.4). Frequently co-occurring words are located close to each other. Words that are placed in the center are close to all the other words. That means that those words occurred with all the other words most frequently. I drew concentric circles to show the distance of the words from the center.

Although there are slight differences in terminology, in both figures, one can find similar words in similar locations. In the center circle, there are "I", "myself", "feeling". In the second circle, there are "child", "baby", "mama", and "pregnancy". In the third circle, there are "alone", "talking", and "being with".

This comparison shows that even though the two BBSs were independent of each other, they were similar in their terminology and the structure of the narratives. Therefore, it can be said that a similar narrative pattern was shared across communities with similar experiences. This form of narrative helped people who had experienced trauma to describe their experience, share it with others, and overcome difficulties of communication among survivors. An established way of storytelling enables people to share their experiences easily. This is because the personal stories of members tend to reflect the community narrative (Rappaport 1993: 245). The narrative framework views mutual help organizations as one potential type of community available to people. An important characteristic of a community is that it has a narrative about itself and about its individual members (Rappaport 1993: 246). Narratives

BBS *A*

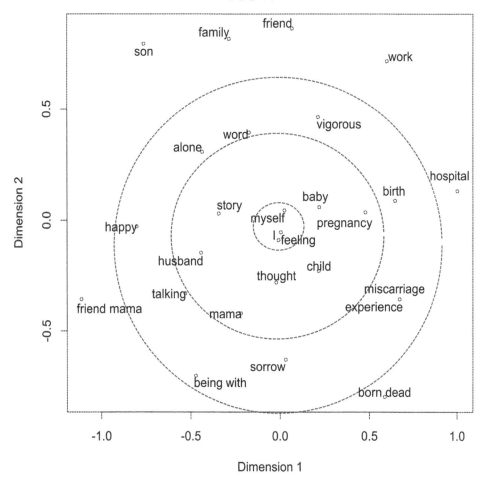

Figure 21.3 MDS chart for BBS A

(and stories) have certain structural features that include event sequences arranged in context over time. Thus, they are different from abstract principles (rules) that tend to be contextual and static. Narratives also serve certain functions, such as communicating to members and others what the community is like, how it came to be that way, and (sometimes implicitly) what behavior is expected (Rappaport 1993: 249).

The *tanjo shi* community published books, held face-to-face self-help groups, and started involving medical workers (Otsuka and Fukuriki 2003). These expanded self-narratives gradually impacted upon the wider society, performing a bridging function between the intimate and the public sphere. As mentioned before, Plummer's intimate citizenship is useful for understanding the case of *tanjo shi*. Although the Habermasian public sphere had not taken off in Japan during the era of the popularized Internet, there were clear elements of intimate citizenship discernible online.

BBS *B*

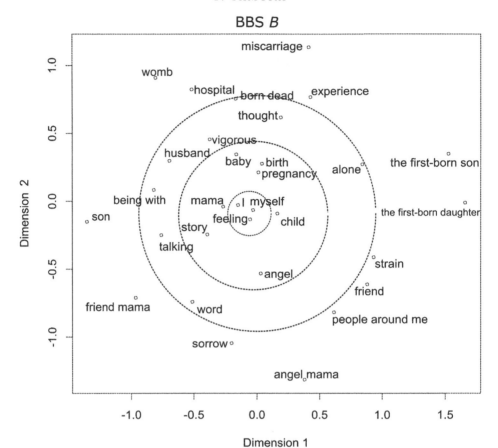

Figure 21.4 MDS chart for BBS B

Narratives and Social Movements

The gigantic earthquake followed by tsunami that occurred on 11 March 2011 (henceforth 3/11) caused an accident at the Fukushima Daiichi nuclear power plant resulting in a nationwide anti-nuclear campaign in Japan. In March 2013, an anti-nuclear protest group called the Metropolitan Coalition Against Nukes (MCAN) began conducting major protests in front of the prime minister's residence (known as *Kanteimae Kōgi* protests), and has emerged as one of the most influential civilian protest groups in modern times (Noma 2012).

The political scientist Gonoi has commented on the "cloudification" of social movements which came along with the spread of the Internet in society. According to Gonoi, the Web (that is, "the cloud") has made it possible for people to exchange information easily since it decreases the cost of sharing information and takes the hassle out of publicizing events. People can download designs for posters, find meeting points, or check the route of demonstrations—all online.

However, "cloudification" does not satisfy all the needs of social movements. First, the diffusion of information via the Internet has some limitations. In the context of the resource mobilization theory, scholars have mainly emphasized the role of the Internet in spreading information and organizing social actions (Eltantawy and Wiest 2011: 1207–1224). Some scholars, however, have suggested that the effectiveness of the Internet has been exaggerated (Masaki 2012: 92–94). MCAN's organizers came to recognize these limitations, because they were able to reach fewer people than they had expected. Therefore, MCAN had to find new ways to contact a greater number of people. For this purpose, they established the *No Nukes Magazine*.

Although the Internet has pros and cons, it has also become an essential instrument for social movements, which can no longer fulfill their missions without it. Bearing the moral and emotional perspective of social actions in mind, the Internet is a place where the exchange of personal narratives can take place. I argue that this aspect of the Internet is closely connected with individuals' participation in activism.

The narrative approach has also been introduced to the field of study of social movements. As Joseph Davis has insisted, a narrative is both a vital form of movement discourse and a crucial analytical concept (Davis 2002: 4). Narratives give coherence and directionality to rapidly unfolding events, help constitute and sustain a collective identity, and configure emotions so as to provide incentives for high-risk participation (Davis 2002: 20). Participants must do more than agree with a particular formulation of grievances or rationale for engaging in ameliorative action. Participants' involvement is perhaps never simply logical and instrumental, but—and in many contexts more so—also imaginative, intuitive, and emotional (Davis 2002: 24). Davis also claims that stories are powerful because they are social practices. Stories involve two parties, a teller (or narrator) and an interpretive audience (listeners/readers), and well-told stories establish a relationship between the two (Davis 2002: 16). This is what we can observe taking place on the Internet.

Through their online activities, individuals talk about their experiences of activism and thereby sustain a collective identity. Participants also learn the vocabulary of activism, share collective stories of activism and narrate this as a narrative of their lives (Davis 2002: 54). We can see this in the communication of activists themselves. Thus, this section presents the results of an analysis of two Twitter feeds and voluntary speeches by protesters. One Twitter feed was that of an organizer of the anti-nuke protests, Misao Redwolf, and the other was that of an active protest participant who operates the @tatangarani Twitter account. The speeches analyzed were recorded and presented by Yasumichi Noma (2012) in his book, *Kinyo Kanteimae Kogi: Demono Koega Seijio Kaeru* (The Protest).

Misao Redwolf, who is an illustrator by profession, has been engaged in anti-nuclear action since 2007. She has now abandoned her professional work almost completely, and devoted her life to organizing protests. I have analyzed her entire Twitter feed, from December 2009 to May 2013. Misao's writing consists of anti-nuke demonstrations, criticism of nuclear power schemes, caring for Fukushima, and personal contemplation and narratives. These writings are comparatively independent and coexistent. Her updates contain many personal narratives about her dedication, loneliness, suffering, disappointment, anger, meditation, and gratitude to collaborators. Her followers can understand her thoughts, style of life, weaknesses, and strengths. We can see that these kinds of self-narratives on the Internet are able to unite an organizer and collaborators in a different way from traditional institutional movements.

Figure 21.6 is a network map of @tatangarani, who is a company employee in Tokyo. She grew up in a rural city of Japan in a rather conservative family, but has a very good relationship with her parents. Prior to 3/11, she had never thought about participating in political protests. Her Twitter feed was filled with posts by friends, and Tweets about girls' parties and fancy foods. However, the triple disaster changed her priorities and pushed her

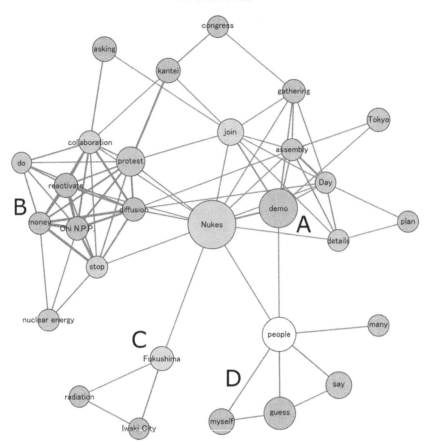

Figure 21.5 Network map of Misao Redwolf

gradually into activism. Figure 21.6 is a network map of @tatangarani after 3/11. It consists of anti-nuke actions, concern for Fukushima, daily life narratives, Japan and the world, asking for the diffusion of protest information, and her awareness of social issues.

These topics are well connected and integrated, except for those belonging to node C (above). When @tatangarani started to write about nuclear power plants, it was suggested that she create two separate accounts, one for her daily life and one for the anti-nuclear issues. However, she decided to keep a single acount, arguing "But, both are the truth and both are me" (Tamura 2015). She accepted her new beliefs and reconstructed her own narrative and identity. She said that writing about her daily life aims to create a connection between her and her followers who have no interest in social actions (Tamura 2015).

In order to study collective stories, I also analyzed voluntary speeches during the weekly *Kanteimae Kōgi* protests. Protesters spoke about "nukes", "Fukushima", "children", "government", "nation", and "Japan". This map also shares the basic elements for the anti-nuclear protest story.

In order to compare these three texts, I developed category labels from frequently occurring words and applied them to the three texts. Applying the same coding rule to different texts makes them comparable. I classified these three texts into five categories: "anti-nuke action",

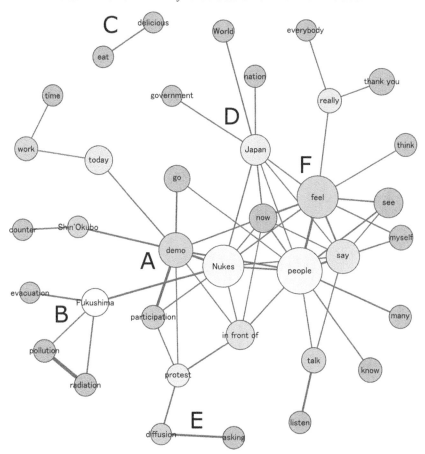

Figure 21.6 Network map of @tatangarani

"radiation exposure", "children", "Japan", and "no category" with the KH Coder software. Figure 21.7 is a graph that indicates the ratio of each category except "no category".[3] Figure 21.8 shows us that the terminology, topics, and structures of those three texts are similar. The organizer, the participant, and the collective narrative shared a model of the story for anti-nuke actions. The participant and the collective narrative show particular resemblance.

MCAN is a loose coalition for action. Almost all participants are connected solely through the Internet, and usually do not know each other offline. Therefore, it can be said that MCAN does not have much organizational unity at all. However, analysis shows that the narratives of the organizers and the participants both share collective terminologies and common patterns describing their protest activities. As Rappaport claims, the personal stories of group members tend to reflect the community narrative (Rappaport 1993: 245). Narratives give coherence and directionality to rapidly unfolding events, help constitute and sustain a collective identity, and configure emotions so as to provide incentives for high-risk participation (Davis 2002: 20).

At the same time, as indicated by Figures 21.5, 21.6, and 21.7, tweets by Misao and @tatangarani contain personal narratives which were not present in the collective narratives. The two Twitter feeds shared common stories but also contained unique individual stories.

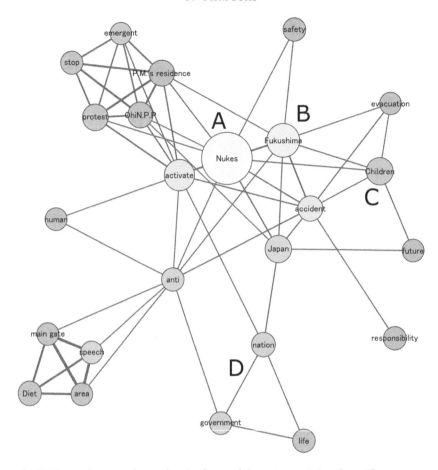

Figure 21.7 Network map of speeches in front of the prime minister's residence

As Julian Rappaport notes, a community has a narrative about itself and about its individual members (Rappaport 1993: 246). In this Japanese social movement and its online communication, we can also see how personal narratives provide a pathway from the intimate sphere to the public sphere.

Conclusion

In this chapter, I have argued that self-narratives have played a significant role in Japanese CMC from its early stages to now. Japanese people could have made use of CMC in a multitude of ways. However, they have largely chosen to talk about themselves instead of discussing public or social issues. From the earliest BBS days, they shared narratives and created intimate spheres, which later opened the way for the development of an "intimate" public sphere. This is a very important—but not widely appreciated—way in which the Japanese redefined and imagined the Internet.

To develop this account, in this chapter I schematically divided Japanese CMC into three eras. The pre-Internet *pasokon tsūshin* era was when the Japanese first began to use digital

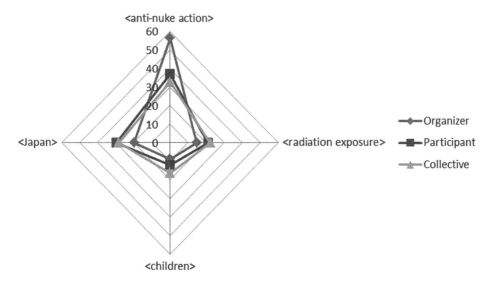

Figure 21.8 Comparison of three texts

networks for their personal communication. They tried and tested the digital network to see whether it could become a place where they could convey self-narratives, as demonstrated with the FLADY case. In the second stage, the popular Internet era, CMC became more widely recognized as a means of sharing self-narratives. People gathered on the Internet intentionally to share their personal experiences. As we saw in the case study of the *tanjo shi* grief community, online communication unites individual grief in the intimate sphere with social action in the public sphere, even involving medical workers. In the third era, of social network services, we find that after the pivotal events of 3/11, Japanese people started to use the Internet for social activism. Even during this era, narratives played a significant role in uniting individuals and developing a collective narrative model for the movement. This can be seen in the narratives discussed above, emerging in Twitter use by activists. Exchanging narratives created forms for communication and united people who shared the same concerns.

Thus, despite the fact that the Internet was an imported technology, we can trace its unique history in Japan by examining the way that Japanese people imagined and redefined its uses. For future research, we would benefit from further studies focusing on forms of communication that do not necessarily produce benefits for society—for example, online racist discourse, which has become a real social problem in Japan, such as the online activities of the *Zaitōkukai*, the most well-known group promoting hate speech against minorities. The term stands for *Zainichi tokken o yurusanai shimin no kai*, which means"Citizens against Special Privilege of Zainichi (foreign residents in Japan)". This group has a similar structure of shared terms, and utilizes the same form of communication as do the anti-nuke groups, but instead shares racist narratives. In response, movements have been established by citizens against racism which use the Internet to share their anti-racist narratives, indicating that there is still much to be said about how Japanese people share narratives about themselves and others via digital networks.

Notes

1. Cumulated results of surveys from 2002 (N=569), 2003 (N=876), 2005 (N=500), 2006 (N=500) Quota sampling. The figure is derived from Tamura (2006).
2. The analysis of the posts occurred in this way. First, the software broke sentences into their smallest parts—morphemes—and classified them according to the parts of speech. Then it found the words that appeared most frequently and those that co-occurred most frequently. Although the KH Coder is unable to analyze syntactic constructions, it does enable the visualization of text characteristics. Frequently co-occurring words are connected by lines and this enabled the visualization of word networks. Each subnetwork (that is, a small network which is roughly understandable as a topic) is connected to the other subnetworks and this constitutes the whole network map.
3. Originally, the total percent of each category was more than 100 because one message can be tagged with plural categories. For the sake of comparison, the numbers are standardized as a percentage of each category.

References

Baym, N. (1994) "The Emergence of On-line Community", in S. Jones (ed.), *CyberSociety: Computer-Mediated Communication and Community*, Thousand Oaks, CA: Sage, pp. 35–68.

Bruner, J. (1987) *Actual Minds, Possible Worlds*, Cambridge, MA: Harvard University Press.

Chiou, W.-B., and Wan, C.-S. (2006) "Sexual Self-Disclosure in Cyberspace Among Taiwanese Adolescents: Gender Differences and the Interplay of Cyberspace and Real Life", *CyberPsychology and Behavior*, 9(1): 46–53.

Davis, J. E. (2002) *Stories of Change: Narrative and Social Movements*, Albany, NY: State University of New York Press.

Denzin, N. K. (1989) *Interpretive Interactionism*, Thousand Oaks, CA: Sage.

Eltantawy, N., and Wiest, J. B. (2011) "Social Media in the Egyptian Revolution: Reconsidering Resource Mobilization Theory", *International Journal of Communication*, 5: 1207–1224.

Engqvist, I., and Nilsson, K. (2011) "Men's Experience of their Partners' Postpartum Psychiatric Disorders: Narratives from the Internet", *Mental Health in Family Medicine*, 8(3): 137–146.

Fleischmann, A., and Miller, E. C. (2013) "Online Narratives by Adults with ADHD who Were Diagnosed in Adulthood", *Learning Disability Quarterly*, 36(1): 47–60.

Goggin, G., and McLelland, M. (eds) (2009) *Internationalizing Internet Studies: Beyond Anglophone Paradigms*, New York: Routledge.

Habermas, J. (1992) *The Structural Transformation of the Public Sphere: An Inquiry into a Category of Bourgeois Society*, trans. T. Burgerm, Cambridge: Polity.

Haker, H., Lauber, C., and Rössler, W. (2005) "Internet Forums: A Self-Help Approach for Individuals with Schizophrenia?", *Acta Psychiatrica Scandinavica*, 112(6): 474–477.

Hanisch, C. (2006) *The Personal Is Political: The Original Feminist Theory*, available at: www.carolhanisch.org/CHwritings/PIP.html (accessed 25 June 2014).

Heilferty, C. M. (2011) "Ethical Considerations in the Study of Online Illness Narratives: A Qualitative Review: Online Illness Narratives", *Journal of Advanced Nursing*, 67(5): 945–953.

Hoshikawa, T. (2001) *Kokyōken no Shakaigaku: Dijitaru Nettowākingu ni yoru Kokyōken Kōchiku he Mukete* (Sociology for the Public Sphere), Kyoto: Hōritubunkasya.

IAjapan (The Internet Association Japan) (1998) *Intānetto Hakusho* (Internet White Paper), Tokyo: Impress Corporation.

Ishii, K., Tsuji, D., Hashimoto, Y., Mori, Y., and Mikami, S. (2000) "Naiyō Bunseki ni Yoru Kojin Hōmupeji no Kokusai Hikaku Jiko Kaiji Jiko Hyoshutsu wo Chūshin ni (Content Analysis on Personal Homepages of Japan, USA, and China)", *Research Bulletin of the Institute of Socio-Information and Communication Studies*, University of Tokyo, 14: 1–82.

Josefsson, U. (2005) "Coping with Illness Online: The Case of Patients' Online Communities", *The Information Society*, 21(2): 143–153.

Kato, I. (1999) "Gurūpu Apurōchi no Mondai to Kongo no Kadai (Problems in Group Approach and Future Tasks)", in K. Kawano (ed.), *Fueminisuto Kaunseringu no Mirai* (Future of Feminist Counseling), Tokyo: Shinsuisha, pp. 53–82.

Kato, I. (2002) "CRken Sonogo (After Study Group for CR)", *Fueminisuto Kaunseringu Kenkyū*, 1: 76–85.

Kawano, K. (1991) *Fueminisuto Kaunseringu* (Feminist Counselling), Tokyo: Shinsuisha.

Kawaura, Y., Yamashita, K., and Kawakami, Y. (1999) "Hito wa Naze Uebu Nikki wo Kakitsudukeru noka: Konpyūta-Nettowāku ni okeru Jiko Hyōgen (What Makes People Keep Writing Web Diaries? Self-Expression in Cyberspace)", *Shakai Shinrigaku Kenkyū*, 14(3): 133–143.

Kirsh, B. (1974) "Consciousness-Raising Groups as Therapy for Women", in V. Franks (ed.), *Women in Therapy: New Psychotherapies for a Changing Society*, New York: Brunner/Mazel, pp. 326–354.

Kumon, S. (1988) *Nettowāku Shakai* (Network Society), Tokyo: Chuōkōronsha.

Lee Bee Hian *et al.* (2004) "Getting to Know You: Exploring the Development of Relational Intimacy in Computer-Mediated Communication", *Journal of Computer-Mediated Communication*, 9(3).

Masaki, I. (2012) *Demo no Medeia Ron: Shakaundo Shakai no Yukue* (Media Theory for Demonstrations: Future of Social Movement Society), Tokyo: Chikuma Shobo.

Matsuoka, M. (2005) *Nippon no Chōsen: Intānetto no Yoake* (Challenge of Japan), Tokyo: RBB Press.

Miyata, K. (2005) *Kizuna wo Tsunagu Medeia: Nettojidai no Shakaikankeishihon* (Media Makes Bonds: Social Capital in the Internet Era), Tokyo: NTTShuppan.

Muto, S., and Shibuya, H. (2002) *Mēru Kaunseringu*, (Gendai no Esupuri 418) [*Email Counselling*], Tokyo: Shibundo.

Nakano, T., and Sakurai, A. (eds) (1995) *Raifu Hisutorī no Shakaigaku* (Life History Sociology), Tokyo: Kōbundō.

Narita, Y. (1993) "Medeia Keiken To Komyunikēshon: Pasokon Tsūshin Netto ni okeru Komyunikēshon Manzoku 1 (Media Experience and Communication)", *Chūkyōdaigaku Shakaigakubu Kiyō*, 7(2): 43–92.

NIFTY (1997) *Denen Kokyōshugi: Nettowāku Komyuniti no Shutsūgen* (Symposium on Digital Network: Arrival of Networking Communities), Tokyo: NTT Publishing.

Nifty Soshō wo Kangaeru Kai (2000) *Hanron (Counterargument): Nettowāku ni okeru Genron no Jiyū To Sekinin*, Tokyo: Kōbōsha.

Noma, Y. (2012) *Kinyo Kanteimae Kōgi: Demono Koega Seijio Kaeru* (The Protest), Tokyo: Kawadeshobōshinsha.

O'Brien, M. R., and Clark, D. (2010) "Use of Unsolicited First-Person Written Illness Narratives in Research: Systematic Review", *Journal of Advanced Nursing*, 66(8): 1671–1682.

Okabe, K. (1986) *Pasokon Shimin Nettowāku* (PC Civil Network), Tokyo: Gijutu to Ningen.

Otsuka, K., and Fukuriki, J. (2003) "Tanjōshi wo Keikenshita Hahaoya no Kōdōbunseki (Behavior Analysis for Mothers who Had Stillbirth): Ryūzan Shizan no Kea wo Kangaeru", *Nihon Kangogakkai Rombunshu Boseikango*, 34: 124–126.

Oyanokai, Ryūzan Shizan Shinseijishi de Kowo nakushita Oyanokai (2002) *Tanjō Shi* (Stillbirth), Tokyo: Sanseidō.

Plummer, K. (2003) *Intimate Citizenship: Private Decisions and Public Dialogues*, Seattle, WA: University of Washington Press.

Polkinghorne, D. E. (1988) *Narrative Knowing and the Human Sciences*, New York: State University of New York Press.

Poster, M. (2013) *The Mode of Information: Poststructuralism and Social Contexts*, Cambridge: John Wiley.

Rappaport, J. (1993) "Narrative Studies, Personal Stories, and Identity Transformation in the Mutual Help Context", *Journal of Applied Behavioral Science*, 29(2): 239–256.

Robinson, K. M. (2001) "Unsolicited Narratives from the Internet: A Rich Source of Qualitative Data", *Qualitative Health Research*, 11(5): 706–714.

Simmons, T. (2008) "The Personal Is Political? Blogging and Citizen Stories, the Case of Mum's Army", *Information Polity*, 13(1): 87–96.

Solanilla, L. (2008) "The Internet as a Tool for Communicating Life Stories: A New Challenge for 'Memory Institutions'", *International Journal of Intangible Heritage*, 3: 104–116.

Somushō (Ministry of Internal Affairs and Communications, Japan) (1998) *White Paper 1998: Information and Communication in Japan*, Tokyo, available at: www.soumu.go.jp/johotsusintokei/whitepaper/ja/h10/pdf/H10_06_C2E82BECF.pdf (accessed 22 May 2015).

Somushō (Ministry of Internal Affairs and Communications, Japan) (2010) *White Paper 2010: Information and Communication in Japan*, Tokyo, available at: www.soumu.go.jp/main_content/000114508.pdf (accessed 22 May 2015).

Spector, M. B., and Kitsuse, J. I. (1987) *Constructing Social Problems*, New York: Aldine de Gruyter.

Swartwood, R. M., Veach, P. M., Kuhne, J., Lee, H. K., and Ji, K. (2011) "Surviving Grief: An Analysis of the Exchange of Hope in Online Grief Communities", *OMEGA: Journal of Death and Dying*, 63(2): 161–181.

Tabuchi, Y., and Norisada, Y. (2013) "Self-Disclosure in the University and on the Internet: Relation with Maladjustment Tendency, Personal Traits, and Internet Usage Time" (in Japanese), *Bulletin of the Faculty of Education, Wakayama University, Humanities*, 63: 205–213.

Tamura, Takanori (2006) "*Nihon no Intānetto ni Okeru Jikomonogatariteki Komyunikeshon to Imikukan* (Communication with Self-Narratives in Japanese Internet and Semantic Space)", Ph.D. thesis, University of Tsukuba, Tsukuba.

Tamura, Takanori (2008) "Denshi Nettowāku jōde Jiko wo Monogataru: Uebu Nikki wo Daizaini (Telling Self-narratives on the Digital Network: Analysis of Web Diaries)", in Y. Kawanabe (ed.), *Noizu to Daiarōgu no Kyōdōtai: Shiminshakai no Gembakara* (Community of Noise and Dialogue: Study on Fields of Civil Society), Tsukuba: University of Tsukuba Press, pp. 249–275.

Tamura, Takanori (2015) "The Internet and Personal Narratives in the Post-Disaster Anti-Nuclear Movement", *The Asia-Pacific Journal*, 13(6–4), available at: www.japanfocus.org/-Takanori-Tamura/4280/article.html (accessed 22 May 2015).

Tamura, Takeshi (2003) *Intānetto Serapi Heno Shōtai* (Invitation to Internet Therapy): *Shinriryōhō no Atarashii Sekai*, Tokyo: Sinyōsha.

Tokyo High Court (2001) *Appeal Court Decision for Nifty-Serve Case*, No. 28071458, Tokyo High Court, 5 September, available at: www.netlaw.co.jp/hanrei/gendaishisouforum_130905.html (accessed 22 May 2015).

Yamashita, K., Kawakami, Y., Kawaura, Y., and Miura, A. (2005) *Ueburogu no Shinrigaku* (Psychology of Weblog), Tokyo: NTTShuppan.

Yoshida, J. (2000) *Intānetto Kūkan Shakaigaku* (Sociology for Cyberspace), Kyoto: Sekaishisōsha.

22

HISTORIES OF BLOGGING

Tim Highfield

Introduction

Writing in 2014, blogging's moment as an innovative and popular social medium—before "social media" became a thing—seems, in Internet time, like the distant past. Long since surpassed in public awareness, and in global user base, by social networking sites and social media like Facebook and Twitter, blogs can seem, particularly to a Western perspective, to be quaint but passé, a signifier of the Web 2.0 era, in the same way that domains like Geocities and Lycos firmly belong to the Internet of the 1990s. Yet, while blogging might not attract the same attention or importance as it did in the mid-2000s, the medium is not dead: blogs occupy a place in the mediasphere, in connection, not competition, with social media, with their respective uses reflecting the strengths and affordances of each platform. Furthermore, the influence of blogging can be perceived in many common features of online content, whether in style or in functionality. Finally, even if the moment for blogs within particular genres peaked before Twitter became a default platform for unfolding commentary, to argue that all blogging is finished is to overlook the ways that blogs are employed for diverse subjects, from activism to fashion, and in non-Western contexts or for international audiences.

This chapter provides a brief sketch of the history of blogging, as platform, genre, and influence. The focus here is not on any one particular use of blogs: some genres of blogging, while notable, are well established in research literature, but the blogosphere was never just a space for talking about politics or celebrity gossip, or acting as an online version of personal diaries. While this chapter does make reference to key events in the public awareness of blogging—especially the ways that older and newer media interacted—this is not the history of the political blogosphere. The public perception (and the mainstream media image) of blogging is important for understanding how practices of blogging were positioned, and evolved, over time. The history of blogging is part of the wider development of the mediasphere, for bloggers were not just bloggers, posting their own thoughts: they were readers of other blogs and media sources, commenting, linking to, and sharing other content, and using other platforms in addition to their own blogs. To study the history of blogs, then, we need to understand not just what blogs are, but what blogs *were*—what did blogging mean in 1997, 2002, 2006, or 2010, and what might it mean beyond this point? "Blog" might be a truncation of "web log", a reflection of initial uses of blogs as personal journals when the form first emerged in the late 1990s, but that in itself does not tell the story of what blogging became.

What Is/Was Blogging?

Defining blogs has proved a complex dilemma, since the uses and genres of blogging demonstrate a wide range of practices (Bruns and Jacobs 2006; Rettberg 2008). These various approaches might not share any overlaps beyond the platform used—and unlike Twitter, Facebook, or Tumblr, blogging research often featured less on an individual platform like Blogger or Wordpress, but, rather, on groups of blogs, which might include sites hosted by individuals as well as blogs set up on services such as LiveJournal, Over-Blog, Windows Live Spaces, and Skyblog. This lack of consistency helped promote the diversity of the blogosphere, allowing users to have more freedom with what they presented than would be found later in more uniform social media; this also meant that no one service became synonymous with "blogging".

Rather, definitions of "blog" focused on common structural elements that set blogging apart from other, contemporary forms of online communication: such defining attributes included presenting posts in reverse chronological order; blog posts as discrete entities within the blog itself (with their own, unique links); the ability for readers to add comments to posts; the use of RSS as automatic notifications of new posts; sections such as blogrolls—lists of links to sites of interest or affiliation, often provided in a static sidebar—and the inclusion of non-textual content (images, videos, audio, as well as topical links to other sites) within blog posts (Schmidt 2007). Some services provided different approaches to these common traits: LiveJournal, for instance, mixed elements of blogging with what would become central characteristics of social networking sites, using danah boyd and Nicole Ellison's (2008) definition, with users curating their own lists of friends and connections on the site.

The name LiveJournal also reflects the personal nature of early blogs. Precursors to the automated publication, centrally hosted, "What You See Is What You Get" (WYSIWYG) editing blogs of LiveJournal and Blogger (both launched in 1999), for instance, include personal home pages manually updated with news and lists of links of interest. By 2002, blogging was established enough to have already received one historical overview (Blood 2002), and while personal diaries remained popular uses of blogging, its genre coverage was growing. If a blog had a topical focus, though, this did not mean that it was not also a personal record: indeed, part of the buzz surrounding blogging was that it provided a means for people not part of the traditional media to share their opinions, expertise, analysis, content, and commentary. Services like Blogger and Wordpress meant that the levels of technical literacy (and finances) required to set up a personal webpage were suddenly diminished, making online channels a space for more voices to be shared, if not heard. Although the democratic potential and reality of the Internet remains a topic of extensive debate (Hindman 2009)—whether for political purposes or just giving marginalized voices a platform to effectively spread their messages—and other social, political, and technical factors also impacted upon who could and did blog, the rise of blogging did reduce some barriers to participation online.

Not only did discourse around blogging involve the potential for anyone to start blogging (although this was not without its critics—see Keen 2007), there was also the possibility that anyone's blog could find itself with an audience of millions. While readership for many blogs remained low (see the critiques by Lovink 2008)—and having a new, extended but unknown, audience was not necessarily the aim for all bloggers—publicly publishing posts online could also bring readers in on delay, who found the content after the fact. At their most extreme— and as with other widely shared material on social media that might go viral (Nahon and Hemsley 2013)—a blogger might suddenly receive an extensive audience (whether temporary or lasting). The blog posts of Salam Pax, for example, during the US-led invasion of Iraq in

2003—initially intended as a personal exchange with a friend—attracted international attention for their civilian perspective from the ground in Baghdad (Zuckerman 2008). During crises, content shared by bloggers might become important primary sources, including as part of citizen journalism initiatives; the publication of media and updates during the terrorist attacks in New York City on 11 September 2001, the Indian Ocean tsunami of December 2004, and the bombings in London in July 2005, for example, made use of blogs, among other channels, for information dissemination (Gillmor 2006).

Blogging and citizen journalism are not the same, but have an overlap in practices (Bruns 2005): citizen journalists may use blogs to share their reports and content, and bloggers might carry out citizen journalism. However, blogs are not the only platforms used by citizen journalists, and many bloggers were concerned with topics other than documenting civic life. Similarly, providing citizen analysis and commentary, as political and news bloggers might do, is not necessarily citizen journalism but more akin to opinion and editorial pieces. Both bloggers and citizen journalists, though, did form part of the same discussions around the legal status and ethical responsibilities for online publications, since unlike journalists, bloggers had no explicit code of ethics; such questions arose as part of blogging's historical trajectory from a new platform with a small user base, to an alternative media with growing public awareness and uncertainty, to an established and known medium.

These questions were not just for political bloggers, though; the public nature of much blogging and the accompanying trends of Web 2.0 and social networking sites encouraged Internet users to post personal thoughts, opinions, and media content online. The popularity of celebrity-oriented blogs such as Perez Hilton and D-Listed, and blog communities like Oh No They Didn't demonstrate the audience for gossip and rumor, but the associated risks of publishing illicit, libelous, and defamatory material, as well as that illegally obtained, can also lead to litigation. Using blogs to share copyrighted material, too, could cause problems; the rise of mp3 blogs in the mid-2000s, and especially their own moment within indie music circles as arbiters of taste, helped to break new bands and make songs available to new audiences (Baym and Burnett 2009; Borschke 2012). This sometimes took place with the approval of bands or labels (or was done by them), but mp3 bloggers would also post material without permission, which could cause sites to be deleted and material removed without warning (Harvey 2013).

The growing popularity of blogging also led to a diverse range of blogging genres: in addition to politics, news, and personal diaries, blogs featured topics from music and food to parenting, lifestyle, education, sport, technology, and travel, while styles of blogging, from sharing lists of links to primarily posting photos or videos, also instigated new genres. The rise of blogging genres could lead to the development of close-knit communities of interest and support, with networks of parenting blogs, including the subgenre of "mummy bloggers", and health-related blogs documenting illnesses, disorders, and disability (Goggin and Noonan 2006; Yeshua-Katz and Martins 2013). Australian and New Zealand feminist bloggers, too, reinforced the connections between bloggers by running a monthly "carnival" wherein one blogger hosted submissions from others in the community (Down Under Feminists' Carnival n.d.).

Blogging was also a support and promotional outlet for other fields; in education, for instance, blogs were used in classes, and academics blogged to promote work-in-progress, share their research and publications, and discuss related topics (Mewburn and Thomson 2013). Lifestyle bloggers, meanwhile, used their blogs to promote products and events, from fashion (Rocamora 2012; Sedeke and Arora 2013) to food (Lofgren 2013); as their audiences grew and individual bloggers' reputations as "new influencers" became apparent (Trammell and

Keshelashviki 2005), lifestyle bloggers in particular were approached by companies for paid promotions. The personal voice, and authenticity of, blog posts appealed as an alternative approach to advertising—and was a reason why the bloggers had attracted an audience—although bloggers posting "advertorials" (especially without disclosing the nature of the post) were not universally approved by their readers (Hopkins and Thomas 2011). These diverse practices also place blogging within a wider Internet history—that of Internet culture and the presentation and distribution of popular culture online, of copyright, privacy, and piracy, of amateur experts, user-generated content, and taste cultures. While blogging was a specific approach to posting content and media online, then, it was not an approach that developed in isolation, free from any other contextual factors.

Although much attention was given to blogging's impact on public discourse through its textual content, allowing individuals a "voice" through the written word, other blogging genres developed that primarily focused on other media forms. Photoblogs, for instance, used the blog format to promote an individual's photographs (Cohen 2005), and many blogs would mix media forms. Podcasts, too, used some of the same technological elements as blogs, in particular RSS, to share audio productions (Jarrett 2009). Other approaches might use blog-related nomenclature without always being blog-like: "vloggers", for example, described video blogs, where users would post videos that contained personal views and commentary in the same way as a blog post. With the rise of YouTube in particular, though, "vlogging" also became used to describe a specific aesthetic, of "a talking head speaking straight-to-camera . . . [discussing] domestic, personal politics" (Burgess and Green 2009: 28). Since the structural elements of the standard blogging definition might not be present here, vlogging in particular quickly evolved to mean something similar, yet detached, to the first blogs.

Blogging genres promoted the formation of communities of interest around topics and approaches. These were not discrete spaces, either, as overlaps and further topical specialization took place. A genre-oriented blogosphere connected several themes, and contained several subthemes within it. The Australian political blogosphere was not just a space for bloggers to discuss partisan politics, but also included sites analyzing political topics from, for example, economic, psephological, and feminist perspectives (for the latter especially, see Shaw 2012a, 2012b). These spaces intersected to extend the scope of commentary and analysis, and to respond to their discussions and leading questions. Similarly, analysis of blogospheres identified by common languages, from Farsi to Arabic, identified the presence of distinct but interconnected communities of interest, covering topics from politics to poetry (Etling *et al.* 2010; Kelly and Etling 2008).

Such overlaps also serve to connect international audiences. While regional blogospheres might primarily communicate in their local languages, there is a subcategory of bridge-bloggers (Zuckerman 2008) who might write about the same topics, and collate information from other bloggers, but in other languages to make this content accessible to other readers. Ethan Zuckerman identified bridge-bloggers in several African nations and Rebecca MacKinnon (2008) studied bridge-bloggers in China, highlighting both the uptake of blogging in non-Western contexts, and the appeal of international commentary (although writing in a non-native language does not necessarily mean that bridge-blogging is the intention; see de Vries 2009). The bridge-blogging function was formalized further by the development of projects such as Global Voices (n.d.), which aggregate and host commentary from international bloggers and promote these views, in a clear and centralized manner, to a global audience (Russell 2009).

Global Voices and similar projects can mix elements of citizen journalism and blogging, providing a means for sharing views and reports from uncertain social, political, and media situations, circumventing surveillance and media controls. Such aims are not a prerequisite for international connections, though: other initiatives that recognized and promoted the global blogosphere, and its common approaches, were based on shared topics of interest. The Music Alliance Pact (MAP), for instance, was launched in 2008 as a collective of mp3 blogs from different countries, each contributing one song per month from artists from their countries and promoting the entire month's list on their own sites (Connor 2008). As well as the USA and the UK, the MAP grew to include bloggers from Australia, New Zealand, Singapore, Korea, Sweden, Chile, and others, presenting the (music/mp3) blogosphere as a global village connected through their enjoyment of music. The taste cultures promoted by the bloggers concerned might determine the type of music promoted, but a project like MAP shows the rise of similar approaches to blogging around the world; the blog as a space for sharing content, promoting subjects, and posting personal commentary was not a Western-only approach, and mp3 blogs, as one generic example, were adopted by international bloggers (see also international coverage of local music scenes, as noted by Baym and Burnett 2009).

Indeed, although their catalysts and topics might vary drastically, global blogging and blogs in languages other than English displayed various common approaches and uses (Russell and Echchaibi 2009). Regional and language-specific platforms provided opportunities for national blog networks to develop; particularly before popular English-language platforms became internationalized, with dashboards in multiple languages, local blogging services were widely used. In South Korea, for instance, popular services included Cyworld, which shared characteristics with blogs while also being more than just a blog host, pre-empting elements of social media platforms (Choi 2006; Kim and Yun 2008). French bloggers, meanwhile, could set up blogs using services provided by mainstream media organizations, such as *Le Monde* newspaper and the Skyrock radio network. Other nations took to English-language platforms en masse: Russian bloggers' adoption of LiveJournal, for instance, reflected the availability of Russian-language interfaces and the perceived benefit of user data being stored outside Russia (see Alexanyan and Koltsova 2009). Indeed, the tension between public communication through blogs, surveillance, and users' data was also a factor for international bloggers, from French bloggers being arrested on suspicion of posting messages, to their Skyblog blogs inciting violence during riots in 2005 (Russell 2007), to bloggers—and other prominent voices on social media—being targeted and arrested during the Arab Spring series of uprisings in North Africa and the Middle East in 2010 and 2011 (Howard and Hussain 2011). These tensions remain a concern for online activity in general, beyond the blogosphere and beyond political unrest.

Perceptions of Blogging

The history of blogging is also a history of changing perspectives and disputes around the value and contribution of blogs, and online communication in general. Blogging fits into the historical narrative around user-generated content and participatory media, and the convergence between old and new media forms (Jenkins 2006). From an alternative practice, blogging's growing popularity saw it become first challenged and criticized, then adopted and integrated into the digital strategies of traditional media; for political and news blogs in particular, the increased attention and apparent status of bloggers within discussions online—as well as bloggers' willingness to critique the work of the mainstream media—led to editorials attacking blogging in general and individual bloggers specifically (Highfield and Bruns 2012). Yet this was also not a universal strategy, and some traditional media, especially those investing in digital presences, were more willing to start blogging.

The rationale behind media campaigns against bloggers, especially Western political blogging, can perhaps be attributed to several key events that demonstrated (in the USA) the power and presence of blogs as new and "dangerous" media; these include the use of blogs, and the Internet in general, for grassroots support in Howard Dean's unsuccessful 2004 Presidential bid; the 2004 resignation of veteran *60 Minutes* anchor Dan Rather after bloggers helped break a story that the program had used erroneous documents in a story about then-President George W. Bush's military record; and the 2002 resignation of Senate Majority leader Trent Lott following the publication of seemingly pro-segregation remarks which were spread by bloggers (Gillmor 2006; Hindman 2009; Munger 2008). The fact that these events from the early 2000s remained watershed moments for the blogosphere's impact also demonstrates that its peak as a new force in the mediasphere was not long-lasting: this is not to say that bloggers had limited achievements, but rather that after this period they were a more known group, and so could be monitored. The same developments happened with social media: tracking topics of interest and buzz on these platforms, as well as in other media, is a key part of journalistic strategy.

Monitoring social media buzz also demonstrates a change in the perception of the users involved in these spaces: despite the potential for new and marginalized voices to be heard through blogs, and for more diversity in discussions, there were also fears that the blogosphere would be an example of cyberbalkanization rather than an open, public forum (Sunstein 2008). Instead of being a revitalized or reimagined public sphere, the blogosphere might fragment into distributed and isolated communities of like-minded voices following principles of homophily: for the political blogosphere especially, separating into ideological clusters could cause an echo-chamber effect, where individuals are only exposed to views they agree with, and which repeatedly get reinforced (see Meraz 2011). These fears were not entirely realized; while political blogs did demonstrate at various points ideological clustering, this was not at the expense of being aware of, and linking to, views from oppositional blogs and media sources, including in critique (Adamic and Glance 2005; Shaw and Benkler 2012). Other criticisms, and derogatory views, of bloggers saw political and news blogs, specifically, dismissed by some mainstream media outlets as being run from bedrooms by people in their pyjamas (see Jones and Himelboim 2010); this was despite the expertise of many bloggers in their fields of interest rather than journalism, and indeed despite the growing influx of professionals into blogging too. Journalist blogs, for instance, became channels for journalists to post material both as part of their professional work on their parent organization's sites, and on personal blogs (Garden 2010; Singer 2005).

For some bloggers, their work could lead them to celebrity status; vloggers such as LonelyGirl15, for instance, became prominent through the originality and nature of their content, although the authenticity of LonelyGirl15 was also disputed and later confirmed to be a commercial promotion (Burgess and Green 2009). Celebrity status could also occur as part of the overall, elite blogging "A-list", or within a blogger's own circles: bloggers could become micro-celebrities (see Marwick and boyd 2011; Senft 2013), due to their status as influencers for their readers. Popular and original blogs could also see their work extend into other forms, such as book deals: the Julie and Julia project, for example, started as a blog dedicated to trying each recipe in Julia Child's *Mastering the Art of French Cooking* (Powell 2002), became a book, and was subsequently adapted into a film (Ephron 2009). While such cases are outliers for the blogosphere at large, since millions of blogs might only receive reader numbers in the tens rather than the thousands, let alone see their posts edited into books, they also demonstrate how sites can achieve clear prominence in the wider public consciousness, beyond a blog-specific (or Internet-only) context. Furthermore, even if bloggers are no longer achieving such popularity, similar trends can be seen with other social media platforms, as books are published based on prominent Twitter accounts and hashtags, from comedic intentions to social justice movements and projects combatting social issues (Bates 2014).

Developments like Google purchasing Blogger, and the integration of blogging into news and commentary sites and portals, demonstrate the acceptance of blogs, and the prominence of blogging within the popular consciousness. Individuals could blog for free, but the decision to invest millions of dollars into blogging platforms and infrastructure shows a recognition of blogs as a component of online culture and the mediasphere. From a new and alternative practice to the mainstreaming of blogging and evolving approaches, blogs—and bloggers as unique voices, new influencers, and topical experts—occupied key positions in the extended mediasphere. As a new social media ecology developed, with the growing popularity of centralized sites such as Facebook and Twitter, public attention moved to these newer platforms; however, even if blogging's major points of public, cultural, or political impact had passed in Western contexts, this does not mean that the blogosphere became a ghost town, as more and more users signed up to Facebook.

Youth Culture Killed My Blog?

The Western blogging moment was exactly that: "peak blog" (to use current but almost inevitably immediately dated parlance) came and went, as blogging transitioned from being something new to an established and accepted practice online. However, the uses and popularity of blogs as active pursuits continued unabated, even with the rise of newer platforms. Furthermore, the affordances that enabled casual Internet users without extensive technical literacies to start blogging continued to develop, leading to the growth of social networking sites and social media which built on blogging's achievements and made them even more accessible to a wider Internet population.

Blogging's appeal lay in part in the ability of users to create their own websites, for free, without needing to know how to code or pay for hosting or domain names, and post to the content they wanted to; these may be as part of explicit networks of friends and other users of interest (such as LiveJournal), or in more discrete arrangements where networks and connections were articulated through lists of links or citations in blog posts. This latter situation, though, did not create the same centralized feel—and content feeds—for networks: multiple friends might all have blogs on Blogger or Wordpress, for instance, but these hosts did not initially offer a way for a user to see all posts by their friends in one place. RSS readers created a means for aggregating these posts, from multiple blogging hosts; the discontinuation of popular RSS services like Google Reader (in 2013) is perhaps reflective of the transition from requiring such aggregators to centralized feeds on single platforms and indeed of different modes of content provision and readership (mobile apps, Facebook pages, Twitter accounts, and more).

The importance of centralization can be seen in the popularity of social media like Facebook, especially in that site's mid-2000s tussle for user numbers with MySpace; by offering users not only the opportunity to create their own profile, and share content and comments for free, but also the ability to connect to friends' Facebook profiles and have friends' posts appear in an aggregated feed, Facebook used successful elements of blogs to shape online social networking. At the same time, neither Facebook nor MySpace was a blogging platform: while MySpace included a blog function, and the reverse chronology of the Facebook news feed (now just one option for displaying content) as well as the space for personal expression and sharing reflected elements of blogs, these platforms were not designed as blogs. Facebook's uses surpassed blog-like activities with the introduction of third-party apps and features like pages and groups; meanwhile, its blog equivalent, the Notes feature, declined in visibility over time and with site redesigns.

The integration of blog-like functionalities into social networking sites, social media, and indeed to other websites, highlights the transition from blogging alone to blogging within: rather than blogs being individual, stand-alone sites, they (or their equivalents) became additional elements of extended websites and online platforms. Users do not employ one single social media platform or app to post content or commentary and make connections with others, but instead are active on the likes of Facebook, Twitter, Instagram, YouTube, Snapchat, Tinder, Tumblr, and Pinterest, and many more (including more niche platforms), simultaneously or through linked profiles, and for different purposes and audiences; similarly, blogs became one aspect of a social media ecology that were read and written, shared and commented on, but not the sole destination or outlet.

This transition is underlined by the growth of Twitter in particular. The 140-character limit for tweets helped encourage Twitter's promotion as a "microblogging" platform (as was also the case for the Chinese-language Weibo), yet while elements such as the reverse chronological display of content have become standard in such spaces, Twitter's uses extend beyond those of blogs (see Weller *et al.* 2013). These are in part due to the different affordances and norms of Twitter and blogs, and the different populations using these platforms; interpersonal communication, including among friends and acquaintances but also encompassing celebrities, politicians, and organizations, are (in a Western context especially) more commonplace on Twitter than blogs for the simple reason that Twitter is more widely used. Indeed, Twitter allows for the personal posting of comments and content, of linking to other content of interest, and sharing other people's thoughts, without the same amount of effort for creating and maintaining a blog (with tweets actively promoting concision rather than long-form commentary).

Tumblr is another social media platform which could be seen as a successor to, or descendant of, blogging in its mid-2000s guise; in mixing functionalities of Twitter and blogging, Tumblr still maintains blogging terminology—its retweeting equivalent is "reblogging"—yet the cultural practices of Tumblr differ from the traditional styles of blogging (Rettberg 2014). While Tumblr users can post long-form writing, the platform is also a space for mixing comments and reactions with photos and other visual material, especially animated gifs drawn and recontextualized from popular culture sources. Of course, as noted earlier, image-driven blogs were popular practices, such as photoblogs; yet Tumblr is not just a space for original content, but is at times more a platform for mixing and appropriating content from various sources to provide commentary and entertainment.

The popularity of platforms such as Facebook, Twitter, and Tumblr demonstrate the move towards social media as opposed to blogging, focusing on smaller pieces of content and commentary, centralized content and audiences, and especially mobile-friendly content (in terms of reading and contributing). Similarly, popular opinion and cultural websites, such as Jezebel and io9, reflect the morphing of blogging and other discussion-oriented platforms— and indeed the integration of social media profiles for comments. The adoption and adaptation of blogging affordances, especially the reverse-chronological display of content as standard, reflects the impact that blogging had on Web development, but what is also clear is that blogging is just one part of a wider, evolving social media ecology (Bruns and Highfield 2012). These different platforms work in tandem, though, rather than competition: when news sites such as *The Guardian* cover breaking news (including crises, press conferences, parliamentary debates, or sports), they employ a live blog format with new posts for each update over the course of the event (Thurman and Walters 2013). The blog serves a further aggregational function, for not only does it let journalists provide more extended posts than would fit in a tweet, but they are also able to embed comments sourced from Twitter and from readers, videos and photos from Instagram, Vine, YouTube, and other sources. Each of these different platforms provides particular functions and affordances, and the live blogs help to curate this diversity by using them in extended and cumulative coverage of breaking news.

Individual and group blogs continue to publish new content, whether promotional, lifestyle-related, personal, or political; what the contemporary social media situation has helped to cause, though, is that blogs in general are no longer the sole—or primary—channels for this content. In addition to a blogger's individual, personal profiles, they might also run pages and accounts for their blogs—or related to their topic of interest—on Facebook or Twitter. New blog posts get promoted on these channels, but other content also gets shared here: social media are not merely an additional way of sharing links to posts, but provide opportunities for new audiences and alternative forms of content. Blogs can carry out similar functions to their earlier iterations, but for different rationales—the aggregational approach of live blogs, for example, is similar to those of filter and link blogs, but here the reasoning is that the blog provides a centralized space to highlight comments of interest, operating in tandem with associated discussions on social media. Blogs also act as equivalents for columns and opinion pieces on popular websites, although the inclusion of comments and blog post-like features on many articles makes the distinction between what is and what is not a blog more fuzzy: under the structural definition of a blog, based on its common elements, blogging might not seem as common a practice in 2015 as it was in 2005. Yet unconsciously surreptitious blogging takes place every day: elements introduced or popularized by blogging influence and shape other forms of online communication, such that, even if a Facebook Timeline might not fit the traditional idea of a "blog", aspects of it still show the traces of advances made by blogging a decade previously.

Conclusion: Blog Days Are Over?

As this overview has shown, blogging in 2014 is very different from blogging in 1997; as with many facets of Internet communication, there has been much change over the past decade and a half at cultural, technological, international, political, and economic levels (among others), and each of these has impacted upon the evolution of blogging. From personal journals to extended analyses of political subjects, economic statistics research, or climate change opinion pieces, from recipe sharing and restaurant reviews, collections of archival images, and tech culture commentary, to make-up tips and promotions, holiday diaries, and music discussions, blogs represent a wealth of subjects and approaches that might share no commonalities beyond being "blogs".

The variety within the blogosphere, and the affordances of blogs in, for example, offering a space for extended posts and comments, mean that, while blogging might not have the same visibility or popularity in 2014 as it did in 2005, the practice is not dead. Blogs are "old" media when it comes to online communication but, just as news and political blogs did not replace journalism (not that it was their aim), Twitter and Facebook have not overthrown the blogosphere. Blogging remains a key practice in multiple contexts. The importance of blogs for activist movements, especially in response to strict media regulations and government control, is in part because of the affordances of the platform, and partly because of security, surveillance, and privacy fears around using popular, centralized social media platforms. Projects like Global Voices, too, underline the contribution that blogging can make in non-Western contexts.

If blogs in the early 2000s were used as personal websites (whether topically focused or documenting an individual's day-to-day life), their adoption for this purpose reflected the key affordances and functionalities they enabled. The ability to post personal, user-generated content at will—whether short or longer-form pieces—without needing extensive technical literacies or infrastructure requirements (if an individual could access the Internet and browse the Web, they could essentially set up a blog) was inviting to many, allowing them to share their comments on any topic. Social networking sites and social media surpassed blogging in popularity, due to their own connections and functions, building on the appealing aspects of blogging, but also centralizing users (and having a more extensive user base) and offering more functions. However, blogging remains an active practice because its own abilities and specializations remain relevant and have not been completely replaced or integrated by social media platforms. Even if other media overshadow blogs in public consciousness, their functions and affordances are still critical—indeed, the historical trajectory of blogging has reached a point where the ubiquity of functions that emerged from blogs, and the established nature of blogs within the mediasphere, mean that blogs are still being created and read, even if they are not recognized or promoted using that label. Given the evolution of blogging over a decade and a half, the term "blog" might mean something very different in years to come—and it might fall out of favor completely—but blogging's influence will continue to help shape new practices in online communication.

References

Adamic, L. A., and Glance, N. (2005) *The Political Blogosphere and the 2004 US Election: Divided They Blog*, available at: www.blogpulse.com/papers/2005/AdamicGlanceBlogWWW.pdf

Alexanyan, K., and Koltsova, O. (2009) "Blogging in Russia Is Not Russian Blogging", in A. Russell and N. Echchaibi (eds), *International Blogging: Identity, Politics, and Networked Publics*, New York: Peter Lang, pp. 65–84.

Bates, L. (2014) *Everyday Sexism*, London: Simon & Schuster.

Baym, N. K., and Burnett, R. (2009) "Amateur Experts: International Fan Labour in Swedish Independent Music", *International Journal of Cultural Studies*, 12(5): 433–449.

Blood, R. (2002) "Weblogs: A History and Perspective", in J. Rodzvilla (ed.), *We've Got Blog: How Weblogs Are Changing Our Culture*, Cambridge, MA: Perseus Publishing, pp. 7–16.

Borschke, M. (2012) "Ad Hoc Archivists: Mp3 Blogs and the Generation of Provenance", *Continuum: Journal of Media & Cultural Studies*, 26(1): 1–10.

boyd, d., and Ellison, N. B. (2008) "Social Network Sites: Definition, History, and Scholarship", *Journal of Computer-Mediated Communication*, 13(1): 210–230.

Bruns, A. (2005) *Gatewatching: Collaborative Online News Production*, New York: Peter Lang.

Bruns, A., and Highfield, T. (2012) "Blogs, Twitter, and Breaking News: The Produsage of Citizen Journalism", in R. A. Lind (ed.), *Produsing Theory in a Digital World: The Intersection of Audiences and Production in Contemporary Theory*, New York: Peter Lang, pp. 15–32.

Bruns, A., and Jacobs, J. (2006) *Uses of Blogs*, New York: Peter Lang.

Burgess, J., and Green, J. (2009) *YouTube: Online Video and Participatory Culture*, Cambridge: Polity.

Choi, J. H. (2006) "Living in Cyworld: Contextualizing Cy-Ties in South Korea", in A. Bruns and J. Jacobs (eds), *Uses of Blogs*, New York: Peter Lang, pp. 173–186.

Cohen, K. R. (2005) "What Does the Photoblog Want?", *Media, Culture & Society*, 27(6): 883–901.

Connor (2008) "Music Alliance Pact: October 2008", *I Guess I'm Floating*, available at: www.iguessimfloating.net/2008/10/music-alliance-pact-october-2008.html

de Vries, K. (2009) "Bridges or Breaches? Thoughts on How People Use Blogs in China", in A. Russell and N. Echchaibi (eds), *International Blogging: Identity, Politics, and Networked Publics*, New York: Peter Lang, pp. 47–64.

Down Under Feminists' Carnival (n.d.) "About", *Down Under Feminists' Carnival*, available at: http://downunderfeministscarnival.wordpress.com/about/

Ephron, N. (2009) *Julie & Julia*, USA: Columbia Pictures.

Etling, B., Kelly, J., Faris, R., and Palfrey, J. (2010) "Mapping the Arabic Blogosphere: Politics and Dissent Online", *New Media & Society*, 12(8): 1225–1243, available at: http://nms.sagepub.com/cgi/doi/10.1177/146144 4810385096 (accessed 19 December 2010).

Garden, M. (2010) "Newspaper Blogs: The Genuine Article or Poor Counterfeits?", *Media International Australia, Incorporating Culture and Policy*, 135: 19–31.

Gillmor, D. (2006) *We the Media: Grassroots Journalism by the People, for the People*, Beijing and Sebastopol, CA: O'Reilly.

Global Voices (n.d.) *What Is Global Voices?*, available at: http://globalvoicesonline.org/about/

Goggin, G., and Noonan, T. (2006) "Blogging Disability: The Interface between New Cultural Movements and Internet Technology", in A. Bruns and J. Jacobs (eds), *Uses of Blogs*, New York: Peter Lang, pp. 161–172.

Harvey, E. (2013) "Collective Anticipation: The Contested Circulation of an Album Leak", *Convergence: The International Journal of Research into New Media Technologies*, 19(1): 77–94.

Highfield, T. and Bruns, A. (2012) "Confrontation and Cooptation: A Brief History of Australian Political Blogs", *Media International Australia*, 143: 89–98.

Hindman, M. (2009) *The Myth of Digital Democracy*, Princeton, NJ: Princeton University Press.

Hopkins, J., and Thomas, N. (2011) "Fielding Networked Marketing: Technology and Authenticity in the Monetization of Malaysian Blogs", in D. Araya, Y. Breindl, and T. J. Houghton (eds), *Nexus: New Intersections in Internet Research*, New York: Peter Lang, pp. 139–156.

Howard, P. N., and Hussain, M. M. (2011) "The Role of Digital Media", *Journal of Democracy*, 22(3): 35–48.

Jarrett, K. (2009) "Private Talk in the Public Sphere: Podcasting as Broadcast Talk", *Communication, Politics & Culture*, 42(2): 116–135.

Jenkins, H. (2006) *Convergence Culture: Where Old and New Media Collide*, New York: New York University Press.

Jones, J., and Himelboim, I. (2010) "Just a Guy in Pajamas? Framing the Blogs in Mainstream US Newspaper Coverage (1999–2005)", *New Media & Society*, 12(2): 271–288.

Keen, A. (2007) *The Cult of the Amateur: How Today's Internet Is Killing Our Culture*, New York: Doubleday.

Kelly, J., and Etling, B. (2008) *Mapping Iran's Online Public: Politics and Culture in the Persian Blogosphere*, available at: http://cyber.law.harvard.edu/publications/2008/Mapping_Irans_Online_Public

Kim, K-H., and Yun, H. (2008) "Cying for Me, Cying for Us: Relational Dialectics in a Korean Social Network Site", *Journal of Computer-Mediated Communication*, 13(1): 298–318, available at: http://dx.doi.org/10.1111/j.1083-6101.2007.00397.x

Lofgren, J. (2013) "Food Blogging and Food-Related Media Covergence", *M/C Journal*, 16(3), available at: http://journal.media-culture.org.au/index.php/mcjournal/article/viewArticle/638

Lovink, G. (2008) *Zero Comments: Blogging and Critical Internet Culture*, New York: Routledge.

MacKinnon, R. (2008) "Blogs and China Correspondence: Lessons about Global Information Flows", *Chinese Journal of Communication*, 1(2): 242–257.

Marwick, A. E., and boyd, d. (2011) "To See and Be Seen: Celebrity Practice on Twitter", *Convergence: The International Journal of Research into New Media Technologies*, 17(2): 139–158, available at: http://con.sagepub.com/cgi/doi/10.1177/1354856510394539 (accessed 8 October 2012).

Meraz, S. (2011) "The Fight for 'How To Think': Traditional Media, Social Networks, and Issue Interpretation", *Journalism*, 12(1): 107–127, available at: http://jou.sagepub.com/cgi/doi/10.1177/1464884910385193 (accessed 19 July 2011).

Mewburn, I., and Thomson, P. (2013) "Why Do Academics Blog? An Analysis of Audiences, Purposes and Challenges", *Studies in Higher Education*, 38(8): 1105–1119.

Munger, M. C. (2008) "Blogging and Political Information: Truth or Truthiness?", *Public Choice*, 134(1–2): 125–138.

Nahon, K., and Hemsley, J. (2013) *Going Viral*, Cambridge and Malden, MA: Polity.

Powell, J. (2002) *The Julie/Julia Project*, available at: https://web.archive.org/web/20110819073749/http://blogs.salon.com/0001399/2002/08/25.html

Rettberg, J. W. (2008) *Blogging*, Cambridge and Malden, MA: Polity.

Rettberg, J. W. (2014) *Seeing Ourselves Through Technology: How We Use Selfies, Blogs and Wearable Devices to See and Shape Ourselves*, Basingstoke: Palgrave Macmillan.

Rocamora, A. (2012) "Hypertextuality and Remediation in the Fashion Media: The Case of Fashion Blogs", *Journalism Practice*, 6(1): 92–106.

Russell, A. (2007) "Digital Communication Networks and the Journalistic Field: The 2005 French Riots", *Critical Studies in Media Communication*, 24(4): 285–302.

Russell, A. (2009) "Introduction: International Blogging—Identity, Politics, and Networked Publics", in A. Russell and N. Echchaibi (eds), *International Blogging: Identity, Politics, and Networked Publics*, New York: Peter Lang, pp. 1–10.

Russell, A., and Echchaibi, N. (2009) *International Blogging: Identity, Politics, and Networked Publics*, New York: Peter Lang.

341

Schmidt, J. (2007) "Blogging Practices: An Analytical Framework", *Journal of Computer-Mediated Communication*, 12(4): 1409–1427.

Sedeke, K., and Arora, P. (2013) "Top Ranking Fashion Blogs and Their Role in the Current Fashion Industry", *First Monday*, 18(8), available at: http://firstmonday.org/ojs/index.php/fm/article/view/4314/3739

Senft, T. M. (2013) "Microcelebrities and the Branded Self", in J. Hartley, J. Burgess, and A. Bruns (eds), *A Companion to New Media Dynamics*, Chichester and Malden, MA: John Wiley & Sons, pp. 346–354.

Shaw, A., and Benkler, Y. (2012) "A Tale of Two Blogospheres: Discursive Practices on the Left and Right", *American Behavioral Scientist*, 56(4): 459–487.

Shaw, F. (2012a) " 'Hottest 100 Women': Cross-Platform Discursive Activism in Feminist Blogging Networks", *Australian Feminist Studies*, 27(74): 373–387.

Shaw, F. (2012b) "The Politics of Blogs: Theories of Discursive Activism Online", *Media International Australia, Incorporating Culture and Policy*, 142: 41–49.

Singer, J. B. (2005) "The Political J-Blogger: 'Normalizing' a New Media Form to Fit Old Norms and Practices", *Journalism*, 6(2): 173–198.

Sunstein, C. (2008) "Neither Hayek nor Habermas", *Public Choice*, 134(1–2): 87–95.

Thurman, N., and Walters, A. (2013) "Live Blogging—Digital Journalism's Pivotal Platform? A Case Study of the Production, Consumption, and Form of Live Blogs at Guardian.co.uk", *Digital Journalism*, 1(1): 82–101.

Trammell, K. D., and Keshelashviki, A. (2005) "Examining New Influencers: A Self-Presentation Study of A-List Blogs", *Journalism and Mass Communication Quarterly*, 82(4): 968–982.

Weller, K., Bruns, A., Burgess, J., Mahrt, M., and Puschmann, C. (2013) *Twitter and Society*, New York: Peter Lang.

Yeshua-Katz, D., and Martins, N. (2013) "Communicating Stigma: The Pro-Ana Paradox", *Health Communication*, 28(5): 499–508.

Zuckerman, E. (2008) "Meet the Bridgebloggers", *Public Choice*, 134(1–2): 47–65.

23

SURVIVAL OF THE MOST FLEXIBLE? NATIONAL SOCIAL MEDIA SERVICES IN GLOBAL COMPETITION

The Finnish Case

Jaakko Suominen, Petri Saarikoski, Riikka Turtiainen, and Sari Östman

In this chapter we argue that in the early 2000s, there was far more room for national services or services that expanded operations country by country. By "national services", in this context, we mean commercial Internet services created by Finns and that are totally, or primarily, owned by Finns. Ever since the rise of large global social media services, such as YouTube, Facebook, and Twitter, the living space of national services has narrowed; they have either vanished or attempted to adapt in various ways to the changing Internet climate. In between, there have been various phases when user cultures have been negotiated in order to become new (for example, "wars" between Jaiku/Qaiku users vs. Twitter users). Likewise, it appears that the infrastructure of Finnish-originated, Internet-related inventions and innovations, which are not strongly considered national, survive longer than individual local, national, or transnational services.

We analyze the life-cycles of various national Finnish social media services and platforms such as IRC-Galleria (a photo gallery whose majority of users were teenagers), Jaiku and Qaiku (microblogging services), and Vuodatus (a blog platform). Through analyzing use, public discourses, as well as ownership of services, we study the role that Finnish services played in a global Internet culture. We consider questions such as: Have the services utilized an internationalization strategy? How has their "Finnishness" been defined in public discourses? Have the services managed to adapt and evolve in the ever-changing conditions of global competition, technologies, and user cultures?

Theoretically, we follow consumer researcher Mika Pantzar's (2000) conceptualizations of product genetics and commodity ecology: to what extent (*missä määrin*) were the above-mentioned social media services able to create a favorable environment for themselves? Pantzar defines six relationship types that two commodities can have. He talks about: 1) conceptual relationship, 2) stake-output (*panos-tuotos*) relationship, 3) competition relationship, 4) collaboration and symbiosis, 5) commensalism, as well as 6) exploitation relationship (a predator-prey model). However, first, we will illustrate the history and the context of the popularization of the Internet in Finland.

History of the Internet and Other Information Networks in Finland

The first trials on data transfer occurred in Finland in the early 1960s, when, for example, the Helsinki telephone society (*Helsingin Puhelinosuuskunta*) experimented with the IBM 1001 data transmission system. Finnish universities received the Univac 1108 computer in 1970, and a network between universities was created for using the machine. In Finland, as in many other countries, television was the key medium, which was paired in public discussions with mainframe computers for the creation of more consumer-oriented online services in the 1970s. While this mainly extended only to experiments with teletext, however—for example, in journalism study literature—the concept of interactivity was introduced in the context of computer-networked communication. In 1980, the information networks were already referred to as highways, even though the concept of the "information superhighway" was only popularized 15 years later (Paasonen 2009).

> An information network, or integrated information network, which transmits all the individual as well as mass communication people need, is the goal of communication technology. The cable is called a motorway of communication, because it has significant potential to serve people as consumers and salespersons, as receivers of messages as well as senders of them.
>
> (Sisättö 1980)

> [*Tietoverkko tai integroitu tietoverkko, joka välittää kaiken ihmisten tarvitseman sekä kohde- että joukkoviestinnän, on viestintätekniikan tavoittelema päämäärä. Kaapelia sanotaan viestinnän moottoritieksi, koska sillä on suuret potentiaaliset mahdollisuudet palvella ihmisiä sekä kuluttajina että myyjinä, sanomien vastaanottajina ja lähettäjinä.*
>
> (Sisättö 1980)]

The state and large telephony companies were not the only ones who experimented with computer networks in the 1980s. Hobbyist efforts with home computers, modems, and bulletin board systems (BBS) promulgated the awareness of online communication. The first bulletin board system was established in Finland in 1982. Finnish University and Research Network (FUNET) was founded in 1984, and Finnish Unix Users registered the .fi country domain in 1986. Finland joined in the Internet at the end of 1988 via Nordic Infrastructure for Research & Education Network (NORDUNET). Only a minority of home computer users utilized BBSs, but the usage distributed the information about the possibilities among wider user communities. On one hand, use of the BBS might have sped up the appropriation of the Internet; however, on the other hand, some of the users might have postponed the start of the Internet use, because they could use similar online services otherwise (Hirvonen 2010).

The Internet became popular in Finland in the mid-1990s. At first, it meant merely rising public interest and introductions of the technology in media, whereas the usage occurred mainly in universities and, later, other educational institutions and workplaces where people became familiarized with the Internet, in many cases before they ever used it at home. Internet cafés didn't have a major role in introducing the Internet in Finland, even though there were some commercial trials for net cafés, as well as in introducing the net café concept as parts of state or EU-funded information society projects typically supporting the idea of invigorating local community activities with the help of computers and networks. In 1996, Internet penetration in Finnish households was below 10 percent, though the share of domestic users increased to about 40 percent of households in 2001. The spread of cellphones occurred much more rapidly than almost any other media technologies before that: in 1995, 20 percent of households owned a mobile phone. In five years, the amount had increased to 90 percent (Nurmela 2006).

State-governed information society projects, and public speeches by leading politicians such as President Martti Ahtisaari and Prime Minister Esko Aho, which claimed Finland to be the global number one information society, further strengthened the self-image of the model country of new technology in the mid-1990s. An essential factor in this debate was Nokia Corporation's international success as a producer of cellphones and mobile networks, which were connected to information network visions. After the economic depression in the early 1990s, economic recovery and success, connected to future-oriented technological success stories and hero stories, created a mentality of a digital technology advanced country which combined new technology, not only to economic operations, but also to the Nordic welfare-state ideology (see also Paasonen 2009).

Already in the 1990s, there were local or national trials with Internet services. The main arguments for their need was based on the idea of the importance of national languages in use, as well as the idea of better service with cultural understanding of local conditions. The developing project of a Finnish Web browser, Erwise (1993), had stayed marginal and unnoticed because it occurred soon after the introduction of WWW. Much more attention was paid to services such as the national search engine www.fi, which focused on Finnish Web domains, and was able to provide better search results among Finnish material than its international competitors. There was also a Finnish Web-based email service, Eemeli. Both of these, however, were lost in competition to Google (established in 1998) and other international service providers in the early 2000s. Eemeli and www.fi still exist as brands, but no longer provide their original services.

The turn of the millennium mattered internationally and saw the burst of the new media economy bubble. In Finland, the stock exchange rates of the new media companies peaked in spring 2000, and thus tumbled downwards after that. However, Nokia Corporation maintained and even improved its position for a few years afterwards. Nonetheless, the situation increased critical voices and suspicions that Finland's celebrated position, especially with regard to Internet penetration and advanced uses of mobile telephony, had been overtaken by other countries.

The end of the new technology boom did not, however, have much of an effect on domestic use of the Internet. In households, the domestication of broadband connections was a significant turning point. Computers and the Internet were no longer used occasionally in specific situations, and machines and connections were open all the time. In 2002, around 10 percent of households had a broadband connection, but during 2005, the share of broadband connections went up to over 50 percent. In the spring of 2005, 70 percent of Finns regularly used the Internet, and for the age group of 15–29 years the share was over 95 percent, so it was no wonder that some of the most popular Internet services were tailored to teenagers and young adults. In recent years, the share of Internet use within the whole population has become over 90 percent. Usage in the oldest age groups is related to whether or not the individual had a chance to learn to use the Internet in their work life. The (faster) Internet connections were more often usually first introduced in families that had children and teenagers (Nurmela 2006).

Community services, as well as tele operators such as Sonera, and Elisa-owned portal pages, such as Sonera Plaza, Saunalahti, and Elisa.net, had acted as sorts of seeds for social media, because portals gathered various content services from browser-based games and news for discussion and chat forums. The portal services activated interaction between users. One of the most popular online discussion forums in Finland has been Suomi24.fi (Finland24), with over a million users weekly. It was established in 1998, originally as a portal called Sirkus.com, and has been successively owned by Telia, Eniro, and Aller Media, which are Nordic tele operators and media corporations. Tele operators bought popular services and added them to their portals as well as introducing subportals for certain target groups. For example, Sonera launched its female-oriented Ellit portal on Women's Day, 18 March 1999.

After the burst of the Internet bubble, the firms were, over the next few years, more careful with their investments and visions. The new rise happened because of the discussion about Web 2.0, which was soon conceptually transformed into social media. Both terms lived side-by-side. However, Web 2.0 was comprehended as a more technologically specific phenomenon, as a base that was topped by social media. The definition of terms in Finland occurred mainly in experts' interviews with newspapers, as well as reports made by researchers and other new media professionals. The reports usually touched upon the commercial potentialities of Web 2.0 and social media, and were targeted to state officers, politicians, and firms. The golden age for Web 2.0 reports were the years 2006–2008, which was subsequently followed by a boom in social media reports. In the Web 2.0 reports, authors usually referred in their term definition to Tim O'Reilly's article *What Is Web 2.0? Design Patterns and Business Models for the Next Generation of Software* (2005), but the definitions of social media were more unique. One of the most referred to Finnish definitions of social media has been presented in a report, *Social Media: Introduction to the Tools and Processes of Participatory Economy*, by Esa Sirkkunen and Katri Lietsala (2008). The report was funded by the Finnish Funding Agency for Technology and Innovations, Tekes, which has been behind some other reports. (Other financiers of such reports have been ministries and the Finnish Innovation Fund, SITRA, which also funded the above-mentioned procurement of a Univac 1108 computer in 1970.)

Sirkkunen and Lietsala (2008: 24–26) based their definition of social media on discussions of participatory cultures and summarized features of social media to five characteristics:

1. There is a space for sharing content.
2. Participants in this space create, share, or evaluate all or most of the content themselves.
3. It is based on social interaction.
4. All content has a URL to link it to the external networks.
5. All actively participating members of the site have their own profile page to link other people to the content, to the platform itself, and to the possible applications.

They added five more characteristics which were not obligatory but common in social media services:

1. It feels like a community.
2. People contribute for free.
3. There is a tagging system that allows folksonomy.

4. Content is distributed with feeds in and out of the site.
5. The platforms and tools are in the development phase and changed on the run.

For Sirkkunen and Lietsala, social media was an umbrella term consisting of different genres such as content creation and publishing tools, content sharing, social network services, collaborative productions, virtual worlds, as well as add-ons.

In the following sections, we will return to the beginning of the era of Web 2.0 and social media, and depict three different cases and their trajectories during the last 10–15 years.

IRC-Galleria: Representation of Finnish Youth on the Net

There are many nicknames that have been created in reference to Finns born in the late 1980s and the early 1990s: "Generation Y"; "Digital Natives"; the "Cookie Dough Generation" ["pullamössösukupolvi", a Finnish term for a weaker generation or a "me" generation]; "Children of the Depression". I disagree with these terms. If my own generation should be labeled as something, it should be the IRC-Galleria Generation. Through IRC, we have grown and learnt the social norms of the Internet, years before the masses discovered Facebook. At its height, the sum total of the idle time of IRC-Gallery users was over 1000 years.

It was in this rather sentimental manner that the journalist Oskari Onninen (2013) began his retrospective article about the Finnish online community and Web gallery known as IRC-Galleria published in *Image*, an urban lifestyle magazine. The community platform was established by active Internet relay chat (IRC) users Jari "jaffa" Jaanto and Tomi "shalafi" Lintelä in December 2000 for allowing Finnish IRC users to post images of themselves. However, Timo Oksanen had already, three years before, set up a portrait gallery of IRC users under the same name.

Over the course of a few years, the service sought to distance itself from its IRC roots and become a more general online community targeted mainly towards 15–25-year-old users. Its

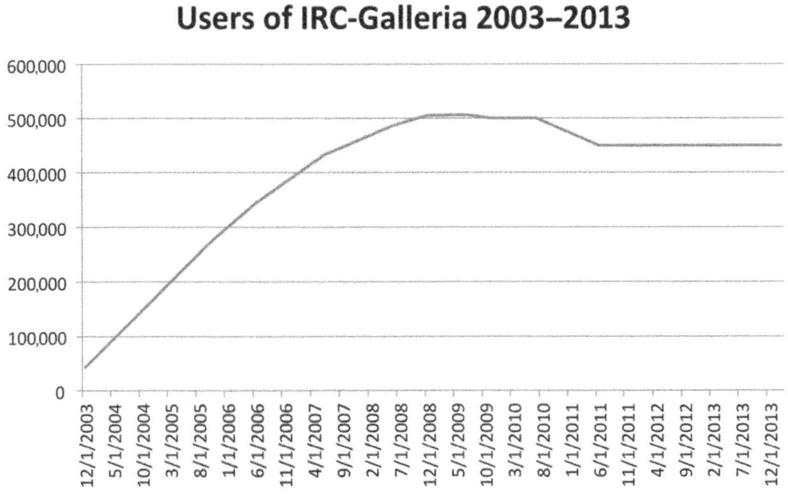

Users of IRC-Galleria 2003–2013

Figure 23.1 Registered users according to IRC-Galleria's own information

main contents were photos published by users and comments related to the photos. The service consisted of other features such as maintaining online diaries and profile pages. In its heyday from 2006 to 2007, IRC-Galleria was described as the most popular Web service in the Nordic countries, and was used by approximately 70 percent of Finnish 15–17-year-olds on a weekly basis. According to some sources, it had more users than similar services in Sweden—Lunarstorm and Bilddagboken—even though Sweden's population is almost double that of Finland. However, such comparisons are not straightforward to conduct, because user statistics vary in different countries. In Finland, it had some competitors, like Kuvake.net and ii2, but they were less popular. In the media, IRC-Galleria was portrayed, at its peak, as a major source of public opinion for Finnish teenagers. Despite the fact that key representatives of the service emphasized that the average age of users was around 20 years, IRC-Galleria was publicly seen to be representative of the teenage online community and "the biggest teen media in Finland". Service providers marketed IRC-Galleria as a platform for conducting surveys. According to newspaper reports, several surveys were conducted with different collaborators about various themes, such as teenage opinion on drugs, cigarettes, girls, and violent behavior, individuals' relationship to money and consumption, activity in politics, and so forth. Likewise, scholars of youth studies began to pay attention to IRC-Galleria and published studies on teenage online behavior, virtual consumption, social networks, as well as about how the users shared photos and represented themselves in their online images.

The service's popularity grew, at first incrementally and then, later, more rapidly. However, only later, in 2007–2008, was the public eye focused on it (see Figure 23.3). IRC-Galleria was also able to compete against MySpace, which never enjoyed much success in Finland and also lost out to competition, mainly from Facebook, due in part to several interconnected, albeit ambiguous, reasons. Even though the rise of the popularity of Facebook started among somewhat older user groups (25–35-year-olds) compared to IRC-Galleria during summer and autumn 2007, younger users more or less surprisingly followed, and gradually became active Facebook users over the next two years. The attractive pull of Facebook increased incrementally, and the developing variety of Facebook features began to attract younger user-groups as well, at least in the short term—even though their own parents also started to

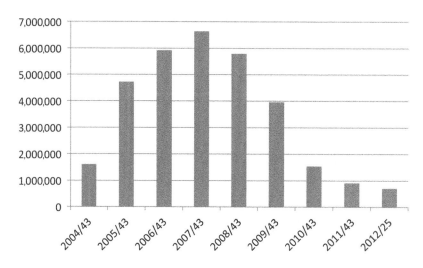

Figure 23.2 Weekly visits to the IRC-Galleria sites according to TNS-Metrix

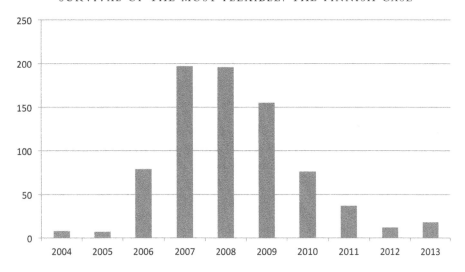

Figure 23.3 Hits of IRC-Galleria in the *Sanoma* newspaper archive

populate Facebook. IRC-Galleria had been sort of its own "parent-free" online space for teenagers, who used nicknames for sharing photos, chatting and getting to know new people.

The founders of the service established a company called Dynamoid for operating and developing IRC-Galleria in 2003, but the company only hired a general manager just prior to 2006 when "serial-entrepreneur" Taneli Tikka was recruited. During his short managing period (2006–2007), IRC-Galleria was sold to Sulake Labs, which operated another Finnish key online service, the Habbo Hotel virtual playworld. Habbo Hotel was targeted at younger users than the typical users of IRC-Galleria, and thus, the two services seemed to provide a promising continuum for the growing user age-groups from 12 (or less) to over 20 years old.

The deal, valued at 15 million euros on the company stock exchange in the spring of 2007, was probably the biggest turning point in the history of IRC-Galleria. The transaction received substantial public attention in Finland, which was somewhat comparable to the international hype generated in autumn 2006 by Google's YouTube investment. Even though at this time the hype's context was national, it also received a similar amount of attention regarding the economic growth of social media and discussion about the possibilities for advertising-based and virtual consumption-based business models, as well as about possible complications for the service related to, for example, privacy issues, stalking, and virtual crimes.

During its heyday, IRC-Galleria attempted to internationalize, country by country, while similar services were introduced in Russia and the Baltic countries, as well as in Germany. However, in Russia, for example, IRC-Galleria remained marginal compared to, for example, the social network service VKontakte which was founded in 2007. The company also produced a photo gallery, "The Dark Portal", for the online game World of Warcraft, but this was not very successful, however (Suominen *et al.* 2013: 115). Its key staff emphasized the service's Finnishness in comparison to its international rivals. Further, IRC-Galleria received the Finnish original emblem "avainlippu" (leader flag) in 2007 from the Association for Finnish Work, and was the first and only online service to receive that recognition, which is usually only granted to Finnish-made industrial products.

However, it should be noted that IRC-Galleria received negative publicity in autumn 2007 after the Jokela school shooting, which occurred on 7 November 2007 at Jokela High School in Jokela, a town in the municipality of Tuusula, Finland. An 18-year-old gunman entered the school that morning armed with a semi-automatic pistol, killing eight people and injuring several others before shooting himself in the head, which caused his death the same evening (Wikipedia 2015a). The perpetrator had uploaded photos on the service, as well as videos on YouTube, and had actively used other online message boards before the massacre. The same type of massacre occurred a year later when a new school shooting, now in Kauhajoki, took place (Wikipedia 2015b). These horrible events were not, however, the reason for the decline of the use of the service. We would argue that Facebook "siphoned off" IRC-Galleria's users as they grew older, when they began to prefer more international network services suitable for versatile use, and both professional and domestic communication, and Facebook provided more services, content, and users. Another possible cause might be that older siblings also introduced Facebook to their younger siblings. We should note, after all, that Facebook managed to transform more quickly than IRC-Galleria as it was international and provided more versatile features than IRC-Galleria.

The decline can be observed from press reports, as well as from IRC-Galleria front pages, archived in the Internet Archive from 2003 onwards. In autumn 2009, IRC-Galleria stopped publishing the exact numbers of users on its front page. Further, its position on the Finnish top website list started to fall at the same time. After the summer of 2012, it was no longer listed on TNS-Metrix, which is the leading and most referred to survey of usage of net services in Finland. Until that point, IRC-Galleria received the highest amount of newspaper hits in 2007 and 2008.

In the press, spokespersons for IRC-Galleria had to explain their services' strengths compared to Facebook and MySpace, the latter having tried to localize its services and having already established an office in Finland in January 2008. The manager, Ville Mujunen, who was responsible for IRC-Galleria for the Sulake Company, claimed in the *Taloussanomat* newspaper that the arrival and localization of MySpace had not affected IRC-Galleria. He argued that international competitors' aggressive and straightforward marketing strategy had not functioned in Finland. He alleged that Facebook, as a trend, was clearly reflected in larger cities, and only admitted that there had been some slight transition in the oldest user groups, over 22-year-olds, from IRC-Galleria to Facebook. According to Mujunen, Facebook focused on managing existing networks of friends, whereas the very active and loyal user group of IRC-Galleria were centered on the creation of new contacts (*Taloussanomat* 2008).

Two and a half years later, some newspapers published stories on the decline of IRC-Galleria use: the amount of weekly visitors had decreased from 800,000 to less than 500,000. Mujunen had to downplay the situation and emphasize interaction between different services: one was able to log in to IRC-Galleria with a Facebook account, and IRC-Galleria was set to profile more like a public meeting point in comparison to the "friend-networking" Facebook. Additionally, due to the economic depression, for this service, as for the others, it was more challenging to obtain advertising, which brought revenue for the service, in addition to selling virtual items to users.

However, the profiling and connections to Facebook were not successful. The teenage masses had already abandoned IRC-Galleria and were not coming back. The University of Helsinki conducted a survey of teenage social media use in Finland in spring 2011. According to the survey report, use of IRC-Galleria had collapsed: whereas only 17 percent of 7–20-year-old participants still used IRC-Galleria often or sometimes, over 80 percent of 16–20-year-olds, and over 70 percent of 13–15-year-olds used Facebook (Aarnio and Multisilta 2012).

At of the time of writing, spring 2014, IRC-Galleria still exists. Its original founders bought back the service from Sulake in December 2011. However, its popularity is only a shadow of what it once was. The journalist Onninen crystallized the feelings of old users of the service when he said:

> Nowadays, browsing IRC-Galleria feels like strolling in the museum of one's own teenage years, where some of the most important things are missing. Alternatively, it is like looking at tattered diary entries from the same age. Only a fraction of that life lived on Gallery is left.
>
> (Onninen 2013)

When applying Mika Pantzar's above-mentioned theories, it appears that IRC-Galleria had, at first, a commensal relationship with other online communities and social network services such as Facebook. All social media services benefited from the boom in social networking sites, media hype, and the need for online content sharing. The relationship, however, altered and became a rivalry. When IRC-Galleria started to lose to the competition, the service sought collaboration and symbiosis with Facebook—for example, permitting log in with a Facebook account. The next brief case consists of similar phases. The Finnish blog platform Vuodatus benefited from the general popularity of weblogs. However, later on, it started to lose popularity, not only to other weblog platforms, but also to other forms of social media services.

Women's Technology: The Finnish Blog Platform

Weblogs had gained popularity in Finland during 2003. Until then, it was uncommon for most people to write or even read weblogs (Suominen *et al.* 2013: 35–36). The blog platform Vuodatus (English translation "tirade" or "outpouring") was established in summer 2004 by Tuomas Rinta. His first public post read: "Now it would be a good time to share a link to somewhere else. How about the nice people of Pinseri—are you interested?" Between 2002 and 2005, the Pinseri page contained a popular and famous list of all Finnish weblogs, and on 15 July 2004, its administrator, Sami Köykkä, wrote a post about Vuodatus, which he called the Finnish version of Blogger. He pointed out that along with the Finnish user interface, there were no longer any language barriers, and starting and maintaining a blog became possible for everyone in Finland (Köykkä 2004; Rinta 2010):

> You can call it a web diary, weblog, blog. Vuodatus.substanssi.net is a new Finnish service that provides its users the possibility to write their thoughts on the Internet for free. Whether you wanted to keep a diary or tell to the world your opinion about it daily, or just to collect your ideas in one place, you can do it here.
>
> (Rinta 2004)

During the test period, the platform had around 200 users (Suominen *et al.* 2013: 62). Early in 2005, the platform was moved under the name Vuodatus.net. Three years later, in 2008, the Finnish media house Alma Media's publishing company, Iltalehti, bought Vuodatus.net for an undisclosed sum from its founder, Tuomas Rinta, who became the development manager for the service. Rinta had stated only a few months prior that the site was not up for sale. Iltalehti, which was a part of Alma Media Corporation, was the publisher of the third largest print newspaper in Finland, as well as one of the most popular online media in Finland. Its biggest rival, *Ilta-Sanomat*, owned by media house Sanoma News, was buying up Web services as well. *Ilta-Sanomat* was the second largest newspaper in Finland, and Sanoma Digital owned, for instance, the blog service Blogilista which was formerly a part of Pinseri (*Digitoday* 2008; Vuodatus.net 2014). Rinta saw that it was the right time to take measures by developing Vuodatus as a business area. There were, even then, tens of thousands of blogs and over one million posts on the service. Vuodatus had thus reached "critical mass", but the Google advertising solution wasn't a profitable source of income for its administrator. However, Rinta assured that the blog platform would remain free for its users and there would no longer be any more advertisements on the site (Aalto 2008).

At that time, after the corporate acquisition (according to the referenced user survey), 90 percent of users of Vuodatus were women. The most popular topics of blog posts were handicrafts and cooking (Aalto 2008). Nonetheless, during the same year, the administration system of Vuodatus underwent a reformation. Adding photos to blog posts became easier and possible to do directly from the photo service Flickr. Rinta "missed his Christmas holidays" while updating the database of the new system. After three weeks of work, albeit with some difficulties, he announced in the bulletin blog that "the administrator is going to sleep now" (ITviikko 2009).

At the end of 2012, Vuodatus was sold to Rohea Oy. It had, at that point, over 300,000 weekly users, of which 94 percent were women, most likely over 25 years of age (TNS Metrix; Vuodatus.net). Sari Östman has argued that early web diaries, the forerunners of weblogs, were a combination of masculine technology and a feminine way of self-reflection. In Finland, publishers have been women, contrary to the situation in the United States (Östman 2007: 43–44). One of the first blog platforms, Blogger, was established in 1999. At that time, Finnish female web publishers were students familiar with information technology. Nowadays, most bloggers are still primarily students, but this group also includes retirees, mothers, working women—people of all kinds (Östman 2007: 52). Women are traditionally more familiar with the concept of diary writing (Gannett 1992: 26–27). In the beginning, weblogs were mostly like diaries moved from personal websites to easy to use platforms. Finnish men could have been uncomfortable also with the image of the blog service's name: "Outpouring" of emotions about everyday life.

Jaiku: Finland's Twitter

The popularity of blogs grew moderately in 2006, but at the same time, the concept of microblogging emerged. Microblogging referred to short messages on approximately the scale of SMS messages, to be sent and commented on around the Web. Microblogging was also related to instant messaging (with services such as Microsoft Messenger) and real-time chat applications, like IRC, which was created by Jarkko Oikarinen at the University of Oulu in August 1988 (Saarikoski *et al.* 2009: 94). Finns had already become accustomed to sending short mobile phone messages, and therefore microblogging was seen as a natural extension of mobile technology. RSS feeds, used to collect and summarize information from blogs and websites, can also be seen as predecessors of microblogging.

Internet entrepreneurs Jyri Engeström and Petteri Koponen started the Jaiku microblog service in February 2006. The founders of Jaiku chose the name because the posts on Jaiku resemble Japanese haiku. They explained that "it collects real time information from the phone address book—about where people are and what they are doing. It works just like instant messaging". Jaiku gained moderate popularity in Finland and the service had almost 10,000 registered users in December 2006. Users were typically active early adopters of social media. At this point, the service was not, however, open to all, and required an invitation to the service to take part. By comparison, the most popular Finnish service in social media was IRC-Galleria, with 345,000 registered users in spring 2006 (Suominen *et al.* 2013: 100–101).

The founders were very active in promoting their service at various events, and Jaiku gained some very positive feedback from this. Jyri Engeström, in particular, who was very well networked internationally, was a popular speaker and became known as a strong promoter of the Web 2.0 concept in Finland. Jaiku is very often compared to Twitter, which was founded by Jack Dorsey in July 2006. A clear advantage of Jaiku compared to Twitter was the possibility of using the Finnish language in communication and a strong sense of solidarity among early adopters (Koistinen 2006a). The most interesting feature of Jaiku was Lifestream, an Internet feed that shared users' online activities while utilizing other programs, such as Flickr for photos, last.fm for music, and the transmission of location via mobile phones. It was also possible to create a chain of comments. On the other hand, Twitter still remained relatively unknown in Finland, while the user base of Jaiku gained a positive reputation. However, at the same time, Twitter received more attention in future years when a number of other microblogging services were established.

The sociologist Ilpo Koskinen noted in *Verkkoviestintäkirja* (The Handbook of Network Communication) (2006) that services like Twitter and Jaiku could be called "moblogs", which refers to mobile blogging and image hosting. Koskinen stated that the moblogs were far more popular in Japan than in Europe, because usage of the Internet by mobile devices was very common in Japan. In addition, he stated that this was an obvious reason for why moblogging in Europe was mainly based on some short-term experiments. In Japan, on the other hand, moblogs worked like real-time browser-based diaries, which provided "trivial insights into the everyday life of the author". Moblogs also work well as tools of citizen journalism when people could quickly take and distribute pictures of important events, even before the arrival of professional journalists (Koskinen 2006: 132).

The concept of Web 2.0 became very fashionable in 2006, and Jaiku was presented as a spearhead of this new network phenomenon. "Users are now producing their own content on the Internet!" read a headline in *Talouselämä* magazine in December 2006. Nowadays, this type of statement would not even make the news at all, but at that time, the content sharing of one's private life in real time was seen as both a new and a revolutionary part of Internet culture. At the same time, the concept of social media began to increase—although at this stage, only slowly. Web 2.0 was defined as a new, more "social network" or "social software". New Finnish services, like Jaiku or Aula—a network community founded by Jyri Engeström together with Marko Ahtisaari—were also labeled as RIA (rich Internet applications) in the computer press. Social media was also even mentioned when experts speculated about what Web 3.0 might be. Many believed it would be connected with mobile phones and smart services in the near future (Suominen *et al.* 2013: 103).

Jaiku was opened to the public in March 2007. The popularity of Jaiku continued among early adopters and its service was widely used at various events and seminars during the following year. A small number of celebrities also began to use the service: perhaps the best known example was A. W. Yrjänä, the leading figure in the Finnish rock band CMX.

In late 2007, Jaiku already had over 40,000 registered users in Finland. There were also a few thousand users outside Finland (Suominen *et al.* 2013: 158–161). The service was noted for its functional simplicity, and as a consequence, it was uploaded as an application for Nokia Symbian-based mobile phones (a beta version was made available in April 2007, and an official version became available in August 2007). IT expert and journalist Kari A. Hintikka stated in October 2007 in *Mikrobitti* computer magazine that, for him, Jaiku was a fine example of a service that produced an augmented reality in real time. Hintikka also mentioned that, on the other hand, he was very skeptical about many of the prophecies of the future of social media. There was too much "hype" and "illusion" in many of the writings he had recently read. Hintikka stated that even many of the experts relied too much on the "Gibson-effect" (a reference to the cyberspace novelist William Gibson, who had been the driving force behind many of the visions of virtual reality in the 1990s, which had later collapsed). Hintikka referred, in particular, to the *Metaverse Roadmap 2016*, a report in which the future of virtual worlds was divided into four different "layers of reality" (Hintikka 2007a: 68; Hintikka 2007b: 77).

During 2007, however, the service gained a new competitor: Twitter. This new American microblogging service was used and tested in the same events and seminars where Jaiku was also presented. The service was much admired, but nonetheless the majority of users still preferred Jaiku. The original inventor of Jaiku, Mika Raento, stated in an interview that although Twitter could also be used on older mobile phone models, Jaiku was still more advanced and user-friendly for Finnish users. The inventor was, no doubt, very proud of his innovation, and perhaps therefore he also assumed that Twitter did not have a chance of success in Finland. But as the popularity of Jaiku grew, there was also some criticism. Jaiku fueled fears about the loss of privacy, for example, when inexperienced users accidentally shared private information with everyone. Mika Raento, nonetheless, stated that these problems were marginal and the service was functioning very well. Further, especially for young people, Jaiku was becoming an important part of their everyday lives (*Digitoday* 2007).

There had been rumors regarding Jaiku's future in the summer of 2007, but the user community was still shocked in October 2007 when they heard that Jaiku had been sold to Google. Shortly after this sale, the founders of Jaiku moved to California to continue their work for Google. During the ensuing years, Google was seriously planning to enter the mobile phone industry. A new Android-operating system designed and produced by Google for mobile devices had been in development for over two years. In 2008, the faith in the future of the service still remained high among Jaiku users, but slowly it became evident that Google had changed their plans and the development of Jaiku was put on hold. This chain of events turned out to be fatal for Jaiku. Thousands of users abandoned Jaiku during 2008 and started to use Twitter instead. The final blow came on 14 January 2009 when Google announced that it would "no longer actively develop the Jaiku codebase", leaving development to a "passionate volunteer team of Googlers". Jaiku lived on as marginal social media for some years, until the service was ultimately shut down in January 2012. Some of the developers of Jaiku started a new microblogging service called Qaiku, which was very similar to Jaiku. A small minority of Jaiku's original users started to use Qaiku. For some years afterwards there was a playful rivalry between the user groups of Qaiku and Twitter (Suominen *et al.* 2013: 195–196).

In interviews, many active users have said that the Jaiku community "had strong community spirit". Kari A. Hintikka remembers that all the early adopters of microblogging that he knew of used Jaiku. It was only after 2008 that core users left the service (Hintikka 2011). Mari Koistinen and Tuija Aalto, who were very well-known early adopters, have said that the service enriched, at the right time, user interaction in the early field of Finnish microblogging. Jaiku was instantly known for its "*Suomi-scene*" (Finland scene). However, when Google purchased Jaiku, the troubles started. Problems in development and technical difficulties during 2008 resulted in Jaiku going into crisis mode.

The history of "Finland's Twitter" demonstrates how the lifespan of a tiny, and yet, popular, microblogging service can be very short in the world of social media. In all likelihood, the growing popularity of Twitter in Finland in 2008 happened because frustrated Jaiku users simply walked away and started to use Twitter instead, while other users simply switched directly to Facebook. This also shows that the formation of communities in social media seems to follow the footsteps of the industry giants.

According to Pantzar's (2000) terminology, the Jaiku case is a combination of commensalism (popularity of microblogs), an exploitation model (the Google transaction), and competition relationship (with Twitter).

Conclusion

Our three main examples show that there has been a need for national social media services, meaning Finnish-developed platforms for Finnish users, in a relatively small country as well. However, what is difficult to estimate is that the unique something "Finnish" in these case services and their life-cycles are not greatly comparable to large states or populated states such as China, Russia, South Korea, or Japan. More comparative studies between similar types of national cases should be done.

Those three services enjoyed particular momentum in the early years of the first decade of the 2000s. The services were based on the earlier popularity of Internet use, new Web 2.0, and the social media boom, as well as a general positive economic trend. On one hand, the need for the services was explained by language reasons: users were eager for Finnish services because of their easier usability and the understanding of local needs, in addition to a desire to create and maintain social networks on a local and national basis, as not everybody was able, or wanted, to use English services. On the other hand, some services, such as Jaiku, weremore likely to target early adopters in the first place and were later aimed at the international market.

The services, however, experienced troubles later on. The popularization also spread as the localization of major international platforms such as Facebook and Twitter narrowed national operating spaces. Even though the services were global, their user interfaces became localized in terms of languages and their well-supported local, communal use. Users moved to other places, which seemed to be more interesting and/or progressive on a global level, and the change caused a vicious circle in which usage further decreased. This was the case, for example, within younger user groups, as well as with pioneers and early adopters. Further, due to the economic recession, possibilities for receiving investments for development or profit from advertising also decreased.

Our three case examples had different main user groups: with IRC-Galleria, it was primarily teenagers; with Vuodatus, female users; and with Jaiku, early technology adopters. However, in every case the services needed some sort of hobbyist interest and zeal at their inception. When the services became more popular, they started to generate more economic interest. The founders typically had a more technical background, but on the popularity curve, the input of "serial entrepreneurs" and other market-oriented professionals was needed. At the same time, the founders' interest or role in the developing services decreased, which caused turbulence in the long run. Even though currently the large international US-based services, such as Facebook and Twitter, are still dominant, a new challenger could appear. If the most popular services were to begin to suffer technical difficulties, privacy scandals, or even provide disturbing advertising, there would be new room, even for new local services, if they could provide an interesting and original user experience.

References

Aalto, T. (2008) *Vuodatus.net Hakee Liiketoimintamallia—Blogialusta Ei Kaupan Vierityspalkki.fi* (Vuodatus.net Seeks a Business Model—The Blog Platform is Not for Sale), available at: http://vierityspalkki.fi/2008/07/24/vuodatusnet-hakee-liiketoimintamallia-blogialusta-ei-kaupan (accessed 7 May 2014).

Aarnio, A., and Multisilta, J. (2012) *Facebook Ja Youtube—Ne On Meidän Juttu! Kansallinen Tutkimus Lasten Ja Nuorten Sosiaalisen Median Ja Verkkopalveluiden Käytöstä 2011* (Facebook and YouTube—They Are Our Thing! National

Study of Uses of Social Media and Net Services Among Children and Teenagers in 2011), Helsinki: Helsingin yliopisto.

Digitoday (2007) "Kontekstitieto Kiehtoi Jaikun Kehittäjää" (Context Information Captivated the Developer of Jaiku), 8 June.

Digitoday (2008) "Vuodatus Kuuluu Nyt Iltalehdelle" (Vuodatus Belongs to Iltalehti Now), 1 October.

Gannett, C. (1992) Gender and the Journal: Diaries and Academic Discourse, New York: State University of New York Press.

Hintikka, K. A. (2007a) "Jaikuilen, Siis Olen Nyt" (I am Jaikuing, Thus I am Now), MikroBitti, August.

Hintikka, K. A. (2007b) "Kohti Metaversea 2016" (Towards Metaverse 2016), MikroBitti, October.

Hintikka, K. A. (2011) interview, 7 July.

Hirvonen, M. (2010) "BBS-Harrastajat 1990-Luvun Tietoverkkokulttuurin Murrosvaiheessa—Näkökulmia Internetin Kulttuuriseen Omaksumiseen" (BBS Users in the Changing Phase of Online Cultures in the 1990s—Perspectives to Cultural Appropriation of the Internet), MA thesis, Digital Culture, Pori: Turun yliopisto.

ITviikko (2009) Suomalainen Blogipalvelu Vuodatus.net Uudistui (Finnish Blog Service Vuodatus.net Updated), 7 January.

Koistinen, M. (2006a) interview, 13 July.

Koistinen, M. (2006b) interview, 26 July.

Koskinen, I. (2006) "Mobiili Multimedia Ja Verkkoviestintä" (Mobile Multimedia and Network Communication), in P. Aula, J. Matikainen, and M. Villi (eds), Verkkoviestintäkirja (Handbook of Network Communication), Helsinki: Gaudeamus, pp. 121–136.

Köykkä, S. (2004) "Vuodatus Aloittaa" ("Vuodatus Starts"), Pinseri, available at: www.pinseri.com/2004/07/15/vuodatus-aloittaa (accessed 7 May 2014).

Nurmela, J. (2006) "Suomalaisten Tieto Ja Viestintätekniikan Käyttö—Sosiologisia Näkökulmia Verkkoviestintään" (Finnish Use of Information and Communication Technology—Sociological Perspectives), in P. Aula, J. Matikainen, and M. Villi (eds), Verkkoviestintäkirja (Handbook of Network Communication), Helsinki: Gaudeamus.

Onninen, O. (2013) "Kaikki Nuoret Tyypit" (All New Kids on the Block), Image, 18 June, available at: www.image.fi/artikkelit/kaikki-nuoret-tyypit

O'Reilly, T. (2005) What Is Web 2.0? Design Patterns and Business Models for the Next Generation of Software, 30 September, available at: www.oreilly.com/pub/a/web2/archive/what-is-web-20.html

Östman, S. (2007) "Nettiksistä Blogeihin: Päiväkirjat Verkossa" (From Net Diaries to Blogs. Diaries Online), Tekniikan Waiheita, 2: 37–57.

Paasonen, S. (2009) "What Cyberspace? Traveling Concepts in Internet Research", in G. Goggin and M. McLelland (eds), Internationalizing Internet Studies: Beyond Anglophone Paradigms, New York: Routledge, pp. 18–31.

Pantzar, M. (2000) "Tuotegenetiikkaa Ja Tavaraekologiaa: Kohti Tavaramaailman Orgaanista Kuvaa" (Product Genetics and Commodity Ecology: Towards an Organic View of Commodity World), in T. Lemola (ed.), Näkökulmia Teknologiaan (Perspectives to Technology), Helsinki: Gaudeamus, pp. 109–127.

Rinta, T. (2004) "Sinä Voit Kutsua Sitä Nettipäiväkirjaksi, Weblogiksi, Blogiksi" (You Can Call It Net Diary, Weblog, Blog), Vuodatus.Substanssi, available at: http://web.archive.org/web/20040715093710/http://vuodatus, substanssi.net (accessed 7 May 2014).

Rinta, T. (2010) "All Good Things Must Come to an End", Vuodatus, available at: http://tuomas.vuodatus.net/lue/2010/11/all-good-things-must-come-to-an-end (accessed 7 May 2014).

Saarikoski, P., Suominen, J., Turtiainen, R., and Östman, S. (2009) Funetista Facebookiin: Internetin kulttuurihistoria (From Funet to Facebook: A Cultural History of the Internet), 1st edn, Helsinki: Gaudeamus.

Sirkkunen, E., and Lietsala, K. (2008) Social Media: Introduction to the Tools and Processes of Participatory Economy, Tampere: Tampere University Press.

Sisättö, S. (1980) (ed.) Kaapelitelevisio (Cable Television), Viestintä Uuteen Aikaan (Communication Up to Date), Helsinki: Weilin+Göös.

Suominen, J., Östman, S., Saarikoski, P., and Turtiainen, R. (2013) Sosiaalisen Median Lyhyt Historia (A Short History of Social Media), 1st edn, Helsinki: Gaudeamus.

Talouselämä (2006) "Käyttäjät Tuottavat Nyt Itse Sisältöä Internetissä" (Users Are Now Producing Their Own Content on the Internet), 15 December.

Taloussanomat (2008) "MySpace Sisään, IRC-Galleria Ulos" (MySpace In, IRC-Galleria Out), 8 January.

TNS Metrix (2012) Weekly Statistics of the Finnish Websites, October, available at: http://tnsmetrix.tns-gallup.fi/public/?lang=en

Vuodatus.net (2014) Vuodatus.net, available at: http://vuodatus.net (accessed 7 May 2014).

Wikipedia (2015a) "Jokela school shooting", Wikipedia, available at: https://en.wikipedia.org/wiki/Jokela_school_shooting

Wikipedia (2015b) "Kauhajoki school shooting", Wikipedia, available at: https://en.wikipedia.org/wiki/Kauhajoki_school_shooting

24

TOWARDS THE SOCIAL AND MOBILE

The Development of the Mobile Internet in China and Japan

Baohua Zhou, Shihui Gui, Fumitoshi Kato, Kana Ohashi, and Larissa Hjorth

Introduction

In this chapter we explore two divergent histories for the rise of social and mobile media—China and Japan. In these two different histories we see how various technological, cultural, social, and linguistic factors have informed the uptake and adoption of social and mobile media. Both countries share some common techno-cultural characteristics, especially the trend towards social mobile media. In particular, convergent social mobile media platforms—WeChat in China and LINE in Japan—are increasingly playing a key role in everyday media spaces.

As we argue in this chapter, social mobile media has become integral in many people's everyday life and interpersonal relationships, especially in and around family communication. It is this intergenerational communication that envelops the mundane intimacies with hybrid forms of new media literacy. Our preliminary findings, drawn from a three-year Australian Research Council discovery project, highlight the significance of mobile media use within both the mundane intimacies (such as conversation with family members) and also broader social and political actions. In order to explore these intergenerational intimate mundane ties we begin with a contextualization of the rise of social mobile media in China, followed by Japan.

Internet and Social Media Development in China: An Historical Overview

In September 1987, 19 years after the birth of the American Advanced Research Project Agency Net (ARPANET), the Internet came to China. The China Academic Network (CANET) officially established the first international Internet email node in Beijing, and sent out the first email from China to Germany on 14 September 1987. The email included the text, "Across the Great Wall we can reach every corner in the world", marking the debut of the Internet in China.

In April 1994, China established its TCP/IP protocol. Later, the first webpage "Tour in China", was launched to introduce Chinese economic, cultural, and trade developments to foreign visitors. At the same time, in order to keep pace with the Information Highway Project being proposed by the American government, Beijing launched its so-called "Golden Projects", or the "Golden Bridge", "Golden Shield", and "Golden Card", which symbolized the official initiation of commercialization and civil use of the Internet in China. From May 1995, Internet business was officially open to the public (CNNIC 2009).

From 1997 to 1998, commercial portal websites such as NetEase.com (www.163.com), Sina.com (www.sina.com.cn) and Sohu.com (www.sohu.com) were established, marking the arrival of the Web 1.0 era in China. As they covered a wide range of information, from politics to economics, from entertainment to sports, these portal websites attracted huge traffic, thus functioning as important news distribution channels for Chinese audiences. The new online news distribution model greatly challenged the traditional information and communication model in content creation, business operation, and capital structure. At the same time, most leading traditional media organizations such as *People's Daily* and *CCTV* also established their online versions.

With blogging arising from 2003, social media gradually grew in visibility. Around 2005, China fully embraced the user-oriented Web 2.0 era in the form of blogging—epitomized in 2006 when "You" was chosen as the *Time Magazine* person of the year. Internet users, young and old, rushed to register their own blog accounts and to keep online diaries. Over the past decade, with the introduction and rise of the mobile Internet, millions of Chinese have embraced the online as part of everyday life.

According to the latest statistical report released by the China Internet Network Information Center (CNNIC 2015), by June 2015 the Chinese online population reached 668 million (ranked number one globally), and nationwide Internet coverage reached 48.8 percent of the population. Among this percentage, mobile phone netizens figured predominantly—88.9 percent (594 million). However, despite the rise of Internet accessibility afforded by mobile media, it should be noted that there are still imbalances according to region, gender, and socio-economic status. For example, the Internet penetration rate in urban China has reached 64.2 percent in 2015, whereas the Internet penetration in regional areas is 30.1 percent (CNNIC 2015).

Today, the Chinese Internet industry consists of roughly three domestic Internet giants referred to as BAT—namely Baidu (www.baidu.com), established in 2000; Alibaba (www.alibaba.com), established in 1999; and Tencent (www.qq.com), established in 1998. These three giants control an enormous amount of user data. In particular, BAT has a wide range of investments, covering various fields of SNS, e-commerce, online gaming, online payment, entertainment, lifestyle, and medical care, and have produced several Internet products with national popularity such as Taobao (an online-shopping website/APP launched by Alibaba in 2003) and WeChat (an Instant Messaging APP launched by Tencent in 2011).

Along with the rapid growth of the Internet in China, control of Internet content has gradually been strengthened. The Chinese government has officially regulated online content and services since 2000. The current Chinese Internet content control system consists of two parts—content censorship over domestic websites, and access blockage targeting websites outside the state's jurisdiction. The famous Great Firewall (GFW) system makes a large number of international websites such as Google, Facebook, and YouTube inaccessible to Chinese netizens. The blockage of foreign websites led by the state acts like a trade barrier that has enabled growth of the domestic industry—for example, Renren.com (the Chinese version of Facebook), Baidu.com (the Chinese version of Google), and Youku.com (the Chinese version of YouTube) (Taneja and Wu, 2014).

In contemporary China, the Internet has become an integral part of official and unofficial forms of everyday life. In March 2015—on behalf of the government—Chinese Premier Li Keqiang introduced the "Internet Plus" policy and elevated Internet development to the level of a national strategy. According to Li:

> We will develop the "Internet Plus" action plan to integrate mobile Internet, cloud computing, big data, and the Internet of Things with modern manufacturing, to encourage the healthy development of e-commerce, industrial networks, and Internet banking, and to get Internet-based companies to increase their presence in the international market.
>
> (2015: 20)

Development of Social Media in China

Although "social media" refers specifically to online applications allowing the creation and communication of user-generated content (UGC) based on the technology and ideology of Web 2.0 (Kaplan and Haenlein 2010), the earliest appearance of social media in China can be traced back to BBS (bulletin board systems) of the Web 1.0 era. In May 1994, the first BBS in China, "the Dawn BBS", was established, providing breakthroughs for a brand new way of communication and discussion among ordinary users. Popular BBSs such as Qiangguo Luntan (www.qglt.com), Tianya (www.tianya.com), and college BBSs, which are still active among some college students, allowed new modes of self-expression and group connection, and also influenced public opinion in transitional China. For example, on Qiangguo Luntan people could discuss and even debate about national policies, such as the one-child policy and the strategies of anti-corruption (Zhou 2008).

In February 1999, Tencent launched its instant messaging tool QQ, which marked the birth of the first nationally popular social media product in China. QQ has been widely favored by its users due to its user-friendly design, rich applications, powerful functions, and stable operating system. By 2015, the number of monthly active QQ user accounts was 832 million with the peak number of concurrent user accounts totaling over 228 million (Tencent 2015). By 2004, the year Facebook was born, "Blog Fever" had fully hit China. Leading companies in the Web 1.0 era such as Sina.com started to provide online blogging services. Tencent also launched the online personal space known as "Qzone" for its QQ users. In Qzone, a user can present his/her online persona by writing blogs, posting photos, sharing thoughts, and linking to outside sites. Qzone has become a popular platform for personal expression and mutual communication between QQ users.

As Qzone has become more popular among its users, more and more social media sites have appeared. In March 2005, Douban (www.douban.com), an UGC social network service based on people's interest and location, was launched. Douban targets well-educated young urban netizens with specialized tastes and provides them a public platform to share, review, and discuss such things as books, movies, and music. It also allows young people to organize cultural activities, make friends, as well as build communities. In December 2005, a Facebook-like real-name social media site for students known as Xiaonei (www.xiaonei.com) was launched, and its name was later changed to Renren (www.renren.com) in 2009 to attract more users beyond college students (as the Chinese "Xiaonei" means "on campus", while "Renren" means "everybody"). By providing online functions such as blogging, photo albums and resource sharing, Renren successfully captured the interest of the first generation of digital natives in China who were born after the 1990s, and enjoyed high popularity for several years.

However, Renren was gradually abandoned by users with the emergence of microblog media-rich sites such as Weibo and WeChat. The launch of Jiepang (www.jiepang.com)—also known as Chinese Foursquare—in 2010 marked the introduction of locative social media in China. Jiepang encouraged users to "check in" online when they visit offline places to win prizes, which also allows them to notify their friends about their movements and experiences, thus creating a new type of place-making among Chinese youth (Hjorth and Gu 2012). However, as other more influential social networking platforms such as Weibo deployed the "check-in" mechanism, Jiepang use declined. Jiepang tried to rebrand itself as an online journal for cataloguing the everyday, but Weibo has continued to dominate.

Weibo and WeChat are undoubtedly the largest and most dominant social media in China today. One of the earliest microblog services (similar to Twitter) in China was Fanfou (www.fanfou.com) established in 2007. However, the launch of Sina Weibo (or simply Weibo) in 2010 attracted many celebrities and cultivated a large number of grassroot opinion leaders due to its strength of town square-like publicity and fast information circulation. Weibo has undermined many traditional media outlets and become the well-deserved new media platform, contributing to democratic influences on the news flow and public discourse in contemporary Chinese society.

Unlike the wide publicity of Weibo (visibility to everyone)—the mobile instant messaging app launched by Tencent in 2011—WeChat deployed various internal applications to

Figure 24.1 A Weibo screenshot

Figure 24.2 A family WeChat group: WeChat has become an important platform for family internal communication.

differentiate functions for connecting. These apps included multimedia instant messaging (text, voice, video, and group chat), creative ways of finding friends ("shake"), and an updated social function known as "Moments". WeChat has now become one of the most influential social media in China (Skuse 2014). In 2015 WeChat's monthly active user number reached 549 million, with a coverage of 90 percent of smartphone holders (Tencent 2015). As a nationally favored mobile Internet app, WeChat has also successfully attracted those "information have-less" or even "information have-nots" (Qiu 2009) to start using the Internet—such as old people and rural residents.

The Impacts of Social Media in China

In the 1990s, the debut of the Internet and BBS opened up a brand new world to Chinese people. At that time, most people were used to highly regulated traditional media sources to gain information. The emergence of BBS challenged the traditional one-way information flow pattern, expanding resources for news information and enlarging the communication and social network of netizens. For the first time, Chinese netizens felt the magic of talking to strangers online and had the chance to express their own opinions freely on public affairs.

The blog bears a revolutionary significance in Internet history, especially in China (MacKinnon 2008). For the first time, blogs made it possible for the writings of the grassroot class in China to be read by others on a large scale. This phenomenon, in turn, indirectly resulted in the growth of online literature mainly focused upon palace drama, time-travel stories, campus love stories, and supernatural stories. Examples include the two leading online literature websites—Qidian.com (www.qidian.com) and Hongxiu.com (www.hongxiu.com). Notably in recent years, a growing number of popular Chinese TV series and movies are adapted from online literature, including *The Legend of Zhenhuan* and *The Secret of Grave Rubbers*.

The popularity of social media such as Renren and Douban can be attributed to the Chinese belief in Confucianism, which emphasizes collectivism and social norms over individual interests (Hofstede 2001). While their American counterparts may focus on developing new relationships and extending their networks in order to bring in social capital, Chinese college students primarily engage in the maintenance of existing, close relationships for bonding social capital (Chu and Choi 2010). Social media, especially Renren, have provided effective ways for accumulating social capital by China's younger generation, most of whom are the only child in their family and thus have a heightened sense of familial ties and obligations.

Due to the advertising and accessibility of its platform, Weibo has become a significant media platform for Chinese netizens to consume and circulate news, to express opinions, and to engage in public and political affairs (Svensson 2014; Zhou 2015). It also serves as an important source of public events, even if the popularity of WeChat does result in the loss of Weibo users. As Kantar Media's (2015) *State of Chinese Social Media in 2015* concludes, Weibo is the "pulse" of China—it both reflects and influences the pulse of China; it amplifies and solidifies the social trends.

On one hand, WeChat has created a unique social networking culture based on mobile multimedia instant messaging. On the other hand, it has built up a low-cost media platform (official account) for individuals and social institutions to express and share. In addition, WeChat integrates many other functions that reflect the rhythms of everyday life. WeChat has become the dominant vehicle for accessing various different online services—from news to entertainment, from e-commerce to payment, from taxi-booking to Lucky Money—seemingly connecting everything and everybody into the network.

In everyday life, the impact of WeChat can be felt as it subtly shapes, and is shaped by, changes in traditional Chinese family communication and intergenerational relationships. With increasingly more Chinese family members accessing WeChat, the popularity of family WeChat groups to share information has emerged, allowing different ways in which families can care for each other and express once unspeakable emotions, especially with the rise in intergenerational geographic mobility (Hjorth and Arnold 2013; Zhou and Xiao 2015).

According to our fieldwork conducted in Shanghai, through the locative and social dimensions of mobile media, parents have more opportunities to give care to their children, especially for translocal families in China. For example, let us consider the mother and daughter participants, Biyu and Ai, who are typical of the respondent found in fieldwork. Biyu's mother, Ai, recounts how mobile media has allowed her to feel emotionally closer to her daughter when she is physically apart through WeChat:

> I want to know about her living, her mood and where she goes and with whom. I worry about her safety. WeChat is a convenient way [. . .] Now I can know what she is doing at the moment. I see where she is. I see her photos. I feel we're closer. It's just like I'm with her.

At the same time, the locative and social dimensions of mobile media also give rise to potential conflicts and problems, especially "over-care" from parents and "worry about worries" of children. Biyu is a typical case in point. She describes her mother as overzealous when it comes to her safety. Ai keeps a "friendly eye" via tracking Biyu's "footprint" on WeChat. "My mom wants to know my every movement", Biyu complains. "Over-care" from parents makes their children recognize the worries of their parents, which, in turn, worries the children.

Figure 24.3 A WeChat "Moment" screenshot: family members living apart use Moment to learn the whereabouts of each other.

Thus young people are also learning how to manage their locative sharing (and non-sharing) on social media as a mode of performance for their parents in order to maintain a harmonious intergenerational relationship.

Over the past 20 years, the Internet in China has played an important part in its economic reform and opening up processes. From PC-oriented Web 1.0 to mobile Internet Web 2.0, the Internet is a crucial technology within contemporary Chinese modernity. It is not only encouraging individual expression, group communication, and civic participation, but also reconstructing the traditional news ecology and power relationships.

In the next section we turn to the rise of the Internet and social media in Japan. Unlike the early beginnings of the Internet in China that relied on PCs, Japan's embrace of the Internet was largely synonymous with the uptake of mobile Internet devices. However, while these technological histories differ, connections can be made around the use of social mobile media to strengthen familial ties through mundane intimacies.

The Internet and the Mobile Phone (*Keitai*) in Japan

The commercial use of the Internet in Japan started in 1993 (see Chapter 11 in this volume). Initially, Internet access was PC-based, consisting of a dial-up connection (with the use of phone line and modem). This system was then replaced in 2001 by high-speed constantly connected line connections known as Asymmetric Digital Subscriber Line (ADSL) by several telecommunication operators (Digital Arts 2015). Along with the development of a faster Internet connection environment for personal computers, Internet connection services via cellphones known as *keitai* appeared. *Keitai* (from *keitai denwa* or handheld phone) is an everyday term for mobile phones and personal handyphones (PHS) that have become ubiquitous in Japanese life from the launch of the first Internet-enabled handsets in 1999 (see Ito *et al.* 2006).

Until the advent of the *keitai*, Internet connections via PC required various kinds of equipment and infrastructure—such as a computer, a phone line, connection equipment (such as a modem), a contract with an Internet service provider—and the configuration of all kinds of settings. A PC-based connection was also expensive as phone-line rental companies billed calls by the minute. Conversely, the dominant mobile Internet service known as "*i-mode*"—an Internet service started in 1999 by NTT docomo—required nothing but a *keitai* to connect to the Internet and charged only for downloads, not for time spent browsing. The simplicity of this system meant that Internet use via *keitai* dramatically increased after 2000.

i-mode advanced its functions with the development of hardware and acquired 40 million subscriptions by 2004—five years after its appearance (NTT docomo 2009). According to NTT docomo (2009), practical services such as "news", "mobile banking", and "ticketing services" were the main services in the beginning, but gradually entertainment-oriented services such as "game", "*chaku-uta*" (downloadable ringtones made up of the melodies of songs), and "*decomail*" (decoration mail) became widely used. *Decomail* updated the image of previous text-only emails since it allowed mail to be enhanced using different templates, images, color, and fonts—attaining wide popularity, especially among young female users (Figure 24.4).

The evolution of these diverse *keitai* services represented by *i-mode* has come to be seen as synonymous with the diffusion of the Internet in Japan. According to the Ministry of Internal Affairs and Communications (MIC), while penetration rates of the Internet in the 1990s were only 21 percent, by 2005 rates had exceeded 70 percent (MIC 2014a). A survey on Internet usage by device conducted by MIC found that the computer was the main Internet

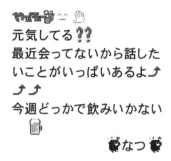

Figure 24.4 Decomail (NTT docomo)

access portal until 2003 (at 40 percent), then becoming a concurrent use of both computer and mobile device in 2005 (57 percent), to the situation today whereby access by computer only has decreased to just 18.6 percent (MIC 2014b). Now it is impossible to untangle the connection between the Internet and the *keitai* in Japan.

Sumaho and Social Media

With the recent spread of smartphones, the Internet has become an embedded part of everyday life for Japanese people, old and young. In Japan, the popularization of smartphones began in the late 2000s when the first iPhone arrived. According to a survey conducted by the Institute for Information and Communications Policy (IICP) in 2013, the utilization rate of smartphones was 52.8 percent, which was 20 points up from the previous poll (IICP 2014). The age group that uses smartphones most frequently is people in their twenties (87.9 percent), followed by those in their thirties (78.7 percent), teens (63.3 percent), forties (58.8 percent), fifties (32.4 percent), and sixties (8.7 percent).

The smartphone is called "*sumaho*" in Japanese and is distinguished from *keitai*. While *keitai* referred to conventional Japanese mobile phones, these devices were more what other countries would define as "smart". *Keitai* devices afforded a convergence of various capabilities including mobile Internet—a capability that many associate with smartphones. A prominent feature of *sumaho* is its flexibility in installing various apps and customizing the set of functions and appearances by an individual's own preferences. Moreover, a touch screen also became an indicator of a *sumaho*. The spread of *sumaho* has resulted in an increase not only in Internet use, but also in more intense social media use among the younger generation. *Sumaho* users use social media more and for longer than conventional *keitai* users (Sekine 2013). That is to say, they no longer talk over *sumaho*, instead they communicate via various social media applications, exchanging short phrases and images. The success of the *sumaho* has also led to the success of LINE. It seems that *sumaho* is creating more opportunities for synchronous communication.

Post-2004 Japan has seen the rise of social media represented by emerging companies such as mixi, GREE, and Mobage. Despite maintaining an invitation-based user registration system until 2010, mixi enrollments had exceeded 10 million by 2007 (Yoshino 2014). mixi allowed users to interact with other mutually accepted members (called "*my miku*") by sharing diaries and photo albums or by interacting in "community" pages with those who share the same interests.

A feature of mixi was how it represented a sharp contrast to large-scale, anonymous Web 1.0 bulletin board systems (BBS) such as 2ch ("*ni-chan*") that had been popular at the beginning of the 2000s. In 2ch users mostly interacted with an unspecified number of other users on an anonymous basis, and, given the anonymity, 2ch became well known for its anarchic and sometimes racist and sexist content. In contrast, mixi offered a sense of security to its users as communication in mixi was based upon a mutually accepted member (*my-miku*) and community members (Yoshino 2014). This type of network promoted trust and respect rather than the trolling characterized by 2ch.

GREE and Mobage harnessed Japan's love of games by focusing upon game services. GREE is known for its world-first mobile social game *Tsuri Suta* (Fishing Star) (GREE 2015). GREE released successive games targeting youth and also sold in-game items (Fujishiro 2010). By 2009, membership surpassed 10 million. Mobage focused on combining social media with games. Its popular games include *Kaitou Royale* (A Royal Phantom Thief), in which the user hunts treasures with other users in the game, and *Hoshikku*, in which users develop the civilization of their star (Fujishiro 2010). Mobage acquired 10 million users in 2008 (DeNA 2015).

During this time, foreign social media such as Twitter and Facebook started to spread in the 2010s, heightened during and after the events of March 2011 (Yoshino 2014). As of 2015, the current social media rates in Japan are 57.1 percent—with 91 percent in the twenties age group, 80.8 percent in the thirties, 76.3 percent in the teens, 60.5 percent in the forties, 36.7 percent in the fifties, and 14.3 percent in the sixties (IICP 2014). The following statistics identify the usage of the three most frequently used social media services among each age group (IICP 2014).

More recently, LINE has begun to dominate the social media landscape in Japan. In particular, its deployment across the generations, and as a metaphor for familial genealogies, can be noted. LINE is a service providing text-messaging among individuals or groups, as

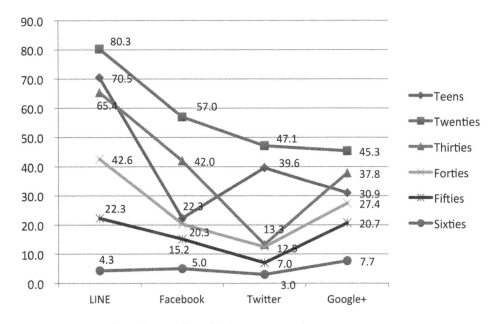

Figure 24.5 Use of popular social media (by age groups)

Figure 24.6 Chat with rabbit stamps on LINE

well as making phone and video calls for no charge. A stamp function—which is an advanced form of *emoji* (pictogram or emoticons) and *decomail*—allows communication without the need for text messaging and this *kawaii* (cute) culture has been key to its success (Figure 24.6). Many of these functions are available in the Chinese WeChat, highlighting the overlaps between the applications and their significance in intergenerational ties in and around social mobile media use in Japan and China.

LINE was developed soon after the earthquake in March 2011. The ex-president of LINE, Mr Morikawa, explained in an interview that they decided to develop LINE because they saw that many people used Twitter as a communication tool for intimates at the time of the earthquake (ITmedia business online 2013). Since 2011 when LINE started its service, it has gained users in many countries, especially Japan. As of 2015, the number of domestic registrants was 58 million, which is over 45 percent of the whole population (LINE 2015). The popularity of LINE has overtaken the role of the aforementioned social media like mixi, GREE, and Mobage. Mr Morikawa cited three characteristics as significant to its success (ITmedia business online 2013):

- Users can communicate with familiar people privately.
- Services are designed especially for *sumaho*.
- Adopting elements such as *emoji* (pictogram), *decomail*, games, and fortune-telling, which were the culture of *i-mode*.

LINE argued that people were exhausted from the multiple communication avenues. By deploying cute characters—which have played an important role in Japanese culture and expressing emotions (Hjorth 2003)—LINE provided the growing amount of *sumaho* users with easy, fun, familiar, and mundane ways to communicate with co-present intimates. Here the *kawaii* functions to personalize and bring an emotional softening to digital encounters.

The Use of Social Media in Family Contexts in Japan

In our fieldwork in Tokyo, seven out of eight participants use LINE most in communicating with their families. Over the three years of working with households, the significance of LINE in intergenerational relationships has grown. In addition, four out of these seven participants have a "family" group on LINE and send messages back and forth with their families. Here, LINE operates as a digital genealogy for offline intimacies. As one participant, 22-year-old Haruko, noted:

My family writes about how they are doing in the family group on LINE. My younger brother tells us when he is coming home from his year abroad and my parents send us photos when they go traveling. It's handy to share photos and videos with everyone in the family. When my younger brother graduated from university, he sent a graduation photo and a message to us to thank our parents. I was deeply moved because at that time we all lived separately. I also sent my future plans to them when I was studying abroad. I felt I was saved at that moment. Before using LINE we didn't share photos when we were traveling. I think we started to use LINE in this way because we started to live separately. Until now we could have sent emails simultaneously to everyone, but we didn't. I like LINE because we can communicate like having a chat.

As discussed elsewhere (Ohashi and Kato 2016), most of the participants in our fieldwork were using more than one social media service. Through a tapestry of social media use afforded by the *sumaho*, they were able to compartmentalize different mundane intimacies and intimate publics. However, currently LINE is the most favored social media service for maintaining relationships with their families. Like the Chinese counterpart, WeChat, LINE plays a key role in the daily rituals that are both intimate as well as mundane. Combined with the use of "stamps", the use of LINE may complement their face-to-face interactions.

Conclusion

In this chapter we have contrasted two very different histories of the rise of the Internet and how it has transformed into its current smartphone context. The development of the Internet in China took place in a rather staged way—from Web 1.0 (that is, the prosperity of portal websites and the popularity of PC) to Web 2.0 (that is, the mobile Internet and the popularity of smartphones). When it comes to Japan, access to the Internet from both PC and mobile phones converged early thanks to the existence of *keitai*. We find that the development of the Internet in China was strongly associated with the effort of the government; while considering the Japanese case, it was not as government-driven as the case in China.

As both Japan and China are culturally, linguistically, and socially diverse, the rise of the Internet, followed by mobile Internet and then social mobile media, has allowed for alternative ways in which to articulate the personal and intergenerational, as well as the political and social. For example, immediately after the earthquake in March 2011, it is said that in the central Tokyo area (including prefectures adjacent to Tokyo), more than five million people could not reach their home on that day because of the damage to public transportation. According to the survey conducted by Weather News (2011), it took about seven times longer to reach home when compared to a person's ordinary commute. While many stayed in their office building, some people tried to walk home. It was reported that during the walk home, many tried to use Twitter to collect information about ongoing changes in transportation recovery. One could, in fact, spontaneously change the route toward one's home based on communication through tweets. Social media enabled coordination at a micro level. Also, as Tamura suggests (in this volume), the experiences of the earthquake motivated people to utilize social media applications to gather and share information about changes in the social and political climate. In addition, mobile media also operated symbolically as a vessel for containing the intimate during times of grief—some people held onto their phones as security when they couldn't make contact with loved ones (Hjorth and Kim 2011).

The political and social influences of the new media have also been observed in China. The emergence of the Internet and social media in China does not merely mean an increase in the quantity of information, but also suggests the possibility of having qualitatively different information and communication to provide diversity and alternatives. It is fair to say that the Internet in China is much more abundant, liberal, and diverse than the state-controlled mass media, and has raised information flows and the expression of opinion to an unprecedented level. A recent nationwide random survey study has found that, after controlling for other variables, Internet use is still significantly related to both civic participation and opinion expression of Chinese people, such that Internet users tend to engage in politics and public affairs more actively compared to Internet non-users (Zhou 2015). Like Japan, the Internet in China is a space in which multiple political and social agendas are conversing.

The mobile Internet in both China and Japan plays a crucial part in everyday life. In particular, the rise of social mobile media like LINE in Japan and WeChat in China highlights the significance of the media in maintaining and fostering intergenerational ties. These are *personal* as they are *political*, *intimate* as they are *public*. Here we see that social mobile media is shaping, as well as being shaped by, familial rituals. However, more work is needed into the growing significance of social mobile media in shaping, and being shaped by, digital kinship.

Acknowledgement

The authors acknowledge support from the Australian Research Council Linkage Project, *Locating the Mobile* (#LP130100848). Baohua Zhou would also like to acknowledge the support of the Chinese National Social Science Foundation Project, "The Influence of Social Media on Public Opinion in Transitional China" (#13CXW021), and Shanghai Social Science Foundation Project "New Media Empowerment" (#2012BXW004).

References

Chu, S. C., and Choi, S. M. (2010) "Social Capital and Self-Presentation on Social Networking Sites: A Comparative Study of Chinese and American Young Generations", *Chinese Journal of Communication*, 3(4): 402–420.

CNNIC (2009) *Chronical Development of Internet in China from 1994 to 1996*, available at: www.cnnic.net.cn/hlwfzyj/hlwdsj/201206/t20120612_27415.htm (accessed 4 August 2015).

CNNIC (2015) *Statistical Survey Report on the Internet Development in China*, available at: www.cnnic.cn/hlwfzyj/hlwxzbg/hlwtjbg/201507/P020150723549500667087.pdf (accessed 4 August 2015).

DeNA (2015) *History of DeNA*, available at: http://dena.com/jp/recruit/career/history/ (accessed 4 August 2015).

Digital Arts (2015) *Nihon Ni Okeru Internet No Rekishi* (History of Internet in Japan), available at: www.daj.jp/20th/history/ (accessed 4 August 2015).

Fujishiro, H. (2010) *Niteiruyoude Chigau Nihon No Sandai SNS* (Japanese Three Major SNS), available at: www.nikkei.com/article/DGXNZO09617270R20C10A6000000/ (accessed 4 August 2015).

GREE (2015) *History*, available at: http://corp.gree.net/jp/ja/corporate/history/ (accessed 4 August 2015).

Hjorth, L. (2003) "Kawaii@keitai", in N. Gottlieb and M. McLelland (eds), *Japanese Cybercultures*, New York: Routledge, pp. 50–59.

Hjorth, L., and Arnold, M. (2013) *Online@AsiaPacific: Mobile, Social and Locative Media in the Asia-Pacific*, New York: Routledge.

Hjorth, L., and Gu, K. (2012) "The Place of Emplaced Visualities: A Case Study of Smartphone Visuality and Location-Based Social Media in Shanghai, China", *Continuum: Journal of Media and Cultural Studies*, 26(5): 699–713.

Hjorth, L., and Kim, Y. (2011) "The Mourning After: A Commentary on Crisis Management in Japan Post 3.11", *Television and New Media*, 12(6): 552–559.

Hofstede, G. (2001) *Culture's Consequences: International Differences in Work-Related Values*, Beverly Hills, CA: Sage.

Institute for Information and Communications Policy (IICP) (2014) *Heisei 25 Nen Jouhou Tsushin Media No Riyou Jikan To Jouhou Koudou Ni Kansuru Chousa Sokuhou* (The Results of a Survey of the Utilization Time of

Telecommunication Media and Information Behavior), available at: www.soumu.go.jp/iicp/chousakenkyu/data/research/survey/telecom/2014/h25mediariyou_1sokuhou.pdf (accessed 30 June 2014).

ITmedia business online (2013) *LINE, Naver Matome Ha Naze Tsuyoinoka?* (Why Are LINE and Naver Strong?), available at: http://bizmakoto.jp/makoto/articles/1309/04/news016_2.html (accessed 4 August 2015).

Ito, M., Okabe, D., and Matsuda, M. (eds) (2006) *Personal, Portable, Pedestrian*, Cambridge, MA: MIT Press.

Kantar Media (2015) *State of Chinese Social Media in 2015*, available at: http://cn-en.kantar.com/media/social/2015/state-of-chinese-social-media-in-2015/ (accessed 4 August 2015).

Kaplan, A. M., and Haenlein, M. (2010) "Users of the World, Unite! The Challenges and Opportunities of Social Media", *Business Horizons*, 53(1): 59–68.

Li, K. (2015) *Report on the Work of the Government*, available at: www.chinadaily.com.cn/china/2015twosession/2015–03/05/content_19729663.htm (accessed 4 August 2015).

LINE (2015) *2015 Nen 4 Gatsu—9 Gatsu Baitai Shiryou* (LINE Media Guide 2015 April–September), available at: https://linecorp.com/ads/pdf/8CCCEF52-B730–11E4-BEB8-ED3AF3F15F22 (accessed 4 August 2015).

MacKinnon, R. (2008) "Blogs and China Correspondence: Lessons About Global Information Flows", *Chinese Journal of Communication*, 1(2): 242–257.

Ministry of Internal Affairs and Communications (MIC) (2014a) *2014 White Paper: Information and Communications in Japan*, available at: www.soumu.go.jp/johotsusintokei/whitepaper/eng/WP2014/chapter-5.pdf#page=1 (accessed 4 August 2015).

Ministry of Internal Affairs and Communications (MIC) (2014b) *Tanmatsu Betsu Ni Mita Internet No Riyoushasuu Hiritsu No Suii* (Survey on Internet Usage by Device), available at: www.soumu.go.jp/johotsusintokei/field/tsuushin01.html (accessed 4 August 2015).

NTT docomo (2009) *i-mode No Rekishi To Shinka* (History and Evolution of i-mode), available at: www.nttdocomo.co.jp/binary/pdf/info/news_release/report/090213.pdf (accessed 4 August 2015).

Ohashi, K., and Kato, F. (2016) "Lines for Connectedness: A Study of Social Media Practices in Japanese Families", in L. Hjorth and O. Khoo (eds), *The Routledge Handbook of New Media in Asia*, London: Routledge, pp. 199–208.

Qiu, J. L. (2009) *Working-Class Network Society: Communication Technology and the Information Have-Less in Urban China*, Cambridge, MA: MIT Press.

Sekine, C. (2013) *20, 30 Dai Ha Internet Wo Donoyouni Chojikan Riyou Shiteirunoka* (The Present State of Long-Time Internet Use Among Young People in Their 20s and 30s), available at: www.nhk.or.jp/bunken/summary/research/report/2013_04/20130403.pdf (accessed 4 August 2015).

Skuse, A. (2014) "Wechat: The Chinese Chat App Stealing Weibo's Thunder", *CNN*, available at: http://edition.cnn.com/2014/02/27/business/tencent-wechat-unseats-sina-weibo/ (accessed 8 August 2015).

Svensson, M. (2014) "Voice, Power and Connectivity in China's Microblogosphere", *China Information*, 28(2): 168–188.

Taneja, H., and Wu, A. X. (2014) "Does the Great Firewall Really Isolate the Chinese?", *The Information Society*, 30: 297–309.

Tencent (2015) *Tencent Announces 2015 First Quarter Results*, available at: www.tencent.com/en-us/content/at/2015/attachments/20150513.pdf (accessed 8 August 2015).

Weather News (2011) "A Survey on 'Stranded Commuters' in Tokyo Metropolitan Area on the Day of Great East Japan Earthquake", *Weather News*, 11 March, available at: http://weathernews.com/ja/nc/press/2011/110411_2.html (accessed 31 October 2015).

Yoshino, H. (2014) "Internet Communication No Bashoka To Datsu-Bashoka (Chapter 2)", in K. Osada and Y. Tadokoro (eds), *Tsunagaru Tsunagaranai No Shakaigaku* (Sociology of Being Connected and Not Being Connected), Tokyo: Koubundou.

Zhou, B. (2008) "Information and Expression on Web 2.0: A Survey Study of Shanghai Netizens", *Journalism and Communication Research*, 4: 75–82.

Zhou, B. (2015) "Internet Use, Socio-Geographic Context and Citizenship Engagement: A Multilevel Model on the Democratizing Effects of the Internet in China", in W. Chen and S. Reese (eds), *Networked China*, New York: Routledge, pp. 19–36.

Zhou, B., and Xiao, M. (2015) "Locative Social Media Engagement and Intergenerational Relationship in China", in L. Hjorth and O. Khoo (eds), *The Routledge Handbook of New Media in Asia*, London: Taylor & Francis, pp. 219–228.

25

PLATFORMS, PRACTICES, AND POLITICS

A Snapshot of Networked Fan Communities in China

Ling Yang

Introduction: Contextualizing Chinese Fandom

Fandom has a long history in China. Traditional Chinese operas, of which Peking opera is the most famous, used to attract fans across the social hierarchy. The late 18th and 19th centuries witnessed the popularization of two images of opera fans: the sophisticated connoisseur who diligently evaluated and recorded the beauty and talents of opera actors, and the lascivious "sugar daddy" who squandered time and money to pursue intimacy with the cross-dressing boy actors (Goldman 2012: 17–22). In the 1920s and 1930s, movie going became "part and parcel of the modern way of life" in metropolises like Shanghai (Lee 1999: 118), which, in turn, produced a large number of movie fans, mostly composed of fashionable youth and petty urbanities. Between 1925 and 1937, over 120 film magazines were launched in China to help movie fans obtain information about domestic and Hollywood film stars (Yue 2009: 47). After having being subdued during the homogeneous and monotonous Mao era (1949–1976), fandom has made a powerful comeback since the late 1970s in tandem with the revival of commercialized mass culture. In the early 1980s, an ardent soccer fan seized national attention by giving up his factory job and family to become the first full-time soccer supporter in China (Tencent Sports 2009). At a time when few Chinese had ever thought about quitting their job or filing for divorce, the daring decision of this soccer fan made him a bizarre yet fascinating icon of personal autonomy during the reform era.

Fandom has gradually evolved from a privilege of the literati and wealthy patrons in traditional society to a common practice among urban consumers in Republican and post-socialist China. However, it was not until the phenomenal rise of Super Girl fandoms in 2005 that the general public began to realize that fandom is more than a usually benign, yet occasionally excessive, pursuit of a personal hobby, but also a remarkable economic force, a booming subculture, and a form of social activism. When individual citizens are connected through the Internet and united by common interests, they can not only determine the outcome of a televised singing contest, but unleash an unprecedented amount of grassroots mobilization, self-organization, and creative energy. Concomitant with the emergence of Super Girl fandoms, the Chinese word "*fensi*", a transliteration of the English word "fans", quickly became the new generic label for fans. Unlike the former umbrella term "*mi*" that denoted an abnormal obsession and a sense of loss, the word "*fensi*", which also refers to string-like rice noodles in Chinese, emits a playful sense of the everyday, as if fandom were a daily necessity like food and water. The negative connotations of the English word "fan", originally an abbreviation of the word "fanatic" (Jenkins 1992: 12), are therefore somehow erased in the translingual borrowing of the term.

It is precisely this ordinariness and ubiquity that has characterized Chinese networked fan communities in the digital era, to the point that Baidu Post Bar, the largest Chinese-language online community in the world, also happens to be the most prominent home base for online fandoms in China. According to the official data of Baidu, released in January 2015, Baidu Post Bar had over one billion registered users, 8.2 million theme bars, an average of nearly 300 million active monthly users, and over 2.7 billion daily visits. Like Chinese netizens in general, the majority of Post Bar users are young people aged between 15 and 35 years old (Incitez China 2015). Considering that the total number of Internet users in China was "merely" 649 million by the end of 2014 (CNNIC 2015), and there are numerous other fan websites besides Baidu Post Bar, even if we deduct those Post Bar users who live outside China and do not identify themselves as fans, the aggregated number of Chinese netizens who are engaged in fan activities would still be staggering.

Currently, based on the nature of their fan objects, online fandoms in China can be divided into four major categories: celebrity fandoms, media fandoms, sports fandoms, and brand communities. Among these four types of fandom, celebrity fandoms are the most visible and stigmatized, as Chinese media have been prone to cover the extreme behaviors of "star-chasers" and portray them as irrational and pathological (Chang 2007; Deng 2010: 143–144; : 56–57). The Chinese idol market used to be reigned over by pop stars from Hong Kong, Taiwan, Japan, and Korea. While transregional East Asian super stars continue to attract a huge number of Chinese fans (Pease 2006; Lin 2013; Tsai 2008), in the past decade, local pop idols such as Li Yuchun and, most recently, the teen boy band TFBOYS have all developed large loyal followings.

Media fandoms are made up of fans of a wide variety of media texts, ranging from novels, television, and films to anime, comics, and games (ACG), and usually have a more equal mix of men and women than the female-dominated celebrity fandoms. Indigenous Web literature (Feng 2013; Lugg 2011), Japanese manga and anime (Pang 2009; Wang 2005), Japanese, Korean, and American television dramas (Deng 2010; Hu 2005; Ahn 2014; Jiang and Leung 2012; J. Yang 2012), as well as domestic and foreign online games (Lindtner and Szablewicz 2011; Wu and Wang 2011) have all gained dedicated followers among Chinese youth.

Sports fandoms are mainly built around elite sport stars and popular sports like soccer and basketball (Clark 2012: 93–99). Although the Chinese men's soccer team has been a national laughing-stock for decades, Chinese soccer fans have found solace in appreciating soccer games played by foreign teams and many have become supporters of European and South American teams. While sports fandoms have been traditionally dominated by men, in recent years the number of female sports fans has also increased noticeably.

Brand communities refer to groups of loyal customers of particular brand names, such as Apple (Wang 2014) and its Chinese rival Xiaomi (W. Li 2014). Hailed as "the world's most valuable start-up", Xiaomi earns its success through building a strong fan base and encouraging customer participation (Dou 2015; Wong 2014). As of August 2015, the company's official Weibo account had drawn over ten million followers.

This chapter aims to provide a short overview of the history, practices, and issues associated with Chinese online fan communities. It starts with an outline of the evolution of Internet platforms and technologies that have facilitated the formation and development of networked fan communities, such as bulletin board systems (BBS), Baidu Post Bar, Sina Weibo, and Tencent QQ. It then dwells on fansubbing (foreign-language media subtitled by fans) and shipping ("*peidui*" in Chinese, meaning "pairing" or "coupling" of celebrities or media characters in original stories), two web-based practices that have far-reaching impacts on Chinese fan cultures and society at large, followed by an examination of conflicts and tensions in online fan spaces. Although fandoms have offered fans an invaluable sense of agency, identity, and belonging, they also constitute a site of fierce contestations, often caused by gender-related issues and government censorship. The chapter concludes with a brief analysis of the continuing relevance and importance of fandoms to Chinese netizens.

Fanning the Internet

China established a fully functional linkage to the World Wide Web in April 1994. Initially, Internet access service was provided only to academic institutions (Herold 2011: 1). Hence, students from elite universities were among the earliest Internet users, and college BBSs (bulletin board systems) became the first platform for online fandoms in China. Starting from 1996, special manga and anime sections began to appear on campus BBSs across the country. The "Comic" section of the BBS of Tsinghua University was particularly influential, as it produced a number of well-known figures in Chinese ACG fandoms, and was one of the rare discussion boards at that time where female users seemed to outnumber male users. One female member of the comic section later went on to establish a personal website named Sangsang Academy, which cultivated and nourished the first generation of Chinese *fujoshi* (literally "rotten girls")—that is, female fans of an originally Japanese genre of male same-sex romance (Banana Sonna 2014). The commercial BBS affiliated to Sitong Lifang Information Technology Company also left a mark on the history of Chinese fan culture, because its "Sports Salon" used to be the most renowned online sports community in China. When Sitong was reshuffled into Sina, the would-be largest Chinese-language portal website in 1998, the moderator of the Sports Salon also joined the new company and later became its Vice CEO (Peng 2005: 52–55).

Around 1997, Internet start-ups like Netease, currently the fourth largest Internet company in China, began to offer free space to individual users to construct their own personal websites. A young TV game fan took this opportunity to create his own hobby-based BBS "Mop" on Netease. Originally a discussion board for a small circle of loyal TV game fans, Mop later evolved into China's leading online forum, and the birthplace of many Internet memes, practices, and cyber celebrities, including the controversial "human flesh search", a "collaborative cyber activity" to search for people who have violated societal norms or social mores (Tsou 2015: 183). Since 1998, individually run literary websites also mushroomed in cyberspace, and many literature lovers began to post their original works on the Internet. In 2000, "The Sky of Dragon" was created by five young men with the intention to become the largest original literature website in the Chinese-language world. While it did become the most trafficked literature website on the mainland within a year, the website soon lost its dominant position in the market due to mismanagement and gradually transformed from a leading publishing platform into the most influential discussion forum for web literature fans (Baidu Encyclopedia 2015a). Today, over 810,000 registered users frequent the website to recommend their favorite web literature works, write literary reviews, and share writing experience.

By 2003, with the diffusion of broadband and the rapid increase of Internet users, many well-known personal websites experienced rising operational costs brought on by the volume of new users. To solve this financial problem, website owners had to either charge their users or sell the websites to external investors. The establishment of Baidu Post Bar, a free, public, query-based, searchable community in December 2003, however, offered another option for fans who had neither the money nor the technical know-how to run their own websites. Any user with basic computer knowledge can set up a post bar at Baidu and become the bar manager after simple registration. The topic of each bar is usually indicated through its name. All the content in a bar is viewable to unregistered users, but many bars allow only registered members to post there. Each bar works like an independent online forum and is connected to other bars through the search and "friendly links" functions.

In 2004, Hunan Satellite TV aired the first season of a reality singing contest called Super Girl. During the contest, enthusiastic viewers began to set up bars at Baidu for their favorite contestants. This fan tradition was carried on in the second season, which turned out to be one of the most popular programs in the history of the Chinese television industry. In August 2005, when the show entered the final round, 3.5 million users visited "Super Girl Bar" daily and left over two million posts (S. Li 2014: 203). This is merely the amount of traffic at a single bar. There were at least 20 highly active Super Girl-related bars in 2005. The congregation of millions of Super Girl fans at Baidu Post Bar and the tremendous amount of chatting, creating, connecting, and mobilizing carried out there mark the birth of a true "participatory culture" (Jenkins 2006). Through utilizing new media technology, forming a knowledge community, and harnessing collective intelligence, Super Girl fans are no longer passive consumers of the entertainment industry, but have become active content producers and distributors, competing interpretive communities, and committed advocates of alternative tastes and values (L. Yang 2012, 2014). While Baidu Post Bar provided the platform for Super Girl fans to fully realize their cultural potential, Super Girl fans also made Baidu Post Bar famous overnight and helped it discover its *raison d'être*.

Soon after Facebook and Twitter were banned in China in 2009, Sina launched a Twitter-like social networking service called Weibo. Yet, unlike Twitter which is "uni-directional and text-only" (Hu 2012: 108), Sina Weibo allows users to upload videos and images, and to comment directly on each other's posts, hence combining elements of BBS and blogs (Sullivan 2014: 27). By September 2014, monthly active users at Sina Weibo had reached 167 million (Sina Weibo Data Center 2015). As of 2015, almost every star and starlet in the Sinophone entertainment industry has opened an account on Weibo for self-promotion and cultivation of their fandom. So have non-Chinese stars and media personalities who intend to expand their Chinese market. Other entertainment industry players, such as television stations and program producers, have also maintained an active presence on Sina Weibo.

The clustering of entertainment celebrities and professionals on a single social platform has radically altered celebrity and media fans' access to the entertainment industry and their relationships with fan organizations. In the past, fans often had to join a fan organization, usually an online forum, to obtain updated news and information about their favorite stars and media texts. The fan organizations functioned as an intermediary between rank-and-file fans and the entertainment industry. While the industry used the fan clubs to promote products and artists, the fan clubs in return received "first-hand information about star activities and free tickets" (Fung 2009: 293). Now, however, fans can bypass the middleman, along with its top-down organizational structure and power struggles, to gain information directly from, and interact with, stars and media producers through the latter's Sina Weibo accounts (Zhou 2013: 146). Moreover, Weibo has given fans a chance to rise to stardom themselves, as ordinary users could also gain a huge following through continuously posting clever and humorous content on their accounts. One such example is "Xiaoye Meizi Learns Mocking (*Xiaoye Meizi Xue Tucao*)", a Chinese fan of Japanese pop culture. Chiefly through reposting and commenting on interesting images from Japanese Twitter accounts, Xiaoye Meizi has accumulated 11 million fans in a period of two-and-a-half years and become a notable promoter of *fujoshi* subculture on Weibo.

The emergence of new platforms does not necessarily spell the demise of older ones, as fans generally utilize multiple platforms to satisfy their diverse needs. Apart from Baidu Post Bar and Sina Weibo, QQ, an instant messaging service launched by Tencent in 1999, has continued to be a favorite networking tool for Chinese fans. Before QQ came out, online fan communities depended solely on BBSs to keep connected. If a BBS was abruptly shut down due to technical problems, the community built around it would also fall to pieces. QQ, however, provided fans a permanent and secure way to keep in touch with each other (Banana Sonna 2014). QQ chat groups, which set a ceiling on the number of group members, are often used to build smaller and more intimate fan circles. Transgressive content that could not be posted on Baidu Post Bar or Sina Weibo is usually circulated through QQ chat groups.

Fansubbing and Shipping

Empowered by Internet technologies, Chinese fans have engaged in a wide range of online fan practices, including connecting with their favorite stars; collecting information about their favorite media texts; participating in fan discussion; producing, distributing, and consuming fan works; making fansubs for foreign media products; and sharing pictures or videos of cosplay. Since a number of English-language studies (see Feng 2013; Kong 2012; Wu and Wang 2011; Yang and Bao 2012; Zhang 2014; Zhang and Fung 2014; Zhang and Mao 2013; Zhang and Zhang 2015) have already documented various activities conducted by fans and enthusiasts on the Internet, in this chapter I focus on fansubbing and shipping, two primary practices that have formed the basis of many media and celebrity fandoms.

As "a new model of content distribution" (Lee 2011: 1131) based on collective knowledge, global collaboration, and voluntary fan labor, fansubbing is not something uniquely Chinese, but a global cultural phenomenon. Yet it is probably only in China, where the state has established a complex and interlocking control system to keep out ideologically harmful foreign cultural content (Fung 2008), that fansubbing has been utilized to such an extent that it has been able to drastically change the cultural landscape of a whole nation. The first Chinese fansub group "Planet" was formed by fans of Japanese manga and anime before 2000. Due to the lack of Japanese translators, Planet had to look for English fansubs of Japanese anime titles and translate from English into Chinese. After Planet disbanded, some former members established a new group "Wander" in 2001. It was this group that invented a new fansub software that greatly reduced the workload of fansubbers (Liu 2011). Since 2002, numerous fansub groups have been set up, offering netizens convenient, free, and timely access to anime programs, television shows, films, and games from Japan, Korea, the United States and Europe. Fandoms of Japanese and Korean stars have also organized their own fansub groups to make fansubs for videos related to their idols (Lei 2012: 68–69). While the popularity of Japanese and Korean dramas in China all began with CCTV screening, it is purely through fansubbing that Anglo-American television series have become trendy cultural products on the Chinese Internet.

All fansub groups rely on the Internet to obtain source content, organize and release fansubs (Zhang and Mao 2013), recruit new fansubbers, and communicate with viewers (Liu and de Seta 2015). In addition to hosting their own online forums for fans to discuss and download fansubbed materials, fansub groups also use Sina Weibo to share information of shows and fansubbing progress. It has been observed that big fansub groups operate like a well-organized company, even though no monetary compensation is involved. With efficient workflow, a strict trainee system, high team spirits, and professional standards, as well as fierce competitiveness, these amateur fansub groups can be more productive than professional translating services (Hu 2009). Another appealing advantage of fansubbing over official translation is that fansubbers frequently add valuable annotations to help audiences understand the cultural context, and spice up their translations with Internet catchphrases and funny personal comments (Tian 2011: 65–74).

Occasionally, fansubbers also attempt to resist and subvert the meaning of the original content. Due to the rise of China on the world stage, it has become a common practice for American television producers to incorporate some Chinese elements in their shows to attract the audience's attention. Some of their references to China are viewed by Chinese fans of American shows as stale and offensive China-bashing. In December 2008, *Boston Legal* (2004–2008), an American legal dramedy, aired a two-hour series finale titled "Made in China", which narrates the purchase of the protagonists' law firm by a large Chinese corporation. To stall this deal, one of the main characters goes to court and argues that the American legal system would be destroyed by the Chinese should the purchase materialize. Angered by this perceived vilification of China, major fansub groups decided to collectively boycott this finale by refusing to fansub it (Deng 2010: 177). After a week's delay, one fansub group finally completed the translation. Yet the group not only embedded a notice at the beginning of the episode, saying that "we strongly advise you not to watch this episode", but deliberately translated all the references to "China" into "C country" (Sohu News 2008).

Since fansubs in China generally come in the form of "hard subs", meaning that subtitles are directly encoded into the video, when releasing the fansubs, fansubbers also distribute the original material. This practice has placed fansub groups into a double bind. On the one hand, they face legal challenges from copyright holders of the original content; on the other hand, they are themselves victims of copyright infringements, as the products of their fan labor can be easily pirated by DVD manufacturers or video websites. In November 2014, the most well-known fansub group YYeTs announced that it had temporarily gone offline to "clean up" its content due to copyright concerns. On the same day, another popular website for fansubbed content, "Shooter", also announced its closure (Olesen 2014). While copyright violation could be used as a convenient excuse for the shutdown of fansub websites, the removal of licensed American television series from mainstream video websites in 2014 (Mozur 2014) and the takedown of 38 Japanese anime titles from the Internet in 2015 (Kyodo News 2015) could only be attributed to censorship. To continue to watch those hit shows, viewers had to search for fansubbed resources in the fan communities formed around those shows or file storage services like Baidu Pan.

Like fansubbing, shipping (derived from "relation-ship") is also a prominent fan practice that has cut across different types of fandom and challenged the dominant ideology of the state. It involves fantasizing two real-life celebrities or fictional characters as a romantic and/or sexual couple. There are generally three kinds of pairings, male or female same-sex pairings, respectively called "Boys' Love" (BL) and "Girls' Love" (GL), and heterosexual pairings or "Boy and Girl" (BG). Shipping often lies at the core of fan gossip, fan fiction (fanfics), fan art, and fan videos (fanvids). While there are a considerable number of BG-style fan works in the ACG fandom, the majority of fan works in celebrity fandoms and television fandoms are BL narratives. Many fans have their own "one true pairing", whereas there are also "one and only" fans who strongly oppose any shipping of their favorite stars or characters. To cater to fans' desire for shipping, Japanese and Korean media producers and entertainment companies often intentionally highlight the bonding between two particular members of a pop band or two characters in a manga or anime series during production and promotion. Yet these "official pairings" are not necessarily the ones most welcomed or accepted by fans. The question of who should be with whom, and in the case of same-sex pairing, who should be the top and who should be the bottom, can be the source of endless debates and feuds in a fandom.

Chinese fans' practice of shipping was borrowed from Japan, where original BL narratives were created in the genre of girls' comics in the early 1970s, and derivative BL works based on the plots and characters of existing media texts and imagined experience of celebrities "have also long been very popular" (McLelland and Welker 2015: 4). The first known Chinese BL fanfic was based on the popular Japanese manga and anime series *Slam Dunk* (1990–1996) and posted on Sangsang Academy in 1999. Since the turn of the century, the practice of shipping has spread from Japanese ACG fandoms into television, celebrity, and sports fandoms. The Taiwanese traditional bromance *The Seven Heroes and Five Gallants* (*Qixia Wuyi*, 1994), the Chinese military drama *Soldiers Sortie* (*Shibing Tuji*, 2008), and the BBC series *Sherlock* (2010–) have all inspired a great amount of BL-oriented fan creativity. There are also a large number of BL fanfics based on Japanese and Korean pop idols, German and Italian soccer players, as well as world-class figure skaters. Ever since trans-Asian pop icon Wang Leehom and classical pianist Li Yundi performed together on CCTV Spring Festival Gala in 2012, there has been a shipping frenzy surrounding the two male celebrities, which even caught media-wide attention (Zhou forthcoming). The first visible wave of GL shipping was triggered by the Super Girl contest in 2005 and 2006 that featured a number of androgynous-looking contestants (Yang and Bao 2012; Zhao 2014). Through fansubs, the American lesbian-themed television show, *The L Word* (2004–2009), has also stimulated a stream of original and translated GL fanfics.

Although shipping and related queer fan practices, particularly BL-oriented activities, are commonly associated with heterosexual women (Yi 2013), there is in fact a significant portion of non-straight fans in certain Chinese queer fandoms. For instance, a 2006 survey of over 2,500 participants of an online forum dedicated to the *The L Word* shows that 45.04 percent of the participants are self-identified lesbians and 30.32 percent are self-identified bisexual female fans (Zhao forthcoming). In the amateur audio drama community devoted to the fan adaptation of original BL works, most of the male voice actors are believed to be gay. One of the most popular writers of original BL is also a young gay man whose sexual orientation has been an open secret in the BL fandom. Some of his works skillfully blur the distinctions between BL fiction and gay literature.

Despite the increased social tolerance of sexual minorities in Chinese society, the government has maintained an ambiguous policy of "no approval, no disapproval, no promotion" towards homosexuality, making it "exceedingly difficult for queers to claim acceptance, visibility, and space" (Engebretsen 2014: 16). The massive dissemination of non-heterosexual fantasies in and across fan communities, however, goes directly against the sexual conservatism of the state. Through playing with non-normative gender roles and sexualities, queer shipping has functioned not only as a viral online campaign for the legitimacy of same-sex attraction, but a gateway to an alternative set of relations, pleasures, and desires beyond dominant social and familial norms. Since queer fan works often contain graphic and deviant sex scenes, they have been subject to both government persecution and communal censorship

(Liu 2009; Yang and Xu forthcoming; Yi 2013). Like fansubbers who have to walk a thin line between their desire to share the work they love and the obligation to protect the interests of the producer, fans of queer fantasy also have to deal with the tension between freedom of expression and the ethics of representation.

Distinctions and Contestations

Thanks to fansubbing and commercial imports, Chinese fans are able to transcend national boundaries to embrace media and cultural content from other parts of the world. The proliferation of media products in the market also compels fans to be more selective of their fan objects, as cultural consumption has increasingly become the key channel of self-fashioning and identity performance in post-socialist China. To assess and defend the value of their fandoms, Chinese fans tend to compare their fan objects with similar ones and draw a sharp distinction between their own fan objects/communities and objects/communities of others.

During the 2005 Super Girl contest, in order to mobilize public support, fans of the second runner-up Zhang Liangying purposefully portrayed themselves as a group of social and cultural elites with substantial clout and impeachable taste, while ridiculing fans of Li Yuchun, the final winner of the show, as a bunch of ignorant, sentimental, and bored female office workers (L. Jang 2012: 56). Those fans of local reality TV shows are now despised by fans of Anglo-American reality shows who believe that Anglo-American reality shows are more original, truthful, and sincere than local ones (Zhang and Zhang 2015: 209). Similarly, fans of American television series also consider American dramas to be superior to Korean and local dramas in terms of quality and scornfully categorize viewers of local dramas as countryside people, bored housewives, the elderly, or children (Deng 2010: 148–149). The online gaming communities involve even more complicated deployment of cultural and social distinctions, as "[w]here one plays, what one plays and who one plays with" are all ways for gamers to distinguish themselves (Lindtner and Szablewicz 2011: 93). Obviously, those "tactics of distinction (vis-à-vis other fan cultures or within the same fan culture)" not only "revolve around claims to authenticity—of being the true fan" (de Kloet and van Zoonen 2007: 326), but operate along axes of age, gender, and education (Fiske 1992: 32).

While the antagonism between different factions of the same fandom and different fandoms of the same genre is also evident in European and American fandoms too (Johnson 2007; Theodoropoulou 2007), the hostility targeted at female-dominated idol fandoms by male-dominated media and sports fandoms seems to be specific to the deeply misogynist Chinese society. Such male-induced hostility is usually manifested via flaming, Internet parody, and a form of cyber-attack called "bar explosion" (baoba), which refers to the act of flooding Baidu Post Bar with trash posts so as to disrupt the normal operation of the said bar. Li Yuchun Bar, once the biggest post bar on Baidu, has been the first victim of bar explosion. The attack was orchestrated by Li Yi Bar (see Figure 25.1), a popular online forum that evolved from the anti-fandom of a smug Chinese soccer player. On 21 June 2007, suspecting that Li Yuchun Bar was behind the suspension of their bar managers, members of Li Yi Bar, together with supporters from other football bars, spammed Li Yuchun Bar with nearly 100,000 trash messages. Technicians of Baidu Post Bar had to reset the posting procedure of Li Yuchun Bar before they could finally stop the attack (Baidu Encyclopedia 2015b).

Since then, fandoms of Korean male idol bands have also suffered from bar explosion. The most well-known cyber-attack on Korean fandoms was the "69 Holy War", in which over 100,000 netizens participated in the hacking of websites for the Super Junior boy band and the "explosion" of Super Junior bars on Baidu. The attack was scheduled on 9 June because

Figure 25.1 A screenshot taken from the homepage of Li Yi Bar at http://tieba.baidu.com/f?kw=__&ie=utf-8 on 26 September 2015. The motto of Li Yi Bar reads: "Work hard! Be the master of your own destiny! All people are 'the Great'!"

it was the day that high school students finished their college entrance exams. Since Super Junior fans are mostly "young girls aged from 15 to 25" and their attackers were also "young men of the same age group" (Yang and Zheng 2012: 647), the incident could hence be read as an allegory of a group of male chauvinists collectively berating women in their tribe for their unruly desire for foreign men.

Baidu WoW Bar was one of the major forces of the "69" crusade. Like Li Yi Bar, WoW Bar has also morphed from an online forum for WoW (World of Warcraft) gamers into a socializing venue for male netizens. Over time, both bars have invented their own unique bar cultures. While WoW bar is known for the Internet satire of "Grass Mud Horse", an ingenious parody of censorship that has garnered much academic attention (for example, Li 2015; Meng 2011; Tang and Yang 2011), Li Yi Bar is famous for a recent Internet "loser" (*diaosi*) meme that expresses widespread disillusion with social mobility among lower-class young men (Szablewicz 2014; Yang *et al.* 2015). Partly through their high-profile cyber-attacks on female online fandoms, and their spectacular display of masculine prowess and male-bonding, both bars have become the two most populous bars on Baidu respectively. The former now boasts a membership of 18.59 million and the latter 6.53 million. In contrast, the combined membership of Li Yuchun Bar and Super Junior Bar has barely reached two million.

Organized male aggression against female fans on the Internet is a partial result of the persistent male dominance in Chinese cyberspace. When the China Internet Network Information Center (CNNIC) conducted its first survey of Internet development in China in 1997, 87.7 percent of Internet users were male, while only 12.3 percent were female (CNNIC 1997). Although the gender gap has narrowed considerably in the past two decades, by December 2014, male Internet users still outnumber female users by about 12 percent (CNNIC 2015). Moreover, the gender-bending appearance of Li Yuchun and Korean male idols like Super Junior has made many male netizens uneasy, as they perceive non-normative gender representations to be a sign of social discord and disintegration. In 2009, WoW Bar invented the "Cult of Spring Brother" to mock Li Yuchun and her female fans. Members of the bar created many manipulated images in which Li Yuchun's head was superimposed on the body of a hyper-masculine man, apparently to prove that Li Yuchun is neither a woman nor a man, but a freak. One member of WoW Bar even created a serialized manga based on a fictional character named "Spring Brother" . The amateur artist's personal blog, where the work was initially posted, used to come under frequent attacks from Li Yuchun's fans. The sabotage eventually died out when the storyline of the manga evolved into something different from a simple parody of Li Yuchun (U17 2010).

Frequently, however, these misogynist male fans have also used their wit and creativity to "mock the powerful and/or the authorities" and therefore assumed the role of fan activists (Yang et al. 2015: 200). One example is a 64-minute machinima produced by a WoW gaming community in early 2010. Drawing on Internet memes and WoW lingo, the video unleashed a protest against exploitation by the gaming industry, government censorship, the pathologization of gamers, and the widespread inequality and corruption in Chinese society. Its passionate questioning of "Why can't we have cheap entertainment that costs only 40 cents an hour?" and the assertion that "What we are addicted to is not the game, but the sense of belonging brought by the game" are thought to have articulated eloquently the innermost feelings of gamers (Szablewicz 2014; Yang and Jiang 2015; Zhang and Fung 2014). Occasionally, more radical resistance to government restrictions of cultural consumption has occurred as well. In 2006, after Japanese anime was banned from prime time on Chinese television, an upset 20-year-old fan of Japanese manga and anime placed a false bomb at a large state-owned bookstore in Beijing, threatening to blow up a metro line if Japanese anime was not screened within a month. In the court trial, the young "anime terrorist" claimed that he had the responsibility to fight against "cultural discrimination against foreign animations in the Chinese cultural market" (Wang 2007).

Although fan activism in China is more often than not a forced reaction to state interference, fans' demands to enjoy their fan objects without restriction is inherently at odds with the authoritarian party-state that ruthlessly stamps out any sign of challenge to its control. The scholarly worry that fans' indulgence in entertainment content will divert their attention from performance of civic duties and political engagement (Zhang and Mao 2013) is therefore misguided, because the panoptic gaze of the state does not distinguish between the political and non-political, nor does it leave anything to chance. As long as an entertainment program becomes sufficiently popular to generate the capacity for grassroots mobilization, be it Super Girl, whose vote-in system carries an overt democratic message, or a comedy show like The Big Bang Theory (2007–) that contains little sex or violence, the state will take action to rein it in, instantly rendering apolitical entertainment into a site of ideological contestation. Yet this is not to claim that all fandoms are politically engaged or engaged with the "right" politics. Like the fractal and divided public opinions on the Internet, the political positions and the degree of political participation vary greatly from fandom to fandom. Take AcFun and Bilibili, for example. The two most important ACG-themed video-sharing sites in China have fostered drastically different political atmospheres. While AcFun has positioned itself as an online stronghold for nationalistic and pro-government "leftist otaku" (zhaizuo), Bilibili has largely avoided getting involved in political issues.

Conclusion

The history of the Internet in China is closely intertwined with fan activities and the formation of networked fan communities. Fans are not only eager users of new media technologies, they are also the inventors, participants, and game changers of Chinese Internet culture and the IT industry. Although fan activities are generally motivated by the desire for entertainment and pleasure, practices like fansubbing and shipping are loaded with political implications. The former tears apart state control of information and cultural content; the latter defies government repression of transgressive and marginalized desires and sexualities. Through escaping, evading, and contesting state censorship, Chinese fans have built dynamic transnational fan cultures of their own in cyberspace and made an enormous contribution to the progressive change of cultural outlook and social morale.

Due to the diversity of fan objects and fan participants, however, Chinese online fan space is demarcated by cultural and gender distinctions, and infused with conflicts between fandoms of different gender make-up, as well as between fandoms and the state. This gendered dimension of Chinese cyber culture has often been overlooked by researchers of the Chinese Internet due to the "bias towards sweeping and dichotomous analytical categories, such as state vs. netizens, politics vs. entertainment, and authoritarianism vs. democracy" (G. Yang 2014: 136). Yet the contentiousness of Chinese fandoms is also accompanied by a tremendous outburst of creativity, vibrancy, and solidarity, things that a fake "harmonious society" would never be able to deliver. Since many online fan communities have allowed members to discuss topics that are unrelated to the fan objects, and members of big fandoms usually come from diverse socio-cultural backgrounds, instead of creating "deliberative clusters" of like-minded people and reinforcing the views they already hold (Sautedé 2013: 337), Chinese fandoms actually constitute an avenue to a heterogeneous and heterodox new world where fans can conduct peer-to-peer communication with people they would never be able to mingle with in the offline life. With the ever-intensifiying government crackdowns on outright political dissent and collective action, seemingly apolitical online fandoms are likely to be embraced by more Chinese netizens as a sanctuary where they can be "empowered to forge new types of consciousness, identity, shared meanings, communities, relationships, space and place" without the unwanted influence of the state (Marolt 2014: 16).

References

Ahn, J. (2014) "The New Korean Wave in China: Chinese Users' Use of Korean Popular Culture via the Internet", *International Journal of Contents*, 10(3): 47–54.

Baidu Encyclopedia (2015a) *Longkong* (The Sky of Dragon), 25 June, available at: http://baike.baidu.com/link?url=ZCCKR-mzOcY1UsqTkXRaNVH3MDW_OcPtGrLDdL6LkpgW7foTu9RsDddn8vzyfKR_02rR3wr26faDEt5-jY5m7_ (accessed 5 September 2015).

Baidu Encyclopedia (2015b) *Baoba* (Bar Explosion), 28 August, available at: http://baike.baidu.com/link?url=HSOlAC7e6PQf1MPJHJtiN1JttdT-N6ZNgNM6f2ZQ5QyfHTKrKmYxphw4TRrEk0zcW0izEwOSkLhEZW8t6tUChK (accessed 5 September 2015).

Banana Sonna (2014) "Zhongguo ACGquan de Fazhan Lishi shi Zenyangde, Younaxie Zhongyao Wangzhan?" (What's the Development History of Chinese ACG Circle, Does It Have Any Important Websites?), *Zhihu*, 13 May, available at: www.zhihu.com/question/22561605 (accessed 5 September 2015).

Chang, S. (2007) "Xinmeijie Huanjing zhong de Shouzhong Yanjiu—Yi Xuni Shequ zhong de Zhuixingzu Weili" (Audience Studies in the Age of New Media—A Case Study of an Online Fan Community), Ph.D. thesis, Tsinghua University, Beijing.

Clark, P. (2012) *Youth Culture in China: From Red Guards to Netizens*, Cambridge: Cambridge University Press.

CNNIC (1997) *Zhongguo Hulian Wangluo Fazhan Zhuangkuang Tongji Baogao (1997/10)* (Statistical Report on Internet Development in China (October 1997)), available at: www.cnnic.net.cn/hlwfzyj/hlwxzbg/hlwtjbg/201206/P020120612485123735661.pdf (accessed 5 September 2015).

CNNIC (2015) *Di Sanshiwu Ci Zhongguo Hulian Wangluo Fazhan Zhuangkuang Tongji Baogao* (The 35th Statistical Report on Internet Development in China), available at: www.cnnic.net.cn/hlwfzyj/hlwxzbg/hlwtjbg/201502/P020150203548852631921.pdf (accessed 5 September 2015).

de Kloet, J., and van Zoonen, L. (2007) "Fan Culture—Performing Difference", in E. Devereux (ed.), *Media Studies: Key Issues and Debates*, London, Sage, pp. 322–341.

Deng, W. (2010) *Mi yu Miqun: Meijie Shiyong Zhong de Shenfen Rentong Jiangou* (Fans and Fandom: The Construction of Identity in Media Usage), Beijing: Communication University of China Press.

Dou, E. (2015) "Xiaomi: The Secret to The World's Most Valuable Startup", *The Wall Street Journal*, 6 April, available at: www.wsj.com/articles/to-lift-brand-xiaomi-fosters-phone-fan-club-1428345473 (accessed 5 September 2015).

Engebretsen, E. L. (2014) *Queer Women in Urban China: An Ethnography*, New York: Routledge.

Feng, J. (2013) *Romancing the Internet: Producing and Consuming Chinese Web Romance*, Leiden: Brill.

Fiske, J. (1992) "The Cultural Economy of Fandom", in L. A. Lewis (ed.), *The Adoring Audience: Fan Culture and Popular Media*, London: Routledge, pp. 30–49.

Fung, A. Y. H. (2008) *Global Capital, Local Culture: Transnational Media Corporations in China*, New York: Peter Lang.

Fung, A. Y. H. (2009) "Fandom, Youth and Consumption in China", *European Journal of Cultural Studies*, 12(3): 285–303.

Goldman, A. (2012) *Opera and the City: The Politics of Culture in Beijing, 1770–1900*, Stanford, CA: Stanford University Press.

Herold, D. K. (2011) "Noise, Spectacle, Politics: Carnival in Chinese Cyberspace", in D. K. Herold and P. Marolt (eds), *Online Society in China: Creating, Celebrating, and Instrumentalising the Online Carnival*, New York: Routledge, pp. 1–19.

Hu, K. (2005) "The Power of Circulation: Digital Technologies and the Online Chinese Fans of Japanese TV Drama", *Inter-Asia Cultural Studies*, 6(2): 171–186.

Hu, K. (2009) "Zhongguo Zimuzu Yu Xin Ziyouzhuyi De Gongzuo Lunli" (Chinese Subtitle Groups and the Neoliberal Work Ethics), *Xinwenxue Yanjiu* (Mass Communication Research), 101: 177–214.

Hu, Y. (2012) "Spreading the News" (trans. R. Flagg), *Index on Censorship*, 41(4): 107–111.

Incitez China (2015) "Baidu Post Bar More MAUs than Weibo in Jan 2015", *China Internet Watch*, 11 March, available at: www.chinainternetwatch.com/12628/baidu-post-bar-more-maus-than-weibo-jan-2015/#ixzz3jWCONIE7 (accessed 5 September 2015).

Jenkins, H. (1992) *Textual Poachers: Television Fans and Participatory Culture*, New York: Routledge.

Jenkins, H. (2006) *Convergence Culture: Where Old and New Media Collide*, New York: New York University Press.

Jiang, Q., and Leung, L. (2012) "Lifestyles, Gratifications Sought, and Narrative Appeal: American and Korean TV Drama Viewing Among Internet Users in Urban China", *International Communication Gazette*, 74(2): 159–180.

Johnson, D. (2007) "Fan-Tagonism: Factions, Institutions, and Constitutive Hegemonies of Fandom", in J. Gray, C. Sandvoss, and C. L. Harrington (eds), *Fandom: Identities and Communities in a Mediated World*, New York: New York University Press, pp. 285–300.

Kong, S. (2012) "The 'Affective Alliance': *Undercover*, Internet Media Fandom, and the Sociality of Cultural Consumption in Postsocialist China", *Modern Chinese Literature and Culture*, 24(1): 1–47.

Kyodo News (2015) "China Bans 'Attack on Titan', Other Popular Japanese Anime from Web", *The Japan Times*, 9 June, available at: www.japantimes.co.jp/news/2015/06/09/national/china-bans-attack-on-titan-other-popular-japanese-anime-from-web/#.VdxQTJOqpBd (accessed 5 September 2015).

Lee, H. (2011) "Participatory Media Fandom: A Case Study of Anime Fansubbing", *Media, Culture & Society*, 33(8): 1131–1147.

Lee, L. O. (1999) *Shanghai Modern: The Flowering of a New Urban Culture in China, 1930–1945*, Cambridge, MA: Harvard University Press.

Lei, W. (2012) *Wangluo Miqun yu Kuaguo Chuanbo: Jiyu Zimuzu Xianxiang de Yanjiu* (Online Fandom and International Communication: A Study Based on the Phenomenon of Fansub Group), Beijing: Communication University of China Press.

Li, H. S. (2015) "Narrative Dissidence, Spoof Videos and Alternative Memory in China", *International Journal of Cultural Studies*, doi: 10.1177/1367877915595477 (accessed 5 September 2015).

Li, S. (2014) "Baidu Tieba Shizhounian, Wei Xingqu Ersheng—Guanyu Tieba Shinian Fensi Wenhua Bianqian De Jiedu" (Ten Years of Baidu Post Bar, Born for Interest: A Reading of the Changing Fan Cultures of Post Bar in the Past Decade), *Xinwen Shijie* (News World), 10: 202–204.

Li, W. (2014) *Canyugan: Xiaomi Koubei Yingxiao Neibu Shouce* (The Sense of Participation: An Internal Guide to Word-of-Mouth Marketing of Xiaomi), Beijing: Zhongxin Publishing House.

Lin, W. (2013) "Jay Chou's Music and the Shaping of Popular Culture in China", in L. Fitzsimmons and J. A. Lent (eds), *Popular Culture in Asia: Memory, City, Celebrity*, Houndmills: Palgrave Macmillan, pp. 206–219.

Lindtner, S., and Szablewicz, M. (2011) "China's Many Internets: Participation and Digital Game Play Across a Changing Technology Landscape", in D. K. Herold and P. Marolt (eds), *Online Society in China: Creating, Celebrating, and Instrumentalising the Online Carnival*, New York: Routledge, pp. 89–105.

Liu, T. (2009) "Conflicting Discourses on Boys' Love and Subcultural Tactics in Mainland China and Hong Kong", *Intersections: Gender and Sexuality in Asia and the Pacific*, 20, available at: http://intersections.anu.edu.au/issue20/liu.htm (accessed 5 September 2015).

Liu, X., and de Seta, G. (2015) "Chinese Fansub Groups as Communities of Practice: An Ethnography of Online Language Learning", in P. Marolt and D. K. Herold (eds), *China Online: Locating Society in Online Spaces*, New York: Routledge, pp. 125–140.

Liu, Z. (2011) "Wutuobang Li Yeyou Kuaile" (There Is Also Fun in Utopia), *Nanfang Zhoumo* (Southern Weekly), 18 November, available at: www.infzm.com/content/64924 (accessed 5 September 2015).

Lugg, A. (2011) "Chinese Online Fiction: Taste Publics, Entertainment, and *Candle in the Tomb*", *Chinese Journal of Communication*, 4(2): 121–136.

McLelland, M., and Welker, J. (2015) "An Introduction to 'Boys Love' in Japan", in M. McLelland, K. Nagaike, K. Suganuma, and J. Welker (eds), *Boys Love Manga and Beyond: History, Culture, and Community in Japan*, Jackson, MI: University Press of Mississippi, pp. 3–20.

Marolt, P. (2014) *Cyberzomia*, Asia Research Institute Working Paper Series, no. 214, available at: www.ari.nus.edu.sg/wps/wps14_214.pdf (accessed 5 September 2015).

Meng, B. (2011) "From *Steamed Bun* to *Grass Mud Horse*: E Gao as Alternative Political Discourse on the Chinese Internet", *Global Media and Communication*, 7(1): 33–51.

Mozur, P. (2014) "China Forces Four U.S. TV Shows Off Web", *The Wall Street Journal*, 28 April, available at: www.wsj.com/articles/SB10001424052702304163604579527683976216624 (accessed 5 September 2015).

Olesen, A. (2014) "A Mournful Farewell to Chinese Copyright Pirates", *Foreign Policy*, 25 November, available at: http://foreignpolicy.com/2014/11/25/a-mournful-farewell-to-chinese-copyright-pirates/ (accessed 5 September 2015).

Pang, L. K. (2009) "The Transgression of Sharing and Copying: Pirating Japanese Animation in China", in C. Berry, N. Liscutin, and J. D. Mackintosh (eds), *Cultural Industries and Cultural Studies in Northeast Asia: What a Difference a Region Makes*, Hong Kong: Hong Kong University Press, pp. 119–134.

Pease, R. (2006) "Internet, Fandom, and K-Wave in China", in K. Howard (ed.), *Korean Pop Music: Riding the Wave*, Folkestone: Global Oriental, pp. 176–189.

Peng, L. (2005) *Zhongguo Wangluo Meiti de Diyige Shinian* (The First Decade of Chinese Online Media), Beijing: Tsinghua University Press.

Sautedé, E. (2013) "The Internet in China's State-Society Relations: Will Goliath Prevail in the Chiaroscuro?" *China Information*, 27(3): 327–346.

Sina Weibo Data Center (2015) "2014nian Xinlang Weibo Yonghu Fazhan Baogao" (2014 Sina Weibo User Development Report), *199 IT*, 27 January, available at: www.199it.com/archives/324955.html (accessed 5 September 2015).

Sohu News (2008) "Meiju Niuqu Zhongguo Yanlun Zhongguo Zimuzu Ti Kangyi" (Chinese Fansub Groups Protest Against American Drama's Distorted Speech About China), *Sohu News*, 25 December, available at: http://news.sohu.com/20081225/n261423529.shtml (accessed 5 September 2015).

Sullivan, J. (2014) "China's Weibo: Is Faster Different?" *New Media & Society*, 16(1): 24–37.

Szablewicz, M. (2014) "The 'Losers' of China's Internet: Memes as 'Structures of Feeling' for Disillusioned Young Netizens", *China Information*, 28(2): 259–275.

Tang, L., and Yang, P. (2011) "Symbolic Power and the Internet: The Power of a 'Horse'", *Media, Culture & Society*, 33(5): 675–691.

Tencent Sports (2009) "Zhongguo Zutan Shida Ganren Qiumi Chiqinghan Su Linglei Fengjingxian" (Ten Most Touching Fans in Chinese Football: Dedicated Men Form Alternative Landscape), *Tencent Sports*, 13 April, available at: http://sports.qq.com/a/20090413/000117.htm (accessed 5 September 2015).

Theodoropoulou, V. (2007) "The Anti-Fan Within the Fan: Awe and Envy in Sport Fandom", in J. Gray, C. Sandvoss, and C. L. Harrington (eds), *Fandom: Identities and Communities in a Mediated World*, New York: New York University Press, pp. 316–327.

Tian, Y. (2011) "Fansub Cyber Culture in China", MA thesis, Georgetown University, Washington, DC.

Tsai, E. (2008) "Existing in the Age of Innocence: Pop Stars, Publics, and the Politics in Asia", in B. H. Chua and K. Iwabuchi (eds), *East Asian Pop Culture: Analyzing the Korean Wave*, Hong Kong: Hong Kong University Press, pp. 217–242.

Tsou, Y. (2015) "Digital Natives in the Name of a Cause: From 'Flash Mob' to 'Human Flesh Search'", in N. Shah, P. P. Sneha, and S. Chattapadhyay (eds), *Digital Activism in Asia Reader*, Lüneburg: Meson Press, pp. 179–194.

U17 (2010) "Zhongguo Yuanchuang Dongman Zuojia Xianzhuang Diaocha—Shengda Danghong Dongman Zuozhe Fangtanlu" (An Investigation of the Current Situation of Original Manga and Anime Artists in China: An Interview with Popular Shanda Manga and Anime Creator)", *U17*, 9 August, available at: www.u17.com/news/1282.html (accessed 5 September 2015).

Wang, J. (2014) "'Guofen' Qunti Qingnian Yawenhua Yanjiu" (A Youth Subcultural Study of Apple Fans), MA thesis, Shaanxi Normal University, Shaanxi.

Wang, Q. (2007) "Buman Xianbo Waiguo Donghuapian Daxuesheng Yangyan Zha Batongxian Shoushen" (Discontented with Restriction on Foreign Animation: College Student Who Threatened to Bomb Batong Line Held for Trial), *Jinghua Shibao* (*Beijing Times*), 4 July, available at: http://media.people.com.cn/GB/40606/5967167.html (accessed 5 September 2015).

Wang, Y. (2005) "The Dissemination of Japanese Manga in China: The Interplay of Culture and Social Transformation in Post Reform Period", MA thesis, Lund University, Sweden.

Wong, K. (2014) "Xiaomi and the Power of the Fan Economy", *btrax*, 22 September, available at: http://blog.btrax.com/en/2014/09/22/xiaomi-the-fan-economy-and-word-of-mouth-marketing/ (accessed 5 September 2015).

Wu, W., and Wang, X. (2011) "Lost in Virtual Carnival and Masquerade: In-Game Marriage on the Chinese Internet", in D. K. Herold and P. Marolt (eds), *Online Society in China: Creating, Celebrating, and Instrumentalising the Online Carnival*, New York: Routledge, pp. 106–123.

Yang, G. (2014) "Political Contestation in Chinese Digital Spaces: Deepening the Critical Inquiry", *China Information*, 28(2): 135–144.

Yang, G., and Jiang, M. (2015) "The Networked Practice of Online Political Satire in China: Between Ritual and Resistance", *The International Communication Gazette*, 77(3): 215–231.

Yang, J. (2012) "The Korean Wave (Hallyu) in East Asia: A Comparison of Chinese, Japanese, and Taiwanese Audiences Who Watch Korean TV Dramas", *Development and Society*, 41(1): 103–147.

Yang, L. (2012) *Zhuanxing Shidai de Yule Kuanghuan—Chaonv Fensi yu Dazhong Wenhua Xiaofei* (Entertaining the Transitional Era: Super Girl Fandoms and the Consumption of Popular Culture), Beijing: China Social Sciences Press.

Yang, L. (2014) "Reality Talent Shows in China: Transnational Format, Affective Engagement, and the Chinese Dream", in L. Ouellette (ed.), *A Companion to Reality Television*, Malden: Wiley-Blackwell, pp. 516–540.

Yang, L., and Bao, H. (2012) "Queerly Intimate: Friends, Fans and Affective Communication in a *Super Girl* Fan Fiction Community", *Cultural Studies*, 26(6): 842–871.

Yang, L., and Xu, Y. (forthcoming) "'The Love that Dare Not Speak Its Name': The Fate of Chinese *Danmei* Communities in the 2014 Anti-Porn Campaign", in M. McLelland (ed.), *The End of "Cool Japan": Ethical, Legal, and Cultural Challenges to Japanese Popular Culture*, Oxford: Routledge.

Yang, L., and Zheng, Y. (2012) "Fen Qings (Angry Youth) in Contemporary China", *Journal of Contemporary China*, 21(76): 637–653.

Yang, P., Tang, L., and Wang, X. (2015) "*Diaosi* as Infrapolitics: Scatological Tropes, Identity-Making and Cultural Intimacy on China's Internet", *Media, Culture & Society*, 37(2): 197–214.

Yi, E. J. (2013) "Reflection on Chinese Boys' Love Fans: An Insider's View", *Transformative Works and Cultures*, 12, doi:10.3983/twc.2013.0424 (accessed 5 September 2015).

Yue, L. (2009) *Dangdai Zhongguo Dazhong Chuanmei de Mingxing Shengchan yu Xiaofei* (The Production and Consumption of Stardom in Contemporary Chinese Mass Media), Changsha: Yuelu Shushe.

Zhang, L., and Fung, A. Y. H. (2014) "Working as Playing? Consumer Labor, Guild and the Secondary Industry of Online Gaming in China", *New Media & Society*, 16(1): 38–54.

Zhang, N. (2014) "Web-Based Backpacking Communities and Online Activism in China: Movement Without Marching", *China Information*, 28(2): 276–296.

Zhang, W., and Mao, C. (2013) "Fan Activism Sustained and Challenged: Participatory Culture in Chinese Online Translation Communities", *Chinese Journal of Communication*, 6(1): 45–61.

Zhang, W., and Zhang, L. (2015) "Fandom of Foreign Reality TV Shows in the Chinese Cyber Sphere", in W. Chen and S. Reese (eds), *Networked China: Global Dynamics of Digital Media and Civic Engagement*, London: Routledge, pp. 197–213.

Zhao, J. J. (2014) "Fandom as a Middle Ground: Fictive Queer Fantasies and Real-World Lesbianism in *FSCN*", *Media Fields Journal: Access/Trespass A Special Conference Issue*, available at: http://mediafieldsjournal.square space.com/fandom-as-a-middle-ground/ (accessed 5 September 2015).

Zhao, J. J. (forthcoming) "Queering the Post-*L Word* 'Shane' in the 'Garden of Eden': Chinese Fans' Gossip About Katherine Moennig", in M. Lavin, L. Yang, and J. J. Zhao (eds), *Queer Fan Cultures in Mainland China, Hong Kong, and Taiwan*, Hong Kong: Hong Kong University Press.

Zhou, E. L. (2013) "Displeasure, Star-Chasing and the Transcultural Networking Fandom", *Participations: Journal of Audience & Reception Studies*, 10(2): 139–167.

Zhou, S. (forthcoming) "From Online BL Fandom to CCTV Spring Festival Gala: The Transforming Power of Online Carnival", in M. Lavin, L. Yang, and J. J. Zhao (eds), *Queer Fan Cultures in Mainland China, Hong Kong, and Taiwan*, Hong Kong: Hong Kong University Press.

Part 6

INTERNETS AND NEW MEDIA FORMS

26

ONLINE ADVERTISING

Christina Spurgeon

An Institutional Perspective

In the context of a professional communication discipline, advertising is generally taken to be a "paid mediated form of communication from an identifiable source, designed to persuade the receiver to take some action now or in the future" (Richards and Curran 2002: 74). Studied in its broader cultural, political, economic, and historical context, advertising is understood in media and cultural studies to be a globally significant and locally varied social institution (Leiss *et al.* 2005), comprising organizations, networks, conventions, norms, and texts, that plays an important role in "shaping the 'mental maps' of individuals and how they think about the world and their place in it" (Cunningham *et al.* 2015: 97). This chapter applies an institutional perspective to the development of online advertising. First, it situates the adaptation of advertising-funded commercial media business models to the Internet within wider debates about the commercialization of the Internet. It considers advertising industry-specific developments that conditioned online media for advertising, and the development of a raft of new subdisciplines and textual practices, as part of a general expansion of advertising. Shifts in the balance of social power afforded by the Internet, between media, advertising intermediaries, and two distinct groups of Internet end users—advertisers and consumers—are considered in this chapter. This analysis also shows how, in North American and European contexts in particular, the institutions of commercial media and advertising have continued to co-evolve in the process of addressing the enduring challenge of advertising avoidance and other expressions of consumer "misbehavior". This chapter draws attention to crucial changes in the social contract between media and consumers that were set in motion with the commercialization of the Internet and which became explicit, and most visible, in the terms of service for social media. End users now concede personal information in exchange for communication affordances as well as access to "free", often user-generated, content. This chapter also seeks to serve as a provocation to media, communication, and cultural studies to pay greater attention to the influence of advertising in accounting for Internet history. This intent is underpinned by an approach to Internet history that treats it as continuous with the histories of media and communications institutions that existed prior to the Internet.

Commercializing the Internet

The history of online advertising is intertwined with the history of the commercialization of the Internet. The early forms of advertising that appeared on bulletin boards and in email prior to the early 1990s were controversial, but nonetheless comparatively crude attempts to use the Internet for promotional purposes. Indeed, many of these efforts were quickly labeled "spam" (Bunton 2013), a term that served to "identify a way of thinking and doing online that was lazy, indiscriminate, and a waste of the time and attention of others" (Bunton 2013: 13). Arguably, also reflected in this assignation was early Internet user resistance, if not hostility, to advertising. Even though advertising was only one element of the problem of spam, it nonetheless constituted an important "shadow history" (Bunton 2013) of the Internet. This chapter is mainly concerned with Web-based advertising, the formal arrival of which has been dated to 1994 (for example, Li and Leckenby 2012: 211–212; McStay 2010: 44) and the appearance of the first banner ads in *HotWired*, which also claimed to be the first commercial online magazine. *HotWired* also led the way in the development of auditing methods for online publications (Hollis 2005) and in the use of real-time analytics to inform online media buying.

Importantly, the "acceptable use" policies which prohibited commercial communication on the Internet prior to the development of commercial Internet service providers (ISPs) and commercial online media had not been promulgated for "ideological reasons" (Spurgeon 2008: 11). Rather, managers of backbone communications links were seeking to contain the escalating costs and network loads that increasing demands for connectivity were placing on a publicly subsidized communications infrastructure that was meant to be dedicated to research. Nonetheless, this concern for containing communications costs helped to frame a shift in thinking about the Internet as a commodity service to a general global information infrastructure that could support all industries (Leiner *et al.* 1997: 107–108), including advertising. Even though the early Internet had the appearance of being non-commercial, it was constructed from private networks. Consequently, its early status is probably more accurately described as pre-commercial rather than non-commercial, with subsequent developments framed as questions of how, not whether, commercialization would unfold. As Brian Winston observed (1998: 333): "[f]rom the late 1980s on, and despite the illusion of independence which had surrounded the enterprise almost from the outset, it was inevitable that this tax-funded and government-managed asset would be handed over to the private sector."

As with Internet adoption in general, graphical web browsers hugely assisted market-based experimentation in developing business models for the new online environment. Media, communications, and IT industry business models were tried, and new ones were developed, with varying degrees of success. Two distinct approaches emerged from this activity that can broadly be described as "closed" (proprietary) and "open". In general, proprietary approaches were concerned with creating conditions of exclusivity from which private benefits (revenue and, ideally, profits) could be extracted. Internet media businesses generated revenues from a range of sources (Sinclair 2012; Spurgeon 2008), including utility-style charges for Internet connectivity, carriage services, and support for communications functionality, such as email and the Web; subscription, premium, and "freemium" charges for niche information and entertainment services, such as games, financial information, and adult content; license fees for Internet applications such as browsers, software, and other downloadable premium content; charges for bundled utility, communications, and content services that drove traffic through commercialized portals and "walled" content gardens; and advertising, the revenue stream of particular interest in this chapter. Open source approaches worked with the "public good" characteristics of information to add value to the "applications" layer of the Internet (Lessig 2006: 145) including, for example, commercial, knowledge-intensive IT services that customized the Linux operating system developed under the General Public License for use on Internet servers. As Lawrence Lessig (2006: 146) observed:

[o]penness—not property or contract but free code and access—created the boom that gave birth to the Internet that we know. And it was this boom that then attracted the attention of commerce. With all this activity, commerce rightly reasoned, surely there was money to be made.

In reality, the new commercial media that developed, globally native, from this mix, blended both open and proprietary approaches to create new media businesses. For example, companies such as Google and Yahoo! relied on open source software such as Linux to run their servers and keep operational costs manageable, as well as revenue from advertising sales.

The Internet was a marketing communications Aladdin's cave. It combined three key marketing channel capabilities: "communication, transaction and distribution; and the vertical integration of marketing communications, including advertising, public relations, promotion and direct marketing" (Vences and Segura 2014: 702).

Rapid commercial development of the Internet was fueled by the exploration of these capabilities. The early years were marked by "opportunism and venture capitalism, as opposed to traditional companies employing traditional scalable marketing and business techniques" (McStay 2010: 17). They were also "boom" years for online advertising, "characterized by experimentation and the rise and fall of a plethora of new online companies and a plethora of advertising formats" (Hollis 2005: 255) and a lively industry debate about the advertising uses to which online media were best suited: brand building or direct response (McStay 2010: 45). The comparative effectiveness of online and offline media was also a focus for early scholarly and industry research (Sundar *et al.* 2012: 355).

In the face of considerable brand advertiser skepticism, expectations about brand advertising, revenue windfalls based on mass media advertising rates and business models (Brown and Daguid 2001: 247; Hemmer 2005: 481) seemed unrealistic. This was an important factor in the dot.com crash at the beginning of the new millennium. When dot.com start-ups could not overcome brand advertiser resistance to advertising in new online channels, they were themselves forced to curtail advertising spending, and online advertising revenues quickly plateaued (Hollis 2005). Even so, advertising or advertising services were the most likely revenue base for new Internet-based commercial media and related services by the time Tim O'Reilly proclaimed the era of Web 2.0 in 2005. Consideration for end-user agency rapidly reshaped advertising media, markets, and practices. As Sally McMillan (2007: 24) remarked: "[c]ompanies that survived the dot-com crash were those that invested in understanding consumer behavior and in facilitating transactions that made sense online."

Disintermediation—the removal of unnecessary "middlemen" from value chains (including advertising agencies)—was an important, related part of Web 2.0 "common sense".

Expansion of Advertising

Internet advertising revenues grew rapidly, and began to be registered in national calculations of main media expenditure from the early 2000s. In 2005, online advertising accounted for an estimated 6 percent of all advertising spending in 88 international markets, including OECD countries (Clift 2015). With the exception of 2009, when global advertising expenditures experienced negative growth as part of the global financial crisis, the total amount of advertising expenditure continued to increase. This aggregate growth of advertising was due to a complex array of factors. For example, consumer economies and societies continued to develop rapidly in many parts of the world at the same time that Internet media channels were proliferating at an exponential rate. There were, and continue to be, important local variations in patterns of advertising expenditure across different media. However, the general trend in favor of an increasing proportion of advertising expenditure in online media was clear. By 2015, the global share of online advertising spending had increased to 29 percent, almost equal to the combined share of print, radio, cinema, and outdoor, and the online share of advertising expenditure exceeded television in a number of markets, including England, Canada, and Australia. The following account of key factors in the rapid expansion of online advertising focuses on the influence of Google and Facebook emanating from the USA. It does not extend to equally significant parallel developments in Asian markets—for example, the impact of Baidu and Weibo in China. Nonetheless, one important difference in the development trajectories of the social contract between commercial media and consumers across these territories is remarked upon in the concluding section of this chapter.

Throughout the twentieth century, advertising played a crucial role in the internationalization of capital, and since the 1980s, in the globalization of brands, consumer cultures, markets, and media (Sinclair 2012). It developed into a highly complex global service industry "which supports the foreign investment of global advertisers and stimulates global media development" (Sinclair 2012: 21). Like the global advertisers and commercial media it serviced, the international advertising industry came to be dominated by a small number of holding companies that were horizontally and vertically integrated across the full gamut of marketing communication disciplines (Sinclair 2012: 37). Even though the Internet seemed well matched to the needs of the global "manufacturing/marketing/media complex" (Sinclair 2012: 1), it also afforded local and hyperlocal possibilities of advertising, as well as individual self-promotion. Small advertisers turned out to be the early adopters of online advertising.

The Web 2.0 focus on end users was extended by the Internet beyond media consumers to another vast pool of hitherto taken for granted media users—small advertisers—concentrated at the "classifieds" end of the advertising market (Spurgeon 2006). Search media such as Google secured a revenue base in the "long tail" (Anderson 2006) of the demand curve for Internet advertising channels. Although far from being the first search media (Batelle 2005), Google quickly became the market leader in online advertising following the launch of its self-service keyword targeting ad program AdWords in 2000. It went on to develop AdSense, which matched online advertisers with online publishers, in 2003. AdSense disrupted established commercial media by making targeted advertising revenue streams available to a host of new online competitors. While the average value to Google of individual transactions on keywords or ads placed in online media was small, the cumulative value of this trade was considerable (Sinclair 2012: 53; Spurgeon 2008). The self-service advertising business model was also subsequently adopted by social media, such as Facebook. The success that the search media had with keyword advertising has been attributed to a variety of factors. Search advertising was likely to be perceived by search media users as potentially useful, rather than as "clutter" (Sundar *et al.* 2012: 362), perhaps aided by low levels of awareness about the distinction between paid and unpaid search results (Hargittai 2007). This apparent end-user acceptance of keyword advertising contributed to a revalorization of "informational" advertising (as distinct from "transformational" advertising, epitomized by television brand advertising) (Rossiter and Percy 1997). Keyword advertising also simultaneously threatened industry disintermediation on one hand, and stimulated the development of new digital specializations such as search engine optimization on the other.

Tapping the "head" of the advertising demand curve, occupied by national and global brand advertisers, was nonetheless important to Internet-based commercial media. As Internet data speeds improved, so too did the online prospects for rich branded media content. Persuading brand advertisers who were familiar with the well-established conventions of analogue print and broadcast media to expand into online media, as well as making it possible for them to do so, was a priority both for native online commercial media and pre-Internet ("old") commercial media that were attempting to make up lost ground online. Conditioning the Internet to be "brand-friendly" (Internet Advertising Bureau n.d.) necessitated new levels of online advertising industry unification and coordination. Various industry stakeholder formations led negotiations to standardize ad formats, audience measurement methods, and metrics in the hope of achieving industry consensus on the still unresolved problems of the "currencies" that would be used for buying and selling online media (Bermejo 2007: 117–198; Micu 2012: 58). The need for representation in public policy processes was also a spur to action. Leadership in this field was quickly assumed by the Internet Advertising Bureau (IAB), which was established as a dedicated industry association in New York City in June 1996. The IAB's initial membership was made up of "more than 125 companies involved in Internet advertising, including virtually all major commercial interactive content providers and consumer online services" (IAB 1996). Its early members also included measurement companies, research suppliers, and traffic companies. Changing its name to the Interactive Advertising Bureau in 2001, the scope of the IAB's focus was also broadened to include mobile and multimedia platforms. The IAB also expanded internationally. At the time of writing, IABs had been established in 44 national territories, under license from the US-based IAB, for the purpose of globalizing online advertising standards, among other things (IAB n.d.).

For a time, it appeared that a confluence of factors might tip the balance of power in the institutional relations of commercial media and advertisers back in favor of advertisers in European and American markets, if not elsewhere. These included the glut of online advertising inventory, which contributed to plummeting advertising rates for online media and general conditions of a media buyers' market (including an extended boom in the growth of specialist media buying agencies; Sinclair 2012: 40–41). Brand advertisers, wary as a result of earlier advertising agency excesses that stemmed from the industry's previous reliance on lucrative two-way commissions, used the opportunity of the Internet to rethink their marketing communications strategies, and were frequently reported to be taking back control of advertising budgets and experimenting with "in-house" solutions (Cappo 2003). The restrictive trade practices of commercial print and analogue broadcast media, which effectively controlled entry into the advertising industry in many markets, also continued to come under regulatory scrutiny (Spurgeon 2015: 72). Such an axial shift in the balance of power between brand advertisers and large media proprietors had not been seen since the early years of television, when US networks turned away from sponsored programming to "spot" advertising as their preferred mode of generating advertising revenue (Sinclair 2012: 51; Spurgeon 2015). This shift in the 1950s broke the nexus between brand advertisers and program production that had first been facilitated by advertising agencies in the early days of broadcast radio. It was partly a political response to the problems of bias, manipulation, and, in extreme cases, corruption, inherent to media systems that were effectively controlled by advertisers. It was also a path-dependent consequence of the one-to-many communication and control architectures of mass media, which concentrated social power, not just cybernetic control, in "senders" (Beniger 1989). For the remainder of the twentieth century, mass media asserted their authority over advertisers as the "gatekeepers of huge audiences" (Couldry and Turow 2014: 1715) and arguably served a wider public interest (often backed up with regulation) by maintaining clear distinctions between advertising and editorial content.

Evidence of brand advertisers taking the opportunity of the Internet to re-assert direct control over marketing communication budgets and, ultimately, media content could be found in many places, including the disintermediation of television as the preferred platform for brand advertising in many territories; a renewed interest in direct and integrated approaches to marketing and advertising techniques (Spurgeon 2008); the erosion of the advertising/editorial binary (Couldry and Turow 2014); and direct involvement in media production, including branded content and "native" advertising (Seligman 2015). Intense competition between advertisers and the media for the attention and engagement of Internet consumers and users dramatically reshaped the development trajectories of commercial media and advertising services, and broke open important questions of definition in the process—for example, "Who is a media company?" and "What is an ad?" While a consensus appears to have emerged in media and cultural studies about the commercial status of search and social media in an expanded field of media and communications firms, there is less certainty about such developments as iTunes, Amazon, and eBay. As the tension between the fragmentation of advertising media and the integration of communication strategies intensified, other major disciplinary distinctions also began to collapse. As McStay pondered, "[i]s a website advertising or is it a virtual shop window?" (McStay 2010: 116).

In any event, the largest commercial media companies ever seen also developed with the Internet. Google quickly became the largest commercial media company in the world by virtue of extensive horizontal and deep and vertical integration of a range of convergent industries, including advertising. Global consolidation of pre-existing marketing communications holding companies also continued. As online moved increasingly to the center of media planning strategies (McStay 2010: 28–32), global media and advertising holding companies, old and new, went about strengthening their networks and offerings in the digital space, often by acquiring many of the independent specialists that had survived the dot.com bubble burst.

Online Advertising Perceptions and Practices

Hovland and Wolburg (2014: 42) observe that historical adoption rates for electronic home-based information and entertainment technologies have always outpaced non-home markets for new technologies. Like radio and television before them, the consequences of the Internet also "radiate exponentially and indefinitely throughout every aspect of society", most notably through "the continuing breakdown in the boundaries of time and space and have ultimately led to further re-definitions in communities and markets" (Hovland and Wolburg 2014: 43). Online media provided new social and communicative spaces for community and commerce. Within a decade of the launch of the Apple Macintosh personal computer, and following the development of graphical web browsers, residential users were connecting to the Internet via ISPs at rates that were unprecedented for any other home-based technology, perhaps with the exception of cellphones.

The Internet dynamically redistributed the loci of control in media systems, which had the effect of massively increasing the range of media and entertainment choices, much of which was user-generated. Internet fora and consumer-produced blogs located beyond the influence, and often the awareness, of brand advertisers increased the visibility of Internet end user and consumer perspectives. Many early new media studies scholarships focused on the consequences and implications of increased end-user capacity to act in networks. Major developments in advertising practices also accompanied the transformation of consumers into prosumers, produsers, and co-creators. End-user influences such as changing media choices, unprecedented demands for advertiser accountability, and new consumer tactics and tools of advertising avoidance, shaped many of these developments.

It was known long before the Internet that the most important channel for selling was word of mouth, due to the perceived independence and high levels of trust invested in this mode of communication (Buttle 1998). This continued to be the case for the Internet, especially for "high involvement" product categories such as consumer electronics (Reigner 2007). Direct selling in various forms including door-to-door sales, while important, was also controversial for reliance on high-pressure techniques and unconscionable contracts (Jolson 1972). Even though returns on investments in mass media advertising were hard to ascertain, and matching media to markets was an imprecise science, print and broadcast media, like branding, proved to be a reasonably effective compromise for dealing with the industrial scale and costs of population-wide selling. Internet channels combined the attributes of peer-to-peer, direct, and mass-media functionality. The data capabilities of the Internet also promised greater accountability for advertising expenditure, but the Internet also increased the ease with which consumers could "misbehave" in their dealings with advertisers.

Consumers have used technology to avoid advertising since the days of VCRs. The Internet brought the problem of advertising avoidance on an expanded variety of fronts into sharp focus. The standard explanations for this behavior, as responses to problems of clutter and interruption, were inadequate to the challenge of the Internet. Research showed that relevance and credibility were also important contributing reasons for avoidance (Kelly *et al.* 2010). Internet users also learned quickly from negative experiences of Internet advertising (Cho and Cheon 2004). Consumer determination to avoid Internet advertising, especially annoying forms such as pop-ups and pop-unders (Li and Leckenby 2012: 212) fed demand for the development of ad blocking and filtering software (O'Reilly 2015). Web browsers supported ad blocking extensions, a feature that was used as a selling point to consumers. Ad placement and server agencies responded by developing work-arounds. Tensions between pro- and anti-ad blocking camps escalated, and drew in online publishers who saw ad-blocking software as a threat to their viability (Fisher 2010).

Advertisers looked at other ways to connect with markets, and to operate "under the radar" of consumer awareness of advertising (Bond and Kirshenbaum 1998). They too learned rapidly, often through trial and error, to use the Internet to actively engage consumers as brand ambassadors and advocates with immense direct-selling capacity—for example, through techniques such as affiliate advertising, permission-based email, and viral marketing. More controversial techniques that combined elements of advertiser-supplied messages and end-user productivity to simulate and stimulate consumer-to-consumer endorsements came to be known as "astroturfing" (fake grassroots), and were targets for end-user backlash when they were uncovered (Gunders and Brown 2010: 54; Hovland and Wolburg 2014: 36). Managing the risks of consumer interaction emerged as an important consideration as branded content strategies were taken into online channels, often extending practices developed in offline media and entertainment contexts. For example, the incorporation of advergaming into web marketing strategies was, in part, a logical development of in-game advertising that had been a part of computer gaming since the late 1970s (McStay 2010: 78–79). It meshed well with the demographic profile of Internet users, but its use, particularly by food brands to target children was, and continues to be, controversial (McStay 2010: 170; Moore and Rideout 2007).

Experimentation occurred with other rich media forms, and moved well beyond product placement into advertiser-created content. It re-energized older normative concerns about the extent to which advertising should be allowed to cloak itself as non-commercial forms of media content. BMW famously commissioned internationally recognized film and television creatives to produce webisodes for online distribution that featured BMW cars as brand heroes and took the form of web cinema to new heights of creative excellence (Clay 2008). Brands took up real estate in virtual worlds such as Second Life and dedicated online brand channels developed for the purpose of cultivating brand fandom. Brand communities with social media functionalities began to link consumers to goods and services, and to each other, in many novel ways. Nike, for example, pioneered customized production of Nike-branded goods within its global brand communities (Spurgeon 2009). Red Bull's sponsorship of Felix Baumgartner's "Jump from the Edge of Space" was celebrated in marketing communications literature as a case study in state-of-the-art integrated branded content in 2012 (for example, Ryan 2014). These developments required brands "to relinquish a degree of strategic control over what their brands stand for, instead listening and reacting to consumer perspectives" (McStay 2010: 28). They marked a more "conversational" approach to communicating with consumers (Spurgeon 2008).

There were a variety of regulatory responses to the Internet that sought to make certain aspects of online advertising accountable and governable, some novel to the Internet and others continuous with pre-existing schemes of regulation (Freedman 2012: 113). Legislation to address spam was promulgated in a large number of national jurisdictions from the early 2000s (Bunton 2013). Even though there were important differences between American "opt-in" and European "opt-out" thresholds (Spurgeon 2008: 93–99), the rapid, internationally coordinated response to the problem of spam demonstrated that when there was the political will to do so, national governments had the capacity to exert direct regulatory influence over advertising, and the Internet more generally. Industry agencies were also proactive in this space. For example, in spite of advertiser and publisher opposition, the Advertising Standards Board in Australia claimed jurisdiction over the Web. At the time of writing, it considered the Web in its entirety to be a marketing communication platform, and had adjudicated complaints about content appearing anywhere from corporate websites to online magazines, even where publishers had asserted that the content in question was "editorial" not "advertising" (Advertising Standards Bureau 2010, 2013).

Another series of issues arose with the data capabilities of online media, generated from the inbuilt registration systems of the physical, code, and application layers of the Internet (Spurgeon 2008: 84), and their use by online commercial media and advertisers. Critical attention focused on the consequences for human subjectivity, culture, and knowledge of reliance on intelligent agents to personalize online media experiences (Poster 2005). For example, while it seemed reasonable to posit the impossibility of objective online search results (Blanke 2005), equally impossible was the prospect of assuring their neutrality, or ascertaining the extent to which organic search results were subtly shaped by the interests of commercial media, which ultimately control questions of relevance, or advertisers whose revenues fund search media. This concern was concretely illustrated in 2008 when Google acquired DoubleClick. This paved the way for the online advertising market to be dominated by Google, especially if DoubleClick favored Google in its online strategies (Hovland and Wolburg 2014: 150). Other important normative concerns for information rights, privacy, and security are considered in the next, concluding, section to this chapter.

Advertising, Data and the Changing "Social Contract" of Commercial Media Use

Reliance on computational power and digital communications grew exponentially with the Internet. So, too, did the amount of data generated from it, and the capacity and sophistication of analysis. Consumer research and surveillance tools were developed by modern advertising (Couldry and Turow 2014: 1713) to improve targeting (for example, market segmentation and demographic or psychographic targeting). Data generated by Internet users about their actual online media usage expanded opportunities for media planning and buying systems to further reduce uncertainty in matching the advertising, media, and target markets (Cannon 2012: 315). Elsewhere in this volume, Yu discusses the role that censorship played in the development of "1984" industries around online media in China. In European and North American contexts, dataveillance capacity was shaped, instead, by commercial media and advertisers who turned to more precise targeting on- and offline to improve consumer receptivity and overcome resistance to advertising (Cannon 2012: 315). By tracking Internet usage, it became possible to micro-target advertising, and indeed personalize Internet media channels in real time (Couldry and Turow 2014: 1711) in at least six different ways: contextual, behavioral, geographic, daypart, affinity, and product category (Plummer *et al.*, 2007, cited in McStay 2010: 44). The volume of data generated by Internet usage also fundamentally changed how effects were measured (Gangadharbatla 2012: 412).

Many new digital, interactive, and online advertising specializations emerged in the dot.com boom, including Internet usage analytics specializations that massively scaled up and technologized orthodox media usage monitoring methods (Lee and Johnson 2012: 277), and serviced data-driven marketers and media buyers. Online publishers led the early adoption of technologies that could "trace people's actions within and across websites, applications (apps), devices and physical locations" (Couldry and Turow 2014: 1714). Advertising networks quickly followed. The industry itself was exercised by the effort to reconcile differences between the methodologies of the two dominant providers, Neilsen Online and CommScore (Lee and Johnson 2012: 283). While efforts were made to ensure that the personal data traded between collecting agencies (usually media) and third parties such as advertisers and researchers was also anonymized, major breaches of personal privacy and security nonetheless occurred (Couldry and Turow 2014). Critical scholarship was concerned with the privacy and security implications of trade in personal data, as well as the rate at which data mining became ubiquitous, and the broader social and cultural implications of intensive database marketing. These developments, McStay observed (2010: 104), constituted users "as objects without authorship".

The amount of Internet data was not just a technological feature of the Internet. It was also made possible by another tectonic shift in the social relations of commercial media. Flew (2006) observed that the policy settlements between public and private interests in broadcasting services that governments had arbitrated throughout the twentieth century had begun to fail in the face of the Internet, and that there remained immense uncertainty about the role of "public interest" considerations in the governmental arrangements for post-broadcasting media. Online engagement was increasingly predicated on click-through "private contractual relations between users and publishers", a shift Sal Humphreys (2009: 54) described as "significant". Advertising scholars had already looked to social contract theory to normalize direct marketing online behavioral targeting as a benign use of personal information, as well as a necessary transaction cost between media users and proprietors (Gordon and De Lima-Turner 1997). Castells (2002: 174) observed that Internet users seemed generally willing to part with personal data in exchange for free content, content creation tools, communications services, server space, and so on. Lessig (2002: 133) argued that Internet users were also willing to part with personal data to facilitate transactions, or what Bill Gates (1996: 181) described as "friction-free capitalism". Other scholars contested the extent of consent, and the use of data in the personalization of commercial media, and pointed to an underlying anxiety about the extent to which personal data was being used "without the knowledge and consent of consumers" (Sengara *et al.* 2009: 39) or obtained through coercive practices of reward and punishment (McStay 2010: 101). Unfavorable terms of service in relation to privacy and personal data, for example, did not generally cause users to leave a social network or media service, because exit costs were too great. Media studies research (Humphreys 2009) suggested this was because leaving a social network was a source of greater social harm to an individual than staying on unfavorable terms, if indeed participants were fully aware of the implications of terms, before hitting the "I accept" button in the first place. All these analyses point to important qualitative differences between the social contract that was taking shape around online commercial media and that which pertained to pre-Internet commercial media in many parts of the world. In short, the effectiveness of online marketing, and the viability of online commercial media, both seem to be increasingly contingent upon deepening processes of "dataveillance" (McStay 2010: 130). Sal Humphreys (2009: 60) expressed the problem for online media in terms of the following question: "Is the cost of participation to be that people must accede to terms and conditions they regard as objectionable?"

In the decade following the advent of online advertising, early heroic accounts of the Internet which celebrated end-user influence began to be tempered with a criticality of hindsight (Curran 2012: 35) and international experience. Although the influence of consumers figured more directly in shaping the social field of commercial media and advertising, the importance, indeed necessity, of end-user productivity to new Internet economies did not deliver equity in the distribution of systemic power or social authority. It remained the case that the capacity of individualized consumers to articulate, coordinate, and organize in the changing media market was not as well resourced or developed as many of the advertisers and commercial media who targeted them. If the challenge of how advertisers and commercial media were publicly held to account was daunting in the mass-media era of the twentieth century, it became all the more complex as a result of the Internet and online advertising in the twenty-first century.

Further Reading

This chapter has scoped online advertising as a very large field of industry practice, public policy, and multidisciplinary scholarship. There are many excellent texts that help to make sense of this field. The following three are particularly useful for pursing the institutional approach developed here.

Hovland, R., and Wolburg, J. (2014) *Advertising, Society, and Consumer Culture*, Hoboken, NJ: Taylor & Francis.
McStay, A. (2010) *Digital Advertising*, London: Palgrave Macmillan.
Sinclair, J. (2012) *Advertising, the Media and Globalisation: A World in Motion*, London: Routledge.

References

Advertising Standards Bureau (2010) *American Apparel, Case Report 0141/10.*
Advertising Standards Bureau (2013) *ACP Publishing, Case Report 0437/12.*
Anderson, C. (2006) *The Long Tail*, New York: Hyperion.
Batelle, J. (2005) *The Search: How Google and its Rivals Rewrote the Rules of Business and Transformed Our Culture*, New York: Portfolio.
Beniger, J. (1989) *The Control Revolution: Technological and Economic Origins of the Information Society*, Cambridge, MA: Harvard University Press.
Bermejo, F. (2007) *The Internet Audience: Constitution and Measurement*, New York: Peter Lang.
Blanke, T. (2005) "Ethical Subjectification and Search Engines: Ethics Reconsidered", *International Review of Information Ethics*, 3: 33–38.
Bond, J., and Kirshenbaum, R. (1998) *Under the Radar: Talking to Today's Cynical Consumer*, New York: John Wiley & Sons.
Brown, J., and Daguid, P. (2001) *The Social Life of Information*, Boston, MA: Harvard Business School Publishing.

Bunton, F. (2013) *Spam: The Shadow History of the Internet*, Cambridge, MA: MIT Press.

Buttle, F. (1998) "Word of Mouth: Understanding and Managing Referral Marketing", *Journal of Strategic Marketing*, 6(3): 241–254.

Cannon, H. (2012) "Media Analysis and Decision Making", in S. Rodgers and E. Thorsen (eds), *Advertising Theory*, New York: Routledge, pp. 313–336.

Cappo, J. (2003) *The Future of Advertising: New Media, New Clients, New Consumers in the Post-Television Age*, New York: McGraw-Hill.

Castells, M. (2002) *The Internet Galaxy: Reflections on the Internet, Business, and Society*, Oxford: Oxford University Press.

Cho, C.-H., and Cheon, H. J. (2004) "Why Do People Avoid Advertising on the Internet?", *Journal of Advertising*, 33(4): 89–97.

Clay, A. (2008) "BMW Films and the Star Wars Kid: 'Early Web Cinema' and Technology", in B. Bennett, M. Furstenau, and A. Mackenzie (eds), *Cinema and Technology: Cultures, Theories, Practices*, New York: Palgrave Macmillan, pp. 37–52.

Clift, J. (2015) "WFA Global Marketer Week 2015: Global Advertising Spend and Economic Outlook 2015–2016", *World Advertising Resource Centre*, available at: www.warc.com/Content/Documents/A104086_WFA_Global_Marketer_Week_2015_Global_advertising_spend_26_economic_outlook2c_20152016.content?PUB=WARC-DATA&CID=A104086&ID=0a93e761–4405–404d-809e-e629dbb22d77&q=&qr= (accessed 1 September 2015).

Couldry, N., and Turow, J. (2014) "Advertising, Big Data and the Clearance of the Public Realm: Marketers' New Approaches to the Content Subsidy", *International Journal of Communication*, 8: 1710–1726.

Cunningham, S., Flew, T., and Swift, A. (2015) *Media Economics*, London: Palgrave.

Curran, J. (2012) "Rethinking Internet History", in J. Curran, N. Fenton, and D. Freedman, *Misunderstanding the Internet*, Oxford: Routledge, pp. 34–65.

Fisher, K. (2010) "Why Ad Blocking Is Devastating the Sites You Love", *ars technica*, 7 March, available at: http://arstechnica.com/business/2010/03/why-ad-blocking-is-devastating-to-the-sites-you-love/ (accessed 9 November 2015).

Flew, T. (2006) "The Social Contract and Beyond in Broadcast Media Policy", *Television & New Media*, 7(3): 282–305.

Freedman, D. (2012) "Outsourcing Internet Regulation", in J. Curran, N. Fenton, and D. Freedman (eds), *Misunderstanding the Internet*, Oxford: Routledge, pp. 95–120.

Gangadharbatla, H. (2012) "Social Media and Advertising Theory", in S. Rodgers and E. Thorsen (eds), *Advertising Theory*, New York: Routledge, pp. 402–416.

Gates, B. (1996) *The Road Ahead*, New York: Penguin.

Gordon, M., and De Lima-Turner, K. (1997) "Consumer Attitudes to Internet Advertising", *International Marketing Review*, 14(5): 362–375.

Gunders, J., and Brown, D. (2010) *The Complete Idiot's Guide to Memes*, New York: Alpha.

Hargittai, E. (2007) "The Social, Political, Economic, and Cultural Dimensions of Search Engines: An Introduction", *Journal of Computer-Mediated Communication*, 12(3): 769–777.

Hemmer, J. (2005) "The Internet Advertising Battle: Copyright Laws Used to Stop the Use of Ad-Blocking Software", *Temple Journal of Science, Technology and Environmental Law*, 24: 479–497.

Hollis, N. (2005) "Ten Years of Learning on How Online Advertising Builds Brands", *Journal of Advertising Research*, 45(2): 255–268.

Hovland, R., and Wolburg, J. (2014) *Advertising, Society, and Consumer Culture*, Hoboken, NJ: Taylor & Francis.

Humphreys, S. (2009) "Discursive Constructions of MMOGs and Some Implications for Policy and Regulation", *Media International Australia: Incorporating Culture and Policy*, 130: 53–65.

Internet Advertising Bureau (IAB) (1996) founded on 20 June 1996, available at: www.facebook.com/IAB/ (accessed 4 November 2015).

Internet Advertising Bureau (IAB) (n.d.) "Our Story", *Internet Advertising Bureau*, available at: www.iab.com/our-story (accessed 1 September 2015).

Jolson, M. (1972) "Direct Selling: Consumer vs. Salesman: Is Conflict Inevitable?", *Business Horizons*, 15(5): 87–95.

Kelly, L., Kerr, G., and Drennan, J. (2010) "Avoidance of Advertising in Social Networking Sites", *Journal of Interactive Advertising*, 10(2): 16–27.

Lee, M., and Johnson, C. (2012) *Principles of Advertising: A Global Perspective*, 2nd edn, Hoboken, NJ: Taylor & Francis.

Leiner, B., Cerf, V., Clark, D., Kahn, R., Kleinrock, L., Lynch, D., Postel, J., Roberts, L., and Wolff, S. (1997) "The Past and Future History of the Internet", *Communications of the ACM*, 40(2): 102–108.

Leiss, W., Kline, S., Jhally, S., and Botterill, J. (2005) *Social Communication in Advertising: Consumption in the Mediated Marketplace*, New York: Routledge.

Lessig, L. (2002) *The Future of Ideas: The Fate of the Commons in a Connected World*, New York: Vintage Books.

Lessig, L. (2006) *Code: Version 2.0*, New York: Basic Books.

Li, H., and Leckenby, J. (2012) "Examining the Effectiveness of Internet Advertising Formats", in S. Schumann and E. Thorson (eds), *Internet Advertising: Theory and Research*, London: Lawrence Erlbaum Associates, pp. 203–224.

McMillan, S. (2007) "Internet Advertising: One Face or Many?", in S. Schumann and E. Thorson (eds), *Internet Advertising: Theory and Research*, London: Lawrence Erlbaum Associates, pp. 15–36.

McStay, A. (2010) *Digital Advertising*, London: Palgrave Macmillan.

Micu, A. (2012) "Theoretical Approaches in Internet Advertising Research", in S. Schumann and E. Thorson (eds), *Internet Advertising: Theory and Research*, London: Lawrence Erlbaum Associates, pp. 37–68.

Moore, E. S., and Rideout, V. (2007) "The Online Marketing of Food to Children: Is It Just Fun and Games?", *Journal of Public Policy and Marketing*, 26(2): 202–220.

O'Reilly, L. (2015) "The Inventor of the Ad Blocker Tells Us He Wrote the Code as a 'Procrastination Project' at University—And He's Never Made Money from It", *Business Insider Australia*, 14 July, available at: www.businessinsider.com.au/interview-with-the-inventor-of-the-ad-blocker-henrik-aasted-srensen-2015-7 (accessed 9 November 2015).

Poster, M. (2005) "Future Advertising: Dick's Ubik and the Digital Ad", in S. Cohen and R. Rutsky (eds), *Consumption in an Age of Information*, Oxford: Berg, pp. 21–40.

Reigner, C. (2007) "Word of Mouth on the Web: The Impact of Web 2.0 on Consumer Purchase Decisions", *Journal of Advertising Research*, 47(4): 436–447.

Richards, J., and Curran, C. (2002) "Oracles on 'Advertising': Searching for a Definition", *Journal of Advertising*, 31(2): 63–77.

Rossiter, J. R., and Percy, L. (1997) *Advertising Communication and Promotion Management*, 2nd edn, New York: McGraw-Hill.

Ryan, D. (2014) "Red Bull Stratos", in *The Best Digital Marketing Campaigns in the World II*, London: Kogan Page, pp. 78–83.

Seligman, T. (2015) "Native Advertising: The Old is New Again", *Computer and Internet Lawyer*, 32(7): 1–9.

Sengara, R., Humphreys, S., Given, J., McCutcheon, M., and Milne, C. (2009) "Future Consumer: Emerging Consumer Issues in Telecommunications and Convergence Communications and Media", *Australian Communications Consumer Action Network*, available at: www.accan.org.au/our-work/research/93-future-consumer-research-report (accessed 17 November 2015).

Sinclair, J. (2012) *Advertising, the Media and Globalisation: A World in Motion*, London: Routledge.

Spurgeon, C. (2006) "Advertising and the New Search Media", *Media International Australia Incorporating Culture and Policy*, 119: pp. 51–61.

Spurgeon, C. (2008) *Advertising and New Media*, Oxford, Routledge.

Spurgeon, C. (2009) "From Mass Communication to Mass Conversation: Why 1984 Wasn't Like '1984'", *Australian Journal of Communication*, 36(2): 143–158.

Spurgeon, C. (2015) "Regulating Integrated Advertising", in M. P. McAllister and E. West (eds), *The Routledge Companion to Advertising and Promotional Culture*, New York: Routledge, pp. 71–82.

Sundar, S. S., Xu, Q., and Xue, D. (2012) "The Role of Technology in Online Persuasion", in S. Rodgers and E. Thorsen (eds), *Advertising Theory*, New York: Routledge, pp. 337–354.

Vences, N., and Segura, R. (2014) "Interactive Advertising Bureau", in K. Harvey (ed.), *Encyclopedia of Social Media and Politics*, Los Angeles, CA: Sage, pp. 701–703.

Winston, B. (1998) *Media, Technology and Society*, London: Routledge.

27

CONTEXTS, PROSPECTS, AND CONTRADICTIONS

Histories of Internet–Based Digital Journalism Research in Africa

Hayes Mawindi Mabweazara

Introduction: Context and Conflicting Positions

Despite the fact that Africa is the least connected continent on the Internet (with an estimated Internet penetration rate of 28.6 percent as of November 2015; Internet World Stats n.d.), traditional journalism has not escaped the complexities and contradictions associated with the 1990s crusade towards the adoption of the Internet in journalism. There is consensus among scholars that journalists on the continent, like their counterparts in the rest of the world, are experiencing the disruptive impact of the Internet on the way they gather, produce, and distribute news (Mabweazara 2015a; Mabweazara *et al.* 2014; Paterson 2013). Serious structural changes are underway—content is undergoing radical changes, old operational and business matrices have been disrupted. Similarly, news consumption habits and practices are finding new definitions on the Web as audiences look for, as well as share, news content "in iterative consumption practices that challenge as well as complement traditional news flows" (Mabweazara 2015b: 11). News organizations are clearly undergoing an unprecedented state of turmoil, as developments that previously seemed fairly distant have gradually become an inescapable reality, threatening established professional ideals as well as the social function of journalism. Inevitably, questions of normativity have taken center-stage as news organizations grapple with the pressures to embrace the complexities of the Web in localized and exogenously influenced ways (Mabweazara 2015b).

Research into these developments, however, remains limited, fragmented, and typically undertaken as isolated and disconnected projects that are sometimes contradictory. The research is, to use James Katz and Mark Aakhus's (2002) phrase, "ordinarily slender". More notably, there is very little exploration of the intersections between the Internet and mainstream journalism practice, despite the fact that, in general, journalists happen to be among the largest Internet users on the continent (Mudhai and Nyabuga 2001; Nyamnjoh 2005).

Against this background, this chapter provides an exploratory overview of research into Internet-based digital journalism in Africa by exploring trends and perspectives taken by different researchers in this field. In doing so, the chapter also highlights developments in the adoption and use of the Internet for information gathering, as well as connecting with news sources by journalists in Africa. By focusing on the broader African context, I do not take for granted the important differences between African countries, nor do I assume any semblance of homogeneity in the countries themselves. My interest is purely in offering an alternative understanding of research approaches taken outside the dominant body of knowledge emerging from Western scholarship, especially Europe and America.

In pursuing the above, I show that the history of Internet-based journalism, as well as research into the connections between the Internet and journalism in Africa, has, in many ways, taken the path of research in other contexts outside journalism itself, which is largely characterized by mixed, and occasionally contradictory, opinions on the opportunities and challenges offered by the Internet in Africa (Obijiofor 1996). Outside digital journalism research, scholarly opinions can generally be seen as divided along three interconnected strands: those who celebrate the Internet's "promise" for Africa in ways that resonate with the deterministic discourses of the so-called "information society"; those who generally express pessimism on the adoption and appropriation of web-based technologies; and those who take a more cautious "sociological" approach that transcends both the celebratory and pessimistic approaches to new technologies. Collectively, these scholars span diverse fields, including politics and development discourses.

Researchers who celebrate the Internet's promise for Africa generally argue that the technology can support the necessary social and economic transformation in Africa and the wider economically developing world (Adamolekun 1996; Etta and Parvyn-Wamahiu 2003). Demands for greater job performance, economies of scale, and competitive advantage are seen as requiring a "modernization" of old systems in order not to be left behind in world developments (Adamolekun 1996: 32). This approach can be seen against the backdrop of the prevalent one-sided assumptions of the Modernization theory, which broadly conceives media technology as a "powerful force for development" (Berger 2005: 3).

Madden (2005: xi) thus posits that unless new technologies, including the Internet, are widely adopted, "Developing countries will remain unable to compete in the New Economy where the sources of advantage are [. . .] the fast adoption of new technological innovation" (see also Adam and Wood 1999; Etta and Parvyn-Wamahiu 2003).

In a similar vein, Wole Adamolekun (1996: 27) argues that "the economy has truly become global and it is only wise [for Africa] to hook on to the information superhighway to remain relevant". For these reasons, Anthea Garman (2003: 2) notes that in Africa "every 'new' technology that comes along is embraced with passion, [and] hailed as a savior for all human ills, and is seen as full of promise alone".

Following this line of thought, Alan Hedley (1999) observes that both technological infrastructure and African people's will to make a difference in using the Internet are growing, and it is possible to reduce the North–South gap to provide greater cultural balance, and improve the quality of life for African people. Francis Nyamnjoh (2005: 4) aptly espouses this determination by arguing that:

> because Africa is part of the world, and because its backwardness is less the result of choice than of circumstance, ordinary Africans are determined to be part of the technological revolutions of the modern world, even if this means accessing the information superhighway on foot, horseback, bicycles, bush taxis and second-hand

cars, or relying on lifts and the generosity of the super-endowed in the latest sports and fancy cars.

These celebratory sentiments have, however, been criticized for being overly ambitious and prescriptive, and for not taking into account the situated nature of the contexts in which the Internet and related technologies are deployed in Africa. Thus, contrary to the foregoing "expressions of faith" in the Internet and its associated technologies, some scholars have argued that developing nations have to be extremely careful in contemplating joining the "bandwagon" in the so-called "information superhighway" associated with the Internet. Adamolekun (1996: 34–35) warns thus:

> If we must know [. . .] [the Internet] is full of several booby traps for unwary and unprepared information wayfarers. The sheer great immediacy and drama we now experience and the speed at which we can view what is happening world wide [. . .] makes it extremely difficult to easily process the data we have on our hands at any given time.

These views are echoed by other equally ambivalent Afrocentric scholars, who argue that, with the emergence of the Internet, Africans are becoming increasingly less analytical consumers and more passive onlookers (Mutula 2005). Other critics further contend that the dominance of English on the Internet has resulted in the cultural marginalization of groups whose languages and cultures do not exist on the Internet. They argue that this could have a homogenizing effect on local cultures (see Okigbo 1995). For this reason, Adamolekun (1996: 35) calls for the need to "Recognize the responsibility to help [African] people under-stand, evaluate and appreciate the advantages and disadvantages of [web-based technologies], and also take due care to use each one appropriately and strategically".

Those adopting a more cautious sociological approach that neither celebrates nor disparages the diffusion of the Internet into various social contexts in Africa assert that "Just as one should avoid a crude technological determinism in exploring the positive potential of new media such as the Internet, one should also not overstate the negative aspects [. . .] and lose sight of the innovative use of these technologies [. . .] on the [African] continent" (Wasserman 2005: 174).

Herman Wasserman further suggests that when assessing the potential that new technologies hold for Africa, "connectivity problems should prevent overly optimistic analyses" (Wasserman 2005: 174). Thus, whether one takes an optimistic or pessimistic view of the Internet in Africa, the question of "real access", including connectivity as well as the necessary skills and technological literacy, should be considered seriously (Wasserman 2005: 165).

For a number of scholars who follow this line of thought, while "it is no exaggeration to say that some African countries are already in the league of multimedia, interaction, real-time, digital and narrow band [and in some countries broad band] information systems" (Adamolekun 1996: 32), it is equally true that, given the socio-economic conditions prevailing in Africa, the Internet and related digital technologies have not yet necessarily permeated all sectors (Okigbo 1995). Thus, as Adamolekun (1996: 30) further observes, many people are still ignorant of new technologies: "they still go about their daily chores the way they know best"—using the well-known and established traditional methods of communication.

Despite the mixed opinions on the opportunities offered by the Internet and related technologies, their potential benefits and contributions are never disputed by both critics and advocates (Adam and Wood 1999; Obijiofor 1996). In the same way, regardless of the challenges faced by Africans, there are significant attempts at adopting and deploying new technologies in different settings although "[their impact] on users has not been well documented" (Adam and Wood 1999: 307), especially in journalism studies.

However, as noted earlier, an exploratory overview of research into the connections between the Internet and journalism in Africa points to the path taken in generic research into the social impact of the Internet outside journalism. Before delving into this point, it is important to highlight that the arrival of the Internet and its associated interactive digital technologies in Africa in the 1990s "sparked celebratory, almost utopian bliss" (Banda *et al.* 2009: 1) among their proponents. Its adoption was generally accompanied by the hype about the continent's possibility of "leapfrogging" some stages of development (Banda *et al.* 2009: 1). In the context of journalism, "the Internet was seen as having the potential to increase journalists' work efficiency and thus overcome[ing] the barriers associated with the 'traditional' means of journalism practice" (Mabweazara 2011: 57).

Taking the cue from developments in the West, a number of African newsrooms, especially in South Africa (one of the most advanced economies on the continent), led the way in harnessing the perceived power of the Internet in newsmaking operations (Berger 2005; Mavhungu and Mabweazara 2014). Although initially simply "shoveling" print content on websites, with very minimal changes, the late 2000s saw most news organizations on the continent adopting distinct web-based news production and dissemination approaches. These included regularly updating their news content, breaking news online, and enabling readers to comment on stories as well as share content via interactive websites and social media platforms such as Facebook and Twitter. Some news organizations even sought to use their websites and emails to get leads and insights from their readers, and sources in the wake of the political standoffs and the challenges posed by repressive media environments (Mabweazara 2011; Moyo 2009).

For most African news organizations, however, online news production in its distinct and defined form (characterized by stand-alone news websites) emerged much later, largely as part of initiatives by exiled journalists, who sought to counter repressive media systems predominantly saturated by state-controlled media in their home countries (Mabweazara 2011; Moyo 2009; Skjerdal 2014). These displaced journalists saw the Internet as offering a window for alternative viewpoints on the issues that journalists report on.

The rest of the chapter thus unfolds by first discussing the "mixed" opinions characteristic of early research into the impact of the Internet on journalism in Africa. It then shifts attention to an emerging corpus of critical research that transcends the tension between advocates and cynics by adopting a more "balanced" approach, sensitive to the multiple factors that shape the adoption and use of the Internet in African journalism. The chapter concludes by drawing attention to scholarly discourses that emphasize the importance of considering localized— uniquely African—structural and functional conditions that shape and constrain the appropriation of the Internet by journalists on the continent.

The Promise of the Web for African Journalism: Advocates and Cynics

Early research into the impact of the Internet on journalism in Africa can loosely be divided between researchers who saw the Web as a "goldmine" that presents African journalists with new opportunities for improved practice (Berger 2005), and those who framed it as challenging and threatening the traditional normative ideals of journalism (Chari 2009). These scholars largely tended "to draw on *utopian* and *dystopian* views about the relationship between [the

Internet] and society, and predictably arrive[d] at diametrically opposed conclusions" (Mare 2013: 84).

Proponents of the Internet collectively submitted that, despite the problems faced by African journalists with regard to accessing and using the Internet and its associated digital technologies, they are making every effort to use the technologies productively in daily professional routines. The researchers argued that the "digital revolution" facilitated positive radical shifts in journalism by positively transforming every aspect of news production and reception. Among these scholars, Guy Berger (2005: 1) examined how South African journalists deploy new technologies and argued that they "are far from being mired in 'backwardness' or passively awaiting external salvation". Supporting this view, Nyamnjoh (2005: 4) posited that Africans were determined to be part of the technological revolutions of the modern world, and researchers simply needed to recognize "the creative ways in which [they] merge their traditions with exogenous influences to create realities that are not reducible to either but enriched by both". Writing from a Kenyan perspective, Okoth Mudhai and George Nyabuga (2001) also observed that journalists were among the early adopters of the Internet, and thus played a key role in publicizing its many positive aspects to other sectors. Focusing on Ghana and Nigeria, Levi Obijiofor (2003: 54) observed that the Internet helped journalists to "save time in their work as well as improving the quality of newspapers by accelerated speed of production, enhancement of newspaper aesthetics and ease of crosschecking spelling errors with the aid of the spell check software".

A number of early researchers also focused on the impact of specific technological features on journalism, especially the interactivity of online newspaper editions. Tawana Kupe (2003) and Mudhai (2004), for instance, highlighted the centrality of the interactivity of online editions of African newspapers, which allow users to comment, give feedback, or vote on controversial issues. This group of scholars argued that the interactivity and participatory cultures facilitated by the Internet enabled journalists in Africa to directly engage with readers, thus altering news production processes and our very understanding of who produces news. These developments were seen as permanently challenging and redefining the traditional definition of journalism, consequently forcing the news media to adapt or face extinction (Esipisu and Kariithi 2007).

Seen through the lenses of Internet advocates, the changes pointed to "a widening exposure of [African] journalists to news and inevitably a growing participation of citizens in newsmaking even if only those citizens with access and the means to deploy the [Internet] are involved" (Mabweazara 2011: 68). This highlights "a subtle but significant gradual dispersion of the newsrooms' monopoly in defining what constitutes news". In other terms, journalists in Africa can be seen as "no longer speak[ing] *ex cathedra* as they used to do before the [Internet era]" (Mabweazara 2011: 68).

For Dumisani Moyo (2009), the ability to engage directly with news, and with other news consumers, gave readers greater influence over the material covered in the newspapers, while at the same time providing journalists with an opportunity to access ideas and leads from the readers. In the same manner, participatory forms of journalism (including "social media" practices such as blogging, tweeting, and Facebook) have equally been hailed as integral to processes of democratization by giving ordinary citizens a voice (Moyo 2009; Paterson 2013).

These "celebratory" views have also focused on the generation of news content by ordinary citizens, who collect and share information through platforms afforded by web-based technologies. Citizens are seen as resisting "formal or institutional ways of packaging information" by "responding to the [interactive and engaging] nature of the technology at hand" (Moyo 2009: 557). The mobile phone, in its pervasive nature across Africa, has particularly been seen as central to citizens' active engagement in newsmaking. Thus, armed with cheap Internet-enabled smartphones and other media tools, ordinary citizens are deemed able to capture "news" in real or close-to-real time—much more immediately and rapidly than professional journalists. This is seen as contributing a great deal to the circulation of public opinion, and to some extent influencing the way mainstream media cover important events such as elections on the continent (Moyo 2009). For these critics, emerging popular interactions on the Internet are not only resulting in new forms of citizenship but also *reinvigorating African journalism*—somewhat "reforming" it by taking it back to reality— reconnecting it with a disillusioned readership (Allan 2014; Mabweazara 2014; Paterson 2014). Thus, the emerging interactive and participatory cultures facilitated by the Internet are seen as "shaking up traditional journalism and turning journalists back to the 'orthodoxy' of the profession. [Thereby] giving journalism *renewed human perspective* that has been lost over the years" (Mabweazara 2014: 76).

Scholars occupying the other side of the divide are generally skeptical and leery of the appropriation of the Internet and its associated digital technologies in journalism. They have tended to emphasize the "normative dilemmas" as well as the disruptive implications of the Internet to the practice of journalism (Mabweazara 2013: 135). Tendai Chari (2009), for instance, argues that the euphoria and opportunities associated with the Internet in Africa have tended to eclipse the ethical dilemmas and challenges associated with the medium. For Chari, the Internet has fundamentally transformed journalism practice as "[j]ournalists no longer feel compelled to adhere to the ethical canons" (2009: 1) of the profession. Factual errors, fabrications, and plagiarism have become much more prevalent than before (Chari 2009). In the same line of thought, Mudhai and Nyabuga (2001) posit that the problem of plagiarizing stories and the difficulties faced in trying to authenticate online sources raises questions of news accuracy and credibility in the "Internet era". Francis Kasoma similarly expresses misgivings by arguing that "the information superhighway has made journalists practice their profession in a hurry as they strive to satisfy the world's craving for more and quicker news" (1996: 95), resulting in "the humaneness of journalism" increasingly giving way to the expediencies of cut-throat financial competition. These critics have generally argued that African journalists should take great caution when using Internet content. Thus, Mudhai (2004) warns that the news media in Africa need to display more commitment towards content creation, rather than taking the shortcut of filling space with stale material from the Internet.

Other researchers observe that the Internet is not only reconfiguring newsroom traditions as noted above, but also redefining professional relationships, especially between cub reporters and senior journalists. They argue that the typical trend whereby newcomers shared information—from contacts and approaches to writing news stories—with veterans and vice versa has been redefined (see Berger 2005). For these critics, the Internet has turned journalists into individualistic people as well as reducing the chances of colleagues communicating face-to-face.

Citizen journalism in particular has received scathing criticism, with some critics derisively arguing that embracing it is "like handing a man off the street a scalpel and authorising him to perform surgery" (Foss 2008), as ordinary citizens are under no obligation to use professional norms such as accuracy and balance. Kathy Goldfain and Nadia van der Merwe (2006: 104–115) argue that the major weakness of citizen journalism "is the lack of quality control", which makes it difficult for the practice to build up the trust enjoyed by traditional journalism.

The foregoing sentiments echo some views from Western journalism scholarship, where scholars have long "accepted the discourse of the Internet as the major player in redefining and rethinking 'traditional' journalism" (Deuze and Dimoudi 2002: 86). Mark Deuze (2003:

203) writes: "we can now identify the effect that [the Internet] has had on the profession and its culture(s)." Writing from an American context, John Pavlik (2005: 245) observes that with the permeation of the Internet into journalism, "new ethical problems are arising or old ethical concerns [are taking] on new meaning". Although these largely varied and polarized scholarly positions confirm and highlight pertinent issues with regard to the implications of the Internet for journalism practice in Africa, they largely overlook the complexities entrenched in the professional and organizational worlds in which African journalists operate. Some of the views appear to miss the deeper and more sophisticated understandings of how journalists on the continent are negotiating their way around the Internet. The following sections accordingly shift attention to research that considers the complexities and contradictions that mediate the appropriation of the Internet in African journalism.

The Critical Turn: Beyond the One-Dimensional Optimist/Pessimist Binary

While belief in the transformative power of the Internet still implicitly underpins some opinions on its potential implications for African journalism, as discussed earlier, the brazen techno-euphoric moment of wonderment and awe characteristic of the mid-1990s no longer occupies mainstream thought on the Internet in Africa. After realizing the shortcomings of exclusively apportioning "power" (or blame) to the Internet, contemporary scholarly dis-courses have warily shifted to cautious positions sensitive to the complexities and contradictions that mediate the appropriation of the Internet in various social sectors. A corpus of research that critically examines the shifting ecology of African journalism and how it is adjusting to the changing structurations of society is emerging (see Atton and Mabweazara 2011; Mabweazara *et al.* 2014; Obijiofor and Hanusch 2011; Paterson 2013). This nascent research emphasizes the "situated nature" of Internet use in journalism practice, especially the influences of localized socio-political, economic, and cultural circumstances in which the technology is assimilated and *appropriated*. It questions the *technist* inclinations of early scholarship, and maintains a critical alertness to the *social shaping* nature of technology. As Martin Conboy (2013: 149) reminds us: "Technology, in isolation, has never made journalism better or worse [. . .] [It] does not drive change. It has to adapt to the patterns of cultural expectation within particular societies at specific moments in time." In this line of thought, the imperatives shaping African journalism in the digital era are seen as "negotiated in converging circum-stances of economic, political and cultural factors" (Allan 2014: ix), all ordinarily seen as commonsensical.

Although much work still needs to be done, this cautious and predominantly sociological generation of scholarship transcends the one-dimensional approach rooted in the simplistic binary tensions between celebratory and critical approaches to the Internet characteristic of early researchers. It foregrounds meanings and understandings acquired through empirically engaging with the complexities of the social context in which African journalism is coming to terms with the changes engendered by the Internet. This "critical sociological turn" acknowledges and takes into account the "localized" socio-cultural, political, and economic realities which shape adoption practices as well as uses of the Internet by journalists in Africa. These localized conditions also point to the lasting setbacks associated with the realities of "access" to digital technologies, thus foregrounding crucial questions of *structure* and *agency*.

This wave of scholarship provides scope for research avenues that dig deeper into the complex imbrications of Internet-based digital journalism practices in Africa. It maps avenues for approaches that capture the nuances of localized appropriations of the Internet by journalists, including the creative ways in which they are merging "their traditions with exogenous influences to create realities that are not reducible to either but enriched by both" (Nyamnjoh 2005: 4).

Awakening to the Challenging Realities of Local Conditions

Researchers adopting the foregoing critical perspective remind us that an understanding of African journalism practice in the digital era cannot be complete without taking into consideration the structural and functional challenges (largely related to the *digital divide*) faced by journalists and ordinary citizens alike. In taking this approach, they warn, however, that we should "avoid falling into the clichéd trap of defining African journalism as permanently in deficit" (Mabweazara 2015b: 14). The critics further point to the fact that the rate at which new digital technologies are adopted in newsmaking contexts across the continent are far from homogeneous, owing to the structural and functional inequalities associated with the notion of the *digital divide*. As Chris Paterson (2014: 259–260) aptly puts it, most journalists in Africa operate in plural and complex contexts where conditions of news production are "sometimes strikingly similar to what might be seen in any global news hub" and, equally, sometimes fairly distant "in terms of its goals and methods".

These conditions, as the researchers argue, offer a critical conceptual point of departure as well as a relevant explanatory framework for evaluating the North–South dichotomies in terms of how news organizations and their reporters are adapting to an era permeated by rapidly evolving changes in Internet-based digital technologies. Obijiofor and Hanusch (2011: 193) contend that questions of limited access to new technologies slow "technological diffusions", and that limited training opportunities in various sub-Saharan African news organizations have a negative impact on journalists' "knowledge and understanding of how to [effectively] use technology in their job". Writing from a South African context, Berger (2005: 10) similarly observes that Internet use "is integrated unevenly into newsrooms, and there are major variations across the region in regard to problems of access. This, and the lack of proper training, constrains the use of [the technology] to its fullest."

In the same vein, Kupe (2003) observes that the bulk of African journalists operate with significantly fewer resources, are poorly paid, and generally have low job security. He further notes that African journalists broadly operate in multicultural countries that are at various stages of constituting themselves as nations in a globalizing world. Equally, they are beset by poor telecommunications infrastructure, prohibitive costs, and general inequitable access to relevant technologies. Thus, while some news organizations and their staffers are weathering the storm and speaking in "celebratory" terms, some are deprived and panic-stricken, hence taking tentative steps into the "digital world".

Other researchers in this paradigm point to the constraints imposed by complex political systems in Africa, which often translate to restrictive legal and regulatory structures for news organizations (Hyden and Leslie 2007). All these local factors coalesce to shape and constrain how news organizations and their journalists appropriate the Internet. The conditions of deprivation, as some scholars note, cultivate localized practices and cultures, which point to determined pursuits for "digital inclusion" and unrivaled efforts to mitigate and circumvent extant operational challenges (Nyamnjoh 2005).

Embracing the "Local" Complexities of the African Context

As already noted, the plurality of the conditions in which African journalists operate has been foregrounded by a number of emerging researchers who challenge popular misconceptions which paint African countries with the same socio-cultural and economic brush. These critics foreground the fact that the continent is diverse and complex, and so is the rate at which digital technologies, including the Internet, are adopted in newsmaking contexts. Levi Obonyo (2011: 5) reminds us that "Africa does not provide a clear picture that is easy to diagnose". Thus, while the realities of local conditions discussed in the preceding section suggest a uniform scenario, the enormity and complexity of Africa makes it difficult to paint the continent's "digital" journalistic cultures with one brush (Mabweazara 2015b).

For some scholars, the scene is equally diverse in terms of the political economy of news organizations. South Africa, for example, stands apart from the rest of English-speaking Africa; its media infrastructure is predominantly well funded, with excellent newsroom infrastructure. It shares a number of characteristics with Western economies. As Goran Hyden and Michael Leslie (2007: 19) note: "[n]o other country on [the] continent has such a well-developed and sophisticated market infrastructure. What is happening there [. . .] has no direct parallel elsewhere in sub-Saharan Africa."

This scenario, as other researchers argue, opens up for debate the longstanding question of the extent to which contemporary journalism can be conceived of as homogeneous across the continent and, indeed, across global regions. By the same token, it remains to be seen whether the normative ideals of Internet-based digital journalism emerging from Western economies apply in Africa, despite the numerous challenges faced by news organizations and their journalists, including the disproportionate distribution of digital technologies (Mabweazara 2015b). Thus, in their critique of new forms of citizen interactions and participatory cultures on the Web, Lynette Steenveld and Larry Strelitz (2010) warn against the wholesale adoption of Western models, which define citizen journalists as "produsers" (Bruns 2007). This approach, as they put it, presumes a citizenry of both consumers and producers of media products, who are relatively well educated, are familiar with, and have unfettered access to the Internet as a form of social communication. Citizens are also presumed to be confident and adept at participating in these new interactive spaces (Mare 2013).

Adding another cautionary dimension to this debate, Moyo (2009) argues that in Africa, the Internet and its associated digital technologies can also be seen as agents of both inclusion and exclusion in terms of citizen participation. Thus, in reminding us of the complexities of the African context, Luke Goode (2009) submits that we should not forget the fact that in Africa, journalism has always existed alongside other forms of "localized" and unique news dissemination and storytelling practices. For these scholars, it is important to examine how the technology is "acquiring new meanings" in the heterogeneity of localized social interactions and appropriations (Mabweazara 2015b: 15). In addressing how Facebook is used in a Mozambican community newspaper, Admire Mare, for example, observes how young working-class people who cannot connect on Facebook make use of a brick wall, "dubbed the physical 'Facebook wall', [where] citizens [. . .] post news tips, [. . .] complaints on service delivery challenges and act as whistle blowers on corruption cases" (2014: 23). This innovative recreation of an online Facebook wall in physical space points to individuals' refusal to "celebrate victimhood" (Nyamnjoh in Wasserman 2009: 291) through creatively refashion-ing available resources to "develop genres of use [that are] in line with their needs and expectations" (Mare 2014: 23).

These observations point to the need to examine how localized circumstances and situations provide ground for the development of uniquely African journalistic experiences. This necessitates engaging directly with questions and debates about how varied contextual factors shape what might be interpreted as "context-dependent practices" (Atton and Mabweazara 2011), as well as how global influences are tamed and localized. Scholars following this line of thought further point to dimensions of "socially shaped" innovations; internal creativity and adaptations in African news production contexts (see Berger 2005; Mabweazara et al. 2014; Paterson 2013). They offer compelling evidence of the agency and creativity displayed by journalists in adopting and using the Internet, which all points to what Nyamnjoh (2005) refers to as the "creative domestication of individual agency". The researchers also point to the importance of closely examining the broader communication ecology, including how it provides insights that can enable us to advance our understanding of developments in Internet-based digital journalism in Africa (Mabweazara et al. 2014).

Considerations of the complexities around the "context" in which African journalists operate also foreground the importance of attending to the intricacies of *local cultural factors*, which "give credibility to additional theoretical ways" (Berger 2005: 1) of assessing how African journalists are adjusting to the Internet era. The notion of *ubuntu*, for example, has recurrently emerged as an overarching African cultural compass for understanding what "Africaness" means (Shaw 2009), and thus illuminating the intricacies of African cultural life, which has implications for the appropriations of digital technologies in newsmaking contexts. It directs our attention to the "cultural orientation to communal values" which "focus our critical lenses to contingent social relationships and worldviews by which aspects of African journalism practice are maintained and defined" (Mabweazara 2015a: 115). Nyamnjoh (2005), for example, highlights how the innovative use of digital technologies in Africa generally hinges on local cultural values of *solidarity*, *interconnectedness*, and *interdependence*. These values make it possible for people to access the Internet (and its associated digital technologies) without necessarily being directly connected. In many situations, as Nyamnjoh (2005) further contends, it suffices for an individual to be connected in order for whole groups and communities to benefit. Consequently, while Internet connectivity in Africa is significantly lower, local cultural values make it possible for others to access the opportunities associated with "connectivity" without necessarily being connected or owning the technologies themselves (Mabweazara 2015a). A number of researchers have highlighted how journalists operating in impoverished newsrooms yield the benefits of digital technologies through sharing the limited and largely antiquated resources available (Mabweazara 2015a). Citing examples from selected South African newsrooms, Berger writes: "even as regards unwired computers, in many cases journalists queue to share these rather than have personal workstations" (2005: 9).

An understanding of these *cultural* dynamics is therefore central to attempts to closely examine how African journalists negotiate their way around the Internet. It further mitigates the pitfalls of exclusively "seeking explanations in the obvious and well-known contextual challenges" (Mabweazara 2015a: 116) facing most African news organizations as discussed above. The local cultural factors point to the "lived materialities of reportorial forms, practices and epistemologies" (Allan 2014: x), which show us where the challenges lie, as well as where the potentials for Internet-based digital journalism in Africa are located. This, however, is not to suggest a localized research agenda of separatism, fixated on *locale* and consequently barring "essential insights from 'outside' intellectual [. . .] experiences" (Mabweazara 2015a: 107). Rather, as Chris Atton and Hayes Mabweazara (2011) point out, we need to reconnect our accounts in Africa with insights emerging from other regions, especially the economically developed north, where research into the intersections between journalism and new technologies has a long trajectory.

Conclusion

This chapter has attempted to provide a broadly contextualized overview of trends and dimensions in the histories of Internet-based digital journalism research and practice in Africa. It has explored the trends and perspectives taken by different researchers in this field, and demonstrates that research on the connections between journalism and the Internet in Africa generally follows the path taken in research outside journalism. The research can largely be divided between three interconnected strands: those who celebrate the Internet's "promise" for African journalism in ways that typically resonate with the techno-deterministic discourses of the 1990s; those who generally express semblances of pessimism on the use of the Internet in journalism; and those who adopt a more cautious sociological approach that bridges, and in some cases transcends, the celebratory and pessimistic binary approaches to the social function of the Internet. The latter penetrates the basic occupational and professional characteristics of journalism in situated African contexts, thereby foregrounding unique contextually rooted understandings of evolving practices, attitudes, and patterns of Internet-based digital journalism on the continent. This sensitivity to *context*, as some researchers point out, also helps to define African journalism in the digital era, as well as position it in "the universals that are [often] deaf-and-dumb to the particularities of journalism in and on Africa" (Wasserman 2009: 287). It allows us to see the appropriation of the Internet by journalists "as a multifaceted experience that can be evaluated against the backdrop of local context factors" (Mabweazara 2015a: 114) as well as essential insights from "outside" forces. These understandings, as the chapter points out at the beginning, remain under-represented in global journalism scholarship.

References

Adam, L., and Wood, F. (1999) "An Investigation of the Impact of Information and Communication Technologies in Sub-Saharan Africa", *Journal of Information Science*, 25(4): 307–318.

Adamolekun, W. (1996) "The Information Superhighway and Traditional Communication: Where We Stand", *Africa Media Review*, 10(2): 22–36.

Allan, S. (2014) "Foreword", in H. M. Mabweazara, M. Hayes, O. F. Mudhai, and J. Whittaker (eds), *Online Journalism in Africa: Trends, Practices and Emerging Cultures*, London: Routledge, pp. ix–x.

Atton, C., and Mabweazara, H. M. (2011) "New Media and Journalism Practice in Africa: An Agenda for Research", *Journalism: Theory, Practice & Criticism* 12(6): 667–673.

Banda, F., Mudhai, O. F., and Tettey, W.J. (2009) "Introduction: New Media and Democracy in Africa: A Critical Interjection", in O. F. Mudhai, W. J. Tettey, and F. Banda (eds), *African Media and the Digital Public Sphere*, New York: Palgrave Macmillan, pp. 1–20.

Berger, G. (2005) "Powering African Newsrooms: Theorising How Southern African Journalists Make Use of ICTs for Newsgathering", in G. Berger (ed.), *Doing Digital Journalism: how Southern African Newsgatherers Are Using ICTs*, Grahamstown: High Way Africa, pp. 1–14.

Bruns, A. (2007) *Produsage: Towards a Broader Framework for User-Led Content Creation*, available at: http://produsage. org/files/Produsage%20(Creativity%20and%20Cognition%202007).pdf

Chari, T. (2009) "Ethical Challenges Facing Zimbabwean Media in the Context of the Internet", *Global Media Journal: African Edition*, 3(1): 1–34.

Conboy, M. (2013) *Journalism Studies: The Basics*, London: Routledge.

Deuze, M. (2003) "The Web and its Journalisms: Considering the Consequences of Different Types of Newsmedia Online", *New Media & Society*, 5(2): 203–230.

Deuze, M., and Dimoudi, C. (2002) "Online Journalists in the Netherlands: Towards a Profile of a New Profession", *Journalism*, 3(1): 85–100.

Esipisu, I., and Kariithi, N. (2007) "New Media Development in Africa", *Global Media Journal: Africa Edition*, 1(1).

Etta, F. E., and Parvyn-Wamahiu, S. (2003) *Information and Communication Technologies for Development in Africa: The Experience with Telecentres* (Vol. 2), Dakar: International Development Research Centre & Council of the Development of Social Science Research in Africa.

Foss, K. (2008) "Ordinary Citizens Redefining News-Gathering", *IOL*, 15 September, available at: http://mini.iol.co.za/news/south-africa/ordinary-citizens-redefining-news-gathering-416470

Garman, A. (2003) "Africa Media", *Rhodes Journalism Review*, 23: 2.

Goldfain, K., and van der Merwe, N. (2006) "The Role of a Political Blog: The Case of www.commentary.co.zw", *Communicare*, 25(1): 103–125.

Goode, L. (2009) "Social News, Citizen Journalism and Democracy", *New Media & Society*, 11(8): 1287–1305.

Hedley, A. R. (1999) "The Information Age: Apartheid, Cultural Imperialism, or Global Village?", *Social Science Computer Review*, 17(1): 78–87.

Hyden, G., and Leslie, M. (2007) "Communications and Democratisation in Africa", in G. Hyden, M. Leslie, and F. F. Ogundimu (eds), *Media and Democracy in Africa*, Piscataway, NJ: Transaction Publishers, pp. 1–27.

Internet World Stats (n.d.) "Internet Usage Statistics for Africa", *Internet World Stats*, available at: www.internetworldstats.com/stats1.htm (accessed 27 February 2016).

Kasoma, F. P. (1996) "The Foundations of African Ethics (Afriethics) and the Professional Practice of Journalism: The Case of Society-Centred Media Morality", *Africa Media Review*, 10(3): 93–116.

Katz, J. E., and Aakhus, M. (2002) *Perpetual Contact: Mobile Communication, Private Talk, Public Performance*, Cambridge: Cambridge University Press.

Kupe, T. (2003) "The Untold 21st Century Story", *Rhodes Journalism Review*, 23: 18.

Mabweazara, H. M. (2011) "The Internet in the Print Newsroom: Trends, Practices and Emerging Cultures in Zimbabwe", in D. Domingo and C. Paterson (eds), *Making Online News: Newsroom Ethnography in the Second Decade of Internet Journalism*, New York: Peter Lang. pp. 57–69.

Mabweazara, H. M. (2013) "Normative Dilemmas and Issues for Zimbabwean Print Journalism in the 'Information Society' Era", *Digital Journalism*, 1(1): 135–151.

Mabweazara, H. M. (2014) "Zimbabwe's Mainstream Press in the 'Social Media Age': Emerging Practices, Cultures and Normative Dilemmas", in H. M. Mabweazara, O. F. Mudhai, and J. Whittaker (eds), *Online Journalism in Africa: Trends, Practices and Emerging Cultures*, London: Routledge, pp. 76–85.

Mabweazara, H. M. (2015a) "Charting Theoretical Directions for Examining African Journalism in the "Digital Era", *Journalism Practice*, 9(1): 106–122.

Mabweazara, H. M. (2015b) "African Journalism in the 'Digital Era': Charting a Research Agenda", *African Journalism Studies*, 36(1): 11–17.

Mabweazara, H. M., Mudhai, O. F., and Whittaker, J. (eds) (2014) *Online Journalism in Africa: Trends, Practices and Emerging Cultures*, London: Routledge.

Madden, G. (2005) "Introduction", in N. C. Lesame (ed.), *New Media: Technology and Policy in Developing Countries*, Pretoria: Van Schaik.

Mare, A. (2013) "A Complicated but Symbiotic Affair: The Relationship Between Mainstream Media and Social Media in the Coverage of Social Protests in Southern Africa", *Ecquid Novi: African Journalism Studies*, 34(1): 83–98.

Mare, A. (2014) "New Media Technologies and Internal Newsroom Creativity in Mozambique: The Case of @verdade", *Digital Journalism*, 2(1): 12–28.

Mavhungu, J., and Mabweazara, H. M. (2014) "The South African Mainstream Press in the Online Environment: Successes, Opportunities and Challenges", in H. M. Mabweazara, O. F. Mudhai, and J. Whittaker (eds), *Online Journalism in Africa: Trends, Practices and Emerging Cultures*, London: Routledge, pp. 34–48.

Moyo, D. (2009) "Citizen Journalism and the Parallel Market of Information in Zimbabwe's 2008 Election", *Journalism Studies*, 10(4): 551–567.

Mudhai, O. F. (2004) "Researching the Impact of ICTs as Change Catalysts in Africa", *Ecquid Novi: South African Journal for Journalism Research*, 25(2): 313–335.

Mudhai, O. F., and Nyabuga, G. (2001) "The Internet: Triumphs and Trials for Journalism in Kenya", paper presented to the *Annual Highway Africa Conference*, Rhodes University.

Mutula, S. M. (2005) "Peculiarities of the Digital Divide in Sub-Saharan Africa", *Program: Electronic Library and Information Systems*, 39(2): 122–138.

Nyamnjoh, F. B. (2005) *Africa's Media: Democracy and the Politics of Belonging*, London: Zed Books.

Obijiofor, L. (1996) "Future Impact of New Communication Technologies: A Bibliographic Analysis", *Africa Media Review*, 10(2): 53–71.

Obijiofor, L. M. (2003) "New Technologies and Journalism Practice in Nigeria and Ghana", *Asia Pacific Media Educator*, 14: 36–56.

Obijiofor, L., and Hanusch, F. (2011) *Journalism Across Cultures: An Introduction*, New York: Palgrave Macmillan.

Obonyo, L. (2011) "Towards a Theory of Communication for Africa: The Challenges for Emerging Democracies", *Communicatio*, 37(1): 1–20.

Okigbo, C. (1995) "National Images in the Age of the Information Superhighway: African Perspectives", *Africa Media Review*, 9(2): 105–121.

Paterson, C. (2013) "Journalism and Social Media in the African Context", *Ecquid Novi: African Journalism Studies*, 34(1): 1–6.

Paterson, C. (2014) "Epilogue", in H. M. Mabweazara, O. F. Mudhai, and J. Whittaker (eds), *Online Journalism in Africa: Trends, Practices and Emerging Cultures*, London: Routledge, pp. 259–261.

Pavlik, J. V. (2005) "Running the Technological Gauntlet: Journalism and New Media", in H. De Burgh (ed.), *Making Journalists*, London: Routledge, pp. 245–263.

Shaw, I. S. (2009) "Towards an African Journalism Model: A Critical Historical Perspective", *International Communication Gazette*, 71(6): 491–510.

Skjerdal, T. (2014) "Online Journalism Under Pressure: An Ethiopian Account", in H. M. Mabweazara, O. F. Mudhai, and J. Whittaker (eds), *Online Journalism in Africa: Trends, Practices and Emerging Cultures*, London: Routledge, pp. 89–103.

Steenveld, L., and Strelitz, L. (2010) "Citizen Journalism in Grahamstown: *Iindaba Ziyafika* and the Difficulties of Instituting Citizen Journalism in a Poor South African Country Town", paper presented at the *World Journalism Education Congress*, 5–7 July, Grahamstown, South Africa.

Wasserman, H. (2005) "Connecting African Activism with Global Networks: ICTs and South African Social Movements", *Africa Development*, 30(1&2): 163–182.

Wasserman, H. (2009) "Extending the Theoretical Cloth to Make Room for African Experience: An Interview with Francis Nyamnjoh", *Journalism Studies*, 10(2): 281–293.

28

CELLPHONE AND INTERNET NOVELS

How Digital Literature Changed Print Books in Japan

Alisa Freedman

Introduction

Digital media has improved individual lives and built communities by providing spaces for people to share stories (for example, see Williams and Zenger 2012). This has been especially true in Japan, where Internet forums, particularly textboards that do not require registration and allow anonymous posts, became popular earlier and mobile technologies developed more quickly than in other countries (see, for instance, Gottlieb and McLelland 2003). Some of the most influential stories created online have described supposedly real events and emotions that resonate with the experiences of readers and make their knowledge and help seem appreciated. Even before social media like Facebook and video-sharing sites like YouTube became public around 2005, users found a sense of belonging on Internet forums like Japan's expansive 2channel (also written as Ni channeru or 2ch) textboard, launched in 1999 by Hiroyuki Nishima and offering hundreds of discussion boards. Online stories that bring authors and readers in close proximity have expanded offline, extending the artistic range of older media and providing new consumer bases. Prime examples are the novels written to be read on cellphones (*keitai shōsetsu*) and *Train Man* (*Densha otoko*), the collaborative effort of 2channel participants, which was turned into bestselling books between 2004 and 2007, and grabbed the attention of the international press. These Internet narratives were also adapted into television dramas and feature films, among other media, and have inspired sequels and spin-offs. These forms of collective writing exemplify the dominant Japanese marketing strategy of "media mix", or the release of one title in various commercial media formats with adaptations timed to maintain popularity, which has been essential to the success of series like Pokémon (see, for example, Steinberg 2012).

This chapter explores how digital novels reaffirmed, rather than undermined, the cultural significance of the print book in Japan and provided models for the commercialization of fan-produced culture worldwide. They exemplified what were becoming conventions of Japanese Internet use, including access patterns, visual languages, user identifications, and corporate tie-ins. At the same time, they encouraged discussions about groups on the fringes of Japanese society, particularly delinquent girls and male *otaku* (avid fans of hobbies). Although these literary trends waned in popularity after around 2008, they have had a lasting influence on how books and authors are defined. I take an original approach by examining cellphone novels and Internet novels together as representing pivotal years in Japan when online culture impacted upon traditional publishing and reading practices and enabled the rise of fandoms. I provide a different reading than the plethora of journalistic reports and academic theses that question the literariness of these narrative forms or view them as fascinating but short-lived popular culture (for instance, Goodyear 2008). With my focus on the history of the intersection of digital and print media, and my attention to literary narratives, aesthetics, and genres, as well as formats, I add to the conversation about the creative, liberating, and community-building potential of mobile and Internet communications (see also Hjorth 2014; Kim 2014).

Cellphone Novels by the Thumb Generation

In 2006, the Ministry of Information and Communications reported that more people in Japan accessed the Internet by cellphones than by computers (69.2 million compared to 66 million, with 48.6 million using both) (Williams 2006). Reasons included affordable cellphone packet plans, use of the Internet for leisure rather than work in a corporate system still reliant on paperwork, and the custom of browsing websites during spare time provided by long train commutes, the main mode of transportation in Japanese cities. On one hand, the term "Galapagos Syndrome" (*garapagosu-ka*), denoting a strain of a global product with features only found locally, was coined in reference to Japanese 3G phones that were too advanced to be used elsewhere; this syndrome reflects both Japan's reputation for fashionable technology and anxiety about being an isolated "island nation" (see, for example, Tabuchi 2009). On the other hand, Japanese cellphones have been in the vanguard of global trends, such as text messaging (short message service—SMS) and emoticons.

SMS texts, 140–160 character messages, became popular in Japan as an inexpensive, private mode of communication in the late 1990s, predominant among female users of "pocket bells", stylish personal pagers and the then least expensive communication tool (pocket bells were first introduced by Nippon Telegraph and Telephone (NTT) in 1968). The nickname "thumb tribe" (*oyayubizoku*), once used for *pachinko* (a kind of pinball) players, was applied as early as 2001 to the generation of youth who text on cellphones with their thumbs. Thumb tribe members became accustomed to discussing their lives and seeking empathy through text messages. SMS altered customs of formal written communication, which has historically relied on set seasonal greetings and "*mahō no kotoba*", magically polite words, to soothe social relationships. Abbreviations developed to save space and convey feelings, but demanded communal knowledge to be understood. For example, SKY, for *Supā Kūki Yomanai*, meaning "super clueless", was popular SMS slang in 2007. Text languages, to which new words have constantly been added, can be viewed as an extension of the shared vocabularies that solidify social groups, such as the 2channel users described later in this chapter. The first *emoji*, or picture character, was a heart mark on the pocket bell in 1995. Colorful, sometimes animated, *emoji* were created around 1999 by NTT designer Kurita Shigetaka, and have been preprogrammed into cellphones starting with DoCoMo *i-mode* (Internet access by NTT, from "*do* communications over the *mobile* network") and differ slightly according to provider. The yellow faces, holiday symbols, and other now iconic *emoji* are part of Japanese "*kawaii*" (cute premised on seeming vulnerable) aesthetics, characterized by big heads, missing noses or mouths, and large eyes to show emotion. A standard set of *emoji* has globalized on iPhones, Windows phones, Skype, Facebook, and other platforms, while including images like the bowing man that are specific to Japan. In 2004, DoCoMo began offering unlimited domestic

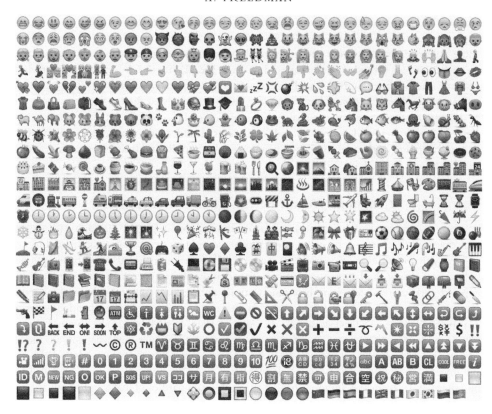

Figure 28.1 Unicode standard 3.0 *emoji* (June 2016)

text messaging in their monthly packet plans, a change that made the writing of novels on cellphones possible.

In January 2002, NEC became one of the first corporations to promote reading novels on cellphones. For an inexpensive flat rate of 100 yen per month, subscribers could receive installments from the "Shinchō Cellphone Library" (*Shinchō keitai bunko*), a limited digital collection of the Shinchō publishing company's paperback books. Advertisements promoted the service as a way to occupy time while waiting for and traveling on trains. One of the first available books was *Train Poster Stories* (*Nakazuri shōsetsu*), an anthology of uplifting tales by popular authors serialized on posters hung from the ceilings (*nakazuri*) of JR East commuter trains from September 1990 to September 1991 to attract passengers during the time of the bursting of the financial bubble by providing free reading material.

The trend for new novels available for cellphone serialization began with *Deep Love: Ayu's Story* (*Deep Love—Ayu no monogatari*) written by a thirty-something man under the pen name Yoshi. A former preparatory school teacher, Yoshi was inspired in 2000 by the increasing use of *i-mode* to open Zavn.net, a website for cellphone access, to publicize his original works, including photographs he took of youth in Tokyo's fashionable Shibuya neighborhood. To promote Zavn.net, Yoshi distributed cards with the URL in Shibuya. In May 2000, he began serializing *Deep Love*, the story of the decline of Ayu, a 17-year-old who engages in *enjo kōsai*, or compensating dating, an issue widely discussed in the mass media at the time. Yoshi self-published *Deep Love* as a book for Zavn.net subscribers. As news of the story spread, Yoshi

Figure 28.2 Book cover of *Deep Love: Ayu's Story* manga, Vol. 1 (written by Yoshi and illustrated by Yoshi Yuu, 2004)

was offered contracts from mainstream publishers, which he declined because they proposed changes to the sexually explicit and violent content and to his casual writing style. He worked with the smaller Starts Publishing (known for Oz-brand women's magazines) to reissue *Deep Love Complete Version: Ayu's Story* (*Deep Love kanzen han ~ Ayu no monogatari*) in 2002, followed by three sequels (Yoshi 2003a, b and c). These books are written horizontally, instead of vertically, and open from the left rather than from the right, as had been the norm in Japan. Thus, by adopting the practice of reading SMS, they changed the appearance of the printed page. They have larger font and wider margins than usual to re-create the experience of reading cellphone screens. *Deep Love* was adapted into five manga series from 2004 through 2006, a film (2004) which Yoshi used Zavn.net to help cast, and two television series (2004 and 2005, TV Tokyo) that aired late at night due to controversial content.

The best-known website for circulating cellphone novels has been Magic Island (*Mahō no i-rando*, "i" in "island" a pun for *i-mode*), opened as a homepage provider in 1999, preceding the launch of Japan's local Amazon bookseller by one year. Starting in 2000, Magic Island included a "book function" (BOOK *kinō*) enabling users to write stories in 1,000-character chapters, up to 500 pages, for free. The first Magic Island novel published as a print book was *What the Angels Gave Me* (*Tenshi ga kureta mono*) by Chaco (2005), who became one of the most prolific cellphone novelists. The book, which sold more than one million copies (Emata 2007: 55), was thanks in part to fans directly contacting publishers (Mahō no i-rando toshokan 2007: 38). Opening in March 2006, the compilation site Magic Island Library (Mahō no toshokan) allowed subscribers to browse, comment on, review, and rank novels (corporate and fan ranking of products, from books and music to horoscopes, is a popular marketing tool in Japan). By May 2007, Magic Island Library offered more than a million titles (Mahō no i-rando toshokan 2007: 38). The establishment of such competitor websites as Wild Strawberries (*No-ichigo*) and Orion⋆ attest to the long-accepted Japanese cultural notion that good ideas should be emulated. The primary publishers of cellphone novels have been Starts Publishing and Goma Books (known for celebrity accounts). In 2007, Magic Island had between 4.8 and 5.2 million registered users, around 70 percent of whom were women, mostly ages 17 and 18, with an increasing number of readers in upper primary school grades and junior high school (Emata 2007: 54–55; Mika 2006). Cellphone novels perhaps filled a gap in Japan for young adult novels, a genre popular in other countries, such as the United States, because of its attention to issues facing teenagers.

Many cellphone novelists are novice writers who do not aspire to literary careers. Almost all hide their identities behind one-word, cute-sounding, easy-to-remember names (such as Yoshi, Chaco, and Mei), combining the tradition of pen names in Japanese literature (especially common before World War II) with handle names on public Internet sites. The author and protagonist of *Love Sky: Sad Love Story* (*Koizora: Setsunai koi monogatari*), ranked third in the 2006 bestseller list, are both named Mika, making this doomed romance between high-school students, one of whom is dying of cancer, seem premised on truth. Use of given names in Japanese society, where most people are called by their surnames, fosters a sense of intimacy. It is important to note that novels by celebrity authors (*geijin bon*) have also been bestsellers. One of the top-grossing books of 2006 was *Tokyo Tower: Mom, Me, and Sometimes Dad* (*Tokyo Tawā ~ okan to boku to, tokidoki, oton*), the autobiographical novel by Lily Franky (his pen name), author, illustrator, musician, and actor, which was made into a film (2006), television special (2006), and series (2007).

Magic Island and similar websites offer a model of "joint creation" (*sōhō tsukuri ageru*) that extends the historical practice of reader comments in Japanese periodicals, such as response columns in 1920s girls' fiction and manner magazines and 1970s girls comics (*shōjo manga*) magazines (see, for example, Frederick 2006; Prough 2010). Yoshiaki Itō, head of production at Magic Island, remarked that the readers and authors play a "game of catch"; authors toss chapters to readers, who then suggest changes and correct mistakes (Emata 2007: 55). Towa, winner of the first Japan Cellphone Novel Prize (2006) for *Clearness* (*Kurianesu*), thanked readers for lightening the mood of the story (Emata 2007: 55).

Professionally published book versions of cellphone novels dominated bestseller lists between 2005 and 2007, with film and television adaptations helping to increase sales. For example, *Red Thread* (*Akai ito*) by Mei (2007a), the story of two junior high-school students who were fated to fall in love and the troubles caused by friends and family, ranked second in 2007 (Asahi.com 2007) and led to the sequel *Red Thread Destiny* (*Akai ito ~ destiny*) (Mei 2007b). In 2007, Starts Publishing published 20 cellphone novels, providing almost one-third of its income (Goodyear 2008); Goma Books and Magic Island together sold three million cellphone novels, beating sales of larger publishing companies (Lytle 2007). As Starts Publishing editor Matsushima Shigeru commented in a press interview:

> [Readers] don't know when and which stories will disappear from cellphones and the Internet. They want to buy the books just because they want the things that have had an impact on their lives close at hand.
>
> (Emata 2007: 55)

According to publishing conventions, books longer than 350 pages are divided into two volumes (upper and lower), each sold separately, with cover art and other design elements showing that they are a set.

The most popular cellphone novels cast underdog teenaged characters in the "pure love" (*jun'ai*) stories that were emerging as a distinct genre marketed to women and men. In many instances, one or more of the characters falls in love for the first time, and the couple needs to overcome obstacles to be together. Stories end or a character dies before love can become soiled with mundane aspects of domestic life. A seminal pure love story was Kyoichi Katayama's *Crying Out Love, In the Center of the World* (*Sekai no chūshin de, ai o sakebu*) (2001), which was adapted into a manga, film, and television series in 2004 and a Korean film in 2005. Published by Shōgakukan in 2001, this tale of a boy in love with a girl dying of cancer became a bestseller in 2004, in part because of the efforts by a Shōgakukan salesman to mobilize the book's fan base and the promotion by such young actresses as Kō Shibasaki, who appeared in the film version. In *Deep Love,* the protagonist Ayu seeks lost innocence and salvation through heterosexual romance with a boy dying of heart disease. Cellphone novels discuss issues rarely covered in pure love stories, such as domestic abuse, prostitution, rape, drug addiction, and suicide. In general, these books provide an insight into the psychology of troubled youth but do not offer solutions to their hardships. As represented by *Deep Love,* many characters cannot overcome traumas that are often caused by their own bad decisions, and their stories tend to end unhappily. The genre turns problems into issues of personal choice, thereby releasing the Japanese government, educational institutions, and public society from blame. They inspire tears but not activism.

Cellphone novels share literary techniques and visual qualities. Most often written in the first person, they convey the sense of reading messages from friends. As Mei, author of *Red Thread*, remarked in an interview with Goma Books, although it takes the average reader one to three minutes per page of a cellphone novel, it takes her hours of writing and revision to make pages seem that simple (Mahō no i-rando toshokan 2007: 9). Three kinds of dialogue dominate the stories, which are almost entirely devoid of narration: daily conversations, inner monologues, and words from the heart conveyed orally and through texts (Mahō no i-rando toshokan 2007: 160). In their guide for aspiring authors, Magic Island suggests using line spacing and paragraphing, along with square brackets and other punctuation, to create tempo and rhythm. They instruct that short sentences are easier to read on cellphones than long ones. Authors should consider sound, such as the ringing of phones and chimes of texts. Magic Island advises that authors write their novels on cellphones so that they can see how they will be read (Mahō no i-rando toshokan 2007: 160). In part due to screen limitations, cellphone novels are full of sentence fragments, which some critics have praised as emulating Japanese literary traditions of enmeshing poetry within prose to heighten emotions (see Dooley 2008), but others have disparaged as poor writing (see Onishi 2008). With the exception of stars (for emphasis and flair), heart marks (to show love), and musical notes (for ringing phones and arriving messages), most cellphone novels have few emoticons.

In other respects, cellphone novels perpetuate longstanding literary conventions, such as using awards to establish authorial careers and publishing of stories in periodicals before releasing them as stand-alone books. The Japan Cellphone Novel Prize (*Nihon keitai shōsetsu taishō*), founded by Magic Island, Starts Publishing, and the large Mainichi Newspaper Company) parallels the Akutagawa Prize (and the companion Naoki Prize for popular fiction) given twice a year to up-and-coming authors for novellas appearing in magazines. While not making pretenses toward producing highbrow literature, Goma Books published versions of classics for which copyrights have expired in the style of cellphone novels, including Ryūnosuke Akutagawa's *Spider's Thread* (*Kumo no ito*). Nun and literary scholar Setouchi Jakucho (1922–) serialized the cellphone novel *Tomorrow's Rainbow* (*Ashita no niji*), inspired by the eleventh-century *Tale of Genji* (*Genji monogatari*) that she had translated (Okamura 2008). Jakucho took the pen name "Purple" (*Pāpuru*), an allusion to Murasaki Shikibu, the *Tale of Genji*'s probable female author (Murasaki means purple). Thanks to global media attention, the fad spread worldwide. For example, the first cellphone novel serialized in North America was *Secondhand Memories* (*Mukashi no omoide*) by Takatsu, a Japanese university student studying in Toronto, on Textnovel (founded in 2008) from 2009 to 2011 and featured in an English-language textbook in Japan (Takatsu 2011). Yet by this time, as I will explain in the conclusion, the Japanese popularity for cellphone novels had waned, with the exception of the light high-school romance *Wolf Boy x Natural Girl* by a 15-year-old girl called "Bunny" (from a *Bambi* character) who began the story while in sixth grade and sold 110,000 copies in 2009 (Nagano 2010).

Train Man and 2channel Romance

Internet books (paper editions of stories created and first available online) developed concurrently with cellphone novels. As explained below, consumed by a different demographic and accessed primarily on computers, Internet novels represent an alternative mode of collaborative writing. The most famous example is *Train Man* (*Densha otoko*)—bestselling Internet book (October 2004), film (June 2005), television series (July–September 2005), stage play (September, 2005), four manga in *shōjo* and *seinen* styles (comics for girls and boys, respectively, 2005), and even an adult video (2005) based on a supposedly real event—was created through anonymous posts on the expansive 2channel forum from March to May 2004. An inspiring love story of an awkward nerd and a fashionable working woman, *Train Man* centers on the couple and the online community who encouraged them.

Train Man attests to the cultural significance of 2channel which comprises more than 600 boards (*ita*) where users, who keep their identities anonymous or use nicknames, can chat about subjects that might be taboo in face-to-face conversations. To stay current and save bandwidth, threads are limited to 1,000 posts; users continue discussions by adding threads. 2channel received around 2.5 million posts a day in 2007 and has been monitored for trends by such corporations as Dentsu Advertising (Katayama 2007). *Train Man* exemplified a productive use of 2channel, which has also been the site of libel and advertisement of crimes. Most notoriously, on 3 May 2000, a 17-year-old calling himself "Neomugicha" (New Barley Tea) posted a warning message before hijacking a bus in Fukuoka and killing a passenger. *Train Man* unfolded on boards for "*doku no otoko*"—that is, single (*dokushin*) men who think they are as unattractive as poison (*doku*).

The story began after a shy 22-year-old, given the handle Train Man on the second day of the discussion, protected a woman from a drunk on a Tokyo train. Although such harassment is common on Tokyo trains, help from a stranger is not, and the woman sent Train Man expensive Hermes brand teacups to show her gratitude. While the choice of Hermes is unusual, gift giving is an accepted way of showing appreciation in Japan. Train Man, who had never had a girlfriend, asked for advice on how to ask the woman, affectionately nicknamed Hermes, on a date. From the start, Train Man appeared as an exceptionally caring person, whom many 2channel subscribers felt a desire to help. The story developed as the online community, mostly men, offered and debated suggestions on how Train Man could make Hermes fall in love with him and as Train Man reported the events of his new relationship and feelings about how his life was changing. The story attracted new writers and readers, and spread outside the "poison man" board.

The story was written in 2channel slang. Aspects of this language that often focuses on the visuality of words and puns include using homophones for Chinese characters, a technique that is not new and was used for transliteration of Western words into Japanese in the nineteenth century. This is evident in "*Nakano Hitori*", a 2channel phrase meaning "one among us" that designates the collective author of *Train Man*. In addition, long vowel sounds are shortened, short ones are lengthened, similar but incorrect characters are used, and two-word phrases are abbreviated into two syllables, a common way of referring to buzzwords and brands. For example, Katayama's novel *Sekai no chūshin de, ai o sakebu* discussed above is called "*Sekachū*". 2channel written language was voiced in the television and film versions of *Train Man*, making words like "*moe*" (affection for two-dimensional characters) part of everyday speech (Galbraith 2009). Along with text messages, 2channel subscribers post ASCII artwork (affectionately nicknamed AA), both "*kaomoji*" (face emoticons) and elaborate pictures comprising letters, punctuation marks, and other printable characters. Encoding for Japanese (Shift JIS) has more keyboard characters than for alphabet-based languages and thus more artistic potential.

Train Man and most of his supporters are self-identified "*otaku*", avid fans who spend time and money obtaining knowledge of and things related to hobbies. Train Man promoted more positive connotations of the term coined in studies of anti-social male behavior in the first half of the 1980s and made notorious by the serial killer Tsutomu Miyazaki in 1989. In *Train Man*, *otaku* are portrayed as participating in global networks that run parallel to, but do not oppose, local groups of family, school, and work, which have formed the backbone of Japanese society. Although applied to other fandoms, *otaku* is now mostly used both playfully and pejoratively to denote ardent collectors of manga, anime, and computer technologies, forms of Japanese popular culture that have globalized. Especially in discussions among fans, *otaku* are divided into subgroups. Train Man represents the "*Akiba-kei otaku*", or the predominantly male denizens of Tokyo's Akihabara electronics district, a subculture that is not too far removed from mainstream urban society. In *Train Man*, *Akiba-kei otaku* are portrayed as manifesting both conspicuous consumption and production, giving rise to new trends and vocabularies through the shared desire for brands and commodities. Members of *Akiba-kei* Internet forums, interviewees in media reports, and bloggers have generally expressed a mix of shame and pride in belonging to these communities—feelings articulated by Train Man. Through the online conversation that often reads as a guide to fashion and dating in Tokyo, Train Man gained confidence by changing his physical appearance. (Fashion plays a large part

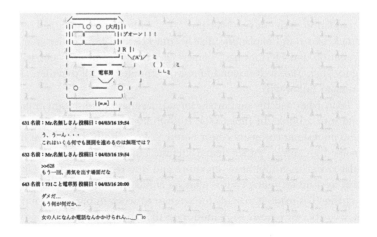

Figure 28.3 Screenshot from the *Train Man* Internet novel

in the story and was the prime factor that distinguishes Train Man from the men that Hermes would ordinarily choose.) Train Man hid, but did not give up his *otaku* identity, and spent as much time on 2channel discussing his hobbies as he did Hermes. In a pivotal point in their relationship, he used his knowledge of computers to impress Hermes, whose nickname is also associated with consumer culture.

On 9 May 2004, Train Man posted on 2channel that he had confessed his love for Hermes. Love confessions are a stock part of Japanese fiction and film, but Train Man unconventionally discussed his fears and feelings with other characters, rather than just making the reader privy to these private thoughts. In the last posts included in the story, 2channel subscribers tell Train Man that he had learned how to be an ideal romantic partner and no longer needed the advice of the *otaku* community, which had benefited from his example. His task was to advance into "mainstream" society, remembering the people who helped him motivate to change but leaving his former life behind. The participants in the online discussion gave Train Man a send-off, implying that, although a hero, he was no longer one of them. Thus, Train Man has influenced the development of a new kind of romantic male hero: the compassionate, motivated *otaku* with disposable income and leisure time. Yet to be this *otaku* hero, Train Man needed to move outside his community and prove that he wanted to and could conform to notions of male behavior that have dominated the popular imagination since the post-war period. Train Man's identity is thus fraught with contradictions.

In May 2004, the 57-day online conversation of 29,862 posts was edited into a six-chapter story of 1,919 posts (6.4 percent of the total discussion) (Andō 2005: 5) and made available on a free website. Fans rendered the website into other world languages, such as the 2006 English translation by "Project.Densha". Each chapter detailed a separate "mission" that Train Man needed to complete to further his romance and included such tasks as inviting Hermes to dinner and holding her hand. Negative posts and pornographic ASCII art were not included. The most positive of several potential endings was chosen and thereby prevented additional interpretations of the story. A note on the last page, presumably by Nakano Hitori, praises Train Man's courage and the 2channel users' sense of community. Beneath is an ASCII-art picture of two Monā cats, the 2channel mascot, along with Giko neko, another ASCII-art cat figure, representing Train Man and Hermes. Hermes remarks that 2channel supporters are good people, as they walk out an exit door, showing her approval of the kinds of *otaku* portrayed and the role that mobility played in their story (Nakano 2004: 364). *Train Man* was made into a "true love story for the Internet generation", to borrow the tagline from the American translation of the novel (Nakano 2007). Although not included on the website, Train Man posted follow-ups explaining that he and Hermes grew closer after she read the 2channel conversation and Hermes has "semi-*otaku*" hobbies but does not state what they are. According to *Train Man* websites and blogs, the couple are still together, although their real identities remain unknown.

As news of Train Man and his supporters spread, Japanese publishing companies vied to turn the website into a book. In June 2004, Nishimura awarded publication rights to 34-year-old Shinchō publishing company editor Gunji Yoko, who had produced five successful books but remained a contract rather than a lifetime employee. Because of the publishing focus on popular rather than highbrow literature and due to financial losses, it has become an industry norm to contract young editors who are familiar with book trends. As exemplified by Gunji, this change has made it possible for women to work in higher-level positions, but, without much security, they need to demonstrate that their jobs are necessary. Gunji was able to acquire the project from Nishimura because she proposed designing the book to resemble an online chat with ASCII artwork and 2channel slang, rather than developing the story into a more conventional novel with elaborate plot lines and character descriptions (Nikkei Woman 2006: 62). For her achievement, she was chosen as 2006 Nikkei Woman of the Year in the hit-maker category. Published at a time of proliferation of 2channel user guides and the popularization of ASCII art, *Train Man* heightened the domination of Nishimura's Internet empire.

Although the story website is still available for free and the URL address is even listed in the back of the book, more than 260,000 copies of *Train Man* sold in the first three weeks after it was released on 22 October; sales reached 1.5 million by the summer of 2005, when the film and television series aired (Ashby 2004; *Densha otoko o kangaeru tomo no kai* 2005: 7;). According to a survey published in the 22 November, 2004 issue of the news magazine *AERA*, 70 percent of the customers who purchased *Train Man* during the first three weeks were men and most likely 2channel participants, but after November 2004, 46 percent of book buyers were female, a change that was in part thanks to advertising campaigns and the spread of the story through television and other media (Suzuki 2005: 79, 72, 111).

Train Man presents a radically different appearance of the page: the 364-page book is entirely composed of online posts; those by Train Man are shaded in gray. A closing discussion on 16 May, a week after Train Man's confession of love, serves as an epilogue. Little explanation is given, implying that the target reader is familiar with the story and format. The story is told almost entirely through dialogue and makes the reader feel as though she is overhearing a conversation among a crowd. This narrative structure allows the plot to unfold in real time, a sense also conveyed in cellphone novels. Because the posts are anonymous and the real Train Man and Hermes are unknown, notions of copyright, royalties, and press releases changed. If Train Man were real, he should receive part of the copyright, which belonged instead to Nishimura. Internet novels published before *Train Man* were not commercially successful. For example, in 2001, director Shunji Iwai compiled a book of posts from the online forum that became the basis of his film *All About Lily Chou Chou* (*Riri shu shu no subete*) (Iwai 2001) about Japanese teenagers who suffered from bullying and other trials of adolescence, and bonded on a fansite for a pop music star. *Train Man* and the books it inspired, however, impart life-affirming messages.

The success of *Train Man* led to companion volumes, sociological studies, and self-help books, marking a case of popular fiction inspiring the examination of Japanese social structures and individual psychology. A prime example is the *Train Man Styling Bible* (*Densha otoko sutairingu baiburu*), which resulted from a contest to refashion *otaku* sponsored by the web company Appeal Click (Kikuchi 2005). In 2005, different publishers created spin-off Internet books in the same format as *Train Man* that were also supposedly based on true stories of *otaku* asking for love and advice, and sharing their relationships on 2channel. For example, *Pervert Man* (*Chikan otoko*) (Itano 2005) began with a post by a nerd obsessed with anime and reptiles who was mistaken for a molester. The collective author's name is given as Itano Sumito, literally "those who live online", and it was made into a film and manga. The Japanese title of the American film *Napoleon Dynamite* is *Bus Man* (*Basu otoko*), which was released on DVD in November 2005 and sometimes marketed in displays near those for *Train Man*.

As the case of cellphone novels, the popularity of *Train Man* is in part due to its claims of realism. The truth claim has made *Train Man* a topic of media discussions about national issues facing Japan and has made changes in the publishing industry more striking. Conversely, it has spurred debate among people who consider themselves members of the *otaku* community about whether Train Man is a positive role model – for example, an outspoken opponent of what he calls "love capitalism" that normalizes heterosexual romance. Honda Tōru's 2005 *Radio-Wave Man* (*Denpa otoko*) (Honda 2005a) and *Radio-Wave Crusade* (*Denpa taisen*)

(Honda 2005b) present dissenting views and ask why Hermes did not change instead, and why an *otaku* like Train Man would rather interact with a live woman than a character encountered online. Conspiracy theories that *Train Man* was created by Fuji Television and Dentsu Advertising in collusion with 2channel's Nishimura, and perhaps the Japanese government, have also circulated in books and online, and critics have meticulously catalogued the aspects of the story that did not seem possible or seem to have occurred too quickly (*Densha otoko o kangaeru tomo no kai* 2005: 459–460).

Through a confluence of marketing forces and media discourses, the height of the *Train Man* phenomenon came in 2005, the year that former Prime Minister Koizumi declared Japan's low fertility rates to be a national problem. Because marriage has been viewed in government and journalistic discourses as a means toward paternity, the trend of men and women marrying late became a public concern. In 2004, the average age of first marriage was 29.6 for Japanese men and 27.8 for women (Masaki 2006). In news magazines devoted to issues of marriage and family, and the concurrent spate of books about heterosexual relationships, Train Man was described as a potential partner for career women, a demographic blamed for marrying after their twenties (see, for example, Sakai and Fukui 2005). As I have argued elsewhere, ultimately, media discourses about Train Man and the communities formed around him reveal contradictions in gender norms and advance the patriarchal family (Freedman 2009).

Legacy of Digital Age Stories

As evident by the above examples, digital media have transformed Japanese literature by redefining authors, readers, characters, books, and enabling collaborative writing. Rather than rendering print media obsolete, cellphones and the Internet have created book formats and added new languages. They exemplify how the Japanese publishing industry has compensated for decreasing sales by increasing titles. There was a 0.4 percent rise in new books in 2007 (Japan Book Publishers Association 2014). Related book types include "light novels" (*raito noberu*), with ties to video games, anime, and other digital culture. Cellphone and Internet novels have furthered publishing conventions. For example, they perpetuate the Japanese custom of first serializing stories in magazines, newspapers, and other "disposable" subscription media, and then, if they are well received, publishing them as books. Awards and ranking are used to promote literary careers. They also demonstrate how faddish attention to social issues can contribute to the dismissal of matters deserving more sustained consideration. As such, much popular fiction, while raising awareness of the need to solve problems facing contemporary Japan, tends to support the social status quo.

Key differences between cellphone and 2channel novels demonstrate the diversity of digital stories and their communities. Cellphone novels epitomize the fast, easy qualities of mobile communication, while 2channel reflects a slower pace of web browsing. *Train Man* was heavily edited after the story was finished, while cellphone authors serialize chapters as they write them. The youth characters of cellphone novels have less access to power than Train Man, who had the leisure, finances, and support network to improve his life. Because of its older readership, empathetic characters, use of 2channel, and occurrence in years of national concern over falling marriage rates, *Train Man* inspired more discussion about changing gender norms than cellphone novels did.

Developments in mobile technologies have made *keitai* writing obsolete. The first cellphone/e-book reader in Japan, Biblio (produced by Toshiba for KDDI—now AU), that held around 5,000 books (7GB), was advertised on trains in 2009. Starting with the iPhone (marketed in Japan in 2008), "smartphones" with larger screens and faster Internet access offer more reading material. Goma Books filed for bankruptcy in September 2009. Other 2channel novels have been edited into compilation sites, including *Husky and Medley* (*Hasukī to medorē*), an audience-supported romance from June to July 2008. A *yuri* (girls' love) manga version was created by fans. Nishimura sold 2channel to the Singapore-based Packet Monster in 2009 and, since 2012, has been the director of Niwango, the company that operates the video-sharing site NicoNico Douga (which went public in 2006). *Otaku* helping their partners, community, and themselves by falling in love has become a popular culture trope, as in *The World God Only Knows* (*Kami nomi zo shirusekai*, 2008–2014), a manga by Tamiki Wakaki, light novel, and anime series. Although limited in their historical lifespan, cellphone and 2channel novels have indelibly changed storytelling in Japan.

Further Reading

Freedman, A. (2009) "*Train Man* and the Gender Politics of 'Otaku' Culture: The Rise of New Media, Nerd Heroes and Consumer Communities" (an extended discussion of *Train Man*), *Intersections: Gender and Sexuality in Asia and the Pacific*, 20: 4.

Goodyear, D. (2008) "I ❤ NOVELS: Young Women Develop a Genre for the Cellular Age" (provides helpful information about cellphone novelists), The New Yorker, 2 December.

The "Project Densha" English translation of the official *Train Man* website can be found at: www.rinji.tv/densha/

References

Andō, K. (2005) *Fūinsareta Densha Otoko* (Cracking the Story of Train Man), Tokyo: Ohta Books.

Asahi.com (2007) "Futsū No Wakamono Ga Keitai Shōsetsu–Besutoserā Mo Zokuzoku" (Average Young Adult Readers Turning to Cellphone Novels: The Bestsellers Continue), *Asahi.com*, 11 February, available at: www.asahi.com/culture/news_culture/TKY200702100253.html (accessed 10 July 2014).

Ashby, J. (2004) "Hey Mr. Trainman", *Japan Times*, 18 November, available at: http://search.japantimes.co.jp/cgi-bin/ek20041118br.html (accessed 8 March 2007).

Chaco (2005) *Tenshi Ga Kureta Mono* (What the Angels Gave Me), Tokyo: Starts Publishing.

Densha Otoko o Kangaeru Tomo No Kai (Train Man Friendship Society) (2005) *Otosan Ni Mo Wakaru?: Junai Manuaru Tettei Kaiseki* (A Complete Guide to Pure Love So That Even Your Father Could Understand), Tokyo: Koara bukkusu.

Dooley, B. (2008) "Big in Japan: A Cellphone Novel for You, the Reader", *The Millions*, 31 January, available at: www.themillions.com/2008/01/big-in-japan-cellphone-novel-for-you.html (accessed 5 July 2014).

Emata Takako (2007) "Kētai hatsu shōsetuka ni naru" (Becoming a First-Time Cellphone Novelist), *AERA*, February, 26: 54–55.

Franky, L. (2005) *Tokyo Tawā ~ Okan To Boku To, Tokidoki, Oton* (Tokyo Tower: Mom, Me, and Sometimes Dad), Tokyo: Fūsōsha.

Frederick, S. (2006) *Turning Pages: Reading and Writing Women's Magazines in Interwar Japan*, Honolulu: University of Hawaii Press.

Freedman, A. (2009) "*Train Man* and the Gender Politics of 'Otaku' Culture: The Rise of New Media, Nerd Heroes and Consumer Communities", *Intersections*, available at: http://intersections.anu.edu.au/issue20/freedman.htm (accessed 11 July 2014).

Galbraith, P. (2009) "*Moe*: Exploring Virtual Potential in Post-Millennial Japan", *Electronic Journal of Contemporary Japan*, available at: www.japanesestudies.org.uk/articles/2009/Galbraith.html (accessed 10 July 2014).

Goodyear, D. (2008) "I ❤ NOVELS: Young Women Develop a Genre for the Cellular Age", *The New Yorker*, 2 December, available at: www.newyorker.com/reporting/2008/12/22/081222fa_fact_goodyear?currentPage=all (accessed 5 July 2014).

Gottlieb, N., and McLelland, M. (2003) *Japanese Cybercultures*, Oxford: Routledge.

Hjorth, L. (2014) "Stories of Mobile Women: Micro-Narratives and Mobile Novels in Japan", in *The Mobile Story: Narrative Practices with Locative Technologies*, New York: Routledge.

Honda, T. (2005a) *Denpa Otoko* (Radio-Wave Man), Tokyo: Sansai Books.

Honda, T. (2005b) *Denpa Taisen* (Radio Wave Crusade), Tokyo: Ota shuppan.

Itano, S. (2005) *Chikan Otoko* (Pervert Man), Tokyo: Futabasha.

Iwai, S. (2001) *Riri Shu Shu no Subete* (All About Lily Chou Chou), Tokyo: Rockwell Eyes.

Japan Book Publishers Association (2014) *An Introduction to Publishing in Japan 2014–2015*, Tokyo: Japan Book Publishers Association.

Katayama, K. (2001) *Sekai No Chūshin De, Ai O Sakebu* (Crying Out Love, In the Center of the World), Tokyo: Shōgakukan.

Katayama, L. (2007) "2-Channel Gives Japan's Famously Quiet People a Mighty Voice", *Wired*, 19 April, available at: www.wired.com/culture/lifestyle/news/2007/04/2channel (accessed 18 October 2013).

Kikuchi, F. (2005) *Densha Otoko Sutairingu Baiburu* (*Train Man* Styling Bible), Tokyo: Sogo Horei shuppan.

Kim, K. (2014) "Genealogy of Mobile Creativity: A Media Archeological Approach to Literary Practice in Japan", in G. Goggin and L. Hjorth (eds), *The Routledge Companion to Mobile Media*, New York: Routledge.

Lytle, J. (2007) "Mobile Novels Outsell Paper Books in Japan", *TechRadar*, 9 August, available at: www.techradar.com/us/news/phone-and-communications/mobile-phones/mobile-novels-outsell-paper-books-in-japan-154848 (accessed 8 July 2014).

Mahō no i-rando toshokan (ed.) (2007) *Kono Keitai Shōsetu Ga Sugoi* (These Cellphone Novels are Awesome), Tokyo: Goma bukkusu.

Masaki, H. (2006) "Japan Stares into Demographic Abyss", *Asia Times Online*, 9 May, available at: www.atimes.com/atimes/Japan/HE09Dh04.html (accessed 13 July 2014).

Mei (2007a) *Akai ito* (Red Thread), Vols 1 and 2, Tokyo: Goma Books.

Mei (2007b) *Akai ito ~ Destiny*, Vols 1 and 2, Tokyo: Goma Books.

Mika (2006) *Koizora ~ Setsunai Koi Monogatari*, Vols. 1 and 2, Tokyo: Starts Publishing.

Nagano, Y. (2010) "For Japan's Cellphone Novelists, Proof of Success Is in the Print", *Los Angeles Times*, 9 February, available at: http://articles.latimes.com/2010/feb/09/world/la-fg-japan-phone-novel9–2010feb09 (accessed 9 July 2014).

Nakano, H. (2004) *Densha Otoko* (Train Man), Tokyo: Shinchōsha.

Nakano, H. (2007) *Train Man*, trans. B. Elliott, New York: Del Rey Books.

Nikkei Woman (2006) "Shinchōsha: 27 Sai, Ano Issatsu No Hon Ga Tenkideshita" (Member of the Shinchō Publishing Company: With this One Book, She Made a Turning Point in Her Career at Age Twenty-Seven), *Nikkei Woman*, January, 1: 62–63.

Okamura, N. (2008) "Author Nun Finds New Outlet in Cellphone Fiction", *Reuters*, 26 September, available at: www.reuters.com/articlePrint?articleId=USTRE48P12I20080926 (accessed 5 July 2014).

Onishi, N. (2008) "Thumbs Race as Japan's Bestsellers Go Cellular", *New York Times*, 20 January, available at: www.nytimes.com/2008/01/20/world/asia/20japan.html (accessed 5 July 2014).

Pāpuru (Setouchi Jakucho) (2008) *Ashita no Niji* (Tomorrow's Rainbow), Tokyo: Mainichi Shimbunsha.

Prough, J. (2010) *Straight from the Heart: Gender, Intimacy, and the Cultural Production of Shojo Manga*, Honolulu: University of Hawaii Press.

Sakai, H. and Fukui, Y. (2005) "Densha Otoko No Mote Otoku Kenkyū" (Train Man's Study of Popular Guys), *AERA*, 27 June: 14–19.

Steinberg, M. (2012) *Anime's Media Mix: Franchising Toys and Characters in Japan*, Minneapolis, MN: University of Minnesota Press.

Suzuki, A. (2005) *'Densha Otoko' Wa Dare Nano Ka—'Netaka' Suru Komiunikesshon* (Who Is 'Train Man'? His Story Has Become the Basis of Communication), Tokyo: Chūō kōron shinsha.

Tabuchi, H. (2009) "Why Japan's Cellphones Haven't Gone Global", *New York Times*, 19 July, available at: www.nytimes.com/2009/07/20/technology/20cell.html?_r=0 (accessed 8 July 2014).

Takatsu (2011) "Secondhand Memories Now Complete", *Espresso Love Blog*, 9 March, available at: http://takatsu.wordpress.com/2011/03/09/secondhand-memories-now-complete (accessed 10 July 2014).

Tamiki, W. (2008–2014) *Kami Nomi Zo Shirusekai* (The World God Only Knows), Vols 1–26, Tokyo: Shokakugan.

Towa (2007) *Kurianesu* (Clearness), Tokyo: Starts Publishing.

Williams, B. and Zenger, A. (eds) (2012) *New Media Literacies and Participatory Popular Culture Across Borders*, New York: Routledge.

Williams, M. (2006) "More Mobile Internet Users than Wired in Japan", *Infoworld*, 5 July, available at: www.infoworld.com/d/networking/more-mobile-internet-*users*-*wired*-in-japan-259 (accessed 7 July 2014).

Yoshi (2003a) *Deep Love Kanzen Dai Ni Bu ~ Hosuto* (Deep Love Complete Edition Part 2: Host), Tokyo: Starts Publishing.

Yoshi (2003b) *Deep Love ~ Reina No Unmei* (Deep Love: Rena's Fate), Tokyo: Starts Publishing.

Yoshi (2003c) *Deep Love Tokubetsu Han: Pao No Monogatari* (Deep Love Special Edition: Pao's Story), Tokyo: Starts Publishing.

Yoshi and Yoshii, Y. (2004) *Deep Love ~ Ayu no Monogatari* (Deep Love: Ayu's Story), Tokyo: Kōdansha.

29

WHERE THE STAKES ARE HIGHER

Transnational Labor and Digital Gambling Media

César Albarrán-Torres

Introduction

The rise, fall, and ultimate comeback of online gambling has been an important, yet often unacknowledged, episode of the history of the Internet. Casual players from Western developed countries have gambled online since the Internet became widely available for household use in the mid-1990s (Ridley 1996; Borch 2009). Wagering activities such as online poker, digital roulette, slots, and sports betting soon took hold of online spaces. The Internet allowed for users in different locations to play each other in real time, as well as an unprecedented 24/7 availability of gambling in domestic spaces. Suddenly, consumers did not have to travel to the casino or local gambling venue in order to play.

Online casinos disrupted cultural notions of gambling, and soon became controversial due to worries around addiction. Large player pools formed in developed countries such as the United States and the United Kingdom, even though digital gambling was, and remains, for the most part, illegal in those jurisdictions. For their more permissive (and sometimes underdeveloped) legal frameworks and looser labor regulations, developing countries became the site for the material establishment of the online gambling industry—and I will explain why in this chapter.

The development of hardware and software that allows user communication in real time, as well as the unstable legal and jurisdictional apparatuses that support online gambling, have been two crucial elements that tie online gambling to grander narratives in the Internet's path to global dissemination. Internet gambling is a prime example of how longstanding cultural practices and industries adapted to online spaces, traversing spatial and jurisdictional borders. This chapter will focus on such processes of adaptation, with a particular emphasis on the legal and labor issues that emerged from the expansion of online gambling practices in developed countries and the hosting of casino servers in developing nations. The study of the global infrastructure and chains of labor that support online gambling platforms is a big gap in current research on online casinos. I argue that the lack of academic work on the processes involved in the sustenance of gaming platforms diminishes our understanding of online casinos as complex transnational networks of labor and digital media.

The current chapter supports these claims by describing and analyzing a concrete case study: the online casinos set up in the Central American country of Costa Rica in the early 2000s, and the government's 2011 regulatory response to even up a disadvantageous situation in which foreign companies paid little or no taxes and offered precarious employment to locals (Asamblea Legislativa de la República de Costa Rica 2011). I argue that a fruitful way of recording the manifold histories of online gambling as digital media is complementing existing research by exploring the conflicts and ethical concerns that result from the "developed world/emerging nations" dichotomy that appears to be present in the history of Internet gambling.

Online Gambling: Current and Future Research Agendas

Despite being a multi-billion-dollar industry (Fiedler and Wilcke 2011) of considerable social significance in the Western world, online gambling has rarely been approached by media and cultural studies scholars. Internet historians have also largely ignored gambling as a driving force behind the expansion of digital networks, online communities, and technological development. This is not the case with other online media practices that are generally deemed as pernicious but culturally relevant. Internet pornography, for example, has received much scholarly attention and been recognized as a key element of online communities and practices (on its history, logistical complexity, and cultural significance, see Jacobs and Janssen 2007). The illegal duplication and distribution of copyrighted content has also produced valuable cultural studies research, such as Shujen Wang's volume *Framing Piracy: Globalization and Film Distribution in Greater China* (2003) or Ramón Lobato's book *Shadow Economies of Cinema: Mapping Informal Film Distribution* (2012).

The complexity of online gambling as media should not be underestimated or overlooked by researchers interested in transnational media ecologies. As John Farnsworth and Terry Austrin state, digital gambling practices such as online poker typify "common patterns of interaction across traditional and new media, as well as mass and personal media forms" (2010: 110). Studying online gambling can shed light on other digital media forms such as video games, virtual worlds, and even financial tools, and how these are made possible through complex processes of creativity and labor.

There are very notable exceptions of scholars who have studied online gambling seriously, particularly from sociology, cultural studies, and political science. We can think, for example, of Fiona Nicoll's work on the intersections of finance, traditional betting, digital gambling, and power, or what she calls "finopower" (2013); Gerda Reith's thorough cultural history *The Age of Chance: Gambling in Western Culture*, published in 1999, before digital gambling became a widespread phenomenon, but that nevertheless forecasts the disruptive nature of the new medium; Thomas Malaby's analysis of economic dynamics and gambling in virtual environments (2006); James Cosgrave's 2006 collection *The Sociology of Risk and Gambling Reader*, or Rebecca Cassidy, Andrea Pisac, and Claire Loussouarn's 2013 book *Qualitative Research in Gambling: Exploring the Production and Consumption of Risk*, which begins to investigate the negotiations between traditional forms of gambling and new game delivery models, such as social casino gaming and mobile apps.

Most of this research focuses, however, on understanding industry dynamics and consumption in developed countries. Much journalistic and some scholarly attention has been placed on the consumption of online wagering, with a particular emphasis on problem gambling and addiction in industrialized Western countries such as Australia, Canada, Italy, the United Kingdom, and the United States (LaPlante *et al.* 2008; Griffiths *et al.* 2010; Griffiths

2013; McGrath Goodman 2014). Other scholars such as Ole Bjerg (2011) and Cosgrave and Klassen (2001) have theorized parallels between digital and land-based gambling and capitalism, but without fully acknowledging the ethical concerns raised by how online wagering is made possible through chains of potential corruption and precarious labor (a notable lack in Bjerg's Marxian approach). Others have analyzed the problematic irruption of online gambling in domestic spaces through desktop computers (Borch 2009) or in public spaces through mobile devices (Albarrán-Torres and Goggin 2014).

The development of online gambling has been quite serendipitous due to conflicting regulatory schemes and cultural attitudes towards commodified risk, which may explain the lack of scholarship on its labyrinth-like history (legal studies have, however, approached this issue; see Lycka 2011). While some developed countries, such as the United Kingdom, allow citizens to gamble online but forbid the establishment of online casinos in their territory, others allow people to access online casinos but restrict advertising, as is the case in Australia (Wilson 2003; Lycka 2011; Laffey et al. 2015). In terms of their suitability for online gambling operations, some emerging economies offer lower (or zero) taxation on gambling and a higher predictability of taxes, cheaper labor, and oftentimes English-speaking staff, as is the case with the Caribbean islands of Antigua and Jamaica, and Central American nations like Belize and Costa Rica (Raventós and Zolezzi 2011: 301).

In order to truly understand global online gambling as a fundamental but unexplored aspect of global Internet histories, it is important to acknowledge the contrasting roles that developed and developing countries have had in the growth of this economic sector. As Gerard Goggin and Mark McLelland recognize, it is important "to describe, analyze, and theorize particular Internet forms, and how users are arranged, publics and audiences are created, and relations of consumption and production are reconfigured" (2010: 11).

Current literature on online gambling focuses on these relations of consumption, but the transnational infrastructures required for its production remain for the most part hidden (for example, some gambling software is designed in the developed world, but hosted and operated elsewhere). It is also key to recognize the power differentials in this process, and the "very different shaping of 'big' and 'little' cultures of the Internet in particular contexts" (Goggin and McLelland 2010: 11). These "cultures of the Internet" also encompass the dynamics through which digital labor is sourced and maintained.

As mentioned, the history of online casinos has seen two parallel narratives: consumption in highly mediatized developed nations, and the problematical hosting of gambling platforms in emerging economies like Costa Rica. Online gambling is particularly popular in so-called Global North countries such as Austria, Canada, Finland, France, Italy, Spain, Sweden, the United States, and the United Kingdom (PokerScout 2013), even though not all these jurisdictions are fully regulated. It is important to note here that in non-Western gambling markets such as Macao and Singapore, governments have proved reluctant to accept online gambling, even though they host a buoyant terrestrial casino industry that rivals Las Vegas.

As it soon became apparent in the late 1990s that legislation and tax regimes in countries like the United States and the United Kingdom—as mentioned, two highly lucrative markets for unregulated online casinos—would not accommodate digital gambling platforms, most servers are located in offshore jurisdictions with lax regulations, such as Costa Rica, Malta, the Isle of Man, Gibraltar, Antigua, and Alderney in the Channel Islands (on Alderney, see Bowers 2012; Connell 2014). Thus, the vast, mostly unchartered and tangled network of online gambling extended all over the world, bringing together consumers in the developed world and service industries in emerging economies.

In many respects, these parallel histories resemble other cases in which digital media is presented as a sanitized, pristine product of the information era, even though its production oftentimes involves chains of borderline unjust labor and possible corruption in developing countries. The lack of general awareness of the production processes involved in the sustenance of digital media practices is not exclusive to online gambling. As happens with online casinos, the production of software and accompanying hardware devices is also seldom acknowledged by tech companies and consumers. As Robbie Fordyce and Luke van Ryn point out, for example: "The labor practices that surround the production of an Apple iPod, iPhone, or iPad remain largely undiscussed in the marketing of these commodities" (2014: 37). The absence of general understanding on how digital media experiences are made possible alienates the many individuals involved in the production of devices and software, and raises ethical concerns among the more conscientious consumers. The mythology of the digital era privileges stories surrounding creative software and hardware design, but generally ignores the material processes required to make these designs a reality.

Academics have discussed the somewhat invisible labor involved in the production of digital media experiences, which sheds some light on the direction that research on transnational digital gambling might take. Media scholars Jack Linchuan Qiu, Melissa Gregg, and Kate Crawford, for example, propose a framework called "Circuits of Labour", after the seminal cultural studies work of du Gay *et al.* on the cultural appropriation of technology. Qiu, Gregg, and Crawford argue that it is ethically fundamental to critically discuss the roles of production, bodies, and materiality as cornerstones of the information era. The case of online casinos is particularly relevant since the circuits of labor involved in their production and sustenance border illegality and, as we will see with the Costa Rican example, has historically depended on the murkiness of unsteady labor conditions.

Using the controversial manufacturing of Apple products in China as a case study, Qiu, Gregg, and Crawford argue that there exists a "global commodity chain" and an "unequal international division of labour" that must be scrutinized (Qiu *et al.* 2014). They also contend that:

> Even the least material forms of labor input—for instance, by employees of software or advertising companies—have a physical dimension: they have to position their bodies in front of the computers and/or telephones, and expect to remain so for certain hours of the day.
>
> (Qiu, Gregg, and Crawford 2014)

In the case of online gambling, forms of "least material" precarious labor include work in server maintenance, software design, and customer support in call centers, mostly staffed by women. Just like other digital enterprises such as software development (which increasingly sources work from emerging economies like India, as noted by Qiu, Gregg, and Crawford), the online gambling industry is not that weightless. Its untold history reveals numerous instances in which the technical infrastructures and regulatory systems that allow play seem to rely on a transnational network of production and consumption. On one end of this chain are hyper-mediated wealthy countries, on the other are emerging nations dependent on service industries.

The history of online casinos is populated with cases in which precarious labor in developing nations has made it possible for players in the developed world to gamble for real money. Brett Neilson and Ned Rossiter argue that "capital has always tried to shore up its own precariousness through the control of labour and, in particular, the mobility of labour" (2005).

As the epitome of ruthless capitalism, as "cathedrals of consumption" (Ritzer and Stillman 2001), online casinos rely on the mobility of labor, as servers have historically relocated around the globe to find more profitable arrangements.

The seemingly ethereal nature of online transactions has, nevertheless, real repercussions in the lives of citizens, as shown by the Costa Rican example discussed below. Online casino operations have perpetuated the image of developing countries, in particular Latin American nations, as an adult playground for Westerners. Here, another equally important example of the ways in which consumption in wealthy countries affect the less fortunate comes to mind. The Foxconn scandal, which involved the revelation of poor labor conditions and even suicides in factories manufacturing parts for Apple products, revealed the oftentimes problematic production processes involved in the sustenance of contemporary digital cultures (Qiu et al. 2014), of which online gambling has been part.

A Tale of Two Worlds: A Brief History of Online Casinos

Online gambling is a buoyant industry that has stayed afloat, despite massive crackdowns, for almost two decades. Online sports gambling first emerged in 1996, establishing operations in Caribbean islands like Antigua and Central American countries such as Costa Rica and Belize. The Caribbean islands were particularly attractive to early gambling entrepreneurs because they had a long history of serving as offshore financial centers, with technical and financial infrastructures well in place (Marshall 2008). The first online poker site to offer real money wagering was the now defunct Planet Poker, founded by the Canadian entrepreneur and poker player Randy Blumer. The inaugural hand was dealt on 1 January 1998. The site became commercially viable just a few months after its launch, but suffered severe problems due to technical shortcomings of current technological networks, such as poor dial-up connections, faulty software, and geographical limitations (Smith 2011). Real-time play proved difficult. In 1999, Paradise Poker (now Sportingbet) challenged Planet Poker's monopoly in the United States and Canada, and thus the relentless proliferation and ruthless competition of desktop-based online poker rooms began. Today, the number of sites is so vast and ever-changing that it is almost impossible to assess the exact number of gambling platforms that exist in the Internet and mobile networks (Farnsworth and Austrin 2010).

Although historically it has been hard to assess the size and reach of the online poker industry, in large part due to operations being set up in countries with murky legal waters, it is clear that it involves large numbers of casual players, mostly from North America and Europe. According to the results of a pioneering and, as of today, unique audit of online poker operators conducted by researchers from the University of Hamburg, in 2010 alone six million people engaged in online poker, suggesting a US\$3.61 billion take to the operators. These figures speak both of a greatly profitable industry and a vast network of users (Fiedler and Wilcke 2011). Ingo Fiedler and Ann-Christin Wilcke (2011) describe how "large player pools and the corresponding network effects have helped the game to grow to a size not to be matched in the offline world". The ten most popular online poker websites in the United States and Europe, according to the online poker traffic rank published by PokerScout (constantly used as a reference in the industry) are: PokerStars, 888 Poker, iPoker, Party Poker, Full Tilt Poker, PokerStars.it (Italy), Bodog, PokerStars.es (Spain), Winamax.fr (France), and Adjarbet (as of 27 March 2016; for an updated ranking, visit pokerscout.com).

As digital media forms, online gambling platforms have come a long way since Planet Poker dealt its inaugural hand in 1998. Planet Poker was a simple platform that presented a bird's-eye view of a poker table. Even though the game featured digital characters, their actions were limited, and play was constantly interrupted because of unreliable dial-up connections (Smith 2011). It was soon evident that online gambling operations for poker and sports betting would need dedicated servers and reliable infrastructures to be able to function. The technical requirements of online casinos soon made some countries, like Costa Rica, more desirable than others for the establishment of gambling companies.

The technical complexity of the transnational networks that make online gambling possible is only made evident when there is a service disruption. For example, in April 2014, a fire in Gibraltar's main power station rendered several online betting sites unable to operate for several hours, much to the desperation of both punters and gambling companies. Among those affected were the UK firms William Hill, Ladbrokes, Betfred, Stan James, and Betfair (Russell 2014). This case is significant as it exemplifies some of the complications that arise when technical infrastructures fail and become evident. Otherwise, for the most part they go unacknowledged internationally.

There are other factors that have turned online casinos into operationally complex networks. Since the mid-2000s, digital gambling has appropriated the production processes and aesthetic qualities of mainstream video games. It is only fitting that poker would expand its possibilities through digital technology, for, as Lev Manovich puts it, "games are one cultural form which requires algorithm-like behavior from the players" (2000: 180). The most advanced online gambling platforms are as technically and socially complex as virtual worlds like Second Life, which, contrary to online casinos, has been the subject of rigorous ethnographic studies (Boellstorff 2008; Parmentier and Rolland 2009). Better broadband connections, more powerful hardware, and increasingly sophisticated game engines have made these possible, and the improvements can be seen in online casinos such as PokerStars, 888, Bodog (poker.bodog.eu) and, most noticeably, in PKR, a mix between Second Life and standard online casinos.

As media, gambling platforms have evolved through their digitization. In the case of poker, for instance, gameplay has gone from being dependent on the materiality of cards and chips to being played on digital interfaces and through informational networks (Hoffer 2007). Where early games were a lonely endeavor, online poker has become an increasingly participatory medium. From being played secretly or with an air of lawlessness, online poker has generated its own cultures of celebrity and aspiration. Because the machines operate as both mediators and players, online poker has evolved from being a game predominantly defined by chance (even if skill is also involved), to one where skill is lauded. The complexity of online poker is defined by communicative acts that take place between humans brought together by non-human actors (machines), and between humans and machines. In complex online poker sites such as the Aldernay-based PKR, role-playing is core because gamblers are highly reliant on how their avatars express tells, bluffs, and emotions. This requires a complex technical infrastructure that spreads globally.

The global expansion of online gambling operations echoes gambling's own sprawling nature. The origins of modern poker, for example, lay in the pioneering drive of nineteenth-century America. Then, the Mississippi River served as a backdrop for a brewing gambling culture that was not devoid of certain drama. Fortunes were made and lost, and recently liberated slaves bet and lost their newly acquired freedom (Kelly 2006). Much as in today's Internet, some gamblers became professionals, and established cultural and financial networks that ran parallel to mainstream cultural assemblages. Poker became a widespread cultural practice in the southern United States in the late nineteenth century, particularly via its dissemination through riverboats on the Mississippi (Humphreys 2010: 494). Gamblers chose to bet on riverboats as they provided a jurisdictionally ambiguous space, much like the offshore physical location of the servers running today's online casinos.

Fear, Loathing, and Gambling in Costa Rica

Less than two years after the pioneering casino Planet Poker was established in 1998, there were approximately 125 online gambling operators established in Costa Rica (Raventós and Zolezzi 2011). These operators offered games such as online poker and digital roulette, as well as sports booking services. By then, these companies employed numerous Costa Ricans and generated a considerable amount of tax-free revenue.

Legal frameworks in Costa Rica were simply unprepared to deal with the trepid expansion of online casino operations. Because local regulations allowed online casino operators to register merely as "technology companies", it is hard to assess the real magnitude of the Costa Rican online casino industry. Costa Rica offers numerous advantages to overseas gambling companies, primarily a more robust technical infrastructure than other countries in the region (for a comprehensive history of the Internet in Costa Rica, see Siles 2008). As in other Latin American countries, the Costa Rican government sponsored Internet-related projects in the 1990s, as information technologies were seen as a key step towards the neoliberal ideal of progress (Siles 2012). In the mid-2000s, some commentators even forecasted a massive growth in the IT sector of the country, thanks to government support and openness, predicting the rise of the Tico Tiger (in reference to Ireland's rise into the Celtic Tiger in the early 2000s). However, these predictions turned out to be overly optimistic (Hoffmann 2004; Paus 2005).

In addition to its more stable infrastructure, US online casinos prefer Costa Rican call center workers because they can deal with a moderate Spanish accent (to cater to the Hispanic market in the United States), and they share a time zone with most online gamblers (Raventós and Zolezzi 2011: 301). Among hundreds, Costa Rica currently hosts the highly popular online casinos Luxury Casino, Royal Panda Casino, All Slots Casino, bet-at-home Casino, Bet365 Casino, and Betvictor Casino, all catering for the United States and Europe, and dealing in American dollars, Euros, and increasingly in the digital currency Bitcoin. Apart from online gambling operations, Costa Rica is also quickly becoming one of the prime tourist destinations for terrestrial gambling in America, with luxury boutique casinos opening near the most popular natural attractions that the country is famous for.

Popular culture depictions of the conflictive nature of offshore casino operations in Costa Rica have surfaced recently. In the summer of 2013, 20th Century Fox released the movie *Runner Runner*, which depicts Costa Rica as a safe haven for corruption and debauchery associated with online gambling. Local authorities and online casino personnel are portrayed as lazy, corrupt, and ignorant, summoning Hollywood clichés in its depiction of Latin American countries as full of "bandidos" and "greasers" (Stam and Spence 1983). Upon its release, groups in favor of the full legalization of gambling in the United States used the film to stress the need for a comprehensive legislative framework to regulate online gambling (Dreier 2013; Lewis 2013). It is worth noting that the movie was released just before the legalization of online casinos in some US states like New Jersey and Nevada later in 2013, a significant development in the power dynamics of the online gambling industry.

Online gambling operations in Costa Rica have faced numerous crackdowns that have affected the local economy and jeopardized hundreds of jobs, which renders the "circuits of labour" (Qiu *et al.* 2014) of gambling more visible. In 2006, for example, the online bookie service BetonSports was put at risk when its CEO, David Carruthers, was arrested in the

United States on charges of conspiracy, racketeering, and tax evasion (Raventós and Zolezzi 2011: 299). Online casinos constantly disappear or are moved to mirror sites when legislative or taxation regimes change in the territories where the servers are located, or when developed countries crack down on digital gambling operations. When there is a crackdown on gambling sites, some operators keep online casinos afloat by getting new domain names or moving servers, which shows the adaptability of digital gambling networks. As a user known as "Renee" wrote in the blog *Tight Poker* after 13 US online casinos (most of them set up in the Caribbean and Central America) were shut down in 2011, gambling operators find ways to endure:

> There is still hope for Internet poker since poker giants, and Internet gambling firms are still trying to find ways to survive. For example, as soon as the online poker sites were indicted, Bodog.com became Bodog.eu, and they would have definitely won over several thousands of players from the poker giants who were indicted.
>
> (Renee 2011)

In other words, the online gambling industry operates in a similar way to the sweatshops or *maquilas* of the fashion and technology industries, which simply move their operations to more suitable territories in terms of low taxes and precarious forms of labor. The 2006 and 2011 crackdowns put at risk the livelihoods of hundreds of Costa Ricans who relied on the online casino industry directly or indirectly. Crackdowns on online gambling sites in the United States reveal the precarious position of Costa Rican IT and call center workers.

In view of this disadvantageous arrangement, by 2009 Costa Rican lawmakers pushed for a thorough regulation of the industry through the proposed *Ley de Regulación de Apuestas, Casinos y Juegos de Azar* (Law for the Regulation of Bets, Casinos and Games of Chance) (Asamblea Legislativa de la República de Costa Rica 2011), which was written with the aid of the United States Department of Treasury, perhaps forecasting the gradual state-by-state legalization of online gambling in the United States. In this proposal, lawmakers claimed that half the global online gambling market was split between the Caribbean island of Antigua and Costa Rica, and that this should translate into tax revenue (Antigua's own struggles over the US ban on offshore gambling servers are chronicled in Cooper (2011) and Jackson (2012)). Legislators also stressed the fact that the online gambling industry provided jobs for the younger generation, and that these jobs should be kept in the country. Lawmakers acknowledged that the lack of regulation in online gambling operations allowed for criminal activities and ties to organized crime and terrorist organizations. The 2009 proposal also pointed to the fact that gambling companies registered as data-processing businesses, so it was difficult to identify illegal cash influxes. Costa Rica enjoys relative political stability compared to other Central American countries, which is why it was possible to promulgate such a law.

This law, then a stand-alone response to predatory investments, was approved in 2011, and had the following objectives:

a. To tax casinos and sports booking call centers, and use tax revenues for public safety and the fight against organized crime.
b. To offer basic regulation on casinos, bets, and games of chance.
c. To keep gambling from establishing ties to organized crime and drug cartels, and from financing terrorism.
d. To establish sanctions against those who do not abide by this law.[1]

What is also interesting and unique about the Costa Rican case is that these online casinos operate only for overseas users. Under Costa Rican law, citizens and permanent residents of the Central American country are not allowed to gamble in Costa Rican online casinos (in theory they could, however, gamble in overseas sites). The casinos block local IP addresses, and monetary transactions technically do not take place in Costa Rica, but overseas. When setting up shop in Costa Rica, gambling companies usually open bank accounts in nearby jurisdictions such as Bermuda or the Bahamas, so all transactions derived from gambling are processed elsewhere to abide by local laws.

The restrictions that the Costa Rican government puts on its own citizens when it comes to the consumption of online gambling are similar to the measures put into place by the Singaporean government to curb local gambling consumption in its highly profitable brick and mortar casinos. In Singapore (a country with high rates of digital media adoption), foreign visitors can freely enter the two main casino resorts, the immensely profitable World Sentosa and Marina World Sands, but citizens and permanent residents have to pay a costly entrance fee—in the vicinity of US$100 a day or US$2,200 a year. This charge is an effort to discourage gambling among the local population, who additionally has to pay copious tax on any winnings. Similarly, the Singaporean government has vowed to place strict regulations on online gambling (Watts 2013). Singaporean land venues are global gambling hubs, just like Costa Rican online casinos, but local consumption is highly regulated, which highlights the strictly service drive of the gambling industry in emerging economies.

Conclusion

This chapter is a pioneering, and thus exploratory, approach to highlighting the complex nature of digital gambling platforms as transnational media. Online gambling is made up of social, media, and technical networks (van Dijk 2012: 25) that bridge consumers in developing nations and workers in emerging economies. In order to keep up with the increasing amount of research on the labor processes involved in the procurement of digital cultures (Neilson and Rossiter 2005; Qiu et al. 2014), research on online gambling must look into how networks of labor and media interlock and adapt to cultural norms and legal regulations. The Costa Rican example discussed here reveals a power struggle between foreign investment and local laws, transnational business models, and local labor conditions in a country heavily reliant on service industries and foreign tourism. The regulatory framework put into place in Costa Rica highlights the unstable nature of labor conditions in some digital economies, and the necessity to discuss these critically.

Ultimately, this chapter is a call for action for future research on how digital gambling comes into being through transnational networks of production that generally involve precarious forms of labor in emerging economies. A big part of truly internationalizing Internet studies (Goggin and McLelland 2010) is acknowledging the "circuits of labour" (Qiu et al. 2014) involved in the production of digital commodities and entertainment. Only then will the comprehensive history of online gambling be told, and the chains of production needed to sustain online media consumption, as well as the digital precariat, be taken into account.

Note

1. Author's translation of the *Ley de Regulación de Apuestas, Casinos y Juegos de Azar* (Asamblea Legislativa de la República de Costa Rica 2011).

References

Albarrán-Torres, C., and Goggin, G. (2014) "Mobile Social Gambling: Poker's Next Frontier", *Mobile Media & Communication*, 2(1): 94–109.

Asamblea Legislativa de la República de Costa Rica (2011) *Ley de Regulación de Apuestas, Casinos y Juegos de Azar*, File 17.551.

Bjerg, O. (2011) *Poker: The Parody of Capitalism*, Ann Arbor, MI: University of Michigan Press.

Boellstorff, T. (2008) *Coming of Age in Second Life: An Anthropologist Explores the Virtually Human*, Princeton, NJ: Princeton University Press.

Borch, A. (2009) "Balancing Rules: Gambling Consumption at Home" in S. F. Kingma (ed.), *Global Gambling: Cultural Perspectives on Gambling Organizations*, London: Routledge, pp. 195–210.

Bowers, S. (2012) "Alderney, the Unlikely Hub for a Global, Online Gambling Industry", *The Guardian*, 4 July, available at: www.theguardian.com/uk/2012/jul/04/alderney-hub-online-gambling

Cassidy, R., Pisac, A., and Loussouarn, C. (eds) (2013) *Qualitative Research in Gambling: Exploring the Production and Consumption of Risk*, New York, Routledge.

Connell, J. (2014) "Alderney: Gambling, Bitcoin and the Art of Unorthodoxy", *Island Studies Journal*, 9(1): 69–78.

Cooper, A. F. (2011) *Internet Gambling Offshore: Caribbean Struggles Over Casino Capitalism*, Basingstoke: Palgrave Macmillan.

Cosgrave, J. (2006) *The Sociology of Risk and Gambling Reader*, New York: Routledge.

Cosgrave, J., and Klassen, T. R. (2001) "Gambling Against the State: The State and the Legitimation of Gambling", *Current Sociology*, 49(1): 1–15.

Dreier, H. (2013) "Online Poker Thriller 'Runner' Quickly Politicized", *Las Vegas Review Journal*, 5 October, available at: www.reviewjournal.com/business/casinos-gaming/online-poker-thriller-runner-quickly-politicized

Farnsworth, J., and Austrin, T. (2010) "The Ethnography of New Media Worlds? Following the Case of Global Poker", *New Media & Society*, 12(7): 1120–1136.

Fiedler, I., and Wilcke, A. (2011) "The Market of Online Poker", The University of Hamburg, *Social Science Research Network*, available at: http://papers.ssrn.com/sol3/papers.cfm?abstract_id=1747646

Fordyce, R., and van Ryn, L. (2014) "Ethical Commodities as Exodus and Refusal", *Ephemera: Theory & Politics in Organization*, 14(1): 35–55.

Goggin, G., and McLelland, M. (eds) (2010) *Internationalizing Internet Studies: Beyond Anglophone Paradigms*, London: Routledge.

Griffiths, M. D. (2013) "Social Gambling via Facebook: Further Observations and Concerns", *Gaming Law Review and Economics*, 17(2): 104–106.

Griffiths, M., Parke, J., Wood, R., and Rigbye, J. (2010) "Online Poker Gambling in University Students: Further Findings from an Online Survey", *International Journal of Mental Health and Addiction*, 8(1): 82–89.

Hoffer, R. (2007) *Jackpot Nation: Rambling and Gambling Across Our Landscape of Luck*, New York: Harper-Collins.

Hoffmann, B. (2004) *The Politics of the Internet in Third World Development: Challenges in Contrasting Regimes with Case Studies of Costa Rica and Cuba*, London: Routledge.

Humphreys, A. (2010) "Semiotic Structure and the Legitimation of Consumption Practices: The Case of Casino Gambling", *Journal of Consumer Research*, 37(3): 490–510.

Jackson, S. (2012) "Small States and Compliance Bargaining in the WTO: An Analysis of the Antigua-US Gambling Services Case", *Cambridge Review of International Affairs*, 25(3): 367–385.

Jacobs, K., and Janssen, M. (eds) (2007) *C'lickme: A Netporn Studies Reader*, Amsterdam: Institute of Network Cultures.

Kelly, J. (2006) "Poker: The Very American Career of the Card Game You Can Learn in 10 Minutes and Work On for the Rest of Your Life", *American Heritage*, 57(6).

Laffey, D., Della Sala, V., and Laffey, K. (2015) "Patriot Games: The Regulation of Online Gambling in the European Union", *Journal of European Public Policy*, pp. 1–17.

LaPlante, D. A., Schumann, A., LaBrie, R. A., and Shaffer, H. J. (2008) "Population Trends in Internet Sports Gambling", *Computers in Human Behavior*, 24(5): 2399–2414.

Lewis, H. (2013) "'Runner Runner': Gambling Groups Use Ben Affleck Film to Push for Online Supervision", *The Hollywood Reporter*, 23 August, available at: www.hollywoodreporter.com/news/runner-runner-gambling-groups-use-613663

Lobato, R. (2012) *Shadow Economies of Cinema: Mapping Informal Film Distribution*, Basingstoke: Palgrave Macmillan.

Lycka, M. (2011) "Online Gambling: Towards a Transnational Regulation?", *Gaming Law Review and Economics*, 15(4): 179–195.

McGrath Goodman, L. (2014) "How Washington Opened the Floodgates to Online Poker, Dealing Parents a Bad Hand", *Newsweek*, 14 August, available at: www.newsweek.com/2014/08/22/how-washington-opened-floodgates-online-poker-dealing-parents-bad-hand-264459.html

Malaby, T. (2006) "Parlaying Value Capital In and Beyond Virtual Worlds", *Games and Culture*, 1(2): 141–162.

Manovich, L. (2000) "Database as a Genre of New Media", *AI & Society*, 14(2): 176–183.

Marshall, D. D. (2008) "Gaining Fluency in Finance: Globalisation/Financialisation and Offshore Financial Centres", *Contemporary Politics*, 14(3): 357–373

Neilson, B., and Rossiter, N. (2005) "From Precarity to Precariousness and Back Again: Labour, Life and Unstable Networks", *Fibreculture*, 5.

Nicoll, F. (2013) "Finopower: Governing Intersections Between Gambling and Finance", *Communication and Critical/Cultural Studies*, 10(4): 385–405.

Parmentier, G., and Rolland, S. (2009) "Les Consommateurs des Mondes Virtuels: Construction Identitaire et Expérience de Consommation dans Second Life", *Recherche et Applications en Marketing*, 24(3): 43–56.

Paus, E. (2005) *Foreign Investment, Development, and Globalization: Can Costa Rica Become Ireland?*, Basingstoke: Palgrave Macmillan.

PokerScout (2013) *PokerScout*, available at: www.pokerscout.com/

Qiu, J. L., Gregg, M., and Crawford, K. (2014) "Circuits of Labour: A Labour Theory of the iPhone Era", *TripleC: Communication, Capitalism & Critique*, 12(2): 564–581.

Raventós, P., and Zolezzi, S. (2011) "Sportsbooks and Politicians: Place Your Bet!", *Journal of Business Research*, 64(3): 299–305.

Reith, G. (1999) *The Age of Chance: Gambling in Western Culture*, London: Routledge.

Renee (2011) "What's Left of US Online Poker After Black Friday and Black Tuesday", *Tight Poker*, 2 June, available at: www.tightpoker.com/news/what%E2%80%99s-left-of-us-online-poker-after-black-friday-and-black-tuesday-2592

Ridley, S. (1996) "You Can Bet on It", *Internet.au*, 13: 41–45.

Ritzer, G., and Stillman, T. (2001) "The Modern Las Vegas Casino-Hotel: The Paradigmatic New Means of Consumption", *M@ n@ gement*, 4(3): 83–99.

Russell, B. (2014) "Most Online Betting Services Back to Normal Following Gibraltar Blaze", *Express*, 21 April, available at: www.express.co.uk/news/uk/471487/Fuel-explosion-in-Gibraltar-causes-huge-fire-and-disrupts-online-betting-sites

Siles, I. G. (2008) *Por un Sueño En. Red. Ado. una Historia de Internet en Costa Rica (1990–2005)*, San Jose, CA: Editorial UCR.

Siles, I. (2012) "Establishing the Internet in Costa Rica: Co-optation and the Closure of Technological Controversies", *The Information Society*, 28(1): 13–23.

Smith, E. (2011) "Planet Poker Era", *Poker History*, 10 August, available at: www.pokerhistory.eu/history/planet-poker-first-online-poker-room

Stam, R., and Spence, L. (1983) "Colonialism, Racism and Representation", *Screen*, 24(2): 2–20.

van Dijk, J. (2012) *The Network Society: Social Aspects of New Media*, Thousand Oaks, CA: Sage.

Wang, S. (2003) *Framing Piracy: Globalization and Film Distribution in Greater China*, Lanham, MD: Rowman & Littlefield.

Watts, J. M. (2013) "Singapore Looks to Restrict Online Gambling", *The Wall Street Journal*, 3 December, available at: http://blogs.wsj.com/searealtime/2013/12/03/singapore-looks-to-restrict-online-gambling/

Wilson, M. (2003) "Chips, Bits, and the Law: An Economic Geography of Internet Gambling", *Environment and Planning A*, 35(7): 1245–1260.

30

THE EMERGENCE OF VERNACULAR DIGITAL MUSIC CULTURES

Andrew Whelan

Many of the ways that remediation via network technology is now understood are given, in part, by the established narratives of the encounter between music and technology, especially from the late 1990s onward. This encounter provides a kind of benchmark to which more recent developments can be indexed. It functions as a template for understanding conflict around emerging technologies and imagining and anticipating the roles, attributes, and temperaments of the various players in such conflict. These include software developers (open-source or otherwise), "new" media entrepreneurs and start-ups, Internet service providers (ISPs), "old" or established media industry interests, their lobbyists, and their legal representation, creative labor, and the audience (both commonly imagined as young, cool, and technologically savvy), consumer advocacy and civil liberties campaigners, state regulatory entities, the more remote international standardization and legal oversight bodies (such as the International Standards Organisation), and so on. The communication channels between these various social worlds, and the affordances of the digital media environment for the development of new forms of value, new directions of financial flow, and new marketing opportunities in a context of surveillance and big data, are similarly foreshadowed in the music/technology narrative.

Given this import, it is worth reflecting on how this narrative is told. It is always seductive to think in terms of "eras" or "epochs". Decades, for instance, although essentially arbitrary, are definitional means of referring to social and cultural formations that are both very broad— "the 60s"—and at exactly that same juncture, oddly narrow. "The 60s" might evoke Swinging London or Apollo 11; it probably means rather different things to the average Kazakh or Mauritian.

It is similarly broad and narrow when, in a representative account of the history of music online, Marcus Boon (2013: 12) breaks down "the age of Napster (1999–2002), the age of Rapidshare and Megaupload and music blogs (2004–9), and that of Bit Torrent (2008–?)", as though these were all neatly discrete. Prior to 1999, the implication seems to be that there was nothing (or at any rate, nothing worth mentioning). These "ages", though, are discontinuous and cumulative; their borders imprecise. Temporality and technology do not march neatly on in lockstep, and both are moreover distributed across economically and culturally distinct social and geographical spaces. Often ostensibly antiquated technologies co-exist with much more recent forms, and moreover continue, sometimes in profound ways, to influence and shape the practices and understandings brought to bear on and through newer technologies. Media ecologies appear to accrete, rather than cleanly supplanting one another.

The standard and often repeated ways of presenting versions of events thus imply, and in a sense impose, a kind of "tempocentricity" (a normalization of the present as the morally correct position for evaluating past phenomena), alongside a particular historical linearity: first one thing happens, and then another thing happens, and similar such things pile up sequentially until we get to where we are now.

Part of the case presented in this chapter is that such histories are partial, and that this partiality can have unproductive consequences for our grasp of the relations between events and the effects of those relations on our current context. The most interesting things about such histories are often what, of necessity, they omit. There is another fundamental issue, though, which should be attended to here. The repetition of specific elements in the music/technology narrative tends to sediment tacit preconceptions: about what music is as a form and as a set of practices, which technologies are to be considered pertinent to it, and how exactly music and technology and their relations are to be understood. It is, to some extent, inevitable that these histories should have this consequence, but it nonetheless warrants care and attention.

For these reasons, this chapter does not offer a standard sequential history of the emergence of digital music, or of the antecedent cultures of music production, distribution, and consumption on the Internet. The conventional way of telling the history of music online assembles various pertinent elements into a coherent narrative. These elements can be given varying degrees of emphasis, as elaborated below. Rather than impose an apparently temporalsequence, this chapter works "around" some of the central dynamics and processes of music online so as to highlight how the standard histories work to legitimate or obscure particular sets of concerns. I will first describe some of the common elements constituting the conventional narrative of music online, before attending specifically to two particularities of the relation between music and technology that tend commonly to be muted or overlooked altogether.

The first of these particularities I will refer to as "configurations of practice", by which I mean approaches to recorded music and cultures of music distribution and access, which exhibit continuities and similarities across times, spaces, and media formats. These continuities are often downplayed; they undercut the "newness" of online music and the rhetoric of online distribution as a rupture or disjunction with that which preceded it. Similarly, the effects of digital music on particular subcultures (as opposed to particular markets) are commonly lauded for their consequences for communities of fans (Baym and Ledbetter 2009; Bennett 2011; O'Reilly and Doherty 2006). Music listeners are often described as "speaking back" to Big Media, seizing control of the means of music distribution, engaging directly (in a fashion imagined as oddly immediate or unmediated) with each other and musicians, and so on (for example, see Jenkins 2006; Kibby 2000). According to these sorts of perspectives, we can embrace online music distribution as in some way politically progressive—a kind of radical consumer sovereignty is endorsed as itself politically redemptive, which is perhaps informative about current understandings of the political. Generally, such framing paradoxically tends to reinforce perceptions of music-as-a-commodity, obscuring from view the vast swathes of leisure, "amateur", or niche music production, distribution, and consumption conducted online. These practices are embedded in specific contexts and cultures of music making and sharing, and should not be understood as spontaneously emergent consequences of technological access; the digital liberation of music-as-a-commodity. These are configurations of practice, which have richer and longer histories than ordinarily assumed.

I will refer to the second of these particularities as the "sociability of digital audio". "Sociability" in this context refers in more than one way. It is not only that strangers often connect with each other, albeit sometimes in a "drive-by" manner, in their shared projects around finding, making, and engaging with music in various ways, such that music is an engine of human sociability. This kind of framing of the sociability of digital music holds digital music as a stable or constant entity, which nonetheless triggers, or, at the least, affords forms of social action around it.

The sociability of digital audio implies not only that music is disembedded, lifted out of previous material and cultural contexts. Music online is highly elastic or "explodable". It separates out, disaggregates at base levels, and recombines in unexpected ways. As I will go on to show, vernacular online music cultures have historically been evidenced in the circulation of discrete and quite miniature audio elements in digital format. This disaggregation of sounds seems to influence musical grammars. This should not be understood as an observation about musical "quality": "more" or "faster" is not necessarily "better" or "worse". Rather, musics encounter each other online at multiple scales and thereby proliferate: digital audio is sociable.

With the objective in mind of an historical overview of music on the Internet from the mid-1980s onward, there is a range of ways in which the standard account could be expressed: across regions or generations; within different genres or subcultures; within national and global markets, industries, and media firms; across copyright and legal regimes; within social contexts with varying access to flows of media content, and so on.

One version would be a history of formats, narrated with reference to file name extension suffixes—aiff, mp3, ra, flac, ogg, etc.—and their adoption, diffusion, and commercial integration. This story highlights the intersections between technics and aesthetics. It is ostensibly a narrative of technological development: proliferating formats emerge and circulate, designed with various technical affordances in mind: file size, media player compatibility (or non-compatibility, in the interests of locking in consumers or "blackboxing" the audio and its potential uses), streaming vs. storage usage, levels of proprietary control (such as digital rights management or DRM), fidelity, and so on. At the same time, this is a narrative inflected by affective cultural claims about the veracity and more importantly the *authenticity* of format: where vinyl is said to be "warm", the lingua franca digital music format, mp3, is described as "lossy".

As a proprietary licensed standard, the mp3 (Moving Picture Experts Group, Audio Layer 3) was originally developed in the late 1980s by a team of electrical engineers led by Karlheinz Brandenburg at the Fraunhofer-Institut for Integrated Circuits in Erlangen, a research entity funded by the German government. The standard draws on long histories of investigation in psychoacoustics and electrical engineering, going back to telephone architecture research conducted in the interwar period at Bell and AT&T (see Denegri-Knott and Tadajewski 2010). The mp3 encoder was released commercially in 1994. The format exploits a psychoacoustic phenomenon known as "auditory masking". This phrase refers to how the human ear's capacity to recognize one sound can be influenced by the presence of another sound. The format uses a compression algorithm to omit sound ranges inaudible to the human ear in the interests of producing a compact and therefore transmissible digital file—hence "lossy". The format affords a variety of rates of compression measured in kilobytes per second or kbps: 320kbps is high (it occupies more space as data and retains more of the original range of sound); 92kbps is low. The VBR (variable bitrate) codec is particularly efficient: it converts audio according to the information density in the original recording, allocating higher kbps to complex or "busy" moments in an audio file so as to retain data quality and thus fidelity.

In specific contexts (such as over a sound system), the lossiness of mp3 is widely held to impact on depth of tone and crispness, particularly at the low end. DJs favour lossless digital formats such as .wav or AAC (Advanced Audio Coding), and are generally reluctant to play mp3s below 320kbps at events. Lower bitrates generate noticeable acoustic artifacts, especially if the file is manipulated (for instance, slowed down) in real time.

The mp3 is in some respects a private format, best experienced in isolation, through headphones. The format is also subject to degradation over time and through extensive duplication: mp3 files can come to exhibit various audible forms of digital file corruption. For audio cultures interested in the aesthetic properties of formats (in the tradition of tape manipulation and looping, or sampling from and scratching vinyl), this has presented new creative possibilities, such as "bitcrushing": repeatedly re-encoding mp3s at low bitrate to degrade the acoustic quality of the file. Some musicians set their audio software to record at very low bitrates, to accentuate the effects of low-quality encoding and foreground the format itself as a carrier with aesthetic attributes (see, for instance, the Microbit Records netlabel, which releases lobit music exclusively; 64kbps is the maximum permitted).

Among the lossless options, flac as a commercial format (a format one could pay to download music in) is marketed as "CD-like" in its accuracy. The high-fidelity format is the one that makes itself inaudible, a perfectly transparent container. The trade-off with lossless formats is in file size, and in addition, consequently, bandwidth. This version of the narrative of music online, the history of format, indexes audiophilic preoccupations which expose both the increasingly close alignment between technological and aesthetic form characteristic of digital media culture, and the reliance on previous formats as both standards of quality and as aesthetically charged and privileged parameters of form (the 12-inch single, the 78, the C60 cassette). For instance, the three-minute pop tune is largely a consequence of the limit set by the vinyl single. Although there is no longer any formal limit in either direction for a piece of popular music (barring radio airplay, which is beyond the reach of the vast majority of music being produced or already in circulation), most popular music remains, in terms of duration, within time spans set by previously dominant formats.

Perhaps less commonly considered, the history of digital music could be written as a story of ever-cheaper computer memory, mass storage devices, and increasingly accessible broadband. Digital music is "virtual", composed, as it were, of zeros and ones, but beyond the rhetoric of the cloud, and the formats and playback software it encounters, it requires hardware: hard drives, servers, routers, and the rest. Downloading four or five songs on a dial-up modem in the early 2000s took hours, with a maximum possible speed of 56kbps (as was ordinary for domestic access in Europe or the USA at that time). With a broadband connection, one can easily download more music than time can be found with which to listen to it. Correspondingly, this implies having a "place" to store all of this audio data: an external drive. In this way, the diminishing revenue streams previously flowing towards the big three record labels are sometimes said to have been diverted towards ISPs and the consumer electronics companies who produce mass storage devices. In some cases (such as Sony), the self-same corporations appeared both to lose out to file-sharing (content) and benefit from it (hardware).

More specifically still, this version can be told as a story about vertical integration, lock-in, and market monopoly, in the form of the iTunes media manager, the iTunes Store, the iPod, and, latterly, the iPhone. While it has always been possible to load music from other sources into iTunes and transfer it to an iPod or iPhone, and although Apple finally abandoned DRM for music in 2009, the pivotal role of Apple in normalizing digital music globally cannot be understated (see Arditi 2014). The iTunes Store opened in 2003; it has been the world's largest retail provider of music since 2010. The format the iTunes Store sells in, AAC, cannot be played on devices other than those manufactured by Apple. Apple devices also cannot play some media formats without conversion, notably the open-source format ogg and the Windows format wma. Consumer advocacy groups in Norway, Finland, Sweden, Denmark, France, Germany, and the UK have disputed Apple's end-user license agreement.

Another version of the history of digital music would concern itself with file-sharing distribution platforms: this story is often told as a kind of enclosure narrative littered with the headstones of peer-to-peer platforms. The list of such sites is long and doleful, including but not limited to: MP3.com (closed 2000), Napster (closed 2001), Audiogalaxy (2002), ShareReactor (2004), LokiTorrent (2005), Kazaa (2006), Razorback2 (2006), Demonoid (2007), OiNK's Pink Palace (2007), Morpheus (2008), TorrentSpy (2008), Foxy (2011), and so on. Successive closures of platforms commonly entail mass migrations, of thousands or in some instances tens of thousands of users, and in some cases considerable disruptions to online communities invested in particular genres, as when users struggle to find each other again on the "new" platform (if indeed there was a consensus as to where to go), with perhaps slightly different user names, and so on (Whelan 2008).

This trajectory runs parallel to the transition, effected more or less successfully, from "piracy" to legitimate business on the part of some of the developers who produced the early file-sharing programs. The original peer-to-peer brands continue to generate revenue. Electronics retailer Best Buy purchased Napster for $121 million in 2008. The first Korean file-sharing site, Soribada, remains the largest, having become a subscription service in 2006. This followed the site's closure by court order in 2002. Soribada is now one of the biggest online music distributors in Korea (see Lee 2005).

A perverse consequence of the broader context of media ownership is that software code and legal code have here moved in unison, mutually propelling each other forward into more ingenious and byzantine logics. Legal formulations galvanize coders to develop software that will evade legal capture or neatly occupy loopholes in the currently existing legal framework. In turn, these advances in software lead the pursuing legal campaign to develop more closed and exhaustively stringent definitions of terms (such as "making available"), in an effort to close the gap (Burk 2014). The imposition of these "reformed" copyright regimes on im-poverished communities outside the Global North is often pernicious, and also indicative of the role historically played by copyright in enforcing marketized ideas of personhood and property (Sundaram 2009).

Copyright-holding bodies went to extraordinary lengths in advancing specific and legally consequential definitions of the musical work as a kind of property (in some jurisdictions it was suggested, for example, that second-hand CD sales should also be criminalized, and in one notable instance that perhaps even *throwing away* a CD could be infringing). The Recording Industry Association of America in particular came to be represented as absurdly litigious. The strategy of suing consumers for sharing music carried disastrous public relations consequences. Various national and international copyright reform strategies were pursued (SOPA, PIPA, ACTA; see Carrier 2013), with copyrights extended and legal powers enforced. In several countries (France, the UK, Ireland, New Zealand), "graduated response" or "three strikes" systems were inaugurated, such that subscribers risk being disconnected by their ISPs if they are found to have persistently made material available online, after having received cease and desist letters from copyright holders. These systems imply close cooperation between ISPs and rights holders: close enough that ISPs would be essentially required to surveil their subscribers on behalf of rights holders, terminating contracts where they are obliged to do so.

This legal history would also describe the emergence of a shadowy world of inter-mediary corporate surveillance and network disruption, where independent companies with names like Web Sheriff and MediaSentry, working on commission or contracted by the major labels, engage in "spoofing" or "decoying": distributing spam or bogus files (in one noted case, mp3s consisting of silence or static, labeled with the track titles of a current Madonna album) in order both to track their movement, and to flood the network with useless "noise". Other monetization strategies include "copyright trolling"; where legal entrepreneurs aggregate the rights for obscure or orphan content and offer them up to litigators, and "spamigation" or "speculative invoicing". The latter involves collecting IP data from file-sharing sites and then mass mailing file-sharers, threatening them with court proceedings and offering an out-of-court payment as a means of settlement (Lobato and Thomas 2012). The skirmishes which the secretive companies in this curious but lucrative sector of the tech/law area have had with hackers have been informative; for instance, in 2007 leaked emails from MediaDefender demonstrated that the major labels quite sensibly (given that p2p users are the most active music fans), albeit covertly, use p2p surveillance data for market research purposes:

> Nicole from pussy cat dolls has a single called "whatever u like". It's not selling well on itunes or playing that great on radio. A song called "Baby Love" just leaked (I don't know how long ago). Interscope wants to know if Baby Love is picking up steam on p2p. They need to make a decision by early next week on whether they should switch to this song as the single. Please get me a score comparison on Monday for these two tracks. Also, please put beyonces, fergie, gwen, and nelly furtado singles as comparisons.
>
> (Enigmax and Ernesto 2007)

This rather undercuts the assertion on the part of the majors that there could be no non-infringing use for p2p.

At the other extreme from this industry of "security", established and run with massive funding from the major players in the content industries, is the international "warez scene", and notable in this context, the "mp3 scene". The warez scene (as in "softwarez") emerged in the early 1980s, a piracy subculture with a complex social hierarchy and an elitist competitive ethos, devoted to "cracking" or removing copy protection from software and then releasing it (Reunanen et al. 2015). The mp3 scene which emerged from this consists of different "crews" who compete with each other to rip and release music and other media at or before its official release date—the phenomenon referred to as "0-day" or zero day. This can be understood as a kind of heroic gifting, after the model of heroic consumption advanced by Evan Eisenberg: "The true hero of consumption is a rebel of consumption. By taking acquisition to an ascetic extreme he repudiates it, and so transplants himself to an older and nobler world" (1988: 15). The gifts produced by mp3 scene crews are not reciprocal. These crews generally hold the "lamers" of peer-to-peer in contempt, although peer-to-peer is the principal means by which they become famous. 0-day can be understood as a parallel iteration of the acquisitiveness and obsession associated with prior forms of engaging with musical materiality, specifically record collecting. While a website like Kick Ass Torrents (from which one might source links to downloadable content) generates significant revenue from advertising, the highly organized and secretive rip crews, who have for years been among the most significant sources of pirated content (one might say the "secondary" sources, one link away from the record labels, and often securing leaks and advance releases from inside the industry supply chain), are essentially engaged in economies of reputational and status competition (see Cooper and Harrison 2001; Huizing and van der Wal 2014; Whelan 2010).

Consider the Floppy Swop netlabel, based in Birmingham and active from 2001 to 2009. This netlabel released art, music, and text files; every release was 1.44 megabytes (mbs) or under in size: the precise size required to fit on a 3.5-inch floppy disk (www.floppyswop. co.uk/). Another netlabel, 4m@-records (pronounced "format", active from 2009 to 2012, www.proc-records.net/INDEX2.html), followed a similar restricted palette, but with a further specification: not only must the audio files of a given release be no more than 1.44mbs, but they must also be accompanied by an image file sized precisely at 198 x 153—the dimensions of a label that could be affixed to a floppy disk. Among the countless netlabels releasing music at no cost, these are two among several who follow this particular format. All the releases produced by these two labels, as is also quite common, are archived and remain freely available. Assertions that floppy disks sound "warmer" than mp3s are not commonly heard. What kind of nostalgia is this exactly?

The Fraunhofer Institute's original mp3 encoder was first made available on a floppy disk, although the "crack" by which it could be used indefinitely by anyone to rip CD audio to mp3 was originally circulated online in the warez scene, specifically, via Usenet and Internet Relay Chat in 1994. The first full, "pirated" copies of commercially released music in mp3 format, however, were circulated on floppy disks. According to Stephen Witt, a crew called CDA (Compress Da Audio; the acronym a play on the filename extension of CD audio as read by a Windows computer) produced and released the first rip, on 10 August 1996. It was a copy of the Metallica song "Until It Sleeps", distributed through the mail, as a compressed file on four 3.5-inch floppy disks (Witt 2015). This early "sneakernet" was not simply proof of concept. Floppy disks sent via snail mail had been the principal distributive system for the software crackers of the early warez scene. As late as 1996, transfer speeds and storage capacity rendered online exchanges of full mp3s implausible for ordinary users (US colleges, notably, provided broadband access to their students, the core early adopters of Napster).

Just as significantly, transmission via postal service was also simply how commercially released audio was (re-)distributed, especially in niche and DIY genres. In an interview with Simon Reynolds (2013), \m/etal\m/inx of the Sickness Abounds mp3 blog described her background in the tape-trading scene or "cassette underground" of the early 1980s:

> I'd buy Metal Forces, Maximumrocknroll, and any other zines I could find and attack the "pen-pal" sections something fierce! I really worked at it as if it was a full-time job. I had over 200 traders from around 30 countries by the time I was 16. We all referred to it as "The Underground." It was our P2P network, but without computers.

With hindsight, \m/etal\m/inx describes the underground with reference to p2p: older "network" forms come to appear "p2p-like". Essentially, the way it was before is the way it is now, "but without computers". Jonas Andersson memorably puts it like this: "the prime conceptual models through which we understand the world in a given era can be derived from the machinic metaphors of that era" (2009: 97 n.10). As with "Until It Sleeps" circulating on floppy disks, people were not remarking at that time on how annoying or simply odd it was that there was not yet p2p; the apparent inevitability is only given retrospectively.

The crucial point here is that these approaches to distribution, which became globally ubiquitous, arose from homologous configurations of practice across multiple media cultures. Through the 1980s, up until the mid- to late 1990s, avid music listeners (and a great many music producers), and devoted warez scene members, were exchanging media among themselves through the post (many certainly continue to do so). How we choose to tell this story is of consequence, as in the conventional narrative, the original mp3 scene rip crews are described as coming in a straightforward way out of warez; the practices of musical networks were supplanted—reinvented, even—by practices developed by networks of sophisticated technology users. The implication of this conventional narrative is that musical cultures are inert; digital technologies are dynamic and reconstitute the cultural practices around them. This is both empirically and conceptually dubious.

Telling the story in this way obscures the role played by recognizably similar configurations of practice across a very wide range of audio cultures, and also glosses the existence of active individuals who were members of both communities (that is, the warez scene, and the cassette underground). It is worth emphasizing this point because of the longstanding, and almost universal, occurrence of informal musical exchange in a variety of media formats, but especially on cassette, and ordinarily with tangential or at best "piratical" connections to formal markets. Cassette exchange has been pervasive in sub- and countercultural music scenes of the Global North (Harrison 2006; Novak 2013; Whitman 2005), but cassette cultures have been documented globally. There is recent work concerning the roles played by cassettes among the Sudanese diaspora (Impey 2013). International networks of cassette exchange played an important role in the 1979 Revolution in Iran (Sreberny-Mohammadi and Mohammadi 1994). The classic ethnomusicological research on cassette culture addresses the Indian subcontinent (Manuel 1993). Similar practices are documented elsewhere, in the absence of both the cassette and the Internet, as with Bluetooth transfer of audio files across mobile phones in the Saharan desert (Kirkley 2011), USB drive exchange in Cuba (Astley forthcoming), and mobile phone memory card circulation in Vanuatu (Stern 2014). Mobile phone ringtones (or rather, music produced, adapted, or formatted for ringtone compatibility) are increasingly popular, and are widely circulated among young people in localities as diverse as Japan (Manabe 2009) and Botswana (Lesitaokana forthcoming). It is safe to infer that similar configurations of practice exist elsewhere. These are social configurations, based around exchanges of the material musical media or carrier. Music here is not a private consumption good; its mobility is a vehicle of cohesion in social relationships.

Taking all of this on board, the assumption that audio cultures were somehow sitting around waiting for someone to invent the mp3 to massify their process, and that, more critically, the optimal form of exchange is essentially a pseudonymous or anonymous, any/many online transfer without further obligation or interaction seems short-sighted to say the least (see David 2010; Giesler 2006; Lessig 2004; McGee and Skågeby 2005).

That this assumption is so pervasive is perhaps connected to the romantic appeal of the story: illicit transfers, secretive rip crews, bad guy copyright enforcers, the liberation of music: a version of the digital sublime. As indicated above, the conventional story is unwittingly informative insofar as a kind of hyper-consumption is privileged as subversive and emanci- patory. A digital commons is to be constituted, a kind of performative, indirect public sphere, via an open archive and the cultural capital thereby instantiated. Unpaid access and content curation becomes a form of resistance, in a kind of militant, librarian politics (see, for example, Land 2007). Market logics for understanding practices around music media are thereby normalized as starting assumptions, and then promptly contradicted by the ordinary practices around music media we encounter in the world around us. We are thus obliged again to work out this riddle of why people are, apparently, suddenly doing something they shouldn't with musical commodities.

We can pursue this logic from the other end, so to speak, considering the musical forms and practices that originated in networked home computing culture. Where we do so, we can see specific features of the sociability of digital audio that are worth reflecting on, not least because of the context they provide for the issues raised above.

A 1985 copy of *PC Mag*, for example, discusses configuring a computer with PC-Talk III software so that it can receive commands for graphics and audio on signing onto BBSs, and mentions one bulletin specifically, on Pardue's BBS, which consists of "well over a minute's worth of computerized Bach" (Stone 1985: 262). If even compressed audio file size was prohibitively large for electronic transfer as late as 1996, how was it possible to listen to a rendering of Bach eleven years previously?

The answer to this question brings us to a distinction between form and content, and thereby to the transmission of form (specifically, code). This distinction is particularly important in understanding another grouping within the warez scene, the "demoscene", and the role that this community played in the development of music online. The warez were circulated with signature "cracktros", intros added by the crew who produced the crack, designed to demonstrate the technical prowess of the originating crew. This is the origin of the demoscene, a European phenomenon of the mid-1980s, where groups compete to produce the most sophisticated demos they can within the capabilities of a particular operating system (notably, the Commodore 64).

Demos were able to include sound because no audio data was actually transmitted. Where an mp3 is a "locked" file whatever its size, and is ordinarily simply played back (unless someone loads it into a software program in order to manipulate it), the music featured in early demos was generated by sets of instructions in code which, when executed, caused the receiving computer to produce sounds in a particular sequence in real time.

Music production for the demoscene gradually developed into a distinct subculture, which is now referred to as "MOD" or "tracker music". MOD refers to the file name extension for a "module file" on a Commodore computer. A MOD file contains a number of short audio samples, and instructions or a "pattern" for how and when those samples are to be played. MODs are produced with music sequencing programs called "trackers". A proto-tracker program called Soundmonitor was available as of 1986 for the Commodore 64. The first MOD tracker program, Ultimate Soundtracker, was released in 1987 for the Commodore Amiga. Shareware clones were soon circulating, notably ProTracker and NoiseTracker. Demoscene members still refer to what would ordinarily be called an album as a "musicdisk", a self-contained and stand-alone program and a collection of songs, possibly with graphics and other information. It is called a musicdisk because, again, these used to be circulated on 3.5-inch floppy disks. Not for the first time, the floppy, rather than the CD, appears as the precursor to the mp3.

The music so circulated was characteristically "bleepy", composed of the simple waveforms generated by 1980s sound chips. It is commonly referred to as "chiptune" (see, for instance, the 8bitpeoples label). As Anders Carlsson describes, however, tracker music is really grounded in the medium rather than the form (2008: 159–160). Tracker programs are used to produce many different styles of music. They are used extensively in electronic dance music (EDM) genres, and the historical significance of the demoscene for electronic music cannot be overstated. Several noted EDM producers of the 2000s and 2010s originated in the demoscene (for example, Bogdan Raczynski, Brothomstates, members of Infected Mushroom and Swedish House Mafia). There is an influential German EDM group called Atari Teenage Riot. In 2008, the hardcore label Noizetek put out an album called *The Final Amiga 500*

Battle, which was originally performed at a Minneapolis rave in 1997. This is not chiptune, but it utilizes the software developed in and by the demoscene.

Lynn Standafer is a well-known EDM producer, releasing under the name Enduser. He uses the Renoise tracker. As is customary, his online presence is spread across multiple locations. One of those is a website called Sellfy. Enduser uses Sellfy to sell downloadable sample packs. A sample pack is a collection of sounds for sequencing and composition. Sample packs are put together by musicians, by audio production software companies, and by members of the same communities who use them. The information for "end.user sample pack 5 (+ bonus set & extended drums)" reads:

> zip file is 211 mb
>
> audio samples to cut up and create with. there are one shots, sequenced breakbeats, synths, atmospheres ... as well as 2 longer drum tracks that have been extracted from tracks which represent what you can do with these sounds. feel free to cut any of it up and use it in your own compositions.
>
> in addition to the sample material, i have recently acquired a live end.user recording from john zorn's stone venue in new york city from 2005. thanks to kurt from ohm resistance for tracking that down.
>
> as always, thanks for the support.
>
> (Enduser 2015)

This is audio in a sociable form, sound produced in order to meet with other sounds in other contexts. From the beginnings of the demoscene, audio has been sociable in this way, produced first solely by code generating sound locally, and then expanding to incorporate the transmission of miniscule samples in module files, which could be opened and adapted by anyone with the appropriate software.

Enduser's sample packs are disaggregated audio, which will be hybridized in future encounters with other audio. Online music is therefore sociable with itself: it is fluid and promiscuous. These miniature sounds that constitute music online as a social practice, in a kind of competitive cottage industry of relatively closed "scenes", predate the encounter with disintermediated recorded music, the archive made available by people like \m/etal\m/inx. In this context, commercially released pieces of music come to be disarticulated from whatever musical and cultural framework they were originally intended for, and abrupt and unexpected juxtapositions and disruptions come to render established musical meanings unstable and increasingly contingent.

One curious aspect of this is a dual process around the "scale" of the musical field. Music producers and others with ready access to online resources and networks value sounds at what Richard Middleton (1990: 189) calls the musematic level (the level of the museme, the minimally meaningful unit of musical expression). These are sounds isolable in the way that a single snare sound or electronic blip or James Brown grunt is isolable. These sounds are in a sense musically atomic, and almost infinitely plastic. Music in its digital form thus becomes "microscopic". This process is simultaneous with an unprecedented increase in the availability of music. Somewhat vertiginously, music becomes both very big and very small online.

I have argued here that the way the story of music online is usually told tends to obscure important aspects of the history. Among such aspects, I have highlighted two. The first I have described as the configurations of practice around music sharing as a mediated social activity. These configurations are longstanding, durable, and open to encounters with new distributive forms and formats. The second I have referred to as the sociability of digital audio, by which I mean that music online "talks to itself", largely because, from its emergence, digital music has by design and affordance been miniature and open to manipulation and reassembly. These aspects are important to attend to, lest the contributions of critically important (but sometimes obscure) social formations and quite mundane technologies and systems (floppy disks, the postal service) disappear from view in the history of music online. This history is plural, and the present conjuncture is the culmination of multiple, intersecting, and ongoing trajectories.

Further reading

Burkart, P. (2014) *Pirate Politics: The New Information Policy Conflicts*, Cambridge, MA: MIT Press.
Sterne, J. (2012) *MP3: The Meaning of a Format*, Durham, NC: Duke University Press.
Wikström, P. (2013) *The Music Industry: Music in the Cloud*, Cambridge: Polity.

References

Andersson, J. (2009) "For the Good of the Net: The Pirate Bay as a Strategic Sovereign", *Culture Machine*, 10, available at: www.culturemachine.net/index.php/cm/article/view/346/359 (accessed 22 June 2009).

Arditi, D. (2014) "iTunes: Breaking Barriers and Building Walls", *Popular Music and Society*, 37(4): 408–424.

Astley, T. (forthcoming) "The People's Mixtape: Peer-To-Peer File Sharing Without the Internet in Contemporary Cuba", in A. Whelan and R. Nowak (eds), *Networked Music Cultures: Contemporary Approaches, Emerging Issues*, Basingstoke: Palgrave Macmillan, pp. 13–30.

Baym, N. K., and Ledbetter, A. (2009) "Tunes That Bind? Predicting Friendship Strength in a Music-Based Social Network", *Information, Communication and Society*, 12(3): 408–427.

Bennett, L. (2011) "Music Fandom Online: R.E.M. Fans in Pursuit of the Ultimate First Listen", *New Media & Society*, 14(5): 748–763.

Boon, M. (2013) "Meditations in an Emergency: On the Apparent Destruction of My MP3 Collection", in K. M. Moist and D. Banash (eds), *Contemporary Collecting: Objects, Practices, and the Fate of Things*, Plymouth: Scarecrow Press, pp. 3–12.

Burk, D. (2014) "Copyright and the Architecture of Digital Delivery", *First Monday*, 19(10), available at: http://firstmonday.org/ojs/index.php/fm/article/view/5544 (accessed 22 June 2015).

Carlsson, A. 2008, "Chip Music: Low-Tech Data Music Sharing", in K. Collins (ed.), *From Pac-Man to Pop Music: Interactive Audio in Games and New Media*, Aldershot: Ashgate, pp. 153–162.

Carrier, M. (2013) "SOPA, PIPA, ACTA, TPP: An Alphabet Soup of Innovation-Stifling Copyright Legislation and Agreements", *Northwestern Journal of Technology and Intellectual Property*, 11(2): 21–31.

Cooper, J., and Harrison, D. (2001) "The Social Organization of Audio Piracy on the Internet", *Media, Culture and Society*, 23(1): 71–89.

David, M. (2010) *Peer to Peer and the Music Industry: The Criminalization of Sharing*, Los Angeles, CA: Sage.

Denegri-Knott, J., and Tadajewski, M. (2010) "The Emergence of MP3 Technology", *Journal of Historical Research in Marketing*, 2(4): 397–425.

Eisenberg, E. (1988) *The Recording Angel: Music, Records and Culture from Aristotle to Zappa*, London: Picador.

Enduser (2015) "end.user sample pack 5 (+ bonus set & extended drums)", *Sellfy*, available at: https://sellfy.com/p/a729/ (accessed 2 July 2015).

Enigmax and Ernesto (2007) "Record Labels Use Piracy Data to Please Fans", *Torrentfreak*, 18 September, available at: https://torrentfreak.com/record-labels-use-piracy-data-to-please-fans-070918/ (accessed 22 June 2015).

Giesler, M. (2006) "Consumer Gift Systems", *Journal of Consumer Research*, 33(2): 283–290.

Harrison, A. K. (2006) "'Cheaper Than a CD, Plus We Really Mean It': Bay Area Underground Hip Hop Tapes as Subcultural Artefacts", *Popular Music*, 25(2): 283–301.

Huizing, A., and van der Wal, J. (2014) "Explaining the Rise and Fall of the Warez MP3 Scene: An Empirical Account from the Inside", *First Monday*, 19(10), available at: http://firstmonday.org/ojs/index.php/fm/article/view/5546 (accessed 24 June 2015).

Impey, A. (2013) "Keeping in Touch via Cassette: Tracing Dinka Songs from Cattle Camp to Transnational Audio-Letter", *Journal of African Cultural Studies*, 25(2): 197–210.

Jenkins, H. (2006) *Convergence Culture: Where Old and New Media Collide*, New York: New York University Press.

Kibby, M. D. (2000) "Home on the Page: A Virtual Place of Music Community", *Popular Music*, 19(1): 91–100.

Kirkley, C. (2011) "Music from Saharan Cellphones", *Sahelsounds*, available at: https://sahelsounds.bandcamp.com/album/music-from-saharan-cellphones (accessed 27 June 2015).

Land, C. (2007) "Flying the Black Flag: Revolt, Revolution and the Social Organization of Piracy in the 'Golden Age'", *Management and Organizational History*, 2(2): 169–192.

Lee, K. S. (2005) "The Momentum of Control and Autonomy: A Local Scene of Peer-To-Peer Music-Sharing Technology", *Media, Culture and Society*, 27(5): 799–809.

Lessig, L. (2004) *Free Culture: How Big Media Uses Technology and the Law to Lock Down Culture and Control Creativity*, New York: Penguin Press.

Lobato, R., and Thomas, J. (2011) "The Business of Anti-Piracy: New Zones of Enterprise in the Copyright Wars", *International Journal of Communication*, 5: 606–625.

McGee, K., and Skågeby, J. (2011) "Gifting Technologies", *First Monday*, special issue 1, available at: www.firstmonday.org/ojs/index.php/fm/article/view/1457 (accessed 3 August 2015).

Manabe, N. (2009) "Going Mobile: The Mobile Internet, Ringtones, and the Music Market in Japan", in G. Goggin and M. McLelland (eds), *Internationalizing Internet Studies: Beyond Anglophone Paradigms*, New York: Routledge, pp. 316–332.

Manuel, P. (1993) *Cassette Culture: Popular Music and Technology in North India*, London: University of Chicago Press.

Middleton, R. (1990) *Studying Popular Music*, Buckingham: Open University Press.

Novak, D. (2013) *Japanoise: Music at the Edge of Circulation*, Durham, NC: Duke University Press.

O'Reilly, D., and Doherty, K. (2006) "Music B(r)ands Online and Constructing Community: The Case of New Model Army", in M. D. Ayers (ed.), *Cybersounds: Essays on Virtual Music Culture*, New York: Peter Lang Press, pp. 137–159.

Reunanen, M., Wasiak, P., and Botz, D. (2015) "Crack Intros: Piracy, Creativity, and Communication", *International Journal of Communication*, 9: 798–817.

Reynolds, S. (2013) "Sharity Blogs *Wire* Piece", *ReynoldsRetro*, available at: http://reynoldsretro.blogspot.com/2013/05/800x600-normal-0-false-false-false-en_30.html (accessed 27 June 2015).

Sreberny-Mohammadi, A., and Mohammadi, A. (1994) *Small Media, Big Revolution: Communication, Culture, and the Iranian Revolution*, Minneapolis, MN: University of Minnesota Press.

Stern, M. (2014) "'Mi Wantem Musik Blong Mi Hemi Blong Evriwan' ('I Want My Music to Be for Everyone'): Digital Developments, Copyright and Music Circulation in Port Vila, Vanuatu", *First Monday*, 19(10), available at: http://firstmonday.org/ojs/index.php/fm/article/view/5551/4130 (accessed 27 June 2015).

Stone, M. D. (1985) "Taking Notice of Bulletin Boards", *PC Mag*, 30 April, pp. 261–262.

Sundaram, R. (2009) *Pirate Modernity: Delhi's Media Urbanism*, London: Routledge.

Whelan, A. (2008) *Breakcore: Identity and Interaction on Peer-to-Peer*, Newcastle: Cambridge Scholars.

Whelan, A. (2010) "Leeching Bataille: Peer-to-Peer Potlatch and the Acephalic Response", in J. M. Prada, A. Lafuente, and J. Borrego (eds), *4th Inclusiva-net Meeting: P2P Networks and Processes*, Madrid: Medialab Prado.

Whitman, M. (2005) "'When We're Finished With It, They Can Have It': Jamband Tape-Trading Culture", MA thesis, University of Chicago, available at: www.whitperson.com/Marc_Whitman_MA_Thesis_May_2005.pdf (accessed 22 June 2015).

Witt, S. (2015) *How Music Got Free: The End of an Industry, the Turn of the Century, and the Patient Zero of Piracy*, New York: Viking.

31

HISTORIES OF INTERNET GAMES AND PLAY

Space, Technique, and Modality

Teodor Mitew and Christopher Moore

Introduction

It would be a daunting task to attempt an authoritative history of the Internet and play, and it is not our intention to sketch such an account, in the singular, even if the space allowed for it. Rather, we have undertaken a preliminary mapping of those elements which, we argue, should participate in the telling of the histories of Internet games. For this approach to work, we must stray from the usual litany of dates and events constructing the illusion of teleological progression leading to a terminus. Instead, we have built our argument around the key elements that, we think, should *always* be present in the telling of histories of Internet games and play.

Consider the experience of playing Internet games using a personal computer (PC) as a process that is constructed and continually performed in space and time. The process inevitably involves a material space, the computer hardware, an Internet connection, and a digital game modulated and mediated for play in these settings. While physical places such as lounge rooms and Internet cafés, and technical strata such as computers connected through low-lag fiber to game servers, can be imagined fairly straightforwardly, the modalities of digital games include a heterogeneous set of elements such as genre, storyline, play-world, player numbers, mode of distribution, and so on. The entire experiential construct of Internet play is in effect a function of the alignment of these key elements into a temporary, but stable, network of nodes, which can be imagined as the proverbial black box of actor network theory (Latour 1999).

Therefore, in approaching Internet games historically, we propose to open the black box and focus on selected historical alignments between game spaces (spatiality), the technical strata (technique), and the genres and modes (modality) of play. Furthermore, if these black-boxed relations can be argued to generate the affordances of Internet games, then it follows that we have to approach all spaces, technologies, and modes of play as operating on the same flat ontological plane. In other words, we cannot take it as a starting point that one of these elements is somehow more real, officially precedent or structurally more important than the others in our historical perspective.

Importantly, our approach is not methodologically unique and has a distinguished pedigree in the history of historiography. Fernand Braudel, perhaps the most notable representative of the Annales School, argued in his seminal history of the Mediterranean (1995) that one cannot tell the multiplicity of histories of that heterogeneous region without accounting for heretofore ignored elements such as climates, landscapes, and currents in all their complex materiality. In Braudel's telling, sea currents, hills, valleys, river estuaries, and deep-water bays are all equally enmeshed in the production of histories, and on the same ontological footing, as the kings, institutions, and other human protagonists we are used to encountering on the pages of history books. Crucially, this approach does not position the affordances of geography as hierarchically more important than human agency; rather, both are co-formative of the compost of entangled agencies forming history.

Similarly, the triad of game spaces, game techniques, and game modalities could be imagined as a prism through which the historicity of Internet play is to be approached. Simply put, in discussing game spaces from a historical perspective we inevitably have to account for the modalities of genre and the technical stratum of play; in discussing the historical influences of broadband connectivity on the experience of Internet play – for example, in terms of distribution, we are inevitably forced to account for the spatial element as well as the changing modalities of genre; and finally, an historical account of the modalities of game play as exemplified by genre has to also account for the roles of spaces and technicities of play in performing that genre.

That being said, the meticulous attention to logistical details necessitated by our approach is the main constraint facing our argument. Inevitably, our approach involves curtailing discussion of some developmental vectors that must be acknowledged and anticipated, not because they are less important, but due to simple limitations of scope. In assembling an analytical framework that positions its three poles of space, technique, and modality around a narrated history of multiplayer PC games, we have necessitated a limited attention to the contribution of other important innovations, technologies, and practices, including mobile telephony and portable devices, from the Nintendo Gameboys to the openness of the Android operating system which lends its particular set of affordances to the development of new markets and multiplayer experiences. Similarly, while we have attempted to frame this as a global history, our attention to the role of gender, race, sexuality, and the extensive involvement of participants in the subcultural formations crucial to the mainstream success of those genres we do consider, are not absent from our consideration, but necessarily limited in detail here.

Modalities of Play

We begin our discussion by focusing on the modalities of genre and game play, followed by the role of game spaces in formatting play, and finally consider the intersecting roles and histories of technical strata in the production, distribution, and serialization of game play online.

In thinking about the history of Internet games and play from the perspective of genre and modes of game play, we are confining our scope to three modalities so large and present in various histories of the Internet that they have come to define entirely new game types and styles of play: the first person shooter (FPS), the real time strategy (RTS), and the role-playing game (RPG). It is through these three modalities of Internet-enabled multiplayer games that we argue the history of the Internet and games is also a history of play that moves outside the boundaries of the interactive experiences of games and their virtual worlds. In effect, this creates a meta-modality, or the play of play, which variously involves what Axel Bruns (2008) considers as produsage, or along the lines of George Ritzer *et al.*'s (2012) revision of Toffler's concept of prosumption, and what Henry Jenkins (2006) and Joost Raessens (2005) refer to as participatory media culture. These are crucial meta-modal forces in determining the cultural dimensions of game genres, play spaces and the success, adoption, and modification of game techniques.

Our contention is that, in this context, the PC platform should be imagined as a nodal extension of the Internet in the home and the Internet café, a spatio-technical integration of domestic and public environments serving as a liberating affordance for players. Through their infiltration of these spaces, initially in the late 1980s and extensively in the 1990s, games provided a consumer vector for the waves of personal new media and entertainment devices and content, contributing directly to the PC industry as a driver of technological and design innovations and choices: take, for example, current generation PC architecture, which has been fragmented thanks to the PC games market's emphasis on graphical processing units to offset the computational demands of modern FPS games. Similarly, the change of modem speeds from 24k to 56k (*c.* 1995), and broadband levels (in the early 2000s), is easily associated with the domestic connectivity demands of massively multiplayer online (MMO) games.

Titles including the hugely popular US-based *Ultima Online* (1997), and one of the first graphical virtual worlds, the French *La 4ème Prophétie* (1999), and *Lineage* (1998), which saw massive success in South Korea and Taiwan, were influential drivers of domestic Internet connectivity. These games provided a model for second wave MMORPGs that relied heavily on broadband connections for content distribution as well as play, including the Icelandic *Eve Online* (2003) and Sony's *The Matrix Online* (2005), and culminated in third-wave massively multiplayer games with intense graphic processing and high stakes competition that demanded conditions greater than 56 kilobits per second, such as *Age of Conan: Hyborian Adventures* (2008), *Warhammer Online: Age of Reckoning* (2009), *Lord Of The Rings Online* (2010), *Star Wars: The Old Republic* (2011), and *Star Trek Online* (2010). These games largely mark the end of big budget massively multiplayer role-playing games, as most transformed from subscription services to free-to-play games with premium purchases quickly after launch, and the player base shifted interest to other emerging genres of PC-enabled Internet play.

The game console obviously enters this field of relations, but is newer to networking and Internet connectivity and therefore largely absent from early online play cultures; it is also less central to technological change than the PC, and more peripheral to the technologies of production, as it is located primarily in the domain of domestic entertainment and the living room. The development of console operating systems and their Internet and network connectivity is parallel to the already compromised design of always-already closed hardware necessarily lagging behind the desktop equivalent due to the constraints of massification and standardization of its production. What is more, arguably it was profound failure at the content and hardware layers of the console industry that contributed to the 1983–1984 collapse of the video game industry (Apperley 2006: 8).

From an historical perspective, the 1980s was a pivotal era for the development of the modalities of Internet games: Commodore released the Amiga 1000, Apple launched the Macintosh, and IBM released the first PC-AT—a high- end domestic PC based on the Intel 80286 chips around which the majority of the PC games industry would be organized. The Internet domain name system was created in this time frame, establishing some of the most recognized Web domains, including .com .gov, .edu, .org, and .net, and this was also the period in which William Gibson (1982) would coin the term "cyberspace", and lay the foundations of cyberpunk, still infecting much of contemporary science fiction.

Simultaneously, the popularity of the multiplayer fantasy game genre was cemented in the early 1980s with the third revision of the *Dungeons and Dragons (D&D) Basic Set*. It was the algorithmic nature of the pen-and-paper tabletop role-playing system of *D&D* which served as the foundation for a modality of play in single player and multiplayer fantasy genre experiences that traces a trajectory through some of the biggest selling PC games in the fantasy MMO and RPG games: from *Colossal Cave Adventure* (1977) and *Zork* (1980), to the *Advanced Dungeons & Dragons* Gold Box Adventures (1988–1990), the first fully multiplayer experiences of *Ultima Online* (1997), the LAN party RPG favorite *Neverwinter Nights* (2002), and the penultimate MMORPG *World of Warcraft* (2004).

This is the socio-technical compost from which the science fiction and fantasy milieus of digital games rapidly evolve, as increased access to online community formations and fandoms was enabled by increased domestic and institutional Internet access from schools, public libraries, and universities. The confluence of the established modalities of the fantasy genre and increased access to domestic Internet connectivity in the 1990s, and broadband and cable connections in the 2000s, enabled new kinds of online role-play, competitive gaming, and simultaneous but geographically distributed play. This in turn was fundamental to a networked modality of genre play, one that is simultaneously virtual and spatially located (King and Krzywinska 2002; Apperley 2006).

Tom Apperley's (2006: 6–7) approach to genre is to overturn common assumptions that games are a consistent medium with a static aesthetic and rigid representational strategies, including drawing attention to "ergodic" (Aarseth 1997: 7) actions involved in the interactivity of video game play. Apperley builds on King and Krzywinska's (2002) critical approach to game genre that looks to the complex layering of assumptions and the totalizing misconceptions of genre as a descriptive category for games derived from literary, film, and video industries and traditions, without looking to the dimensions of interactivity in the genealogical trajectories of video games.

The RTS, FPS, and RPG game modes are common interfaces for both fantasy and science fiction because of the way the spatiality of the game is organized and the particular formatting of the player's point of view. For example, *Starcraft* is science fiction experienced through the RTS genre, and its multiplayer modality has served to orient the techniques of online multiplayer and format the cultural spaces of competitive leagues becoming the foundation for a global interest in e-sports (Dhoedt 2014). Digital game ethnographer T. L. Taylor suggests it is in part the formatting of multiplayer RTS and FPS games via Internet spaces, and the techniques of control over the material interface of mouse and keyboard, incorporating the player's body in the cybernetic assemblage (2013: 38), that arguably result in the often overtly misogynistic and "insider" nature of the experience (2013: 29).

The *World of Warcraft* franchise might owe a great debt to Tolkien and Chaucer, but its fantasy themes are clearly rooted in the Hollywood *oeuvre* of, frequently B-grade, fantasy movies of the 1970s and 1980s, including *Conan the Barbarian* (1982), *Legend* (1985), *Willow* (1988), *Labyrinth* (1986), *Red Sonja* (1985), *Krull* (1983), *Dragonslayer* (1981), and *The Dark Crystal* (1982). The point here is that the movies themselves shared similar cultural tropes with the literary pulp fantasy of Edgar Rice Burroughs, Robert E. Howard, Fritz Lieber, the Sword and Sorcery genre, and a further lineage of historical fiction (Sir Walter Scott), each serving as an expression of an escapist milieu and a reaction to the reality of the times. Similarly, the techniques of the fantasy modality shine through the collaborative world that is the experience of *World of Warcraft*, not only in terms of the representational and generic elements, but also the technicity of the adventuring "party". The party mechanic is core to the experience of the networked virtual reality of the fantasy role-playing game in both single player and multiplayer modalities and spaces.

The spatiality of networked fan cultures of fantasy RPGs enabled the personalization of game content through modification and the provision of user-generated content, a practice transported directly from the technique of the pen-and-paper era. Bioware's *Neverwinter Nights* (2002) used digital distribution of content and access to legitimate modding tools to enable players access to the technicity of the meta-player, similar to the modal experience of the Games Master (GM), creating virtual spaces to adventure in, and community spaces via the Web, to build and share an enormous amount of content. The collaboration and participation was made possible by the technical affordances of the game, and the modalities of its distribution, creating hundreds of thousands of communally experienced stories and interactions.

The human-algorithmic hybrid nature of the Dungeon Master (DM), or GM, in pen-and-paper games, required a player dedicated to operating the role-playing game system for its other players by interpreting and applying the game rules, which usually requires dice rolls to determine outcomes and resolve player-nominated strategies. This technique of the RPG modality continues to inform the spaces and technologies of contemporary MMO experiences and defines the RPG milieu, its vocabulary, and its terminology: hit points, gold pieces, experience points, etc. The DM is an interface between players and the game, the techniques of world building and algorithmic logic, the content experience and the spaces they occupy. Bioware's modding and content-creation toolset for *Neverwinter Nights* extends the DM, and provides a technique of meta-spatiality, giving control over all elements of the narrative and play experience of the game to the player; control over story, events, actions, and other storytelling dynamics provided a more personalized experience than is possible using the pre-programmed and automated narrative processes of automated storytelling game engines (Tychsen *et al.* 2005).

Space and Spatiality

If there is contrast in the way play is encountered and performed in different types of spaces, we are able to make the argument that the history of Internet play is also a history of spaces. Take, for example, the new capacities for mobile Internet technologies and mobile Internet-enabled devices to reformat any space, no matter how formalized and institutionalized, into a playful one of a game space through the act of play (Moore 2011).

In accounting for the spatial element in the experience of the modalities of play, we have to consider the situated experiences of the human player and the materiality of play spaces formatting the affordances of those experiences. Here, space is understood not as a Cartesian shell populated by the subjectivity of human players, or limited to interaction between a player, input devices, algorithm, and screen, but as a fundamental element in the continuous performance of the experience of play. Consider the material dimensions formatting the social conventions and underpinning the cultural experiences of a local area network (LAN) or Internet café. These are connected physical spaces hosting access to the digitally networked game spaces, which demonstrate multiple layers and modalities of play, which includes, but is not limited to, the multiplayer game mode.

Spaces like the living room or bedroom occupied by the personal computer; the cramped and confined spaces of the ad hoc LAN room strewn with cables, tables, PC cases, and large CRT monitors; the sprawling vistas of cloned desktop machines of LAN cafés; the flat-screen booths with PC towers crammed with high-capacity graphics cards of the Korean PC Baang.

Each of these techniques informs the spatial configurations and has its own affordances co-performing the experience of play, each of them is always already infused with *a* culture and *a* set of practices entangling and performing the player as firmly as the player directs protagonists on the screen via the cybernetic controls of keyboard and mouse.

Arguably, the Internet has repositioned play as a central fixture of mainstream entertainment. As Jesper Juul has observed (2010), trends in technical and cultural convergence have culminated in the ubiquitous presence of games, increasingly public and mobile in their play (Moore 2011), and from this commonality have renormalized both games and play in contemporary and popular culture for audiences of all ages. Were it not for the Internet's ability to connect machines and humans, we would not have globally shared the "massively" single player experience of the open world of *Grand Theft Auto 5* (*GTAV*) (2015) and its sprawling narrative and equally massive virtual space, which sold 45 million copies across previous and current generation video game consoles, earning more than $2 billion US dollars in revenue in 2014 (Grubb 2015; McWhertor 2015).

Later in 2015, the publication of *GTAV* on the PC digital distribution platform Steam, developed by the Valve Corporation, saw a peak simultaneous player base of 300,000 gamers, all occupying the same, but individually realized, virtual worlds concurrently before the release of the game's official multiplayer element, connecting players together in an open world environment (SteamSpy 2015). The different modalities of the Internet-enabled single-player and multiplayer experience of *GTAV* occupy multiple spatialities and techniques that exist well outside the direct cybernetic interface of the virtual world, creating an intersecting vector through which all "play" has the potential to "move" (Moore 2011).

This movement extends beyond the controller and screen to the participatory media cultures of games and gamers (Raessens 2005), whose affective investment in the labor of play activities is shared via the materiality of play, capturing and rendering it through the techniques of screenshots, memes, reviews, blog posts, forums, and software and hardware modifications. This has led to the establishment of new genres of niche paratextual and creative industries enabled by the Internet (Consalvo 2009; Moore 2012, 2014) and the Web: from the hand-crafted game memorabilia, unique hardware modifications, and unofficial game-related merchandise sold via Etsy and Ebay, to the constant stream of images contributed under the Instagram and Flickr #cosplay hashtag, and the millions of hours of live streamed gameplay via Twitch TV and the YouTube genre of *Let's Play* videos that have come to dominate the economics of televisualized and remediated play (Dredge 2013). The Internet, the hardware layer of networking technologies, and the software layer of the Web have enabled these new modalities of play to combine to produce and regulate spatialities of commercial consumer culture within systems of major global production and social relations.

Significant scholarly attention has considered the arrangements of techniques and modalities of LAN play, which built on the Internet protocols of high-speed and low-latency network communication to create a multiplicity of play spaces. These spatialities include the commercially run Internet cafés and PC Baangs (Chan 2006; Swalwell 2009), the massive Nordic LAN competitions, including "Assembly"—the world's largest LAN "party" held annually in Helsinki, Finland (Tyni and Sotamaa 2014), as well as the smaller scale ad hoc LAN "parties" which involve the incorporation of PC and console technologies in the temporary reformatting of more domestic spaces (Jansz and Martens 2005). In American culture the Internet café played only a minor role where the LAN "party" was more present and less geographically persistent (Taylor 2013), but not so in Europe and Asia where a different cultural history of online games is encountered; a set of cultural experiences based not on the distributed suburban spatiality of most American and Australian cities, but rather on much more communal and urban spaces (Chan 2006).

The success of LAN-driven game genres, supported by the participatory media cultures of software and hardware modification (Postigo 2007), has produced multiple generations of new modalities of play; from the very first FPS multiplayer experiences of *Doom* (1993) to the recent rise of another entirely new game type enabled by player modding communities, the massively online battle arena (MOBA), and its mediation via the Internet, especially social media and online streaming, achieving critical mass for the global e-sports tournament industry.

E-sports are a modality of LAN culture and Internet technologies that were popularized in the 1990s (Taylor 2013), but extend precedence to competitive modalities and social practices of play in ritualized public spaces from early gambling halls, pinball parlors, amusement arcades, and eventually video game arcades and Internet cafés. Notably, the modalities of e-sports feature both the atomized domestic spaces of living rooms and bedrooms televised via Twitch TV and YouTube, and the same virtual spaces used to televise the large hyper-mediated public events of global e-sports leagues and finals matches resembling rock concerts. In both cases, low-latency bandwidth enables the performance of these modalities in front of highly scalable global publics—an excellent example of the triad of modality, space, and technique in all histories of Internet, games, and play.

In addition, e-sports attract massive global audiences for games that began, or were inspired by, player-contributed modifications of other games, including Valve's *Dawn of the Ancients 2* (*DOTA2* 2013), *League of Legends* (*LoL* 2009) and Blizzard's *Heroes of the Storm* (2015). The publisher of *LoL*, Riot Games, attracted a global audience of 32 million people for the Season 3 World Championship in 2013, with its Twitch TV live coverage peaking at 8.5 million simultaneous viewers (McCormick 2013). In this example, new public spaces and modalities of play, and the cultures of their consumption and production, are entirely indebted to the availability, affordability, and sociality of Internet-enabled technologies (Taylor *et al.* 2014; Taylor and Witkowski 2010).

Taylor *et al.*'s actor network theory analysis of the temporal and spatial arrangements of LAN events illustrates the interconnected assemblages of participants, researchers, games, and gaming platforms as public gaming sites—an approach that reveals prior-held convictions and fears regarding the notion that online games are detrimental to real-world sociality is "inaccurate and limiting" (2014: 777). Their approach documents clear tensions in two modalities of play, both in terms of the gender construction and spatiality of the hyper-feminized and masculinized representations of video game content and its physical instantiation in the limited access women have to "public" game sites, and the levels of hostility demonstrated to women in these heavily male-dominated spaces:

> Not only were women clearly a minority across these sites, but the sociospatial organization of their attendance often made it difficult to approach them. At LAN events in particular, female attendees who were part of larger, male-dominated groups (usually the girlfriend, wife or relative of one of the male attendees) were typically positioned at the end of that group's row of computers, often playing a single-player game while the other (male) group members played in multiplayer games together.
>
> (Taylor *et al.* 2014: 774)

Histories of Internet games and play are therefore always already unfolding on networks preconfiguring how play is framed and understood. They are also histories of digital distribution, new technologies, new spaces, and modalities of consumption, as the technical layer of the Web interfaces between players and the "bricks-and-mortar" realm. The range of modalities of production that have occurred from this transition include crowd-funding, serialization of game content via downloadable content (DLC), and the move to open player *beta* periods of pre-release testing and prepaid access to unfinished games. Both the success of digital distribution and the extent of game piracy is preconfigured by the rise of Internet, software, and hacker cultures, a pattern that emerges again in still earlier iterations and precursors like the BBS.

The Internet has enabled new authorized channels of distribution, reformatting the public spaces of the Web as commercial ones. Non-corporate publics, however, have taken the affordances of digital technologies in opposite directions, formalizing the practice of file-sharing emerging from the ideological and anti-authoritarian regimes of hacker culture, from the very outset of the Internet up to its current iteration in torrent sites like The Pirate Bay (see Figure 31.1), which replicates modalities of the "zero day" pirate websites and warez Internet communities of the late 1990s and early 2000s:

> The Warez scene in a sense is focused on engaging a kind of meta-game that involves modding game software products. Game piracy has thus become recognized as a collective, decentralized and placeless endeavor (i.e., not a physical organization) that relies on torrent servers as its underground distribution venue for game warez.
>
> (Scacchi 2010)

The technicity of early Internet piracy involved software "cracks", small files used to circumvent anti-copying devices on material media, such as serial codes and registration numbers. The product of hackers and the warez community, who managed networks of disk piracy to access content, these disks become the basis for the "sneaker" net at LAN events, as files were traded on physical disks before broadband access and high-speed LAN networks were fast enough to support both file-sharing traffic and the networked game data.

Technique and Technicity

Until the advances of fast Internet speeds and the density of broadband connections to support the distribution of large digital files, game piracy also manifested within physical distribution vectors including the CD and DVD "burner", which replicated the originally purchased disk ad infinitum to be sold by street and market vendors across Eastern Europe and Asia. Throughout South-East and East Asia in the early 1990s this practice was completely institutionalized as an open market of pirated copies of music, movies, and games, and was even regulated into similarly discrete vendors. Copyright infringement in China, especially with regard to Western media and software, is even today only minimally policed (Ma 2015), with copyright having little cultural foundation in political or social life. The country has only recently started ratifying the major international intellectual property rights treaties (Bates and Liu 2010).

China's regulations on the sale of Western video game consoles included heavy taxation and strong restrictions. Following the 2000 ban on console games (Aslinger 2013: 62), these conditions created an intensive focus on PC games with local network and Internet play, from casual online games like *QQ Speed* (Tencent QQ Games 2008), to the retelling of *Journey to the West* in the popular *Fantasy Westward Journey* (Net Ease 2004), and massively multiplayer online games *Demi-Gods and Semi-Devils* (Sohu Games 2007) and *League of Legends*

Figure 31.1 A screenshot of The Pirate Bay PC games offering

(*LoL*, Riot 2009). The local industry has operationalized culturally specific spatialities as a result of adopting PC and Internet technologies that produce a complex modality of strongly regulated but highly popular networked environments.

In responding to the problems of standardizing the technologies of multiplayer, and managing online content and attending to the modalities of Internet piracy, in 2003 the Valve Corporation created a new online space for the digital distribution of games, called Steam (Crossley 2011). Steam is a technique of destabilizing the fixed modalities of PC games and serializing their development over time through consecutive patching delivered via peer-based Internet connections, simultaneously connecting PC players of games like *Counter Strike* (1999) and *Half-Life* (1998) multiplayer to the already established infrastructure of global servers (Bishop 2011).

No longer confined to the department store or the video games retail chain outlet, or even the massive national chains like Walmart, the virtualization of consumption via Steam and other digital distribution channels has become the ground for new commercial social spaces (Newman 2012). These are spaces of consumption and of a social interaction that simulate the experience of North American-style mall culture, Japanese pachinko halls, or the communal aspects of arcade culture. Steam also shares a sense of the "arcade" with Walter Benjamin's *Arcades Projects* (1999), a spatiality for exploration, and an enclosing technique of architecture lending itself to new modes of consumption and non-linear narratives of experience, perfect for Benjamin's juxtaposed reflections and montaged accounts.

With Steam, Valve has developed the platform to serve a daily user base of 12 million players (Steam 2016), transforming a content delivery platform into a social network, a library, a cinema, a gallery, and a video game arcade. Steam is a retail interface to networked digital space for the curation and presentation of traces of achievements and accolades, screenshots and machinima, mods, friends, groups and communities, forums, blogs, reviews, links, and jumping-off points and other "pieces of the digital urban nomadism", and the collected traces of urban life similar to those including handbills, tickets, photographs, advertisements, diaries, and newspaper cuttings (Featherstone 1998: 909).

Alongside Steam, the Apple iOS game store, and the online stores of the major video game consoles, it is Facebook and other serialized digitally distributed online game content and RPG environments like MMORPG *World of Warcraft* (Blizzard 2004) and the single-player RPG *Skyrim* that have catered to traditional marginalized video game audiences (Fahs and Gohr 2012; Martey *et al.* 2014).

In addition, Steam's distribution model largely eliminated problems of access to physical stores and scarcity-bound game copies, which helped to reduce piracy and support the development and sale of "indie" and independent games (Bergquist 2011). Before the arrival of Steam, the Internet was relied on for non-mainstream games and access to cracks, hacks, and mods that would enable play (Best 2011). Today, access to "pirate" content resides on the same torrenting sites as the games themselves (see Figure 31.1), with sites such as The Pirate Bay acting as convenient spaces for locating the large files of contemporary games, and the legion of warez, crackz, and serials sites that form the dark underground of the Internet.

The materiality of the physical copy enabled a modality of sharing, connecting the spatiality of street markets and sociality and culture of disk-trading at LAN events and Internet cafés, connected to the virtual spaces of the Web. This is why we are making the argument that a history of the Internet and games is a history of the relationship of the spaces for play, and enabling play, and how their intersection has created new global markets in the digital distribution of games. As Internet speeds increased, the spaces of piracy and gaming were increasingly virtualized, and yet still retained physical connections to the games industry, from gold farming hostels (Heeks 2010: 11) to bitcoin-mining operations which use the graphics hardware designed for the specialty PC gaming markets on a technically sophisticated level usually associated with Silicon Valley.

Conclusion

Our aim with this brief overview is to draw attention to the persistence and integrated nature of questions of game modality, spatiality, and technique in the histories of the Internet, games, and play. In using this approach, we have addressed the contention that the Internet has simultaneously facilitated the dematerialization of the physical copy associated with accessing games, and rematerialized play as investment in the new global market in a mix of official and unofficial channels of consumption, from licensed merchandising to fan-produced cosplay and other expressions of participatory media culture.

The degree to which the technologies of the Internet, especially the diffusion of high-speed broadband Internet connections, have made new game spaces possible, including those for the reconfigurations of the modalities of play, is matched only by their enclosure within the formalized modes of industrial production, as beta-testers, mod-creators, community leaders, and so on (Moore 2005). The "play" *of* and *with* games is a result of the spatial, modal, and technical triad of Internet affordances, which supports the movement and appropriation of content outside the boundaries of the game's own representational strategies and technical interactions. This modality of play has been officially incorporated within the techniques of game development, through the technical and legal responses to physical and digital piracy, in terms of new spaces of consumption such as Steam and Facebook, as well as new methods of digital distribution extending game and play spaces to new material settings.

Those parts of the game industry which organized along a re-creation of the cinema or television studio model encompass a more traditional spatiality grounded in a highly successful model of production. Crucially, this production model presupposes a legal regime of property built around physical goods, often linked vertically and horizontally in the games industry between manufacturers like Nintendo, which also produce and distribute game titles, to studios who work with publishers and distributors.

Prior to the appearance of Steam, Xbox Live, the Playstation store, and other Internet-enabled marketplaces, this model operated within a highly regulated legacy media paradigm that construed the downloading and modification of digital copies as a transgression of the model. It is important to note how unstable this studio mode of production is, and has been since the mid-1980s, following the crash of the Atari game console in 1983 (Bogost and Montfort 2009). The Australian games industry has undergone profound structural change following the global financial crisis, in which the major game studios, previously reliant on the global rates of currency exchange, have closed, while concurrently seeing a massive rise in the success of "indie" and independent titles made available via Internet-enabled digital distribution platforms including Xbox Live, Steam, and the Apple iOS game store (McCrea 2013).

Parts of the games industry most like a legacy media studio were the most adamant in terms of technical anti-copying measures, while on the other hand, the phenomenon of Valve was conceptualized at the intersection between technique, space, and mode. Steam was positioned by Gabe Newell, Valve CEO, as a response to the notion of piracy that addressed the core triad of technique, spatiality, and modality in reconceptualizing copyright infringement not as the fault of consumers, but as a result of markets delivering poor service to consumers. In other words, in taking account of the triad of space, technique, and mode of play, Steam shifted the paradigm of Internet play to a new frame of reference, addressing the main artificially imposed inefficiencies of the previous regime.

Valve's long-term success here has been to codify the provided labor of gamers, incorporating them into the official techniques of industrial production, and in the process codify a new type of player (the beta tester) as a secondary market in unfinished games. By changing the modalities and techniques of play, this process also established a new space for the serialization of game content that eradicates the notion of "finished" games. Steam has dissolved the game commodity as a self-enclosed static object, without diminishing its materiality, replacing it with a new type of fluid object commodified as a service, and changing and revitalizing the Internet games industry as a result. As such, games have colonized mainstream entertainment via the affordances of Internet and Web technologies. This process offers new modalities of mediation, from YouTube to Twitch TV, and a veritable multitude of emerging play traditions of fan expression such as cosplay, as well as more traditional expressions of fandom including fan art and fiction that are translated to physical spaces of experience such as game LANs and popular culture conventions.

This shift in the triad of space, technique, and modality has profound effects, and one of the key things to understand and point out is that the effects are not only in terms of the economics of distribution, genre, and hardware. The effects also manifest in terms of structure, institution, narrative, experience, and interaction, and we need only look to the most successful contemporary games to observe how game development and public play have been integrated within an open-ended processual experience.

It is true that titles and series like *The Elder Scrolls Skyrim*, *Total War*, and *Half Life*, with their modding communities and massive degrees of user-contributed online textual resources, have resulted in successful niche paratextual and creative industries, but this history of the

Internet, games, and play, is also the history of new means for the commodification of play. It is also the case that the technical packaging of entertainment supports new modes of quantification and analysis, where the conditions of participation include improvements to the play based on the surveilled and incorporated activity of its participatory media cultures. The future of Internet games continues to be anticipated within the prism of space, technique, and modality with new innovations and explorations of game structures, interactions, and interfaces of a range of emerging Virtual Reality (VR) technologies for the PC with the Oculus Rift and HTC Vive, and mobile devices with the Samsung Gear VR. At the time of writing, the third wave of VR innovations nears commercial release, and has the potential to offer radically embodied modes of mediation and interaction that will take extensive advantage of the locative features and Internet-enabled devices to deliver entirely new massively multiplayer experiences. Games like *Hover Junkers* are being designed entirely for VR, which is entirely controlled in a one-to-one analogue movement fully colonizing and transforming the physical play space.

References

Aarseth, E. (1997) *Cybertext: Perspectives on Ergodic Literature*, Baltimore, MD: John Hopkins University Press.

Apperley, T. (2006) "Genre and Game Studies: Toward a Critical Approach to Video Game Genres", *Simulation and Gaming*, 37(1): 6–23.

Aslinger, B. (2013) "Redefining the Console for the Global, Networked Era", in B. Aslinger and N. B. Huntemann (eds), *Gaming Globally: Production, Play, and Place*, New York: Palgrave Macmillian, pp. 59–73.

Bates, B. J., and Liu, T. (2010) "A Cultural Approach to DRM Implementation in China", *Westminster Papers in Communication and Culture*, 7(1): 7–26.

Benjamin, W. (1999) *Arcades Projects*, ed. R. Tiedemann, trans. E. Howard and K. McLaughlin, Cambridge, MA: Harvard University Press.

Bergquist, M. (2011) "Economics in the Small and Independent Game Industry", Ph.D. thesis, Norwegian University of Science and Technology.

Best, M. (2011) "Participatory Gaming Culture: Indie Game Design as Dialogue Between Player & Creator", Ph.D. thesis, Universiteit Utrecht.

Bishop, T. (2011) "How Valve Experiments With the Economics of Video Games", *Geek Wire*, available at: www.geekwire.com/2011/experiments-video-game-economics-valves-gabe-newell/ (accessed 11 July 2015).

Bogost, I., and Montfort, N. (2009) *Racing the Beam: The Atari 2600 Platform*, Cambridge, MA: MIT Press.

Braudel, F. (1995 [1949]) *La Méditerranée et le Monde Méditerranéen à l'époque de Philippe II* (The Mediterranean and the Mediterranean World in the Age of Philip II), trans. S. Reynolds, Berkeley, CA: University of California Press.

Bruns, A. (2008) *Blogs, Wikipedia, Second Life, and Beyond: From Production to Produsage*, New York: Peter Lang.

Chan, D. (2006) "Negotiating Intra-Asian Games Networks: On Cultural Proximity, East Asian Games Design, and Chinese Farmers", *Fibreculture Journal*, 8, available at: http://eight.fibreculturejournal.org/fcj-049-negotiating-intra-asian-games-networks-on-cultural-proximity-east-asian-games-design-and-chinese-farmers/ (accessed 11 July 2015).

Consalvo, M. (2009) *Cheating: Gaining Advantage in Videogames*, Cambridge, MA: MIT Press.

Crossley, R. (2011) "The Valve Manifesto", *Develop Online*, available at: www.develop-online.net/analysis/the-valve-manifesto/0117024 (accessed 11 July 2015).

Dhoedt, S. (2014) *State of Play* (documentary), Seoul Film Commission.

Dredge, S. (2013) "PewDiePie Unseats Miley Cyrus as World's Most Popular YouTube Channel", *The Guardian*, 8 November, available at: www.theguardian.com/technology/2013/nov/08/pewdiepie-miley-cyrus-youtube-videos (accessed 13 July 2015).

Fahs, B., and Gohr, M. (2012) "Superpatriarchy Meets Cyberfeminism: Facebook, Online Gaming, and the New Social Genocide", *MP: An Online Feminist Journal*, 3(6), available at: http://academinist.org/wpcontent/uploads/2010/06/030601_Superpatriarchy.pdf (accessed 9 July 2015).

Featherstone, M. (1998) "The Flâneur, the City and Virtual Public Life", *Urban Studies*, 35(5–6): 909–925.

Gibson, W. (1982) "Burning Chrome", *Omni*, July.

Grubb, J. (2015) "Grand Theft Auto V Beats Skyrim's Record for Concurrent Players on Steam", *VentureBeat*, 15 April, available at: http://venturebeat.com/2015/04/14/grand-theft-auto-v-beats-skyrims-record-for-concurrent-players-on-steam/ (accessed 8 July 2015).

Heeks, R. (2010) "Understanding 'Gold Farming' and Real-Money Trading as the Intersection of Real and Virtual Economies", *Journal of Virtual Worlds Research*, 2(4): 1–27.

Jansz, J., and Martens, L. (2005) "Gaming at a LAN Event: The Social Context of Playing Video Games", *New Media and Society*, 7(3): 333–355.

Jenkins, H. (2006) *Convergence Culture: Where Old and New Media Collide*, New York: New York University Press.

Juul, J. (2010) *Casual Revolution*, Cambridge, MA: MIT Press.

King, G., and Krzywinska, T. (eds) (2002) *ScreenPlay: Cinema/Videogames/Interfacings*, London: Wallflower Press.

Latour, B. (1999) *Pandora's Hope: Essays on the Reality of Science Studies*, Cambridge, MA: Harvard University Press.

Ma, Y. M. (2015) "Stop Online Piracy Act: The Next Step in Copyright Protection or Censorship of Online Expression", *Law School Student Scholarship*, paper 655, available at: http://scholarship.shu.edu/student_scholarship/655

McCormick, R. (2013) "'League of Legends' eSports Finals Watched by 32 Million People", *The Verge*, 19 November, available at: www.theverge.com/2013/11/19/5123724/league-of-legends-world-championship-32-million-viewers (accessed 9 July 2015).

McCrea, C. (2013) "Australian Video Games: The Collapse and Reconstruction of an Industry", in B. Aslinger and N. B. Huntemann (eds), *Gaming Globally: Production, Play, and Place*, New York: Palgrave Macmillian, pp. 203–207.

McWhertor, M. (2015) "Grand Theft Auto 5 Sells 45M Copies, Boosted by PS4 and Xbox One Versions", *Polygon*, 3 February, available at: www.polygon.com/2015/2/3/7973035/grand-theft-auto-5-sales-45-million-ps4-xbox-one (accessed 9 July 2015).

Martey, R. M., Stromer-Galley, J., Banks, J., Wu, J., and Consalvo, M. (2014) "The Strategic Female: Gender-Switching and Player Behavior in Online Games", *Information, Communication & Society*, 17(3): 286–300.

Moore, C. L. (2005) "Commonising the Enclosure: Online Games and Reforming Intellectual Property Regimes", *Australian Journal of Emerging Technologies and Society*, 3(2): 100–114.

Moore, C. (2011) "The Magic Circle and the Mobility of Play", *Convergence*, 17(4): 373–387.

Moore, C. (2012) "Invigorating Play: The Role of Affect in Online Multiplayer FPS Game", in G. A. Voorhees, J. Call, and K. Whitlock (eds), *Guns, Grenades, and Grunts: First-Person Shooter Games*, London: Continuum, pp. 341–364.

Moore, C. (2014) "Screenshots as Virtual Photography, Digital Media Objects and the Production of Online Persona", in P. Arthur and K. Bode (eds), *Advancing Digital Humanities: Research, Methods, Theories*, London: Continuum, pp. 141–160.

Newman, J. (2012) "Ports and Patches: Digital Games as Unstable Objects", *Convergence*, 18: 135–142.

Postigo, H. (2007) "Of Mods and Modders: Chasing Down the Value of Fan-Based Digital Game Modification", *Games and Culture*, 2: 300–313.

Raessens, J. (2005) "Computer Games as Participatory Media Culture", in J. Reassens and J. Goldstein (eds), *Handbook of Computer Game Studies*, Cambridge, MA: MIT Press, pp. 373–388.

Ritzer, J., Dean, P., and Jurgenson, N. (2012) "The Coming of Age of the Prosumer", *American Behavioral Scientist*, 56(4): 379–398.

Scacchi, W. (2010) "Computer Game Mods, Modders, Modding, and the Mod Scene", *First Monday*, 15(5), available at: http://uncommonculture.org/ojs/index.php/fm/article/view/2965/2526 (accessed 9 July 2015).

Steam (2016) "Steam User and Game Stats", *Steam*, available at: http://store.steampowered.com/stats/ (accessed 31 March 2016).

SteamSpy (2015) "Grand Theft Auto V", *SteamSpy*, available at: http://steamspy.com/app/271590 (accessed 9 July 2015).

Swalwell, M. (2009) "LAN Gaming Groups: Snapshots from an Australasian Case Study, 1999–2008", in L. Hjorth and D. Chan (eds), *Gaming Cultures and Place in Asia-Pacific*, London: Routledge, pp. 117–140.

Taylor, N., Jenson, J., de Castell, S., and Dilouya, B. (2014) "Public Displays of Play: Studying Online Games in Physical Settings", *Journal of Computer-Mediated Communication*, 19: 763–779.

Taylor, T. L. (2013) *Raising the Stakes*, Cambridge, MA: MIT Press.

Taylor, T. L., and Witkowski, E. (2010) "This Is How We Play It: What a Mega-LAN Can Teach Us About Games", *FDG '10*, Monterey, CA, 19–21 June.

Tychsen, A., Hitchens, M., Brolund, T., and Kavakli, M. (2005) "The Game Master", *Proceedings of the Second Australasian Conference on Interactive Entertainment*.

Tyni, H., and Sotamaa, O. (2014) "Assembling a Game Development Scene? Uncovering Finland's Largest Demo Party", *Game Journal*, 1(3): 109–119.

Part 7

PUBLICS, POLITICS, AND DIGITAL SOCIETIES

32

DIGITAL MEDIA AND SOCIO-POLITICAL CHANGE IN THE ARAB REGION

Ilhem Allagui

Three central factors have influenced Internet development in the Arab region in the last 25 years. The first is regulation, manifested by governments' common concern to keep access to, and usage of, information and communication technologies (ICTs) under the control of the state. The second has been the region's uneven resources that enable investments in ICT infrastructure and activities, and the third is the emergence and diffusion of social media. The oil-rich economies and politically "stable" monarchies of the Arabian Gulf were able to build the most advanced ICT infrastructure, offering a sophisticated Internet experience to users. The less well-resourced Arab countries struggled to build an adequate Internet infrastructure, and most of them did so under international pressure, or in the context of free trade agreements (Abdulla 2007). With modest technology and slow connectivity, the Internet user experience in developing countries was flimsy. This is still true in conflict zones such as Yemen, Iraq, and Syria. Yet almost all Arab countries have succeeded in the last decade in implementing at least a functional technology for private and corporate usage; this was fostered in large part by the massive adoption of social media.

The Arab uprisings, which started with the Tunisian riots in the wake of Bouazizi's self-immolation in December 2010, proved that information technologies could be empowering tools despite the varying quality of infrastructure and state control. Amazed at how citizens of a small country succeeded in overthrowing an authoritarian regime of more than two decades using digital technologies, the international community responded in awe by labeling it the "Internet revolution", the "new media revolution", the "Twitter revolution", and the "Facebook revolution".

This chapter narrates the highlights of Internet history in the Arab region in relation to its social and political transformations. Using key cases where digital technologies enabled actions and change of significant impact, the article argues that the uprisings are a construct of several *actors* and not *technologies*. The insurrections were the work of activists online and offline; those who survived and others who martyred themselves for their countries. Impressed by how fast the old regimes were overcome in Tunisia, Egypt, Libya, and Yemen, and idealizing social media and technology, people trusted that the "revolutions" would carry on for themselves. They did not. The technology is *enabling* and leading to collective actions in inconsistent ways. It enabled popular movements to overthrow authoritarian regimes, and is also now enabling the Mujahidin of the Islamic State (IS) to expand their troops and achieve the objectives of their socio-political agendas.

This chapter uses anecdotal case studies to discuss socio-political changes occurring in Arab societies. Although there are certainly other cases worth studying, I put forward examples that relate to blogging in preparation for the uprisings, as well as social networking and online activism. I have also chosen to include a short section on social media usage by the extremist jihadist in the frame of political transformations and to argue that technology can be both constructive and destructive.

Prior to discussing the uptake and usage of the Internet for socio-political motivations, I outline how the Internet came to be adopted in similar and different manners across the countries of the Arab region.

Internet Development: Trends and Patterns

By 2020, the Arab region will celebrate three decades of Internet adoption. The literature seems to agree that the first Internet connections in the Arab region were recorded in Tunisia (1991), Kuwait (1992), Egypt and the United Arab Emirates (UAE) (1993), with Jordan, Morocco, Algeria, and Lebanon connecting in 1994. Despite being early adopters, these governments were soon concerned about losing control of information flow. In addition to surveillance, other significant reasons for initially low Internet adoption were the high cost of hardware and connectivity for the average citizen, as well as a lack of computing skills, relatively high illiteracy rates in some countries, and a dearth of Web content in Arabic (Wheeler 2009). Jon Anderson (2009) argues that the first generation of Internet developers in the Arab region were students, young elites who had studied in the West and brought back technological abilities in different areas such as building online communities, developing programs and policies, and launching websites and forums. These were early adopters of the Internet, and the first to capitalize economically and socially via cyberspace in the region.

By 2014, 36 percent of people in the Arab world used the Internet (Mohamed Ben Rashed School of Government 2014), and the number is expected to reach 51 percent by 2017 (Arab Knowledge Economy Report 2014). However, until 2005, the Internet penetration rate in the majority of Arab countries was less than 10 percent. In those early days, Internet usage was predominantly tied to news available online. In fact, the top traffic of the Arabic websites was recorded for news websites that belong to TV broadcasters or newspapers (United Nations Economic and Social Commission for Western Asia 2003). Thus, early Internet usage could be described in light of the media system in the Arab countries as follows:

1. The resource-rich Gulf countries of Bahrain, UAE, Qatar, and Kuwait that prioritized investing in Internet infrastructure and encouraged Internet adoption. Bahrain, Kuwait, and the UAE heavily invested in and supported the media market while at the same time applying regulation and censorship. By 2002, Qatar recorded the lowest number of media available online (five) compared to Bahrain (seven), the UAE (13) and Kuwait (14) (United Nations Economic and Social Commission for Western Asia 2003).

2. The more populous, but less well-resourced, countries were:
   a. those such as Oman and Morocco that had limited free media but were doubtful about the impact of the Internet on the productivity and progress of their countries. Criticism of the governments is tolerated but not of the sultan or the king. In Oman, for instance, when new Internet forums appeared in the mid-2000s, users used their

real names when challenging the regime and debating economic and political debates (Valeri 2015).

b. those with tightly controlled media such as Tunisia, Egypt, Libya, Algeria, Yemen, and Syria that were fearful of the threat the Internet posed to their rulers.

c. those that lacked the resources to build an adequate Internet infrastructure, such as Lebanon, Jordan, Palestine, Iraq, and Yemen. These societies either had relatively free media systems, especially Lebanon and Jordan, or were in conflict zones.

By 2007, the Arab Internet sphere had been completely reconfigured. Syria, Libya, and Algeria had joined the least connected group of Yemen, Iraq, and Palestine, whereas Saudi Arabia, Morocco, Jordan, Lebanon, Oman, Egypt, and Tunisia had become moderately connected. These nations enjoyed a connectivity rate approaching 20 percent, although their governments have adopted a strategy of one step forward and two steps back, sporadically blocking websites and censoring content.

This remained true until 2010, which marked a year of setback in several Arab countries, followed by a surge of unprecedented Internet connectivity. In 2011, another divide emerged within the middle cluster, splitting countries into two groups: Lebanon, Oman, Saudi Arabia, and Morocco reached approximately 50 percent Internet penetration rate, while Egypt, Jordan, Tunisia, and Palestine witnessed Internet penetration rates between 30 and 40 percent, with Palestine moving up from among the least connected to join the high middle group, performing even better than Jordan and Tunisia by 2014 (Figure 32.1).

The uprisings and resulting popular awareness orchestrated by a dominant media discourse about the value of social media have propelled the adoption of ICT in the region. For instance,

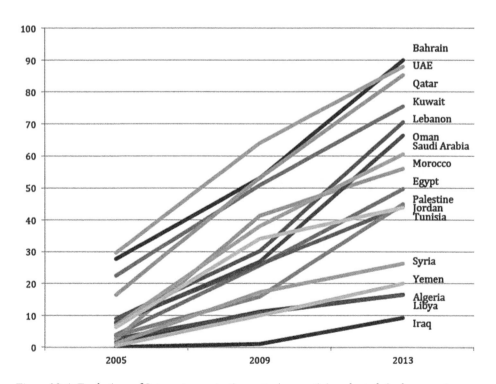

Figure 32.1 Evolution of Internet penetration rate (percent) in selected Arab countries

in 2011, Sudan registered a 37 percent growth in mobile number subscriptions, Yemen 22 percent, and Lebanon 20 percent. Morocco recorded the highest growth rate at 46 percent, followed by Sudan and Yemen, both around 40 percent. Egypt recorded a 30 percent increase, and Tunisia 26 percent. Overall in 2011, the region recorded about 30 percent growth in the number of Internet users compared to 2010, which is unprecedented for the region (Madar Research and Development 2012).

Before the surge of smartphones, the household increase of connectivity to the Internet also means an increase in computer ownership. The rates of computer ownership and connectivity per household indicate the proportion of Arab users who use ICT in the comfort of their homes. Figure 32.2 shows that the percentage of households with a computer at home is slightly higher than the percentage of households having access to the Internet at home. In several countries, the Internet is not a main reason for computer use. The figure also illustrates that households in the countries where the uprisings occurred were the least well equipped with both the Internet and computers.

In 2001, the region was considered the second highest growing in the world (after China) in terms of computer purchases (World Bank 2002). Back in 2000, Egypt, Saudi Arabia, and the UAE recorded the highest investment in IT hardware, software, and computing services compared to the rest of the Middle East and North Africa (MENA) countries. These three countries recorded about 60 percent of the total expenditure of US$2 billion, the majority of which (more than 90 percent) consisted of hardware sales. This helped the Gulf countries to be ahead of the rest in activities like e-government or e-commerce. As for Egypt, attractive IT-related activities included offshore engeneering and design, or remote education activities. A few other countries took advantage of other opportunities in the provision of IT services. Companies in Jordan made a reputation in data conversion tasks and others in Morocco specialized in call center services. Both countries recorded growth from developing such export opportunities (World Bank 2002). In the rest of the Arab region, growth has been minimal, if it occurred at all, due to persisting economic struggles and unstable political conditions.

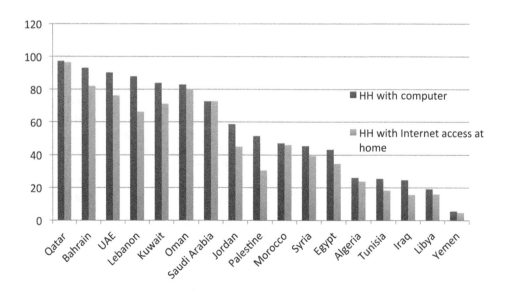

Figure 32.2 Percentages of households with Internet and computers (2013)

First introduced as an alternative to the high cost of purchasing individual hardware and online access, Internet cafés were the milieu where people discovered the Internet and started chatting or building online communities. However, state surveillance and control practices have pushed users away from these Internet cafés; users were subject to surveillance and monitoring practice, they were asked to give full identification details and contacts, their navigation habits were monitored, and emails and messages were regularly inspected (Deibert *et al.* 2010).

Internet cafés were also the birthplace of Arab blogging from within the region. Bloggers used public computers and community centers, not simply because of the high cost of household connectivity, which was an almost unbearable cost for the average citizen. Rather, blogging arose from a shared experience in the cafés, as users shared their work and learned about blogs that engaged in political activism. The first users of Internet cafés talked about culture, music, and dating in chats or bulletin forums; they were impressed how they could talk to other users in different countries, and chatted about a variety of topics. Online forums contributed to "collectively navigate complex identity and gender issues" by citizens where an offline space dedicated for such discussions was unavailable (Hussain and Howard 2012: 206). Issues discussed on forums included those related to gender and religious beliefs, as well as various other contentious subjects within politics and culture. In Bahrain, for instance, the impact of blogs was minimal until the mid-2000s, although online forums were still active and "highly influential over politics", while also documenting these political events through news and reports (Karagueuzian and Badine 2013: 307). Online forums and chats became less popular when technology enabled users to have their own "pages": users discovered that they could write their own diaries on easy-to-use platforms and share them with the rest of the world.

Bloggers were not necessarily political activists working towards a political agenda or affiliated with any political party. Most of them were simple citizens concerned with local issues. For example, one of the bloggers I met during the Freedom Online Tunisia Forum in 2013 was a teacher from southern Tunisia. The first issue he wrote about was the dreadful state of the streets in his neighborhood and city. He also criticized the high cost of water and the lousy cultural scene in his city, but while using cynicism and humor. He couldn't complain aloud in real life; and when online, although he felt more comfortable talking about these issues, he had to use a framing that would not offend those who are monitoring. The Internet enabled such bloggers to voice their concerns and aspirations while being mindful of the state control.

Blogging and the Rise of Online Activism

This chapter is not about political activism in the Arab region. It is not the space to talk about the history of unions, the Brotherhood, or any other political party that contributed to the revolutions or reshaped their directions. This chapter is about how Internet development has brought about a new culture in relation to socio-political change. I have highlighted above how the uprisings have caused the growth of Internet connectivity rates in most of the Arab countries. Here, I will continue with the history of blogging in the region, and review key cases that contributed to the transformations.

Blogging about politics is the emblem of twenty-first-century Arab activism. Since freedom of expression is restricted by controlled media environments, users found in blogs (in Arabic, *mudawanet*) the prospect for political change and social transformation (Douai 2009). As noted above, the first blogs were not political: originally, the first generation of bloggers preferred to write about their personal lives as if maintaining diaries. Politics was not their main topic;

feelings, thoughts, marriage, and faith were more popular subjects of discussion (Etling *et al.* 2009). Zuckerman (2008) argues that Arab bloggers were first attracted to blogging to build "bridges" with other cultures and interact with international communities. Internet pioneers and early bloggers in the region are tech-savvy programmers and developers, but also diaspora Arabs (Anderson 2013). They may have studied abroad before going back home tooled with computer knowledge and expertise (Anderson 2013) to share and experiment with other less skilled users and initiate web-forums, "chats", and news bulletins prior to blogs and other genres.

Bloggers used the format to explore a variety of issues, but political blogging has played a central role in Arab political identity construction. Arab regimes of the twenty-first century have so far expunged the public sphere where ideas are supposed to be forged, solidified, or reconstructed in an environment of free thought and exchange (Habermas 1989). The dearth of such physical spaces drove young people—both tech-savvy and otherwise—to discover and appreciate the digital version of this agora. New forms of civic participation have arisen, and "amateur" experiences (in contrast to sponsored ones or those affiliated with political parties) of online activism commenced and have become more significant after the invasion of Iraq. Thanks to the blogging environment in Iraq, users witnessed a new way of swaying public opinion and seeking international support.

For instance, *Salam Pax* is an important chapter in Arab blogging. Started as a diary recounting the lives of everyday Iraqis after the American invasion, *Salam Pax* garnered international attention. Whether blogs led to democracy is not the question, as Adrienne Russell comments on the Iraqi blog *Riverbend*: "[blogs] may or may not be fostering political representative democracy in Iraq, but it is definitely strengthening traditional forms of communication there, such as oral-style micro storytelling, as the key ingredient to larger cultural conceptions" (2009: 2).

Upon realizing how threatening political blogging could be, Arab leaders have reacted consistently by censoring, arresting, torturing, and intimidating bloggers. In fact, Arab countries have adopted similar methods to block Internet access and filter content. They have limited ISP numbers, encouraged a monopoly of telecom operators, and kept Internet content under scrutiny. Muzammil Hussain and Philip Howard argue:

> [M]any Arab governments have responded to the new information technologies in consistent ways: censorship strategies have been developed with similar objectives of cultural control, Internet service providers are held legally responsible for the content that flows over their networks, and government agencies work aggressively to support (often "Islamic") cultural content online.
>
> (2013: 12)

In 2009, the Commission to Protect Journalists (2009) published the ten worst countries to be a blogger. Four of the ten countries were from within the Arab region—namely Syria, Saudi Arabia, Tunisia, and Egypt.

Governments have been vigilant against blogging. Borhane Bessaiess, one of Tunisian ex-president Ben Ali's consultants, confessed on television that Ben Ali used to regularly visit *Tunisnews*, a blog operated from Switzerland. Bessaiess adds that bloggers were the real revolutionaries who started the Tunisian revolution (Nessmanews 2014).

Long before the uprisings, Zouhair Yahiaoui, activist and founder of the blog *TUNeZINE*, was among the first Arab victims of the crackdown on Internet dissidence, and one of the most recognized for his contribution to and battle for online activism (Hofheinz 2005). He was arrested on 4 June 2004, and detained in prison under accusations of disseminating false news and criticizing the regime and its corrupted practices. After serving his sentence, he left prison and died shortly after of a heart attack in 2005.

In 1997, Bahraini Galal Olwai was arrested and detained for 18 months for sending information over the Internet to opposition party Bahraini Liberal Movement. In 2003, both Algeria and Syria detained citizen journalists for posting articles or emailing newsletters, acts that were perceived as threatening the internal security of the country (Wheeler 2009). Around the same time, Egyptian activists, concerned about the 2005 Egyptian presidential elections, turned to blogs to share breaking stories of torture, corruption, and abuse by the police force, as well as to plan and organize protests (Hussain and Howard 2012). As David Faris argues:

> Digital activism in Egypt stretches back nearly a decade [2001]. The work of these earlier blogger-activists was pioneering in the sense that it helped transform public debate about a number of issues that became focal points during the Egyptian revolution itself.
>
> (2012: 22)

Other prominent and influential blogs include *Amarji* by Syrian activist Ammar Abdulhamid that was launched in 2005, *Mideast Dispatches* by Dahr Jamail in 2003, *The Angry Arab* by Lebanese Asaad Abu Khalil (2003), *Haitham Sabbah* by Palestinian Haitham Sabbah (1999), and *Misr Digital* by Egyptian Wael Abbas (2005) (Karagueuzian and Badine 2013).

Before the Tunisian turmoil of 2010, the failed phosphate mining in Gafsa in 2008 encouraged Tunisian bloggers to be more aggressive online, reinforcing the network of bloggers internally and abroad. Gafsa is a governorate in the Tunisian south containing the cities of Redeyef and Omm Larayes, known for their coalfields. The economic condition in Gafsa is similar to other less-developed interior regions, where youth employment is high and prospects few. The Phosphate Gafsa Company conducted a hiring contest that many suspected would lack fairness and transparency. Disappointment over the employment announcement sparked protests that led to brutal and violent confrontations with police officers. More youth died in the 2008 Gafsa riots than those of Sidi Bouzid in 2010 to 2011, and by all measures the confrontation was more violent and bloody. However, people did not hear about the events in Gafsa; there was no coverage by Tunisian media, private or public. The blog coverage, though minimal, reached some international news sources by posting films and photos captured on cellular phones on the Web .

Some Tunisian immigrant associations tried to break the blockade of the media imposed by the authorities. Support committees appeared in Nantes, home to an immigrant community originating from Redeyef, as well as in Paris through the Fédération des Tunisiens pour une Citoyenneté des Deux Rives (Tunisian Federation for Citizenship on Both Shores). The Tunisian Workers Communist Party posted a daily review of the events on its website, albadil.org (now inactive). The effects of these support initiatives abroad were ultimately rather limited. The only professional images were broadcast on the opposition satellite television channel *Al-Hiwar Attounsi*, broadcast from London (Gobe 2011). Gafsa events were an important time for bloggers to come together and knit ties that successfully constructed a network that would lead to and facilitate the Tunisian uprisings (Allagui and Kuebler 2011). The Gafsa riot represented an important step in preparing bloggers for the uprisings; they came together and built strong ties online and offline, best illustrated by their white anti-censorship marches on 22 May 2010, six months before the revolts, in downtown Tunis, Paris, and Montreal (Ben Gharbia 2010).

Similarly, in Egypt, online activists used blogging to denounce abusive government practices. For instance, Egyptian blogger Wael Abbas posted cellphone videos of torture and physical abuse, not just to raise awareness about practices which people already knew about, but to encourage others to report similar practices, and document and share such content with fellow citizens for maximum impact (Seib 2012). Videos taken by mobiles were posted afterwards on YouTube, Vine, and other platforms. The use of cellphones to capture and share moments of the uprisings intensified as events unfolded, leading the government's senior officials to respond using the same means. They instructed Vodafone, the government Telecom entity and the principal service provider in Egypt, to send subscribers messages warning them to ignore rumors and fabricated images, and encouraging them to stay away from gatherings.

Blogging has proved to be an effective channel for speaking out about local concerns and practicing citizens' rights. The most popular Arab blogs enabled discussions about local issues rather than pan-Arab issues (Lynch 2007). In order to have impact and drive change, blogs cannot work independently, but must fit into a network of agents, actors, and institutions that work constructively together. Citizen journalism is an evident outcome of this. When working in harmony, the "tools provide infrastructure for networks that in a political context can be the foundation of a revolutionary movement" (Seib 2012).

Social Networking and the Free Flow of Information

The end of the 1990s marks the second phase of the history of the Internet instigated by social networking. While the end of the first millennium was crowned by the remarkable rise of Web commercialization, the debut of the second millennium has propelled Internet users into an era of digital socialization. Finding information, making online transactions, entertaining and expressing oneself, exploring and negotiating intimacy on the Web, all belong to first millennium practices. Sharing content and engaging in symbiotic digital relations are trends of the new millennium. A 2013 study reports that the most common uses of social media in the region are to read about and look at what friends or family are doing online, to get advice and ideas, and to network and connect with new people (Shediac *et al.* 2013). Social networking has enhanced Internet usage; it has introduced new ways of digital personalization and socialization, as users instantly share any content they wish with whomever they want. To those hostile, doubtful, or concerned about public exposure and privacy, social networks offer customization features that give the impression that users have control of their content, despite the threats posed by iCloud's exposure or big brother surveillance. However, the social media usage of this group of "uncomfortable users" is less intense when compared to those comfortable voicing their political opinions (Dennis *et al.* 2015).

The marriage of the Internet with Web 2.0 features enabled a transformed mediated political and social experience in the Arab region. Up until this point, strategic information that needed to circulate in the public spheres of democratic societies—public policies or government spending reports, for example—was inaccessible to Arab citizens. The Internet and social media offered a path for those who believe in transparency to revive—if not give birth to—civic societies in Arab countries. Social networks have thoroughly changed the channels of public dissemination of information. Users access news on social networks, traditional media push their news on social media, critics and public personalities challenge the news, criticize political parties, and express opinions on social media. Increasingly, traditional media also turn to social media to get news, follow trends, and fill in their talk shows and programs. In Tunisia, for instance, the travel expenditure and food bills of the temporary (or transitional) president

Moncef Marzouki, also candidate for the presidential elections held in 2014, circulated on Facebook and were criticized as excessive, causing damage to his reputation. This information, once impossible to access in any Arab country, went viral in traditional media.

To get their news, Internet users tend to check their social networks. They also share news through Twitter, Facebook, and WhatsApp with their network of friends, family, followers, and colleagues. Frequent users report that social media is an important news source; however, they also confess that they have reservations about the quality of news they get, which varies between professional news and less reliable, amateurish, news (Dennis *et al.* 2015).

Within their network of friends, people were comfortable sharing updates during the uprisings, feeling as though they were in their own communities. The tools of technology and social media enabled and facilitated interconnectivity. As Manuel Castells points out:

> The digital social networks based on the Internet and on wireless platforms are decisive tools for mobilizing, for organizing, for deliberating, for coordinating, and for deciding. Yet, the role of the Internet goes beyond instrumentality: it creates the conditions for a form of shared practice that allows a leaderless movement to survive, deliberate, coordinate, and expand.
>
> (Castells 2012: 229)

Digital communication has played an important role in changing the political landscape. In Saudi Arabia, for instance, digital tools

> have provided an open media space for political discourse with no offline equivalent but have also allowed social elites to closely manage the production and consumption of political content, [whereas in Egypt] the regime has used digital media for monitoring, though not restricting, dissent, and online civil society and journalism have flourished.
>
> (Hussain and Howard 2012: 202)

During the Tunisian revolt, the government banned access to Facebook and video sites such as YouTube and DailyMotion prior to the revolts (then, in a late attempt to calm the revolts, ex-president Ben Ali ordered the ban to be lifted in January 2011). The Egyptian government's attempts to control communication through mobile phones were not limited to text-message users. When the government found this approach had failed, officials cut off Internet access in the country, demonstrating once again their unwillingness to change by adopting an authoritarian approach. For five days, Egyptians could not access the Internet; however, users adopted counter-strategies—namely, through proxies to communicate with allies overseas—and continued to exert pressure on the government.

Internet Usage and Socio-cultural Transformations

In the Arab Middle East, research into Internet usage has developed in the shadow of the Western theoretical framework (Matar and Bessaiso 2012) and methodological tradition. Using an audience research perspective, early literature looked at Internet usage among Arab populations and concurred that entertainment (listening to music, watching movies, and playing games) and communication (emailing, chatting, networking with family and friends) were the main usages of the Internet (Allagui 2009; Hofheinz 2005; Wheeler 2004). In addition to extending social contacts, Arab users are interested in accessing online news and discussing almost everything on popular forums such as *Maktoob*, *Jeeran*, and *Kooora*, as well as finding and providing guidance on contemporary Islamic life (Anderson 2003; Hofheinz 2005). Until 2010, and before the spark of the Arab uprisings, most studies describe Arab Internet users as content consumers moving between online entertainment and social networking (Hofheinz 2011).

Arab women have not yet reached global standards in terms of their usage of the Internet and social networks, and their usage is still below their male counterparts. However, their roles in the turmoil as activists are indisputable (Arab Social Media Report 2011, 2012). The Internet and digital technologies can free Arab women from social and cultural ties typical traditional and patriarchal societies. James Katz and Ronald Rice suggest that technology offers the possibility to expand one's self-expression and become free from cultural legacy. As they note: "New technology can allow people to integrate and explore aspects of their lives and to expand their personal possibilities, freeing themselves from local culture influences" (2002: 266).

In 1997, UNESCO called on Arab women to use the Internet in order to express their own voices; in 2002, Queen Rania of Jordan invited Arab women to use the Internet to "reshape their lives" (Wheeler 2004: 143). Women's education in the region has prepared them for the digital millennium. In several countries of the region, Arab females outnumber men in attending universities. A new generation of digitally connected women have enhanced gendered Internet experiences. With the adoption of the Internet, networked relationships and personal interests have been reconfigured. Newly connected women slowly showed an interest in politics, specifically local politics, and cared little about reaching out to the world. As Wheeler wrote about Kuwaiti women whom she interviewed about a decade ago: "[They] barely mentioned the concept of the 'global voice'; the only specific online political activity noted was the campaign for women's suffrage in Kuwait" (2004: 160).

Clearly, things have changed in ten years, and the Arab revolutions are evidence of the active role played by women in denouncing abuses, organizing demonstrations, and raising their voices to inform, communicate, and negotiate (Allagui 2014; Arab Social Media Report 2011). However, their preference for local politics remains consistent. Tunisian Lina ben Mhenna maintained a blog that reported on the progress of marches and sit-ins in all regions of the country, and Tawakkol Karman was the first journalist in Yemen to conduct reporting via the Internet (Nippon 2014). Online activists like Asmaa Mahfouz and Israa abdel Fattah, founder and co-founder of the April 6th Youth Movement, played central roles in the spark of the revolution in Egypt by using the Internet to call on Egyptians to occupy Tahrir Square on 25 January 2011. This is very different from the early days of the Internet when female users were mainly interested in entertainment forums such as *lakii* (for you), and *Hawaaworld* (Eve's World).

Today, aside from search engines and portals that are entry gates to the Web, social networking sites dominate the top-visited websites in the Gulf region (see Table 32.1). In Lebanon, Jordan, and Egypt, news websites with local interest are what predominantly attract Internet users, regardless of their gender.

When compared to the situation in the late 1990s, entertainment websites, as well as religious websites, have disappeared from the top ranking where they were in the late 1990s. This does not deny users' interest in music, movies, and games, but the platforms have changed; instead of 6arab.com, users visit YouTube, and instead of *Maktoob*, they may go to Facebook or other social networking sites. Table 32.1 also shows that in Egypt, Lebanon, and Jordan, news sites dominate the top 25. This could be explained by two reasons: first,

Table 32.1 Categories of the top 25 visited websites in selected Arab countries

Country	News sites	Social networks	Forums	E-commerce	SE/portals	Entertainment	Football	Other
Algeria	2	4	1	4	7	-	1	6
Bahrain	4	7	-	3	6	1	1	3
Egypt	9	5	-	1	7	-	1	2
Jordan	9	6	-	2	4	1	1	2
Lebanon	9	6	-	2	6	1	-	1
Morocco	4	5	-	3	5	-	4	4
Qatar	3	6	1	2	8	-	-	5
Saudi Arabia	4	6	-	5	7	-	1	2
UAE	4	6	-	5	7	-	-	3

the long publishing tradition in these countries; and, second, users are politically savvy due to their countries' situation. Moreover, there is relatively more freedom of expression than before, and people consult local news sites that are now considered to be more reliable. For the Arabian Gulf countries, the top news sites are from India and the Philippines, catering to the needs of the large expatriate population that wants to read news from their home country. The news-reading habits of local citizens are different from those of expatriates. In Qatar, for instance, ictQatar (2014) reveals that most Qatari nationals get their news first from WhatsApp (34 percent), then Twitter (25 percent), and Facebook (12 percent). However, non-Qatari expatriates first check Facebook (52 percent) as a source for news, then WhatsApp (21 percent) and Twitter (12 percent) (2014). Thus, news consumption has shifted from traditional online media such as websites, to new, "on-the-go" applications and social networks, media made possible by high smartphone penetration rates in the Arabian Gulf countries. The new trend of "on-the-go" media news is also evidenced in the launch of news applications such as AlJazeera's AJ+, for instance, reflecting a new trend of news consumption on smartphones.

Mujatweets and Social Media Usage by Extremists

Table 32.1 above also shows that Islamic websites have disappeared from the top-visited sites in Arab countries. In the last decade of the twentieth century, Arab cyberspace saw the emergence of Islam digitization. Websites such as *Islamonline* and *Islamnet* offered digital versions of the *Quran*, *prophet's hadiths*, and Islamic *fatwas*, extending the reach of Islam (*Dawaa*) to believers and non-believers. Describing those who benefited the most from Internet technologies, el Gody (2007) includes political activists—leftists, Islamists, civil society, and human rights groups—who were marginalized and long-deprived of freedom of expression. Then he cites religious groups who use the Internet to spread their ideologies. The third group comprises social groups who challenge traditions and social norms, and who use the Internet to get their voice out.

A few Saudi *muftis* see social media as incompatible with sharia and religious values due to the potential spread of lies and threat to social and religious values; otherwise, Islamic groups have used the Internet extensively as a channel of information, communication, and dissemination to a young audience they found were craving such content. For example, 74 percent of the Arab Digital Generation[1] in Gulf Cooperation Council countries and North Africa, and 63 percent of them in the Levant find that the Internet brings them closer to their religion. More than six out of ten report that they are exposed to religious content that increases their knowledge, and more than seven out of ten think that this religious content allows them to endorse their beliefs and strengthen their faith (Strategy& 2012).

Since the Arab Spring, not only have Islamic groups capitalized on social media for their proselytism efforts (Ibahrine 2013), but conservative extremist groups, too, have used social media to spread their religious and political agendas. Social networks have demonstrated the capacity to mobilize activists, and have now become soft tools in the Islamic State *mujahidins'* hands to recruit troops, intimidate opponents, and promote their message. The audience they attempted to reach was not a hard one to uncover, as they are willing to interact with online users they don't know. In fact, Internet users in the MENA region are more likely to meet online people they don't know in person, and to accept friendships and connections from people they don't know, than any other region (Rassed 2014).

While officially starting in Iraq and Syria under the brand ISIS (Islamic State of Iraq and Syria), the movement has now been rebranded as IS (Islamic State) because of its expansion plans for the rest of the region, especially since Egypt's Sinai jihadists have pledged their allegiance to the IS through YouTube. *Mujatweets*, a collection of professional promotional videos produced by the IS publishing house, Al Hayet Media Centre, is distributed through social networks, exposing the jihadis' life with the objective to convince others, preferably Muslims resident in the West, to join. After YouTube blocked the ISIS account following the posting of violent executions, *Mujatweets* have been distributed through Dailymotion. Twitter has closed the official account of ISIS, but the predominant messages on the allies' social media accounts (mainly on Twitter) consistently call for *jihad*.

The ISIS social media campaign is aggressive and professional, experts say (Campaign Middle East 2014). A marketing and propaganda PR machine organizes Twitter accounts, distributes videos on DailyMotion, posts questions and answers on ask.fm, and produces a mobile application that followers download in order to receive news, content, and updates. Instagram, Tumblr, and Internet memes are also used as part of their marketing tactics, as well as a call to action ("Join me for the next program") that makes the videos look professional, almost entertaining, and "Hollywood style" (Rose 2014).

Hence, while social media has been celebrated for enabling socio-political transformation during the Arab uprisings, they are now also blamed for promoting the IS jihadists' objectives: "Social media has repeatedly been blamed for radicalising recruits and mobilising support for Isis" (Burke 2014).

Conclusion

The Arab uprisings have brought about liberalization of civil society in places such as Tunisia. While this is not totally true in Egypt or other Arabian Gulf countries, the Internet in Tunisia is now a much less regulated space than before the uprisisngs, where non-government organizations, bloggers, and citizens alike can discuss, share, engage, and participate in democratic discussions about public policy, political practices, and economic and social development issues. In such a case, civil society activities are seldom subject to state censorship and the control of one country. Led by civically engaged people, they care about and protect the population from political and social abuses. Their presence and contribution today is a gain from the development of the new technologies, the uprisings, and is protected by both the legitimacy of their actions and the constitution.

Throughout the region, governments have been forced to revise policies with regard to media, freedom of expression, censorship, and security. Clearly, after the Arab uprisings, where new media platforms were converted into tools for social and political action, governments had little choice but to adjust to the demands of the new digitally connected Arab citizens. While in some countries, such as Egypt and others in the Arabian Gulf, governments tightened their control and regulation of the Internet and social media usage, Tunisia went a step further in the opposite direction and joined the Freedom Online Coalition, launched in December 2011, committed to advancing Internet freedom, privacy, and freedom of expression online. Of the 23 countries in the coalition, Tunisia is the only Arab member. Although the number of Internet users is still under the world average in some Arab countries, those who use the Internet feel empowered through their engagement and involvement in political and social spheres. The majority of Arab users find that they can better understand politics since using the Internet, according to the Arab Media Survey (Allagui and Breslow 2013); almost half of users feel empowered and have more political influence since they started using the Internet; and 49 percent think they have more say about government policies. Users also feel less concerned with surveillance and control, as six out of ten respondents reported that they aren't worried about governments checking their online navigation.

This is a significant change compared to the situation prior to the uprisings, when no more than three out of ten agreed with these statements. As Figure 32.3 below illustrates, less than 20 percent of UAE respondents surveyed in 2009 felt they had influence in politics, a proportion that jumped to 50 percent in 2013, post-uprisings; a similar proportion was recorded in the same year by the Arab Media Survey (Allagui and Breslow 2009, 2013).

Thus, one can only agree with the positive impact of the Internet on Arab political lives. However, the developments witnessed in the events of the Arab uprisings cannot resolve the question of whether the technologies drive democratization. The causal relationship between technology and democracy depends on what democratization means within different societies, and what best suits the relations between the governed and the governing models. Research

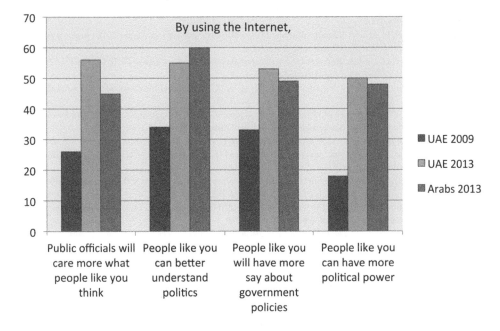

Figure 32.3 The Internet and perceptions of governance

shows that people in some monarchies like the UAE are quite happy and confident about their governments; even non-UAE Arab youth see the UAE as a model nation (ASDA'A Burson-Marsteller Arab Youth Survey 2013). In addition, the populations' priorities and commitment to fight for change of governance depends on how much they are willing to give up in order to gain. For instance, freeing Hosni Mubarak and dismissing all charges against him did not spark a new turmoil in Egypt, which can be interpreted as a compromise from a silenced majority. After the clashes between pro-Muslim Brotherhood and their opponents, some Egyptians preferred the return of the military regime to reinstate civil security and stability.

Socio-political transformations in the Arab region are still in progress. Clearly, technology is enabling, with a significant capacity to bring about effective change. In this chapter, I only looked at selected cases and selected countries because it would have been unfeasible to cover the history and developments of the Internet in the 22 countries of the Arab League in such a limited space. While this sounds a limitation, it is also an opportunity that enabled me to highlight some of the positive changes occurring in some regions—namely, in Tunisia, post uprisings. Regrettably, tight Internet regulation and the remaining structures of oppression in some Arab countries have obstructed the celebratory role of technology and the path towards democracy.

Note

1. Strategy& (2012) defines the Arab Digital Generation as those born between 1977 and 1997. This group represents 40 percent of the MENA population.

References

Abdulla, R. A. (2007) *The Internet in the Arab World: Egypt and Beyond*, New York: Peter Lang.

Allagui, I. (2009) "Multiple Mirrors of the Arab Digital Gap", *Global Media Journal*, American edition, 8(14): 14–23.

Allagui, I. (2014) "Waiting for Spring: Arab Resistance and Change, Editorial Introduction", *International Journal of Communication*, 8: 983–1007.

Allagui, I., and Breslow, H. (2009) "Emirates Internet Project Report", *Internet Usage in the UAE: Report of Findings*, American University of Sharjah, United Arab Emirates.

Allagui, I., and Breslow, H. (2013) "Emirates Internet Project Report", *Internet Usage in the UAE: Report of Findings*, American University of Sharjah, United Arab Emirates.

Allagui, I., and Kuebler, J. (2011) "The Arab Spring and Role of ICTs, Editorial Introduction", *International Journal of Communication*, 5: 1435–1442.

Anderson, J. W. (2003) "The Internet and Islam's New Interpreters", in D. F. Eickelman and J. W. Anderson (eds), *New Media in the Muslim World*, Bloomington, IN: Indiana University Press, pp. 41–55.

Anderson, J. W. (2009) *Cyberspace, Civil Society and the Internet Biographies in the Middle East*, Conference presentation at Lund University, available at: www.academia.edu/3473353/Cyberspace_Civil_Society_and_Internet_Biographies_in_the_Middle_East

Anderson, J. W. (2013) "Online and Offline Continuities, Community and Agency of the Internet", *CyberOrient*, 7(1), available at: www.cyberorient.net/article.do?articleId=8355

Arab Knowledge Economy Report (2014) "Madar Research & Development and Orient Planet", *Orient Planet*, available at: www.orientplanet.com/akereport2014.pdf

Arab Social Media Report (2011) *The Role of Social Media in Arab Women's Empowerment*, Dubai: Dubai School of Government, 1(N3).

Arab Social Media Report (2012) *Social Media in the Arab World: Influencing Societal and Cultural Change?*, Dubai: Dubai School of Government, 2(N1).

ASDA'A Burson-Marsteller Arab Youth Survey (2013) *ASDA'A Burson-Marsteller Arab Youth Survey*, available at: http://arabyouthsurvey.com

Ben Gharbia, S. (2010) "Anti-Censorship Movement in Tunisia: Creativity, Courage and Hope", *Global Voices*, available at: https://advox.globalvoices.org/2010/05/27/anti-censorship-movement-in-tunisia-creativity-courage-and-hope/

Burke, J. (2014) "Indian Police Arrest Owner of Pro-Islamic State Twitter Account", *The Guardian*, 13 December, available at: www.theguardian.com/world/2014/dec/13/india-isis-twitter-mehdi-masroor-biswas-shamiwitness

Campaign Middle East (2014) "Isis: Media Marketing and Murder", *Campaign Middle East*, 1 September, available at: http://campaignme.com/2014/09/01/15570/isis-media-marketing-murder/ (accessed 5 December 2014).

Castells, M. (2012) *Networks of Outrage and Hope: Social Movements in the Internet Age*, Cambridge: Polity Press.

Commission to Protect Journalists (2009) "10 Worst Countries to Be a Blogger", *Commission to Protect Journalists*, 30 April, available at: http://cpj.org/reports/2009/04/10-worst-countries-to-be-a-blogger.php (accessed 6 November 2014).

Deibert, R., Palfrey, J., Rohozinski, R., and Zittrain, J. (2010) *Access Controlled: The Shaping of Power, Rights, and Rule in Cyberspace*, Cambridge, MA: MIT Press.

Dennis, E. E., Martin, J. D., and Wood, R. (2015) *Media Use in the Middle East, Northwestern University in Qatar*, available at: www.mideastmedia.org/survey/2015/chapter/social-media.html#subchapter4

Douai, A. (2009) "Offline Politics in the Arab Blogosphere: Trends and Prospects in Morocco", in A. Russell and N. Echchaibi (eds), *International Blogging: Identity, Politics and Networked Publics*, New York: Peter Lang, pp. 133–150.

el Gody, A. (2007) "New Media, New Audiences, New Topics, and New Forms of Censorship in the Middle East", in P. Seib (ed.), *New Media and the New Middle East*, New York: Palgrave Macmillan, pp. 213–234.

Etling, B., Kelly, J., Faris, R., and Palfrey, J. (2009) "Mapping the Arab Blogosphere: Politics, Culture and Dissent", *Berkman Center for Internet & Society*, available at: http://cyber.law.harvard.edu/sites/cyber.law.harvard.edu/files/Mapping_the_Arabic_Blogosphere_0.pdf

Faris, D. (2012) *Dissent and Revolution in a Digital Age: Social Media, Blogging and Activism in Egypt*, New York: Tauris.

Gobe, E. (2011) "The Gafsa Mining Basin between Riots and a Social Movement: Meaning and Significance of a Protest Movement in Ben Ali's Tunisia", *Archives ouvertes en Sciences de l'homme et la societe*, available at: https://halshs.archives-ouvertes.fr/halshs-00557826

Habermas, J. (1989) *The Structural Transformation of the Public Sphere: An Inquiry into a Category of Bourgeois Society*, Cambridge, MA: MIT Press.

Hofheinz, A. (2005) "The Internet in the Arab World: Playground for Political Liberalization", *Internationale Politik und Gesellschaft*, 3: 78–96, available at: www.fes.de/ipg/IPG3_2005/07HOFHEINZ.PDF (accessed 8 December 2014).

Hofheinz, A. (2011) "Nextopia? Beyond Revolution 2.0", in I. Allagui and J. Kuebler (eds), *The International Journal of Communication*, 5: 1417–1434.

Hussain, M. and Howard, P. (2012) "Opening Closed Regimes: Civil Society, Information Infrastructure, and Political Islam", in E. Anduiza, M. J. Jensen, and L. Jorba (eds), *Digital Media and Political Engagement Worldwide: A Comparative Study*, Cambridge: Cambridge University Press, pp. 200–220.

Karagueuzian, C., and Badine, P. C. (2013) "Youth, Peace, and New Media in the Middle East", in S. Hafez and S. Slyomovics (eds), *Anthropology of the Middle East and North Africa: Into the New Millennium*, Bloomington, IN: Indiana University Press, pp. 301–322.

Ibahrine, M. (2013) "Islam and Social Media", in K. Harvey (ed.), *Encyclopedia of Social Media and Politics*, Vol. 9, Thousand Oaks: Sage Publishing, pp. 737–741.

ictQatar (2014) "How Qatar Uses WhatsApp, Snapchat and Other Social Media", *Rassed Research Briefing, ictQatar*, 1 December.

Katz, J. E., and Rice, R. E. (2002) *Social Consequences of Internet Use: Access, Involvement, and Interaction*, Cambridge, MA: MIT Press.

Lynch, M. (2007) "Blogging the New Arab Public", *Arab Media & Society*, pp. 1–30, available at: www.arabmedia society.com/?article=10 (accessed 1 December 2014).

Madar Research and Development (2012) "Arab ICT Use and Social Networks Adoption Report", *Madar Research and Development*, available at: www.kacst.edu.sa/en/about/publications/Other%20Publications/Arab%20ICT%20Use%20Report%202012.pdf

Matar, D., and Bessaiso, E. (2012) "Middle East Media Research", in I. Volkmer (ed.), *The Handbook of Global Media Research*, Oxford: Wiley-Blackwell, pp. 195–211.

Mohamed Ben Rashed School of Government (2014) "The Arab World Online 2014: Trends in Internet and Mobile Usage in the Region", *Mohamed Ben Rashed School of Government*, available at: www.mbrsg.ae/getattachment/ff70c2c5-0fce-405d-b23f-93c198d4ca44/The-Arab-World-Online-2014-Trends-in-Internet-and.aspx

Nessmanews (2014) "Nessmanews", *Nessma TV* (broadcast), 7 November.

Nippon (2014) "Unchaining the Potential of Women Worldwide: An Interview With Nobel Laureate Tawakkol Karman", *Nippon*, October, retrieved on 1 December 2014 at www.nippon.com/en/people/e00070/

Rassed (2014) "The Attitudes of Online Users in the MENA Region to Cybersafety, Security and Data Privacy", *Rassed, ictQatar*, July, available at: www.ictqatar.qa/sites/default/files/cybersafety_security_and_data_privacy_-_full_report_1.pdf

Rose, S. (2014) "The Isis Propaganda War: A Hi-Tech Media Jihad", *The Guardian*, 12 October, available at: www.theguardian.com/world/2014/oct/07/isis-media-machine-propaganda-war (accessed 20 November 2014).

Russell, A. (2009) "Introduction: International Blogging—Identity, Politics, and Networked Publics", in A. Russell and N. Echchaibi (eds), *International Blogging: Identity, Politics and Networked Publics*, New York: Peter Lang, pp. 1–10.

Seib, P. (2012) *Real-Time Diplomacy: Politics and Power in the Social Media Era*, New York: Palgrave MacMillan.

Shediac, R., Shehadi, R. T., Bhargava, J., and Samman, H. (2013) "Generations A: Differences and Similarities Across the Arab Generations", *Strategy&*, available at: www.strategyand.pwc.com/reports/arab-generations

Strategy& (2012) "Understanding the Arab Digital Generation", *Strategy&*, available at: www.strategyand.pwc.com/reports/understanding-arab-digital-generation

United Nations Economic and Social Commission for Western Asia (2003) *Promotion of Arabic Content on Digital Networks* (Arabic), Vol. 3, Beirut, Lebanon: United Nations Publication.

Valeri, M. (2015) "Simmering Unrest and Succession Challenges in Oman", *The Carnegie Endowment for International Peace*, 28 January, available at: http://carnegieendowment.org/2015/01/28/simmering-unrest-and-succession-challenges-in-oman/i0s3

Wheeler, D. (2004) "Blessings and Curses: Women and the Internet Revolution in the Arab World", in N. Sakr (ed.), *Women and Media in the Middle East: Power Through Self-Expression*, London: IB Tauris, pp. 138–161.

Wheeler, D. (2009) "Working around the State: Internet Use and Political Identity in the Arab World", in A. Chadwick and P. Howard (eds), *Routledge Handbook of Internet Politics*, Abingdon: Routledge, pp. 305–320.

World Bank (2002) "Republic of Tunisia: Information and Communication Technologies. Contribution to Growth and Employment Generation", *World Bank*, Vol. 1, Washington, DC, available at: http://hdl.handle.net/10986/19063

Zuckerman, E. (2008) "Meet the Bridgebloggers", *Public Choice*, 134: 47–65.

33

INDONESIA'S INTERNET BLUEPRINT

Shifting Experience in Media Culture

Endah Triastuti

Introduction

This chapter looks back on the period before Indonesia emerged as a digital nation. It shows how the development of information and communication technologies (ICTs) is affected by a range of interrelated factors, such as infrastructure, politics, economy, geography, and education levels. Within the Indonesian context, it is argued that implementation of Internet technology and communications was intertwined with various social factors and power discourses exercised by both government and corporations (see, for example, Gurumurthy 2004).

The discussion will take into account the Indonesian government's view of media communication, particularly ICTs during their early development. It draws on Willbur Schramm's idea that the development of media communications accelerates economic and social development in emerging countries, and thus helps people create a path to modernity (Schramm 1964: 5–6). Later on, our discussion will include Robert Stevenson's argument that we also need to give attention to the negative vision of modernity. As Stevenson argues, power holders in emerging countries tend to control communication technologies, and this has a negative impact on a nation's economic and social development (Stevenson 1986).

Stevenson's argument is relevant to the Indonesian government's strategies in establishing Indonesia's communication infrastructure under the Suharto New Order regime.[1] This is because the earlier design of the state's media communication systems was heavily focused on promoting education programs and bolstering economic growth—for instance, when, after 1962, Suharto's authoritarian regime established a media monopoly designed to turn the nation into a controlled space (Kitley 1994: 103; Lim 2002). That is to say, the state used news broadcasts, information, and even entertainment programs to promote state officials and specific constructions of the nation state (Hill and Sen 2005: 5–6; Jurriëns 2009: 54–57, 152–153; Kitley 2003: 100). All programs and content that were considered damaging to the national idelogy were banned. The state structured, centralized, and filtered information flows in a way consistent with the panoptic modality of power (Lim 2002).[2] When Indonesian people were introduced to the Internet, there was a great expectation that new media would usher in better democracy (Hill and Sen 2005; Lim 2005). Or, in effect, that people would be able to participate in public discourse, despite the fact that traditional media were still tightly controlled (Lim in Couldry and Curran 2003: 284). Against this backdrop, in this chapter I draw on Nick Couldry's argument that advances in technology, and changes in social and spatial media, shift the experience of being media users. He argues that in a media-convergent world, power is dispersed throughout media culture. Drawing on Couldry's argument, I show how the authoritarian system of media control during Suharto's reign shifted to a form of shared power where media users apply contextual tactics to reclaim autonomy. In the contemporary period, we can observe the various struggles taking place within media culture in Indonesia that are still dealing with the effects of the centralized media system imposed during Suharto's regime.

With this background in mind, this chapter is, on one hand, intended to examine the various factors that contributed to the ongoing development and innovation of the Internet in Indonesia. On the other hand, this chapter also aims to recognize circulations of power through media culture after the collapse of the authoritarian regime, especially in the era of ICTs. I argue that engagement with the Internet in Indonesia involves struggle, forms of appropriation, oppression, and resistance to the former regime's effort to impose the idea of the nation using traditional media such as radio and television.

In what follows, I start with an overview of early media infrastructure and policy, then give an outline of the establishment of Internet infastructure in Indonesia, divided into four sections, based on the key actors who played important roles within each overlapping period. These are the Scholars' Period, the Hobbyists' Period, the Bureaucrats' Period, and the Entrepreneurs' Period. I conclude with a brief discussion of the development of social media from the mid-2000s as it played out in a highly linguistically and ethnically diverse nation.

Early Media Infrastructure and Policy in Indonesia (1980s to end of 2000)

Indonesia is an archipelagic country of 13,677 islands, with a total land area of about 739,000 square miles. It comprises peoples with various cultural, religious, and ethnic backgrounds. In response to this complex situation, former Indonesian leaders have imposed various policies aimed at forming new loyalties to the state (Bertrand 2004).

The two first post-colonial Indonesian presidents, Sukarno (1945–1967) and Suharto (1967–1998) believed that the media played an important role in nation building (for example, Loven 2008).[3] Hence, media infrastructure building in Indonesia can be understood as a political project and part of its national culture (for example, Hill and Sen 2005; Kitley 2000; Schlesinger 1991). Both radio and television were deployed for building social capital, establishing a sense of connectedness and widening access to political information. Sukarno and Suharto both regulated the media, and used media as a tool to support national unity and preserve cultural nationalism, through their distribution of airtime and control over programing (Kitley 2000; Taylor 2003).

When Sukarno established his "old" regime in 1945, he harnessed Radio Republik Indonesia (RRI) as a means for making political broadcasts (Sen and Hill 2000: 80). Creating a monopoly system on the radio, he disseminated information for propaganda purposes and saw the main role of RRI as cultivating a sense of the nation against minority concerns. Twenty years after RRI was born, Sukarno introduced the idea of national television, and promoted Televisi Republik Indonesia (TVRI) as the ultimate instrument for nation building, as stated in the first paragraph of the Presidential Decree (KEPRES, KEPutustan PRESident) no. 27, 1963).

When Suharto took over Sukarno's reign in 1966, both RRI and TVRI underwent significant shifts. At managerial level, Suharto placed both networks under the control of the

Information Ministry (Departemen Penerangan) in 1974. Although RRI's monopoly in news production remained, Suharto allowed hundreds of private radio stations to operate. There were 217 private radio stations in Indonesia in 1974 (Lindsay 1997), and 1,000 after the fall of Suharto in 1998 (Jurriëns 2009). Although most private radio stations in Indonesia are located in big cities, and use Bahasa Indonesia as the official language (Hill *et al.* 2010), local stations remain, catering to different ethno-linguistic audiences (Reid in Lindsay and Tan, 2003: 17). The state not only allowed a number of private radio stations to operate and run their own programs, but also allowed private stations to be supported by advertising under broadcasting regulations (Lindsay 1997). The flourishing of private radio in Indonesia indicated that Suharto slowly accentuated the economic roles of the media.

Focusing his presidency on economic development, Suharto developed a domestic satellite system known as Palapa in 1976 (Parapak in Thomas 2005). On the one hand, Palapa envisioned national unity and integrity (Barker 2005; Hill and Sen 2005; Kitley 2000) in the interest of manifesting an archipelagic outlook (*wawasan nusantara*) (a notion mentioned in Hoey 2003). On the other hand, it affirmed Suharto's impulse to sustain his authoritarian regime by controlling both communication flows and content. For decades, under Suharto's regime, this communication technology system served as a panoptic system of surveillance through ensuring a monopoly that controlled the information flow and its content across the nation (Kitley 2000). Within this panoptic surveillance system, Suharto presided over a government that enforced Java-centrism and nurtured the supremacy of Javanese culture (Beittinger-Lee 2013; Desai 2013; Jenkins 2010). During his regime, he adopted a strong hierarchical structure that dictated policies, regulation, and national planning, reaching down from Jakarta at its center to the smallest villages of the archipelago. This situation recalls arguments that communication technology has the potential to create new forms of domination (Stevenson 1988), enabling elite control of information flows (Crawford 2007: para 4).

In the 1990s, Suharto shifted policies to reform television regulations, granting access to commercial broadcasters, demonstrating the state's efforts to restructure Indonesia's broadcast service to meet economic imperatives (Kitley 1994).[4] It is clear that the role of the media under the New Order (1965–1998) slowly shifted from a political role in nation building to an economic role.[5] Yet, even though state authorities under Suharto's regime changed a number of regulations and loosened their control over Indonesia's media system, there was insufficient confidence to launch the Internet infrastructure promptly. The idea of the Internet created anxieties among state officials, who realized that it would undermine the monopoly of state-controlled media (McChesney 1999: 119–120). The Internet was seen as a challenge to authoritarian governments, as it potentially opened up liberating space for its users (1999). Thus, the regime showed initial resistance to incorporating the Internet within Indonesia's media framework, fearing the possibility that it might undermine the state's panoptic control of information (Hill and Sen 2005: 31).

Indonesia's neighbors, specifically Singapore and Malaysia, were early adopters in establishing Internet infrastructure. Gradually, the view that technology plays an important role in increasing economic growth became a significant factor that motivated the government to begin to invest in Internet technology. Below, I identify five key periods, pointing out how a range of interrelated factors influenced the establishment of Internet infrastructure in Indonesia, and, to some extent, delayed the development of a nationwide service network.

The Scholars' Period (1972–1989)

The first period is the Scholars' Period, referred to as such because it started within Indonesia's universities. This period is marked by the commencement of the Inter UNIversity Net project

(UNInet) in 1982. This project had been initiated around 1970 by scholars from UI through the establishment of the computer science centre (PUSILKOM) at UI, Jakarta. The UNInet system was hosted in the PERtamina and Pemda DKI offices in Jakarta.

UNInet was a joint project involving a number of public universities in Indonesia, and marks the beginning of Indonesia's networking era. In the early 1980s, this network enabled the staff at PUSILKOM to send electronic messages (Luhukay and Budiardjo 1983). In 1986, UNInet created links within a number of Indonesian universities including UI, Bandung Institute of Technology (ITB), Bogor Agriculture Institute (IPB), Gajah Mada University (UGM) in Yogyakarta, Surabaya Institute of Technology (ITS), Hasanuddin University (Unhas) in South Sulawesi, and the Directorate General of Higher Education in the Ministry of Education and Culture (Lim 2005: 66). In the same year, the University of Indonesia was able to make the first international connection between the Korean Advanced Institute of Science and Technology (KAIST) in Korea, and Seismo, Seizmic Research, Arlington-Virginia, USA, through a Unix-to-Unix-Copy Protocol (UUCP).

Unfortunately, in the late 1980s, UNInet project activities were completely closed down. According to Samik Ibrahim (2010), one of the actors who set the stage for Internet development in Indonesia, this was due to the government's incomprehension of the significance of the project's innovations, compounded by a poor budgeting system that could not fund the expensive project of wiring the whole country (see also Hill and Sen 2005).

The Hobbyists' Period (1980s–2004)

Despite the setback faced by UNInet users, a small group of researchers and scholars from the Institute of Technology, Bandung (ITB) independently established a low-cost secure Internet connection, based on a speed of 9.6 kilobits per second throughout Indonesia, using radio packet technology under the Computer Network Research Group (CNRG). This was the first Internet connection used by the Science and Technology Network project (Ilmu Pengetahuan dan TEKnologi NETwork (IPTEKNET)). This project laid the foundations for the establishment of ITB as a hub for Indonesia's other universities for educational purposes (Lim 2005; Purbo 2002).

This small group of scholars basically comprised university-based technical hobbyists who were interested in developing cheaper Internet connections for more social purposes. They implemented the new technology in a variety of ways, such as establishing a low-cost Wide Area Computer Network AMPRnet (Amateur Packet Radio Network). I nominate this period as the hobbyist or "skunkworks" period, skunkworks being a term designating "a concentration of a few good people, applying the simplest, most straight forward methods possible to develop and produce new products" (Rogers 1995: 221).

The hobbyists opened up possible alternatives for establishing the Internet in Indonesia by attempting to devise low-cost-connection-BBS (bulletin board systems) that were generally accessible. BBS was introduced in the 1980s in Indonesia, and was warmly welcomed by hobbyists in Jakarta, who become highly engaged with the new technology. However, BBS had several issues, mainly related to the insufficient fixed-line telephone connection infrastructure.[6] Additionally, the cost of dial-up connection was high (Lim 2005). In the late 1990s, Telkom, for example, charged 165 rupiahs per minute, about US$1 per hour for an Internet connection, and charged a fee of around US$75 for renting a new line. For the average working class person in Jakarta back then, whose minimum wage was 819,100 rupiahs (US$91) per month, Internet connection fees were still beyond affordability for most people, let alone in other regions.

Indonesian hobbyists aimed for a new breakthrough by maximizing the fact that BBS basically extends radio's basic features to transmit text over voice using telephone lines. In 1987, senior hobbyist Robby Soebiakto introduced the idea of setting up computer technology with packet radio,[7] which is based on the radio communication system (Purbo 2002). This technology enabled users to send textual data using radio waves and has become known as the Amateur Packet Radio Network (AMPRNet). Through this innovation, students in ITB who joined the Amateur Radio Club (ARC) and the Computer Network Research Group (CNRG) initiated the practice of using packet radio technology as a foundation for Internet connections. These early experiments in radio opened up opportunities for computer communications pioneers to create Internet connections in a number of public universities in Indonesia.

The Bureaucrats' Period (1983–1997)

The third key period concerning the establishment of the Internet in Indonesia is the Bureaucrats' Period. During this period, the state demonstrated a deliberate intention to exploit technology in order to foster economic growth (Makka 1996). Under the control and sponsorship of the Bureau for the Assessment and Application of Technology (*Badan Pengembangan dan Pengawasan Teknologi*), the Minister for Research and Technology, B. J. Habibie, initiated the IPTEKNET project in 1989 (Hill and Sen 2005) to establish a self-sustaining Internet service provider (ISP) which would become the embryo of the commercial era of Internet connections in Indonesia (Owen *et al.* 2001).

Less than ten years after the IPTEKNET project commenced, *Time* magazine recorded 1995 as Indonesia's year of the Internet, as the state officially took a leap forward. Unfortunately, during this time, uncertainty regarding Internet regulations came under discussion. Hill and Sen argue that the ambiguity in Internet regulations and management reflected what they called government failure. May 1995 was acknowledged as the commencement of the Internet in Indonesia, yet the state was unable to maintain the previous strict departmental arrangements and divided Internet regulation between two different departments—namely, the Department of Information and the Department of Tourism, Post and Telecommunication. It complicated matters further by appointing the Department of Research and Technology to build the actual Internet infrastructure (Hill and Sen 2005: 49).

However, the state's decision to involve two departments in the administration of the Internet can be viewed from a different angle, since the complex nature of the Internet needed different kinds of administration. Additionally, the early administration of the Internet infrastructure was consistent with the four program objectives of a US$34.5 million World Bank loan initiated in 1998. This loan was intended to expand telecommunications infrastructure in Indonesia, and covered the basic communications medium using the postal network, and the new communication media by introducing the Internet. Thus, in order to support these goals, the World Bank required the state to involve several institutions in the new venture—namely, the Ministry of Tourism, Post and Telecommunications, PT Pos Indonesia, IPTEKNET, and Badan Perencanaan Pembangunan Nasional (National Development Planning Agency of the Republic of Indonesia). That is to say, the Internet was recognized as definitely not an "ordinary" medium compared with the "traditional media" that came before.

The early commercialization of the Internet gradually demonstrated its capacity to increase Indonesia's economic growth, but the maze of bureaucratic complexities governing the medium showed that the Internet is not always a liberating technology. In February 1996, the Deparpostel Minister, Joop Ave, insisted that "the government remains consistent, in that [licences] will not be given to conglomerates" (Hill and Sen 2005: 64). However, most small businesses had no financial cushion, and thus entered financial arrangements with Suharto's cronies such as Bustanil Arifin (head of the national logistic board), Admiral Sudomo (the former Commander of the Command for the Restoration of Security and Order), and Probawo Subianto (Suharto's son-in-law), who held capital ventures. Together with other ISP businesses led by Indonesian conglomerate Liem Sioe Liong, these big ventures became market leaders in Internet provision, such as RADNET, CBN, Centrin, and LinkNet. That is to say, even though the Internet led Indonesian society into the first stages of an information-literate society, and dislodged the state's panoptic surveillance capacities (Maddison 2007), the fact that the Internet infrastructure was connected with powerful elites decentered more marginalized groups, such as the "technically competent young IT entrepreneur" (Hill and Sen 2005: 63), revealing that the Internet is not necessarily free from the culture of authoritarianism.

The Entrepreneurs' Period (1994–recently)

The first ISP, IdOLA (Indonesia Online Access), launched by PT Aplikanusa Lintasarta—a subsidiary of PT IndoSat—in late 1994, was already providing access to the World Wide Web in 17 cities by the end of 1996. Among those ISPs launched in 1996, IndoNet was serving five cities, and WasantaraNet, of the government's postal service PT Pos Indonesia, connected 22 cities by the end of that year. Other major providers appearing in 1995 and 1996 were MegaNet, RADNET, Sistelindo, and MelsaNet, followed in 1997 by CakraWeb and IndoGlobal (Kosasih 1999; Samik-Ibrahim 1996–2002), not to mention numerous smaller ISPs. After the first commercial ISPs were launched, the establishment of the Internet infrastructure in Indonesia accelerated (Mahdi 1995). In 1999, the Director General of Post and Telecommunications issued 50 ISP licenses. In 2007, there were 298 ISP licenses. This means that within less than ten years, the number of ISPs in Indonesia provided by the state increased almost six times. However, there was a huge gap in terms of Internet development between rural and urban areas (Pisu 2010; Udhiarto and Anggono 2007). Rural areas, mostly outside Java, lagged behind other urban, mostly Javanese areas, in part because of the high cost of connection in remote areas (The World Bank 2006: 61) and geographical issues (Global Business Guide Indonesia 2013). As Internet connections were very limited and expensive, it was mainly people who worked for local government or foreign companies who could access the Internet (Sikhakane and Lubbe 2005; Udhiarto and Anggono 2007). Additionally, the Indonesian government did not remedy the lack of Internet cafés outside Java by providing well-established dial-up Internet connection across the archipelago.

Responding to market demand for Internet access, soon after the fall of Suharto in 1998, warnet businesses flourished, especially in Indonesia's big cities and close to universities. "Warnet" are venues where Internet users can purchase time on Internet-enabled computers.[8] As a result, and as a direct commercial response to the bottleneck in private connections, the first Internet café (Warung Internet (WARNET))[9] began to operate, offering users Internet access at a relatively low cost.

Scholars have claimed that Internet cafés meet the needs of low- and middle-class consumers from big cities in Java (Wahid et al. 2005: 4). During this time, the market established several types of warnet. According to Rusdiah (2013) there are at least three types of warnet or Internet cafés, reflecting their capital (equipment), licenses (unlicensed and licensed), connection (dial-up, broadband, and VSAT), and services (browsing and games). Clearly, in the early 2000s people saw warnet as a good business opportunity. According to Asosiasi WARNET Indonesia (Indonesian Internet Kiosk Association), in 2007, 40 percent of 20 million Internet users in Indonesia accessed the Internet from an Internet café. In 2011, there were at least 260,000 warnets across Indonesia, mostly located in Java (Deloitte Access Economics 2011: 6).

After 2000: Indonesia's Love Affair with Social Media

The most flourishing and outstanding period in the development of Internet use in Indonesia commenced in 2005, when the state released the 2.4 GHz wireless radio frequency to enhance wireless Internet connections. This policy reduced the costs involved in Internet set-up, thus encouraging the development of an Internet industry, and increasing the number of Internet subscribers and users. Data shows that every year Internet penetration in Indonesia is increasing.

Yet despite this effort, due to difficulties in servicing and connecting a sprawling archipelagic national territory, the state has still been faced with difficulties in bringing the Internet to Indonesia's remote areas.[10] It appears that the number of Internet users differs widely across each region in Indonesia (Rusdiah 2013).

Significantly, mobile Internet has proven more "friendly" to Indonesian people who live in rural areas. The state enhanced opportunities to access the Internet by finalizing Telecommunications Law No. 36/1999 that implemented the Anti-Monopoly Law in the telecommunications industry. The law effectively ended the monopoly of the Indonesian telecommunication sector by two giant telecommunication providers, PT Telkom and PT Indosat. In early 2006, the Indonesian government authorized a number of providers, such as PT Natrindo Telepon Selular, Hutchison CP Telecommunications, Telkomsel, and Excelcomindo, to build a mobile Internet infrastructure in Indonesia. These new entrants of wireless Internet providers did not only make a quick grab for the Indonesian Internet market share, but have also increased access to telecommunication (The World Bank 2006). Mobile technology is gaining popularity across the board in Indonesia, both in urban and rural areas (see, for example, Lim 2013).

In 2014, there were 266 million people using mobile phones to access the Internet. The boom in mobile phones as a means of social networking has been apparent. In 2013, Indonesia was Facebook's fourth biggest market with 70 percent of Indonesian Facebook users acessing it through their mobile (Carter-Lau 2013).

Over the following years, online activities involving social media have become the number one activity on the Internet in Indonesia (Semiocast 2013). In 2015, APJII reported that participating in social media, including browsing and searching for information, is the most common activity on the Internet in the country. In fact, 92.9 percent of the Internet population in Indonesia are very active Facebook users, whereas 7.5 percent of all tweets globally come from Indonesia, making it the third largest Twitter-using country, with 385 tweets posted every second.

Social media is already changing the language of politics as digital platforms become the new space of democracy (Lim 2013; Nugroho 2011). They provide networks of civic engagement where open discussion is allowed (see, for example, Kaskus—Indonesia's largest online community—which has more than two million members and 70,000 posts each day, and Isa Dan Islam—an interfaith, open discussion community). In contemporary Indonesian social media space, political dissent is also expressed (see Anda Bertanya Habib Riziek Menjawab's Facebook fan page, or Change.org), and opposition parties are empowered—for example, TemanAHOK (Ahok's friends), Gerakan Anti Pelecehan Seksual terhadap Wanita (women's rights against sexual harassment), or LGBT Indonesia. The character of the Internet itself has encouraged the state to change its view regarding media regulation. Although the media had previously been used as a control tool, the country partly won its democracy through people power engaging with the Internet.[11] Furthermore, in 2014, for example, new president Jokowi won the Indonesian presidential election due to the support he had gained from campaign activity mostly on social media (see, for example, Safitri 2015).

The Indonesian love affair with social media demonstrates that in an era of media complexity, people engage with media in multiple ways. As Couldry puts it, in a media-saturated world the audience is "relocated" from the "sitting room" to "a variety of social contexts". Media power can no longer be considered direct and massive; instead it is dispersed across the "whole spectrum of talk, action, and thought that draws on media" (Couldry 2005: 196).

Conclusion

This brief history of Internet infrastructure development in Indonesia illustrates that technological innovations involve multiple interconnected factors such as political, cultural, linguistic, and technical issues. Although in its beginnings the Internet was envisaged by the state as another media vehicle for its nation-building agenda, as the Internet developed in relation to various infrastructure and economic factors, actual users found ways to deploy the technology for their own ends. The roll-out of mobile Internet technology in the 2000s massiveley increased the opportunities for people in Indonesia to engage with the new technology.

The brief surviving records of early Internet communities illustrates the beginning of the era of social media, where Indonesian netters, both male and female, started their engagement with the Internet. Within this engagement, social media users showed their ability to negotiate and to recreate the global and national domination through their practices on the Internet. People's engagement with the Internet in Indonesia is in line with Couldry's argument that the Internet offers multiple impacts, rather than those solely related to its technological features (Couldry and Curran 2003).

The establishment of Internet infrastructure and practices is associated with a new potential to share power via cyberspace. The centralized media system closely controlled by the government during Suharto's era has now been fundamentally challenged. The boom in social media use in Indonesia, and its uses for various political ends, indicates the potential of Internet users to take over—at least to some extent—government's power and control over media use. Today, anyone with access to a computer or a phone can promote themselves, express opinions, and share ideas over a multitude of formats and platforms.

Even though claims about the impact of the Internet in Indonesia should not be over-emphasized (see, for example, Lim 2005; Margolis and Resnick 2000), it is evident that the new technology has the ability to increase civic engagement that leads to social and economic transformation. Since 2013, for example, Indonesia has seen the birth of home-grown sharing platforms such as Go-Jek, a start-up that provides a platform for motorbike ride-sharing, which shows the rise of the sharing economy in Indonesia and its changing consumption patterns. The last presidential election in 2014 showed the public's ability to coordinate a massive and rapid response. In this sense of power shifting, various parties in Indonesia have the ability to influence the media at various levels.

However, my study also acknowledges that while media do not obviously and directly exert power over their audiences' everyday lives, "Across social life as a whole, a huge number of activities involving everyone (including those who are not 'in power') contribute to sustaining particular power relations (Couldry 2005: 194).

My study is evidence of the fact that power is still circulated in media culture through symbolic forms. Among the most vivid evidence for this is the trend for using an informal register, which we may call "hanging out language", across Indonesian cyberspace that is informally known as Bahasa Gaul (Gaul language). Gaul language is derived mainly from Jakartan language (Smith-Hefner 2007: 186; see also Sneddon 2003). I argue that this brings forward the important role of Java as the center of politics, the economy, technology, and the media industries, as well as the center of the growth of this new set of language practices, and the Internet. Hence, with respect to Indonesian cyberspace, these symbolic forms are manifested as a subject of hegemonic struggle as a response to power relations that are rooted in a system of language standardization (Blackledge 2000; Keane 2003; Squires 2010).

In the case of Indonesia's cyberspace, the evolution of the Internet illustrates the wider power relations within media culture in Indonesia (see Couldry 2005). Through various strategies, Indonesian Internet users improvise in their various uses of the Internet, as well as social media, to undermine their domination within Indonesian media culture. Thus, my study shows, in line with Homi Bhabha's (2004) argument, that within discourses of power, there is always a liminal space where subordinates are able to negotiate power distribution.

Notes

1. At the outset, I refer to Schlessinger's assertion (in Kitley 2000: 6–7) that state ideology during Suharto's authoritarian government (1965–1998) was all-pervasive, particularly in media regulations and nation building.
2. In his book *Discipline and Punish: The Birth of the Prison* (1977), Foucault discusses Jeremy Bentham's terminology of the Panopticon. Foucault argues that, in power, discourse control does not necessarily result from a coercive action. Instead, control can be achieved through a disciplinary mechanism, by creating a belief of constant and total surveillance. As follows, systematic control is internalized, forming a hegemony of power (Foucault 1977: 200–203). The form of hegemony as a result of Suharto's authoritarian government is incarnated in Indonesian cyberspace after reformation in 1998.
3. Nation building was viewed both as a literal process of building (bridges, roads, high-rises, monuments, industry) and as a process of "building" a national consciousness (through education, sports, propaganda, etc.) (Barker 2005: 1).
4. Philip Kitley (1994) notes the series of policy changes started in the 1980s, with the banning of advertisement programs from TVRI (1981), the managing policies of the home video entertainment industry (1983–1987), the legislating of the home use of satellite dishes and video (1986–1990), the establishing of a restricted broadcast service (1987), and the structuring of the commercial broadcast services (1993–present).
5. According to Kitley (1994), this major policy change indicated the Indonesian government's readiness to open up economic and political liberalism that was expected to improve Indonesia's financial circumstances.
6. In 1981 and 1982, the national fixed-line phone density rate was only 0.57 per 100 inhabitants. Compared with other South-east Asian countries, Indonesia's national fixed-line phone density at that time was extremely low. That is to say, although fixed-line phone connection was in high demand, product and service availability was very low, because of the expensive registration fee, but also because people had to queue up to register their applications. Even in 2005, PT Telkom, which has built Indonesia's telecommunications infrastructure for many decades, provided nine million units of fixed-line connection (The World Bank 2006). With a population of more than 215 million, national fixed-line density rate in that year was only 4 percent, which was below the world's average fixed-line density rate that reached 10 percent. Indonesia's fixed-line density rate was even less than Singapore's rate, which in 2002 had already reached 46.6 percent. There is a lot of fuss made about telecommunication infrastructure establishment in Indonesia. The main issue has been central and peripheral: as a capital city, Jakarta has been well infrastructured, compared with small, remote, and hinterland villages, of which 64.4 percent have not been touched by basic telecommunications such as the fixed-line telephone.
7. Komunitas Indonesia Open Source, available at: http://opensource.telkomspeedy.com/ (accessed 27 March 2009).
8. In 1998, the average cost to use the Internet for an hour was 700–1,200 rupiahs, and increased from 3,000 to 5,000 rupiahs in 2008. In 2012, AUD$1 was around 10,000 rupiahs.
9. Most writers use "Internet café" as the English translation for "Warung Internet" in Indonesia. In my opinion, by using the word "café", those writers have misrepresented the word "warung" to the reader. Today, there are many cafés in Indonesia, meaning a cozy place to enjoy drinking coffee. These cafés serve free or discount-price Internet hot-spot connections for their customers. In contrast, Warung Internet does not serve coffee or food; it only provides a PC with an Internet connection.
10. The Indonesian government established programs on the accessibility of the Internet for rural people around 2011, such as "Desa PINTER", Internet stalls, and mobile Internet for remote areas, namely the Mobile Pusat Layanan Internet Kecamatan (Mobile District Internet Service Center) program, and "Desa Digital" (digital rural village), which was implemented in early 2013.
11. Sen and Hill (2001) acknowledged the Internet as the main democracy tool in the fall of Suharto in 1998. Lim (2012) offered a more convivial point of view by stating that the birth of Internet Indonesia is a process that has different outcomes, and of a different nature (for example re-formation in 1998 and Laskar Jihad).

References

Barker, J. (2005) "Engineers and Political Dreams: Indonesia in the Satellite Age", *Current Anthropology*, 46.

Beittinger-Lee, V. (2013) *(Un)Civil Society and Political Change in Indonesia: A Contested Arena*, New York: Routledge.

Bertrand, J. (2004) *Nationalism and Ethnic Conflict in Indonesia*, Cambridge: Cambridge University Press.

Bhabha, H. K. (2004) *The Location of Culture*, New York: Routledge.

Blackledge, A. (2000) "Monolingual Ideologies in Multilingual States: Language, Hegemony and Social Justice in Western Liberal Democracies", *Estudios de Sociolingüística: Linguas, Sociedades e Culturas*, 1(2): 25–46.

Carter-Lau, P. (2013) "Indonesia: The social media capital of the world", On Device Research, available at: https://ondeviceresearch.com/blog/indonesia-social-media-capital-world.

Couldry, N. (2005) "The Extended Audience", in M. Gillespie (ed.), *Media Audiences*, Buckinghamshire: Open University Press, pp. 184–196.

Couldry, N., and Curran, J. (2003) *Contesting Media Power: Alternative Media in a Networked World*, Lanham, MD: Rowman & Littlefield.

Crawford, M. (2007) "Information Revolution", *Inside Indonesia*, 30 September, available at: www.insideindonesia.org/information-revolution.

Deloitte Access Economics (2011) *The Connected Archipelago: The Role of the Internet in Indonesia's Economic Development*, Sydney: Deloitte Access Economics.

Desai, R. (2013) *Developmental and Cultural Nationalisms*, New York: Routledge.

Foucault, M. (1977) *Discipline and Punish: The Birth of the Prison*, Harmondsworth: Penguin.

Global Business Guide Indonesia. (2013) *Improving Internet Access in Indonesia, Global Business Guide Indonesia*, available at: www.gbgindonesia.com/en/services/article/2012/improving_internet_access_in_indonesia.php

Gurumurthy, A. (2004) "Gender and ICTs", *Bridge: Institute of Development Studies*, available at: www.bridge.ids.ac.uk/sites/bridge.ids.ac.uk/files/reports/CEP-ICTs-OR.pdf.

Hill, C., Corbett, C., and Rose, A. S. (2010) "Why So Few? Women in Science, Technology, Engineering and Mathematics", *American Association of University Women*, available at: www.aauw.org/resource/why-so-few-women-in-science-technology-engineering-mathematics/.

Hill, D. T., and Sen, K. (2005) *The Internet in Indonesia's New Democracy*, Oxford: Routledge.

Hoey, B. A. (2003) "Nationalism in Indonesia", *Ethnology*, 42: 109–126.

Ibrahim, S. (2010) email interview, 20 May.

Jenkins, D. (2010) *Suharto and His Generals: Indonesian Military Politics, 1975–1983*, Sheffield: Equinox.

Jurriëns, E. (2009) *From Monologue to Dialogue: Radio and Reform in Indonesia*, Leiden: Kitlv Press.

Keane, W. (2003) "Public Speaking: On Indonesian as the Language of the Nation", *Public Culture*, 15: 503–530.

Kitley, P. (1994) "Fine Tuning Control: Commercial Television in Indonesia", *The Australian Journal of Media & Culture*, 8(2): 103–123.

Kitley, P. (2000) *Television Nation and Culture in Indonesia*, Ohio RIS Southeast Asia Series, no. 104, Athens, OH: Ohio University Press.

Kitley, P. (2003) "Civil Society in Charge? Television and the Public Sphere in Indonesia after *Reformasi*", in P. Kitley (ed.), *Television, Regulation and Civil Society in Asia*, London: Routledge, pp. 97–114.

Kosasih, S. (1999) "Dunia Cyber: Sejarah Internet", *Suara KalTim*, (3): 24 July.

Lim, M. (2002) "Cyber-Civic Space in Indonesia: From Panopticon to Pandemonium?", *International Development Planning Review*, 4: 383–400.

Lim, M. (2005) "@Rchipelago Online: The Internet and Political Activism in Indonesia", Ph.D. thesis, University of Twente.

Lim, M. (2012) interview.

Lim, M. (2013) "Many Clicks But Little Sticks: Social Media Activism in Indonesia", *Journal Of Contemporary Asia*, 43(4): 636–657.

Lindsay, J. (1997) "Making Waves: Private Radio and Local Identities in Indonesia", *Indonesia*, 64: 105–123.

Lindsay, J., and Tan, Y. Y. (2003) *Babel or Behemoth: Language Trends in Asia*, Asia Research Institute, National University Of Singapore.

Loven, K. (2008) *Watching Si Doel: Television, Language and Identity in Contemporary Indonesia*, Leiden: Kitlv Press.

Luhukay, J., and Budiardjo, B. (1983) "Uninet: An Inter-University Computer Network", *Asia Electronics Symposium*, 19–20 October, Jakarta.

McChesney, R. W. (1999) *Rich Media, Poor Democracy: Communication Politics in Dubious Times*, Urbana, IL: University of Illinois Press.

Maddison, Z. V. (2007) "Information's Role in Emerging Democratic Societies: The Case of Indonesia", *Information for Social Change*, 25.

Mahdi, W. (1995) "The Internet Factor in Indonesia: Was That All?", 54th Annual Meeting of the Association for Asian Studies, Washington DC, 4-7 April, available at: http://waruno.de/PDFs/wm_IDinetsaga.pdf.

Makka, A. M. (1996) *Bjh: Bacharuddin Jusuf Habibie, His Life and Career*, Jakarta: Pustaka Cidesindo.

Margolis, M., and Resnick, D. (2000) Politics as Usual: *The Cyberspace "Revolution"*, Contemporary American Politics, vol. 6, Sage Publications.

Newey, A. (1999) "Freedom of Expression: Censorship in Private Hands", in J. Cooper (ed.), *Liberating Cyberspace: Civil Liberties, Human Rights, and the Internet*, London: Pluto Press, pp. 13–43.

Nugroho, A. Y. (2011) *Citizens in @Ction*, Manchester: Manchester Institute of Innovation Research.

Owen, D. E., Sulaiman, I. F., Baldia, S., and Mintz, S.P. (2001) *Indonesia: Information and Communications Technologies (ICT) Assessment*, Jakarta: USAID/ECG.

Pisu, M. (2010) *Tackling the Infrastructure Challenge in Indonesia*, OECD Economics Department Working Papers.

Priandoyo, A. (2007) "Berapa Biaya Pengurusan Telepon Kabel Telkom?", Anjar Priandoyo's Shortcut, available at: https://priandoyo.wordpress.com/2007/06/18/berapa-biaya-pengurusan-telepon-kabel-telkom/.

Purbo, O. (1995) "The Indonesian Government Networking Status", *The United Nations ESCAP Meeting*, Bangkok: AIM APIC.

Purbo, O. W. (2002) *An Indonesian Digital Review: Internet Infrastructure and Initiatives*, Padjadjaran University Repository, available at: http://ftp.unpad.ac.id/orari/library/cd-al-manaar-digilib/bahan/3.%20INFOTEK/1.%20ARTIKEL/4-indonesiaan%20Digital%20Review.pdf.

Rogers, E. M. (1995) *Diffusion of Innovations*, New York: Free Press.

Rusdiah, R. (2013) "Internet Center (Warnet) Diffusion in Rural Villages to Sustain Economic Development or Part of Global Big Data Trend?", *Information Systems International Conference*, Bali, Indonesia.

Safitri, D. (2015) "Indonesia and the Danger of Social Media Democracy", *Jakarta Post*, 27 June.

Samik-Ibrahim, R. M. (1996–2002) "Perintisan WWW di Indonesia", *IKI-20230: Sistem Operasi*, available at: https://rms46.vlsm.org/1/51.html.

Schlesinger, P. (1991) "Media, the Political Order and National Identity", *Media, Culture & Society*, 13(3): 297–308.

Schramm, W. (1964) *Mass Media and National Development: The Role of Information in the Developing Countries*, Stanford, CA: Stanford University Press.

Semiocast (2013) "Twitter reaches half a billion accounts", Paris: Semiocast, available at: http://semiocast.com/en/publications/2012_07_30_Twitter_reaches_half_a_billion_accounts_140m_in_the_US.

Sen, K., and Hill, D. (2000) *Media, Culture and Politics in Indonesia*, Oxford: Oxford University Press.

Sikhakane, B., and Lubbe, S. (2005) "Preliminaries into Problems to Access Information: The Digital Divide and Rural Communities", *South African Journal of Information Management*, 7(3).

Smith-Hefner, N. J. (2007) "Youth Language, Gaul Sociability, and the New Indonesian Middle Class", *Journal of Linguistic Anthropology*, 17(2): 184–203.

Sneddon, J. N. (2003) *Indonesian Language: Its History and Role in Modern Society*, Sydney: University of New South Wales Press.

Soegijoko, S., Purbo, O.W., Merati, W., Sutikno, P., and Achmad, I. (1996) *Computer Networking in Indonesia: Current Status and Recommendations for its Developments*, The Asia Pacific Networking Group Meeting, Singapore.

Squires, L. (2010) "Enregistering Internet Language", *Language in Society*, 39(4): 457–492.

Stevenson, R. L. (1986) "Radio and Television Growth in the Third World, 1960–1985", *International Communication Gazette*, 38(1): 115–125.

Stevenson, R. L. (1988) *Communication, Development, and the Third World: The Global Politics of Information*, New York: Longman.

Sulistyanto (2008) "The Development of the Internet in Indonesia: Challenges and Prospects to Go Online", Komunikasi dan Media, available at: http://sulistyanto70.blogspot.co.id/search?updated-min=2008-01-01T00:00:00%2B07:00&updated-max=2009-01-01T00:00:00%2B07:00&max-results=6 2015.

Taylor, J. G. (2003) *Indonesia: Peoples and Histories*, New Haven: Yale University Press.

Thomas, A. O. (2005) *Imagi-Nations and Borderless Television: Media, Culture and Politics Across Asia*, New Delhi: Sage.

Udhiarto, A., and Anggono, B. D. (2007) *Bridging Digital Divide by Empowering School in Rural Area: Case Study in Kebumen Region, Central Java, Indonesia*, Putrajaya International Convention Center.

Wahid, F., Furuholt, B., and Kristiansen, S. (2005) "Global Diffusion of the Internet III: Information Diffusion Agents and the Spread of Internet Cafés in Indonesia", *Communications of the Association for Information Systems*, 13.

The World Bank. (2006) *Indonesia: Connecting the Archipelago*, The World Bank, pp. 1–11, available at: http://siteresources.worldbank.org/INTINDONESIA/Resources/Publication/280016-1152870963030/2753486-1162359048143/TelkomBriefs.pdf.

34

HISTORIES OF THE INTERNET AND POLITICAL COMMUNICATION IN LUSOPHONE AFRICA

Susana Salgado

Introduction

The Portuguese-speaking African countries offer particularly interesting case studies when the objective is to examine the political influence of the Internet.[1] Angola, Cape Verde, Mozambique, and Sao Tome and Principe[2] share the same language and a similar historical background of nearly five centuries of Portuguese colonization, and although with very different degrees of success, these countries are also commonly considered new democracies. In the early 1990s, the third wave of democratization (Huntington 1991), which had started in 1974 with the Carnation Revolution in Portugal, spread to Africa, and several sub-Saharan African countries initiated democratic reforms, mainly by adopting new constitutions, multi-party regimes, and elections as the means to select rulers. These four countries also share the particular feature of having started their democratization processes simultaneously with the worldwide expansion of the Internet.

The development of the Internet can be addressed from many different angles; for example, the history of the medium itself includes not only the elements that have affected its development, but also the implications of its historical evolution in different contexts. Different regions of the world, different areas of society, and different social and age groups are likely to induce different experiences, adaptations, perceptions, histories, and therefore outline different understandings and paradigms of the Internet's evolution and its effects. In addition, histories of the individuals' use of the Internet and their lives intersect and contribute to building not only the history of a country, but also the history of the Internet.

These countries' histories represent valuable illustrations of different Internet histories and of different Internet development paces. The Internet has influenced communicative practices in general, and political communication in particular, by adding different dimensions to power discourses and facilitating collective action, for instance. Particularly in developing countries, the Internet has the potential to enhance active citizenship and promote political participation by providing citizens with alternative ways to demand more freedom and social justice.

The Internet has been often presented as an important driver of democratization. A first preliminary observation of these four countries' democratic development points to very different levels of democratization achieved in the last decades, and therefore demonstrates that the impact of technology is greatly mediated by other factors and that technology by itself does not have the power initially attributed by some technological determinist but also rather utopian views (Grossman 1995; Ferdinand 2000, among others).

Through individual and collective histories from Lusophone Africa, and supported by knowledge obtained from interviews, observation, and media analysis, this chapter looks at new online political communication opportunities in countries experiencing democratization processes. It addresses both the role of independent online news media outlets and blogs in environments facing constraints to freedom, and the use of the Internet in citizens' participation and political change.

Online Political Communication Accounts

The Background

When compared to the rest of the world, the percentage of Internet users in Lusophone African countries, and especially in Angola and Mozambique, is small. Internet access is still very limited outside the main cities, which ends up contributing to accentuating inequalities between regions and social classes. Mozambique is the country with the least people connected to the Internet—only 4.3 percent in 2012. In Angola, the percentage of Internet users was 14.8 percent, and in Sao Tome and Principe it was 20.2 percent in the same year. Cape Verde is the country where the most people have access: 32 percent of citizens were already using the Internet in 2012 (Internet World Stats 2015; Salgado 2015).

Some of the main obstacles to Internet access and use are the high prices and the low quality of most service providers. But the major constraints are still closely related to the poor living conditions that large sections of these countries' populations still face (lack of decent housing with electricity, for example) and low levels of functional, communicational, and media literacies in general. What is demanded of citizens in an information society is much more than knowing how to read and write. The level of competence required to use efficiently the new information and communication technologies involves different types of literacy, such as functional literacy, which refers to comprehension and interpretation skills, and communicational and media literacy, which means that citizens should have the ability to analyze and create different messages in different media genres, and should be able to identify the medium most suited to communicate their ideas (Salgado 2014: 111).

Technology in general, and more recently the Internet in particular, have been pointed out as having the role of facilitators that drive other innovations, democratization, and economic development (Lerner 1958; Mudhai *et al.* 2009; Nwokeafor and Langmia 2010; Salgado 2012, just to provide some examples related to developing nations). The 2015 United Nations General Assembly's debate recently reinforced the goal of achieving universal access to the Internet by the end of 2020, because, according to this organization, the Internet is directly linked to human development in all of its different facets, including economic and political. This view is not new, and a very similar perspective is shared by the World Bank (2009) in a report that demonstrates that access to affordable and reliable high-speed Internet and mobile communications are central to economic growth and job creation in developing countries.

Several international organizations have been fundamental in the history of building the Internet in sub-Saharan Africa, particularly in respect to infrastructure and capacity building; however, for the time being, access to technology and information is still extremely differentiated, and these gaps have tended to accentuate the already existing great differences among social and political groups in these societies.

Although the Internet contains in itself the potential for further development, the ways in which it is used and its histories seem to be strongly conditioned by context. Allowing for substantial cross-country differences, there is still a long way to go in the African Portuguese-speaking countries regarding the democratization of Internet access, especially taking into consideration some persisting structural constraints, such as the lack of electricity and telephone lines or broadband access in some remote and rural regions. Indeed, there are strong inequalities in access to the Internet and technologies in general, both between the four countries and within them. Until a few years ago, apart from more wealthy people, the Internet users in these countries were civil servants and other workers in the service sector who had Internet access in their jobs. This gap is clearly reflected in the blogger communities: most bloggers are from the middle and upper classes, and have an academic level considered very high when compared with the rest of the population; there are blogs, for example, by politicians, journalists, academic researchers, historians, and artists (Salgado 2012).

Most usage was also, and still is in many places, confined to the capital city and to major cities. However, even though Internet access is still limited, it has grown in recent years due to the availability of cheaper access to services and the implementation of projects designed to promote Internet access for the general population. Efforts to equip schools, universities, libraries, and other public services with computers and Internet access have increased and, in some cases, small cities and villages were included. Other options are cyber cafés and free-access media centers and libraries.

In Angola, a project was put in place to provide all provinces with media libraries, including in the least populated provinces, and to distribute mobile media libraries throughout the country while more definitive structures are not in place. The mobile structures are thus supposed to facilitate the access of the general population to new technologies and allow citizens, including students, to do all kinds of research on the Internet (Angop 2015). In 2015, Angola had six media libraries in Luanda, Benguela, Huambo, Lubango, Saurimo, and Soyo, six mobile media libraries scattered across the country, and plans to establish six more of these structures by the end of the year. The government expects to have at least one of these media centers fully operational in each of Angola's 18 provinces by 2017 (Deutsche Welle 2015).

This project is part of the N'gola Digital program regarding the "Information Society and Technologies of Information and Communication" of the Angolan Ministry of Telecommunications and Information Technologies, which has as its main objectives to provide communities with computers connected to the Internet, and to organize workshops on how to use computers and software at different levels of proficiency. More recently, Movicel, an Angolan mobile phone company, developed a partnership with Facebook, the app "Internet.org", to provide free Internet access to a limited selection of websites related to news, health, employment, weather, and, of course, Facebook (*O País* 2015).

In Cape Verde, the history of the Internet began in 1996 and since then its use has become increasingly affordable to a growing number of people. In 2009, a study by the National Statistics Institute (Instituto Nacional de Estatística (INE)) revealed that in Cape Verde 45.7 percent of the population lived less than 15 minutes away from an Internet connection spot; the percentage was 61.6 percent in the capital city Praia, but in the interior municipality São Salvador do Mundo, only 6.8 percent (Instituto Nacional de Estatística 2009). São Salvador do Mundo is situated in the central part of Santiago, the same island where the capital city Praia is located. The fact that the Cape Verdean authorities have decided to implement a program to offer free wireless Internet access near the city halls in most cities helped to improve the overall numbers. But also contributing to increasing the number of users and democratizing access is the fact that Cape Verde already has its schools, universities, libraries, and public services in general connected to the Internet.

According to the International Telecommunication Union (ITU), Cape Verde is part of the very small group of African countries with a relatively high proportion of the population online: in 2014, these were Seychelles (50 percent), South Africa (49 percent), Mauritius and Kenya (39 percent), and Cape Verde and Nigeria (38 percent). Cape Verde was not, however, highlighted in this report for its household penetration; only four out of a total of 38 countries in Africa had more than 30 percent of households with Internet access in 2013, and they were: Seychelles (51 percent), Mauritius (45 percent), South Africa (39 percent), and Ghana (32 percent) (ITU 2014: 87–88). Internet penetration levels and the use of new technologies among young people aged 15–24 is around 65 percent in Cape Verde. Finally, access to mobile broadband in Cape Verde and the level of prices of ICTs (the fifth lowest in Africa behind Seychelles, Mauritius, South Africa, and Botswana) were also important drivers of the rapid increase of Internet access in this country (National Communications Authority (Agência Nacional das Comunicações) 2013).

In Sao Tome and Principe the price of having Internet at home was, in 2011, more than 100 euros per month, which is extremely high for a country where 61.7 percent of the population was, in 2009, considered poor (World Bank 2009). The installation of fiber optic in 2012 made better services available, and lowered prices slightly in this country. Companies and international authorities, such as the Chinese government, have been assisting the government in Sao Tome and Principe in opening digital centers and in providing computers with Internet access to libraries throughout the country. This was the case in the Mé-Zóchi district, where a digital center with 30 computers was inaugurated in the village of Trindade, in March 2013, as a joint initiative of the Mé-Zóchi district and the National Institute of Research and Knowledge (Instituto Nacional de Investigação e Conhecimento (INIC)), and funded by the Taiwan Embassy in Sao Tome with US$60,000. The Mé-Zóchi district has around 15,000 inhabitants, and especially for the underprivileged, this is the only opportunity to acquire digital skills and qualifications. This was not the only project of this kind supported by the Taiwan Embassy: there was also a digital center in the district of Cantagalo, and before Trindade and Cantagalo, the Taiwan Embassy had also supported the library in Principe Island (*Jornal Digital* 2013). Another noteworthy example is the 'Internet4all' program, implemented in 2004 by the company Bahnhof to train local communities in the use of the Internet.

The price of Internet services is an issue in Mozambique too. According to a report by Beyond Access,[3] for over 95 percent of its population, Mozambique's Internet services are unaffordable. Its fixed broadband connections are the fourth most expensive in the world, and while mobile services are less expensive, a subscription costs over 65 percent of the average family's income (Beyond Access 2014). Nevertheless, the number of Internet service providers has been growing, which means an increase of companies, institutions, and individuals with Internet access. At the end of the 1990s, the Mozambican National Communications Institute had recorded only one ISP operating in the country, the Eduardo Mondlane University, and in 2014, there were more than 20. But Internet services are heavily concentrated in Maputo, the capital city, and many are reluctant to expand to interior and smaller cities, on the grounds of insufficient demand and unreliable electricity services (Balancing Act 2014).

The introduction of submarine cables in 2009 and 2010 has made access to cheaper international connectivity possible in Mozambique, but despite this, only a small minority of the population is able to purchase computers and have Internet access at home. Most people use the Internet at their workplaces or in Internet cafés and telecenters. There have been several initiatives by the government and NGOs to provide the country with these infrastructures. For example, in 2006, eight centers were set up to provide access to ICTs in rural communities, through the Social Communication Institute in cooperation with several international organizations as part of a government initiative. More recently, the government has been working with strategic partners to explore the potential of libraries to serve as points of Internet access.

In these countries, the Internet is not systematically controlled, and until now only the Angolan government has tried to regulate access and use of the Internet: in April 2011, it approved in parliament a law that allows authorities to control users and online content, and created a committee to analyze the existing Press Law and to work on the regulation of the Internet. In Mozambique, even though a number of sites remained untouched after criticizing the government, there were reports of government agents monitoring the email accounts of members of opposition political parties (Salgado 2014).

A Young Female Blogger and Opposition Politician in Mozambique

For her work as a politician, Maria Ivone Soares was one of the nominees for "African emergent personalities" in 2014, distinguished by the news magazine *The Africa Report*. Maria Ivone Soares has been considered a rising star in the context of opposition politics in Mozambique (see, for instance, Africa Intelligence 2015). For many of her party members and supporters of Mozambican National Resistance (RENAMO), she embodies part of the hopes of accomplishing sustainable changes in Mozambican politics in the near future. She represents a new generation, and embodies a different approach to politics based on dialogue and communication, in which the use of new media has been key.

The Mozambique Liberation Front (FRELIMO) has been ruling Mozambique since independence in 1975 and has won every election after the democratization process started at the beginning of the 1990s. FRELIMO and RENAMO have been the two main parties in the Mozambican party system, but more recently a new influential political force entered the game: RENAMO dissidents created a new political party, Democratic Movement of Mozambique (MDM), which participated in the 2009 election and managed to elect eight of 250 parliamentary deputies.

Mozambique has had regular elections since 1994, but FRELIMO has been consolidating its position the political scene. For instance, in the 2009 election, FRELIMO won with 75 percent in the presidential and legislative elections, while in 2004 the party had fewer votes: 62 percent in the legislative elections and 63.7 percent in the presidential election. While FRELIMO is wining supporters, RENAMO's voting results took the opposite course. In 2004, the party had 29.7 percent in the legislative election and 31.7 percent in the presidential election, and in 2009 its votes decreased to 16.41 percent in the legislative election and 17.68 percent in the presidential election.

The high level of distrust between FRELIMO and RENAMO has been hindering the country's democratization process. On several occasions, RENAMO questioned and refused to accept the election results, and threatened to boycott elections. RENAMO has also been involved in occasional guerrilla attacks and the RENAMO leader, Afonso Dhlakama, has been in hiding for some time in central Mozambique. Aside from these local skirmishes, the country has been living in peace since the General Peace Agreement was signed in 1992 between RENAMO and FRELIMO, ending a 16-year-long civil war. The tension is none-theless fully extended to political elites: for example, FRELIMO and RENAMO parliamentary groups frequently reject each other's proposals, regardless of the public value of the proposed policies. This constant lack of agreement has important consequences for political inclusion and the quality of public debate. It also diverts attention from the important issues that concern the population to party quarrels and disputes between political leaders, which end up being the focus of most of the mainstream media coverage.

Maria Ivone Soares is Afonso Dhlakama's niece, but also one of RENAMO's members of parliament, former RENAMO spokesperson, and former leader of the party youth. She has been an active blogger (mariaivonesoares.blogspot.com; rabiscosdasoares.blogspot.com; politic andomoz.blogspot.com), because she sees the potential of this means of communication to raise young people's criticism about the challenges that the country faces in maintaining a multi-party democracy. Maria Ivone Soares is outspoken and pointed to (for instance, by the sociologist Carlos Serra 2007) as an example of courage for assuming her identity in the blogosphere. Only in very few cases do people reveal their identity in the Mozambican blogosphere, and in the case of women, this is even rarer.

Although the Internet is not controlled on a systematic basis, there are reports of bloggers being ordered to cease their activities. Because of this, and also due to the relatively new environment of freedom, some bloggers prefer to maintain anonymity (Salgado 2012). Anonymity encourages the expression of opinions and is an important key driver for political participation in contexts such as this, where citizens are not accustomed to freedom and tolerance. Anonymity is also essential in contexts with constraints to freedom, where there might be persecutions of those who have a different opinion from the authorities or do not share the same views as the majority.

At the same time as the possibility of anonymity is regarded as a driver of political participation, it is also criticized for transforming spaces of participation, such as online news comments and blogs, into slander spaces used to insult opponents and to offend others. The personal attacks and defamation shielded by anonymity that often take place in these online spaces inhibit some citizens from participating in public life, particularly women, and hinder debates in general. Assessing whether anonymous comments and blogs are positive or negative to democratization processes is extremely complicated: although, on one hand, distortion of information and provocations are noticeable in many of these spaces, on the other hand, people tend to reveal more and feel more comfortable about exposing problems than they would be in situations where their face was shown and their name revealed.

Maria Ivone Soares is against anonymity in the blogosphere, but understands that some prefer to write under the protection of nicknames or in secrecy because they fear reprisals. In her blogs, she publishes posts about her position on issues, debates, and political decisions, but also poetry and personal thoughts. She also writes opinion articles regularly, and acknowledges the importance of independent news media in the Mozambican democratization process. According to her, independent news media outlets contribute to diminishing the information deficit regarding Mozambique's real problems and bring new approaches to issues and facts, because independent journalists try to balance news coverage, incorporating different and sometimes contradictory points of view, in addition to the official version of the FRELIMO government (Salgado 2014: 77).

With her political actions and behavior, Maria Ivone Soares intends to be a role model for young people, and girls in particular, inspiring them to speak freely about what is wrong in the country, and giving voice to all those who cannot speak for themselves. One of the reasons why she decided to use new media is because, in her view, the multi-party democracy has been threatened in Mozambique, and the challenge is to arouse a posture of critical thought within the younger generations. Given the absence of spaces for opposition politicians to express their alternative ideas, blogs are a privileged space for free expression of opinions.

Activists and Political Prisoners or Troublemakers in Angola?

Although the Lusophone African blogosphere is awash with posts on politics, human rights issues, and opinions, including criticisms of political authorities, blogs are not a privileged means for collective action and mobilization, as they are mainly used as a means of individual expression. When the objective is to organize protest or support actions, other online tools are usually preferred, such as emails, SMS messages, and social networks.

In Angola, the right to freedom of association, although recognized in the Constitution, is not fully observed in practice. When the people who organize collective popular actions support the president, José Eduardo dos Santos, and the Popular Movement for the Liberation of Angola (MPLA) party and government, there are no obstacles, and they are even assisted by the MPLA party structures. In contrast, when opposition parties or groups and movements that are critical of the president or of the government have tried to initiate actions, they have been quickly repressed by the authorities.

In June 2015, 15 to 17 young democracy activists were arrested and their documents and computers confiscated during a meeting in Luanda where they were gathered to discuss the situation in Angola. They were accused of an attempted *coup d'état* and of planning to harm the president. After the arrest, the Angolan organization Association for Justice, Peace and Democracy (AJPD) announced that they had been subjected to physical and psychological torture. The non-governmental organization Amnesty International issued a press release condemning what they called "another attempt by the Angolan authorities to intimidate anyone who thinks differently" (Amnesty International 2015). The case brought to mind the events that followed a protest action on 27 May 1977 against the then president, Agostinho Neto, which resulted in the death and disappearance of several people.

This new case involves a group of young educated people who have been very critical of the regime, because, according to them, Angola is a dictatorship, not a democracy. Angola started a democratization process at around the same time as the other Portuguese-speaking African countries in the early 1990s, but given the very low degree of its democratic consolidation and the many setbacks for freedom in general, there has been some ongoing discussion, both in the international press and in scholarly research, on whether the term "democracy" should be applied to the Angolan regime (for instance, Chabal 2002; Chabal and Vidal 2007; Salgado 2014).

The group of activists was composed of nearly 20 people (some went missing immediately after the meeting), including: rapper Luaty Beirão, who went on a hunger strike for 36 days to protest against these imprisonments; Manuel Nito Alves, a very young activist who was imprisoned for a couple of months in 2013 for wearing an anti-President dos Santos T-shirt, and who adopted the name of one of the leading voices (Nito Alves) against the former president, Agostinho Neto, in 1977; and university professor Nuno Dala. They were arrested and accused by the Criminal Investigation Services of the Interior Ministry of "preparing actions with the intention of changing the country's order and public security" (*Público* 2015a).

The so-called Angolan Revolutionary Movement was inspired by the Arab Spring movements and mainly calls into question the permanence of President José Eduardo dos Santos, who has been in power since 1979 and is one of the longest ruling leaders in Africa.

They also argued for the observance of human rights and demanded improvements in public policies, as well as the end of corruption and poor governance. More recently, demonstrations were organized to demand an end to police violence against demonstrators.

The group was behind the organization of several demonstrations against President José Eduardo dos Santos, and its members were very active in the growing online protests, noticeably in different social networks and discussion forums. Opposition political parties and political and social movements not aligned with the MPLA government do not have access to mainstream media to convey their messages, and if they appear in the news, they are framed negatively as delinquents and troublemakers. Regarding the Angolan media system, the state-owned media are completely controlled by the MPLA, and private ownership does not necessarily mean being independent of the MPLA government, President José Eduardo dos Santos, and his close supporters. In recent years there has been an important attempt by the MPLA political elite to further control the media system, through the purchase and launch of private news media outlets. Such a strategy allows conveying an external image of plurality in the media and content suppliers, while completely filling the space allowed to private initiative, to prevent the actual alternative voices (independent from the MPLA) of getting access to their own spaces of expression. This should be interpreted as a form of constraining dissent and any contestation (Salgado 2014: 67).

In fact, the Internet and online media have become powerful tools to gain sympathizers and mobilize more supporters for political and other causes, especially when there are no alternatives within the mainstream media system. But they are also a means for regimes to control opponents and follow their activities closely. In fact, Evgeny Morozov (2011) has recently insisted on the idea, somewhat against the current, that Internet freedom is, in most cases, an illusion. He has drawn attention to evidence that confirms that the Internet can be used as an instrument by authoritarian regimes to maintain their power and to oppress citizens even more: in several places, dictators have been using the Internet to launch misinformation campaigns and have been pursuing dissidents through their online trails.

This group of Angolan political activists was closely monitored, and all their online tracks apparently followed by the regime to prevent new popular demonstrations and to control their actions in general. Their social network accounts were full of references to demonstrations and to the need to organize "strong movements and eventually evolve to political party interventions". Words and phrases such as "revolution", "fight against the regime", "end corruption", "end censorship" are common. In addition to the online surveillance, these young activists have also complained about the presence of "moles" (people working for the secret services) in some of their meetings.

Between 2011 and 2013, a few demonstrations were organized in Luanda by these activists, but the frequency of these events was dramatically reduced—not because of a lack of mobilization, but simply because the authorities were able to prevent them from happening. In the first events, the authorities allowed the demonstrations to start, but soon after, the police force intervened to identify and arrest some of the demonstrators, dispersing the remainder. More recently, the protests have been put down by the security forces even before they start, and due to this sometimes violent repression, many citizens are afraid of joining the protests (*Público* 2015b).

In Angola, following the events in Tunisia and Egypt, in March 2011, the protest began on the Internet when emails and an anonymous website (http://revolucaoangolana.webs.com) announced the "New Revolution of the Angolan people", calling on people to demonstrate against the MPLA and the president. The MPLA government, not willing to tolerate any comparisons between Angola and the northern African countries, reacted strongly, ensuring that public order would be maintained at any cost, despite the fact that the Angolan Constitution grants all citizens the right to demonstrate peacefully. In March 2011, and in several other demonstrations and demonstration attempts that followed (for example, in July 2011, March 2012, December 2012, March 2013, June 2013), the authorities responded with a heavy police presence. On some of these occasions, counter-demonstrations in favor of the government were organized to take place at the same time.

It is thus not surprising that the Angolan government has also prepared new legislation designed to control and restrict the online environment. In 2011, the National Assembly approved a bill criminalizing the use of the Internet and mobile phones to send any type of information without the prior written consent of everybody mentioned in its contents. This new law, presented as a data protection measure, establishes imprisonment time and allows the security forces to conduct searches and confiscate data and documents without a court order. It was also carefully designed to prevent protests initiated and coordinated through the Internet from happening.

In an effort to prevent online activism, there were also attempts to block social networks in Cameroon, Uganda, and Swaziland; however, Angola was at the forefront with regard to drafting repressive legislation. This attempt to regulate online activity comes in line with the MPLA government's restrictive posture towards the media in general. It also shows that, although Internet penetration levels are not particularly high, the number of people with access is already enough to shake the political situation slightly. Until a few years ago, almost no one dared to criticize the president in public; however, more recently the Internet and the pro-democracy and freedom initiatives have encouraged more people to show their discontent.

Online Political Activism in Cape Verde: Young People, New Media

In Cape Verde at the beginning of 2015, a similar group of young people decided to join forces to engage in politics actively as a civic movement. They have subsequently been successful in organizing demonstrations and mobilizing the Cape Verdean youth, among others. It all started with the deep disappointment among young citizens about their job prospects, the direction the country was going, and the behavior of the ruling elites in general.

The civic action movement Movimento de Acção Cívica, MAC#114, is a political, yet non-partisan, movement, founded by a group of young jobless graduates, young professionals, and students with the objectives of involving young people in the political decisions that affect their lives and of making the youth more aware of their rights. The group, founded and led by 33-year-old sociology graduate and farmer Rony Moreira, has opted for a decentralized leadership model present throughout the main Cape Verde cities, and wants to function as a "pressure group" committed to raising civic awareness among young people and the underprivileged in general.

Rony Moreira was formerly affiliated with the African Party for the Independence of Cape Verde (PAICV), and a youth leader who was expelled for criticizing some of the party leaders' positions, which in his opinion were not following the ideals of a left-wing party committed to promoting equality of rights and opportunities for all and to allocating the country's public resources in a balanced way. Some of the other names involved in the movement are: Adilson Correia, from Assomada (a city in the interior of Santiago island), who is 29 years old and an electronics teacher; Vacilísio Gomes, 28 years old, a political science and international relations graduate student at the University of Mindelo, in São Vicente island; and Jassy Sousa, an international relations graduate from Sal island. They share the goal of mobilizing Cape

Verdean public opinion so as to debate issues that concern the population, such as unemployment, insecurity, poverty, injustice, and inequality (interview with MAC#114 members, by newspaper *A Semana*).

Cape Verde is usually pointed out as an example in Africa of the successful implementation of a democratic regime, because the development of democratic institutions has been sustainable and long-lasting. With very few resources and a very dry climate, Cape Verde is considered a poor country. Successive governments in the democratization period have tried to circumvent some of these difficulties by making important investments in human resources formation. Cape Verde is currently one of the few sub-Saharan African countries with a medium human development index (in the same group as South Africa, Botswana, and Namibia),[4] and is pointed to as one of the most free countries, both for journalists and the general population. Despite the overall good indicators in terms of both human development and democratic consolidation, Cape Verde currently faces important challenges, such as increasing levels of criminality across the country, mainly related to drug and alcohol abuse and growing youth unemployment. The country's strategic location along drug-trafficking routes is another major concern, given that this could mean a rapid increase in criminality and insecurity in general, influencing negatively both the unemployed youth and the rising tourism sector, one of the most important economic sectors in the country.

Despite successful democratic consolidation, some issues regarding a strong political bipolarization between the two main parties, PAICV and Movement for Democracy (MpD), and the obstacles that fringe political actors face to be included in debates and to be covered by the mainstream media, have been raised. In addition, the existence of corruption in the form of vote buying represents an institutionalized strategy of electoral campaigning. There is political and party competition, but translated into strong bipolarization between the two main political parties that have been alternating in power. Small political forces complain about the political bipolarization that prevents them from achieving better results in elections and denounce the use of public resources by the two main political parties. Also lacking in Cape Verde is the deepening of a culture of criticism, in which the population feels less apprehensive about questioning the government's decisions and action, as well as structures that mobilize and organize all those citizens who are unhappy with the current state of affairs and the way governments, parties, and members of parliament have been conducting politics.

What is at stake for MAC#114 is the right to equal opportunities and social justice— basically, the idea that the distribution of opportunities, wealth, and privileges needs to be fair in Cape Verde. So it is no coincidence that the trigger that became their first great battle and propelled the first street protests was the approval of new regulation regarding the Statute of Political Position Holders in Parliament. The new proposed statute included more privileges, such as a 65 percent salary increase considered immoral by these activists, given the situation in which most of the people live. They were also against the fact that members of parliament are not obliged to restrict their employment, which opens the door to situations of intermingling of business, political, and even media interests.

The "114" in the name of the movement is related to article 114 of the Rules of Procedure at the National Assembly. It is invoked whenever an MP wants to defend their honor and was included in the name of the movement because these activists want to restore the honor of the unemployed and the underprivileged Cape Verdean citizens. Although it is a movement clearly identified with Cape Verdean youth, its support structure has widened quickly, and it now includes people from different social, religious, and political sectors of society.

Probably inspired by other political movements, such as the *Indignados* in Portugal and Spain, MAC#114 stands for a participatory model of democracy, a more inclusive configuration of power that takes into account different interests in the policy-making process, with citizens' political involvement going beyond their vote in elections. MAC#114 also criticizes the type of "clientelist democracy" that both PAICV and MpD have supposedly been implementing, in which social mobility and job opportunities are related to belonging to these parties. Basically, the ideas of participation, equitable distribution of resources, social justice, and equal opportunities drive this political movement, and are supported by the objectives of raising citizens' awareness about their rights and democratic ideals in general, while providing them with the necessary structures of mobilization as tools to affect changes in politics.

In Cape Verde, the media system is an accurate picture of the bipolarization of the political system. The two political parties that have alternated in government (PAICV and MpD), have at one time or another controlled the broadcasting sector (state-owned television and radio stations), while the weekly private newspapers are divided in support of these two parties. In terms of news content, the newspapers' political orientation is noticeable in opinions and commentaries, but also in how information is selected and presented. For instance, the smaller political forces often complain about the difficulties in getting their messages across in the mainstream media (Salgado 2014: 168). The press's monitoring role is therefore somehow compromised, and at the same time, the two main parties' institutional communication is usually very strong.

With no access to the mainstream media agenda, MAC#114 has taken to social networks, especially Facebook, which has become its most important communication tool when it comes to both informing about the movement's objectives and mobilizing people for collective action. Use of the Internet as a means of influence, and as a tool to express opinions, is not new in Cape Verde. Since its use started to expand, the Internet has been used by different political and social actors, first through blogs, and then increasingly through social networking websites, to read and comment on the news, and to publish blogs on different topics. MAC#114 is the first example of systematic use of the Internet for citizens' mobilization.

An Online Journalist in Sao Tome and Principe

The Santomean journalist Abel Veiga has made the Internet his working environment. Because he launched the first online paper in 2000, he is considered one of the "fathers of digital journalism" in the archipelago. *Téla Non* was not only the first online paper in Sao Tome and Principe, but it was also the only daily newspaper in the country. *Téla Non* was also the first to allow readers' comments and to promote discussions about news and issues in general, and is one of the very few independent media outlets operating in the country.

Sao Tome and Principe's media system reflects the characteristics of a very small and very poor country, with extremely high newspaper prices for the general population, a very small advertising market and extremely low newspaper-reading rates. Independent news media are rare in Sao Tome and Principe. In addition to the high level of politicization of the news media, two other reasons explain this: severe economic difficulties, and widespread self-censorship among the small journalistic community (the Union of Journalists estimates that the number of journalists was around 100 in 2012).

When compared with online newspapers in other Portuguese-speaking African countries, *Téla Non* is indeed one of the online papers with more comments from readers. They are given the opportunity to comment on the issues raised by the news stories, but readers also use the space to request and exchange different kinds of information among themselves, making this website an actual forum for citizens. Although on a smaller scale when compared with consolidated democracies and more developed countries, the immediate result of these different online publications is that more information and new perspectives on issues, actors, and events are available, including foreign experiences and foreign evaluations of national experiences (Salgado 2014).

Téla Non is widely read by politicians, journalists, students, civil servants, and the remaining small fraction of the population with Internet access (the price of having Internet access at home was around 100 euros per month in 2011), but most of its readers are located abroad. These include business people with interests in Sao Tome and Principe, and the diaspora community that is a very important audience for *Téla Non*, especially from countries such as Portugal, Brazil, Angola, Cape Verde, the United Kingdom, France, and the United States of America. In fact, the number of average monthly website users from Portugal was three times higher than Santomean users in 2012.

In addition to the important international exposure of this online newspaper, *Téla Non's* content also reaches parts of the population in Sao Tome and Principe without Internet access through other news media outlets and such means as friends, colleagues, and word of mouth. So, despite major limitations in access to the Internet for a large part of the population, content published online can reach wider audiences through other means of communication (some television and radio shows present summaries of the online press headlines), or even through interpersonal communication. Important and controversial news stories are often printed and distributed, and, for instance, in the city of Sao Tome, some taxi drivers print some of *Téla Non's* news stories for their clients to read during the ride. Due to scarce human resources some private radio stations feed their news reports with *Téla Non's* news content, functioning in this way as "resonance boxes".

This is all the more important as *Téla Non* has a vital role in setting the media agenda, because it covers some of the events and issues that the state-owned media prefer to ignore. Abel Veiga sees online media, both newspapers and blogs, as extremely important for improving the quality and the plurality of information in Sao Tome and Principe. The Santomean online informational environment has contributed to offer different—and sometimes contradictory—versions of issues and events, and it has also stimulated competition between news media outlets, which has contributed to improve the overall quality of news content. All of this has had a positive influence on both freedom of information and freedom of expression in the country.

In the Santomean context, Abel Veiga has a bold vision of the role of the news media. For him, democracy means open debate and plurality of views, so only with the existence of such conditions can any country be considered democratic. The Constitution has guaranteed freedom of expression since 1991 and freedom of the press is also ensured by law. However, there are constraints that limit the levels of freedom in the country: "Journalists are often intimidated, which results in high levels of self-censorship. There are no beatings, but journalists deal with threats, professional retaliations, judicial processes" (interview conducted by the author of this chapter on 29 June 2011; for more information, see Salgado 2014: 93–108).

Those in power are accustomed to control the media in Sao Tome and Principe. The state-owned television and radio stations are instruments used by the ruling parties, and most of the private news media are also controlled indirectly. There are very few independent news media outlets and there have been many different attempts to silence their voices or to persuade them to support the party in power. Its international impact makes *Téla Non* particularly interesting for politicians. In addition, *Téla Non* has always had a critical approach that arises from its stated mission of monitoring the conduct of elected officials and politicians in general. This objective is nevertheless often perceived by politicians as a hidden agenda to overthrow governments and political leaders. Abel Veiga believes that *Téla Non*'s open nature, promoting participation and debates, is essential to its mission, and argues that the objective is to act on behalf of the population, showing and discussing what is wrong, not to overthrow any government.

Political instability is an issue in Sao Tome and Principe. Since its transition to a multi-party system in 1991, this country has had many more governments and prime ministers than elections: in 20 years there were 19 prime ministers, and no government lasted a full parliamentary term. This is one of the effects of strong disagreements between political parties and even stronger personal (more than ideological) divergences among the political elites (Salgado 2014: 83). The fact that Sao Tome and Principe is a very small country does not help, because most people know each other personally. There are many grudges accumulated over the years, and relations between politicians and the independent news media are often conflicting.

The constraints to journalistic work are worse in the case of the independent media. Their access to political sources is very limited, because governments prefer to release information through the state-owned media to ensure control of the actual news content, and in some cases, the political elites even order information blackouts against the independent media. The argument used is that the media need to speak with a single voice to prevent political instability, and that too much plurality and debate would, in fact, be harmful for democracy. Abel Veiga completely disagrees with these arguments, and sees the politicians as the only ones responsible for political instability. In his view, plurality is an extremely important value, and online newspapers and blogs have been contributing to improved freedom in Sao Tome and Principe, and promoting debate on issues. Many of these publications have been developed outside the political elites' control, which makes them particularly important in a democracy-building context.

Prospects and Different Democratic Developments

These histories of the Internet illustrate the state of democratic development of Mozambique, Angola, Cape Verde, and Sao Tome and Principe. These are histories of individuals and groups in respect to their ideals and goals, and their use of the Internet, but these are also accounts of freedom of the press, plurality, freedom of expression, freedom of association, and of struggles for equal rights and social justice.

The Internet has enabled alternative power dynamics, which in these cases have more or less conflicted and challenged the status quo. These actors, movements, and publications emerged and flourished in their national contexts due to the Internet. They represent new ways of mediating political communication and power in contexts where the Internet is more than just a new media vehicle for political information. Enhancing creative practices and shaping interplays, it provides opportunities to go beyond established discourses, and contributes to creating new power configurations. However, the impact on democracy is not always the same: in some cases, the Internet has forced some openness, while in others it has caused further repression. It is, thus, a mistake to assume that a country is only going to be more democratic and free because of the Internet.

Some of the most democratizing features of the Internet are related to the democratization of information: not only has the Internet the potential to multiply information producers, but it can also facilitate access to more diverse sources of information. The Internet therefore offers the potential for decentralized information production and distribution, allowing more ideas and opinions to circulate, which in itself is a valuable tool in democracy. The Internet also has the potential to boost citizen mobilization and participation. How the Internet's potential is explored and how the available information is used varies according to context.

The Internet opens up new possibilities that are the result of technological innovation and development, but the ways in which it is used are strongly shaped by the surrounding environment. In Cape Verde, it has allowed activists to mobilize the population and influence policy making, but in Angola it was used as a surveillance weapon against the pro-democracy activists. In Mozambique, the Internet serves as means of communication for an opposition politician, and in Sao Tome and Principe as a medium for an independent press. Some of the Internet's most important distinctive features—interconnectivity, immediacy, interactivity, anonymity, the possibility of becoming "viral"—can be useful to both dictators and democrats. The Internet is shaped by actors according to their histories, goals, and ability to use it.

Notes

1. This chapter is part of a larger research project funded by the Portuguese Foundation for Science and Technology and developed between 2008 and 2014, which included extensive fieldwork and interviews with local actors.
2. Guinea Bissau is not included in this study.
3. Beyond Access is an initiative of IREX, an international non-profit organization with support from the Bill and Melinda Gates Foundation.
4. The human development index is one of the United Nations Development Programme's tools to assess the overall quality of life of human beings. It is a statistic derived from combined indices on life expectancy, education, and income in each country, and is used to compare and rank countries. Countries are usually divided into three groups: high, medium, and low human development. Most of the sub-Saharan African countries are in the "low human development" group.

References

Africa Intelligence (2015) "Maria Ivone Soares, Renamo's star", *Africa Intelligence*, 1 October, available at: www.africaintelligence.com/ION/who-s-who/2015/10/01/maria-ivone-soares-renamo-s-star,108050284-ART

Amnesty International (2015) "Ativistas Detidos em Angola têm de ser Imediatamente Libertos", 22 June, *Amnesty International Portugal*, available at: www.amnistia-internacional.pt/index.php?option=com_content&view=article&id=2163:2015–06–22–19–23–52&catid=43:angola&Itemid=109

Angop (2015) "Bié: Província Ganha Mediateca Móvel", *Angop: Agência Angola Press*, 22 April, available at: www.portalangop.co.ao/angola/pt_pt/noticias/lazer-e-cultura/2015/3/17/Bie-Provincia-ganha-mediateca-movel,099252ba-f1f8–414e-a908–7e533926d6d0.html (accessed 28 October 2015).

A Semana (2015) "Mac#114, o Movimento que fez 'Tremer' a Classe Política Cabo-Verdiana", *A Semana*, 15 May.

Balancing Act (2014) "Internet Access on the Increase in Mozambique", *Telecoms, Internet and Broadcast in Africa*, 329, available at: www.balancingact-africa.com/news/en/issue-no-329/Internet/Internet-access-on-t/en (accessed 29 October 2015).

Beyond Access (2014) "Boosting Access to Affordable Internet in Mozambique", *Beyond Access*, available at: http://beyondaccess.net/2014/07/11/affordable-Internet-mozambique/ (accessed 29 October 2015).

Chabal, P. (2002) *A History of Postcolonial Lusophone Africa*, Bloomington, IN: Indiana University Press.

Chabal, P., and Vidal, N. (eds) (2007) *Angola: The Weight of History*, London: Hurst Publishers.

Deutsche Welle (2015) "Acesso 'Sem Filtros' à Internet em Angola", *Deutsche Welle*, 3 June, available at: www.dw.com/pt/acesso-sem-filtros-à-Internet-em-angola/a-18495315?maca=bra-cb_po_globalvoices-14551-xml-mrs (accessed 28 October 2015).

Ferdinand, P. (ed.) (2000) *The Internet, Democracy and Democratization*, London: Frank Cass.

Grossman, L. K. (1995) *The Electronic Republic: Reshaping Democracy in the Information Age*, New York: Viking Press.

Huntington, S. (1991) *The Third Wave: Democratization in the Late Twentieth Century*, Norman, OK: University of Oklahoma Press.

Instituto Nacional de Estatística (2009) *Questionário Unificado de Indicadores Básicos de Bem-Estar* (Questionnaire on Well-Being Indicators), Praia: Instituto Nacional de Estatística.

International Telecommunication Union (ITU) (2014) "Measuring the Information Society Report", *International Telecommunication Union*, Geneva, available at: www.itu.int/en/ITUD/Statistics/Documents/publications/mis 2014/MIS2014_without_Annex_4.pdf (accessed 29 October 2015).

Internet World Stats (2015) "Internet Usage Statistics for Africa", *Internet World Stats*, available at: www.Internet worldstats.com/stats1.htm (accessed 29 April 2015).

Jornal Digital (2013) "São Tomé e Príncipe: Trindade já Dispõe de um Centro Digital", *Jornal Digital*, 4 April, available at: www.jornaldigital.com/noticias.php?noticia=35764 (accessed June 2013).

Lerner, D. (1958) *The Passing of Traditional Society: Modernizing the Middle East*, New York: Free Press.

Morozov, E. (2011) *The Net Delusion: The Dark Side of Internet Freedom*, New York: PublicAffairs.

Mudhai, O. F., Tettey, W. J., and Banda, F. (eds) (2009) *African Media and the Digital Public Sphere*, New York: Palgrave Macmillan.

National Communications Authority (2013) "Cabo Verde Sobe Cinco Posições no Ranking Global da UIT Soobre índice de Desenvolvimento das TIC", *National Communications Authority of Cape Verde*, available at: www.anac.cv/index.php?option=com_content&view=article&id=323 (accessed 29 October 2015).

Nwokeafor, C. U., and Langmia, K. (eds) (2010) *Media and Technology in Emerging African Democracies*, Lanham, MD: University Press of America.

O País (2015) "Internet Grátis Chega a Angola", 29 June, available at: http://opais.co.ao/Internet-gratis-chega-angola/ (accessed 29 October 2015).

Público (2015a) "Activistas Detidos Numa Casa em Luanda por Perturbação da Ordem Pública", 22 June, available at: www.publico.pt/mundo/noticia/activistas-detidos-numa-casa-em-luanda-por-perturbacao-da-ordem-publica-1699733?page=-1

Público (2015b) "A Repressão Está Agora a Chegar a um Nível Diferente em Angola", *Público*, 23 June, available at: www.publico.pt/mundo/noticia/a-repressao-esta-agora-a-chegar-a-um-nivel-diferente-em-angola-1699860?page=-1

Salgado, S. (2012) "The Web in African Countries: Exploring the Possible Influences of the Internet in the Democratization Processes", *Information, Communication & Society*, 15(9): 1373–1389.

Salgado, S. (2014) *The Internet and Democracy Building in Lusophone African Countries*, Surrey: Ashgate.

Salgado, S. (2015) "Political Participation, Alternative Media and Citizen Journalism in Lusophone Africa", in B. Mutsvairo (ed.), *A Connected Continent: Perspectives on Participatory Politics and Citizen Journalism in a Networked Africa*, Hampshire: Palgrave, pp. 187–201.

Serra, C. (2007) "Um Caso Inédito: Maria Ivone Soares" (A Unique Case: Maria Ivone Soares), *Diário de um Sociólogo* (Diary of a Sociologist), 19 September, available at: http://oficinadesociologia.blogspot.com.au/2007/09/um-caso-indito-maria-ivone-soares.html

World Bank (2009) "IC4D, Information and Communications for Development 2009: Extending Reach and Increasing Impact", *Global Information and Communications Technology Department of the World Bank and IFC*, available at: http://web.worldbank.org/ (accessed 3 September 2015).

35

AMPLIFYING CYBERACTIONS

A Short History of e-Resistance in South Korea

Kwang-Suk Lee

Introduction

Both the distorted rootedness of technology (structure) and overzealous digital culture (agency) have been deeply influential in the formation and development of digital society in South Korea (hereafter "Korea"). Although Korea's "neo-authoritarian" control and regulation have sought to rigorously suppress online users' culture on the Internet, their autonomy from below, through their roles in setting the agenda on socially sensitive issues, has evolved rapidly. Today, the neo-authoritarian state has persistently been subservient to the interests of big business and neoliberal deregulatory policy, rather than to the defense of the public interest. Furthermore, the government's power apparatus has become highly advanced, and has hidden its suppressive mechanisms with the help of information and communication technologies in a manner comparable to the disciplinary society of the previous military regimes (Lee 2007).

Nevertheless, individual agents' autonomous activities have co-evolved with these particular structural factors in forming the history of the Internet in Korea. This chapter aims to investigate the specificities of users' online culture in the developmental mode of digital technology and the Internet in Korean society since the early 1980s.

The present study examines the dialectic tensions arising within digital culture between the dominant power of Korea's neoliberal governments and the autonomous political subjects from below in the histories of the Internet in Korea. It does so by chronologically patterning the two moments of control and autonomy between the regulatory power and the new political subjects; in terms of theory, based on the socio-cultural approach to Internet development, this study seeks to investigate the brief history of Korean digital activism. By doing so, it aims to disclose how, even within a seemingly rigid code of control, political tension has existed between the codification of power and social influences from the intervention of human agents. This chapter focuses more on the subcultural wave of Internet history in Korea, which has largely been unnoticed in institutional and policy studies of Korea's Internet history.

In theoretical terms, this study aims at an integrative historical approach that seeks to observe not merely the top-down historical engines driving technological futures—such as information technology (IT) policies, governmentality, market activities, and other power conditions influencing digital technologies—but also the evolving phases of digital culture autonomously constructed by Internet users from below. The latter also implies that individuals and communities on the Internet have the autonomous momentum of altering digital culture's trajectory in the direction of alternative and democratic options. Even if culture and ideology enter history as effective forces in the technical sphere, this chapter argues that "no matter how firmly custom or instrumentality may appear to organize and contain [technology], it carries the seeds of its own subversion" (Marvin 1988: 8).

Above all, along with describing users' autonomy, this study aims at emphasizing the local dynamics of underground digital culture reacting against social control. In other words, relying on the contingent interests of agency seen in histories of Korea's Internet since the early 1980s, this study attempts to understand the web of meanings in which Internet users interact with, and even counteract, the socially determinist vision of the dominant stakeholders of digital technology. In searching for the tendencies of the structure and agency struggles in the local setting of Korea's Internet, this chapter will reveal dynamic relationships of control and autonomy by displaying some patterns related to significant issues raised in analyses of electronic activism. This study concludes that throughout the historical evolution of cyberactivism, online users' activities can be considered significant, both in creating innovations in digital culture and in increasing the democratic attitude of society. In this respect, the present study construes the Internet and mobile platforms as part of the active public sphere, which informs us about the suppressive aspects of power and the socially supportive networks that enable online users to unite against social control on the Internet.

Cyberactivism Against the Darkness of "Digital Korea"

Over the last several years, digitization has been a key feature of the latter stages of Korea's "compressed modernity"—a phrase encapsulating the way in which the country has leapfrogged conventional development stages, moving from being a traditional agrarian society to an industrial society to an information society in just a few decades.[1] The rapid IT growth curve stands in contrast to stories that give an inside view of Korean society. While broadband and mobile Internet have become crucial communication media, promoting freedom of socio-political expression in Korea, online space is also becoming an electronic dungeon patroled by the neo-authoritarian government due to its anxieties about online users' freedom of expression. In 2009, when Frank La Rue, a UN special rapporteur, visited Korea, he noted "ironic" aspects of Korea's IT development, including its advanced broadband Internet, arguing "it is crucial to protect and promote the right to freedom of opinion and expression in cyberspace paralleling technological advancement in Korea" (in People's Solidarity for Participatory Democracy 2009).

With the advent of the Lee Myung-bak administration (2008–2012) and the ensuing Park Geun-hye administration (2013–), Korea's IT success can be seen as Janus-faced: the face not publicly touted includes the government's attempts at hyper-panoptic social control, the spy agency's scandal of manufacturing electoral consent through Twitter, the vulnerable condition of online human rights, the chronic cronyism between the state and IT-involved conglomerates, the suppression of online activism against the neo-authoritarian civilian government, and other ugly conditions of a neo-authoritarian state. The incorporation of Korean information technology into a new capitalist mode of production and into bureaucratic mechanisms designed to regulate each Korean citizen is the dark side of Korea's "broadband nirvana" (Lee 2012). The interventionist role the government has played in the process is far from the normative role of the state as a public mediator guaranteeing citizens' equal rights; such a government should defend citizens' freedom of expression and information rights against predation.

The main section of this chapter discusses the recent history of Korean digital and new media developments in relation to electronic activism. It will explore how undemocratic and bureaucratic trends during these periods have eroded the health and the potential of advanced digital culture in Korean society, and how Koreans have taken a leading role in transforming the "crisis of *res publica*" (Kang 2011) through an active, and even subversive, digital culture. This section outlines a genealogy of online forms of political protest: how they have changed from an embryonic phase (relying on PC-based online communication during the period between the early 1980s and the mid-1990s), through an evolving phase ("thumb culture" and the Internet during the period between the late 1990s and the mid-2000s), to a trans-forming phase of resistance (mobile culture and social media during the period between the late 2000s and the present). The latter two phases represent typical cases of "cyberactivism" or "net activism" that attempt to translate the principles of direct action or protest into pro-social electronic actions created by the Internet and mobile phone users. As Manuel Castells describes the contemporary network-based social movement: "The space of the movement is always made of an interaction between the space of flows on the Internet and wireless communication networks, and the space of places of the occupied sites" (Castells 2012: 222). This electronic fabric of resistance has allowed online users to express their anger concerning political and social issues, and to criticize the neo-authoritarian Korean governments throughout recent history.

The Embryonic Phase of Cyberactivism

Korean scholars have barely begun to discuss the concept of Internet activism or cyberactivism in the early era of online space, up until the 1980s when the System Development Network, described as Korea's first Internet system, began its operations, and the online communication service using PC communications was launched. However, during the period between the early 1980s through the mid-1990s, Korea had already engendered new digital "tribes", such as PC-based communicators, amateur hackers, young software program developers, private BBS operators, and online community dwellers, most of whom were libertarian and crypto-anarchist in their advocacy of decentralized technology (*Geongbo Sidae* (Information Age) 1991a: 92–93; 1991b: 74, 77). For instance, more than 300 private BBS groups operated in 1991 alone (Kang 2007: 499–510). Originating from the BBS culture, the online-based community groups expanded enormously in cyberspace.

From 1995 onward, the rapid change was facilitated by the Korean government's policy drive to shift the national economy from traditional labor-intensive industries to cultural or knowledge-based economies (National Computerization Agency 2005). Thanks to the widespread dissemination of high-speed Internet since the mid-1990s, Koreans have discovered the freedoms afforded by electronic conduits of cultural expression. In Korea, up through at least the early 1990s, the grid of military-authoritarian practices that threatened citizens' rights was pervasive: for instance, the national ID system identifying each Korean, the use of paramilitary violence to break labor unions, the use of closed-circuit television for policing, the widespread practice of government eavesdropping, and politically motivated investigations of activist citizens. During the dark days of these repressive military regimes, Korean citizens were eager to have more political rights, such as freedom of speech, expression, and assembly (Lee 2009: 191–192).

After entering into a stable phase of civilian government, the public's interest shifted from focusing on demands for political democracy to the protection of cultural expression. This shift can be viewed as an extension of democratic concerns into a new cultural arena. With the widespread dissemination of digital communications in the 1990s and 2000s, Koreans have discovered the freedom afforded by electronic conduits of cultural expression. The eruption of socio-cultural exchange spurred by the mobility and interconnectivity of new communication technologies has acclimated citizens to speaking out in their own voices and expressing their own values. The ecology of the citizens' autonomous culture has shifted from the street barricade struggle of resisting authoritarian regimes by throwing stones and Molotov cocktails to resisting the dominant discourses of society through electronic forms of cultural expression, such as the PC-*Bangs* (Internet cafés), electronic forums, blogs, online computer game rooms, Cyworld, a popular Web-community site, and text messaging with mobile phones.

With the number of high-speed Internet subscribers rising to ten million in 2000, many Koreans had already begun to spend a good deal of time on electronic networks—playing online games in Internet cafés, decorating their blogs, communicating with each other using mobile devices, connecting with hobby or interest groups through Internet portal sites, and exchanging audiovisual materials with others. At this embryonic phase of online culture, however, we can hardly discern any links between online and offline protests, except for one case in 1991. KETEL, then the biggest PC communications service provider, intended to merge with PC COM. KETEL was a non-commercial database service offered by the *Korea Economic Daily* since 1985, and, through the merger, PC COM sought to absorb pre-existing KETEL users into a larger body of commercial subscribers (Larson 1995: 85). This sparked the anger of KETEL users, and finally led to a rally with a candlelight vigil protest in front of the KETEL building. This is the first example of a linkage between online and offline protest against the commercialization of electronic space. However, online users' voices went largely unheard, mainly due to the low rate of participation of online users in the real-world protest. There were some other significant cases of early electronic civil disobedience: the online users' virtual sit-ins at the BBS sites of the major TV broadcasters, who had tried to minimize the social impact of the Daegu subway fire in 1995; the online petition campaign led by *BatongMo*[2] (an abbreviation of a users' group for political justice in communications) for enacting the Special Punishment Law on the 1980 Gwangju Massacre[3] crimes court in 1995; and the black ribbon campaign led by the *Chong-paup Tongshin Jiwondan* (a communications support group for a general strike) in 1996.[4]

In the early phase of online users' cyberactivism, a sequential link existed between online events and offline events, but the link was intermittent: an online event happened, and afterward the offline event erupted—the online and offline events were not so much instantaneous as sequentially delayed, or sometimes each was in its own silo. For instance, online users were accustomed at that time to organizing regular and irregular online and offline meetings (called *Jeongmo* and *Beon-gye*, respectively, in Korean). Although the KETEL candlelight vigil protest represented a sequential link between online and offline events for the first time, it was too ineffectual to encourage most cyberactions to emerge into the physical sphere. Tying politico-social agendas in electronic space to street politics was rarely achieved until the early 2000s, when the Internet became popular.

The Evolving Phase of Cyberactivism

In Korea, the social formation of cyberactivism was brought about by reactions against an upsurge of economic neoliberalism and the political conservatism of monopolistic capitalists and national policymakers, as well as by the citizens' strong feelings about socio-cultural agendas. Although authoritarian and suppressive characteristics in the area of human rights and freedom of speech, reminiscent of the military regimes, have diminished, the civilian government's neoliberal market policies have given more economic power to the *Chaebols*— Korean-style family-owned multinationals such as Samsung and LG—increasing the government's symbiosis with them (Lee 2012). Meanwhile, through technological advances, such as the national installation of broadband Internet networks and the population's expanding use of mobile handsets, Korea's citizens began asserting public opinions and cultural styles, things once represented only by conservative big media. The Korean citizens' movement enacted e-resistance by weaving together a spontaneous, indeterminate, informal, and complex network of singularities in order to act as a commonality. The new mood of online activism grew rapidly with the swift mobilization of citizens for rallies in major downtown streets during the 2002 presidential election, and later culminated in online flame wars and offline candlelight vigil protests against the presence of US troops in Korea.

In the 2002 Korean presidential election, an election campaign using mobile phones and the Internet was very effective in organizing citizens and uniting them in the agenda of political democratization (Lee 2009). Using their own cellphones, which were technologically in the age of "thumb culture" at that time, Korea's younger citizens mobilized and encouraged friends, families, and peers to vote for the progressive candidate. The younger generation, those in their twenties and thirties, with access to instant messaging and email, engaged in a "mobile politics" that made use of wireless devices (Kim 2003).

Prior to the widespread distribution of electronic media that could be used for self-organized resistance, conservative big media had been the main influence on public opinion. The new wave of network-based cyberpolitics, however, began to allow anonymously scattered citizens to mobilize one another to protest against the politically conservative government and big media. For instance, to produce alternative discourse on the Internet, in 2000, the netizens themselves launched *OhmyNews*, a Korean online news site with the editorial principle that "every citizen is a reporter", and it enlisted 38,000 "citizen reporters" who published about 150 stories on the site each day in the early 2000s. At that time, the website drew half a million visitors a day, and it has become one of the alternative Internet media framing the public agenda against the conservative big media.

With the rapid growth of online citizen journalism, electronic networks have been increasingly used to mobilize enormous rallies of Korean citizens focused on socially sensitive issues. In June 2002, a citizens' rally commemorating the tragic death of two teenage girls struck by a US military vehicle was initiated for the first time by one citizen's online posting expressing anger at the presence of US armed forces in Korea. The temporary rage was gradually transmitted to online forums and cafés where citizens posted their opinions, discussed the political and military conditions in Korea that caused the tragedy, and set the date for an offline rally. The staging of several rallies sparked a wave of anti-US protests, and later forced the government to scale down its plan to send Korean troops to Iraq.

The online-offline protest linkage first came into view in the 2002 rally, and culminated in the 2008 *chotbul* (candlelight) vigil protests against the Lee Myung-bak administration, which aimed to reopen the Korean beef market to US imports (once the third-largest importer of American beef). Anger against the Lee government's propaganda finally brought tens of thousands of demonstrators to the streets, expressing Koreans' fear of eating meat tainted with potentially fatal mad cow disease, as the demonstrators placed no faith in the Lee administration's reiterated assurances that the beef would be thoroughly inspected and safe (see, for example, Hansen 2008). During the negotiations with US trade representatives, the

Korean government repeatedly concealed the details of its agreements with the USA from the Korean people, despite the requests of civil society groups that such information be made public. Further, the government disseminated disinformation claiming that the bilateral trade negotiation would be wholly beneficial to Korea's citizens and its national economy, even though the risks involved could threaten local sustainability. The behind-closed-doors policy-making processes have provoked civil society's resistance to the undemocratic aspects of the government's policies.

During the three-month long *chotbul* vigil protests in 2008, patterns of organization among Korean netizens were mobile, rapid, network-based, interconnected, and nomadic, enabling them to speak freely in their own voices in both online and offline spaces.[5] In Korea, wired and wireless technology contributed to a common agenda by uniting citizens' micro-narratives of anger across physical space. Korean netizens demonstrated distinctive abilities "to capture the new technologies of power" (Poster 2004: 329). Their methods of cyberactivism were creating a new paradigm for the social participation of citizens. This new paradigm—spontaneous but unified action through the electronic network—has become popular, and even threatened Lee's tenure as president at that time.

The 2008 *chotbul* protests against the government's propaganda eventually failed to change the government's desire to reopen the Korean beef market, and afterward the Lee government reacted with anti-democratic legal actions against tens of thousands of protestors who had expressed criticism of the government both on the street and on the Internet, charging them with vandalism, libel and slander, unlawful assembly, and other irrational civil suits. While the 2008 candlelight vigil protests became known as a significant national occasion of cyberactivism, Korean citizens had to continue to confront the counterattacking forces of the neo-authoritarian state until the end of Lee's presidency in 2012, and afterward, with the advent of Park's presidency in 2013.

The Transforming Phase of Cyberactivism

By 2013, broadband Internet subscribers in Korea exceeded 8.6 million out of a population of 50 million. As of December 2012, there were more than 53.6 million registered mobile phone users. In the wake of the smartphone's debut in November 2009, there are now more than 40 million registered smartphone users and tablet PC users (ZDNet Korea 2015). Following the smartphone's rapid adoption in Korea, one can easily observe many social media users accessing Twitter and Facebook with their smartphones. Above all, Twitter has rapidly become a crucial social networking service for renewing Koreans' political practices. Twitter users in Korea have increased exponentially, and as of December 2013 exceeded 6.42 million (Oikolab 2013).

These new material conditions of smartphones and social networking site (SNS) culture have increasingly collided with the neo-authoritarian government's threats to the citizens, due to its anxieties about past online-offline massive rallies since the early 2000s (Hong 2009; Jo 2010; Paik 2008). After Lee's presidency began in 2008, his administration dramatically intensified surveillance techniques aimed at controlling each citizen. For instance, the investigative authorities began to ask for targeted citizens' location data, as well as personal calling data, without a warrant (Joint Korean NGOs 2010).

In response, online users have aimed at regenerating their counterforce to challenge wider social control of Korean society through the voters, whom they sloganized as the "2040 *Saedae Younhap*" (the political alliance among the age cohorts from their twenties to their forties). The 2040 generation, in particular, had voted for Lee Myung-bak, who, it was said during the 2007 presidential election, would revitalize the national economy and promote employment of the younger generations; instead, this segment of society has deteriorated into a zombie-like subproletariat (Shaviro 2002), living with precarious job conditions and a net take-home pay of about US$650 a month. Due to their disillusionment, this age cohort decided to rouse from the political lethargy that had beset them since the *chotbul* protests, and to rectify their wrongly cast votes for President Lee by intervening in regional elections to seek political reform.

As smartphones and tablet PCs have grown in popularity in Korea, the 2040 *Saedae Younhap* has used social media as a key platform through which to advance a political agenda, such as urging their friends and followers to vote for progressive politicians. Among popular social media, the political leverage of Twitter has been demonstrated in three local elections: a regional election in June 2010, a by-election in April 2011, and the Seoul mayoral race in October 2011. During the elective process, many SNS users urged friends to go out and vote, and even posted *Injeung shots* (authentication shots), their self-taken photos outside ballot stations on Twitter and Facebook, to encourage others to vote. Thanks to the rapid spread of smart devices, including Apple's iPhone, since November 2009, SNS culture has also emerged as a key factor both in Korean elections and in the formation of public opinion. Celebrity online activism has also become a new phenomenon, mainly in the form of "socialtainers"[6]—entertainers expressing their socio-political opinions freely in both the online and the offline sphere.

A police state and citizens' political lethargy have given rise to satiric political parodies among Internet and mobile users. Under the Lee administration, TV comedy shows such as Gag Concert, and satiric podcasts such as *Naneun Ggomsuda*, commonly abbreviated to *Naggomsu* ("I'm a weasel", i.e. "I'm a petty-minded creep"), have gained a cult following among the 2040 generation, who have lost their aspirations for political freedom since the *chotbul* protests. Since its first arrival, *Naggomsu* heralded a new emergent parody genre fueled by the popular use of the smartphone in Korea—one which is able to massively spread critical discourses through its complete integration with mobile media. *Naggomsu* has become one of the world's most popular political podcasts on Apple's iTunes, with two million weekly downloads and six million hits on average per episode over the years since its launch in April 2011.

The unscripted podcast program consists of talk shows, rant sessions, and comedy skits lampooning the Lee government (and now the Park government) and the Conservative Party. The episodes were hosted by *Daanzi Ilbo* parody website owner Kim Ou-Joon and had a supporting cast that includes former Democratic Party lawmaker Jung Bong-joo, journalist Joo Jin-u, and political commentator Kim Yong-min. In December 2011, Jung, one of the four hosts, was found guilty of spreading rumors about President Lee's connection to an alleged stock market fraud. Many believe that the guilty verdict was a political verdict designed to stifle the *Naggomsu* podcast. Through Twitter and other social media platforms, online users have voiced their anger against limits on freedom of speech. In provoking these protests, *Naggomsu* had been a key player in advancing a cultural politics against the wrongdoings of the Lee government and encouraged young SNS users to build alternative discourses through podcasts on the basis of mobile culture.[7]

During this period, social media have also acted as a counterweight to the conservative mainstream media, which are largely cronies of the Lee and Park administrations and the ruling party. Social media have given rise to new emergent alternative media such as *Newstapa* (Rebuilding Investigative Journalism) and *Reset KBS!*, during a general strike at KBS, MBC, and YTN TV protesting Lee's meddling in 2012 through a large-scale reshuffling of key executives, program producers, and journalists. Along with a large fan-base for political podcasts such as *Naggomsu*, mobile culture has fueled the rapid growth of the online news program *Newstapa* since its launch in January 2012. Due to the government's control over public broadcasting, some of the expellees from the major TV networks and other small-size production team members have come together to produce an investigative news program about social issues. For instance, *Newstapa*'s investigative journalism in its earlier episodes exposed harmful effects of a so-called "green growth" policy, the Four-River Refurbishment Project under the Lee government, now ranked as the top environmentally destructive project. While gaining a good reputation as an influential online news channel, *Newstapa* uses multiple online outlets to broadcast its programs to more netizens, including its own webpage, YouTube clips, and podcast episodes, and the younger generations download and watch its weekly episodes using their smartphones. As of February 2016, *Newstapa* has finally become the most influential alternative media for citizens in Korea. Social media have also played a key role in the growth of this alternative news source, both in spreading the news program's schedule and in introducing public fundraising among SNS users to support the systematic and consistent production of the news program.

As shown by Koreans' Twitter use in 2012 being twice the world's average, as well as by Korea having some of the world's top political podcasts such as *Naggomsu* and *Newstapa*, some conceptual redefinition of online activism is needed to describe the more real-time based mobile network connections in Korea. Therefore, this study upgrades the concept of cyberactivism by adding the emergent pro-social activism propelled by e-mobilities—the material bases of wireless Internet and smart devices. Further, by 2012, mobile culture in Korea had developed into a sphere for raising citizens' political consciousness by developing alternative media, as well as linking anonymous netizens collectively. Given this, the contemporary phase of online activism in Korea could be called "mobile activism". As exemplified in *Naggomsu* and *Newstapa*, online events in this phase erupt and become an influential agenda without having a popular status in the offline world. We can also observe an upgraded phase of cyberactivism by way of today's combined trends of e-protest: the viral and expansive power of online activism (e.g. pro-social e-mobilities), political podcasts and guerrilla/citizen journalism (e.g. *Naggomsu* and *Newstapa*), and their followers' SNS activism (e.g. cultural–political fan clubs).

With the advent of the Park presidency in 2013, the radical use of social media has rapidly become tainted due to attempts by agents of the intelligence services to influence the 2012 presidential election in favor of Ms. Park. The National Intelligence Service (NIS) has been accused of spreading more than 1.2 million tweets, both to smear her opponents and to sway the presidential election. In coordination with the NIS, the military's secretive Cyberwarfare Command also carried out a similar online campaign during the presidential election (Choe 2013). The political scandal has become the antithesis to an optimistic view of SNS culture as one that empowers online users' autonomous activities. Since that election, SNS-mediated activism in Korea has rapidly dwindled, and the Park administration has diluted the command-level involvement in manufacturing consent on Twitter by assigning it to political scapegoats in the lower ranks (Kim 2013).

The Double-Edged Future of Cyberactivism in Digital Korea

The present study has traced the evolving phases of cyberactivism in Korea since the popular distribution of electronic networks and mobile communications. In general, one can make the following observations on the evolution of electronic resistance in Korea.

First, wired and wireless connection is a socially significant phenomenon in that it reflects an advanced medium allowing us to communicate and entertain on the move, and its history in Korea highlights the ambivalent aspects of electronic connection as an extension of the dominant structure in society and its subversive possibilities. From the latter perspective, the traditional tactics of resistance, such as barricade protests, political forums, colloquiums, and teach-ins, have been revitalized and remediated by the electronic activism of Internet and mobile phone users who use them as tools for public participation in democratic society.

Second, relying on the new conditions of resistance, very active online interconnectivity has arisen in order to share social agendas and to resist the suppressive agenda of the power elite. As shown in the evolving phases of cyberactivism since the 1990s, the rise of new media-based activism has enabled citizens to speak freely in their own voices, in both online and offline spaces, and to reach out to others through interconnectivity. The wave of network-based public opinions began to allow anonymous, scattered citizens to spread counter-discourses against the politically conservative government and big media. In addition, from 2011 onwards, the new conditions of e-resistance, such as the popular use of smartphones, were favorable to a horizontal and leaderless coalition among SNS users owning the electronic gadgets. This network of resistance is quite expansive and open to embracing new groups that have various political and cultural voices, with or without a resultant eruption in offline space. The networked multitude is well skilled in using digital technologies such as podcasts and SNS.

Third, the flipside of this situation also exists. Although digital media seem to guarantee more connections among users in a seamless way, connectivity through digital media in Korea generates repetitive and superficial links among online users sharing similar opinions, rarely encouraging them to reach out to others such as social minorities or to participate in activism in society. We call this "disconnection" in real terms. To describe the divergent tendencies of network-based social connectivity, we term it "intermittent conjunction" (*dansok*), an irregular and unstable mixture of virtual connectivity and disconnection among users. With regard to this concept, Korea is prototypical, exhibiting a condition in which the double-edged phenomenon of disconnection and interconnectivity has become normal. Heavy smartphone use has tended to nurture electronic desire and the over-exertion of cathartic chatting. To make things worse, a gloomy trend of "disconnection" has rapidly increased since the online smear campaign against Ms. Park's political opponents in 2012. The double-sidedness of electronic connectivity could lead the pro-activist momentum of the SNS culture in Korea to seriously deteriorate. The present author is concerned that this emergent phenomenon of *dansok* in users' online activities in Korea is a negative factor making cyberactivism lethargic and susceptible to actual agendas in the real world, even while electronic media have become more and more pervasive and innovative in Korea.

Fourth, in the meantime, Korea has seen the rapid growth of online citizen journalism since 2000. Electronic networks are increasingly used for producing alternative discourses on the Internet, and for mobilizing enormous rallies of citizens to speak out on socially sensitive issues. In the midst of the collapse of the public role of the public broadcasting system in Korea, online citizen journalism and alternative journalism have offered significant platforms on which to build alternative paradigms of social justice countering the mainstream media and the power elites. For instance, the growth of alternative news sites such as *OhmyNews*, *Naggomsu*, and *Newstapa* has played a key role both in spreading fact-based news and in informing investigative news.

Finally, under the recent neo-authoritarian phase of the Park administration, the structural mechanisms of formal democracy have become debilitated, and both old and new media have become distorted and sluggish in the political sphere. However, cyberaction framing a public agenda to counter the conservative big media still seems to be alive in the public space, even though its effects are diminishing. For instance, activist art or artistic activism, emphasizing a "relational aesthetics" (Bourriaud 2002) in which artistic and creative expression speaks to a sociopolitical context, is emerging as one of the most significant communicative acts to protect freedom of expression and oppose censorship. A group of participatory artists is involved in expressing themselves on issues of social justice, such as political freedom of expression, environmentalism, gender equality, minority politics, and other human rights issues by using their own creative and electronic media tools. Along with online media users and activists, contemporary artists will gradually take a leading role in spreading the basic ideas of social justice through technology-mediated artistic creativity and performance as the realities of offline media outlets become worse (for example, Lee 2015, 2016).

Notes

1. For instance, as international reports like the International Telecommunications Union's *Measuring the Information Society 2011* (2011) and the Organization for Economic Co-operation and Development's *Communication Outlook 2013* (2013) testify, Korea has become one of the global trendsetters, and an example to the world in the deployment and penetration of high-speed Internet access, as well as an important locus of innovation in mobile and consumer digital technologies and practices. At 91 percent of the population, Korea has the highest rate of mobile broadband subscriptions (ITU 2011: 12), as well as the fastest average consumer Internet connection speed, and the highest amount of IP traffic (Goldsmith *et al.* 2011).

2. *BaTongMo* later developed into the Korean Progressive Network Center, also known as JinboNet, a leading advocate for human rights in the information society in South Korea.

3. On 22 May 1980, the military regime brutally quelled the uprising, massacring as many as 2,000 people—striking workers, protesting students, and citizens—and took control of Gwangju. General Doo-hwan Chun, who then came to power in a military coup, used the demonstrations in Gwangju as a pretext for furthering his repressive policies. The Gwangju uprising is seen as the most tragic event in the history of post-war Korea.

4. At dawn on 26 December 1996, the ruling party pushed through an anti-democratic labor bill in the absence of opposition party members. The black ribbon campaign, in addition to launching a general strike by the trade unions, was planned to mourn the death of democracy in the political scene, while it benchmarked the idea of the universal blue ribbon campaign for protecting freedom of speech on the Internet.

5. Some cyberculture and new media studies scholars in Korea have analyzed this new mode of cyberactivism, which allowed social minorities to express their anger toward social issues and to criticize the government's bureaucratic and myopic view of market-driven policies. To evaluate the *chotbul* vigil protest, special issues of academic journals considered various theoretical and practical aspects of online activism (e.g., *Culture/Science* (Vol. 55, Fall 2008); *Changbi* (Creativity & Critique) (Vol. 141, Fall 2008); *Philosophy & Reality* (Vol. 79, Winter 2008)) as did both edited and single-authored books (e.g. *Dangdae-Bipyung* (Contemporary Critique) 2009; Hong 2009; Joe 2009).

6. "Socialtainers" in Korea have been growing as SNS stars by shifting the public's feelings, while using social media such as Twitter and Facebook as effective means of emotional communication with their fans and followers.

7. *Naggomsu* did, however, have a downside—its political cult and populist elements, such as its self-aggrandizing and sensationalizing talk-show style, including abusive language, its massive online and offline fan clubs, and its collectivist response to the podcast-related agenda. The political podcasts have gradually taken on the tone of a collective emotional catharsis as an escape from citizens' political lethargy, rather than as actual political reform.

References

Bourriaud, N. (2002) *Relational Aesthetics*, Paris: Les Presses Du Réel.

Castells, M. (2012) *Networks of Outrage and Hope: Social Movements in the Internet Age*, Cambridge: Polity Press.

Choe, S-H. (2013) "Prosecutors Detail Attempt to Sway South Korean Election", *New York Times*, 21 November.

Dangdae-Bipyung (Contemporary Critique) (ed.) (2009) *Dangshineun Wei Chotbul-eul Kisheunayo?* (Why Did You Put Out the Candlelight?), Seoul: Sancheckja.

Geongbo Sidae (Information Age) (1991a) March, Seoul: Geongbo Sidae.

Geongbo Sidae (Information Age) (1991b) December, Seoul: Geongbo Sidae.

Goldsmith, B., Lee, K-S., and Yecies, B. (2011) "In Search of the Korean Digital Wave", *Media International Australia*, 141: 70–77.

Hansen, M. (2008) "Stop the Madness", *New York Times*, 20 June.

Hong, S-T. (ed.) (2009) *Chotbul siwhi wa Hankook Shahwei* (The Chotbul Rally and Korean Society). Seoul: Moonwha/Gwahak (Culture/Science).

International Telecommunications Union (ITU) (2011) *Measuring the Information Society 2011*, Geneva: ITU.

Jo, D-W. (2010) "Real-Time Networked Media Activism in the 2008 Chotbul protest", *Interface*, 2(2): 92–102.

Joe, J-H. (2009) *Minerva-euh Chotbul* (Candles of Minerva), Seoul: Galmuri.

Joint Korean NGOs (2010) *NGO Report on the Situation of Freedom of Opinion and Expression in the Republic of Korea since 2008*, submitted for the official visit of the Special Rapporteur, available at: http://act.jinbo.net/drupal/sites/default/files/KoreaJointNGOreportonFoE.pdf

Kang, M-K. (2007) "Internet-ih Sahweimunhwasa" (The Socio-Cultural History of the Internet), in S. Y. Yoo, *et al.* (eds), *Hankook Media Sahweimunhwasa* (The Socio-Cultural History of Media in Korea), Seoul: Korea Press Foundation.

Kang, M-K. (2011) "The Crisis of Res Publica and Staggering Democracy in South Korea", paper presented to the *Conference for Rethinking Media and Democracy, Media and Society Division, Korean Society for Communication and Journalism Studies*, 28 October, Seoul, Korea.

Kim, S. (2013) "South Korea's Ex-Spy Chief Indicted in Election Scandal", *AP News*, 14 June, available at: http://bigstory.ap.org/article/skoreas-ex-spy-chief-indicted-election-scandal

Kim, S-D. (2003) "The Shaping of New Politics in the Era of Mobile and Cyber Communication: The Internet, Mobile Phone, and Political Participation in Korea", in K. Nyíri (ed.), *Mobile Democracy: Essays on Society, Self, and Politics*, Vienna: Passagen Verlag, pp. 317–325.

Larson, J. F. (1995) *The Telecommunications Revolution in Korea*, Oxford: Oxford University Press.

Lee, K-S. (2007) "Surveillant Institutional Eyes in South Korea: From Discipline to a Digital Grid of Control", *The Information Society*, 23(2): 119–124.

Lee, K-S. (2009) "The Electronic Fabric of Resistance: A Constructive Network of Online Users and Activists Challenging a Rigid Copyright Regime in Korea", in D. Kidd, C. Rodriguez, and L. Stein (eds), *Making Our Media: Global Initiatives Toward a Democratic Public Sphere* (Vol. II: National and Global Movements for Democratic Communication), Cresskill, NJ: Hampton Press, pp. 189–206.

Lee, K-S. (2012) *IT Development in Korea: A Broadband Nirvana?*, London: Routledge.

Lee, K-S. (2015) *New Art Activism: Post-Media Sidae Moonhwa Jeongchi* (New Art Activism: The Cultural Politics in the Era of Post-Media), Seoul: Ahngraphics.

Lee, K-S. (2016) *Oksang-euh Mihak Notes: Pagook-ae maseo-neun Yesoolhengdong Tamsagi* (Aesthetic Notes from the Edge: Art Activism Responding to a Social Crisis), Seoul: HyunsilBook.

Marvin, C. (1988) *When Old Technologies Were New: Thinking About Electric Communication in the Late Nineteenth Century*, Oxford: Oxford University Press.

National Computerization Agency (2005) *Hankook Aiti Jeongcheck-euh Kwageo-wa Mirae* (Past and Present of Korea's IT Policy), Seoul: NCA.

Oikolab (2013) *The Number of Twitter Users in Korea*, available at: http://tki.oiko.cc/

Organization for Economic Co-operation and Development (2013) *OECD Communication Outlook 2013*, Paris: OECD.

Paik, W-I. (2008) "Chotbul siwhi wha Daejoong" (The Candlelight Demonstration and the Peoples), *Donghyang kwa Geonmang* (Trend and Perspective), 74: 159–188.

People's Solidarity for Participatory Democracy (2009) "UN Special Rapporteur Faced 'Ironic Korea' IT Power but Freedom of Opinion and Expression Oppressed", *People Power*, 21 October, available at: www.peoplepower21.org/English/39923

Poster, M. (2004) "The Information Empire", *Comparative Literature Studies*, 41(3): 317–334.

Shaviro, S. (2002) "Capitalist Monsters", *Historical Materialism*, 10(4): 281–290.

ZDNet Korea (2015) "Smartphone Users Exceed 40 Million", *ZDNet Korea*, 20 January, available at: www.zdnet.co.kr/news/news_view.asp?artice_id=20150120151312

36

FROM *YULUN* (PUBLIC OPINION) TO *YUQING* (PUBLIC INTELLIGENCE)

Their History and Practice in China's Information Management

Hu Yong

Introduction

The expressions of *yulun* (舆论, public opinion) and *yuqing* (舆情, public intelligence) have existed in Chinese since ancient times (Wang 2006). Etymologically speaking, the character 舆, *yu*) that the two terms both share derives from the word 舆人 (*yuren*), which meant a group of common people of lower social status in ancient China (Hu 2013). Thus, *yulun* and *yuqing* were used to refer to the opinions of civilians, with connotations and denotations very different from those of their modern implications.[1]

The concept of *yulun* originates in the East. It is a concept more of a political function than merely a collection of individual opinions. That is, the source of public opinion does not come purely from the preferences of a private person but from his concerns and open discussions about public affairs. To put it simply, public opinion can be defined as the majority view on a public issue after it has been discussed in a rational-critical way in the public arena. Public opinion is also a way for citizens to get involved in promoting good governance. It can be a continuous force for social and political change. As a force independent of the political power, it is holding the latter responsible and thus creating a continuous tension between the ruler and the ruled. Meanwhile, public opinion is "the enlightened outcome of common and public reflection on the foundations of social order", an outcome that "encapsulated [social order's] natural laws" (Habermas 1991: 96). As such, it can be seen as a source of political legitimacy. This idea is of vital significance to both the ruling elites and the common people, because the establishment and defense of legitimacy is closely related to public opinion, while the same is also true of its criticism and deconstruction. Accordingly, public opinion constitutes a field of struggle between the state and society. However, as this chapter demonstrates, the concept of *yulun* has been turned into a politically loaded term to serve the purpose of ideological and social control under the regime of the Chinese Communist Party (CCP).

On the other hand, *yuqing* (public intelligence) is a native Chinese concept. It is a product of public opinion control in the Internet age. Born in the Chinese context, *yuqing* is usually mixed with *yulun*, i.e. public opinion, in academic circles. Its meaning has also been intentionally obscured by the government, with the aim to manage information flow. Obviously, *yuqing* is not public opinion itself, and does not possess the original political functions of public opinion either. Instead, it is a kind of intelligence on public opinion, similar to the "internal references" (*neican*) for high-level Party officials in the pre-Internet eras.[2] It operates as both a sanctioning and screening mechanism of *yulun*. It was originally developed to serve the ruling elites' need to understand public attitudes and sentiments on the ground in order to solve social problems for the purpose of maintaining social stability. But, gradually, it has morphed into organized control of public opinion, and become a standard Party and government practice to contain and even eliminate public opinion.

The Evolution of *Yulun* (Public Opinion) in China

As mentioned above, *yulun* derives from the word *yuren*. *Yuren* in ancient books refers to the people of lower social status in general, which reflects the fact that most Chinese people in history had neither the abilities nor conditions to discuss and participate in state affairs. Although the Western discourse of "public opinion" was transmitted to China in modern times (Ni 2010),[3] the word itself, under the tumultuous social and political circumstances of colonization and wars, has been undergoing semantic changes and various interpretations, and has been gradually localized to meet the demands of social development in different periods of time (Ni 2012). For example, in the late Qing Dynasty, when the concept was first introduced into the Chinese lexicon, "*yulun*/public opinion" was a symbol of the people's morale (Chen 1903). It stood in confrontation with the political power and exercised supervision over the latter. This was in agreement with the Western concept. However, with the emergence of newspapers and periodicals directly founded by political parties, *yulun* began to succumb to political propaganda and served ideological purposes, particularly between the CCP, founded in 1921, and the Kuomintang (KMT), reformed in 1924 (Tang 2010).

Guided by the Leninist concept of the revolutionary vanguard party since its foundation, the CCP has attached great importance to guiding and controlling public opinion. It has established and mobilized Party newspapers (党报, *dangbao*)[4] as important tools for developing and guiding public opinion and exercising social control. The Party newspaper theory developed under Mao Zedong held the view that:

> The Party newspaper is another important working mechanism besides meetings; it must have great party spirit [党性, *dangxing*]; it must maintain close ties with the masses; and it must rely on the masses as well as the whole Party to operate instead of relying on any individuals.
>
> (Chen 2006)

"Public opinion" was no longer an ideologically neutral term, but turned into a weapon, which was shaped by the Party, and after 1949, the Party-State, for political mobilization and social control. Under Mao's instruction, it needs to be "unified" and "uniformly generated" from top to bottom and implanted into people's mind, completely deviating from its original connotations (Mao 1977: 157–159; Ding 2011; Wu 2011). During the Cultural Revolution, such "uniformity of public opinion" was brought to an extreme and transformed into the idea that "the proletariat must exercise the all-round dictatorship over the bourgeoisie in all the fields of the superstructure".[5]

With the reform and opening-up policies initiated by Deng Xiaoping in the late 1970s, China went through dramatic political, economic, and social changes. The diversification of property rights and market-oriented economic reforms directly contributed to the formation of a relatively autonomous society. People began to regain their consciousness of individuality, and the authorities in power loosened their control over the mass media, which made it partially possible for the realization of public opinion similar to that in the Western sense—namely, mass communication created an open space where citizens could gather to discuss common concerns. However, this did not last long before hope for a more open society was crushed in 1989. In the post-1989 era, "media oversight" and "supervision by public opinion" were replaced by "public opinion channeling" (舆论引导, *yulun yindao*) and "guidance of public opinion" (舆论导向, *yulun daoxian*). In January 1994, Jiang Zemin put forward the view that "Propaganda and thought work aim to arm the people with scientific theories, guide them with correct public opinion, shape their minds with noble ideas and inspire them with good cultural works" (Jiang 2001). Here, the word "correct" was added as a prefix to "public opinion", naturally indicating that there must be "incorrect" public opinion. To maintain "correct guidance of public opinion" is, in nature, to encourage and indulge Party-sanctioned opinions, while opposing or even suppressing other ones. This created the conditions for the future "struggle of public opinion" (Qian 2013).

In the eyes of the Chinese authorities, public opinion can be "reflected", and, at the same time, "channeled", by the mainstream media. It can be used as a tool to improve the State's ability to govern and refine the Party's ideological work. In this sense, public opinion equals the Party's ideological and political work. Public opinion is never accepted as an independent force. Its power of critique vis-à-vis authority is regarded as troublesome, or potentially so, for the ruling party. Compared to the Mao era, there is a little more space of popular expression, particularly with the arrival and diffusion of the Internet, but no more chances for the public to be listened to.

Yulun/public opinion is regarded as flood and monsters that must be controlled, but never unleashed. Otherwise, the Party-State fears, the political situation would be "out of control", meaning threatening the legitimacy and rule of the Party. Therefore, public opinion must help create "a positive atmosphere"; and "heterogeneous ingredients" must be kept an eye on from contaminating or penetrating Chinese society. In spite of all the market-oriented reforms, the mass media is still operating as the Party-State's ideological apparatus and is owned by the Party-State. Thus, we have witnessed a parallel development of both carefully controlled public opinion and limited media reforms. Public opinion, as we understand it in the Habermasian sense, has never been fully developed in China. What is there to see is "Chinese-style public opinion", which is not originated from civil society but produced by mass media under the guidance of propaganda departments (Hu 2014). The public remains invisible and their voices are silenced.

Unfortunately, there has been a lack of self-reflection among Chinese academia who use the term "*yulun*/public opinion" uncritically, and "guidance of public opinion" indiscriminatingly. They have published tens of thousands of papers on the so-called "guidance of public opinion" to parrot the Party line, and take for granted the responsibility of news media and journalists to "guide" public opinion. However, they have failed to define who "the guided" are supposed to be, what kind of relationship between the guided and the guider of "public opinion" and why people need to be "guided" (Guo 2010; Liu 2013; Zhao 2014).

This kind of stale status of public opinion continued into the early stage of the Internet in China (1994–1998). But soon it was forced to change to adapt to new technological development, with the establishment of major news portals and the flourishing of online forums. The rapid development of the Internet coincided with that of the fastest growth of the economy in Chinese history, incurring dramatic changes in Chinese people's daily lifestyles and consumption patterns. With them came the right consciousness, particularly among the urban middle class. They have begun to realize their individuality, self-worth, and rights as never before. This has led to an outpouring of self-expression, facilitated by new media platforms, such as forums, blogs, and microblogs.

The Rise of Online Public Opinion and *Yuqing*

The year 2003 was called "the year of the Internet public opinion" (Min 2014). That year saw heated discussion on various forums caused by SARS, the case of Liu Yong,[6] the incident of Sun Zhigang,[7] etc. Social incidents led to strong currents of public opinion, so overflowing that traditional media had to respond to them and adjust their agenda. Public opinion, which had long been silenced and "represented" by power, suddenly became prominent on the Internet. The new interactive medium enables anyone, anywhere, to observe their social surroundings and inject a thought, a criticism, or a concern into public discussions. Different forms of networks in the public sphere are in the making, through which everyone can speak, question, and investigate without turning to traditional media. New political discussions are initiated, old issues are rearranged, and fresh horizons are opened up. In sum, people who were once "subjects" and part of a passive audience now become potential contributors to political dialogue and actors on the political stage. A new online field of public opinion is born.

This is in parallel with the traditional and "mainstream" field of public opinion generated by the mass media under the guidance of various propaganda departments. The "two public opinion fields", to use the words of the former head of Xinhua News Agency, Nan Zhenzhong, coexist, and begin to divorce from each other (*People's Daily* 2011). Great disparities can be found in the two fields in terms of content, discourses, and approaches. The Internet public opinion field is keen on promoting civic engagement and cultivating a vibrant public culture. It explores new ways to make the ruling power more accountable. Meanwhile, what the official public opinion field strives to depict is how the government is doing its best to create a harmonious society.

The coexistence of two public opinion fields implies the reversal of the traditional single-centered discourse, as well as the preliminary formation of a pluralistic society in China. The people behind the two public opinion fields are those who not only express different views, but also demand different rights and interests. On observing China's current politics, it is impossible to avoid the profound effects of the conflicting views caused by the clashes between the two public opinion fields. Neither can one underestimate the negative effects on the building of a positive consensus for a desirable society due to the respective closed state of the two fields. Therefore, in recent years, the suggestion of "opening up the passage between the two public opinion fields" has been more frequently offered in the "big media"—national Party papers and central news organizations, such as Xinhua News Agency and *People's Daily*. It has even been defined as a strategic objective of the central Party media's overall transformation, which can be embodied by the actions taken by the Party's traditional organs, such as newspapers and periodicals, radio and television stations, as well as those organs' new media outlets, such as the official microblogs, official WeChat public accounts, and mobile news applications. At the same time, to open up the passage between the two fields is the "mission" of the *yuqing* monitoring industry rising later and one of the sources of its legitimacy (see below).

With the penetration of the Internet and a rapidly increasing Internet population, varieties of contradictions, conflicts, demands, and criticism of power are assembling more obviously on the Internet, searching for different avenues for free speech, which has given rise to "online social power" (Hu 2012). On the contrary, "the mainstream public opinion field" constituted by the traditional media has been losing its momentum slowly, and has even had its agenda set by the netizens. With the structural shift in the public opinion field came a sense of threat, quietly spreading inside the establishment. The Internet is no longer (in top Party leader Hu Jintao's eyes) "a place to collect and distribute the ideological and cultural information and an amplifier of public opinion" (Hu 2008) that the authorities used to cater to with good intentions. Since 2013, in the official context, the Internet has been gradually turned into "the main battlefield of ideological struggle and the main front of ideological and theoretical construction".[8] With the analogy of "battlefield" and "front", "public opinion struggle" is causing much frenzy among the ideologues and in the Party's dogmatic media (Jing 2013; Li 2013; Z. Zhang 2013). Subsequently, various measures have been taken to limit online expression and the offline influences of online public opinion.

The first measure is through increasing legislation. On 8 June 2010, the Information Office of the State Council issued the first White Paper on China's Internet Status, stating that since 1994, a series of laws and regulations concerning Internet administration have been enacted.

> China adheres to rational and scientific law-making, and reserves space for Internet development. Relevant laws and regulations pertaining to basic Internet resource management, information transmission regulation, information security guarantee and other key aspects define the responsibilities and obligations of basic telecommunication business operators, Internet access service providers, Internet information service providers, government administrative organs, Internet users and other related bodies.

The White Paper lists as many as 15 related laws and regulations. Since then, the speed of China's Internet legislation has been accelerated, with a comprehensive set of laws and regulations established to regulate the Internet. According to the China Internet Network Information Center (CNNIC), the number of laws, rules, and guidelines related to the Internet reached 76 at the end of 2014, a 262 percent year-on-year increase (Cao 2015). New national security and anti-terrorism laws are enacted; a draft cybersecurity law is unveiled; and amendments are proposed to the two important regulations concerning Internet intermediaries, *Measures on the Administration of Internet Information Services* (互联网信息服务管理办法), and *Provisions on the Administration of Internet News Information Services* (互联网新闻信息服务管理规定). All these provide a legal framework for the overarching project of media and information control in the digital age.

The second measure is dubbed "technical protection". Since 1989, propaganda departments have been exercising strict control over the import of foreign publications and the purchase of satellite television receiving antennas for watching programs from outside China. Likewise, with the dawn of the computer network, the Chinese government has set up a system of filters to control public access to the Internet, a new channel to get information. Such filtration has extended to all levels of the Internet, such as applications, access points, Internet service providers, and the backbone networks. The so-called Great Firewall affects all kinds of information spaces, such as websites, emails, forums, BBSs in universities, social networks, blogs and blogging services, instant messaging, and search engines.

The third response relies heavily on administrative measures. In face of the "decentralization" of the distributed networks created by Web 2.0, the government has been dedicated to the establishment of control centers to "re-centralize" in order to maintain its controlling power. The Cyberspace Administration of China (CAC), established in 2014, became the top regulator in charge of managing all aspects of the Internet in China. It is given authority to conduct widespread censorship and surveillance of networks and users under a broad mandate to preserve "Internet sovereignty" as a core function of national security.

The significance of this "re-centralization" lies in two aspects. On one hand, it is capable of taking strict control of the number of designated "opinion centers" and denying the right of becoming "opinion centers" to those unauthorized, be it big Vs (Weibo's most prominent users who are verified account holders, usually popular actors, writers, or columnists, who attract millions of followers), NGOs, lawyers, or journalists. The denial may come from a formal regulatory regime, such as policies, licenses, and official media endorsement. It can also be exerted through a subtler and invisible mechanism composed of censorship, surveillance, and information control.

One the other hand, in response to the new pattern of public opinion—namely, the division of two public opinion fields—the Party-State intentionally organizes a "national team" to "grab the microphone back" from civil society. The national team is composed of official social media accounts and mobile applications operated by mainstream media, and social media accounts of various government agencies and departments—for example, both local public security bureaus and the Communist Youth League have formidable presence on social media. Their job is to mass-produce "Chinese-style public opinion" on the Internet, with the notorious Internet commentator system[9] in assistance, so as to restore the capability to set the agenda in case of disruptive emergencies and sensitive issues.

Under these circumstances, *yuqing* came into being. As intelligence on online public opinion, it is supposed to detect the sentiment of the online masses on issues of common concern. It is defined by the people involved as a summary of mental and emotional output generated by the public at any random moment. But this deliberately downplays the terminological shift from *yulun* to *yuqing*, tacitly serving to define a shift in social consciousness. The creation of a unique Chinese expression *yuqing* in replacement of *yulun*/public opinion aims to serve political purposes and propagate official ideology. Such a word becomes an "ideograph", to use the term coined by rhetorical scholar Michael Calvin McGee, which is meant to give the impression of a clear meaning without a clear definition and used as a building block of an ideology (McGee 1980). *Yuqing*, in this sense, is an ideograph representing in condensed form the normative, collective commitments of members of a public. It appears in public argumentation "as the necessary motivations or justifications for action performed in the name of the public" (Condit and Lucaites 1993: xiii–xxii).

Yuqing also strips away the institutional arrangements on which the concept depends for existence. That is, the need for understanding what is going on in people's minds, as represented by a series of *yuqing* analyses, is of great intelligence value to government and businesses alike. Especially for local governments, in face of the dual pressures of preserving stability at the grassroots and supervisions from above, public perception is a tough issue to deal with, sometimes causing over-interpretation and over-reaction. It is not uncommon for local governments at and above the county level to buy an "intelligent search engine system" to monitor *yuqing*, as well as purchase third-party monitoring services (Zhu 2015).

What *yuqing* monitoring is trying to do is measure and quantify public opinion and present relevant analysis and recommendations. Thus, it is giving rise to many indexes—sentiment index, rationality index, "positive energy" (正能量)[10] index, the degree of pessimism, the degree of apathy, and so forth. Accordingly, *yuqing*, in Chinese academia, is only treated as an almost static social-psychological existence in itself;[11] it remains in a steady state at a given point in time. But the contemporary research on public opinion, being increasingly concerned with the mechanisms of shaping public attitudes and constructing public belief, is closely interdependent with the study of public sphere (the source of public opinion) and puts emphasis on the process of public deliberation and communication (Pan 2001).

The distinctions between *yuqing* and *yulun* are similar to that between process and state of being. A "state of being" is to be observed, analyzed, and measured; no matter how difficult it is, there exists the possibility. However, a "process" is related to social structure; it is highly volatile and hard to be traced, collected, or assessed. By breaking it down into smaller components or segments, *yuqing* monitoring bodies believe that it is still possible for the process to be analyzed and compiled together to form a bigger picture that is *yulun*. That picture will be presented to the power in the form of distilled "intelligence" to manage deviances and maintain stability. As a result, the driving force behind many of the analyses of *yuqing* is not the public, but social controllers.

As a product of the Internet, *yuqing* is the power's response to an increasingly active online population. It is part of the Chinese government's strategy to improve its governance by mending fences before cracks get too big and by providing services to prevent further damage to the already leaning fences. Therefore, the typical customers of *yuqing* analyses are those in power. The Chinese government is the biggest customer of the booming *yuqing* industry, as the next section details. The government expects to know about the conditions of the people and gather their collective wisdom so that it can solve many institutional problems, remedy social malaise, and build a new structure for so-called "social management".[12] *Yulun*, however, has become a too heavily loaded political term to those in power, as they tend to regard public opinion as a threat from the people to challenge, undermine, or even topple their control. As a result, *yuqing* collection and analysis is regarded as essential to improved social management, while *yulun* (especially adversary to the regime) is to be channeled and guided. *Yuqing* is thus a social control technique in China's new mentality of governmentality. It has led to a new intelligence industry in the Web 2.0 era.

Yuqing Industry in China

The arrival of Web 2.0 gave birth to more new media platforms, numerous content producers, and a huge amount of data, which makes information monitoring more urgent for the Party and government. In particular, the information that they are monitoring is not news from the official media, but expressions and activities gathered from forums, *tieba* (贴吧, an online community based on keywords, created by Baidu, the biggest search engine in China), blogs, microblogs, and other online venues.

Currently, the *yuqing* industry is operated by three major providers: the Party and government departments; flagship media organizations of the Party; and universities and research institutes. As the major consumers of Internet *yuqing* monitoring, the Party and government departments have established their own specialized monitoring branches. In June 2004, the Bureau of *Yuqing* Information (舆情信息局) of the Propaganda Department of the Central

Committee of the CCP was formally founded. Relying on the central and local propaganda and ideological work system, this bureau specializes in the collection, analysis, and reporting of the country-wide *yuqing* (Wang 2009). Subsequently, the propaganda departments of most provinces, autonomous regions, and municipalities directly under the central government set up *yuqing* information units of different levels—e.g. department (*chu*), division (*ke*), office (*shi*), or center (*zhongxin*) etc. Besides the Party's propaganda system, other organs, such as the subordinate units of the State Council—the Ministry of Education, the Ministry of Public Security, and the State Council Information Office—the political and legal system (政法系统, *zhengfa xitong*), and other institutions and even state-owned enterprises, have all constructed their own *yuqing* information collection and report systems (Wang and Fang 2010). The work of *yuqing* becomes an essential standard practice of the government, and an intelligence network has been extended throughout the country in public service institutions, state-owned enterprises, and other quasi-official organs.

The second major player in the *yuqing* collection and analysis industry is the Party's flagship media organizations, such as *People's Daily* and Xinhua News Agency. These media organizations have established their own *yuqing* monitoring offices or centers, such as People's Daily Online Yuqing Monitoring Office, Xinhua Internet Yuqing Monitoring and Analysis Center, and Global Times Yuqing Investigation Center. These organizations specialize in collecting and analyzing national, local, or disciplinary *yuqing* information based on their own information and news resources. *Yuqing* reports come daily, weekly, and monthly to Party and government organizations at all levels. The leading organizations, for example, People's Daily Online Yuqing Monitoring Office, also provide a ranking list of responses by local governments and their effectiveness, and issue yuqing magazines such as Online Yuqing.

The third category are the *yuqing* research organizations based at universities or academic research institutions, for example, the Internet Information Research Institute of the Communication University of China, the Institute of Public Opinion Research of Remin University of China, and Yuqing Research Laboratory of Shanghai Jiao Tong University. They mainly provide medium- and long-term research reports on online *yuqing* studies and special research reports on emergency management. Many of these organizations are also devoted to developing theories of *yuqing* in an emerging discipline in Chinese academia, the so-called "*yuqing* studies".

The year 2014 saw an unstoppable eruption of *yuqing* as "An interdisciplinary and multifaceted industry. Its products and services cover varieties of activities, including technical support, reputation restoration, risk management and response to crisis, etc" (T. Zhang 2013). Its estimated output value has amounted to the scale of billions (T. Zhang 2013). The number of practitioners has reached two million (Gao 2013), with 1.2 million vacancies still unfilled (Bai 2013). The Ministry of Human Resources and Social Security and the Ministry of Industry and Information Technology have been cooperating with the *yuqing* organizations of People's Daily Online and Xinhua Net respectively in training, assessing, and certifying *yuqing* analysts.[13] The leading companies in the *yuqing* industry are thriving in the capital market.

Some have pointed out that the thriving scene at present is temporary and a "bonus" during China's social transition, when its legal system is being adjusted (Zhu 2015). Meanwhile, the *yuqing* service market is quite chaotic. For example, there are no accepted standards and specifications, no laws and regulations, no industry entry requirements, no supervision bodies, and no future blueprint on *yuqing*-related products and services. In addition, the price system is in complete disorder. The lack of regulations means irregular and unlawful conduct is found regularly among practitioners, such as paid online post deletions and illegal Internet public relations. All of these are putting the *yuqing* industry and its practitioners to a severe test.

In the hope of solving these problems, some industry insiders have tried to form a Sunshine Consensus on Online Yuqing Research, define *yuqing* as a third-party service independent of netizen opinions and government regulation, and develop *yuqing* monitoring into a "sunshine industry" (*People's Daily* 2014). But the reality is that the confluence of politics and business in the expanding *yuqing* industry cannot be stopped by the parties of interests themselves. Frankenstein's creature is out on the run.

On the whole, the demand for, and supply of, *yuqing* reinforce each other to create a downward spiral for the Chinese online speech environment. Most Party and government organizations and state-owned enterprises and public service institutions require localized *yuqing* analyses to meet their low-level fire-fighting style of social management. Their aim is to locate, block, and respond to negative public opinion while it is still in the formative stage. At the same time, a lot of *yuqing* organizations and practitioners cater to, and even encourage and guide, their clients (including the Party and government organizations and state-owned enterprises) to delete posts unfavorable to them, or hire a large number of "online water armies" and Internet marketers to interfere in the online public discourse, in order to maximize their profits. This inevitably leads to artificially altering so-called public opinion. Take Nanjing Qingdun Information and Technology Limited Company as an example. It was founded in 2007 and accepted millions of renminbi investment from Nanjing Yuhua District Government in 2009 (Qingdun 2016a). The company's "Service Process of Crisis Communication and Response to Yuqing" states that, apart from engaging in deleting negative posts, it is capable of manipulating 10,000 active accounts on the mainstream forums, releasing positive news, and providing an automatic system targeting more than 1,000 opinion leaders on microblogs by forwarding positive posts to them (Qingdun 2016b).

Yuqing monitoring, originally as an extension of the State machinery of governance, has now been incorporated into a commercial industry, sucked completely into the opposite side of public opinion, and become a synonym for Internet surveillance and information control. The campaigns of "cracking down on the online rumors" in 2013 and "cleaning the Internet by eliminating pornography and illegal publications" in 2014 (Xu 2014) can both be regarded as purging actions based on the collection and judgement of *yuqing*. Both are targeted at online speeches critical of the government and at those who dare to speak out. The result is the decline of the Internet as an avenue for online public opinion, with Sina Weibo as the primary example. According to a social media analytics company, Zhiwei Data, Sina Weibo activities have dropped to the level of early 2011, more than 30 percent below its peak (Huxiu 2013). Now *yuqing* organizations can collect information on localized crises as they happen, and relevant government departments will interfere immediately by channeling, suppressing, or deleting negative online opinions to prevent them from escalating into a much bigger discourse. In doing so, they have destroyed a healthy ecology of online public opinion, which has resulted in a habitual silence of speech and an enhanced sense of self-censorship. The seemingly rigorous, objective, impartial, and scientific way of intelligence gathering and information analysis by the numerous monitoring tentacles of the gigantic *yuqing* octopus is truncated at its own hands. This trimmed-down information flow is again captured by *yuqing* monitoring bodies, so "a clear and bright cyberspace" reported by certain *yuqing* organizations (Zhu 2013) is simply the realization of a self-fulfilling prophecy.

The weakening of public opinion and the silence of netizens caused by interference from *yuqing* suppliers and consumers can remarkably reduce usable data traffic for monitoring organizations. With fewer clusters, gaps, peaks, and outliers, there will be no early warning sign of future instability, which will ironically decrease the value of the *yuqing* industry itself. What is worse, if information about crises is eliminated, social contradictions and problems will be covered up, and real public opinion will consequently be hidden from those in power. In this sense, it is *yuqing* that wipes *yulun* out.

Conclusion

"Rights" consciousness has been on the rise in China. Farmers, workers, and the new middle class have become increasingly aware of their civil rights and been courageous enough to fight for them. With the emergence and popularization of the Internet, China is slowly developing a public sphere, with "Internet public opinion" taking shape in parallel and counterbalance with so-called "mainstream public opinion". However, in a highly centralized society, such an alternative force has provoked the Party's desire to tighten speech control, and nurtured its ability to invent ingenious methods of micro social management. This has led to the emergence of *yuqing* studies and a booming *yuqing* industry as intelligence, surveillance, and policing agencies on the perceptions and sentiments of online public opinion. The monstrous *yuqing* monitoring system has transformed its function from intelligence gathering and analysis on "social conditions and public opinion" into manipulation and fabrication of Internet public opinion. In the end, the *yuqing* system has "successfully" constructed an orderly and harmonious cyberspace with positive "public opinion". However, in doing so, it has brushed aside and buried real online public opinion on issues and conflicts between and among regions, social classes, religions, ethnicities, and the state and society.

The operations of the *yuqing* monitoring system reflect the paradox of China's Internet management regime: more information is available to average Internet users, but less authenticity on the real attitudes and sentiments of the masses. The change of lexicon and practice from *yulun* to *yuqing* is a result of change in China's information governance and social management. Through the use of *yuqing*, the Party-State intends to keep pace with the times to try to promote good governance at all levels. However, *yuqing* has been used to put down sparks on the prairie, rather than promoting fundamental changes based on the perceptions and sentiments of the masses. *Yuqing* monitoring has morphed into an organized mechanism of social control. It serves the needs of the Party and government to contain and even eliminate public opinion.

Notes

1. The practice of collecting opinions among civilians has been prevalent in China since ancient times. However, it was a top-down practice conducted by those inside the power mechanism, so it was in fact a ruling technique. There used to be another tradition of *qingyi* (清议, righteous elite opinion), by which state affairs could be discussed and officials could be assessed. But that practice was limited within the circle of *shidafu* (士大夫, scholar-officials) rather than open to the public. None of the above traditions in ancient China could be equal to public opinion in its contemporary sense.

2. *Neican* (内参, internal references), according to Yin Yungong, director of the Research Center of the Theoretical System of Socialism with Chinese Characteristics under the Chinese Academy of Social Sciences, refers to "a working mechanism for reporting information internally for considerations. In the Chinese journalism and communication system, 'neican' is a unique phenomenon of information transmission, as well as an important part of the system. 'Neican' should also be seen as a vital means of managing state affairs under the leadership of our Party and government, and knowing about public opinion and the realities . . . The readers of 'neican' are mainly those in the leadership of the Party, the government and the army" (see Yin 2012). *Neicans* are often biased, saying what the writers expect the superiors to hear, and downplaying or omitting unpleasant news. To some extent, "Internet *yuqing*" can be regarded as an upgraded version of *neican* in the Internet age. But, interestingly, today's *yuqing* practitioners believe that what they provide is more objective than *neican*.

3. Ni Lin holds that Chinese language has been influenced by Japanese language in translating "public opinion" into "*yulun*" (Ni 2010). It is a concept of "return graphic loan word" which is defined as a classical Chinese-

character compound being used by the Japanese to translate modern European words and then reintroduced into modern Chinese (see Liu 2002).

4. "A newspaper is not only a collective propagandist and a collective agitator, it is also a collective organizer" (Lenin 1986).

5. See Liang 1975. Liang Xiao is the pen-name for the Great Criticism Group of Beijing University and Qinghua University.

6. Liu Yong was a mafia ringleader in Shenyang, Liaoning Province. When he and his followers were convicted of murder, he was given a life sentence by the provincial court. This sentence triggered a huge public uproar. Eventually, it was reversed and Liu Yong was sentenced to death by the Supreme Court of China.

7. In April 2003, *Southern Metropolis News* published a story about Sun Zhigang, 27, a graphic designer who was picked up by police during a random identity check and died in custody, after being attacked by staff and inmates. The story caused the first mass protest in China's budding online space. The detention and repatriation regulation, under which Sun had been held, was abolished, and a decade of rights advocacy began.

8. In August 2013, Xi Jinping made a speech at the National Conference on Propaganda and Thought Work, in which he emphasized that "the Internet has become the main battlefield of public opinion struggle", and "we should make online opinion work a top priority in ideological and thought work" (Xinhua Net 2015).

9. Internet commentators, known more widely as the 50 Cent Party, are those hired or ordered by the government and the Party to create favorable articles and "polluted" information on the Internet, or post comments favorable towards Party policies and/or against the Party's vocal opponents on forums, social media networks, and all kinds of news outlets, in an attempt to shape and sway public opinion on various issues.

10. A propaganda term referring to positive and uplifting content and attitudes as opposed to critical and negative ones (see Bandursky 2014).

11. Habermas strongly opposed interpreting "public opinion" from the perspective of social psychology, because that would wipe out all essential sociological and politological elements embodied in public opinion, paralyzing the political function and publicness of public opinion. Habermas agreed with Lazarsfeld's point of view— that is, "Public opinion is the corollary of domination . . . something that has political existence only in certain relationships between regime and people" (Habermas 1991: 242).

12. Chinese political jargon coined by the Party to indicate a system for preventing and managing social unrest.

13. In September 2013, *People's Daily* cooperated with the Ministry of Human Resources and Social Security in training "online *yuqing* analysts". In April 2014, Xinhua Net and the Ministry of Industry and Information Technology launched the training of "online *yuqing* management professionals" (Wan and He 2014).

Further Reading

Arendt, H. (1998 [1958]) *The Human Condition* Chicago: University of Chicago Press.

Hu, Y. (2008) *The Rising Cacophony: Personal Expression and Public Discussion in the Internet Age* (*Zhongsheng Xuanhua: Wangluo Shidai De Geren Biaoda Yu Gonggong Taolun*), Guilin: Guangxi Normal University Press.

Xu, J. (2011) *Core Concepts of the Modern Chinese Thought* (*Xiandai Zhongguo Sixiang De Hexin Gainian*), Shanghai: Shanghai People's Publishing House.

References

Bai, C. (2013) "Brief Analysis of the Status and Development Paths of China's Online *Yuqing* Monitoring Industry" (*Luelun Woguo Wangluo Yuqing Jiance Chanye De Xianzhuang Yu Fazhan Lujing*), *People's Forum*, 26: 58–59.

Bandursky, D. (2014) "'Positive Energy', a Pop Propaganda Term?", *China Media Project*, 12 November, available at: http://cmp.hku.hk/2014/11/12/37042/

Cao, Y. (2015) "Government Revs Up Cyberspace Rules", *China Daily*, 29 October, available at: www.china daily.com.cn/china/2015–10/29/content_22312223.htm

Chen, L. (2006) *The Ideological System of the Marxist View on Journalism* (*Makesi Zhuyi Xinwenguan Sixiang Tixi*), Beijing: China Remin University Press, pp. 616–618.

Chen, T. (1903) "On the Corruption of the Hunan Official Paper" (*Lun Hunan Guanbao Zhi Fubai*), *Subao* (苏报), 26 May.

Condit, C. M., and Lucaites, J. L. (1993) *Crafting Equality: America's Anglo-African Word*, Chicago: University of Chicago Press, pp. xxii–xiii.

Ding, B. (2011) "Historical Review of Public Opinion Forms Since the Foundation of New China" (*Dui Xinzhongguo Jianli Yilai Yulun Xingtai De Lishi Kaocha*), *Contemporary Communications*, 1: 8–11.

Gao, J. (2013) "Online *Yuqing* Analyst Has Grown into an Officially Certified Profession: With as Many as 2 Million Practitioners" (*Wangluo Yuqing Fenxishi Cheng Guanfang Renke Zhiye Congyezhe Da 200 Wan*), *Xinhua Net*, 3 October, available at: http://news.xinhuanet.com/newmedia/2013–10/03/c_132769821.htm

Guo, C. (2010) "Research on the CCP's Governance Capacity Construction and Public Opinion Guidance Mechanism" (*Zhongguo Gongchandang Zhizheng Nengli Jianshe Yu Yulun Yindao Jizhi Yanjiu*), Ph.D. thesis, Party School of the Central Committee of CCP, available at: http://cdmd.cnki.com.cn/article/cdmd-80000–2010 138010.htm

Habermas, J. (1991) *The Structural Transformation of the Public Sphere: An Inquiry into a Category of Bourgeois Society*, trans. T. Burger and F. Lawrence. Cambridge, MA: MIT Press.

Hu, J. (2008) "Speech at the Inspection on the *People's Daily*" (*Zai Renminribao Kaocha Gongzuo Shide Jianghua*), *People's Daily*, 20 June, available at: http://politics.people.com.cn/GB/1024/7408514.html

Hu, S. (2013) *Outline of the History of Chinese Philosophy* (*Zhongguo Zhexueshi Dagang*), Shanghai: East China Normal University Press.

Hu, Y. (2012) "Three Trends in Public Opinion Online in China" (*Zhongguo Wangluo Yulun De Sanda Bianhua*), *ChinaFile*, 29 February, available at: www.chinafile.com/three-trends-public-opinion-online-china

Hu, Y. (2014) *Information Wants to Be Free* (*Xinxi Kewang Ziyo*), Shanghai: Fudan University Press.

Huxiu (2013) "Exclusive: Sina Weibo Activities Dropped to the Level of Early 2011, More than 30% Below its Peak" (*Dujia: Xinlang Weibo Huoyuedu Yijing Jiangzhi 2011 Nianchu De Shuiping, Ju Gaofengqi Chixu Xiahua Chaoguo 30%*), *Huxiu*, 9 July, available at: www.huxiu.com/article/16983/1.html

Jiang, Z. (2001) "Speech at the National Conference on Propaganda and Thought Work" (24 January 1994) (*Zai Quanguo Xuanchuan Sixiang Gongzuo Huiyishang De Jianghua*), *On the Construction of the Party*, Beijing: Central Party Literature Press.

Jing, P. (2013) "Dare Draw Sword in the Ideological Arena" (*Yishi Xingtai Lingyu Yao Ganyu Liangjian*), *Beijing Daily*, 2 September, available at: http://news.sina.com.cn/c/2013–09–02/025928105797.shtml

Lenin, V. (1986) *The Collected Works of Lenin*, Vol. 5, Bejing: People's Publishing House.

Li, C. (2013) "A Tight Hold of Public Opinion Work Initiative" (*Laolao Zhangwo Yulun Gongzuo Zhudongquan*), *People's Daily*, 4 September, available at: http://opinion.people.com.cn/n/2013/0904/c1003–22797334.html

Liang, X. (1975) "The Proletariat Must Exercise Dictatorship Over the Bourgeoisie", *Peking Review*, 21 March, 12: 13–16.

Liu, C. (2013) "Theory of Public Opinion Guidance" (*Yulun Yindao Lun*), Ph.D. thesis, Wuhan University, available at: http://cdmd.cnki.com.cn/Article/CDMD-10486–1013210108.htm

Liu, H. (2002) *Translingual Practice: Literature, National Culture and Translated Modernity—China, 1900–1937*, trans. S. Wei *et al.*, Beijing: SDX Joint Publishing Company.

McGee, M.C. (1980) "The 'Ideograph': A Link Between Rhetoric and Ideology", *Quarterly Journal of Speech*, 66(1): 1–16.

Mao, Z. (1977) "In Refutation of 'Uniformity of Public Opinion'" (*Bo "Yulun Yilv"*), in *Selected Works of Mao Zedong*, Vol. 5, 1st edn, Beijing: People's Publishing House: 157–159.

Min, D. (2014) "China's Internet Media and Internet Communication in 2003—The Year of the Internet Public Opinion Stirred Up by the Sun Zhigang Incident" (*2003 Nian De Zhongguo Wangluo Meiti Yu Wangluo Chuanbo: Sun Zhigang Shijian Xianqi "Wangluo Yulun Nian"*), *People's Network*, 15 April, available at: http://media.people.com.cn/n/2014/0415/c40606–24898329.html

Ni, L. (2010) "Thought Evolution of Public Opinion in Modern China" (*Jindai Zhongguo Yulun Sixiang Yanqian*), Ph.D. thesis, Shanghai University, available at: http://cdmd.cnki.com.cn/Article/CDMD-11903–2010 252826.htm

Ni, L. (2012) *Thought Evolution of Public Opinion in Modern China* (*Jindai Zhongguo Yulun Sixiang Bianqian*), Shanghai: Shanghai Jiaotong University Press.

Pan, Z. (2001) "A New Starting Point of Public Opinion Research—Start with Chen Lidan's Work *Public Opinion Studies—Research on Public Opinion Guidance*" (*Yulun Yanjiu De Xinqidian—Cong Chen Lidan Zhu Yulunxue—Yulun Daoxiang Yanjiu Tanqi*), *Journalism and Communication Review*: 87–99.

People's Daily (2011) "Opening Up the Passage Between the 'Two Public Opinion Fields'" (*Datong "Liangge Yulunchang"*), *People's Daily*, 13 July, available at: http://yuqing.people.com.cn/GB/209170/15147976.html

People's Daily (2014) "A Sunshine Consensus on Online *Yuqing* Research" (*Wangluo Yuqing Yanjiu Yangguang Gongshi*), *People's Daily*, 27 February, p. 20.

Qian, G. (2013) "Parsing the 'Public Opinion Struggle'", *China Media Project*, 24 September, available at: http://cmp.hku.hk/2013/09/24/34085/

Qingdun (2016a) "About Qingdun Guanyu Qingdun", *Qingdun*, 1 January, available at: www.yu-qing.com/aboutus/

Qingdun (2016b) "Response to *Yuqing*" (*Yuqing Yingdui*), *Qingdun*, 1 January, available at: www.yu-qing.com/product/yingdui/

State Council Information Office of the People's Republic of China (2010) "The White Paper on China's Internet Status" (*Zhongguo Hulianwang Zhuangkuang Baipishu*), *Xinhua News*, 8 June, available at: http://news.xinhuanet.com/politics/2010–06/08/c_12195221.htm

Tang, X. (2010) "*Qingyi*, Public Opinion and Propaganda—Journalists and Society in Late Qing and Early Republic" (*Qingyi, Yulun Yu Xuanchuan—Qingmo Minchu De Baoren Yu Shehui*), *Journal of East China Normal University: Philosophy and Social Sciences Edition*, 6: 64–70.

Wan, X., and He, H. (2014) "The Value and Market Space of *Yuqing* Business in the Media Transition" (*Yuqing Yewu Zai Meiti Zhuanxingzhong De Jiazhi Ji Shichang Kongjian*), *Chinese Journalist*, 7: 67–69.

Wang, G., and Fang, F. (2010) "Construction of China's *Yuqing* Information Work System: Current Status, Dilemmas and Trends" (*Woguo Yuqing Xinxi Gongzuo Tixi Jianshe: Xianzhuang, Kunjing, Zouxiang*), *Library and Information Science*, 6: 36–39.

Wang, L. (2009) "Differences of *Yuqing* Research and Public Opinions Research" (*Yuqing Yanjiu Yu Minyi Yanjiu De Chayixing*), *Journal of Tianjin University* (*Social Sciences Edition*), 4: 336–340.

Wang, X. (2006) *Studies on Collection and Analysis Mechanism of Yuqing* (*Yuqing Xinxi Huiji Fenxi Jizhi Yanjiu*), Beijing: Xuexi Press.

Wu, T. (2011) "Learning from the Journalism Experience of the Soviet Union: A Historical Review" (*Dui "Xuexi Sulian Xinwen Gongzuo Jingyan" De Lishi Kaocha*), *Chinese Journal of Journalism and Communication*, 7: 102–107.

Xinhua Net (2015) "Make Full Use of the Internet Thinking, and Develop Online Ideological and Theoretical Construction" (*Chongfen Yunyong Hulianwang Siwei, Zuohao Wangshang Sixiang Lilun Zhendi Jianshe*), *Xinhua Net*, 4 December, available at: http://news.xinhuanet.com/politics/2015–12/04/c_128499383.htm

Xu, W. (2014) "Cleaning the Internet by Eliminating Pornography and Illegal Publications: Four Special Operations in 2014" (*2014 Nian "Saohuang Dafei" Gongzuo Jiang Jizhong Kaizhan Sige Zhuanxiang Xingdong*), *Xinhua Net*, 31 March, available at: http://news.xinhuanet.com/politics/2014–03/31/c_1110032789.htm

Yin, Y. (2012) "The Kinds of 'Neican' Deng Xiaoping Usually Read?" (*Deng Xiaoping Changkan Najilei Neican?*), *Communist Party of China News*, 15 November, available at: http://dangshi.people.com.cn/n/2012/1115/c85037–19594559–1.html

Zhang, T. (2013) "*Yuqing* Monitoring: A Response to the New Development of the Internet" (*Yuqing Jiance Yingdui Hulianwang Xin Fazhan*), *People's Daily*, 10 October, available at: http://media.people.com.cn/n/2013/1010/c14677–23143328.html

Zhang, Z. (2013) "Resolutely Sticking to the Battlefield of Ideological Struggle" (*Maozai Yishi Xingtai Douzheng Zhendishang*), *Liberation Army Daily*, 18 September, available at: http://politics.rmlt.com.cn/2013/0918/151891.shtml

Zhao, C. (2014) "Research on the Party's Competence for Public Opinion Guidance in Multifaceted Public Opinion Fields" (*Duoyuan Yulunchangzhong Dangde Yulun Yindao Nengli Yanjiu*), *Journal of Political Science*, 1: 42–51.

Zhu, H. (2013) "Internet Cleanup Has Produced 'First Glimpse of Clear Skies'" (*Hulianwang Shengtai Zhili Qingkong Chuxian*), *People's Daily*, 30 October, available at: http://politics.people.com.cn/n/2013/1030/c1001–23376633.html

Zhu, H. (2015) "*Yuqing* Business: Promoting Good Politics and Good Governance in a Different Way" (*Yuqing Yewu: Tuijin Liangzheng He Shanzhi De Lingpixijing*), *Southern Media Studies*, 55: 29–38.

INDEX

Italic page numbers indicate tables; bold indicate figures.

Printed and bound by CPI Group (UK) Ltd, Croydon, CR0 4YY

01/11/2024

01782600-0001